KEN SCHULTZ'S

Fishing Encyclopedia

Worldwide Angling Guide

VOLUME 1

KEN SCHULTZ'S

Fishing Encyclopedia

Worldwide Angling Guide

Ken Schultz

IDG Books Worldwide, Inc.
An International Data Group Company
Foster City, CA • Chicago, IL • Indianapolis, IN • New York, NY • Southlake, TX

IDG Books Worldwide, Inc.
An International Data Group Company
919 E. Hillsdale Boulevard
Suite 400
Foster City, CA 94404

For general information on books from IDG Books Worldwide's in the U.S., please call our Consumer Customer Service department at 800-762-2974. For reseller information, including discounts and premium sales, please call our Reseller Customer Service department at 800-434-3422.

For information on a multimedia version of this book, available from Tricom Intrtactive, Inc., please go to this Web site: intellipedia.com

To contact the author, please visit: www.kenshultz.com

Library of Congress Cataloging-in-Publication Data

This edition of *Ken Schultz's Fishing Encyclopedia,* which is published in 7 volumes, contains the entire contents of the work as previously published in a single volume: *Ken Schultz's Fishing Encyclopedia,* ISBN 9780028620572

This is Volume 1 of 7

Schultz, Ken, 1950–
Ken Shultz's fishing encyclopedia: worldwide angling guide/ Ken Schultz. — 1st ed.
p. cm.
ISBN 0-02-862057-7
Volume 1: ISBN 9781684427635 (hardcover) | ISBN 9781684427642 (paperback)

1. Fishing—Encyclopedias. 2. Fishes—Encyclopedias. I. Title.
SH411.S38 2000
799.1'03—dc21 99-033719
CIP

Manufactured in the United States of America

First Edition

Table of Contents

Introduction

"Ah, the gallant fisher's life! It is the best of any;
'Tis full of pleasure, void of strife, And 'tis beloved by many."

—IZAAK WALTON

"All men are equal before fish."

—HERBERT HOOVER

WHILE PRODUCING THIS FISHING ENCYCLOPEDIA I SPOKE TO MANY HUNDREDS OF informed anglers. Nearly all of them thought the compilation of all things piscatorial was too overwhelming to contemplate because the angling universe is so enormous and diverse.

Certainly a modern fishing encyclopedia—if it truly provides a full field of knowledge—runs counter to the short and specialized tenets of today's journalism. Yet it is precisely because there is so much to the sport of fishing, plus an increasing profusion of specialized equipment and confusing terminology, that it was necessary to bring order and perspective to all of this in one definitive book.

Ken Schultz's Fishing Encyclopedia & Worldwide Angling Guide has been a long time in the making. I started thinking about it in 1991. Since work began in earnest in 1995, the project became even more expansive than expected, and indeed there were times when it was nearly overwhelming. As a result, the book (now a series of books) grew much bigger than originally planned, becoming 50 percent larger than any fishing encyclopedia that has heretofore been published.

As a result, however, this encyclopedia contains the equivalent of thirty standard-length books, meaning that there is ample space to devote to the species, equipment, techniques, locations, and ancillary matters that encompass the angling universe. Consider that nearly one-third of the encyclopedia series is comprised of the most comprehensive information on worldwide angling opportunities ever assembled. There is absolutely no place to find these details together; indeed, some elements of the *Worldwide Angling Guide* cannot be found anywhere else at all.

Likewise, the coverage of angling methods and equipment has never been addressed more comprehensively between the covers of any other book. In fact, *Ken Schultz's Fishing Encyclopedia* contains the most modern, illuminating, and extensive discourses on the basic elements of fishing tackle—baitcasting, big-game, conventional, flycasting, spinning, and spincasting—ever found in one place. Each of these entries undoubtedly contain more than all but the most scrupulous person will want to know.

Great lengths were also taken, however, to make sure that the less obvious subjects in the angling universe were included and reviewed in comprehensive fashion. For example, nowhere else is there a more extensive review of the principles, methods, and pros and cons of catch-and-release—perhaps the most important angling conservation development of the twentieth century.

Topics like fisheries management, angling-related travel, choosing guides and charter boats, and the care and preparation of fish for consumption, which are among many unglamorous subjects taken for granted elsewhere, receive complete explanation and review here. Likewise the otherwise oft-ignored subjects of ethics and etiquette—increasingly important issues as human pressures increase—are included.

Although there's an enormous amount of information in this series of books, every topic was approached with the intent to take nothing for granted and to present information in straightforward language. Angling is not like nuclear physics, and if it was half as complicated as some people try to make it, no one would enjoy it or have success. The extensive insertion of cross references is thus intended to direct you through a continuing stream of appropriate topics, so you can take any subject as far as you want to go. Some cross references appear within entry text next to topics that are more thoroughly reviewed elsewhere; many cross references appear at the end of entry text, either to direct you to the appropriate subject entry or to note related topics.

We've tried to make things easy to find and to place subjects where you're most likely to look for them, even if you're unsure of the proper terms or spelling. As an example, you'll find rainbow trout under the "T" entries (trout, rainbow) rather than under the "R" entries. Also, at the back of each book is a weights and measures conversion chart; this will be convenient for many readers since there's a liberal mix of metric and U.S. customary weights and measures throughout this book, just as there is at boat docks, fish camps, and tackle shops throughout the world.

Because the text is encyclopedic in format, however, it does not provide a full sense of the joy or spirit of sportfishing—the pleasure that makes it "beloved by many," as Izaak Walton said. Perhaps the accompanying photos help convey this. Photos and line art, incidentally, were planned and selected to reflect the broad, eclectic places and situations that so many anglers experience, as well as to reflect the great diversity of its participants. Angling is a very democratic recreation; as the quotation from President Hoover implies, the fish don't care who hooks them.

It is a special delight to publish this encyclopedia at the close of the twentieth century—a period with the most phenomenal sportfishing growth in the history of mankind—and at the advent of a new millennium. Knowing that the decades ahead will require proper stewardship of aquatic resources—something that anglers in particular have always demonstrated personal and financial support for—this text has been written and edited with sensitivity to conservation issues while also being realistic about the role that humans play as the highest predators and the diverse motivations they bring to angling.

In a sense, the sport of fishing is like a book with as many footnotes as main text. It is full of variables, especially individual skills, weather issues, peculiarities among species, habitat differences, and so forth. You may notice that the words "usually" and "generally" occur often in portions of the text. This isn't meant to be vague; it's because there are often no hard-and-fast rules in catching fish, no matter what you may have heard to the contrary. There are norms, but straying from norms is common for one reason or another, as any angler who has been humbled at a "hot" site at the "best" time of the season can attest.

While there is a wealth of reliable information here, a caveat is in order with regard to the contents of the *Worldwide Angling Guide*. Many of the countries profiled have not in the past provided, or do not currently provide, or may not in the future provide stable travel environments, especially to tourists of certain nationalities. Jungle fishing opportunities are especially among those that may present danger. Angola, Colombia, and Zambia come immediately to mind in this regard. Civil unrest can likewise make travel in certain places dangerous; recent troubles in Kenya, Indonesia, Russia, Uganda, and the Balkans serve as examples. The adventurous angler needs to use good judgment.

Things change the environmental order and aquatic resources, too. Yugoslavia hadn't been wrecked by bombs when that entry was written; Nicaragua and Honduras were leveled by Hurricane Georges right after those entries were written. Environmental changes sometimes radically alter the presence or availability of certain gamefish species, and in the more remote pockets of the world only native people and intrepid explorers are likely to know it.

On a final note, it is tempting to say, as marketers and publicists are wont to do, that this book contains everything an angler will ever need to know about fish and fishing. But new developments in fishing tackle will surely come along, changes in some habitats or in fish populations will alter the techniques and equipment used, and certainly natural changes will take place in some of the world's best angling spots. However, a lot of the fundamentals—the underlying principles of fish behavior, the function of basic equipment, and angling methodology—will be constant, making most of the information in this book relevant to the discerning angler even in years to come.

I expect to add to this body of knowledge in time, so if you think there's something that should have been included, if you have knowledge about fishing in a country that wasn't covered, or if you can suggest an improvement to any aspect of this book, please visit my website—www.kenschultz.com—and post a message about it.

Now, turn to any page and become absorbed.

—Ken Schultz

"If I fished only to capture fish, my fishing trips would have ended long ago."

—ZANE GREY

Acknowledgments

PRODUCING A BOOK OF THIS MAGNITUDE REQUIRED THE INVOLVEMENT OF A tremendous number of people and a great array of talents. This encyclopedia would not have gone beyond a mere suggestion, however, had it not been for the endorsement and encouragement of Natalie Chapman, a former publisher at Macmillan General Reference, now IDG Books Consumer Reference, whose confidence and vision made this book possible, and who gave me free rein to produce it as necessary. I'm also indebted to publisher Marie Butler-Knight, who took this project over in mid-stream, marshaled all the resources, and fervently shepherded the book to completion. Sincere appreciation is also extended to Renee Wilmeth and Kristi Hart, who directed the publisher's nitty-gritty editorial and production work with outstanding dedication and professionalism, plus a reassuring enthusiasm; to Pamela Benner, who paid excellent attention to details in the copyediting process and made good suggestions; and to many other directly involved personnel, particularly Beth Jordan, Faunette Johnston, and Jeanine Bucek.

This book could also not have been completed without the special assistance of my wife, Sandy, and my daughters, Alyson, Megan, and Kristen. They each helped in a variety of ways, especially by being patient. Sandy's assistance with a host of matters was very beneficial, and Kristen was particularly vital, pitching in for a second time during a desperate period with important research and writing assistance.

In order to make this encyclopedia truly comprehensive and of worldwide significance it was imperative to involve a host of contributors with expertise in technical fisheries matters, regional angling opportunities, and specialized sportfishing topics. I'm grateful for their participation and excellent contributions, the bulk of which made up the *Worldwide Angling Guide*. In particular, appreciation is extended to the incomparable Ed Migdalski, who provided technical scientific fisheries advice and vetted all of the fish art.

I'm also indebted to the late, and incomparable in his own right, A. J. McClane. His fishing encyclopedia of 1965 and 1974, though now outdated, was not only a phenomenal reference work, but a monumental achievement in an era before personal computers, electronic mail, fax machines, scanners, laser printers, and the various modern technology that made putting this book together far easier than it was in his time. Unlike me, he was unable to write and edit on a laptop computer in cars, planes, airports, hotel rooms, and other places, or receive electronically transmitted text. More significantly, McClane set a very high bar for what a real fishing encyclopedia ought to be, and provided a template for such a book for the twenty-first century. Without his accomplishment, it would have been much more difficult to plan and publish this book. (Aside to historians: four contributors to this project—Ed Migdalski, George Reiger, Jack Samson, and Bill Scifres—were also contributors to McClane's encyclopedia.)

Just as McClane, the contributors to this book, and the people at IDG Books Worldwide are the best in their fields, so is *Field & Stream* the largest and best fishing and hunting magazine in the world, and I've been privileged to be part of this publication continuously since 1973. I appreciate the confidence and opportunities provided me over that time by its editors. Those opportunities laid the groundwork for this encyclopedia. I'm especially grateful to Editor Slaton White and Managing Editor Mike Toth for allowing me leeway over the last several years that I've been working on this project.

Information, suggestions, encouragement, technical advice, reference paraphernalia, reviews and critiques, and assorted material assistance were received from so many individuals and organizations that some will likely be overlooked in these acknowledgments, for which I apologize.

I'm very grateful to the following individuals:

Blaine Anderson
John Anthon
Dick Ballard
Ron Ballanti
LaVerne Barnes
Cameron Baty
Susan Baumgartner
Gene Bay
Dick Bengraff
Virginia Benoit
Walt Boname
Toby Bradshaw
Eric Burnley
Cyril Calendini
Bill Chapman, Jr.
Jim Chapralis
Larry Columbo
David Cosby
Gary Dollahon
Lou Duarte
Todd DuPuis
Jack Erskine
Mike Fine
Paul Fuller
Riccardo Galigani
Ken Gangler

Guy Geffroy
Lois Gerber
Alessandro Giangio
Barry Gibson
Gary Giudice
Fred Golofaro
Jerry Gomber
George Gowen
Garry Gurke
Judy Hammond
Bill Hilts, Jr.
Bruce Holt
Dr. James Imai
Jimmy Kano
Nick Karas
Glenda Kelley
Gary King
Jason Klein
Bob Lang
Steen Larsen
Mike Leech
Bill Liston
Chun Liu
George Loechl
Paulo Loes
Frank Longino
Jim Matthews
John Mazurkewicz
Tom Melton
Paul Merzig
Ed Mesunas
Bill Miller
Gail Morchower
András Nagy
Andy Newman
Stuart Newman
Donald J. Orth
Tom Pagliaroli
Sheldon Pasternack
Dennis Phillips
Stanko Popovic
Norville Prosser
Jim Reist
Al Ristori
Milt Rosko
Gail Ross
Sharon Rushton
Pat Salimeno
Marty Salovin
Glenn Sapir
Christine Moore Serrao
Vin Sparano
Ron Speed, Sr.
Roy Stiner
Mick Thill
Roger Tucker
Jerry Valentine
Mike Walker
Ben Wechsler
Mark Weintz
Fenner Weller
Jim White
Anthony M. Williams
Dick Wood
Peter Yaskowski

I'm also grateful to the following companies and organizations (and specific people where noted in parenthesis):

American Sportfishing Association (Mike Hayden)
American Wire (Michael Shields)
Arkie Lures
The Atlantic Salmon Federation
Bay de Noc Lure Co.
Bead Tackle (Peter Renkert)
Bear Advertising (Dick Bear, Mark Malkin)
Big Jon (Jerry Livingstone)
Bullet Weights (Douglas Crumrine)
Bushnell Sports Optics (Barbara Mellman)
Cabela's Inc. (Tony Dolle)
Classic Fishing Products (Mike Richards)
C-Map USA (Pam Oldham)
Computrol, Inc.
Cossack Bait Products (Garry Shaw)
Cuba Specialty Mfg. Co. (Craig Osterhus, Dana Pickup)
Daiwa Corp.
Earie Dearie Lure Co. (Helen Galbincea)
EZE Lap Diamond (Donna Long)
Fin-Nor (Niels Stenhoj)
Flambeau Products Corp. (Jason Sauey)
Florida Keys and Key West Visitors Bureau
Flow-Rite of Tennessee (Don Zielinski)
Furuno
Future Fisherman Foundation
Garmin International (Steve Featherstone)
G. Loomis (Gary Loomis, Steve Rajeff)
Gudebrod
International Game Fish Association (Jim Brown)
Hudson River Foundation
Interphase Technologies
K-C Tackle (Raymond Packer)
L. L. Bean (Mary Rose MacKinnon)
L&S Bait Co. (Eric Bachnik)
Lowrance Electronics (Darrell Lowrance, Steve Schneider)
Luhr Jensen & Sons (Phil Jensen, Barry Ternahan)
Magellan Systems Corp. (Don Meyer)
Mann's Bait Co.
Marado Inc.
Old Town Canoe (Jim Kaiser)
O. Mustad & Sons USA (John DeVries)
National Freshwater Fishing Hall of Fame
Nomadic Expeditions (Denise Gogarty)
Normark Corp. (Ron Weber, Craig Weber)
The Orvis Company
Outdoor Technologies
Owner America Corp. (Kat Shitanishi)
Penn Fishing Tackle
Pradco (Joe Hughes, Bruce Stanton)
Scientific Anglers
Shakespeare Fishing Tackle (Mark Davis)
Sheldon's Inc.
Shimano American Corp.
Si-Tex Marine Electronics
Storm Lures (Sharon Andrews, John Storm)
Sufix USA, Inc.
Techsonics Industries
Len Thompson Lures (Richard Pallister)
Top Brass Tackle (Eric Cosby)
Tru-Turn Hooks (Wes Campbell)
Wisconsin Pharmacal
H. D. Wood Advertising
Worden's Lures
The Worth Co.
Wright & McGill Co. (George Large)
Yakima Bait Co. (Rob Phillips)
Zebco Corp. (Jenni Foster)

Gratitude is also due the following government agencies and government-funded programs (and the people noted in parenthesis), which provided research and reference materials, and, in some cases, other forms of assistance:

Alabama Cooperative Extension Service (Richard Wallace)
Alabama Department of Conservation and Natural Resources (Stan Cook)
Alabama Sea Grant Extension Program
Alaska Department of Fish and Game (Jon Lyman)
Alaska Sea Grant College Program (Kurt Byers)
Alberta Department of Environmental Protection

Arizona Game and Fish Department
Arkansas Cooperative Extension Program, Univ. of Arkansas (Nathan Stone)
Arkansas Game and Fish Commission (Keith Sutton)
Auburn University Marine Extension (Richard Wallace, William Hosking, Stephen Szedlmayer)
Brazil Embratur
British Columbia Ministry of Environment, Fisheries Branch
California Department of Fish and Game (A. Petrovich)
Canada Department of Fisheries and Oceans
Canadian Consul General
Cayman Islands Department of Tourism
Colorado Department of Natural Resources
Connecticut Department of Environmental Protection
Delaware Division of Fish and Wildlife
Florida Department of Environmental Protection, Marine Research Institute and Division of Marine Resources (Jim Lewis)
Florida Game and Freshwater Fish Commission, Division of Fisheries (Henry Cabbage)
Georgia Department of Natural Resources (Chris Martin)
Great Lakes Fishery Commission
Guam Department of Agriculture (Gerry Davis)
Hawaii Department of Land and Natural Resources, Division of Aquatic Resources
Idaho Department of Fish and Game (Jack Trueblood)
Illinois Department of Natural Resources
Indiana Department of Natural Resources (Jon Marshall)
International Center for Living Aquatic Resources Management/Food and Agriculture Organization of the United Nations
Iowa Department of Natural Resources (Steve Suman)
Kansas Department of Wildlife and Parks (Mike Miller)
Kentucky Department of Fish and Wildlife Resources (J. Beth Garland)
Louisiana Department of Wildlife and Fisheries
Louisiana Sea Grant College Program
Maine Department of Inland Fisheries and Wildlife (V. Paul Reynolds)
Manitoba Department of Natural Resources, Fisheries Branch (Carl Wall)
Maryland Department of Natural Resources (Eugene Deems, Jr.)
Maryland Sea Grant College Program (Jack Greer)
Massachusetts Division of Fisheries and Wildlife
Michigan Department of Natural Resources, Fisheries Division
Michigan Sea Grant College Program (Martha Walter)
Minnesota Department of Natural Resources (Tom Dickson)
Mississippi Department of Wildlife, Fisheries and Parks (Jim Walker)
Missouri Department of Conservation (John McPherson)
Montana Division of Fish, Wildlife, and Parks
Nevada Department of Conservation and Natural Resources
New Brunswick Department of Economic Development and Tourism
New Brunswick Department of Natural Resources, Fish and Wildlife Branch (Peter Cronin)
Newfoundland Department of Natural Resources
New Hampshire Fish and Game Department (Patricia Fleurie)
New Jersey Division of Fish, Game and Wildlife (Dave Chanda)
New Mexico Department of Game and Fish (Ruth Anderson)
New York Department of Environmental Conservation (Robert Brandt)
New York Sea Grant Program (David MacNeill, Mark Malchoff)
NOAA/Gray's Reef National Marine Sanctuary (Beth Kostka)
NOAA/National Marine Fisheries Service
NOAA/National Weather Service
North Carolina Division of Boating and Inland Fisheries (Fred Harris)
North Carolina Sea Grant
North Dakota Game and Fish Department (Terry Steinwand)
Nova Scotia Department of Fisheries (Murray Hill)
Nova Scotia Department of Lands and Forests (Barry Sabean)
Ohio Department of Natural Resources
Ohio Sea Grant College Program
Oklahoma Department of Wildlife Conservation (Nels Rodefeld)
Ontario Ministry of Economic Development, Trade & Tourism (Tom Boyd)
Ontario Ministry of Natural Resources
Oregon Department of Fish and Wildlife (Randy Henry)
Oregon Sea Grant (Pat Kight)
Parátur, State of Pará, Brazil
Pennsylvania Fish and Boat Commission
Portuguese National Tourist Office (Maria Joáo Ramires)
Prince Edward Island Department of Environmental Resources
Quebec Department of Recreation, Fish and Game
Rhode Island Division of Fish and Game
Rhode Island Sea Grant
Saskatchewan Department of Environment, Fish and Wildlife (Bruce Howard)

South Carolina Department of Natural Resources (Greg Lucas)
South Carolina Sea Grant Consortium (John Tibbetts)
South Dakota Department of Game, Fish and Parks
Spain Ministry of Commerce and Tourism
Tennessee Wildlife Resources Agency (Dave Woodward)
Texas Parks and Wildlife (Steve Lightfoot)
Tourism British Columbia
Tourism New Brunswick
Tourism Newfoundland and Labrador
Tourism Nova Scotia (Randy Brooks)
Tourism Prince Edward Island (Carol Horne)
Tourism Quebec (Siegfried Gagnon)
Tourism Saskatchewan (Gerard Makuch, Nadine Howard)
Travel Alberta (Peter Gregus)
Travel Manitoba (Dennis Maksymetz, Colette Fontaine, Gord Richardson)
University of Connecticut Sea Grant Marine Advisory Program (Nancy Balcom)
University of Delaware Sea Grant College Program
University of Florida Cooperative Extension Service
University of New Hampshire and University of Maine Sea Grant College Program
U.S. Fish and Wildlife Service
Utah Department of Natural Resources (Gerry Schlappe)
Vermont Department of Fish and Wildlife (John Hall)
Virginia Department of Game and Inland Fisheries (Mitchell Norman)
Washington Department of Fish and Wildlife (Nina Carter, James Chandler)
Washington Sea Grant Program (Kris Freeman)
West Virginia Division of Natural Resources (Hoy Murphy)
Wisconsin Department of Natural Resources (David Kunelius)
Woods Hole Oceanographic Institute (Tracey Crago)
Wyoming Game and Fish Department
Yukon Territory Department of Renewable Resources (Susan Thompson)

Finally, I'm also grateful to four student interns, whose early work compiling and organizing research materials was of much help—Kristen Schultz of Oberlin College, Alyson Schultz of Boston University, Mathew Kane of Hamilton College, and John Kuhner of Princeton University—and to Megan Schultz of Ithaca College, for website development and advice.

—Ken Schultz

About the Author, Artists, and Contributors

PRINCIPAL AUTHOR AND EDITOR

Ken Schultz has been a staff fishing writer and editor for *Field & Stream* since 1973. His feature articles and columns for that publication appear monthly, and he contributes to the magazine's nationally syndicated weekly radio show and to its website. Schultz is a frequent author of the outdoors column of the *New York Times*, and he previously was a syndicated newspaper columnist for Gannett. He has authored a dozen books on sportfishing and angling travel topics, has been a featured guest on CNBC, ESPN, and The Nashville Network, and appears regularly in assorted fishing segments for the Outdoor Life Network. A widely traveled angler, Schultz is a former holder of seven line-class world records and was inducted into the Fishing Hall of Fame in 1998. He lives in Forestburgh, New York.

THE ARTISTS

Steve T. Goione is a rising star in the world of fishing and boating art, working in mixed mediums to present his lifelong passion for angling in a dynamic and realistic style. Although he drew the distinctive pen-and-ink illustrations for this book as well as the cover, Goione is primarily a creator of fine art. From his studio in Toms River, New Jersey, he produces commissioned fishing scenes for private collections and limited-edition prints, and he has created original artwork for Sea World in Florida. Goione has also made a mark among boat builders and owners for commissioned renderings of big-game sportfishing craft, and he recently created original artwork for the latest products of Hatteras Yachts. A frequent guest artist on the big-game fishing tournament circuit, Goione appears at exclusive contests each year from Nantucket to Venezuela, and his work is regularly featured at fund-raising events for prominent conservation organizations.

David Kiphuth, whose renderings of fish appear in this book, has had a varied career in the field of art, having been a professional illustrator since 1969. His work has included portraiture, architectural renderings, maps, and book illustration. Kiphuth has created archaeological and scientific book and exhibit renderings for the Yale Peabody Museum, the Yale Department of Anthropology, and Yale University Press. He formerly maintained a studio and gallery in Branford, Connecticut, where he created and sold wildlife and nature art and animal portraits. Since 1989, he has been the staff illustrator for the *Gazette Newspapers* in Schenectady, New York. He lives in Saratoga Springs, New York.

THE CONTRIBUTORS

Brett Albanese of Virginia is a Ph.D candidate at the Department of Fisheries and Wildlife Sciences at Virginia Polytechnic Institute; he formerly worked at the Mississippi Museum of Natural Sciences.

Ken Allen of Maine is Associate Editor of *Maine Sportsman* and a prolific writer, photographer, newspaper columnist, book author, and guide.

Michael Babcock of Montana is Outdoors Editor of the *Great Falls Tribune.*

Ken Bailey of Alberta is Manager of Field Operations in central Alberta for Ducks Unlimited Canada; he is a prolific writer and President of the Outdoor Writers Association of Canada.

Dick Ballard of Missouri is President of Dick Ballard's Fishing Adventures and a foremost authority on Amazonian angling; he's sent anglers fishing around the world for 18 years, and established the first travel service for Bass Pro Shops.

Scott Bannerot of Pennsylvania and Florida has a Ph.D. in fisheries science and has worked in marine biological research and consulting; he is a photojournalist and a charter boat captain.

John A. Barnes of Bermuda is the Director of Agriculture and Fisheries for Bermuda; he authors a weekly fishing column in the Bermuda *Mid Ocean News*, and is an IGFA representative.

Rob Barraclough of Indonesia and England works in the oil industry and is a charter boat captain and freelance writer.

Carlos M. Barrantes of Costa Rica established the first two sportfishing camps in Costa Rica; he is an IGFA representative and was the first President of the Costa Rican Fishing Federation.

Cody Beers of Wyoming works for the Wyoming Game and Fish Department as Associate Editor of *Wyoming Wildlife* magazine and Editor of *Wyoming Wildlife News and Wild Times*; he is also a freelance writer and photographer.

Bob Berry of California is one of the world's top fish carvers and sculptors, and swept all divisions of the 1986 world championship of fish carving; he is a foremost competition judge, a former professional taxidermist, and author of the book *Fish Carving.*

Mike Bleech of Pennsylvania is a writer and photographer whose work has appeared in most major U.S. fishing and hunting magazines.

Larry Blomquist of Louisiana is Publisher of *Breakthrough*, the world's largest taxidermy trade magazine, and one of the top competition judges in North America; he is a retired award-winning taxidermist, and former President of the National Taxidermists Association.

Fred Bonner of North Carolina is Editor of *Carolina Adventure* magazine; he is also a syndicated newspaper columnist, fisheries biologist, and an IGFA representative.

Judith Bowman of New York has been a foremost sporting books dealer for over twenty years; she produces two sporting book catalogs a year, with special emphasis on fishing.

John Brownlee of Florida is Senior Editor of *Salt Water Sportsman* and a former charter boat captain; he has served on the South Atlantic Fishery Management Council, is former Chairman of the Florida Conservation Association, and is an IGFA representative.

Eric B. Burnley of Virginia is the author of *Surf Fishing the Atlantic Coast* and a radio show host; he is a charter boat captain and Regional Editor of both *Salt Water Sportsman* and *The Fisherman* magazines.

Erwin Bursik of South Africa is Publisher of *Ski-Boat* and *Flyfishing* magazines of Durban, a member of the executive board of the South African Deep Sea Angling Association, and an IGFA representative.

Mac Campbell of Great Britain works for *Angling Plus*, a match fishing magazine, and has previously worked for *Sea Angler*, *Trout Fisherman*, and *Angling Times*.

Jim Casada of South Carolina is the author of many books, including *Modern Fly Fishing*; he is Senior Editor of *Sporting Classics* magazine, and outdoor columnist for the Rock Hill *Herald* and Greensboro *News and Record*.

Göran Cederberg of Sweden has been Editor of several international fact-packed large-format angling books, including *The Complete Book of Sportfishing*; he contributes regularly to north-European publications and has been chief editor of a Swedish sportfishing magazine.

Matthew D. Chan of Virginia is a Ph.D candidate at the Department of Fisheries and Wildlife Sciences at Virginia Polytechnic Institute; he formerly worked as a fisheries biologist for the U. S. Army Corps of Engineers.

Dawn Charging of North Dakota is Outdoors Director for the North Dakota State Tourism Department; she is also a writer and photographer whose family owns a successful fishing resort on Lake Sakakawea.

Homer Circle of Florida has been Angling Editor of *Sports Afield* magazine for 34 years; the dean of American outdoor writers, he is the recipient of numerous media and achievement awards, a former member of the Arkansas Game & Fish Commission, and a renowned television and video host.

Barry Ord Clarke of Norway is a professional photographer and writer and the author of several books on fly fishing and fly tying; he contributes regularly to most European fishing magazines, and is fishing consultant to Norway's largest private sporting estate.

Soc Clay of Kentucky is an accomplished and prolific fishing writer and photographer whose work has appeared in every major outdoor periodical in North America.

Angelo Cuanang of California is a Pacific Regional Editor for *Salt Water Sportsman* and a freelance writer and photographer.

Paula J. Del Giudice of Nevada is Outdoor Columnist for the *Las Vegas Sun*; a freelance writer, photographer, and book author; and former President of the Nevada Wildlife Federation.

Arthur De Mello of Uganda is a representative for the IGFA in Uganda.

Hansjörg Dietiker of Switzerland is Editor of the Swiss Anglers Magazine *Petri-Heil*, and an IGFA representative.

Philippe Dolivet of France is the Chief Editor of the French fly fishing magazine *Plaisirs de la Pêche* and a professional photographer; he is a fly fishing instructor and competitor, an ichthyologist, and an IGFA representative.

Gary Edwards of Wyoming is a longtime fishing guide and a television show host; he is the former Editor and Publisher of *Salmon Fever* magazine, and a former fly rod world record holder.

D'arcy Egan of Ohio has been a sportswriter for *The Cleveland Plain Dealer* for over 20 years; he authored the book, *Guide to Ohio Fishing*, and is host of the American Outdoorsman Radio Network.

Bill Ensor of New Brunswick works for the Fish & Wildlife Branch of the New Brunswick Department of Natural Resources; he was formerly marketing manager of fishing and hunting for the New Brunswick Department of Tourism, and is a long-time fishing guide.

Jack Erskine of Australia is a foremost big-game tackle designer and technical innovator who has helped design many of the modern rods, reels, and drag systems in use today.

Stan Fagerstrom of Oregon is one of the world's best known trick and accuracy casters, and has been featured at sport shows worldwide for half a century; he is also a book, magazine, and newspaper writer.

Jan Fogt of Florida is Editor of *The Bahamas Sportfishing Guide* and was the founding editor of *Bahamas Blue Water Magazine*; she is a contributing editor for *Sport Fishing* and *Marlin* magazines, and is also a book author.

Frank Fry of the Yukon Territory has worked with the Yukon Territory's Department of Natural Resources on various fishing projects.

Mike Garzillo of New Hampshire has been a newspaper columnist for 24 years; he is a regular contributor to various publications and a former regional editor for *Outdoor Life*.

Alessandro Giangio of Italy writes for Italy's premier fishing magazine, *Pesca in Mare*, and has been published worldwide; he has authored five books, is owner and master instructor of the Fishbuster Trolling School and Sportfishing Travel, and has a charter boat in Huatulco, Mexico.

Jerry Gibbs of Vermont is Fishing Editor of *Outdoor Life*, where his career as a staff writer has spanned three decades and made him one of North America's most respected angling authors; he has written several books and has been inducted into the Fishing Hall of Fame.

Barry Gibson of Massachusetts is Editor of *Salt Water Sportsman* and a longtime Maine charter boat captain; he is a former member of the New England Fishery Management Council, and former advisor to the International Commission for the Conservation of Atlantic Tunas.

Jerry Gomber of New Jersey has over twenty-five years of experience in design, development, and marketing of fishing rods and reels; during that period he has been responsible for several successful product innovations.

George Gruenefeld of Quebec and Saskatchewan is Editor of *Canadian Outdoor Publications*; he has written for many magazines in Canada and the U.S., is a book author, and was formerly Outdoors Editor for the *Montreal Gazette*.

Chris Hanks of the Northwest Territories is an anthropologist, freelance writer, and author of the book *Fly Fishing in the Northwest Territories*.

Steve Harper of Kansas is the Outdoors Editor of the *Wichita Eagle* and author of the book *Kansas Day Trips*; in 1995 he was named Conservation Communicator of the Year by the Kansas Wildlife Federation.

Dan Heiner of Alaska is an advertising agency executive and former editor and writer for *Alaska Outdoors* magazine; he is the author of four books on Alaska fishing, including *Fly Fishing Alaska's Wild Rivers*.

Bob Hodge of Tennessee is the Outdoors Editor of the *Knoxville News-Sentinel*; he was named the state's Best Outdoor Writer for 1996-97 by the Tennessee Sportswriters Association.

Grant Hopkins of Ontario is the outdoor columnist for the *Ottawa Citizen*, a frequent contributor to *Ontario Out of Doors*, and retired from the Royal Canadian Air Force.

John Husar of Illinois is the longtime outdoors columnist and general sportswriter of the *Chicago Tribune* and co-host of a Chicago radio show; he has worked for newspapers in Kansas, Texas, and New Mexico, and has covered the last nine Olympics.

Jim Imai of California has a Ph.D in physics and is Professor of Physics at California State University, Dominguez Hills; he is a Consulting Physicist for the Daiwa Corporation, and a leading authority on the design and performance of fishing reels and rods.

James Kano of Ontario is the Marketing Director of Japan Communications in Toronto and Outdoor Coordinator for the Press and Tourism division of the Ontario government; his articles have appeared online and in newspapers, guide books, and magazines.

Nick Karas of New York is the retired outdoor columnist for (New York) *Newsday* and a charter boat captain and ichthyologist; he has written for many national magazines and authored a dozen books, including *The Striped Bass* and *Brook Trout*.

Lee Kernen of Wisconsin is the retired Director of Fisheries for the State of Wisconsin; he is also a writer, fishing guide, and fisheries consultant.

Ronnie Kovach of California is a radio and television show host, educator, magazine writer, guide, and author of five books, including *Bass Fishing in California*, *Trout Fishing in California*, and *Saltwater Fishing in California*.

Steen Larsen of Denmark is one of Europe's leading sportfishing writers and photographers; he is a book author and lecturer, and contributes widely to many European angling publications.

Dick Lewers of Australia is Technical Editor of *Encyclopaedia of Australian Fishing*, author of seven books on angling, a former IGFA representative, 35-year columnist for *Modern Fishing Magazine*, and past President of the Australian National Sportfishing Association.

Bill Loftus of Idaho is the Outdoors Editor of the *Lewiston Morning Tribune* and the author of two guidebooks to Idaho.

Maurice Loustau-LaLanne of Seychelles is the Principal Secretary in the Ministry of Tourism and Transport for the Seychelles, and an IGFA representative.

Carl. F. Luckey of Alabama is a writer specializing in antiques and collectibles; he has authored ten books, including his best-selling, 618-page work, *Old Fishing Lures and Tackle*.

Joe Macaluso of Louisiana is an award-winning outdoors sportswriter/editor for the *Baton Rouge Advocate;* his weekly fishing reports have appeared in Louisiana newspapers since 1976.

Rosanne Macfarlane of Prince Edward Island recently received her Masters degree in Biology at

Acadia University; she works for the Department of Fisheries and Environment.

Dennis Maksymetz of Manitoba is Manager of Tourism Marketing for the Industry, Trade and Tourism division of the Manitoba government.

Don Mann of Florida is a longtime contributor to *Florida Sportsman*, a record-holding big-game angler, and book author; his articles and photographs have appeared in many publications.

Al Marlowe of Colorado has written numerous articles for outdoor magazines; he authored a trail guide for the Flat Tops Wilderness area and a fly fishing guide for the Colorado River.

Peter B. Mathiesen of Missouri is Executive Editor and Producer of the *Field & Stream Radio Hour*; he is also a magazine writer, photographer, and video and television show producer.

John McCoy of West Virginia is Outdoors Editor for the *Charleston Daily Mail*, Regional Editor for *Field & Stream*, and a frequent contributor to regional and national magazines.

Tom Meade of Rhode Island writes about the outdoors for the *Providence Journal-Bulletin*; he is the author of *Essential Fly Fishing*, and writes for various magazines.

Ed Migdalski of Connecticut is the retired Director of Yale University's Outdoor Education and Club Sports Programs, retired Ichthyologist for the Yale Peabody Museum, and holder of the current world record for the largest strictly freshwater fish (piraruçu) ever caught on rod and reel.

Kent Mitchell of Georgia has covered outdoor sports for the *Atlanta Journal-Constitution* for three decades; he has received the Communicator of the Year Award from the Georgia Wildlife Federation, and has authored three books on martial arts.

Bill Monroe of Oregon has covered the outdoors for his state's largest daily newspaper, *The Oregonian*, for 18 years.

Gary W. Moore of Vermont is a freelance writer and photographer; he is former Commissioner of the Vermont Fish and Wildlife Department and former Chairman of the Vermont Water Resources Board.

Sam Mossman of New Zealand is Special Projects Editor for *New Zealand Fishing News* magazine; he is the author of three books and hundreds of magazine articles, and has held five world and numerous New Zealand fishing records.

Perry Munro of Nova Scotia is a writer and artist who contributes to *The Atlantic Salmon Journal* and various other magazines; he is also an outfitter, master guide, operator of Maple Mountain Lodge, and a Director of Trout Unlimited Canada.

Iain Nicolson of Angola is an IGFA representative and has a Ph.D. in molecular genetics; he and his family pioneered fishing for blue marlin in Angola and collectively established six world fishing records.

Chris Niskanen of Minnesota is the Outdoors Editor of the *St. Paul Pioneer Press*.

Donald J. Orth of Virginia is a Professor of Fisheries Science in the Department of Fisheries & Wildlife Sciences at Virginia Polytechnic Institute.

Tom Pagliaroli of New Jersey is an advertising agency executive, freelance writer, and photographer whose work has appeared in various regional and national publications.

Ali Pasiner of Turkey is an attorney, the author of two fishing books, and a consultant to the Turkish version of the *Encyclopaedia Britannica*; he is also a writer, editor, and representative of the IGFA.

C. Boyd Pfeiffer of Maryland is a longtime journalist and photographer, a regular columnist for many angling magazines, and the author of numerous books on fishing topics, the latest of which is *Fly Fishing Salt Water Basics*.

Larry Porter of Nebraska has been on the sports staff of the *Omaha World-Herald* for over three decades and their outdoors writer since 1990; he has been named Nebraska Sportswriter of the Year three times, and is a former professional tournament angler.

Steve Price of Texas is a longtime Senior Writer for *Bassmaster* magazine and contributor to a wide variety of national sporting magazines; he is an accomplished photographer and author of several books.

Gareth Purnell of England is Editor of Britain's leading angling magazine, *Improve Your Coarse Fishing*, and former News Editor of *Angling Times*; he has fished annually in the World Freshwater Angling Championships since 1993.

George Reiger of Virginia is Conservation Editor of *Field & Stream* and *Salt Water Sportsman* magazines and the most widely respected conservation writer in North America; he has been a staff writer for *Field & Stream* since 1972, is the author of seven books on angling and marine ecology, and the recipient of numerous honors and awards.

Tim Renken of Missouri has been the outdoors writer for the *St. Louis Post-Dispatch* since 1963; he previously worked for the Nebraska Game Commission.

Len Rich of Newfoundland is the author of two books and many outdoor magazine articles; he operates Awesome Lake Lodge in Labrador, is a former Hunting and Fishing Development Officer for Newfoundland and Labrador, and is a past representative of the Atlantic Salmon Federation.

Tom Richardson of Massachusetts is Managing Editor of *Salt Water Sportsman* magazine, as well as a freelance writer and photographer.

Al Ristori of New Jersey is Saltwater Fishing Editor of the *Newark Star-Ledger*, Regional Editor of *Salt Water Sportsman*, Conservation Editor of *The Fisherman* magazine, and the author of several books;

he is also a charter boat captain and has served on the Mid-Atlantic Fishery Management Council.

Jim Rizzuto of Hawaii is Hawaii Editor for *Salt Water Sportsman* and *Western Outdoors*, a longtime columnist for *West Hawaii Today* and *Hawaii Fishing News*, and the author of the books *Modern Hawaiian Gamefishing* and *Fishing Hawaii Style*.

Nels Rodefeld of Oklahoma is an avid angler and hunter who frequently covers Oklahoma's hunting and fishing scene.

Milt Rosko of New Jersey is a writer for *Big Game Fishing Journal* and various other publications and a longtime authority on saltwater sportfishing; he is a photographer, book author, magazine feature writer, and lecturer.

Terry Rudnick of Washington has been writing articles on Northwest fishing subjects for more than 25 years; he is the author of the book *Washington Fishing, the Complete Guide*, and co-author of *How to Catch Trophy Halibut*.

Bob Sampson, Jr. of Connecticut is a writer, photographer, science teacher, and fisheries biologist; his work has appeared in numerous national and regional magazines.

Jack Samson of New Mexico is the retired Editor-in-Chief of *Field & Stream* and a former Associated Press columnist; he is Saltwater Editor of *Fly Rod & Reel* magazine, author of twenty books, and the first angler to catch both Atlantic and Pacific sailfish and all five species of marlin on a fly.

Ray Sasser of Texas is the Outdoor Editor of *The Dallas Morning News* and a freelance contributor to various magazines; he has been writing about outdoor sports for over 25 years.

Carl Werner Schmidt-Luchs of Germany is a contributor to *Blinker*, the largest angling magazine in Europe; he is a photographer, writer, and author of a dozen angling books.

Kristen Schultz of Massachusetts is a writer who recently graduated from Oberlin College; she works for an engineering consulting firm.

Bill Scifres of Indiana has been the Outdoor Editor of the *Indianapolis Star* since 1953; he is a book author, freelance writer, and photographer.

Eric Sharp of Michigan is Outdoor Editor of *The Detroit News*, and was formerly Outdoor Editor of *The Miami Herald*.

Luis Sier of Argentina is a newspaper columnist, a former magazine publisher, and an outfitter who operates several Argentinian fishing camps.

Jeff Simpson of South Dakota is an information officer for the State of South Dakota, a book author and freelance magazine writer, and former project developer for Cowles Creative Publishing.

DeWayne Smith of Arizona is an information officer for the Maricopa County Parks and Recreation Department; he covered the outdoors for over 30 years for *The Phoenix Gazette*.

Ryan Smith of Virginia is a research assistant with the Department of Fisheries and Wildlife Sciences at Virginia Polytechnic Institute.

Michael Snook of Saskatchewan is a freelance writer, conservationist, outdoor educator, and television producer.

Frank Sousa of Massachusetts is a writer for the *Springfield Sunday Republican* and the *Union News*, Editor/Publisher of *Northeast Woods and Waters*, and a freelance writer and photographer.

Vin T. Sparano of New Jersey is Senior Field Editor and retired Editor-in-Chief of *Outdoor Life*, for whom he worked for over three decades; he is a former syndicated columnist for *Gannett Newspapers*, and the author/editor of fourteen books, including *The Complete Outdoors Encyclopedia*.

Vladimir Stakic of Yugoslavia is Deputy Editor-in-Chief of the Yugoslavian angling magazines *Ribolovacka Revija* and *Ribolovacke Novine*, a freelance writer, and the author of three books of short stories.

Bob Stearns of Florida has been the staff boating/saltwater fishing writer of *Field & Stream* for 20 years and is the Electronics Editor of *Salt Water Sportsman*; the author of two books, he is a renowned fly fishing and light tackle expert, and has held two fly rod world records for sailfish.

Larry Stone of Iowa has been a writer and photographer for over three decades, and writes about the outdoors for the *Des Moines Register*.

Keith Sutton of Arkansas is Editor of *Arkansas Wildlife magazine*, a conservation publication of the Arkansas Game & Fish Commission, and a prolific freelance writer and photographer.

Ferenc Szalay of Hungary is Editor-in-Chief of *Magyar Horgász*, Hungary's premier fishing magazine; he is also President of the Hungarian National Committee for Match Fishing and Executive Board member of the Federation Internationale de la Pêche Sportive en Eau Douce.

Allan Tarvid of Texas is a contributing editor for *Sport Fishing* magazine and has authored hundreds of articles on electronics for sporting and commercial fishing and emergency service use; he has been a fishing guide and search and rescue diver.

Rikk Taylor of British Columbia is Editor and Publisher of *British Columbia Sport Fishing* magazine.

Mick Thill of Illinois and England is one of the world's top professional match fishing anglers and the first and only person to medal in the open water and ice fishing World Freshwater Fishing Championships; he is also a prominent float designer, and coach of the U. S. World Championship fishing teams.

Albert A. W. Threadingham of Fiji is an IGFA

representative for the Fiji Islands and Governor of the Hawaiian International Billfish Association and the Pacific Ocean Research Foundation; he is a former world-record fish holder.

Raj Tilak of Maryland and India is co-author of the book *Game Fishes of India and Angling*, and author of more than 200 research publications; he is experienced in fisheries and wildlife management, with extensive knowledge of gamefishes and their ecology in India.

Anssi Uitti of Finland works for the Finnish outdoor magazine *Metsästys ja Kalastus*, and his articles have appeared in *Urheilukalastus* (Sportfishing) and *Perhokalastus* (Flyfishing) magazines.

Luis Umpierre of Puerto Rico is a physician, Editor of *Notipesca* (Fishing News), President of the Puerto Rico Sportfishing Association, and advisory member of the Caribbean Fishery Management Council.

Rudy Van Duijnhoven of Holland is a freelance photographer and author; his work appears monthly in *BEET-Sportvissers* magazine, and he is European Correspondent for Fly Fishing in *Salt Waters* magazine.

Carlo Vernocchi of Italy and Zanzibar introduced modern big-game fishing to the Zanzibar archipelago of Tanzania in 1992; he is an IGFA representative and charter boat captain.

Victor Villavicencio of Manila is a representative for the IGFA in the Philippines.

Tsutomu Wakabayashi of Japan is the General Manager of the Japan Game Fish Association; he has written for several Japanese fishing magazines, and is an IGFA representative.

Steve Waters of Florida is the outdoors writer for the *Fort Lauderdale Sun-Sentinel* and occasionally writes for national magazines; he was formerly a newspaper writer and video executive in New York.

Tom Wharton of Utah has been Outdoor Editor of the *Salt Lake Tribune* since 1976; he has co-authored five books, and is past President of the Outdoor Writers Association of America.

Jesse E. Williams of New Mexico is the retired Chief of Public Affairs for the New Mexico Department of Game and Fish, and a former Colorado wildlife manager and environmental education supervisor.

Juergen Willms of the Yukon Territory has worked with the Yukon Territory's Department of Natural Resources on various fishing projects.

Jorge Xifra of Paraguay operates El Pescador, a sportfishing outfitting service; he is a writer, television show host, IGFA representative, and holder of four world fishing records.

Photo Credits

All photographs by Ken Schultz except for the following:

Daiwa 103
Fin-Nor 173
Steve Goione 100
Bruce Holt 6, 8
Nick Karas 67
G. Loomis 115
Marado 105, 114
Penn Fishing Tackle 176, 186
Milt Rosko 168
Jack Samson 192, 194, 195
Travel Alberta 16
Zebco 106, 108, 110, 111, 113

A

ABEAM
A nautical term referring to an object that is to one side of a boat and at a right angle to the fore-and-aft line.

ABOARD
On board a boat; on or within a boat.

ACIDITY
The concentration of acid in water or in a solution as described by the pH *(see)* scale. The neutral value of pH is 7.0; the lower the pH value below 7.0, the greater the acidity. The acidity of a given body of water depends on various natural and man-made influences. Highly acidic water is intolerable to fish, and even moderate levels of acidity may reduce fish populations and adversely affect plants and other animals.

ACTION
"Action" is the term used to designate where a fishing rod flexes along its blank *(see)*.
See: Rod, Fishing.

ADIPOSE EYELID
A translucent tissue partially covering the eyeball of some species of fish.
See: Fish.

ADIPOSE FIN
A small fleshy fin without rays found on the back of some fish, behind the dorsal fin and ahead of the caudal fin. Only a small percentage of fish have an adipose fin; among gamefish these include various trout, salmon, grayling, whitefish, and piranhas.
See: Fish.

AERATOR
An aerator is a device that supplies oxygen to water, usually within a livewell, cooler, or some type of container that holds gamefish or live baitfish. As an item of fishing equipment, aerators are comprised of a pump that brings in fresh (raw) or recirculated water and splashes it onto standing water to both mix and oxygenate the water.
See: Livewell.

AFT
A nautical term meaning at or near the stern of a boat.

AIRBOAT
A flat-bottomed aluminum boat driven by a propeller revolving in the air, an airboat is primarily associated with travel in the swamps and saw grasses of the Everglades, where it is impossible to travel any distance in a quick manner in conventional boats. Some people use them to access hunting and fishing areas, although anglers often leave the boat and wade. Large airboats can accommodate several people and are used by some guides; wearing ear protection is advised, as the motors are extremely noisy.

Airboats have also been used on snow- and ice-covered lakes in the north to facilitate travel to and from places where there is an occasional need to cross (or the possibility of crossing) open water or unsafe ice, especially when the trip cannot be made in a boat sporting a lower unit or would be imprudent with an ATV or snowmobile.

AIRPLANE TEASER
A common term for a bird- or airplane-shaped teaser used in offshore fishing, especially for marlin and tuna.
See: Trolling Lures, Saltwater.

ALABAMA
Anglers looking for diversity, both in fish species and types of water, find it quickly in Alabama. The state has more than a million acres of freshwater open to fishing, including more than two dozen large man-made impoundments, seven major river systems, and 20 smaller state-managed lakes. In southern Alabama, the 400-square-mile Mobile Delta provides brackish water conditions, where freshwater and saltwater fish often swim together; and along the Gulf Coast, Mobile and Perdido Bays offer pier, jetty, and flats fishing as well as quick access to offshore opportunities.

The largemouth bass is easily the state's most popular freshwater species, and specimens over 16 pounds have been recorded. In northern Alabama, particularly in several Tennessee River impoundments, smallmouth bass fishing is rated among the best in the world. Spotted bass, black and white

crappie, white bass, several varieties of sunfish, and five species of catfish are present in lakes throughout the state; and in years past, Alabama held world records for both smallmouth and spotted bass. Additionally, striped bass and hybrid striped bass have been introduced successfully to a number of the larger impoundments.

In the brackish water of the delta, as well as in coastal bays, speckled trout, red drum (generally known locally as redfish), and flounder are present, while just offshore at various buoy markers and old oil rig platforms small-boat anglers and charter captains alike chase Spanish and king mackerel, cobia, grouper, amberjack, red snapper, and even an occasional tarpon. Farther offshore along the deep chasm known as DeSoto Canyon and the 100-fathom curve, marlin, wahoo, and sailfish can be taken.

This angling bounty, particularly in freshwater, is primarily the result of Alabama's generally mild weather. Although occasional snow may blanket portions of the state's northern counties, the water temperature remains warm enough to keep the fish active year-round. Additionally, the Tennessee River marks the northern limit of threadfin shad, the smallmouth's favorite prey, and the southern limit of naturally occurring smallmouth. The result is a river system with some of the most consistent trophy smallmouth fishing in the nation.

Freshwater

Tennessee River. With headwaters in northeast Tennessee, the Tennessee River flows southward and enters Alabama just south of Chattanooga. From there the river makes a westward loop through several northern Alabama counties, cuts through a corner of Mississippi, and reenters Tennessee. In Alabama, the Tennessee River has been dammed to form four large reservoirs containing more than 180,000 acres of water. These include Lakes Guntersville, Wheeler, Wilson, and Pickwick.

At 69,000 acres, Guntersville is the largest reservoir in the state. It enjoys an excellent reputation for its largemouth bass and crappie fishing, and during the early 1980s was considered one of America's top bass lakes. This reputation was largely the result of a heavy growth of Eurasian milfoil that infested much of the open water, as well as abundant stump and tree cover. An extensive aquatic vegetation eradication program by the Tennessee Valley Authority in the late 1980s, however, caused a significant decline in the quality of the bass fishery. Fortunately, as the vegetation has slowly regenerated, the fishery is likewise improving.

Wheeler, Wilson, and Pickwick Lakes are famous for their smallmouth bass fishing, particularly in the tailraces below each dam. A then-world record 10.8-pound smallmouth bass was caught in 1950 in the fast water below Wheeler Dam, and today 6- to 8-pounders are regularly caught in these waters each year.

A favorite fishing method in the tailraces is drifting live shad minnows downstream in the current, using spinning tackle, 6- to 10-pound line, and BB-size split shot for weight. The shad are simply hooked through the lips and then kept just above the rocky bottom as the boat drifts with the current. Anglers who learn to read the currents by observing water released from the dam and who steer their boats along the edges where the "slick" calmer water meets the faster flow, are consistently successful.

Other smallmouth techniques for drifting the tailraces include slowly trolling downstream with shallow-running crankbaits, bouncing jigging spoons along the bottom, and casting/drifting small $^{1}/_{8}$-ounce plastic grubs or hair jigs. Largemouth and spotted bass, white bass, catfish, and freshwater drum are also caught this way throughout the year; in winter, jig-drifting techniques often produce excellent sauger catches.

During the summer months, night fishing with spinnerbaits is another productive and popular angling technique for smallmouth. Although the fish remain in relatively deep water during the day, at night they move up on flats and bars less than 10 feet deep to feed. The best flats are those edged by deeper channels, and the most successful technique is usually a slow, steady rise-and-fall retrieve near the bottom.

In spring, channel catfish move onto the flats to spawn, producing excellent opportunities on Pickwick Lake. Most anglers use cut bait and simply anchor at the mouths of tributary creeks or shallow flats, out of the main current flow.

Coosa River. The Coosa River enters Alabama in the northeast corner of the state from Georgia and flows southward for about 175 miles to its confluence with the Tallapoosa River, near the capital city of Montgomery. There the two rivers become the Alabama River, which flows into the Gulf of Mexico.

The Coosa, like all major rivers in the state, has been dammed for flood control and electrical power. The resulting lakes include—from north to south—Weiss, Neely Henry, Logan Martin, Lay, Mitchell, and Jordan. Collectively, they are among the state's most heavily fished waters due to their proximity to Gadsden, Birmingham, and Montgomery. Nevertheless, they continue to provide excellent angling opportunities for Alabama's most popular species: largemouth bass and crappie.

Interestingly, however, three of the lakes have gained nationwide reputations for one particular species. Weiss Lake, especially, has been one of the South's premier crappie lakes for decades, and each spring anglers from as far away as Illinois and Indiana—to say nothing of hordes of locals—converge on the 30,200-acre impoundment to take home coolers full of the tasty panfish.

Live minnows fished under a float are the preferred bait, but many crappie are caught with small bucktail jigs. Crappie are also occasionally caught

by bass anglers fishing small crankbaits. The best places are shallow stump fields throughout the lake, shallow channel drops, wide flats in the tributary creeks, and logjams in the upper Coosa River. Although the majority of fish are caught in water 6 feet deep or less, most anglers use an adjustable float to present baits at different depths until the crappie are located.

While Neely Henry, an 11,200-acre impoundment immediately below Weiss Lake, offers very good bass and crappie fishing, the most well-known largemouth fishing lake on the Coosa chain is the third lake, Logan Martin. Here anglers will find a variety of water conditions, including river current, flats, tributary creeks, and major lake points, that provide year-round opportunities not only for largemouth but also for spotted, white, and hybrid striped bass, as well as for channel, flathead, and blue catfish.

All three fish can be very productive at certain times; spring is undoubtedly the best time, because bass, crappie, and catfish are moving shallow to spawn. Fall fishing is popular and productive as well, with spinnerbaits, crankbaits, and soft-plastic lures the favored choices.

Lake Jordan (pronounced "Jurdan" by many locals) is best known for its spotted bass population. At 6,900 acres it is the smallest of the Coosa River lakes, but it offers excellent combinations of deep and shallow water mixed with abundant rock and stump cover that make it ideal for spotted bass. Local anglers often do well fishing this cover from the shoreline, while others prowl the Coosa's various tributaries, particularly Welona, Weoka, Shoal, and Proctor Creeks.

Both spinning and baitcasting equipment are used for spotted bass, with soft-plastic worms, crankbaits, and spinnerbaits all popular and successful. Spotted bass, especially heavier ones, fight much harder than comparable-size largemouths, making heavier lines and rods somewhat more desirable. These fish tend to stay deeper than largemouths but are often more active.

Chattahoochee River. Along the Chattahoochee River, which forms the boundary between Alabama and Georgia for part of its length, anglers focus on two impoundments: West Point Lake and Lake Walter F. George, also known as Lake Eufaula. Only a small portion of West Point Lake is in Alabama.

After the lake's impoundment in 1974, West Point anglers enjoyed some of the finest largemouth bass fishing in the South, but this gradually changed as the lake's early boom cycle ended. As it declined, however, tens of thousands of hybrid striped bass were stocked in the mid-1980s, and not only did they thrive and create an entirely new sportfishery, their popularity took much of the angling pressure off largemouths.

Today the lake produces excellent catches of both species. Live-bait fishing is popular for both hybrids and largemouths, although artificial lures, especially crankbaits, continue to produce well. West Point does not have the well-defined creek and river channel structure so prevalent downriver on Eufaula, but it does have abundant flats and long, gently sloping points that seem to attract bass whenever water is released through the dam to produce electricity. This makes Carolina-rig fishing with short plastic worms and lizards a popular technique, and places like Wehadkee, Stroud, and Veasey Creeks are well known to every West Point angler.

Lake Eufaula was one of the earliest big-bass lakes in the nation and helped usher in the era of modern bass fishing. It enjoyed a resurgence in its largemouth bass fishing in the mid-1990s, although not quite comparable to its storied heyday of the late 1960s and early 1970s. However, good fishing today—along with many access sites, a national wildlife refuge, and various parks and public-use areas—makes this one of the more popular destinations for anglers from throughout the Southeast and Midwest.

Today, 10-pound and larger bass are caught each spring in Eufaula's tributary creeks, primarily with spinnerbaits and plastic worms. The most notable tributaries include Cowikee, Barbour, White Oak, and Pataula, all of which include different types of stump, brush, and vegetative cover, as well as steep-sided channel drops. Many creeks, coves, points, flats, and other good-looking spots to fish beckon along its 640 miles of shoreline. Crappie, white bass, and other species thrive here too.

This lake is 85 miles long, offering numerous places to explore. The northern sector, above Cowikee Creek, is riverine, whereas the southern sector is typical of impoundments, with wide-open areas. Created in 1963, Eufaula is a substantial hydroelectric and flood control reservoir; almost daily, current is created along the entire lake as power is generated or water is pulled for diversion.

An angler prepares to land a largemouth bass on Lake Eufaula.

A

Late winter and spring are especially popular with both local and visiting anglers, and are known for large bass. Frequent cold fronts make fishing unpredictable, however, with success dropping off dramatically until several days of stable conditions prevail.

Early in the season, especially when bass are spawning, anglers favor shallow flats, particularly those with stumps, brush rows, and vegetation. Although many of these are in major creeks, some are in the main lake—in the open-water sections—and extend for great distances. Another preferred area is along riprap banks. In mid- to late spring, bass move to river and creek ledges and deeper water, when anglers rely heavily on vertical spoon jigging and worm fishing.

Hybrid striper fishing kicks into gear in the summer, with good fishing in some locales (often the same daily) early and late in the day. Topwater activity is common in the fall, from hybrids as well as white bass and largemouths. The latter move shallower in the fall, and October and November provide good fishing again.

Some fish are capable of changing sex during their lives; some deep-dwelling fish possess both female and male sexual organs.

Tallapoosa River. The Tallapoosa includes two significant impoundments, Lakes Harris and Martin, that deserve careful fishing consideration. Harris has become one of eastern Alabama's better-known bass and crappie lakes, while Lake Martin is best known for its spotted bass.

When impounded in 1983, parts of Harris looked like a flooded forest, and it was this flooded timber that provided much-needed habitat for subsequent stockings of Florida-strain largemouths. Overall, the lake retains much of its original winding river configuration, with tributary creeks providing the flooded timber, flats, and backwater areas. Better catches are consistently reported around Fox, Hunter, and Wedowee Creeks, especially with plastic worms, jigs, spinnerbaits, and deep-diving crankbaits.

When viewing Lake Martin for the first time, many people are amazed by how closely it resembles lakes much farther north. The water is clear, and in the lower section there are dozens of tree-covered islands.

Here the spotted bass is king, and anglers work the rocky drops and island points with small plastic worms that require some finesse, and light lines, noisy topwater plugs, and, in colder weather, fast-moving spinnerbaits ripped along steep, rocky bluffs. The latter technique surprises many, yet it lures not only spotted bass but also largemouths up from deep water with vicious strikes.

Tombigbee, Warrior, and Alabama Rivers. These three rivers offer seven reservoirs, perhaps the best known being Lewis Smith Lake on the Warrior River near Cullman. Despite its deep, clear waters, Smith Lake produced a succession of world-record spotted bass, including an 8-pound, 15-ounce fish in 1978. A collection of Smith Lake spotted bass was then introduced into several California lakes, which a few years later produced the first 9-pound spotted bass on record.

Today Smith Lake rarely produces spotted bass larger than 7 pounds. One reason may be the introduction of a now thriving striped bass population. The debate over whether striped bass are eating all the forage formerly enjoyed by the spotted bass, or eating baby spotted bass fry, has raged ever since the stripers were introduced.

To catch big stripers, anglers drift live shad through deep channels, or present jigs and topwater plugs when the fish are surfacing in autumn. Most big spotted bass are caught in February and March as they move shallow to spawn, or at night by anglers familiar with the lake's many rocky coves and points.

The Tombigbee River was dammed and in some places dredged in the late 1970s by the U.S. Army Corps of Engineers to produce the Tennessee-Tombigbee Waterway, designed to open shipping and commerce between rural western Alabama and the Gulf of Mexico. In the process the Corps produced several lakes, including Columbus Lake in Mississippi, and Aliceville, Gainesville, and Demopolis Lakes in Alabama.

These impoundments, especially Aliceville, have produced outstanding bass fishing. Aliceville was stocked with Florida-strain bass in 1980 and nine years later produced two bass weighing more than 14 pounds. All three lakes offer large areas of shallow, weedy, or timber-filled backwater sloughs that provide excellent spawning habitat and are not affected by barge wakes in the main Tenn-Tom navigation channel. Topwater lures, spinnerbaits, and soft-plastic worms and lizards have produced well here, especially in the spring and fall.

Mobile Delta. The vast 400-square-mile Mobile Delta of southern Alabama offers a distinctly different type of fishing, albeit for the same popular species of largemouth bass, crappie, and sunfish. Anglers here, however, can also catch channel bass (redfish), flounder, or speckled trout in the lower portions of the delta, where its freshwater mixes with incoming saltwater from the Gulf of Mexico.

The delta extends approximately 40 miles northward of the Interstate Highway 10 Causeway Bridge. Several major rivers drain into this huge basin, along with numerous smaller streams. The result is a bewildering collection of look-alike waterways, shallow bays, and cypress- and gum-filled swamps. In addition, anglers here must contend with tidal fluctuations that will quickly turn a shallow bay into a mud flat.

Bass anglers in the delta use the same lures and techniques as elsewhere in the state. Notable hotspots include areas with such names as Big Lizard Creek, Twelve Mile Island, Negro Lake, Six Bits Creek, and Squirrel Bayou. Good delta maps are a must for any serious angler.

Public Lakes. Alabama's public lake program ranks among the best in the Southeast, with nearly two dozen small lakes created specifically by the Department of Natural Resources to provide fishing opportunities in areas not readily served by larger reservoirs. They are extremely popular among local anglers, and have been used as models for other state-sponsored public lake programs.

These public lakes are intensely managed for largemouth bass, crappie, flathead catfish, and redear sunfish (shellcrackers). Bass over 13 pounds have been caught in some of the lakes. Most do not allow outboard power, and while small boats may be available for rent, bank fishing has been encouraged by the construction of smooth access areas and piers, as well as special fish attractors within casting distance of the banks. The lakes, none of which is more than 200 acres in area, have a concessionaire on site to sell permits, tackle, and picnic supplies.

Saltwater

With only 5 miles of coastline bordering the gulf, one would expect Alabama's saltwater fishing to be nearly nonexistent, but such is not the case. As previously mentioned, anglers in the Mobile Delta regularly catch flounder, trout, and redfish; in fact, in early spring, bass anglers fishing the lower delta often have to stop using plastic worms because they are so often hit by flounder.

The bays. Alabama's primary saltwater opportunities include Mobile Bay, Perdido Bay, and the Gulf of Mexico. Mobile Bay offers fishing for the same popular inshore species found in the Mobile Delta. The most productive areas are private piers along the shoreline, which produce flounder consistently; and the oil and natural gas rigs, which are located in more open water. Much of the Mobile Bay floor is flat and featureless and doesn't hold many fish.

Plastic grubs like those used by freshwater anglers for bass are excellent for both flounder and speckled trout. Bait anglers use live shrimp or pinfish for both trout and redfish.

Perdido Bay, which is about 20 miles long—with numerous smaller cuts and bayous along its shoreline—runs along Alabama's southeastern tip and opens into the gulf at Alabama Point. The actual entrance to the gulf is quite small, which produces strong tidal currents, and here anglers enjoy some of the bay's best fishing. Redfish, speckled trout, grouper, and even Spanish mackerel and bluefish swim outside this cut; the most productive fishing takes place along both jetties that line the entrance into the bay.

The jetties can be fished on foot or by boat with both artificial lures or live and cut baits. Spoons are effective for both mackerel and bluefish; minnow-imitation jerkbaits catch trout; and redfish hit plastic grubs, especially when the hook is tipped with a piece of shrimp. Live shrimp can be fished under corks to take flounder, grouper, and an occasional redfish.

Gulf of Mexico. For many anglers, piers offer the first and easiest chance to fish saltwater, and there are several along the Alabama coast between the Mobile and gulf shores. The piers are open 24 hours and sell not only bait and tackle, but also refreshments for those who choose to stay longer than just a few hours. Croaker, flounder, and mackerel are taken most often, generally on various types of cut bait with sinker rigs that keep them close to the bottom.

More than 100 artificial reefs and piles of debris are scattered just off the Alabama gulf coast and within easy reach of small boats. These structures have Loran-C identification numbers and are pinpointed on nautical charts, thus offering anglers the opportunity to try for such species as amberjack, red snapper, cobia, and even sharks.

Party boats as well as deep-sea charters are available in each major city along the coast. With charters, anglers can make arrangements to stay inshore to fish the artificial reefs, or venture farther offshore. Inshore charters troll primarily for king mackerel, or work the bottom for red snapper, while offshore boats look for marlin, sailfish, wahoo, swordfish, and dolphin, which are usually present from late spring to early autumn. Generally, party boats and inshore/offshore charters provide all bait and tackle.

ALASKA

It was with good reason that the native peoples named this huge northern landmass *Alyeska*—The Great Land. With 586,412 square miles of total area, and more if the Aleutian Islands are included, Alaska is about one-fifth the size of the lower 48 states combined. Within that area is a bounty of more than 3,000 rivers, more than 3 million lakes, and some 34,000 miles of coastal shoreline—numbers that stagger the imagination, underscore the wealth of opportunities for anglers, and translate into some of North America's premier fishing.

Even though it has now been many decades since "modern" anglers first began exploring the state and probing its waters, much of today's Alaska remains a largely untamed wilderness. With more than 17,500 square miles of inland water alone, it is safe to say that even most longtime residents haven't fished all of what Alaska has to offer.

The Last Frontier, as this state is also known, provides very few roads and/or highway systems, so there is no ready access to many of the state's opportunities. Moreover, much of the state's better fishing is far from populated regions, so it is often necessary to travel great distances.

"Weather permitting," is an expression that holds much meaning for Alaskans, reinforcing the relative inaccessibility of the state's premier fishing locales, especially because so many sites are reached via boat or floatplane.

Anchorage's Lake Hood, the busiest floatplane base in the world, is emblematic of Alaska's

Anglers commonly but carefully share Alaskan streams, and fish, with brown bears.

continuing love affair with, and reliance upon, small, light, float-equipped aircraft. Floatplanes are virtual necessities for transporting anglers to various "bush" destinations. During summers, Alaskan skies are inundated with these small aircraft, a good percentage of which are bound for one of Alaska's premier fishing destinations.

Fortunately, small runways, if not airports, exist in the majority of Alaska's scattered towns and villages, with cities such as Anchorage, Kenai, Fairbanks, Nome, Kodiak, Juneau, and Ketchikan serving as hubs for traveling anglers.

So vast is Alaska that the Department of Fish and Game issues a separate regulations book for each of five regions. A first-time visitor would likely find the task of deciding where to go daunting. There are two ways to approach fishing in Alaska:

- Decide what species you want to fish for, then learn where and when these fish can be found and how to catch them.
- Decide what region you want to visit, then learn what fish are found there and when and where they're usually present.

Five of the six species of Pacific salmon (kings, reds, chums, pinks, and silvers) return to Alaska's freshwater each summer to spawn and are easily the main attractions for most visiting anglers. Substantial populations of rainbow trout, Dolly Varden, arctic charr, lake trout, arctic grayling, and northern pike also draw many anglers, and there are opportunities to catch cutthroat trout, inconnu (sheefish), and steelhead. In saltwater, halibut reign supreme, and Alaska annually produces not only plenty of these flatfish, but also gargantuan specimens. There's also fishing for other bottom dwellers, as well as some effort at catching saltchuck salmon.

Although Alaska has an abundance of waters and freshwater species, the popularity of the relatively few sites that are easily accessed has resulted in extreme pressures on them, and regulations necessarily have become more restrictive. Likewise, catch-and-release fishing—both voluntary and mandatory—has increased, particularly for rainbow trout and grayling. Most top lodges, guides, and outfitters—of which there are many here—practice and advocate this philosophy.

Anchorage: Highway-Accessible Fishing

Anglers traveling via automobile or motor home and operating on a modest budget can experience fair to excellent fishing via Alaska's limited roads and highways, but it won't be as seductive as the experiences provided by a professional pilot/lodge/guide, unless they're able to get far enough away from Alaska's often crowded, highway-accessible areas. Highway travelers will encounter a much greater number of competing anglers than people who fly into the bush.

In essence, there are two roads leading out of Anchorage. The northern road quickly branches in one direction toward Denali National Park via the Parks Highway, and in the other direction easterly through Glennallen to Tok and then to the Canadian border. The second highway heads south from Anchorage around Cook Inlet's Tumagain Arm and then curves up through the scenic Kenai Mountain Range, paralleling south-central Alaska's Kenai Peninsula.

Although limited camping spots are scattered along Alaskan highways, frequently—and especially during fishing seasons—the number of anglers and vacationers on Alaska's roads can be astounding. These highways, many of which have only two lanes, can become ultracongested with slow-moving motor homes and heavy traffic. On summer weekends these roads can be particularly crowded.

Fortunately for the stalwart angler, many smaller, partially paved, dirt and/or gravel trails of various configuration lead away from Alaska's outlying communities. Obtaining references from residents of such places is one way for auto travelers to discover decent fishing. In fact, float tube and canoe fishing opportunities are not difficult for auto travelers to find, and are more abundant than any individual can experience in a lifetime. Anglers with plenty of time and the desire to explore and search for good near-road fishing will find it.

Kenai Peninsula

Despite its vast number of annual visitors, the Kenai Peninsula, and particularly Alaska's prodigious Kenai River, continues to be one of the Last Frontier's top 20 angling destinations. This river is easily Alaska's best-known and most frequented fishery. The Kenai area is one of few in the state with relatively easy access to excellent, and varied, fishing within a short distance from a highway.

The Kenai River begins at Cooper Landing, at the outlet of picturesque, aqua blue Kenai Lake. It is approximately two hours by automobile south of Anchorage. All Kenai Peninsula streams and rivers eventually drain into the frigid saltwater of nearby Cook Inlet.

Beginning in late May, anglers find good to excellent fishing on the Kenai for king (chinook) salmon. Late June and early July generally signal the arrival of numbers of sockeye (red) salmon. In late July, pink (humpbacked) salmon appear, especially during even-numbered years, and in mid-August the first silver (coho) salmon enter the river. The Kenai also supports rainbow trout and Dolly Varden, and a smattering of whitefish; one or more of these species are present in many smaller nearby lakes and streams. In the fall, some of the southernmost Kenai Peninsula streams and rivers host a limited number of steelhead.

The Kenai River is suited to two fishing methods, with one method favored in the lower reaches, the other in the upper reaches. The lower Kenai is a large, deep, and somewhat smooth-flowing river—nearly an estuary at its lowermost parts. This region has the largest runs of the world's biggest strain of king salmon. Here, anglers mostly use spinning or conventional tackle while backtrolling *(see)* from drifting or idling powerboats. In contrast, the upper Kenai is broken and swift flowing, and offers superior rainbow trout, sockeye salmon, Dolly Varden, and silver salmon fishing. These somewhat shallower and swifter currents lend themselves to drift boat and inflatable raft fishing. Anglers typically climb out, secure their craft, and fish from sandbars, or wade. The upper Kenai parallels Sterling Highway in several places, and it's common to see travelers lined up along the roadside, gazing down on inflatable rafts filled with anglers. The waters of the upper Kenai are an unparalleled aqua blue, and owe their distinctive coloration to a blend of ultraclear tributaries with others bearing millions of minuscule particles of silt-laden glacial runoff. There is also a middle section of the Kenai—the area just below Skilak Lake and downstream to Sterling—but it contains difficult-to-negotiate, turbulent areas (especially at and around Naptowne Rapids), where anglers are advised to use a professional guide.

As mentioned earlier, the lower Kenai River is world famous for its strong summer runs of Pacific salmon, particularly for double runs of both king and sockeye salmon, and for outsized kings that haul like a runaway freight train. This is universally the foremost spot for monster king salmon; most of the International Game Fish Association's (IGFA) line-class world records were established here. Each year, especially during June and July, many thousands of visitors arrive from all over to experience this site, some with dreams of breaking its all-tackle 97-pound, 4-ounce chinook salmon record. The majority of those who fish here during the king salmon run are nonresidents, but this trend reverses when the sockeye are in.

At times anglers line the banks of the lower Kenai River in astounding numbers. It's also common to see numerous boats on the Kenai; especially on the lower river during June and July, boat traffic can be bumper to bumper.

Several excellent lakes exist on the Kenai Peninsula. Kenai, Hidden, Crescent, and Jean Lakes are just a few, and they offer reasonably good to excellent fishing. Some Kenai Peninsula lakes are reachable by foot after a few hours of hiking. Anglers with less time or hiking interest can access some lakes by floatplane.

Perhaps a handful of peninsula streams feature good numbers of Dolly Varden, particularly during late summer. One is the famed Russian River, which joins the Kenai where the state ferry crosses. The Russian is considered one of the prettiest flows in all of Alaska. When it is not too crowded with anglers, the river can produce superlative rainbow trout and sockeye fishing. The Moose River at Sterling, and the Swanson River and Lakes system farther south, also offer excellent fishing. Other respected and frequented flows on the Kenai Peninsula are Kasilof River, Deep Creek, Anchor River, and Upper and Lower Russian Lakes.

For saltwater aficionados, the ports of Homer, Seward, and Whittier are departure sites for saltwater salmon, halibut, lingcod, salmon shark, and rockfish angling. All three are commercial fishing centers, and, in season, Dungeness and Alaska king crab may be available here. Halibut is the main interest, however; Homer calls itself the "Halibut Capital of the World," and Cook Inlet has produced monster fish, including line-class world records. Around Deep Creek and Ninilchik, halibut anglers launch in surf to reach the fishing grounds.

The Kenai Peninsula is replete with fishing lodges and services, and several stores and smaller shops that cater to travelers have sprung up along its highways, beginning at Cooper Landing and extending down to Sterling, Soldotna, and Kenai where anglers can procure food, gasoline, lodging, and sundry items, as well as flies, lures, and fishing tackle.

Susitna River Drainage

The mouth of the big, burly, and seemingly always silty Susitna River, which empties into Cook Inlet northwest of Anchorage, is a culmination of several diverse and interesting south-central Alaska tributaries, all of which drain to the ocean via the "Big Su" amidst one of the most awe-inspiring backdrops in Alaska: Mt. McKinley and the majestic, snowcapped Alaska Range. This is easily among the most breathtaking mountain scenery in the state. People commonly refer to the Susitna River as the "Big Su" because it's an unmistakable landmark, especially from the vantage of an airplane. It's one of those rivers you just can't help noticing.

Several miles upstream from where the Big Su

When spawning, big Alaskan king salmon turn crimson and seek out shallow gravel bars.

meets saltwater, it is fed by the formidable Yentna River, which, in turn, is fed by the sizable and swift-flowing Skwentna River. The Skwentna is a paradox in that it is frequently extremely silty, but remains an important and productive south-central Alaska sportfishery.

A few miles upstream are two of this region's jewels. The first of these is the remarkably clear-flowing and lovely Talachulitna River, or Tal, as it's commonly called. This crystalline combination of lovely dry-fly pocket water and cascading riffles plays host to kings, chums, sockeyes, silvers, pinks, Dollies, grayling, and many distinctively spotted rainbow trout. The second is nearby Lake Creek, a virtual twin to the Tal, located across the canyon and downstream a few miles. It yields fair to good numbers of kings, chums, sockeyes, pinks, silvers, rainbows, and grayling, as well as some Dollies.

Extending northeast and northwest from Anchorage, Alaska's Matanuska and Susitna Valleys are dotted with myriad lakes of varying sizes, several of which are suitable for float-tube fishing. Numerous smaller, less-frequented but entirely fishable wilderness streams are scattered throughout this region.

Alexander Lake is representative of several swampy, low-lying areas in the Susitna drainage region where good to excellent northern pike fishing exists. Nearby Hewitt Lake and Fish Lake are other good, fairly easily accessed spots for pike fishing. Other respected waters in this region include Little Susitna River, Theodore River, Deshka River, Chulitna River, Talkeetna River and its tributaries, and Lake Louise, which is part of the Tyone River system located slightly farther to the east.

Although anglers can reach several Susitna drainage waters by automobile via the George Parks Highway, several others are best accessed via boat or floatplane. Two benefits of fishing in south-central Alaska are the area's mild climate relative to other places across the state, and its proximity to Anchorage. Although they are scattered, frequently rustic, and oftentimes accessible only via boat or floatplane, numerous fishing lodges and services exist along the banks of several of the area's waters.

Katmai Region

Covering an area larger than the state of Connecticut, Katmai is a vast, exceptionally beautiful region, graced with myriad pristine lakes and clear-flowing, untamed rivers and streams.

King Salmon, located about 275 miles southwest of Anchorage, is the gateway to famed Katmai National Park and Preserve and also the Brooks River, easily one of the loveliest, most frequented, and most photographed wilderness flows in all of The Great Land. There are typically many Alaskan brown bears at Brooks Falls—approximately midpoint on the river—attracting well over half of all of those who journey from points around the globe to visit these two sites.

The Valley of Ten Thousand Smokes, which was volcanically active in 1912 when Mount Katmai blew its top and when thousands of steam vents suddenly appeared across the region, is another favorite attraction for visitors, whether fishing is on their agendas or not.

Access to Brooks Camp and the Brooks River is primarily via floatplane, although at least one charter boat operation affords access to Brooks via a two-hour upstream journey against the formidable currents of the Naknek River.

The Brooks River, which connects Brooks and Naknek Lakes, is just $1^1/_2$ miles long. However, with its ultraclear waters, beautiful and lush mountain backdrops, and leaping salmon at picturesque Brooks Falls beginning in July, plus numbers of Alaskan brown bears roaming the banks, the Brooks is not only one of the most scenic rivers in the state, but also one of Alaska's most productive and revered fisheries.

Catch-and-release fishing is largely the name of the game on the Brooks, where rainbow trout, grayling, lake trout, sockeye salmon, and silver salmon are the main attractions. However, of the visitors who experience Brooks Camp each summer, more than half are strictly bear viewers and photographers. The Brooks Camp concession, which is less than half a mile from the river and has operated since 1950, offers visitors buffet meals, hot showers, and limited rental cabins. Two major bear viewing platforms, both of which have been improved and enlarged, are set along the banks.

The region has excellent numbers of lake trout, rainbow trout, Dolly Varden, arctic charr, arctic grayling, and four species of Pacific salmon, available according to season. The numerous fishing lodges in Katmai are at highly commendable sites. One of these is where the Kulik River spills into sizable Nonvianuk Lake, and the other is in the stretch between pristine Colville and Grosvenor Lakes. In season, fishing in these locations can be a virtual panacea, especially for fly anglers.

Other notable waters in the region include American Creek, Naknek Lake's Bay of Isles, and the prodigious Naknek River. Several smaller, lesser-known streams here are excellent in season.

At the northernmost boundary of Katmai National Park is the big, wild, and extremely fertile Alagnak, or Branch, River. This meanders roughly 70 miles across a big, rolling tundra before it eventually joins the Kvichak River (the outlet of Lake Iliamna to the north), some 4 or 5 miles upstream of where the now-combined flow empties into Bristol Bay.

The Alagnak, which drains both Nonvianuk and Kukaklek Lakes, offers excellent fishing with a variety of tackle, and superb fly fishing. The braids of the Alagnak, a wild and varied 25-mile-long midsection stretch of broken and ribboned water, is an especially sought-after location. Anglers prefer the lower portions of the Alagnak for salmon; trout and grayling anglers venture farther upstream. Of late, overuse on the Alagnak River has spurred greater limitations on drift permits. Accompanying the rise in regulatory efforts are stricter catch-and-release policies as well, but lodges here have not experienced a significant drop in clientele because of this.

Lake Clark/Lake Iliamna Region

With some 20-plus world-class flows all draining into one exceptionally large inland body of water, it's no wonder Alaska's Lake Clark/Lake Iliamna region is famous worldwide, earning a strong reputation as one of Alaska's premier fisheries. Like many of Alaska's preferred sportfishing regions, however, Iliamna's extremely wild, untamed, and remote landscape is largely floatplane country.

Alaska's largest lake, Iliamna covers 1,022 square miles, yet few boats are seen here, in part because of its reputation for sudden and dangerously high winds. Iliamna is so large that it creates its own weather patterns, and with so much big water flowing into it, anglers focus their attention on the rivers.

Iliamna's major tributary, the Newhalen River, drains Lake Clark to the north and ranks as one of the most productive salmon and trout fisheries in all of Alaska. In July, the number of sockeyes in the Newhalen can be astounding, second only to that in the Kvichak River, which is Iliamna's outlet and connects directly to Bristol Bay.

Over the years, such flows as Lower and Upper Talarik Creeks, Gibraltar, Dream Creek, the Copper River, the Iliamna River, the Tazimina River, the Kvichak, and the Newhalen have all received widespread attention, drawing a lot of anglers for excellent trout, grayling, charr, and salmon fishing. A handful of smaller and lesser-known streams in the region are just as productive as the more well-known locations, and these have generally remained anonymous to prevent over-crowding and excessive pressure.

Although a mere 250 miles from Anchorage, this area is wild and desolate, and the weather can be highly unpredictable. Most visiting anglers require lodge, guiding, and outfitting services, which are scattered throughout the region, particularly on Iliamna's northern shores.

Alaska Peninsula

One of North America's last sportfishing frontiers, the Alaska Peninsula easily ranks as one of the most wild, remote, and difficult-to-access fishing regions in all of The Great Land. Although its geographical beginnings lie only several hundred miles southwest of Anchorage, typical weather patterns across Shelikof Strait frequently keep the majority of Alaska's pilots, private and commercial, well at bay.

"The Peninsula," as it is known, has miles upon miles of lonely wilderness rivers and streams to explore. It also has miles upon miles of wilderness beaches, where visitors can discover such things as Japanese glass fishing floats and bleached-out whale carcasses. Aniakchak Crater, which erupted in 1931, thus creating Surprise Lake in Aniakchak National Monument and Preserve, lies in this region.

Few anglers have tread this largely untouched and untamed region, but many of those who have fished here are compelled to return. Imagine a small aircraft secured by ropes against possible rough winds and parked not far from a wilderness stream. The backdrop: arguably the most formidable and rugged mountains on earth. This is the Alaska Peninsula experience, yet only recently have anglers begun to appreciate this undisturbed region of Alaska and the quality of its fishing (it has long been recognized for trophy Alaskan brown bear and moose hunting). The peninsula boasts some of the best charr and Pacific salmon fishing in the state, as well as excellent steelhead angling.

The better waters of the Alaska Peninsula include Becharof Lake, the Ugashik Lakes, Ugashik Narrows, King Salmon River, Painter Creek, Cinder River, Sandy River, Wildman Lake, Meshik River, and Chignik River. There's also good fishing in various streams and rivers extending all the way to Dutch Harbor and Unalaska in the Aleutian Islands, both located at the extreme far end of the Alaska Peninsula and offering outstanding saltwater and estuary angling opportunities.

The Alaska Peninsula is a terrific halibut angling

site, and in recent times Unalaska Island has been the focal point of a growing sportfishery. Waters around Unalaska have produced numerous halibut over 300 pounds, including record-class fish of 395, 440, and 459 pounds, the latter an all-tackle world record.

The peninsula is known for severe wind and weather conditions, and only a handful of fishing services and lodges exist throughout the region.

Wood River/Tikchik Lakes Region

This highly respected southwestern Alaska fishery consists of approximately a dozen interconnected lakes and their clear-flowing tributaries, which are primarily accessed via Dillingham. The Wood River, located at the southerly end of this lake system, is the major drainage in the area and connects the lakes to the formidable Nushagak River, which empties into Bristol Bay.

The primary flows include the Agulowak, which links Lake Nerka with Lake Aleknagik; the Agulukpak, connecting Lakes Beverly and Nerka; and the lovely Wind and Peace Rivers to the north. These and numerous lesser-known streams provide exceptional wade and drift fishing amid unsurpassed scenery, including steeply descending, cascading waterfalls in northernmost portions.

While northern pike fishing is excellent in the bays of many of the region's major lakes (spots where anglers rarely probe), the major attraction to the Wood River/Tikchik Lakes Region is the exceptional stream angling, especially dry-fly fishing. This is because of easy-to-wade waters, clear-flowing streams, and plenty of rainbow trout, grayling, arctic charr, and Dolly Varden. Strong runs of Pacific salmon frequent these streams as well.

Some area lakes boast superb arctic charr and Dolly Varden, taken by anglers who drift in boats and cast smolt and streamer imitations on sinking lines. Frequently, swarms of arctic terns and seagulls, which swoop to the surface to snatch an easy meal, best indicate where and when to begin casting to schools of charr.

The famed Togiak River, which meanders to Bristol Bay and partially drains the Togiak National Wildlife Refuge, is known for exceptional rainbow trout and silver salmon fishing. Anglers access the river mainly via flights from Dillingham to the village of Togiak. The Aniak River, which is best accessed by flying directly from Anchorage to the village of Aniak, is another highly respected flow in this portion of the state, and it is great rafting water. Several other lesser-known, smaller wilderness rivers and streams run through this region, many of them difficult to access without a professional guide/pilot.

Fishing lodges are scattered throughout southwestern Alaska and the Wood River/Tikchik Lakes Region.

Western Region

Located about 420 miles southwest of Anchorage, and descending to the saltwaters of Kuskokwim Bay, is the immense, rolling, wilderness region widely referred to as Western Alaska, one of the Last Frontier's better sportfishing destinations.

Two of the main attractions in this difficult-to-access area are the Goodnews and Kanektok Rivers. Both originate high in the vast Togiak National Wildlife Refuge and drain westerly through 80 miles of untouched Alaskan wilderness before eventually meeting Kuskokwim Bay and the Bering Sea—the Goodnews at the native village of Goodnews Bay, and the Kanektok at the native village of Quinhagak. In addition, several smaller, exceedingly difficult-to-access streams entice a small number of adventurous anglers. Rainbow trout, Dolly Varden, grayling, and all five species of Pacific salmon are common to this area.

Western Alaska is a vast, rolling, descending wilderness region that is best experienced from a competent, seasoned lodge/tent camp with the necessary boats and equipment. Their experienced, professional guides are familiar with the territory. Not only have they learned the various and always changing river and stream channels and surrounding terrains, they are also accustomed to interacting with indigenous peoples often encountered here.

Although it may be possible to access this region directly from Anchorage, the normal hub is Bethel.

Kodiak Island

For years Kodiak Island was known for brown bear hunting and commercial fishing, but during the 1990s it earned a well-deserved sportfishing reputation.

This 115-mile-long island is about 275 miles south of Anchorage. Typically, commercial flights from Anchorage transport anglers to the city of Kodiak, an established commercial fishing port on the northeast corner of the island. From there, numerous air services fly anglers to the island's streams and rivers.

A road system leading from the city extends to some half-dozen good to excellent drive-to rivers and streams with the potential for better than decent salmon and charr angling. Among these are Buskin River, American River, Sargent Creek, Olds River, Chiniak River, and Pasagshak River.

Of all the excellent wilderness flows on Kodiak Island, the Karluk River, which drains Karluk Lake and winds some 22 miles to the salt at Tanglefoot Bay, is the island's premier attraction and draws the most anglers, who journey to the Karluk from around the globe.

The river is accessible only by boat or aircraft. There are very few small, scattered trails in this area, although a midriver access point, called Portage, is reachable via a 5-mile hike from Larsen Bay. King, sockeye, and silver salmon, plus steelhead, rainbow trout, and chrome-bright Dolly Varden, are the favored species.

The tidally influenced Karluk is wide, fairly

shallow, and relatively easy to wade, making it an excellent site for fly fishing. Lodging along the Karluk is extremely limited, however. Recently, various native groups have begun charging a per diem fee to Alaskan residents and out-of-state anglers alike.

The Ayakkulik ("Red") River, located about 80 miles southwest of the city of Kodiak, is another highly notable fishery accessible only via floatplane or helicopter. Renowned especially for excellent September silver salmon fishing, the Ayakkulik also receives good numbers of October and November steelhead. In summer, Dollies, sockeyes, and pink salmon are usually also abundant.

The Fraser River (also known as the Dog Salmon River), which empties into Olga Bay at the far southwest corner of the island, is another attractive Kodiak flow with strong runs of red, pink, and silver salmon, as well as a major run of chum salmon.

Brown bears are frequently encountered in many places across Kodiak Island but especially in drainages that host Pacific salmon. Presently, only a handful of scattered small to medium-size lodges and fishing operations exist on Kodiak Island, most of them in the proximity of saltwater coves, bays, and lagoons that also attract commercial fishing ventures. These waters support abundant halibut, with the potential for huge specimens.

Southeast Region

A maze of picturesque and pristine islands, canals, coves, and saltwater bays extends along the southern boundaries of the Tongass National Forest in Southeast Alaska, an area frequently called Alaska's Panhandle. Weather permitting, its waters can be both a freshwater and saltwater angler's delight.

In this immensely forested region, a backpacker—or those anxious to get away from crowds—may easily do so. It is not a do-it-yourself fishing region, however; extreme tidal fluctuations and frequently inclement weather make it prudent to use the services of an established lodge or outfitter, preferably one who resides in the particular area you want to fish.

In good weather, many places in Southeast Alaska can be especially scenic; typically, however, comparatively frequent rains make it far wetter and less inviting than much of the remainder of the state. Temperatures are usually modest in comparison with those in Alaska proper, yet one similarity exists: There are very few roads in this region. Floatplanes and boats provide the majority of access.

The Situk River—a tidally influenced flow featuring kings, reds, silvers, steelhead, and sea-run Dolly Varden—is a few miles from Yakutat, to the north, and is one of the region's better-known and respected fishing sites. However, several less-frequented but excellent wilderness streams and rivers crisscross the region, carving through the thickly carpeted Tongass National Forest to the Gulf of Alaska.

Prince of Wales Island, which lies in the southerly part of the region, across Clarence Strait from Ketchikan, is one of Southeast Alaska's premier locales for those who wish to experience a wide array of angling opportunities using all types of fishing techniques. Several excellent freshwater streams exist on Prince of Wales Island; chief among these are the Thorne, Karta, Klawock, and Sarkar. Chum, pink, and silver salmon, plus steelhead, some indigenous rainbows, sea-run Dolly Varden, and sea-run cutthroat trout make up the island's principal freshwater attractions.

Not to be overlooked throughout this region are saltwater angling opportunities. Halibut, lingcod, and mint-bright, migrating Pacific salmon are the leading marine quarries. Halibut fishing here is unsurpassed. Rich halibut fishing grounds are within easy reach of the Southeast Alaska towns of Ketchikan, Wrangell, Petersburg, Sitka, Juneau, and Yakutat, and many of the biggest specimens, as well as existing line-class world records, have been produced in the region.

Sea-run salmon are caught by boaters drifting or trolling in the coves and bays, and these bright sea lice–fresh fish are as hard-fighting as any salmon an angler will encounter.

Paradoxically, as remote as this area is, Southeast Alaska is easily reached via commercial airliner. Widespread cities extend along the entire southeast and include Juneau, Sitka, Ketchikan, Yakutat, Petersburg, Wrangell, and Craig, all of which are accessible by air and only some of which require connecting flights. There is ferry service to some locations as well. One interesting and popularly accessed site is at Blind Slough near Petersburg, on Mitkof Island.

Interpretations of Egyptian wall paintings indicate that fishing for fun was practiced in the period from 2470–2320 B.C.

Southeast Alaska offers exceptional photographic opportunities. The area is replete with scenic splendor, and sightings of bald eagles, whales, sea otters, and myriad sea life are common. Many of the streams here flow cold and crystal clear, so a pair of lightweight gloves and a hat will help maintain body temperature, especially during morning and evening fishing forays. And don't forget rain gear.

Fairbanks Region

A handful of fair to good rivers and streams exist in the Fairbanks region; some of these are accessible via either gravel or paved roads, while others are accessible only via floatplane or boat. Two highways extend northerly from Fairbanks. The Steese Highway, which runs northeast some 140 miles to Circle, parallels the Upper Chatanika River for approximately 70 miles. The Livengood Road, a dirt and gravel road that runs northwesterly, crosses several noteworthy streams, among which are the Chatanika River, Washington Creek, the Tatalina River, the Tolovana, and the Hutlinana. These feature good grayling, decent salmon, and excellent Dolly Varden fishing at various times of the year. Some area waters hold small to medium-size sheefish. Minto Flats, a group of stillwater swamps and sloughs about 40 miles northwest of Fairbanks, is reached via the Livengood Road and is one of Alaska's premier sites for northern pike.

All of the streams nearer the road are fairly heavily fished, so hiking in some distance can greatly increase an angler's chance of encountering less human competition. The Livengood Road terminates at Manley Hot Springs, where boats are available for rent to those anglers wishing to pursue northern pike in nearby sloughs.

Two main rivers extend through the city of Fairbanks: the Tanana River, which is a large, deep, glacially influenced flow, and the Chena, which runs clearer and merges with the Tanana. Both are commonly used by boaters from the Fairbanks area. Closer to Fairbanks, the Chena runs slow and deep; its mid- and upper portions, especially the north fork, are much more attractive. A modicum of kings, a smattering of chums, myriad grayling, some burbot, and lots of pike constitute the majority of the Chena's angling opportunities.

Yukon-Tanana Drainage

This enormous region, extending all the way from the Brooks Range in the north to the Alaska Range in the south, and from the Canadian border in the east to the Bering Sea in the west, is among Alaska's least-frequently visited fisheries. Its enormity is blamed for its lack of appeal. Fortunately, however, many of its fishable waters are in the eastern portion, where adequate road access does exist.

Among the overlooked rivers, for example, is the Nation River,—an excellent kayaking flow that joins the Yukon River some 30 miles west of the Canadian border after meandering through prime big-game country (e.g., moose, caribou, Dall sheep, bears, and wolves). It is among the most-respected record arctic grayling water in all of Alaska, yet because of its distance from populated areas, it remains a little-known river.

The mighty Yukon River—which flows westerly for more than 1,300 miles through the state of Alaska to the Bering Sea, where there is an 80-mile-wide delta—does not get significant angling attention. In a state with so many other places that are less foreboding and simpler to fish, and that offer more services, this is easy to understand. Despite its numbers of king, sockeye, and silver salmon, as well as grayling, sheefish, and pike, the Yukon is considered too silty, too deep in many places and too shallow to navigate in others, or simply too wide to be a prime Alaskan sportfishery. A few intrepid anglers do explore portions of the Yukon, however, and it is known that prodigious numbers of pike—some of them huge—inhabit the sloughs and backwaters along the river as well as its large tributaries.

In fact, anglers devote more attention to the Yukon's numerous tributaries. The majority of these are clear-running, and many offer good to excellent angling. The Charley, the Kandik, and the Tatonduk are examples of little-frequented wilderness Yukon tributaries that have excellent grayling, sheefish, and pike fishing. This area is an intriguing, though wild and highly diverse component of the state, where everything from pike in slack water to arctic grayling in ultraclear dry-fly pocket water may be encountered.

Spending a week floating with a professional outfitter down the Yukon from Eagle, Alaska, to Circle would provide ample opportunity to catch various species while experiencing a multitude of river environments and thus employing diverse angling tactics. Such an adventure might afford a glimpse into Alaska's mining history, and particularly its Klondike gold rush days—especially if you ventured into the river's tributaries.

For many individuals, it is the Yukon's salmon that inspire and awe and wonder. Some of these fish struggle more than 2,000 miles upstream, often through extremely strong currents, before they begin to spawn.

Seward Peninsula/Norton Sound

Nome and the Seward Peninsula are storied gold rush country, but this is also a region with superb fishing opportunities. Here, the grayling, chum salmon, silver salmon, and Dolly Varden angling is often excellent. Trophy northern pike abound in many surrounding lakes and at sloughs off several of the main flows.

Although remoteness can easily be found, numerous local mining roads enable fairly easy access to fishing sites scattered about this region's periphery. Three main roads out of Nome provide auto access to many of its waters. One road leads to Teller, another to Taylor, and the third to Council. Excellent area streams include the Nome River, Eldorado Creek, the Pilgrim River, and the Sinuk River; all are home to grayling, pike, silver salmon, and charr.

The vicinity of Norton Sound teems with several Pacific salmon species, but few anglers ever experience these waters due to its remoteness. About 80 miles east of Nome is the Fish River, which drains into Norton Sound at Golovin Bay. Beginning in midsummer, this flowage can be an angler's paradise. Grayling, silver salmon, and charr are the river's leading species, although pinks and chums are generally present, too. Plenty of pike, including trophy specimens, thrive in the weeds near main river channels and also in the many backwater sloughs. The village of White Mountain is not only a favored rest stop for mushers competing in Alaska's annual sled-dog race, the Iditarod, but it is also a jumping-off site for anglers headed to the Fish/Niukluk drainage, as supplies and guides are available there.

Eastward about 40 miles or so are three notable fishing rivers: the Kwiniuk, which has an abundance of salmon, charr, and grayling; the fairly remote Shaktoolik, known for its grayling, charr,

pink, chum, and silver salmon; and the usually clear-flowing Unalakleet River, which is largely accessible by boat, originates from the village of Unalakleet, and boasts all five salmon species as well as charr, grayling, and northern pike.

Nome, White Mountain, and Unalakleet provide offbeat, adventurous backcountry angling experiences. Choices of guides and outfitters are typically few and far between, although the native guides generally know the rivers intimately.

Northwest Region

In this lightly visited corner of the state, also referred to as the Arctic region, three of Alaska's major rivers—the Kobuk, the Selawik, and the Noatak—nearly converge as they complete their westward flow and eventually drain into Kotzebue Sound near the village of the same name. All three are premier fishing sites, and wind through largely treeless country on a long, meandering, wilderness journey. The Selawik is a large, deep, typically smooth-flowing drainage best known for big sheefish and pike. The Noatak is known mostly for remoteness, scenery, and substantial numbers of dime-bright Dolly Varden, charr, and grayling. The Kobuk, which features chum salmon, Dolly Varden, grayling, sheefish, and pike, is a bit of a mixture of the other two and is considered one of the state's better sheefish waters.

The Wulik River meets the Chukchi Sea approximately 40 miles north of Kotzebue near Kivalina. This is a premier Alaskan sea-run Dolly Varden river. The region also includes several extremely remote lakes.

Migratory sheefish—or tarpon of the north, as they are called (even though they aren't aerial, as their lofty nickname would suggest)—do at times put up a good thrashing, especially as they come to hand or net. They can grow to more than 50 pounds, but typical sheefish specimens weigh 7 or 8 pounds. Although the official Alaska state record sheefish, caught in 1986 on the Pah River, weighed 53 pounds, natives of the villages scattered throughout this region suggest that a new record inconnu is possible here.

The village of Selawik is an excellent source of local guides, as is Kotzebue, which is located at saltwater's edge. However, finding an experienced pilot who has the appropriate plane and also knows the region (as well as the habits and likely whereabouts of sheefish), might be a challenge, although several air services exist in the Kotzebue area.

As with other regions, the only practical means of transportation is the floatplane, as there are very few roads. Several scattered towns and villages lie along the banks of the wild Koyukuk River, a couple of hundred miles farther inland to the east, as well as on the Kobuk River and farther south on the Yukon. Anglers who fly into the region from Anchorage or Fairbanks rest up and resupply at Bettles, McGrath, Galena, or Kivalina before venturing out to the Kobuk or the Noatak, or to other wilderness fishing sites. For the most part, anglers have most of this wide-open country to themselves, perhaps shared with a grizzly bear here and there and some moose.

The Brooks Range

Of all angling destinations in The Great Land, none is less frequented or more distant from populated areas than the remote Brooks Range, that 700-mile-long, east-west extension of the Rocky Mountains consisting of steep, sparse, scenic mountains and extremely wide-open places. It's a virtually treeless mountain range that separates Alaska's oil-rich north slope from the Yukon River Valley.

Most access to this region is via airplane from Bettles, Fairbanks, or Fort Yukon. Services and facilities are extremely limited. The majority of Brooks Range inhabitants, who are oil company employees, access the region either via the James Dalton Highway or local air-taxi from Barrow. Although summer days are exceptionally long and generally cool, the arctic summer season itself is relatively short, and its harsh weather conditions are notorious.

The Panama Canal, known for inter-ocean boat passage, enabled tarpon to move from the Atlantic to the Pacific, where they previously did not exist but are now established.

The Brooks Range is best known for Dall-sheep and caribou hunting, not for fishing, although there's excellent grayling, lake trout, and arctic charr angling in several of the region's remote streams and lakes. Some rivers and streams on the northernmost slopes, which drain to the Beaufort Sea, receive good numbers of sea-run Dolly Varden, as well as a smattering of chum and pink salmon. Anglers will not find king salmon, sockeye salmon, or silver salmon in Alaska's Arctic Slope; however, Dolly Varden, Arctic charr, lake trout, and grayling fishing in this region is often very good and wondrously scenic.

Some notable charr streams in the Brooks Range include the Chandler, Killik, Anaktuvuk, and Hulahula Rivers. Schrader, Porcupine, and Chandler Lakes, plus the Anaktuvuk River Lakes and Etivluk River Lakes, are all known for excellent lake trout fishing. The Jim River, Colville River, and Sagavanirktok produce good grayling fishing, but there are many such waters on either slope.

ALBACORE *Thunnus alalunga.*

Other names—longfin tuna, long-finned tunny, longfin, true albacore, albacore tuna, albie; German: pigfish; French: *germon;* Hawaiian: *âhi pahala;* Japanese: *binchô, binnaga;* Portuguese: *albacora;* Spanish: *albacora, atún blanco.*

A member of the Scombridae family of tuna and mackerel, the albacore is an excellent light-tackle gamefish. Its profitability and quality as a commercial fish, and its popularity as a gamefish, make it one of the most valuable fish in the United States. Called the "chicken of the sea" because of its white meat, the albacore is commercially harvested in

Albacore

large quantities and marketed fresh, smoked, deep-frozen, and canned. It is called true albacore in some places, not to be confused with false albacore *(see: albacore, false)* or little tunny *(see)*.

Identification. Albacore have long pectoral fins that reach to a point beyond the anal fin, as well as small finlets on both the back and the belly that extend from the anal fin to the tail. Albacore are colored dark blue, shading to greenish blue near the tail, and is silvery white on the belly. A metallic or iridescent cast covers the entire body. The dorsal finlets are yellowish, except for the white trailing edge of the tail, and the anal finlets are silvery or dusky. The deepest part of the body is near the second dorsal fin; in other tuna, it is near the middle of the first dorsal fin.

Extremely long, sickle-shaped, black pectoral fins set albacore apart from other tuna; pectoral fins of certain other adult tuna may also be moderately long, but they never extend all the way to the anal fin. This distinction is not as marked in young albacore; in some cases, a juvenile albacore may have shorter pectoral fins than a similar-size yellowfin tuna *(T. albacores)* or a bigeye tuna *(T. obesus)*. The albacore can also be distinguished from other tuna by its lack of stripes or spots on the lower flanks and belly, and by the thin white trailing edge on the margin of the tail fin.

Size. The average weight for albacore is between 10 and 25 pounds. The all-tackle record is 88 pounds, 2 ounces, although commercially caught fish have weighed as much as 93 pounds. The albacore can grow to 5 feet in length.

Distribution. Albacore are found worldwide in tropical and temperate seas, including the Mediterranean, but they also make seasonal migrations into colder zones such as New England, southern Brazil, and the northern Gulf of Mexico. In the western Atlantic, albacore range from Nova Scotia to Brazil, although they rarely range north of New York and are absent from the Straits of Florida; in the Pacific Ocean, they range from Alaska to Mexico. Albacore are abundant in the Pacific but less common in the Atlantic, although in the latter, larger size classes (31 to 50 inches) are associated with cooler bodies of water, whereas smaller individuals tend to occur in warmer waters. In the North Pacific, they migrate annually between Asia and North America.

Habitat. Albacore favor tropical, subtropical, and temperate waters, commonly in the 60° to 66°F range. These fish seldom come close to shore and prefer deep, wide-open waters.

Life history/Behavior. A schooling fish, the albacore is migratory and pelagic; that is, it lives and feeds in the open sea. It roams widely, varying in location from within a few miles of shore to far offshore, as currents and water temperatures dictate. Its availability can change widely from year to year. Albacore have been described as one of the world's fastest migrant fish, and tagging studies have tracked them across entire oceans. Fish tagged off California, for example, were captured 294 days later off the coast of Japan, nearly 5,000 miles away. This is equivalent to a migration of more than 17 miles a day in straight-line fashion.

Albacore spawn from July through October along the west coast of North America, and in the summer season in the Southern Hemisphere of the mid-Pacific. A single female can shed between 1 and 3 million eggs in one spawning effort.

Food and feeding habits. The albacore diet consists of fish, squid, and crustaceans. Albacore feed in schools, which sometimes consist of other tuna-family members, and these schools are typically found around floating objects such as sargassum. Although they will feed at middle depths, they ordinarily feed close to the surface.

Angling. Anglers avidly pursue albacore wherever these fish occur. In California and Mexico, they are the most prominent tuna and are largely caught between 20 and 100 miles offshore, where the waters are mild and deep blue.

Unless warm currents bring albacore to within a few miles of shore, it is usually necessary to run long distances off North America's coasts to find them. They favor those areas where cooler water interfaces with warmer water. Charter boat captains

sometimes use satellite images of ocean temperatures as a guide, and look for seamounts or the edges of canyons (the latter especially on the East Coast of the U.S., as there are no canyons off the West Coast). Locating these fish is the hardest part of the sport, so anglers invest considerable effort trolling for them. Once a school is found, some anglers stop trolling and immediately begin chumming in an effort to keep the tuna nearby, catching them on live or dead baitfish. Others continue trolling. Charter and private boats, however, usually converge where the albacore are concentrated, so these spots are often a hotbed of activity.

Like all tuna, albacore strike hard and make powerful runs. They are a popular light-tackle quarry (4/0 reels and 20- to 50-pound tackle are standard) and are commonly caught by anglers fishing with such baits as mullet, sauries, squid, herring, anchovies, sardines, and other small fish. In some cases, chunking or chumming with dead bait is preferable; in others, light-lining with live bait is more effective. Fishing with live anchovies is popular on the West Coast. Fly fishing is also possible, usually when a chum slick has been established to attract schools of albacore within casting range.

In the northeastern U.S., trollers fish with both lures and rigged baitfish, and there's a strong preference for using green trolling lures and natural baits (whole ballyhoo or strips) dressed with green skirts. When albacore action is hot and a school is encountered, multiple hookups can occur on a boat with many trolling rigs set out; this can become a wild adventure, with lines tangling, rods bent double, and everyone onboard involved in a pandemonium rush.

See: Big-Game Fishing; Chumming; Chunking; Trolling; Tuna.

ALBACORE, FALSE

"False albacore" is a popular term for little tunny *(see)*.

ALBERTA

The most westerly of Canada's Prairie Provinces, Alberta is in many ways diverse. From the arid short-grass prairie in the south to the aspen parkland farm country of the central region, and from the wild lands of the Rockies to the mixed-wood northern boreal forest, the Wild Rose Province is as varied as it is beautiful. And within each ecological zone is a unique and challenging fishery.

The prairies are a dry, flat landscape dissected by warm, slow-moving rivers that have carved deep scars across the landscape. Walleye, sauger, pike, goldeye, and sturgeon swim the lower reaches of these rivers, while rainbow and brown trout inhabit the upper end, where the prairies meet the foothills. On-stream and off-stream reservoirs, built to store the irrigated water that is the lifeblood of the prairie, provide underutilized opportunities for growing walleye, pike, and whitefish populations.

For angling, the central Alberta parkland region is the least bountiful sector of Alberta, but it is nonetheless blessed with a few premium locations, especially the Red Deer and North Saskatchewan Rivers. Their tremendous fish populations are the most diverse in the province. The transition zone between parkland and boreal forest is cottage country, with numerous lakes known for their pike, walleye, and perch fishing.

The forested northern half of Alberta contains the majority of the province's 800 fish-inhabited lakes. Northern pike, walleye, and lake trout thrive here, with arctic grayling running some of this vast region's rivers. Much of this part of Alberta is inaccessible by road, but a handful of fly-in lodges offer world-class angling.

The mountains and foothills on Alberta's west side give birth to some of Canada's most pristine creeks and rivers. Originating in the ice pack of age-old glaciers, these sinuous waters harbor cutthroat and brook trout in the cold upper stretches, giving way to highly productive brown trout and rainbow trout waters where the land starts to level out. The city of Calgary sits on this divide, it's heart lanced by the famous Bow River.

The extreme western and southwestern boundaries of Alberta are occupied by Jasper, Banff, and Waterton National Parks. Rainbow, brook, and lake trout are the featured fishing targets in these locations. Visiting anglers can combine pursuit of these species with enjoyment of unparalleled scenery. Neither disappoints either the first-time or the veteran visitor.

The Prairies

Alberta's prairie region lies due north of Montana, bordered on the east by Saskatchewan and on the west by the Rocky Mountain foothills. The Milk River, the only watershed in Alberta that flows south into the United States, parallels the Montana border before sending its water south, eventually linking with the Missouri River. The Milk earned its name from the high silt load that gives it its at times milky-white appearance. The provincial record sauger was taken from the Milk River, and it is this species that attracts most anglers. It is fished in various ways, in pools, eddies, and behind structure. Pike to 10 pounds also cruise these waters.

A little farther north, the lower Oldman and Bow Rivers meet at an area known locally as "the Forks," to form the South Saskatchewan River. Pike, walleye, sauger, and goldeye can all be found throughout much of this water. Any presentation that can get live bait down to the bottom of pools and outside bends is sure to produce. The lake sturgeon, Alberta's largest fish species, can also be found in the South Saskatchewan. A 105-pound provincial record sturgeon came from these waters.

An angler casting on a lake in Banff National Park projects the quintessential idyllic fishing scene.

Locals recommend a three-way swivel setup, using a 2/0 or 3/0 hook baited with worms and enough weight to keep your offering stationary in the current. Summer evenings tend to produce best.

The lower Bow River offers fine opportunities for large brown and rainbow trout between Carseland and the Bassano Dam, though much of this stretch is inaccessible to angling where it passes through an Indian reserve. Fly anglers enjoy tremendous success using streamers, nymphs, or dry flies, depending largely on the season, water conditions, and weather.

The bulk of the remaining quality angling opportunities across Alberta's parched prairie region occurs on the many irrigation reservoirs that provide stock water. Most hold northern pike, walleye, and lake whitefish, with the occasional rainbow trout that's made its way from the Bow or Oldman through the irrigation supply canals.

Travers, Badger, Chin, Stafford, Crawling Valley, and Milk River Ridge Reservoirs, along with manmade Keho, McGregor, and Newell Lakes, have the potential to produce trophy fish. The provincial record pike, 38 pounds, comes from Keho Lake.

These southern reservoirs, despite being relatively featureless and populated with notoriously finicky fish, are quickly gaining a reputation as Alberta's best walleye fisheries. This species grows quickly in the warm, productive waters common here. In recent years more fly anglers have been pursuing trophy pike. They've been wading or drifting in May or June through shallow bays that have an early growth of vegetation.

The Parkland

Alberta's parkland region is a patchwork of native aspen groves and grasslands interspersed with rolling fields of wheat, barley, canola, and hay. A number of pothole-studded moraines created by receding glaciers some 10,000 years ago pockmark the landscape. The predominant rivers here are the Red Deer, Battle, and North Saskatchewan.

The Red Deer River in this region produces pike and walleye to 10 pounds, sauger, Rocky Mountain whitefish to 3 pounds, and goldeye to 2 pounds. Fishing on the bottom with stationary bait is most effective, and casting from shore also yields pike.

In recent years brown trout fishing has increased immediately upstream and downstream of the city of Red Deer. Fly anglers have had good success quietly wading the shoreline in the evening, casting dry flies to rising fish. A number of browns in the 24- to 30-inch range have been taken. Look for a wide variety of mayfly and caddisfly hatches throughout the season. In the lower stretches of the Red Deer the occasional sturgeon have been taken on dead-still live baits.

The Battle is the region's smallest river but is well known locally for producing big walleye. These fish are extremely migratory, so it's always a difficult river to predict. Spring and fall, when the fish stack up in pools, are the most consis-

tent seasons. Forestburg Reservoir, a hydroelectric impoundment, has yellow perch in addition to pike and walleye. Some big goldeye are caught annually below the reservoir, in the lower reaches of the Battle, mainly on wet flies.

The North Saskatchewan River is arguably Alberta's most productive and underutilized fishery. Running predominantly east-west, and bisecting the capital city of Edmonton, the North Saskatchewan offers quality fishing for walleye in excess of 10 pounds, along with northern pike, sauger, goldeye, burbot, and a few brown trout. Look for fish at creek mouths, above and below islands, on outside curves, and in pools and eddies.

Prior to 1989, the provincial record walleye came from the North Saskatchewan just downstream of Edmonton. During the summer months, fishing with bait rigs, jigs tipped with worms, or bait-tipped three-way rigs is favored, and you never know what to expect on the hook. Lake sturgeon are also common throughout much of this stretch of the river. Stationary bait rigs crammed with worms are preferred for them.

Productive lakes are scattered across the southern portion of the parkland region. Pine Lake, outside Red Deer, yields good walleye, pike, and perch. Sylvan, Gull, Pigeon, and Wabumun Lakes all offer pike, walleye, perch, and lake whitefish. Because of heavily developed water-sports activities on these lakes, they are largely underfished. Pine Lake is the best bet for walleye, while Wabumun gives up pike approaching 25 pounds every year.

These lakes are well known for ice fishing, attracting many winter-only anglers. Lake whitefish are the primary target species, with Gull and Pigeon Lakes the most popular waters. The power plants on Wabumun keep portions of the lake open year-round. These areas attract pike that can be taken throughout the winter months by casting spoons, crankbaits, or flies.

Just outside Edmonton are a number of small, pothole lakes stocked with rainbow trout. Though subject to periodic winterkill, Chickakoo, Eden, Hasse, Cottage, Star, and Black Nugget Lakes are all proven producers. Slow-trolling wet flies and small streamers behind rowed boats or float tubes is popular here, while various baits suspended under a float work well through the ice. East of the city, Hastings and Coal Lakes offer fine perch fishing, particularly in winter.

Within an hour's drive northwest of Edmonton are several lakes with good walleye, pike, and perch populations. Lac St. Anne, Lac la Nonne, Jackfish Lake, and Lake Isle offer good fishing year-round. Another 30 miles farther west, Chip Lake attracts anglers from around the province in search of the burbot that move up from the lake into the Lobstick River in winter. Worms or minnows fished still on the bottom through the ice will almost guarantee a hookup with this tasty table fish.

Within 150 miles northeast of Edmonton is a cluster of lakes known across the province for their walleye, perch, and pike fishing. Though populations of fish are down somewhat from previous years, all still offer fine angling opportunities. Pinehurst Lake near Lac la Biche is probably the best, particularly for walleye; but Touchwood, Spencer, Seibert, Ironwood, Beaver, Moose, and Muriel Lakes are all worth the trip. Look for walleye on sunken reefs and along natural dropoffs during the heat of summer; in spring, fall, and on summer nights search up on the flats. Slow, vertical presentations work best on schooled fish. Perch can be found adjacent to submerged weedbeds, where jigs tipped with minnows will produce. Ice fishing is very popular in this area.

Lake whitefish are found in most of these waters, too. Largely incidental catches in open water, they are more commonly targeted through the ice.

Cold Lake, on the Saskatchewan border, is best known for its lake trout but also has pike, walleye, perch, and whitefish. North of Edmonton, Missawawi, Kinosiu, Mann, and North Buck Lakes are all known for their winter perch fishing. Try small jigs tipped with minnow pieces, fished over sunken weedbeds.

The Boreal Forest

The northern half of Alberta is dominated by mixed-wood boreal forest—a mosaic of aspen poplar, white spruce, and black spruce interspersed with many wetlands of varying sizes. Road access across much of this region is extremely limited, although oil and gas development and its associated roads are opening up more and more of the north each year.

The fishing jewel of this region is Lesser Slave Lake. One of Alberta's largest lakes, it encompasses some 1,160 square kilometers. Located southeast of the town of Peace River, Lesser Slave offers tremendous fishing for walleye to 12 pounds, yellow perch to 2 pounds, and northern pike to 25 pounds. Access to most of the lake is good, with numerous boat launch facilities. The best walleye fishing is in the lake's west basin in spring; the east end picks up after July.

Good pike fishing in Lesser Slave exists wherever deep water is adjacent to forage-fish-holding structure, but the east end of the lake near the town of Slave Lake is a consistent producer. Perch can be found just about anywhere you find walleye, though the mouth of the river, on the lake's extreme east end, has developed a worthy reputation for lots of jumbo perch. Try slow jigging or bait rigging.

Lesser Slave has enviable reputation for terrific ice fishing as well. Anglers travel from afar to tackle trophy pike, walleye, perch, and burbot through the ice. Hilliard's Bay, near the west end, is the most popular winter fishing location. Numerous camping and motel facilities around Lesser Slave Lake cater year-round to anglers.

Other drive-to fishing lakes in the central and western portion of Alberta's north include Utikuma, Peerless, Graham, Cadotte, Fawcett, God's, Sturgeon, Snipe, Iosegun, Baptiste, and Lawrence. Most offer good walleye, pike, perch, and lake whitefish angling all year long. Peerless Lake, a six-hour-drive north of Edmonton, is a notable exception. It offers outstanding lake trout fishing, with 20- to 30-pounders not uncommon. These fish move up shallow in spring and fall, and in summer they congregate in deep cool holes.

Several other lakes in the region offer fine angling opportunities for stocked, but self-sustaining, trout species. The best of these include Dollar Lake, north of Valleyview, which produces brown and rainbow trout to 10 pounds; and Edith and Chrystina Lakes near Swan Hills, which have brook trout up to 5 pounds. Most of the stocked trout ponds are suitable for spinning or fly fishing. On summer evenings it's possible to pick up some nice rising fish on mayfly or caddisfly patterns.

Of the fish-bearing rivers in the northwest, the mighty Peace River is the largest. It is inhabited by pike, walleye, and goldeye in the lower section, and rainbow trout, bull trout, and grayling in the upper stretch. While outstanding at times, and with little angling pressure at any time of year, the Peace is susceptible to carrying high silt loads that leave it unfishable for much of the spring, early summer, and periods following heavy rainfalls.

According to The Guinness Book of Records, the oldest known boat is a 27-foot wooden eel-catching canoe discovered on a Baltic island. It was dated circa 4490 B.C.

Southeast of the city of Grande Prairie, the Wapiti, Simonette, and Smoky Rivers all offer quality angling for pike and walleye in their lower sections, and bull trout, arctic grayling, and whitefish in the higher reaches. The best fishing is from late June through October. Concentrate on pools for pike, walleye, and bull trout; work the riffles and slicks for grayling and whitefish.

The Little Smoky River, near the town of Fox Creek, is arguably Alberta's best arctic grayling water. Much of it was designated catch-and-release-only a number of years ago, and the results have been outstanding. Grayling up to 20 inches are not uncommon, although 10- to 16-inch fish predominate.

South of the Little Smoky, the Berland and Wildhay Rivers hold populations of rainbow trout, bull trout, and grayling. Each has innumerable unnamed tributaries that also offer good fishing.

The Athabasca River, which bisects the northern half of Alberta southwest to northeast, offers quality angling wherever there is access. The lower stretches hold big walleye and pike, and the provincial record walleye was taken out of the Pembina River, a tributary to the Athabasca. In the Athabasca's upper stretches look for bull trout, rainbows, grayling, and whitefish.

The eastern portion of northern Alberta, off the Fort McMurray Highway, has fewer accessible waters. The best among them are Wabasca, Calling, Winnefred, and Christina Lakes. All offer year-round fishing for pike and walleye, though the best months are May, June, September, and October.

Though much of scenic northern Alberta is not accessible by road, a number of fly-in camps offer spectacular fishing. Most are accessed out of either Fort McMurray or Fort Smith, the latter a small town on Alberta's border with the Northwest Territories. The best waters serviced by these camps include Andrew, Lealand, Bistcho, Margaret, Island, Gardiner, and Namur Lakes. Trophy northern pike fishing is available at all these, with walleye and/or lake trout also available. The best bet for lakers is Andrew, in the northeast.

None of the fish in these fly-in lakes see many anglers; as a result they are rather unsophisticated. Trolling is very popular, especially with spoons and minnow plugs. Because of the northern latitude of these lakes, the window of opportunity for fishing is relatively narrow. Ice out occurs from late May to mid-June most years, with the lodges shut down by mid-September.

The Rocky Mountains and Foothills

Alberta is probably best known across North America for its trout fishing, a reputation built largely on the magnificent angling available on the Bow River. However, the Bow is just one of many streams and rivers that offer world-class angling and originate in the Rockies.

Another is the Oldman River and its many tributaries, in the extreme southwest. In the upper stretches of the watershed, bull trout and cutthroat trout dominate. As these rivers wind eastward, rainbows and brown trout thrive. This is truly a fly angler's paradise. Cutthroats are aggressive feeders, falling for virtually any well-presented dry fly; high-floating attractor patterns always produce. Bull trout inhabit the deepest pools and are best taken on large leech or Muddler minnow patterns. Rainbows and browns are much more selective feeders here; the prudent angler will try to match the various caddis, mayfly, or stonefly hatches. Hardware anglers will find success with small, in-line spinners. Top tributaries include the Crowsnest, Castle, Livingston, and St. Mary's Rivers.

Moving north along the foothills, the next major system is the famous Bow River. Originating in Bow Lake in Banff National Park, the Bow tumbles and slides its way down and through Calgary. Bull trout, brook trout, and Rocky Mountain whitefish inhabit the higher reaches, while the nutrient-rich lower stretches have rainbow trout and brown trout, the latter being the fish that made the Bow famous.

The most productive stretch of river is between Calgary and the Carseland Dam, some 30 miles downstream. Anglers can expect 20-inch specimens on most floats through this section. Although the river is best known for its dry-fly fishing, anglers must be prepared to fish nymphs and streamers most of the time for optimal results. This stretch can be drifted effectively in two days; access points allow for one-day floats if preferred.

Veterans of the Bow float with two rods: a 4- or 5-weight rigged with floating line for nymphing and throwing dries, and an 8-weight with a high-speed sink-tip line for streamers. Weighted flies are the norm here. Popular patterns include Woolly Buggers, Zonkers, and Muddlers in the streamer class, and a Gold-ribbed Hare's Ear and San Juan Worm for nymphing. The predominant hatches are plenty and varied, so a wide selection of dry flies is required. August on the Bow is tough and unpredictable, but can offer some outstanding hopper fishing.

Continuing north, the Red Deer system is praised for its wonderful brown trout streams. The Raven and North Raven Rivers (Stauffer Creek) are perhaps the best known in the area, but the Prairie, Dogpond, Fallen Timber, Little Red Deer, and the Red Deer proper—and their tributaries—should not be overlooked. These rivers and streams are relatively small, though they have the potential of giving up 5-pound fish in stretches you can leap across. Attractor patterns like the Royal Coachman and H&L variants will turn fish throughout the season, as will leech patterns worked through the deeper pools and runs.

Farther along is the North Saskatchewan River system. The jewels here include the Ram and North Ram Rivers, which are renowned for cutthroat trout. The North Ram is especially productive, due mostly to its catch-and-release designation, with 18- to 20-inch cutts not uncommon. The main stem of the North Saskatchewan harbors browns, cutts, brookies, bull trout, whitefish, and even a few remnant native lake trout. Farther below, as the river slows and widens, pike and walleye dominate. The best places to fish are from shore at creek mouths and deep pools. This river is very turbulent in spots and is best floated by only the most experienced. A number of tributaries in the North Saskatchewan system offer fine angling opportunities for rainbows, cutthroats, and brook trout.

The Athabasca River watershed south of Highway 16 offers anglers easy access to quality grayling and bull trout angling. The late season—August and September—is best. Bull trout hang in the deepest pools, while grayling can be taken from the riffle and slick areas on a variety of spinners or dry flies. The McLeod, Pembina, and Embarras Rivers and their tributaries are top locations.

The entire length of the Rockies is dotted with high mountain lakes that offer virtually untapped angling for stocked cutthroat, golden, rainbow, and brook trout for those capable of the typically arduous hikes required. A horse-pack or helicopter trip allows the high-country angler to bring in a float tube, which is the most effective way to fish these waters.

ALBRIGHT KNOT

A fishing knot used for making line-to-line connections.

See: Knots, Fishing.

ALDERFLIES

See: Dobsonflies, Fishflies, and Alderflies.

ALEWIFE *Alosa pseudoharengus.*

Other names—herring, sawbelly, gray herring, grayback; French: *gapareau, gaspereau;* Spanish: *alosa, pinchagua.*

A small herring, the alewife is important as forage for gamefish in many inland waters and along the Atlantic coast. It is used commercially in pet food and as fish meal and fertilizer, and it has been a significant factor in the restoration of trout and salmon fisheries in the Great Lakes. The landlocked alewife can at times be a nuisance because of periodic mass die-offs, especially in the Great Lakes; for reasons not fully understood, but believed to be related to the rise in water temperature, landlocked alewives die and drift to shore in the spring and early summer.

Identification. Small and silvery gray with a greenish to bluish back tinge, the alewife usually has one small dark shoulder spot and sometimes other small dusky spots. It has large eyes with well-developed adipose eyelids. The alewife can be distinguished from other herring by its lower jaw, which projects noticeably beyond the upper jaw.

Size. Alewives can grow up to a half pound in weight and to 15 inches in length; they usually average 6 to 12 inches in saltwater and 3 to 6 inches in freshwater.

Distribution. Sea-run alewives extend from Newfoundland and the Gulf of St. Lawrence to South Carolina. Alewives were introduced into the upper Great Lakes and into many other inland waters, although some naturally landlocked populations exist.

Habitat. Alewives are anadromous, inhabiting coastal waters, estuaries, and some inland waters, although some spend their entire lives in freshwater. They have been caught as far as 70 miles offshore in shelf waters.

Alewife

A

Life history/Behavior. The alewife is a schooling fish and is sometimes found in massive concentrations detectable on sportfishing sonar. In late April through early June, saltwater alewives run up freshwater rivers from the sea to spawn in lakes and sluggish stretches of river. Landlocked alewives move from deeper waters to nearshore shallows in lakes, or upstream in rivers, spawning when the water is between 52° and 70°F. Saltwater females deposit 60,000 to 100,000 eggs, whereas freshwater females deposit 10,000 to 12,000 eggs. They deposit the eggs randomly, at night, and both adults leave the eggs unattended. Young alewives hatch in less than a week, and by fall they return to the sea or to deeper waters. Adult landlocked alewives cannot tolerate extreme temperatures, preferring a range of 52° to 70°F—the same temperatures they spawn in.

Food and feeding habits. Young alewives feed on minute free-floating plants and animals, diatoms, copepods, and ostracods; adults feed on plankton, as well as insects, shrimp, small fish, diatoms, copepods, and their own eggs.

Angling. Having virtually no sporting value, alewives are almost never deliberately caught by anglers. They may be caught on tiny spoons or jigs or snagged, however, to be used as live baits. They are also used as chum, and as crab and lobster bait. In freshwater, alewives are a popular live bait in trout and salmon lakes, but they are difficult to keep alive and fresh.

See: Bait; Herring.

ALGAE

The term "algae" refers to a large, heterogenous group of primitive aquatic plants that lack roots, stems, or leaf systems and range from unicellular organisms to large networks of kelp. Algae exist in both freshwater and saltwater. They can be blue-green, yellow, green, brown, and red; there are more than 15,000 species of green algae alone. All species of algae photosynthesize.

As the primary or lowest plant forms, algae are important in sustaining marine and freshwater food chains *(see)*. In freshwater, algae occur in three different types often encountered by anglers: plankton, filamentous, and muskgrass. Plankton is a diverse community made up of suspended algae (phytoplankton), combined with great numbers of minute suspended animals (zooplankton). Filamentous algae consist of stringy, hairlike filaments, often erroneously described as moss or slime because of their appearance when they form a mat or furlike coat on objects. Muskgrass, or stonewort, algae are a more advanced form that has no roots but attaches to lake or stream bottoms.

See: Aquatic Plants.

ALGAE BLOOM

An algae bloom is a dense concentration of algae, usually occurring under high nutrient concentrations as one species becomes so abundant that it obliterates other species, making the water appear cloudy (often brown, yellow, or pea-soup green). Sometimes causing scum and odor, an algae bloom is often blown into shallow areas; during a bloom each ounce of water contains millions of microscopic algae cells. Although a bloom may indirectly provide food for fish, it is an indication that a problem exists in the body of water, and to solve it the source of nutrients must be reduced.

Algae blooms occur in both freshwater and saltwater; the most prominent in saltwater is known as a red tide *(see)*. Some algae blooms can be harmful to human health, especially via toxins in seafood, and may cause fish and invertebrates to die; they appear to be occurring more frequently in the coastal zones and estuaries of the United States. The widely reported pfiesteria *(see)*, responsible for killing billions of fish, is an algae bloom.

See: Eutrophic.

ALIEN SPECIES

A species occurring in an area outside of its historically known natural range as a result of intentional or accidental dispersal by human activities. There are also known as exotic or introduced species.

See: Exotic Species.

ALKALINITY

The capacity to buffer or withstand great fluctuations in the pH *(see)* of water. The neutral value of pH is 7.0; the higher the pH value above 7.0, the greater the alkalinity. Fish prefer a pH close to the neutral value. The alkalinity of a lake generally depends on the minerals in its watershed. Watersheds with soils rich in lime and related materials provide more buffering to lakes, whereas those poor in lime, such as bedrock, provide very little buffering and are more susceptible to changes in pH from acid deposition or acid runoff.

ALLISON TUNA

A term for yellowfin tuna *(see)*, mainly used in Bermuda *(see)*.

ALLOCATION

Distribution, by fisheries management agencies, of fishing opportunities among user groups and individuals. This term is often used with reference to the harvest or allowable catch. In saltwater, allocations are made between recreational anglers and commercial fishermen.

See: Fisheries Management.

ALL-TACKLE WORLD RECORD

The largest individual of a given species of sportfish caught on sporting tackle within the parameters established by the International Game Fish Association *(see),* the certifying organization. An all-tackle world record may also be a line-class world record *(see).*

See: Records.

AMBERJACK, GREATER *Seriola dumerili.*

Other names—amberjack, jack, amberfish, jack hammer, horse-eye bonito, horse-eye jack, Allied kingfish (Australia); French: *poisson limon, sériole couronnée;* Hawaiian: *kahala;* Japanese: *kanpachi;* Spanish: *coronado, pez de limón, serviola.*

Sought after by anglers because of its qualities as a gamefish, the greater amberjack is the largest of the jacks, the most important amberjack to anglers, and, like most of its brethren, a strong fighter. Although it is considered a fair food fish, and a substantial commercial fishery for this species exists in some locales, anglers account for most of the catch. The greater amberjack is high on the list of tropical marine fish suspected of causing ciguatera *(see)* poisoning, although this problem may be isolated to certain areas, as greater amberjack are regularly consumed without incident in some places.

Identification. The greater amberjack is greenish blue to almost purple or brown above the lateral line, and silver below the lateral line. A dark olive brown diagonal stripe extends from the mouth across both eyes to about the first dorsal fin; these are commonly referred to as "fighter stripes" and are prominent in live fish, especially when they are excited. A broad amber stripe runs horizontally along the sides, and disappears after the fish dies. The fins may also have a yellow cast. The greater amberjack has short foredorsal fins, a bluntly pointed head, and no detached finlets.

The greater amberjack bears a resemblance in smaller sizes to the bluefish (as well as other jacks), but it can be distinguished by its more deeply concave tail. Also, it has small teeth in bands instead of the large, triangular teeth of the bluefish. The amber stripe sometimes causes anglers to confuse the greater amberjack with the yellowtail, but it can be distinguished by the 11 to 16 developed gill rakers on the lower limb of the first branchial arch; the yellowtail has 21 to 28 gill rakers.

The first dorsal fin consists of 6 or 7 small, fragile spines connected by a membrane; juveniles have an additional detached spine before the first dorsal fin. The second dorsal fin has 1 spine and 29 to 35 soft rays. The anal fin has 3 spines, the first 2 of which are detached, and 19 to 22 soft rays. In adults, the 2 detached spines are sometimes covered with skin. There is a low keel on the caudal peduncle.

Size. Averaging roughly 15 pounds in weight, and commonly ranging up to 40 pounds, the greater amberjack often exceeds 50 pounds and has been reported to attain weights exceeding 170 pounds. The all-tackle record is 155 pounds, 10 ounces. It can reach a length of more than 5 feet.

Distribution. Although greater amberjack range in the Atlantic Ocean as far north as New England, they exist mostly in southern waters. They are known to occur in the Indo-Pacific area around Japan, China, and the Philippines, in the central Pacific off Hawaii, throughout the western Atlantic Ocean (abundant off the coasts of Florida and in nearby Caribbean waters), in portions of the eastern Atlantic Ocean (Madeira and southern West Africa), and in the Mediterranean Sea in tropical and temperate waters.

Amberjack in some waters are resident fish, but others are migratory coastal pelagic fish that swim with the current edges and eddies. Amberjack tagged in the Atlantic off South Florida have been recaptured as far south as Venezuela.

Habitat. Greater amberjack are found mostly in offshore waters and at considerable depths, as well as around offshore reefs, wrecks, buoys, oil rigs, and the like. They can be caught anywhere in the water column, to depths of several hundred feet, but they are mostly associated with near-bottom structure in the 60- to 240-foot range. This trend is due in large part to the habits of anglers. In some locales, they are caught in inshore waters, even as shallow as under 30 feet, but are usually associated with offshore environs.

Greater Amberjack

Life history/Behavior. The greater amberjack often occurs in schools, but it is not primarily a schooling fish and occasionally remains solitary. Migrations appear to be linked to spawning behavior, which in the Atlantic occurs from March through June. Evidence suggests that spawning may occur in offshore oceanic waters, but few studies have been conducted, although spawning fish are known to congregate over reefs and wrecks. Juveniles have been taken from June through September in offshore waters.

Food and feeding habits. Greater amberjack feed on fish, crabs, and squid.

Angling. With the exception of tuna, amberjack are as hard-fighting a fish, pound for pound, as any found in saltwater. Those anglers who have engaged in a tug of war with a large amberjack know well how their forearm muscles have been strained and how their back and shoulders ache after the duel. Amberjack are especially popular with party and charter boat anglers, as well as those in private boats.

Amberjack are a wide-ranging fish and are likely to be found in various locales, providing good fishing from spring through summer. They are most commonly associated with such intermediate to deep habitats as reefs, rocky outcrops, wrecks, buoys, and other structure. They usually band in small groups, so it is typical to catch an amberjack and have others follow it to the boat. Leaving it hooked or tethered may keep the school around and provide further success.

Amberjack caught off the Florida Keys.

Amberjack are fast swimmers and voracious predators. Fishing with cut or live baits is very popular, as is vertical jigging with bucktails, jigs with soft-plastic bodies, or metal jigging spoons. Lures are sometimes adorned with a strip or chunk of meat. Popular live baits include herring, menhaden, mullet, and especially pinfish and blue runners. In water under 120 feet, some anglers opt for chumming.

Because these fish take a lure or bait very hard, there is seldom a question that a strike has occurred. When fishing in deep water, it is often critical to muscle big amberjack immediately after the fight begins, as they usually head deep for cover and, if they get to it, will break the line on a rock. It often seems as though the more you pull, the harder the amberjack pulls. With a good-size fish on, using the boat to pull the fish away from a reef or wreck to play it in obstruction-free water can be helpful.

It is a chore to turn a big amberjack immediately and coax it away from cover. Where big specimens lurk, anglers depend on heavy tackle, knowing that these fish make determined runs and fight all the way to the boat, even when brought up from deep water. Many amberjack anglers like stand-up fishing *(see)* with 30- to 50-pound-class outfits and a good harness; a two-speed reel is especially helpful for gaining on these bruisers. Anglers deep fishing for snapper and grouper may find themselves overmatched when an amberjack comes along.

On the few occasions when amberjack are encountered near the surface, anglers can cast baits or plugs, spoons, or flies from a boat or from shore. Trollers use deep-diving plugs when appropriate, and some fish with planers and downriggers.

See: Bottom Fishing; Jacks; Jigging; Reef; Wreck.

AMBERJACK, LESSER *Seriola fasciata.*

Other names—amberjack, jack; French: *sériole babianc;* Spanish: *medregal listado.*

The lesser amberjack is the smallest amberjack, seldom encountered by, and relatively unknown to, anglers.

Identification. The lesser amberjack has an olive green or brownish back above the lateral line and is silver below the lateral line. A dark olive brown diagonal stripe extends from the mouth across both eyes to about the first dorsal fin. It is very similar in appearance to the greater amberjack *(see: amberjack, greater)* but has a deeper body profile and a proportionately larger eye, and eight spines in the first dorsal fin.

Size. Reports on the size of this species vary markedly, from up to 12 inches in length to under 10 pounds.

Distribution. In the western Atlantic, the lesser amberjack ranges from Massachusetts to Brazil; in the eastern Atlantic its range is uncertain due to previous confusion with other species, although it has been found off the Madeira Islands.

Lesser Amberjack

Habitat. Lesser amberjack are believed to live deeper than other amberjack, commonly in water from 180 to 410 feet deep, and to spawn in offshore waters.

Food and feeding habits. Lesser amberjack feed on fish and squid.

Angling. There is no concerted fishery for this species.

See: Jacks.

AMERICAN SPORTFISHING ASSOCIATION

Known as the ASA, this nonprofit trade association in Washington, D.C., has the goals of ensuring healthy and sustainable fisheries resources and increasing sportfishing participation. Primarily supported by the sportfishing industry, it also has individual memberships, and is involved in education, conservation, promotion, and marketing with regard to sportfishing.

The ASA's educational arm, the Future Fisherman Foundation, was created in 1986. It implements several national sportfishing education programs, including the "Hooked on Fishing—Not on Drugs" campaign in over 500 schools, a national 4-H sportfishing program, and a complete Sportfishing and Aquatic Resources Education program for educators and youth organizations.

The ASA also created and helps to fund the Fish America Foundation, which has directed millions of dollars to volunteer projects, endorsed by state and/or federal natural resource agencies, and is aimed at preserving waterways and enhancing fish populations without regard to geographic location or species limitations. It is the only program of its kind and has operated since 1983.

AMIDSHIP

The center section of a boat, between the bow and stern.

AMPHIPODS

A large group of crustaceans, most of which are small, compressed creatures (such as sand fleas and freshwater shrimp). These may be of food importance to juvenile fish.

AMUR, WHITE

See: Carp, Grass.

ANADROMOUS

Fish that migrate from saltwater to freshwater in order to spawn. Fish that do the opposite are called catadromous.

Literally meaning "up running," anadromous refers to fish that spend part of their lives in the ocean and move into freshwater rivers or streams to spawn. Anadromous fish hatch in freshwater, move to saltwater to grow to adulthood or sexual maturity, and then return to freshwater to reproduce. Salmon are the best-known anadromous fish, but there are many others, including such prominent species as steelhead trout, sturgeon, striped bass, and shad, and many lesser-known or less highly regarded species. Around the world there are approximately 100 species of anadromous fish.

Complicating an understanding of anadromy is the fact that some anadromous species have adapted, either naturally or by introduction, to a complete life in freshwater environments. These species, which include salmon, striped bass, and steelhead, make spawning migrations from lakes, where they live most of their lives, into rivers to spawn. In such instances, these fish are originally saltwater in origin. They remain anadromous when moved into purely fresh water, although they use the lake as they would the ocean. There are also species of freshwater fish that are native to freshwater and that migrate from lake to stream or river to spawn. These are not technically anadromous, but adfluvial.

Fish that originate in saltwater but have freshwater forms are often called "landlocked," whether or not they have a clear path to and from the sea. Sometimes these fish are physically blocked from reaching the ocean. Fish in a reservoir or lake may be unable to leave. Fish in some streams, like those in high-mountain areas, have a clear passageway to the sea but no means of returning because of waterfalls. Coldwater species may be effectively landlocked in the colder headwaters of a stream because temperatures are too high for them in the lowland parts of that stream or in the ocean in that area. Dolly Varden, for example, are landlocked in the southern tip of their range, but anadromous forms are common farther north.

Sometimes the terminology used to discuss the freshwater forms of saltwater fish is confusing. Atlantic salmon that exist in freshwater lakes without access to the sea are popularly called landlocked salmon or landlocked Atlantic salmon. Sockeye salmon that exist in freshwater lakes without access to the sea are often called Kokanee salmon. Other species, like striped bass and arctic char, are called by the same name in saltwater or freshwater.

Another complicating factor in understanding this topic is the fact that some anadromous

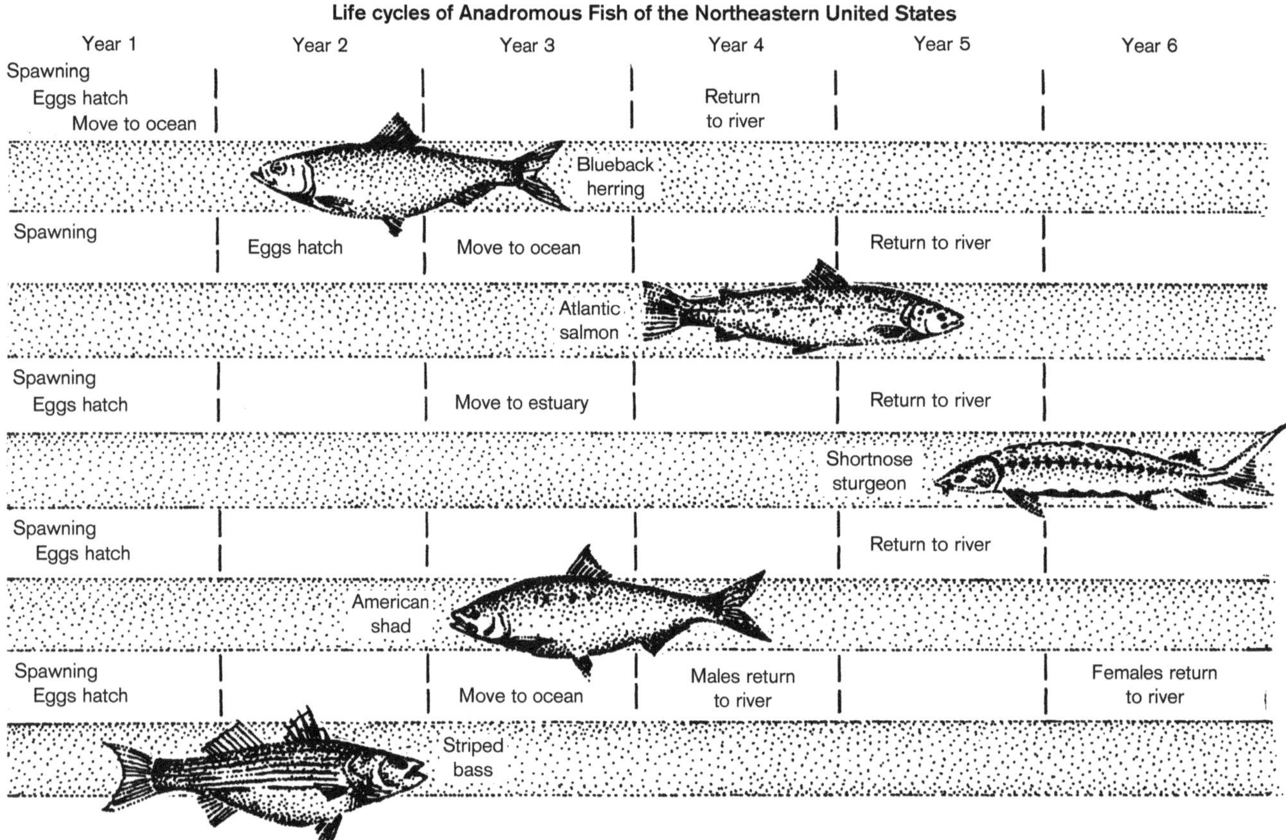

species of fish exercise anadromy optionally. For example, in coastal streams, the young of some steelhead trout may go to sea or may remain in the stream until maturity and then spawn without ever having left freshwater. Trout near the headwaters of a stream are more apt to remain in freshwater. Those that remain are sometimes thought to be genetically different from those that migrate.

Anglers have some difficulty distinguishing by appearance whether an anadromous fish has been to sea. Size is usually an indicator—the large fish having been to sea—but it is not necessarily a determining one. Scientists can tell by aging the fish, often by checking the growth rings on a scale *(see: fisheries management)*. Appearance may be an indicator. Young trout and salmon, for example, undergo a change in appearance before or during their seaward migration. They become more silvery; red colors fade or disappear; and scales get looser. Usually the fish grow so much faster in saltwater that the difference between freshwater growth and saltwater growth is quite apparent on the scales under a microscope. On most subspecies of trout and species of Pacific salmon, the parr marks (large vertical or oval rounded spots on the sides) will gradually disappear whether or not the fish goes to sea. None of these is an infallible indicator. Trout that enter a lake or reservoir, and some of those that remain in large rivers, will show much the same changes and be difficult to tell from a sea-run individual. When a trout leaves the ocean and reenters freshwater, it will gradually regain some of the appearance of stream trout. In general, the sea-run trout has grown faster and is therefore younger than a stream trout of the same size.

There obviously must be important advantages in living an anadromous existence, or the habit would not have developed independently in such widely differing creatures as lampreys, sturgeon, shad, salmon, and striped bass. The advantages must be great enough to pay for the extra energy and risk involved in the migration from freshwater to saltwater and back again. Greater safety for the eggs in freshwater and a better food supply in the ocean appear to be the chief benefits for many fish, but more favorable year-round temperatures may also be a factor.

Being anadromous has numerous advantages and disadvantages both for the fish and for other animals, as well as for the environment in general. Anadromous fish need to make spawning migrations, which, if they are long, create physical hardship on the fish. And if the hazards of the migratory journey become increasingly great and too few spawners are able to make the trip, the existence of the population can be threatened. This is precisely what has happened to many runs of salmon in the Pacific Northwest. Furthermore, if the quality of their spawning habitat has been adversely impacted (pollution, thermal variation, flow impediment, etc.), then they are at great risk there as well. The chemical pollution of Atlantic Coast rivers affected the spawning of striped bass and was a major contributor to the collapse of striped bass stocks in the 1970s and 1980s.

Characteristics of anadromous fish. There are varying degrees of anadromy. In the most extreme cases, fish move from hundreds of miles at sea to hundreds of miles up a river. In the least extreme cases, some borderline species move from brackish water a short distance into freshwater to spawn. Anadromous fish stay in freshwater for varying lengths of time, usually dependent upon the species. Young anadromous fish migrate to the ocean for the first time when their growth and development are at a stage that allows them to survive there. The different anadromous species do not all go to the same place(s) in the ocean; each species migrates to the areas that fulfill their own needs for food and growth. The length of time that they stay in the ocean also varies with each species, and may vary within the species as well; this is usually dependent upon the time necessary to reach adult size or sexual maturity.

Most anadromous fish return to the same river in which they were born. However, some stray to other rivers, which may or may not be accidental. How they find their way from great distances in the ocean to the proper river is yet a mystery *(see: migration),* although there are several theories. One is that they use their sense of smell to detect small amounts of certain chemicals coming from their freshwater rivers. Another is that the fish follow ocean currents until they get close to their home river. And another is that they have internal "compasses" like those found in bees and homing pigeons.

Adult anadromous fish build up a considerable amount of fat while they are in the ocean. Their purpose for returning to freshwater is to reproduce, and some species, like the Pacific salmon, have little need to continue eating. They may still strike out of instinct, however, at other animals and at lures or bait. Many anadromous fish die after they have spawned. All Pacific salmon die. The U.S. Fish and Wildlife Service reports that less than 10 percent of all Atlantic salmon live to spawn a second time. However, several species, including striped bass and American shad, spawn several times.

Unique physiology. Anadromous fish are among those species that are able to cope with extreme changes in the salinity of the water they inhabit. Such species are scientifically labeled "euryhaline," which derives from *eury,* meaning broadly, and *haline,* meaning salty. Not all euryhaline species are anadromous; many live in estuaries where tidal action results in rapid changes in salt content. Some flounder, for example, which normally live in a marine environment, have on occasion been known to move many miles into freshwater. Tarpon and some sharks are also euryhaline, but not anadromous.

At some time in their lives, all anadromous fish must be able to move from freshwater to saltwater, and at a later date they must move back again. Most aquatic creatures cannot adjust to any great change in salt content. The bodies of all fish have a higher salt content than that of freshwater, and freshwater tends to be absorbed by their bodies. The amount of freshwater that would enter the body would soon be fatal if there were no mechanism to eliminate it. Freshwater fish cope with this problem by producing large quantities of very dilute urine. This water removal requires energy, which in turn requires additional food.

Most saltwater fish have the opposite problem. Bony fish have a salt content much lower than that of the ocean water, and if there were no mechanism to prevent it, the water in their bodies would permeate outward until the body salt content was in balance with that of the ocean. (In this connotation, the term "salts" includes the sum total of all salts, not just sodium chloride.) Such fish have to drink saltwater to overcome this dehydration and require a mechanism for getting rid of the excess salts. The process is complex and energy consuming; it involves special salt cells in the gills and mouth lining and a kidney that can excrete very concentrated urine. Sharks and hagfish solve the problem differently; their salt content is greater than that of bony fish, and it is naturally in balance with ocean water.

To be able to live in both freshwater and saltwater, a fish must obviously be equipped to cope with either of these two sets of problems and must be able to shift physiological gears as often as habits and circumstances dictate. The requirements are severe, but there are rewards. There is a great deal of estuarine habitat that changes salinity with the tide, and the only fish that can make extensive use of it are those euryhaline forms, which can thrive in rapidly changing salinity. Furthermore, freshwater fish that can withstand an ocean excursion are able to move from stream to stream, and their progeny quickly become established in nearby coastal streams, some of which might otherwise have no fish at all.

Even though an adult fish may be able to adjust to changes in salinity, its eggs and newly hatched young usually lack this ability; thus, the anadromous parents require a freshwater environment at spawning time.

See: Catadromous; Fisheries Management.

ANAL FIN

The median, unpaired, ventrally located fin that lies behind the anus, usually on the posterior half of the fish.

See: Fish.

ANATOMY *(Body, Function, and Relation to Angling)*

Size

Fish range widely in size. On the bantam side of the spectrum are tiny Philippine gobies less than half an inch long, the smallest of all animals with backbones. They are so diminutive that it takes literally thousands of them to weigh a pound, yet they are harvested commercially for use in many foods. At the behemoth end of the spectrum are giant whale sharks 65 to 70 feet long. The largest whale sharks can weigh as much as 25 tons, but they are so docile they may allow inquisitive scientists to pull alongside them with boats and then climb aboard to prod and poke as they give the big plankton-eaters a close examination. Between these extremes are seemingly limitless shapes and sizes among an estimated 21,000 species. This number exceeds the combined numbers of species of all other vertebrate animals—amphibians, reptiles, birds, and mammals.

Another giant of the sea is the mola, or ocean sunfish, which also goes by the name of headfish because its fins are set far to the rear on its broad, almost tail-less body. Molas, which have the unusual habit of basking at the surface, lying on their side as though dead, may weigh nearly a ton but are not a quarry for anglers. Also in saltwater such highly prized game species as bluefin tuna, swordfish, and certain sharks and marlins reach weights of more than a thousand pounds, with some shark and marlin specimens weighing considerably more.

The white sturgeon, one of the largest of freshwater fish, formerly reached weights of well over a thousand pounds in the Columbia and Fraser Rivers, but is now uncommon over 400 pounds. In the 1800s, monstrous sturgeon of over 2,000 pounds were reported, but fishery workers have not verified such legends. European sturgeon, especially along the Siberian coast from the Volga River, also once attained tremendous proportions but no longer do so. Some of the Asian and South American catfish may weigh 100 pounds or more. The arapaima, or pirarucu, found in Peru, Brazil, and Guyana, will reach about 200 pounds. The prehistoric-looking alligator gar of the southeastern United States can attain a weight of 300 pounds.

Fish size is of special interest to anglers. Many anglers aspire to match their skills against the larger specimens of various game species; competitive events often place a premium on large individual catches; and other rewards, both materialistic and intangible, accrue to those who have caught fish deemed to be of large, if not trophy, caliber.

Records for freshwater and saltwater fish caught on rod and reel are maintained by the International Game Fish Association *(see)* based upon specific standards and on weight. Yet, in many cases, fish are known to grow much larger than sport-caught records indicate. Two all-tackle record tarpon taken on rod and reel, for example, each weighed 283 pounds, which is admittedly sizable but much smaller than the 350-pounders that have reportedly been caught in nets. On the other hand, record rod-and-reel catches greatly exceed the average size

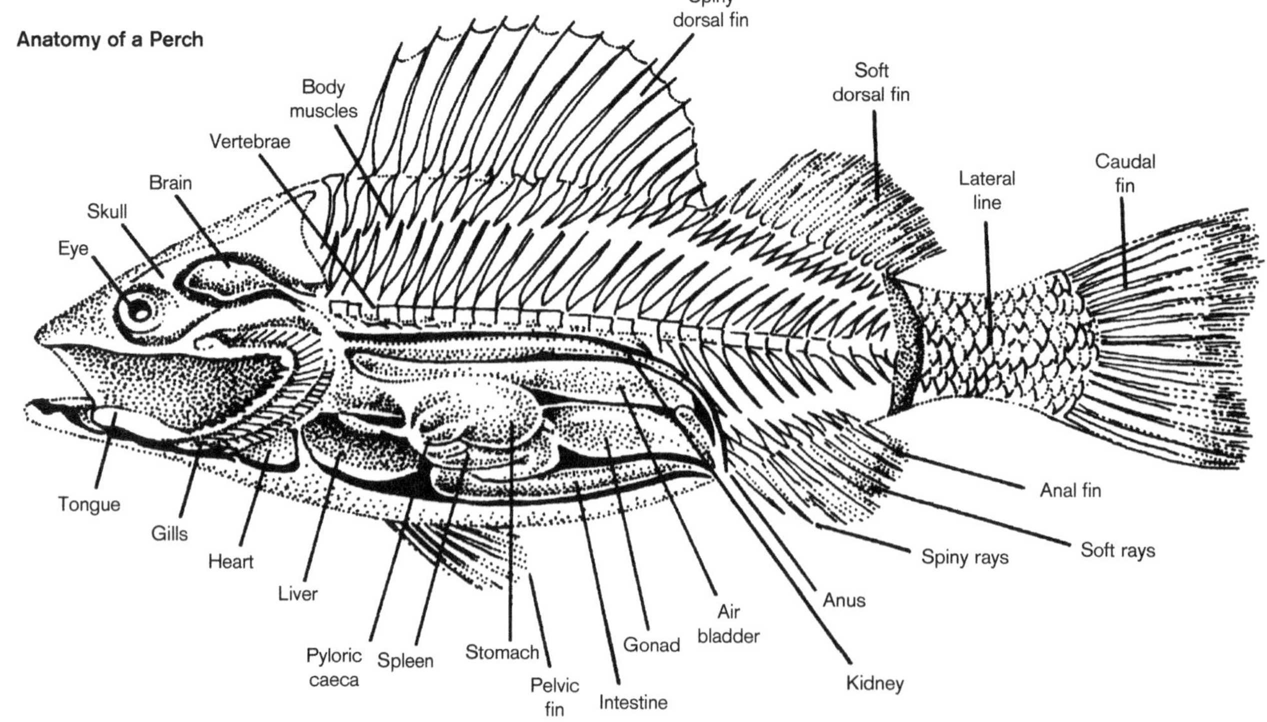

Anatomy of a Perch

Anatomy of a Shark

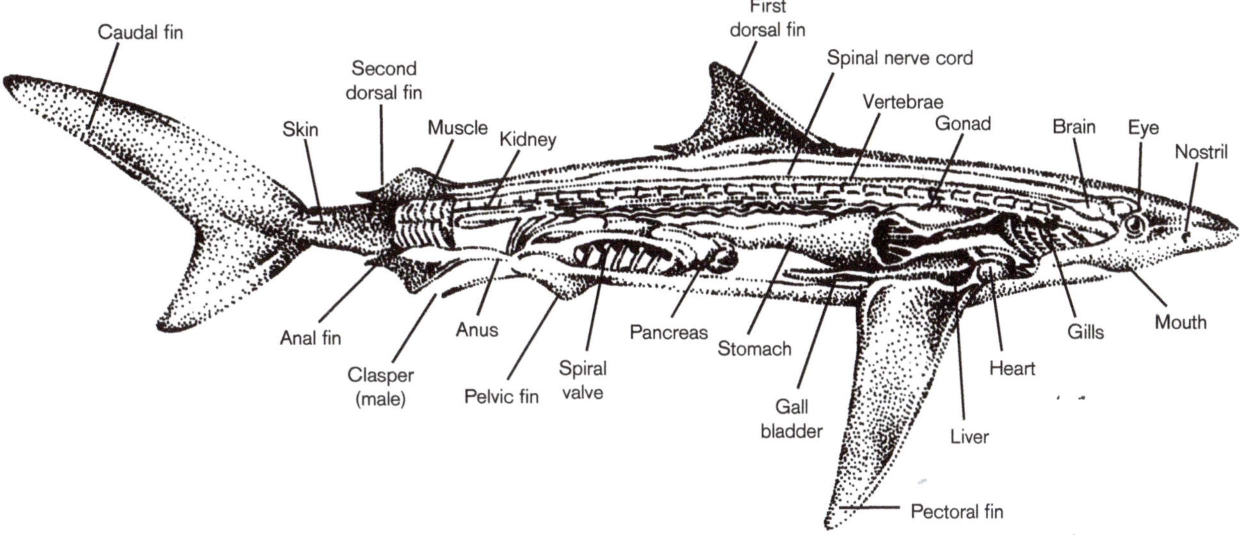

of most species. Most brook trout taken by anglers, for example, weigh less than half a pound, but the sport-caught record for the species is 14 pounds 8 ounces.

A fish does not have to be gigantic to provide fun, however. In this regard, tackle plays an important role. Anglers, using ultralight tackle in ponds and lakes, find it challenging to catch quarter-pound bluegills, rarely if ever hooking one that approaches a pound in weight, let alone the species top record of 4 pounds 12 ounces. Indeed, line-class record categories were long ago established for each species to recognize the angler's fishing skill by virtue of a notable catch for a particular weight of tackle.

Size is a relative issue both in terms of a fish's fighting ability and in its desirability as a catch. Although most larger fish are more difficult to subdue than smaller ones, that is not always the case. Size is also not necessarily comparable between different species; a 10-pound steelhead, for example, provides far better sport than a 10-pound walleye, and a 10-pound bonefish is much more challenging than a 10-pound barracuda. Growing season and geographic location may be a factor as well. A 10-pound largemouth bass in Florida, where a favorable growing season can allow a bass to grow large fast, is akin to perhaps a 6-pound largemouth bass in Minnesota in terms of age and availability within the bass population, the result being that they are catches of similar accomplishment despite being of different size.

Form

The typical fish, such as the yellow perch, largemouth bass, striped bass, and grouper, has a compressed body that is flattened from side to side. In others the body is depressed from top to bottom, as in flounder, rays, and other bottom-hugging types. Still others are spindle-shaped or streamlined, like mackerel, tuna, and trout; and some, such as eels, have an elongated or snakelike body. All fish fit into one of these four categories, but each form in turn may differ with various adaptations in certain portions of its anatomy.

These differences fit the fish for specific environments or particular ways of life. For example, the streamlined tuna is an open-ocean fish that moves constantly, indulges in long migrations, and pursues fast-swimming schools of smaller fish. Its bullet-shaped body is well adapted for such a life. On the other hand, the flounder's depressed body allows it to be completely undetectable as it lies flat on the sandy or muddy bottom, an adaptation that protects it from enemies as well as allows it to grasp unsuspecting prey. Marlin, sailfish, and swordfish are large fish with a long snout (bill) used as a club to stun prey or as a sword in defense. Eels and cutlassfish have slim, snakelike bodies, enabling them to negotiate seemingly inaccessible areas to hunt for food or to escape enemies.

Among the most unusual fish in shape are those that live in the deep sea. Many have luminous spots or stripes along their body, and fins may be reduced to slim filaments, some bearing bulbous and luminous tips. Many have long barbels around the mouth, with lighted tips that serve as lures for attracting smaller prey within reach of their strong jaws. In some, the tail is long and snakelike. Most have very large mouths and an array of long, dagger-sharp teeth that help in holding their catches. The mouth is generally stretchable, as is the stomach. When the fish has the good fortune to capture a meal in the dark depths where food, as a rule, is scarce, it attempts to devour the prey regardless of size. These deep-sea fish are seldom among the species caught by anglers.

Scales

A typical fish's body is covered with thin scales that overlap each other like the shingles of a roof. They are prominent outgrowths of skin, or epidermis, in

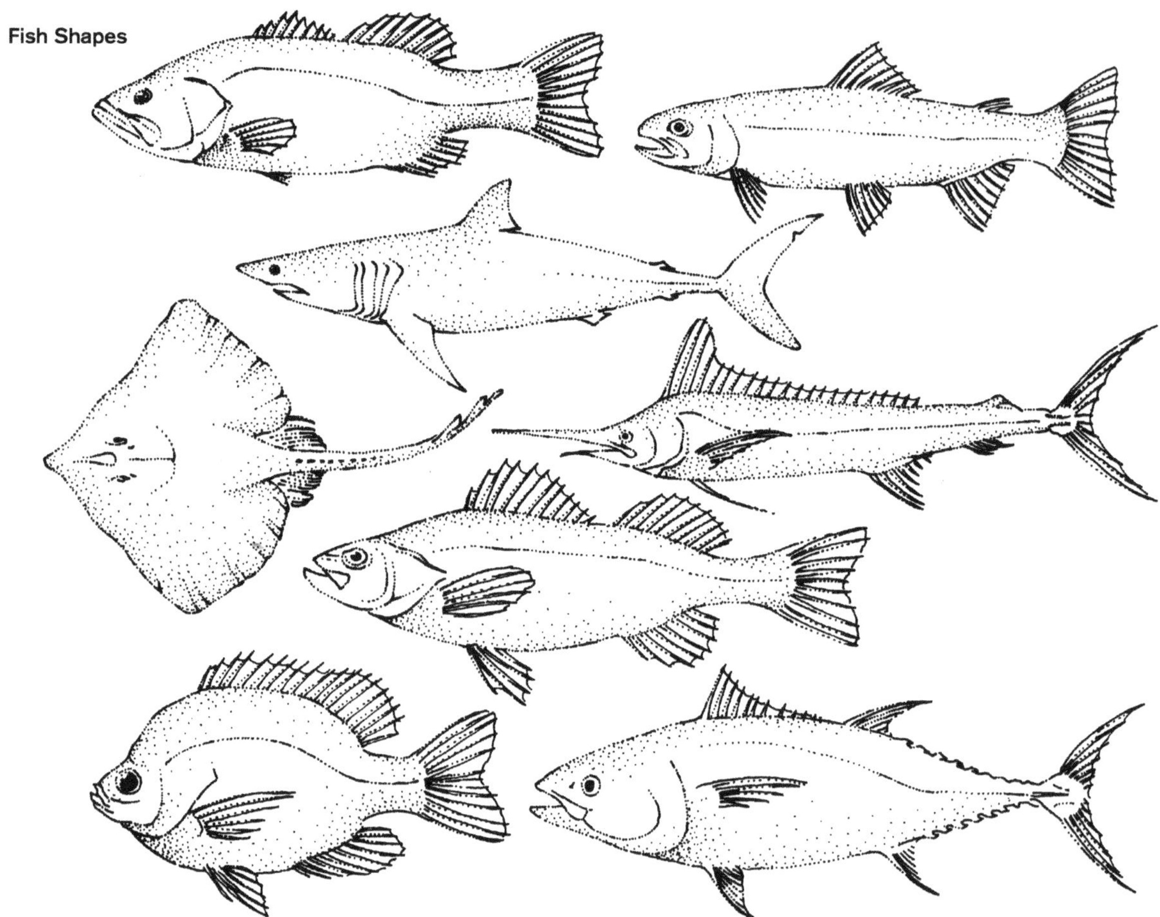

Anatomical differences among fish are most obvious in general body shape but also include body and tail fins.

which numerous glands secrete a protective coating of slime, often referred to as mucous. The slime is a barrier to the entry of parasites, fungi, and disease organisms that might infest the fish, and it seals in the fish's body fluids so that they are not diluted by the watery surroundings. The slime also reduces friction so that the fish slides through the water with a minimum of resistance; it also makes the fish slippery when predators, including the human variety, try to grab hold. Some fish, such as lampreys and hagfish, give off copious amounts of slime.

As a fish grows, its scales increase in size but not in number. Lost scales may be replaced, however. The ridges and spaces on some types of scales become records of age and growth rate. These can be read or counted like the annual rings in the trunk of a tree to determine a fish's age—the fish's growth slowing or stopping during winter when food is scarce and becoming much more rapid during the warm months when food is plentiful. Experts in reading scales can tell when a fish first spawned and each spawning period thereafter. They can determine times of migration, periods of food scarcity, illness, and similar facts about the fish's life. The number of scales in a row along the lateral line can be used to identify closely related species, particularly the young. Growth rings occur also in the vertebrae and in other bones of the body, but to study these requires killing the fish. A few scales can be removed without harm to the fish.

Most bony fish have tough, shinglelike scales with a comblike or serrated edge (ctenoid) along their rear margin, or with smooth rear margins (cycloid). The scales of garfish are hard and almost bony, fitting one against the other like the bricks on a wall. These are called ganoid scales. Sturgeon also have ganoid scales, some of which form ridges of armor along portions of their sides and back.

Sharks have placoid scales, which are the most primitive type. These scales are toothlike, each with a central spine coated on the outside with enamel and with an intermediate layer of dentine over a central pulp cavity. The skin of sharks, with the scales still attached, is the shagreen of commerce, widely used in the past and still used today in primitive areas as an abrasive, like sandpaper, or to make nonslip handles for knives and tools.

The scales may be variously modified on different species. Some fish do not have scales at all. Most species of catfish, for example, are "naked" or smooth-skinned. Their skin is very slippery, however, and some of the rays in their fins are modified as sharp spines. Paddlefish and sculpin have only a few scales. The scales of mackerel are minute. Trout also have tiny scales. Those of eels are widely separated and buried deep in the skin.

Scale Types

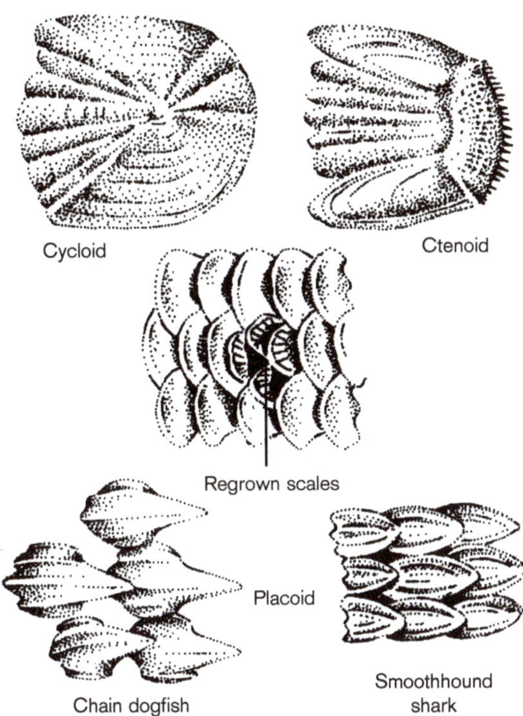

Cycloid scales have smooth rear margins, whereas ctenoid scales have comblike margins; placoid scales, found on sharks, are toothlike. Scales generally are layered, overlapping in rows like roof tiles.

Coloration

The beautiful coloration of fish can be appreciated only when observing them alive, for at death the brilliance and intensity of color begin to fade immediately. Unquestionably, many fish equal or surpass in appearance the most spectacular colored bird or butterfly, and some of the blends and contrasts of body color are impossible to describe with justice.

The color in fish is primarily produced by skin pigments. Basic or background color is due to underlying tissues and body fluids. Iridescent colors are present in body scales, eyes, and abdominal linings of some fish. The rainbowlike reflecting hues of certain kinds of fish are caused by skin pigmentation fragmenting through the irregular ridges of transparent or translucent scales.

All fish are not highly colored, however; the range extends widely from fish with bright colors to species that are uniformly drab in brown, gray, and even pitch-black. In nearly all species, the shades and acuteness of color is adapted to the particular environment a fish inhabits.

In oceanic fish, basic color may be separated into three kinds: silvery in the upper-water zone, reddish in the middle depths, and violet or black in the great depths. Those that swim primarily in the upper layers of ocean water are typically dark blue or greenish blue on the dorsal portions, grading to silvery sides and white belly. Fish that live on the bottom, especially those living close to rocks, reefs, and weedbeds, may be busily mottled or striped. The degree of color concentration also varies depending on the character of the fish's surroundings. For example, a striped bass caught from a sandy area will be lighter in general coloration than one captured from deeper water or from around dark rocks.

The same natural rules apply to freshwater fish. A northern pike, pickerel, or muskie is patterned in mottled greens because its habitat is primarily aquatic plants where it is well camouflaged in alternating light and dark shadows. The bottom-dwelling, dark-backed catfish are almost impossible to detect against a muddy background.

Many anglers are bewildered by the color variances in trouts. Often the same species taken from different types of localities in the same stream may differ in coloration to a startling degree. For example, a trout taken from shallow, swiftly running water over sand and pebbles will be bright and silvery in comparison to a relative that lives under a log in a deep, quiet pool. The steelhead, a sea-run rainbow trout, is another good example of color change. When it leaves the ocean to enter western rivers, it is brilliantly silver; but as it remains in freshwater, the characteristic coloration of the rainbow trout develops: dark greenish blue back, crimson lateral band, and profuse black spots over most of the body.

Regardless of the confusing differences under varying conditions, anglers who know the basic color patterns can easily identify any trout. Each species has recognizable characteristics that do not change. The brook trout, *Salvelinus fontinalis,* for example, always has reticulated or wormlike markings on its back, whereas the under edge of the tail fin and the forward edges of the pectoral, ventral, and anal fins are white.

Most types of fish change color during the spawning season; this is especially noticeable among the trout and salmon tribes. As spawning time approaches, the general coloration becomes darker and more intense. Some examples are surprising, especially in salmon of the U.S. Northwest. All five species are silvery in the ocean, but as they travel upstream to their spawning grounds, they gradually alter to deep reds, browns, and greens—the final colors so drastically different that it seems hardly possible the fish were metallic bright only a short time earlier. Each type of salmon, however, retains its own color characteristics during the amazing transition.

In some types of fish, the coloration intensifies perceptibly when the fish is excited by prey or by predators. Dolphin, a blue-water angler's delight, appear to be almost completely vivid blue when seen from above in a darting school in calm waters.

The color exhibited by most fish is adapted to their particular environments, and a wide range of colors exists, as is evident when comparing the brook trout (top), bonefish (middle), and channel catfish (bottom).

When a dolphin is brought aboard, the unbelievably brilliant golden yellows, blues, and greens undulate and flow magically along the dolphin's body as it thrashes madly about. These changes in shade and degree of color also take place when the dolphin is in varying stages of excitement in the water.

A striped marlin or blue marlin following a surface-trolled bait is a wondrous spectacle of color to observe. As it eyes its quarry from side to side and maneuvers into position to attack, the deep cobalt-blue dorsal fin and bronze-silver sides are at their zenith. This electrifying display of color is lost almost immediately when the fish is boated.

Fins and Locomotion

Fish are propelled through the water by fins, body movement, or both. In general, the main moving force is the caudal fin, or tail, and the area immediately adjacent to it known as the caudal peduncle. In swimming, the fins are put into action by muscles attached to the base of the fin spines and rays. Fish with a fairly rigid body, such as the filefish, trunkfish, triggerfish, manta, and skates, depend mostly on fin action for propulsion. Eels, in contrast, rely on extreme, serpentlike body undulations to swim, with fin movement assisting to a minor extent. Sailfish, marlin, and other big-game fish fold their fins into grooves (lessening water resistance) and rely mainly on their large, rigid tails to go forward. Trout, salmon, catfish, and others are well adapted for sudden turns and short, fast moves. When water is expelled suddenly over the gills in breathing, it acts like a jet stream and aids in a fast start forward.

A fish can swim even if its fins are removed, though it generally has difficulty with direction and balance. In some kinds, however, the fins are highly important in swimming. For example, the pectoral fins of a ray are broad "wings" with which the fish sweeps through the water almost as gracefully as a swallow does in the air. The sharks, which are close relatives of the rays, swim swiftly in a straight line but have great difficulty in stopping or turning because their fins have restricted movement.

Flyingfish glide above the surface of the water with their winglike pectoral fins extended. Sometimes they get additional power surges by dipping their tails into the water and vibrating them vigorously. This may enable them to remain airborne for as long as a quarter of a mile. Needlefish and halfbeaks skitter over the surface for long distances, the front half of their bodies held stiffly out of the water while their still-submerged tails wag rapidly. An African catfish often swims upside down, and seahorses swim in a "standing up" position.

Many kinds of fish jump regularly. Those that take to the air when hooked give anglers the greatest thrills. Often, however, there is no easy explanation for why a fish jumps, other than the possibility that it derives pleasure from these momentary escapes from its watery world. The jump is made to dislodge a hook or to escape a predator in close pursuit; or the fish may try to shake its body free of plaguing parasites. Some spe-

Caudal (Tail) Fin Types

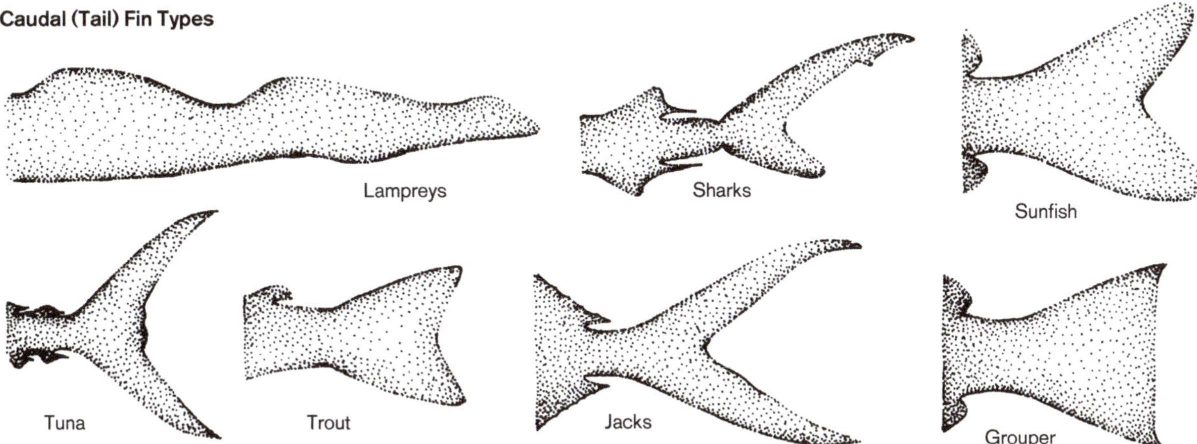

cies make their jumps by surging at high speed from deep water. Others swim rapidly close to the surface, then suddenly turn their noses skyward and give a powerful thrust with their tails as they take to the air. Sailfish and other high jumpers may leap several feet into the air when hooked, often leaping as many as 20 times before being brought to the boat.

Speed

Fisheries professionals are frequently asked how fast fish swim. This is a difficult question to answer precisely, because fish have a cruising speed, a maximum sustainable speed, and a top speed over relatively short distances.

Statistics for cruising (ordinary travel) speed have been taken mostly from tagged fish released at one point and recaptured at another. For example, some bluefin tuna tagged off Cat Cay, Bahamas, were recaptured in Norwegian waters. Two of these crossed the ocean in less than three months. Another completed the trip in the remarkable time of 52 days. These facts, which contradict the belief that all bluefin tuna migrating from the Bahamas spend the summer in western Atlantic coastal waters, indicate that bluefins swim swiftly, but obviously we do not know whether the recaptured specimens swam a direct course or indulged in detours. Also, ocean currents can be a help or a hindrance.

Maximum sustainable speed, that is, the speed that a fish can maintain for long periods, is almost impossible to judge unless measured experimentally on small fish by determining the length of time they can swim in approximately the same spot when currents of the same velocity are flowing by. Boats traveling alongside big-game fish have clocked their rate of speed. In addition, some anglers have attempted to gauge the speed of gamefish by improvising speedometers on their fishing reels or by using stopwatches to time the runs of hooked fish. The speed of a sailfish has been estimated to be as high as 100 yards per 3 seconds, or 68 miles per hour. All the speeds indicated by such experiments are approximate at best because many factors have to be considered, including size of the individual, temperature of the water, currents, the area of the mouth where the fish was hooked, physical condition of the particular fish hooked, and so on.

All members of the tunalike fish, such as the bluefin tuna, bonito, and albacore, are also extremely fast. Other species having a reputation for great speed are marlin, wahoo, dolphin, and swordfish. Generally, speeds of 40 to 50 miles per hour are attributed to these fish. In freshwater, the top speed of salmon has been estimated at 14 to 30 miles per hour, and the cruising speed at 8 miles per hour. The top speed for largemouth bass is about 12 miles per hour.

Air Bladder

The air bladder, located between the stomach and backbone, is also known as the swim bladder, which is misleading because the air bladder has no function in the movement of locomotion of fish in any direction. The mixture of gases that it contains is not normal air, so the correct name should be "gas bladder."

The air bladder is present in most bony fish; it does not appear in lampreys, hagfish, sharks, rays, or skates. The air bladder performs several functions. It may be well supplied with blood vessels, as it is in the tarpon, and act as a supplementary breathing organ. The tarpon has an open tube that leads from the upper side of its gullet to the air bladder. (The tarpon also has a set of gills.) Some species of fish use the air bladder as a compartment in which to store air for breathing. The fish falls back on this reserve when its usual supply of oxygen may be shut off. The air bladder plays a part in aiding equilibrium of density between the fish and the water. (It has no function of adjustment of pressure to changing levels.) In other words, the volume of water occupied by the fish should weigh about as much as the fish does. The air bladder is a compensator between them. For example, the pickerel is capable of "floating," its body motionless, anticipating its prey. The catfish, on the other hand, has no air bladder; it spends most of its life on the bottom.

The saltwater flatfish also has no air bladder, and it dives to the bottom swiftly if it escapes the hook near the surface of the water. (A fish does not raise or lower itself by increasing or decreasing the size of the air bladder.) It has also been definitely established that the air bladder is an efficient hearing aid in many types of fish. It is commonly known that the noises some fish make are produced by the air bladder.

Incidentally, there are some exceptions to the general rule, and that includes the primitive lungfish that are represented by five living species. These "living fossils" are found in Africa, South America, and Australia. The African lungfish's air bladder is purely respiratory in function; this fish cannot use its gills for breathing. If the African lungfish cannot reach the surface to gulp air, it soon drowns.

Skeleton and Muscles

A fish's skeleton is composed of cartilage or bone. Basically, the skeleton provides a foundation for the body and fins, encases and protects the brain and spinal cord, and serves as an attachment for muscles. It contains three principal segments: skull, vertebral column, and fin skeleton.

The meat or flesh covering the fish's muscular system is quite simple. All vertebrates, including fish, have three major types of muscles: smooth (involuntary), cardiac (heart), and striated (skeletal). Functionally, there are two kinds: voluntary and involuntary.

In fish, the smooth muscles are present in the digestive tract, air bladder, reproductive and excretory ducts, eyes, and other organs. The striated muscles run in irregular vertical bands, and various patterns are found in different types of fish. These muscles compose the bulk of the body and are functional in swimming by producing body undulations that propel the fish forward. The muscle segments, called myomeres, are divided into an upper and a lower half by a groove running along the midbody of the fish. The myomeres can be easily seen if the skin is carefully removed from the body or scraped away with a knife after cooking. These broad muscles are the part of the fish that we eat. Striated muscles are also attached to the base of the fin spines and rays, and maneuver the fins in swimming.

Superficial Muscles

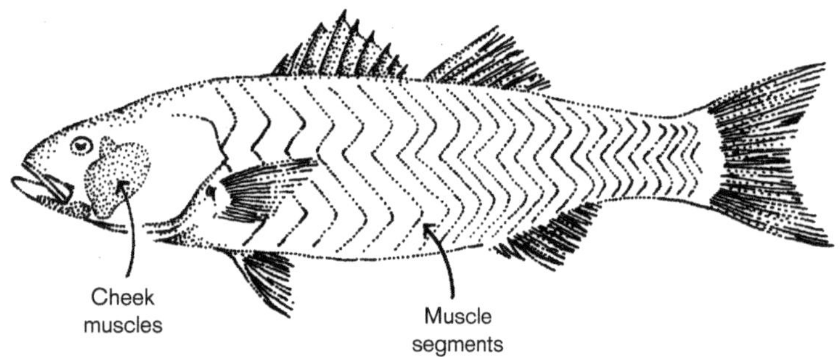

Broad striated muscles make up the bulk of the body of a fish; they run in irregular vertical bands and various patterns, and are functional in swimming.

Teeth, Food, and Digestion

A tremendous diversity exists in the form and size of fish teeth. The character of the dentition is a clue to the fish's feeding habits and the kind of food it consumes. Of all the fish, some sharks display the most awesome array of teeth: profuse and well structured for grasping, tearing, and cutting. The barracuda's teeth are different from any shark's, but they also draw attention because of their ferocious appearance. They are flat, triangular, closely set, and extremely sharp. Such teeth are ideally adapted for capturing live fish, the barracuda's main diet. Small victims are usually swallowed whole; the larger ones may be cut in two and each piece swallowed separately. The bluefish, well known for its ability to chop up a school of baitfish, has teeth of a similar nature but smaller in size.

Some fish possess sharp, conical teeth (called canine, or dog, teeth); pike, pickerel, and muskies are good examples. Such teeth cannot cut but do a good job of grasping and piercing. Fish fortified with canine teeth generally hold a baitfish until its struggles diminish before swallowing it—a fact taken into consideration by anglers before setting the hook. Anglers must exercise extreme caution when removing hooks from sharks, bluefish, barracuda, pikelike fish, and other fish with dangerous dentition.

The yellow perch, sea bass, catfish, and other species have multiple rows of numerous short and closely packed teeth that resemble the tips of a stiff brush. Such an arrangement meets the fish's need to grasp a variety of food off the bottom or hold prey in a sandpaper-like grip until ready to be eaten.

Some kinds of fish have sharp-edged cutting teeth called incisors located in the forward part of the mouth; some are saw-edged, others resemble human teeth, and still others are variously fused into parrotlike beaks. Parrotfish, for example, have such teeth and thrive on small organisms nibbled from corals, rocks, and reefs. Some bottom-dwelling fish, such as skates, rays, and drum, have molarlike teeth that are well adapted for crunching crustaceans, mollusks, and other organisms.

Many fish, including some of the more common types such as carp, minnows, and suckers, have teeth in their throats. These pharyngeal teeth are sharp in some species, molariform in others, and only remnants in still others. There are fish that have teeth on the roof of the mouth (vomerine and palatine) and on the tongue. Pike, pickerel, and muskies, for example, have vomerine teeth that are profuse and closely packed, whereas other fish, such as certain trout, have comparatively few teeth on these areas. One of the distinguishing features between a true trout and a char (rainbow trout versus brook trout, for example) is the presence or

absence of vomerine teeth. The vomerine bone in the center of the char's mouth has only a few teeth, located on its forward end, whereas the vomer of a true trout is much longer and has teeth all along it. Some fish have teeth on the very edges of their mouths (premaxillary and/or maxillary). And many planktonic feeders, such as the menhaden, have no teeth at all; instead, their long gill rakers help in retaining the microscopic organisms they take into their mouths.

Fish are a tremendously diversified group of animals that feed on an extensive variety of foods. Some, when mature, feed exclusively on other fish; others feed entirely on plants. The sea lamprey, a parasitic, highly unattractive eel-like fish, uses its funnel-shaped mouth, lined with radiating rows of sharp teeth, to attach itself to the body of a live fish; then, using its toothed tongue, it rasps a hole in its prey and sucks out blood and body fluids.

In general, the food plan of a fish's life is to eat and to be eaten. Such a scheme involves a food chain. Nutrients in the water nourish various types of free-flowing aquatic plants (phytoplankton) that are eaten by a variety of microscopic animals (zooplankton). A tiny fish feeds on zooplankton, and the bigger fish feeds on the smaller fish. There are many steps in this food chain, as larger fish eat smaller ones until the chain may end with, for example, a bluefin tuna. The tuna eventually expires and sinks to the bottom, where it is eaten by worms, crabs, and other bottom dwellers. Lastly, bacteria return the nutrients to the water in a soluble inorganic form, which the phytoplankton again utilize. The food chain is then complete.

Insects, worms, snails, mussels, squid, and crabs are some of the important larger invertebrates that provide food for fish. Amphibians, reptiles, birds, and mammals, as well as other fish, are also included in the diet of fish. Largemouth bass and muskies, for example, commonly eat frogs and occasionally small turtles or snakes. Gar have been caught that contained bird remains in their stomachs. And goosefish—bottom dwellers with huge mouths—will capture such unusual prey as a diving duck.

Fish also differ in the way they feed. Predators entrap or cut their prey by using their well-developed teeth. Grazers or browsers feed on the bottom. Fish that feed on tiny organisms sifted from the water by using their long gill rakers are known as strainers. Suckers and sturgeon have fleshy, distensible lips well suited to suck food off the bottom and thus are suckers. Some lampreys depend on the blood and fluids of other fish to live; they are categorized as parasites.

Here are a few examples of the structural adaptations of fish that assist them in feeding: catfish and sturgeon have whiskerlike feelers for touching and tasting food before accepting it; sailfish, marlin, and swordfish may stun their prey with their clublike bills before devouring it. The paddlefish employs its long, sensitive, paddlelike snout to stir up the bottom organisms on which it feeds. Gar have elongated snouts filled with needlelike teeth that make a formidable trap for capturing prey. The goosefish, also known as the angler, has a long, slim appendage with a piece of skin at its tip, located on the forward part of its upper snout; this appendage can be wiggled like a worm and acts as a lure to entice prey.

Generally, fish that live in a temperate zone, where seasons are well defined, will eat much more during the warm months than they will during the cold months. In this zone a fish's metabolism slows down greatly during winter. The body temperature of most fish changes with the surrounding environment, and it is not constant as it is in mammals and birds.

The digestive system of fish, as in all other vertebrates, dissolves food, thereby facilitating absorption or assimilation. This system, or metabolic process, is capable of removing some of the toxic properties that may be present in foods on which fish feed.

The basic plan of the digestive tract in a typical fish differs in some respects from that of other vertebrate animals. The tongue cannot move as it does in higher vertebrates, and it does not possess striated muscles. The esophagus, or gullet (between the throat and stomach), is highly distensible and usually can accept any type or size food that the fish can fit into its mouth. Although choking does happen, and has been particularly noticed in pickerel and pike, a fish rarely chokes to death because of food taken into its mouth.

Fish stomachs differ in shape from group to group. The predators have elongated stomachs. Those that are omnivorous generally have saclike stomachs. Sturgeon, gizzard shad, and mullet, among others, have stomachs with heavily muscled walls used for grinding food, just as the gizzard of a chicken does. Some of the bizarre deep-sea fish possess stomachs capable of huge distention, thereby enabling them to hold relatively huge prey. On the other hand, some fish have no stomachs; instead, they have accessory adaptations, such as grinding teeth, that crush the food finely so that it is easily absorbed.

Intestinal structure also differs in fish. The predators have shortened intestines; meaty foods are more easily digested than plant foods. In contrast, herbivores, or plant eaters, have long intestines, sometimes consisting of many folds. Sharks and a few other fish have intestines that incorporate a spiral or coiled valve that aids in digestion. Lampreys and hagfish have no jaws and do not have a well-defined stomach or curvature of the intestine. Lampreys need a simple digestive system because they are parasites that subsist on the blood and juices they suck from other fish. During the long migration from the sea upriver to spawn, the various species of salmon never feed. Their digestive tracts shrink amazingly, allowing the reproductive organs to fill up the abdomen.

Dame Juliana Berners' 1496 pike fishing tip: "Tie the cord to a goose's foot and you shall see good hauling, whether the goose or the pike shall have the better." It is believed the goose was used for trolling.

Gills and Breathing

Like all other living things, fish need oxygen to survive. In humans, the organs responsible for this function are the lungs. In fish, the gills perform the job. However, in some scaleless fish, the exchange of gases takes place through the skin. In fish embryos, various tissues temporarily take up the job of breathing. Some fish are capable of obtaining oxygen directly from the air through several adaptations, including modifications of the mouth cavity, gills, intestine, and air bladder.

A fish's gills are much-divided thin-walled filaments where capillaries lie close to the surface. In a living fish, the gills are bright-red feathery organs that are prominent when the gill cover of the fish is lifted. The filaments are located on bony arches. Most fish have four gill arches. Between the arches are openings through which the water passes. In the gills, carbon dioxide, a waste gas from the cells, is released; at the same time, the dissolved oxygen is taken into the blood for transport to the body cells. This happens quickly and is remarkably efficient—about 75 percent of the oxygen contained in each gulp of water is removed in the brief exposure.

Different kinds of fish vary in their oxygen demands. Trout and salmon require large amounts of oxygen. The cold water in which they live can hold a greater amount of dissolved oxygen than can warm water. Further, many live in fast-flowing streams in which new supplies of oxygen are churned into the water constantly. Most types of catfish are near the opposite extreme; their oxygen demands are so low that they thrive in sluggish warmwater streams and also in ponds and lakes where the oxygen supply is low. A catfish can, in fact, remain alive for a long time out of water if kept cool and moist. Like carp and similar kinds of fish, catfish can be shipped for long distances and arrive at the market alive.

A few fish, such as the various walking catfish, climbing perch, bowfin, gar, gourami, and others, can breathe air. Air-breathers use only about 5 percent of the oxygen available to them with each breath of air. The best-known air-breathers are the lungfish that live in tropical Africa. Their "lung" is an air bladder connected to the lungfish's mouth by a duct, its walls richly supplied with blood vessels. A lungfish gets new supplies of oxygen by rising to the surface and gulping air. It will drown if kept underwater. When the stagnant pool in which it lives dries up, which happens seasonally, the lungfish burrows into the soft mud at the bottom and secretes a slimy coating over its body. It continues to breathe air through a small hole that connects to the surface through the mud casing. When the rains come again and the pool fills, the lungfish wriggles out of its cocoon and resumes its usual living habits.

Lampreys have seven paired gill sacs or bronchial pouches. A lamprey does not take in water through its mouth as other fish do, even when its mouth is not in the act of sucking blood and juices out of its prey. Water, from which the lamprey secures its oxygen, is both taken in and expelled through the gill sacs.

The sea lamprey is a parasitic eel-like creature that exists by sucking out the blood of fish. It attaches itself to the side of its host by means of a funnel-shaped mouth lined with radiating rows of sharp teeth. With its toothed tongue, it rasps a hole in its victim and proceeds to draw out the fish's life blood and body fluids. Surprisingly, fish do not fear the lamprey by sight. The lamprey swims along serenely by the side of a lake trout (or other fish) and simply reaches out, clamping its suction mouth onto the unsuspecting prey. After feasting, it departs and the trout usually dies. If by chance the prey survives, it carries a wound that invites infection.

Rays and skates usually have five paired external gill slits (rarely six or seven) located on the bottom side of the head. Sharks also have the same number of gill slits, but they are located laterally (on the side). In sharks, the water used for respiration is taken in through the mouth and expelled through the gill slits. Rays and skates, however, draw in water through the spiracles located on top, or close to the top, of the head (an excellent adaptation for bottom-dwelling fish). The water flows over the gills and out the gill slits located on the underside of the head.

Because a fish has no opening between its nostrils and mouth cavity as humans do, it has to breathe through its mouth. When the fish opens its mouth, a stream of water is drawn in. During this intake of water the gill cover is held tight, thereby closing the gill opening. Then the fish closes its

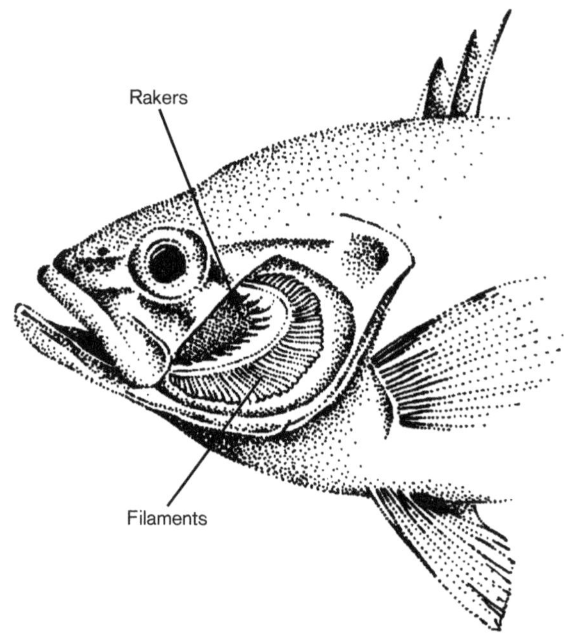

This cutaway view shows the first gill arch of a sunfish. The rakers, which strain the water, are on the left; the filaments, which transfer dissolved oxygen to the blood, are on the right.

mouth and drives the water over the gills and out the external openings by using special throat muscles. As the water passes over the gills, the exchange of gases takes place; that is, oxygen (which has been absorbed from the air by water exposed to it) is taken in through the walls of the fine blood vessels in the gill filaments, and carbon dioxide is given off. The blood, well oxygenated, then travels through the fish's body.

The rapidity with which a fish breathes varies with different species. A human in good health under normal circumstances breathes about 20 to 25 times a minute. Some types of fish have a breathing rate as low as 12 a minute, yet others take as many as 150 breaths per minute. If the fish is exerting itself, or if the oxygen content of the water becomes low, the rate of breathing will be faster, and the fish pants like a runner after finishing the mile.

Although gills play a major role in the respiratory organization of a fish, they also serve another purpose. Gill rakers, located along the anterior margin of the gill arch, aid in several ways. By projecting over the throat opening, they strain water that is passed over the gills. Solid particles are prevented from passing over and injuring the gill filaments. Gill rakers may be short and knobby, as in the pickerel, which is primarily a fish-eater. The shad, on the other hand, feeds on minute organisms. Its gill rakers are numerous, long, and thin, and they serve to sieve out the tiny organisms on which the shad feeds. In between these two extremes in size and shape, gill rakers of various sizes can be found in different types of fish. The number of gill rakers on the first gill arch is sometimes used as an aid in identifying or separating species that closely resemble one another.

Blood Circulation

The circulatory system of a fish, which consists of the heart, blood, and blood vessels, carries to every living cell in the body the oxygen and nourishment required for living; it carries away from the cells the carbon dioxide and other excretory products.

In function, the fish's muscular heart is similar to that of other vertebrates, acting as a pump to force the blood through the system of blood vessels. It differs from the human heart in having only two rather than four compartments—one auricle and one ventricle. The fish's heart is located close behind the fish's mouth. Blood vessels are largest close to the heart and become progressively smaller, terminating in a network of extremely fine capillaries that meander through the body tissues. The blood of a fish, like blood in all vertebrates, is composed of plasma (fluid) and blood cells (solid).

A fish's circulatory system is much simpler than that of a human. In humans, the blood is pumped from the heart into the lungs, where it is oxygenated; it then returns to the heart and receives a good thrust to travel throughout the body. In contrast, fish

Vascular System of a Fish (arteries white, veins black)

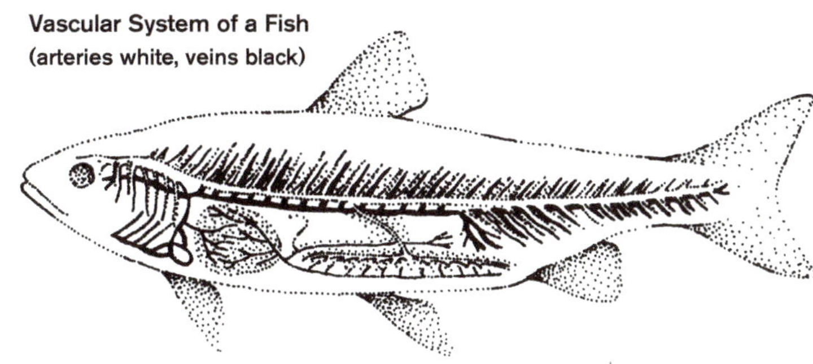

blood passes from the heart to the gills for purification and then travels directly to all other parts of the body.

Fish are often referred to as "cold-blooded" creatures, but this is not entirely true. Some are "warm-blooded," although they cannot sustain a constant body temperature as humans do. Instead, the fish's body temperature approximates that of its surrounding medium: water. Fish blood is thicker than human blood and has low pressure because it is pumped by a heart with only two chambers. Consequently, the flow of blood through a fish's body is slow. Because the blood flows slowly through the gills where it takes on oxygen, and because water contains less oxygen than air, fish blood is not as rich in oxygen as is human blood. Also, because of the slow flow of blood through the gills, the blood cools and approaches the temperature of the water surrounding the fish.

Senses and Nerves

A fish's eyes are adapted or modified for underwater vision, but they are not very different from human eyes. Fish do not have true eyelids. Human eyelids prevent the eyes from becoming dry and also protect against dirt. A fish's eyes are always covered by water; therefore, they require no lids.

The metallic-looking ring, called the iris, encircling the dark center, or lens, of the fish's eye cannot move as it does in the human eye. The human iris can expand or contract depending upon light conditions. Because light never attains great intensity underwater, a fish needs no such adaptation. The big difference between a human eye and the eye of a fish occurs in the lens. In humans it is fairly flat, or dishlike; in fish it is spherical or globular. Human eyes are capable of changing the curvature of the lens to focus at varying distances—flatter for long-range focusing and more curved for shorter range. Although the eye of a fish has a rigid lens and its curvature is incapable of change, it can be moved toward or away from the retina (like the focusing action of a camera). Scientists note one outstanding similarity between the eye of a human and the fish's eye. In both, six muscles move the eyeball. The six muscles are controlled by the same six nerves and act the same way to provide eye movement.

Although fish have no eyelids, they do sleep. Schooling fish commonly separate periodically to rest. Then they become active again and the schools reassemble. Some fish lie on their sides when they rest; others lean against rocks or slip into crevices. Some kinds wriggle their way into the soft ooze at the bottom to take a nap, and some of the parrotfish secrete a blanket of slime over the body at night. The preparation of this "bed" may take as long as an hour.

Important to anglers is the fact that a fish can distinguish colors. Experimenters have found, for example, that largemouth bass and trout quickly learn to tell red from other colors when red is associated with food. They can also distinguish green, blue, and yellow. There are indications that some kinds of fish prefer one color to another and also that water conditions may make one color more easily distinguished than others. Although lure action is most important, anglers can increase their chances of taking a fish by presenting lures of the proper color.

Many kinds of fish have excellent vision at close range. This is made especially clear by the archerfish that feeds on insects. By squirting drops of water forcefully from its mouth into the air, it may shoot down a hovering fly or one resting on grass or weeds. As an archerfish prepares to make its shot, it approaches carefully to make certain of its aim and range. An archerfish is accurate at distances up to about 3 feet and is sometimes successful with even longer shots.

The four-eyed fish, one of the oddities of the fish world, lives in shallow, muddy streams in Central America. On the top of its head are bulbous eyes that are half in and half out of the water as the fish swims along near the surface. These eyes function as four eyes because of their internal structure—the lens is egg-shaped rather than spherical. When the fish looks at objects under the water, light passes through the full length of the lens, and the foureyed fish is as nearsighted as any other fish. When it looks into the air, the light rays pass through the shorter width of the lens, giving the fish good distance vision.

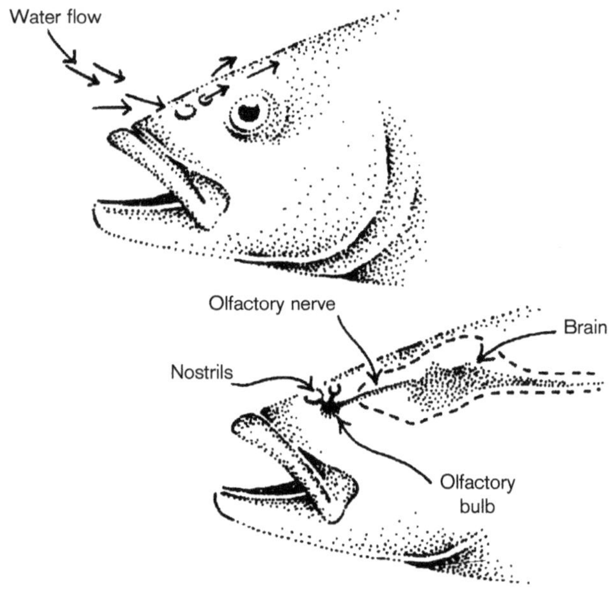

Fish that live in the dusky or dimly lit regions of the sea commonly have eyes that are comparatively larger than the eyes of any other animal with backbones. Fish that live in the perpetual darkness of caves or other subterranean waters usually have no eyes, but those inhabiting the deep sea, far below the depth to which light rays can penetrate, may or may not have eyes. The reason that most deep-sea fish have well-developed eyes is the prevalence of bioluminescense. Deep-sea squid, shrimp, and other creatures, as well as fish, are equipped with light-producing organs. The light they produce is used to recognize enemies or to capture prey.

Many fish with poor vision have well-developed senses of smell, taste, and touch. Improbable as it may seem, fish do possess nostrils. Four nostrils are located close to the top of the snout, one pair on each side. Each pair opens into a small blind sac immediately below the skin. Water, carrying odors, passes through the sacs, which are lined with the receptors of smell. Some fish, including sharks, possess an extremely acute sense of smell.

Fish have taste organs located in the skin of the snout, lips, mouth, and throat. A fish's tongue, unlike the human tongue, is flat, rigid, and cartilaginous and moves only when the base below it moves; nevertheless, it does possess taste buds that indicate to the fish whether to accept or to reject anything taken into its mouth.

There is a close relationship between the senses of smell and taste in fish, just as in humans. Many types of fish are first drawn to food by its odor. For example, catfish and sturgeon, which are first attracted by food odor, will feel and taste the food with their chin barbels before taking it. These whiskerlike appendages contain taste buds. Some catfish have taste buds all over their bodies; certain kinds can actually taste with their tails.

Although fish obviously do not possess outer ears as humans do, they are still capable of hearing. The human ear is composed of an outer, middle, and inner ear; each part interacts with the other for both hearing and maintaining equilibrium. Fish possess only an inner ear, found in the bones of the skull. Outer and middle ears are not necessary in fish, because water is a much better conductor of sound than air. In many fish, these ear bones are connected to the air bladder. Vibrations are transmitted to the ear from the air bladder, which acts as a sounding board.

The lateral-line system, a series of sensory cells usually running the length of both sides of the fish's body, performs an important function in receiving low-frequency vibrations. Actually, it resembles a "hearing organ" of greater sensitivity than human

Smell receptors are located in the nostrils, and water (carrying odors) is drawn into sacs that are lined with the organs of smell. Olfactory nerves connect the nostrils and brain.

ears. The typical lateral line is a mucous-filled tube or canal under the skin; it has contact with the outside world through pores in the skin or through scales along the line or in between them. A nerve situated at intervals alongside the canal sends out branches to it. In some cases the lateral line extends over the fish's tail, and in many fish it continues onto the head and spreads into several branches along the outer bones of the fish's skull, where it is not outwardly visible. The fish utilizes its lateral line to determine the direction of currents of water and the presence of nearby objects as well as to sense vibrations. The lateral line helps the fish to determine water temperature and to find its way when traveling at night or through murky waters. It also assists schooling fish in keeping together and may help a fish to escape enemies.

Many fish are noisy creatures. They make rasping, squeaking, grunting, and squealing noises. This came as a great surprise to military forces during World War II when their sound-detecting devices, designed to pick up the noises of submarines, instead were literally jammed by fish noises. Some fish produce sounds by rubbing together special extensions of the bones of their vertebrae. Others make noises by vibrating muscles that are connected to their air bladders, which amplify the sounds. Still other fish grind their teeth, their mouth cavities serving as sound boxes to amplify the noises. Many fish make sounds when they are caught. Grunts and croakers got their names from this habit.

Some fish are capable of generating electricity. To our present knowledge, no other animal possesses organs that can perform such a function. The electric eel can produce an electric current of shocking power. In a properly constructed aquarium, it can be demonstrated that electricity expelled by an electric eel is strong enough to operate light bulbs. The current also stuns enemies and prey, and acts as a sort of radar system. Sensory pits located on the fish's head receive the reflections of these electrical currents from objects close by. The electric ray and electric catfish are also capable of producing electrical currents strong enough to stun prey. South African gymnotids and African mormyrids are among other kinds of fish that produce electric shocks of lesser strength. The electrical field set up around them serves as a warning device to any intruding prey or predator.

Since fish have a nervous system and sense organs, it would appear that they could feel pain. The fish's brain is not highly developed, however. There is no cerebral cortex (the part of the brain in higher animals that stores impressions), and so the fish has little or no memory. It is not uncommon, for example, for an angler to hook the same fish twice within a short time. Many fish are caught with lures or hooks embedded in their jaws. Fish are essentially creatures of reflex rather than action produced or developed by using the brain. In all probability, physical pain in fish is not very acute, and if any impression of pain is made in the brain, it is quickly lost.

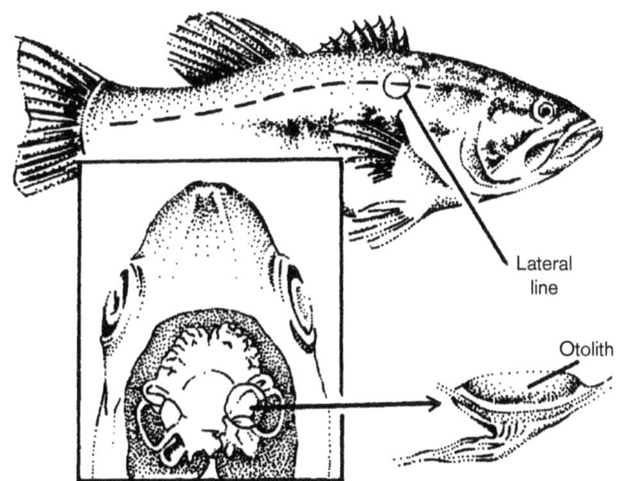

Hearing is accomplished primarily through nerves in the lateral line but also through sound waves detected by the otolith.

Reproduction

The fish, like most animals, begins life as an egg, and, as in all other vertebrates, the single-cell egg cannot develop unless it is fertilized by a sperm produced by the male. Fish sperm is most commonly referred to as milt.

Eggs may be fertilized either externally or internally. External fertilization takes place when the egg is penetrated by the sperm after the egg leaves the female's body. The vast majority of fish are reproduced by this system. Internal fertilization occurs when the male introduces the sperm into the female's body, where it makes contact with and fertilizes the egg. Some sharks and the livebearing toothed carp (popular aquarium fish) are ovoviviparous; that is, the egg is fertilized internally and held within the female without attachment to her until it is ready to be extruded alive. In other species, such as some of the sharks and sculpin, a few catfish, and the skate, the egg is penetrated by the sperm inside the female's body, but it does not hatch until some time after being released from the female.

Reproduction and associated activities in fish are generally referred to as spawning. The spawning season, or breeding period, is that time when the eggs of the female and the milt, or sperm, of the male are ripe. This period may last only a few days, as in some warmwater species like the largemouth bass. Or it may extend into weeks and even months in coldwater species such as the whitefish and the arctic char. Fish that live in tropical waters of fairly constant temperature may spawn year-round.

Depending on the species, spawning may take place in a variety of environments. But, regardless of where the spawning occurs, all fertilized eggs require special conditions for successful

development. Sunlight, oxygen, water agitation, salt and chemicals, water temperature, and other factors have an influence on egg development. In the marine environment, spawning may take place in the open ocean or close to shore. In freshwater, spawning may occur in rapidly moving rivers and streams where the parents leave the eggs, or in quiet waters where the fish makes a nest and then protects it. Some fish leave the saltwater to travel up rivers and streams to spawn. Eels leave saltwater to enter freshwater but return to the sea to spawn.

Fish such as mackerel, which travel in the open ocean in large schools, take part en masse in external fertilization. They form huge groups and release their reproductive cells indiscriminately into the water. No attempt is made at pairing. The fertilized eggs are at the mercy of temperature, winds, currents, water clarity, salinity, and other factors. In this open-sea type of spawning, the eggs of most species float freely. In other species, the fertilized eggs sink to the bottom, where they are greedily fed upon by bottom-dwelling species. In either system, the parents show no concern for the eggs.

"Like a fish out of water" is a phrase that does not apply to some fish that are very much at home on land; among them are spiny eels, mudskippers, climbing perch, and snakeheads.

The striped bass, a popular sportfish, is an example of a fish that leaves the saltwater to spawn in rivers and streams. Its eggs are fertilized more or less freely, and a single female may be attended by as many as 50 males. The nonadhesive eggs are slightly heavier than water and are rolled along the bottom by the current. The parents protect neither eggs nor young.

Six species of salmon, one on the North American East Coast and five along the Pacific, enter freshwater rivers to spawn. Often they travel hundreds of miles before reaching the spawning site. Unlike the striped bass, they pair off and build a type of nest. These nests, called redds, are built in clear water that is well oxygenated and runs over pebbly areas. The eggs sink in between the pebbles of the nest, where they are safe from predators. The parents, however, do not protect eggs or young. If the nest gets covered by silt, the eggs suffocate.

Trout and bass, among the most popular sportfish, have contrasting spawning habits. Bass usually select quiet, sheltered spawning areas, in water 2 to 6 feet deep. The male excavates a depression in the sand or gravel bottom or among the roots of vegetation. The nest averages 2 to 3 feet in width and 6 inches in depth. It is constructed by the male who fans the spot with his tail and transports the small pebbles away in his mouth. Depending on her size, a female largemouth bass usually carries from 2,000 to 26,000 eggs, although there are cases on record of a female carrying as many as 40,000 eggs. The pugnacious male guards the nest, eggs, and young until the school scatters.

In contrast, the female brook trout usually digs her nest in riffles or at the tail end of pools. She turns on her side and with rapid movements of her tail pushes around the gravel, pebbles, and other bottom materials. When the nest, or egg pit, is of proper size and depth, both male and female assume a parallel position over the area; when ready, the eggs and milt are extruded at the same time. Young females may carry 200 to 500 eggs, and larger ones may carry over 2,500.

As soon as the spawning procedure is completed, the female brook trout hollows out another nest a short distance upstream from the first nest. The disturbed pebbles from the second excavation travel downstream, covering the eggs of the first nest with a layer of gravel. Several nests may be required before the female has shed all her eggs.

Time requirements for incubation of eggs depend on the species of fish and the water temperature. For example, largemouth bass eggs hatch in about five days in water about 66°F. The incubation period for brook trout is about 44 days at 50°F, and about 28 days at 59°F. A sudden 10° drop in temperature during the breeding season is usually enough to kill bass eggs or the newly hatched fry.

Attached to a typical newly hatched young fish, called a larva, is an undigested portion of the yolk. This is usually enough food to last until the little fish can adjust to its aquatic world, before it must begin hunting food for itself. Some kinds of fish start to resemble their parents soon after emerging from the egg and may themselves spawn within the year. Others require years of development before they mature.

Young flounder and other members of the flatfish family start life in an upright position, looking like any other little fish. But during the course of development, the skull twists and one eye migrates to the other side of the head until finally both eyes are on the upper side of the fish. Another startling example of differences in appearance between young and adult occurs in the prolific American eel (large specimens deposit 15 to 20 million eggs). The adult eels leave lakes, ponds, and streams to spawn in midwinter in the Sargasso Sea southwest of Bermuda and off the east coast of Florida. In its larval stage, the American eel is thin, ribbonlike, and transparent. Its head is small and pointed; its mouth contains large teeth, although at this stage it apparently takes no food. The larval form lasts about a year. Then it metamorphoses to the elver, at which time the length and the depth of the body shrink but increase in thickness to a cylindrical form resembling the adult eel. The large, larval teeth disappear, and the head also changes shape. The elver, however, does not take on the adult color, and it does not begin to feed until it reaches North American shores. Averaging 2 to $3^1/_2$ inches in length, the elvers appear in spring.

Carp and sturgeon are two of the big egg producers among freshwater fish. When a female sturgeon is full of roe, the eggs may account for as much as 25 percent of her weight. The salted and processed eggs of sturgeons are prized as caviar, as is the roe of salmon, herring, whitefish, codfish, and other fish.

Bullhead and many tropical fish lay their eggs in burrows scooped out of the soft mud at the bottom. Gourami make a bubble nest, the males blowing bubbles that rise to the surface, stick together, and form a floating raft. After the nest is built, the female lays her eggs; the male then blows each egg up into the bubbles, where it remains until it hatches. The male stands guard under the raft to chase away intruders.

Male seahorses carry their eggs and also their young in a belly pouch. A female South American catfish carries her eggs attached to a spongy disc on her belly. Sea catfish males use their mouths as brooding pouches for their eggs; once the young are born, the pouches serve as a place of refuge until the young are large enough to fend for themselves.

Many species of fish make nests. Some nests are elaborate, much like those made by birds. The male stickleback, for example, makes a neat nest of twigs and debris and defends it with his life. Other fish simply sweep away the silt and debris where the eggs are to be laid and keep the nest clean and the water aerated until the eggs hatch.

During the spawning season, the sex of most fish is easily discernible. Because of the huge quantity of eggs she carries, the female is usually potbellied compared with the male. As the reproductive apparatus becomes ripe, a slight press on the belly will cause the whitish milt of the male or the eggs of the female to be seen in the vent. When the milt and eggs are in advanced stages of ripeness, they can be forced out by massaging the belly firmly from the head toward the vent. Hatcheries force out the reproductive products in this manner. The eggs are exuded into a pan, and then the milt is forced over them. Milt and eggs are gently mixed, and fertilization takes place. Except in spawning conditions, the sex of many fish cannot be determined unless the belly is dissected and the immature eggs or milt sac is found.

As spawning time approaches, some kinds of fish develop outward signs that make the sexes easily distinguishable. Male trout and salmon acquire hook jaws. Smelts, suckers, and most species of minnows have on their head and snout small horny tubercles that disappear shortly after spawning has finished. Males of many species possess larger fins or extensions on the fins. And color is often different in the sexes. The male may sport much brighter and more intense coloration than the female. Some fish have permanent differences in their anatomy; for example, the male bull dolphin has an extended or square forehead, whereas the female's forehead is rounded. Males of many species develop large fins or extensions on some of the fins. Male sharks, skates, and rays have tubelike extensions of the pelvic fins that function in mating.

Age and Growth

Although birds and mammals cease to grow after becoming fully mature, fish continue to grow until they die, provided food is abundant. Growth is fastest during the first few years of life and continues at a decreasing rate. It accelerates during warm-weather months when food is abundant. During the cold months, fish do not feed much; their metabolism slows down, and growth is retarded.

Scale Annulli

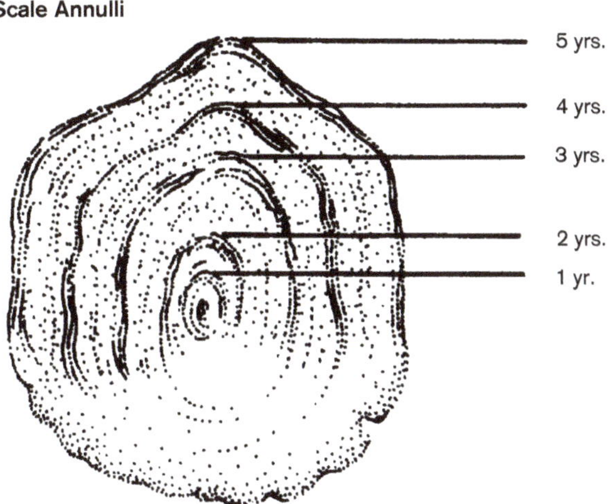

Annual growth rings from this scale indicate a five-year-old fish.

Proper determination of age and growth in fish is important in order to regulate the harvest. In both sport and commercial fish, the age and growth rate must be known in order to reap the crop wisely. Fisheries are controlled by rules and regulations based on facts in the life history of fish.

Generally, fish in warm climates reach sexual maturity and grow faster than their cousins farther north, because the growing seasons are longer and the food supply is not shortened by cold weather. For example, a largemouth bass in Florida may spawn after one year; in Wisconsin the same species does not spawn until the third year; and in Canada the largemouth bass may not reach maturity until the fourth or fifth year. Under average conditions, the largemouth bass may attain 3 inches in length in the first five months, 5 to 6 inches in one year, 8 to 10 inches in two years. By the third year, they may be 12 or more inches.

A fish's growth rate is also influenced by its environment. A pond or lake can support only a limited poundage of fish, just as a piece of farmland produces only a limited harvest of vegetables or other crops. In some bodies of water, fish never attain natural size because there are too many of them for the available food supply. Yellow perch are found stunted because only a few, if any, predators, such as bass and pickerel, are present to feed on them. Stunting may also take place because not enough fish are caught, or perhaps because anglers return all the small ones to the water unharmed.

The age of fish that live in temperate climates can be determined fairly accurately from various bony portions of their anatomy, because definite changes in seasons cause annual marks to appear in the bone. These year zones of growth are produced by the slowing down of metabolism in the winter and its rapid increase in the spring. In some species the annual ridges, called annuli, are especially pronounced and easy to read in the scales and cheekbones. In fish with tiny scales, these annuli are difficult to see, even under a microscope. Spines, vertebrae, jawbones, and earbones have to be studied to determine the fish's age. In cross-section, these various bones may show annual rings that appear similar to the rings in the cross-section of a tree trunk.

In tropical areas with seasonal rainfall, the age of freshwater fish can be denoted by seasonal growth marks caused by dry and wet seasons. In uniformly warm waters, such as the equatorial currents, fish demonstrate little, if any, seasonal fluctuation in growth, and age determination is difficult.

Migration

Migration is the mass movement of fish (or any other animals) along a route from one area to another at about the same time annually. This group travel is induced basically by factors of food and spawning. At times, mass movement may take place for other reasons, but such travel should not be confused with migration. Sudden adverse conditions, such as pollution, excessive sedimentation, or water discoloration caused by unusually severe storms, may force large groups of fish to leave the affected area.

Some fish, called "tide-runners," move with the tide to shore and then out again while searching for food. This movement is simply a daily feeding habit and is not considered migration. Some fish remain in deep water during the day and move to shore at night for feeding. In some lakes the entire population of a certain species may move at times from warming shallows to deeper, cooler waters to survive. The lake trout and the walleye are good examples of sportfish that make seasonal movements of this sort.

The bluefin tuna, one of the largest of the oceanic fish, migrates about the same time each year between the coasts of southern Florida and the Bahamas, where it spawns, to waters off Nova Scotia, Prince Edward Island, and Newfoundland. On reaching these far northern waters, the bluefin will find and follow huge schools of herring, sardines, mackerel, or squid in the same localities, year after year. If the temperature rises higher than usual, or other water changes take place, the bait schools will depart from their customary haunts, and the bluefin will follow.

Inshore fish such as the shad and the striped bass may travel varying distances along the coast before arriving in freshwater rivers or brackish stretches that meet the requirements for their spawning activities. Some species do not travel along a coast or migrate north and south; instead, they move offshore into deeper water in cold weather and inshore during warm weather. Others combine a north-south movement with an inshore-offshore migration.

The California grunion, a small, silvery fish, is an example of a unique and precisely timed migration. It spawns at the turn of high tide and as far up the beach as the largest waves travel. This action takes place during that period when the water reaches farthest up shore. The grunion deposits eggs and sperm in pockets in the wet sand. Two weeks or a month later, at the time of the next highest tide, when the water reaches the nests and stirs up the sand, the young are hatched and scramble out to sea before the tide recedes and prevents them from escaping.

Members of the salmon family participate in what may be termed classical migration. All have the same general life pattern. The eggs are hatched in shallow streams; the young spend their early life in freshwater, grow to maturity in the ocean, and then return to the stream of their birth to spawn. The length of time spent in freshwater and saltwater habitats varies among the species and among populations of the same species. All five species of northwestern Pacific salmon die after their first spawning. The Atlantic salmon drops back to saltwater; those fish that survive the hazards of the sea return to spawn again. Salmon migrate varying distances to reach their spawning sites. The chum and the pink salmon usually spawn a few miles from saltwater and often within reach of the tides. The chinook, largest of the salmon family, may cover thousands of miles and surmount many obstacles before reaching its ancestral spawning grounds. And after spending from one to about four years far out to sea, each individual returns to spawn in the river where it was born.

ANCHOR

A heavy object, usually of lead or metal, that is fastened to a chain and/or line and set on the lake, river, or ocean bottom to keep a boat in position.

Although anchor use varies substantially among anglers, every boat should carry one, at least for deployment in an emergency. Many boaters pay little attention to and don't fully understand how to use this device. Indeed, many freshwater anglers, especially those whose techniques involve only casting or trolling, and those who use electric motors for constant boat positioning and manipulation, rarely use an anchor and may even disdain the use of one. An anchor can be an important accessory for anglers, however, as proper anchoring helps ensure that the boat remains in exactly the right spot.

If a boat loses power, and, due to current or wind direction, is in danger—of drifting aground, into shore, onto a reef or shoal, into other boats, over a small dam, or into a weir, among other possibilities—a readily available anchor, quickly placed into the water, can be used to hold a boat in a safe position, or to slow the drift enough to avoid trouble until power is restored or help arrives.

People who stillfish, and those who drift, are among the primary users of anchors, although anglers casting to specific areas may use an anchor to temporarily maintain position until that locale has been thoroughly fished. Anchors may be necessary under windy conditions, to permit more thorough fishing of a certain location or to set up a chum slick in offshore waters. Some river anglers use heavy chains as an anchor to slow their downstream drift and permit sufficient casting while drifting. Some use heavy blocks as a part-anchor/part-drag system, which enables them to slowly drift while stirring up aquatic life on the bottom and presenting some form of live bait in the stirred-up water.

In freshwater, most anglers anchor in fairly shallow water, especially when fishing rivers and small lakes and ponds. Most fish out of small boats and use small anchors. Sometimes these anchors are homemade, serving their purpose mostly because of their weight and a lack of wind or heavy current. Larger boats used in freshwater, and most fishing boats employed in saltwater, have greater anchoring needs. In these scenarios, both the type of anchor and the method of setting and retrieval become critical.

For larger vessels, it is wise to carry a second anchor as insurance against mishaps with the first. If you are forced to break off the first one, it's convenient to have a backup, either when you wish to continue fishing or when you need more holding power in dangerous or emergency situations.

Basic Anchor Types

Of the great variety of anchor types, a relatively small number are used by anglers. Some modern and newly designed anchors are hybrids, and some are slight variations of the standard designs. The weight and/or the design of the anchor usually determine its holding power, but a heavy anchor is not essential for holding a big boat; bottom conditions, sea conditions, anchor design, how the anchor was set, the amount of rode (anchor line) let out, and other factors all play a role.

Improvised. Small-boat owners have used cement blocks, cement- or sand-filled cans and jugs, sash weights, pieces of iron, truck tire chains, and other makeshift and economical dead weights as anchors. Most of these are suitable only for small to medium-size boats, generally under 20 feet in length, and in fairly calm water. They may not hold sufficiently in heavy waves or in current and typically have little ability to grab the bottom and dig in, although they may hold if they snag behind a big object, such as a rock. Large homemade anchors, including blocks and iron chunks, can be used on large boats, but they are not efficient and will bounce and roll in heavy waves; if they fall into water deeper than the rode, they will exert a downward force on the bow, which could be dangerous, and they are also back breakers when retrieved.

Many river anglers use an improvised anchor, especially chain, which functions primarily as a weight to slow their downstream movement. This is particularly helpful in sections of water with riffles, rapids, or shoals. Chains are noisy and may spook fish in some waters; an option is an industrial-strength jug, filled with sand or mud, that bounces along quietly like a piece of wood.

Anchor Types

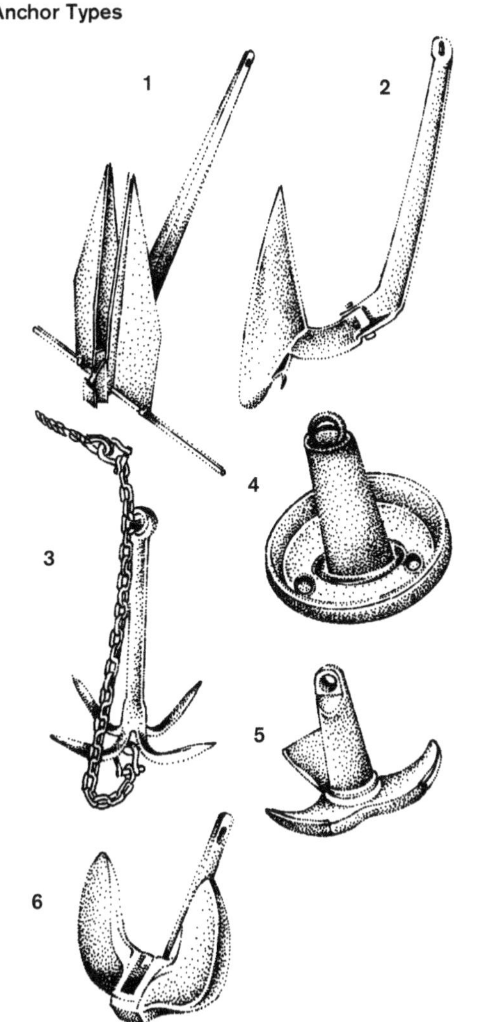

Common anchor types include: Danforth or fluke (1), plow (2), grapnel (3), mushroom (4), river (5), and Navy (6).

Mushroom. This is a cheap anchor, usually made of lead and sometimes having a vinyl or plastic coating. It has a 360-degree cupped lip and an upside-down mushroom appearance. It is solid, fairly small, and stows easily. It is more popular among small-boat owners in freshwater than in saltwater, and it primarily holds due to its weight (usually 8 to 10 pounds, but some are 15 pounds) rather than any intrinsic grabbing ability. Although commonly carried in boats of 15- to 18-foot lengths, such as bass boats, mushroom anchors are mainly useful under ideal conditions, especially where there is a soft bottom; they are not adequate in fast-moving water and cannot hold a heavy boat well, especially in a marl or hard bottom, unless that bottom has plenty of large rocks. When they settle into a muddy bottom, mushroom anchors are prone to

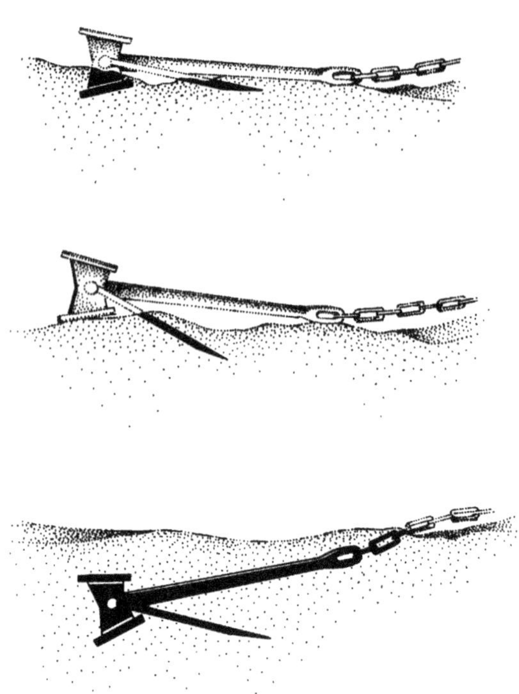

The flukes on a Danforth anchor lie flat when they reach bottom (top), dig in as pressure is applied (middle), then bury the anchor (bottom) for a very secure hold.

bring a lot of the bottom up with them, making for a heavy load to lift out of the water.

Mushroom anchors are regularly used for permanent harbor moorings because they exert a lot of suction once buried into an appropriate bottom. Anglers, who often drop anchor for short periods and mostly when there is wind, wave, and/or current action, do not usually face the ideal conditions that permit mushroom anchors to get a quick and lasting hold.

Danforth. Also known as a lightweight burying anchor, or a fluke anchor, the Danforth has a high holding-power-to-weight ratio and is a favorite of many boaters. It is easy to operate and folds flat for relatively convenient storage, although the large surface area makes it cumbersome in the smaller compartments of many freshwater boats. Their light weight (3 to 10 pounds) makes deployment and retrieval easy, and most have a trip feature for releasing the anchor.

The Danforth is made of steel or aluminum (the latter being lighter) and features two long, flat, and pointed flukes that dig into the bottom as upward pressure is applied on the rode. It is especially effective in mud, sand, and clay and may actually bury itself if left long enough, as rode pressure forces the flukes deeper. On rocky terrain the flukes may skip over the bottom instead of digging in, and the flukes tend to pick up debris when they're retrieved. They may also be hard to use in extremely soft bottoms with a lot of grass. Some newer aluminum versions feature an adjustable shank that can be changed to suit different bottoms.

Navy. This design combines movable flukes with a lot of weight. They are made of lead, sometimes coated with vinyl, and feature bulb and pivoting weight design. Navy anchors hold especially well in soft bottoms and are fairly popular, especially in freshwater, but they have a poor holding-power-to-weight ratio. They are manufactured in 5- to 20-pound sizes, the larger of which do not hold as well as much lighter Danforths.

Plow. This device, which is newer than many of the designs described here, sports a broadhead-like blade and a design that rights the anchor and causes the blade to furrow into the bottom, eventually burying itself if the bottom is soft enough. It has application over diverse bottoms and is especially good in sand and moderate grass. Some versions have a shank that pivots, which reduces the tendency of the anchor to pull out when there's a sharp change in the angle of pull.

These anchors range from 15-pounders, for 25-foot boats, up to 60-pounders. Because they're large, they are hard to store in bow anchor compartments with limited space. For this reason, some boaters fasten them securely to a bow roller.

Grapnel. This is a metal gang-hook anchor that sports four to six upward-sweeping claws. It has no value on soft bottoms but is excellent on rocky bottoms, as the claws readily catch onto objects. Grapnels are of moderate weight and are manufactured in small versions that serve backup duty or are used to scour the bottom for dropped equipment. Grapnels can get seriously hooked on the bottom, becoming impossible to retrieve. This potential problem can be avoided by attaching a trip line to the bottom of the anchor so it can be overturned. They are slightly bulky for small-boat storage, and the many hooks have a way of snagging things in the boat as well as rubbing against the boat.

River. This is a lead anchor, usually vinyl coated, with three wide, cupped blades. It is heavy, weighing from 10 to 30 pounds. It has no benefit in soft bottoms but is meant to hold in rocky bottoms and varying current conditions. Other anchor types—including mushroom, twin-fluked lead navy models, and improvised versions—are also used in rivers, and some boaters use a bow cleat to secure these. The anchor cleat is fastened on the bow deck plate, and the rode runs through it, aided by rollers.

Size. After choosing an anchor style that most suits the types of bottom you'll encounter, you will also have to think about getting the proper size to accommodate your boat. Size should be calculated with potential rough-water conditions (days when it is blowing a lot) or maximum current in mind. Generally, anchor recommendations for boats are based on "working" conditions, that is, rough water and gusty winds in the 20-knot range. Storm conditions require larger sizes. Marine supply stores usu-

Homemade cement and chain anchors are used with these New Brunswick river guide boats.

ally have anchor selection charts that suggest how much holding power is needed for different conditions, and which anchor and corresponding size would be best.

Rode Type and Length

Holding power is determined not only by the design, weight, and size of the anchor but also by the amount of rode you have out. The elements between the anchor and boat, which includes line and chain, are all part of the rode. For many people, particularly freshwater boaters, this is simply known as anchor line. Many boaters in freshwater, and some in saltwater, use only line, without chain, connected directly to the anchor. This is satisfactory for most simple anchoring chores, which depend on light anchor devices and a short rode. Some amount of chain is almost always useful, however, because its weight aids in lowering the angle of pull, it will not suffer when contacting abrasive bottom elements, and it does not get as gritty and dirty as does terminal line.

The vast majority of line used for anchoring is nylon, either twisted or braided. Nylon is preferable to other materials because it resists rot, decay, and mildew if stored out of the sunlight, and its elasticity (between 15 and 30 percent) provides a desirable amount of shock absorption. Twisted nylon is more elastic than braided nylon, but it does not lay as flat and takes up more space. The line is connected to a short length of galvanized chain—usually 6 to 8 feet long but perhaps greater, depending on the size of the anchor and the manufacturer's recommendations. The chain may be vinyl coated to protect the boat and is attached directly to the anchor.

For boats up to 25 feet long, the line diameter should be no less than $^{3}/_{8}$ inch. This size will be more than adequate for most freshwater anglers, especially in smaller craft, and those who anchor fairly shallow. It may be too light for 25-foot boats that run offshore and anchor in deep water, as the line could be subjected to excessive tension. Then, it may be advisable to use $^{1}/_{2}$-inch- or $^{9}/_{16}$-inch-diameter line, which is also easier to handle. Lines that are larger still are recommended for bigger boats.

The necessary length of rode depends on where you will be anchoring and the worst conditions in which you might have to anchor. Small boats usually carry no more than 15 or 20 feet of rode. Although this length is adequate for calm stillwater conditions, it might not be sufficient for the strong current on a river. Generally, the larger the boat, the deeper the water, the more demanding the water conditions, the longer the rode needed. When you have a lot of rode out, however, there is a greater tendency for the boat to swing, especially in wind or current. In some cases a short rode might be adequate, but you would need a heavy anchor to maintain position.

In boating, the term scope is used to describe rode length as it relates to water depth and the height above the water of the anchoring point on the boat. The minimum scope ratio should vary between 5:1 and 10:1, the greater ratio being reserved for rough weather; the U.S. Coast Guard recommends a ratio of 7:1. For example, if the water is 17 feet deep and the anchor point on your boat is 3 feet above the surface (producing a total vertical distance to the bottom of 20 feet), you should let out 140 feet of rode. If the tide rises 3 feet while you are anchored, the ratio would be reduced to 6:1.

Many boaters, especially in freshwater, let out a little more rode than is required for the anchor to contact bottom. In calm waters and protected areas, the boat might remain in position, but this setup will never do in rough water, wind-blown locations, places with current, or emergencies.

Because anchors require a low angle of pull to dig in and to stay in place, scope has a significant impact on efficiency. The less the scope, the higher the angle of pull, and the greater the chance that the anchor will be pulled out of the bottom. In simpler terms, the more parallel to the bottom the angle of the rode becomes, the more an anchor will dig in, especially an anchor with flukes. This tendency is especially true in heavy seas and large swells because they put a great demand on the anchor.

Practical limitations to this do exist, however. Anchoring in 100 feet of water, as is common in

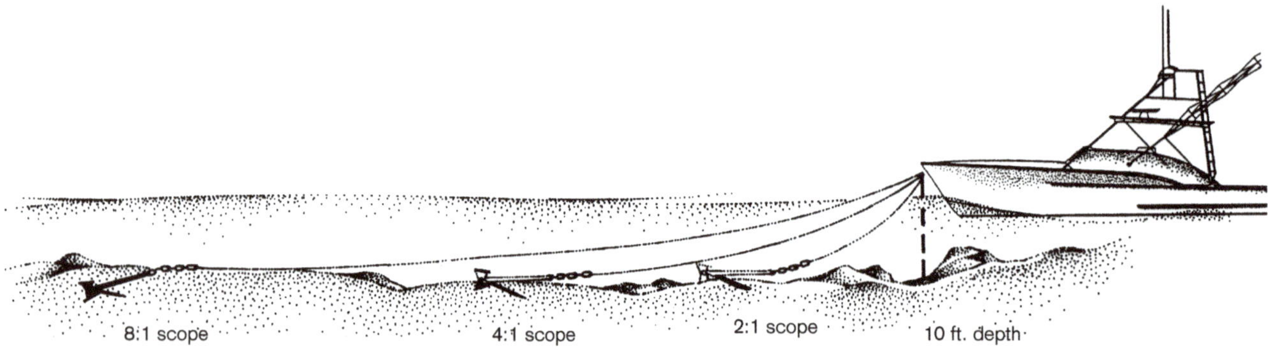

Scope is the ratio of the length of anchor rope to depth of the water from an anchoring point, with a 7:1 ratio recommended by the U.S. Coast Guard. In general, the greater the length of anchor rope, the better the anchor can grab and hold. Shorter lengths produce greater upward pull on the anchor. In the scenario depicted, with a bottom depth of 10 feet, deploying 80 feet of anchor rope will achieve an 8:1 scope.

saltwater, requires 500 to 700 feet of rode if the line material is nearly all nylon; to anchor in 300 feet would theoretically require perhaps 2,000 feet of rode, an amount that presents storage problems as well as retrieval difficulty. To overcome this problem, boaters employ a rode comprised of all galvanized chain, or one that has a longer length of chain (15 to 50 feet) combined with nylon line. The chain, which is attached directly to the anchor, sinks rapidly to the bottom, thereby establishing a lower angle of pull. This enables a great reduction in overall rode length.

When you have a lot of rode out, there is more chance of a strong fish wrapping your fishing line around it. In a big boat, it may not be possible to walk around the foredeck to fight the fish, and this could become problematic. For big tuna and sharks caught while chumming at anchor, it may be necessary to maneuver the boat to fight and land the fish. In this case, an anchor ball (also known as a mooring buoy) is clipped to the rode and dropped in the water, and the boat detaches and moves off. This allows the angler to follow the fish, which may help in landing it and will also aid in preventing it from swimming around the rode.

Setting and Retrieving

The following instructions pertain mostly to the temporary anchoring that characterizes most fishing by boat. Additional and more secure measures may be necessary for permanent mooring setups, as in harbors or for overnight stays. Also, in crowded spots the standard scope may be impractical, allowing too much swinging room.

When you're beaching a boat for a short stay, it may be wise to place an anchor on the shore or, at the least, to tie a rope to some object on the shore. Keep in mind that a falling tide could leave the boat stranded ashore. A rising tide would float the boat, potentially causing it to bang against the shoreline. It might be best to anchor near shore, in enough water to float the boat, rather than to beach it, especially if there is an onshore wind or a lot of wave activity. The bow should be facing into the wind or waves, and the anchor should be set far enough from shore to give the boat room to swing; it may be necessary to tilt the engine up to keep the propeller from dragging. Of course, if the wind direction changes and the boat swings away from shore, you may have to swim out to get into it.

General techniques. Setting out an anchor is not simply a matter of dropping the anchor overboard and waiting until it grabs. The most important thing is to set the anchor so that the boat is in the position you desire. Precise positioning is sometimes absolutely critical for fishing success, when you anchor in a river and want to cast your lures or bait into the head of a downstream pool, for example, or when you anchor over a ledge to fish immediately below the boat.

First, taking into consideration the effects of wind and current, position the boat reasonably close to where you ultimately want it to rest. Make sure you are not standing on the rode and that it is not likely to entangle with anything as you let it out. Lower the anchor into the water without tossing it; in shallow waters, throwing it in with a big splash is like setting off a bomb, scattering alarmed fish far and near. Pay out the rode through your hands, as this practice keeps the line (and especially heavy chain, if used) above the sinking anchor so that it doesn't wrap around the anchor and foul it. This problem is more likely to happen to anchors with flukes.

If you don't want to drift over the desired fishing spot, at this point, you can set position in two ways. Either pay out the proper length of rode until the scope is right and the boat is where you want it to be; or, drift under power well below the place that you want to anchor, using the boat to help dig in the anchor, then motor forward until the proper position and scope are attained. The latter method assumes you're not anchoring over a desirable fishing spot (as when setting up a chumming drift), as this tactic would spook the fish.

If you're letting out a lot of rode, it's a good idea to pull on it to ensure that the anchor is holding. You can use the boat to help dig in the anchor, and

A

A plow anchor is retrieved using an anchor ball, which is not visible but attached to the line and ring on this anchor; note the chain and how it is affixed to the anchor.

in current you can help a dragging anchor grab by motoring slowly forward temporarily so that there is no resistance on the rode.

To retrieve an anchor, do not pull the boat by hand toward the anchor unless it is a small light boat or you don't have far to go. The main reason is to spare your back the strain inherent in this kind of hauling. If you're pulling up to leave a spot, then, using the motor, maneuver the boat over the rode and pull directly upward. If that is not successful in freeing the anchor, motor upstream of it and use the power of the boat, which will easily free many anchors. This is also how you can free anchors that are designed to be tripped with an opposite direction pull. If you plan to continue fishing nearby, using the motor may not be an option, as it could spook the fish.

Another retrieval option is to use a trip line. This is a second line, fastened to the crown of the anchor and used to pull the anchor from the back end. Obviously it has to be attached to the anchor beforehand. A method of setting a trip with a Danforth anchor is to shackle the end of your chain directly to the mud palm of the anchor (you have to drill a hole in it first), run the chain up to the head of the shank and then bind it there with heavy-duty cord so that the line of pull is from the shank, as would ordinarily be. When the anchor is stuck, use the boat to pull it from the opposite direction, which will break the cord and give you a pull from the mud palm.

As mentioned earlier, it may be worthwhile to have a second anchor, perhaps a lighter one, for backup use, or for use when you just want to sit tight for a break; a light anchor for this purpose is referred to as a "lunch hook." Big sportfishing boats should carry a magnum-model anchor for extreme, or storm, conditions. Small-boat owners sometimes use a clever variation of this to anchor and maintain position near a jetty; they set the main anchor off the bow, back down to the jetty, and then throw a long slender piece of wood (like a green tree branch or a broomstick) into the jetty rocks, where it gets wedged. Attached to the center of the stick is a length of 200-pound-strength fishing line. Then they move the boat the appropriate distance from the jetty, cleat off the bow anchor, and then cleat off the heavy line attached to the stick, all of which helps to keep the boat in the proper position.

Deep-water retrieval. Getting an anchor to the bottom in deep water is usually no problem, but hauling up long lengths (300 to 1,000 or more feet) of rode with a heavy anchor at the end of it would be a most unpleasant chore if you had to do it hand-over-hand.

When an anchor is set extremely deep and is hard to budge, or when it is very deep and it would

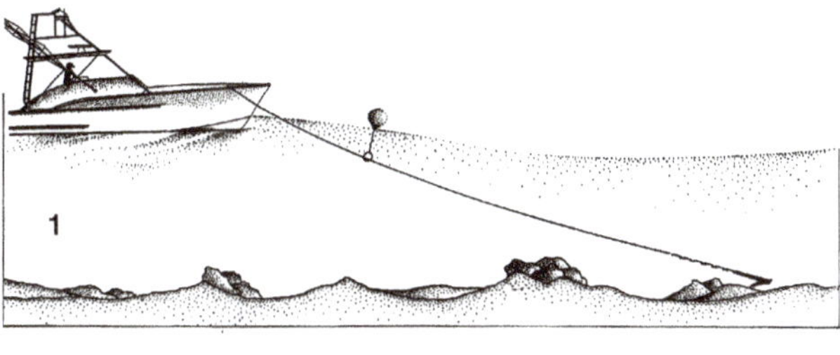

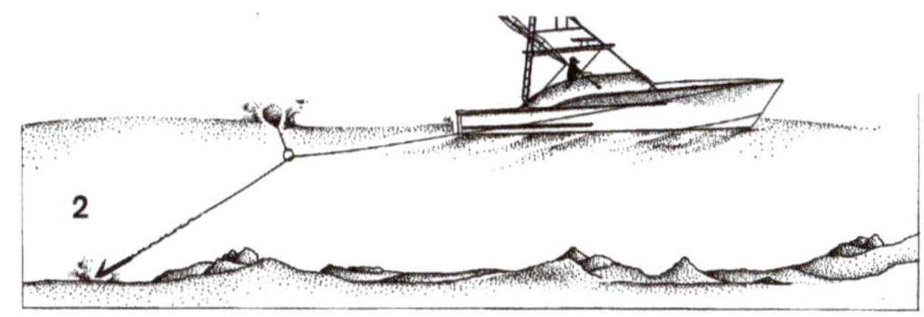

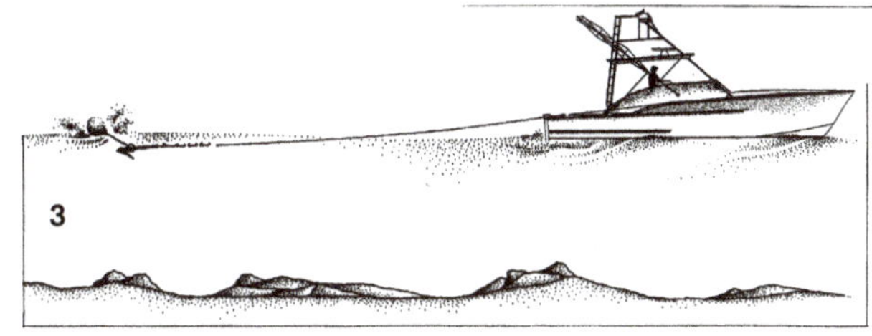

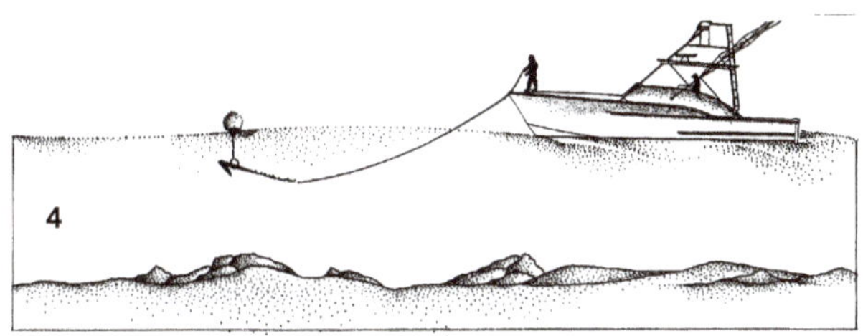

To free a deep, heavy anchor without breaking your back, use a poly anchor ball on a large ring and the maneuver depicted here. Begin by placing the ball so it slides freely on the anchor rope (1). Head directly away from the anchor position, swinging wide so as not to run over the rope (2); the buoyancy of the ball and the movement of the boat will free the anchor. As the boat continues to move forward, the ball will slide down the line to meet the anchor when it is pulled to the surface (3), with the anchor lodging in the anchor ball ring. Slowly head toward the anchor and ball, easily retrieving the rope (4).

A

be an immense strain to raise it completely by hand, the best method is to use a vinyl anchor ball *(see)*, which is also known as a mooring buoy, attached to a short length of line and a spring clip. Fasten the clip to a ring on the cleated rode and drop the ball into the water. Then motor forward, being careful not to run over the rode. Keep moving at a constant speed, which will free the anchor, then pick up speed as the anchor rises and begins to drag the ball. The anchor shank will slide into the ring. Slow the boat and then slowly motor back to the ball while retrieving the rode.

Quick-release anchoring. One of the most useful anchoring techniques for fishing is the quick-release system. This is nothing more than a standard anchor with chain and line; the end of the rode is attached to an anchor ball. A short length of rope from the ball to the boat provides the quick-release feature. The end of the rope can be either looped over a cleat or attached to a boat snap for easy one-handed getaways. This setup is appropriate when you want to stay in a particular spot yet maintain the flexibility necessary to quickly pull away when you hook a large fish and have to move the boat to fight it. When many boats are concentrated in the same area, this system guarantees your position when you return (make sure that your buoy is clearly marked). You'll want a quick release from the anchor to get after a strong fish (like a tuna) and perhaps steer it away from other vessels and their anchor lines. Being able to return to your exact prior spot saves reentering time, of course, but it may also be important in locating fish, especially if you've been chumming. Very often a school of fish will hang around the spot for a good while after the chumming stops. Or, you can tie the chum bag to the ball (if it's not too likely to be eaten by a large shark while you're gone), thus improving the odds that the fish will still be there when you get back.

The ball or buoy used for a quick-release anchor system should be large enough so it won't be dragged under by a strong current, especially if attached to a long rode (rope also has a lot of drag in a strong current). It must be large enough so that you can spot it in choppy seas and thus find it when you return. One of the best devices for this purpose is a plastic-covered, foam-filled boat fender. These come in a variety of sizes and in bright colors for easier spotting.

The famous "Animal of Stronsa," which washed ashore in the Orkney Islands in September 1808, was described as a sea serpent with three pairs of limbs; scientists say it was the remains of some very large shark.

Freeing a hung anchor. Some methods of freeing an anchor have already been discussed, but what do you do when your anchor is really dug in and the standard methods don't free it? A good anchor is not a cheap item, so before you give up and cut the line or try to break it loose via sheer engine horsepower (which can be dangerous), a few tricks are worth a try.

One option is to pull from several different directions, especially upcurrent and upwind. Start with whichever force is stronger, and use the engine to move the boat as far upstream from the anchor as the rode length will permit. Then carefully apply a little more power with the rode secured to a cleat. Don't gun the engine; if the line breaks under considerable strain, it could snap back. And pay careful attention to the seas; you don't want to bury the bow or stern while trying to free an anchor that is worth far less than the boat.

If that doesn't work, the next method is almost always successful. Pay out enough rode to obtain a scope that's as close to 10:1 as possible, tie it securely to a sturdy cleat, and put the engine in gear, heading away from the anchor at a slow speed until the rode is tight. Then take up a heading that allows the boat to circle the anchor while maintaining a tight pull on the rode. Increase the power somewhat, but not so much that you place the rode under dangerous strain. Keep up the strain as the boat makes a complete 360-degree circle around the anchor. You might have to make the circle up to a half-dozen times, but almost always the anchor will eventually come free without any damage to it. It's more a matter of technique than brute force, but you can save many anchors of all types by using this method.

Reducing sway. It may be useful at times, especially for precise positioning and to minimize swaying, to deploy two anchors. In relatively protected waters, you can do this by having a bow anchor and a stern anchor, and several companions who can help. Set out the bow anchor first, drifting far back while paying out bow anchor rode; then lower the stern anchor and, while heading forward and simultaneously keeping tension on the stern rode, retrieve bow rode until you get to the desired position.

Another way to use double anchors, and one that is common for larger boats and for positioning over ledges and reefs in saltwater, is by setting the anchors at 45-degree angles off the port and starboard bows. You have to set one anchor first and drop back to where you want the anchored boat positioned, then cleat that rode off and move forward to a point to port or starboard and even with the first anchor, then let out the second anchor, paying out the rode for that anchor until the boat comes taut on the first rode. Tie each rode to a different cleat so that you can release either rode if necessary. You may have to try this more than once to get the correct positioning, but the important thing is to ensure a 45-degree angle of pull; you don't want both anchors set primarily dead ahead.

Reducing sway may be as simple as changing the point where the anchor rode is secured to the boat, usually from the bow to a position somewhere closer amidships. The best way to do this is with a bridle, a length of line slightly greater than the length of the boat. You tie one end to the bow, and the other end to the stern. Then tie the rode to the boat somewhere near the center of the bridle, thus forming a Y, with the centerline of the boat at approximately right angles to the rode. This causes the broad side of the boat to face into the wind and/or current. You may find it necessary to shorten either the bow or stern section so that the rode itself isn't exactly in the middle. Once you get the hang of this, you can either eliminate boat sway almost completely, or at least reduce it to a level at which you can still fish effectively.

More on positioning. There are ways to change your position once you are firmly anchored. Letting out more rode, for example, is a good way to drop back with the wind or current to cover a greater area. River anglers often lengthen the rode in order to drift farther into a pool, and reef or wreck anglers do likewise to position themselves over different areas. In addition to dropping back when the road is tied to the center of the boat, you can change position by altering the tie-off point. Cleating the rode off-center, usually a few feet down from the bow centerline, you can use the angle of the boat in the water and the direction of the wind or current to bring you to the position you would ordinarily be in if the rode were attached dead-center. This will not work in rough water and heavy winds, but in moderate conditions it can help you spread out horizontally to fish directly over different portions of a ledge, wreck, or reef.

If you have a small boat and primarily fish shallow water, you should still carry ample rode, but in sections rather than in a continuous piece. The main section for shallow water use might be only 25 feet long, but you can carry extra rode in 25-, 50-, and 100-foot lengths. If each section has a loop on one end and a stainless steel snap on the other, the sections can be quickly connected in series to produce a single long line from 50 to 200 feet long. Even if you anchor in just 10 feet of water, this gives a possible scope of 20:1.

The idea behind an extremely long rode is to enable the boat to move forward and backward over a considerable distance by alternately shortening or lengthening the amount of rode, or to deliberately swing the boat back and forth over a wide area with a paddle, electric motor, a pushpole, or even a gas outboard. Silent power is obviously best for the latter maneuver if you're fishing for game that's particularly sensitive to motor noise.

You can, for example, use a long rode to maneuver a boat up and down a river, creek, or canal in which the tide or current is too strong for the electric motor. The idea in this instance is to anchor at the top of a particular productive stretch of water, keeping the rode short at the beginning. Once you've worked the top of the run to your satisfaction, let out just enough rode to reach the next likely productive stretch downstream.

Bit by bit you can continue to work downcurrent, until you reach the end of the rode. At that point, if the current is not too strong and the boat is not too large, you can haul the boat back to the top of the run by hand and work the entire area (or at least the most productive sections) over again, if warranted.

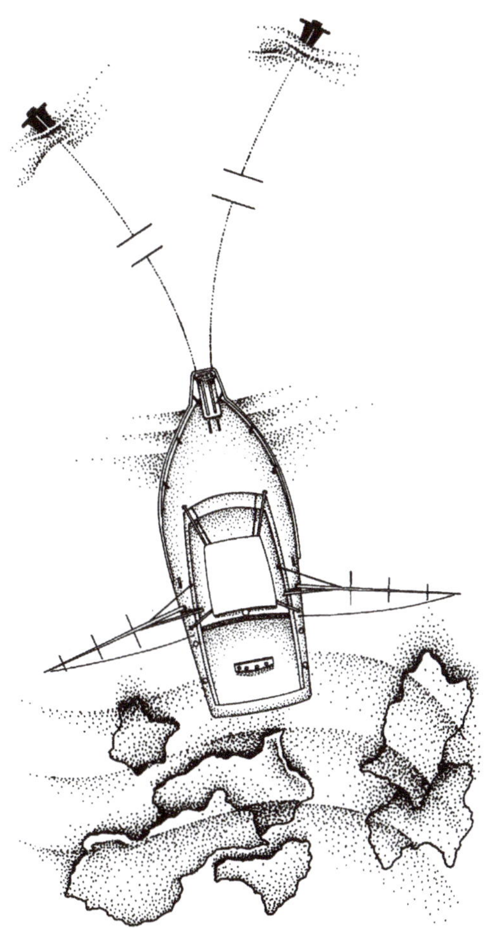

Using two anchors, as depicted for precisely locating the stern of this boat over a reef, is a good way to minimize sideways movement and maintain an exact position.

In stillwater, weak current, and moderate winds, a long rode makes it possible to cover ample water from a quasi-stationary position by deliberately swinging back and forth. Sometimes the wind, like current, can be used to move the boat in one direction. Often, however, swinging the boat over a wide arc requires some source of power. An electric motor enables you to reposition the boat and cast at the same time.

In many situations, fish move up and down shorelines or along shallow depth contours, but not always along precise or relatively narrow underwater pathways. Sometimes you're able to see the fish as they move, or at least detect positive signs of their presence. In other cases, it's just a matter of covering as much of the potentially productive water as possible by blind casting. The large swinging radius of a long rode makes appropriate positioning and repositioning possible, and with stealth.

Safety

Anchor rode should be attached only to the bow of the boat, and to a strong cleat, except under the absolute best of circumstances. It can be extremely dangerous to anchor stern first. Even when the

A

surface of the water is calm, the wake of a passing boat could send a deluge of water over the stern of a boat, causing the boat to capsize. In a river, a boat anchored stern first is susceptible to being pulled down and into the water if another boat should drift into the rode.

In dangerous situations, it may be wise to keep a sharp knife handy in case you have to quickly detach the rode from the boat. And do not coil rode on the bow of the boat. It should be stowed safely away until needed. In heavy seas, rode could be swept into the water and quickly wrapped in the propeller(s), imperiling the boat.

Finally, no matter how much rode you have, always make sure that the end of it is firmly attached to a cleat. People have lost an anchor and all of their rode because it was unattached.

ANCHOR BALL

An anchor ball is a large colorful vinyl ball, also known as a mooring buoy, that is tied to the surface end of anchor line, or rode. This buoy is sometimes used as a fender or for mooring large boats in open water in harbors; in fishing applications, it is used by anglers who anchor in deep water and chum, primarily for tuna or sharks, but also for other species. In offshore chumming, an anchor is set out, and chum and hooked baits drift with the current. When a large fish is caught, it may be necessary to maneuver the boat to fight and land the fish. In this event, the rode is uncleated and the anchor ball, clipped to the rode, is then dropped into the water, enabling the boat to move off. After the fish is landed, the boat returns to the anchor ball (which should be marked for identification) and reattaches to the rode. In this way, the anchor does not have to be hauled in and reset, and proper position in a suitable place is maintained, which can be important when there are many boats in the same area. See: Anchor.

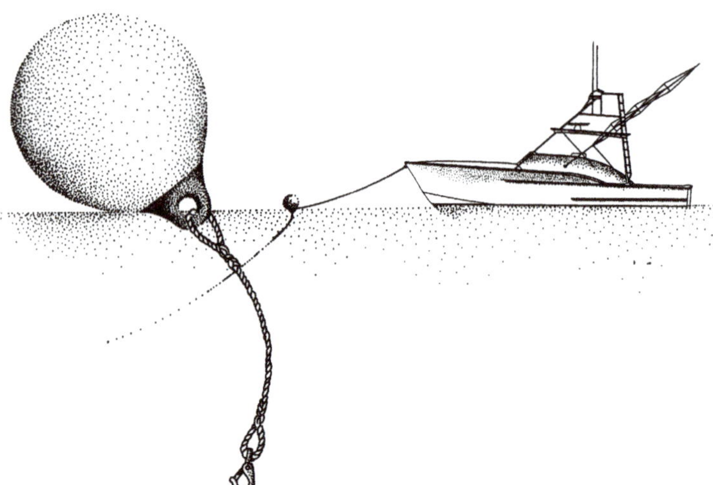

Large boats are often tethered to an anchor ball in a harbor or when fishing offshore, which allows for quickly disengaging from the anchor and easily returning to it.

ANCHOVIES

Northern Anchovy *Engraulis mordax.*

Other names—pinhead, North Pacific anchovy, California anchovy, bay anchovy; French: *anchois du Pacifique nord, anchois de California;* Spanish: *anchoveta de California, anchoa del Pacifico.*

Striped Anchovy *Anchoa hepsetus.*

Other names—broad-striped anchovy; French: *anchois rayé;* Spanish: *anchoa legìtima.*

Northern Anchovy

Striped Anchovy

Similar in appearance, these anchovies differ mostly in range, although the northern anchovy can be slightly longer. The northern anchovy is one of the most important forage fish in the Pacific and is used as bait for tuna and other large gamefish. A minor percentage of northern anchovies harvested are processed for human consumption, marketed in pickled or salted forms. The striped anchovy is also an important forage fish for game species, although it is too small and fragile to be used often for bait.

Identification. Anchovies are silvery fish that look like miniature herring. They have overhanging snouts and long lower jaws that extend behind the eyes. The striped anchovy has a ribbonlike stripe along each side and some yellow about the head. Anchovy species are difficult to differentiate, but the fin rays and pattern of pigmentation on the striped anchovy distinguish it; it has 14 to 17 dorsal fin rays, 15 to 18 pectoral fin rays, and 20 to 24 anal fin rays, as well as melanophores outlining all its dorsal scales.

Size. The northern anchovy can reach 9 inches, although 4 to 5 inches is more common; the striped anchovy can reach 6 inches, but the average length is less than 4 inches.

Distribution. In the eastern Pacific, the northern anchovy is found from northern Vancouver Island south to Cabo San Lucas, Baja California. Two subspecies are recognized, namely *E. mordax mordax,* which extends from British Columbia to Baja California, and *E. mordax nanus,* found in California's bays. In the western Atlantic, striped anchovies are found from Massachusetts (sometimes Maine or even Nova Scotia) south to Fort Pierce, Florida, but not in the Florida Keys and rarely in southern Florida. They also occur in the northern Gulf of Mexico, the Gulf of Venezuela, and south to Uruguay.

Habitat. Both northern and striped anchovies form dense schools and favor shallow coastal waters, including bays and inlets. Striped anchovies are able to tolerate a wide range of salinities.

Life history/Behavior. Northern anchovies spawn through the year, although they do so mainly in winter and early spring. Spawning occurs in nearshore and offshore environs, predominantly in depths of less than 10 meters and in temperatures of 10° to 13°C. Striped anchovies spawn from April through July in harbors, estuaries, and sounds. The eggs of both species are elliptical and float near the surface, hatching within a few days after being released. The young mature in three to four years.

Food. Both anchovies feed on plankton.

ANGELFISH, QUEEN *Holacanthus ciliaris.*

Other names—French: *demoiselle royale;* Spanish: *isabelita patale.*

The queen angelfish is not widely sought by anglers, although it is an attractive incidental catch. It has some food value, although it is more popular as an aquarium fish.

Identification. The queen angelfish has a moderately large body that is deep and compressed. It can be distinguished from its nearest relatives, butterflyfish, by its stout spines, blunter snout, and the spines on the gill cover. It has 14 dorsal spines, and the spine at the angle of the preopercle is relatively long.

Most noteworthy about the appearance of the queen angelfish is its coloration. It is speckled yellowish orange and blue, and the amount of blue varies with the individual and differs in intensity. It has a bright blue border on the soft dorsal and anal fins, with the tips of the fins colored orange and the last few rays of them colored bluish black. It also has a yellowish orange tail, as well as a dark bluish black spot on the forehead, ringed with bright blue, which forms the queen's "crown."

The coloring of the young queen angelfish's is dark blue and very similar that of young blue angelfish, but the rear edges of the dorsal and anal fins are not yellow, as they are in the blue angelfish. There are bluish white bars on the body of the queen angelfish, as with the blue angelfish, but these are curved on the queen angelfish instead of straight.

Angelfish in the Caribbean are generally brighter in color than those along the coasts of North and South America.

Size. Although reported to reach a length of nearly 2 feet, queen angelfish probably do not exceed 18 inches, and they average 8 to 14 inches.

Distribution. Queen angelfish are a common to occasional presence in Florida, the Bahamas, and the Caribbean; they are present in Bermuda and the Gulf of Mexico, and south to Brazil, as well as on coral reefs in the West Indies.

Habitat. Queen angelfish inhabit coral reefs in shallow water, although juveniles prefer offshore

Queen Angelfish

reefs, and mature fish sometimes frequent depths of 20 to 80 feet. They often are indistinguishable from the colorful sea fans, sea whips, and corals they swim amongst.

Behavior. The queen angelfish is usually found alone or in a pair, but not in groups.

Food. Adults feed primarily on sponges, but also consume algae and minute organisms.

Angling. Queen angelfish are an incidental but spunky catch for bottom anglers using baits or baited jigs.

ANGLER

A person who catches—or tries to catch—fish for personal use, fun, challenge, and leisure by using sporting equipment, essentially some type of rod, usually but not always equipped with a reel, to which a line and a hook or lure are attached, and by fair and sporting methods that afford the quarry an opportunity to avoid capture. Although the word "angler" is genderless, it is used interchangeably with "sportfisherman." It has a more specific meaning than "fisherman," although both words may connote the same thing when used in reference to the employment of sporting equipment.

See: Angling; Commercial Fisherman; Fisherman; Fishing; Recreational Fisherman; Sportfisherman; Sportfishing.

ANGLERFISH

"Anglerfish" is a common name for the goosefish *(see),* also called monkfish, bellyfish, frogfish, and sea devil.

ANGLING

The act of catching or trying to catch fish for personal use, fun, challenge, and leisure using sporting equipment, essentially with some type of rod, usually but not always equipped with a reel, to which a line and a hook or lure is attached, and by sporting methods.

Angling is used interchangeably with sportfishing but has a more specific meaning than fishing, although both words may connote the same thing when used in reference to the employment of sporting equipment. The term angling is distinguished from commercial or recreational fishing by virtue of the equipment employed, an implicit understanding of fair chase, and the exercise of sportsmanship. When angling, the equipment used affords the quarry some opportunity to elude capture; thus using a net to encircle and capture fish may be fishing, but it is not angling, and methods that do not have some element of fair play are not truly angling. Angling also implies the intent to keep fish (if fish are kept) for personal use rather than for sale or trade, although some saltwater fish that are caught by sporting means may legally be sold.

What constitutes sport or sporting equipment is open to individual interpretation and encompasses a wide range of equipment and circumstances. Even anglers disagree as to whether certain tactics, tackle, and techniques exclusively used in angling actually qualify as "sport." This is a debate, in part grounded in attitudes and ethical considerations, that defies settlement, and which muddies any attempt at strict definition.

See: Angler; Commercial Fisherman; Fishing; Recreational Fisherman; Sportfisherman; Sportfishing.

ANGOLA

The seventh largest country on the African continent, Angola is well situated along the eastern Atlantic Ocean to provide access to lightly explored saltwater fishing. Bounded by Namibia on the south and the Democratic Republic of the Congo (formerly Zaire) on the north, Angola is larger than Spain and Portugal combined, and has some 1,650 kilometers of coastline that lies between the Equator and the Tropic of Capricorn.

A warm tropical current flows southward along this extensive coastline, from the Gulf of Guinea, whereas the cold Benguela Current sweeps northerly from the South Atlantic. This mixture of currents results in an abundance of forage fish, particularly various species of sardines and scads. The forage fish in turn attract exceptionally large Atlantic sailfish, plenty of dorado, and a still-new fishery for big blue marlin, particularly offshore from the capital city of Luanda.

There is great potential for gamefishing here; however, sportfishing has been limited since the country became independent in 1975 and subsequently endured a lengthy civil war. In the early 1970s the waters off Luanda regularly produced the largest Atlantic sailfish in the world. International Game Fish Association (IGFA) world records were dominated by catches made off Luanda before 1975. Despite advances in angling techniques and equipment, the exploration of other sailfish locations, and a low overall angling effort in Angola in the latter twentieth century, this country still holds the all-tackle world record for Atlantic sailfish, and has produced other existing or former record catches.

In the early 1970s, anglers fished from small speedboats, trolling ballyhoo, mullet, and strip baits. With the arrival of independence, most sailfish enthusiasts fled the country, and recreational fishing for sailfish declined sharply. It was only in the late 1980s that a few people started sailfishing again. However, every passing year sees the arrival of more sportfishing boats and increasing numbers of anglers.

The seas off Luanda are usually calm, as storms are very rare and strong winds virtually unknown. The sea is choppy only in the afternoon, and few days are lost to bad weather. This all makes

for comfortable fishing conditions, although the humidity can be high in the rainy season (February through April).

Sea temperatures vary greatly according to season and location along the coastline. Off Luanda, the peak water temperatures of summer (March and April) reach the mid-80s, and in winter (July and August) they drop to the mid-60s. These waters are normally warm from September to June.

Although sailfish are not present in the quantities touted for other hotspots, the size of its sailfish—the largest Atlantic specimens in the world—make Angola (mainly the Luanda area at present) *the* place to pursue this species. The previously mentioned record, a 141-pounder, was caught in February of 1994, and at least a half- dozen fish weighing between 128 and 132 pounds were registered in competitions between 1994 and 1998. These are impressive statistics, as fewer than 80 sailfish overall are known to have been caught during that time. Unfortunately, competitions in Angola as of the late 1990s were still kill events; only one boat opted for catch-and-release angling.

Sailfish are present off Luanda from October to May, but only appear in significant numbers between January and March. The big sails are usually caught in February and March, but this can vary; some years can be very poor, with few sailfish seen or caught due to abnormally cool water temperatures. Inconsistent arrival times from one season to the next also make this fishery problematic. Sails are caught at a distance of 5 to 12 miles from the head of Luanda Bay. A few miles south of Luanda the highly productive 100-meter dropoff is only a couple of miles offshore, whereas due east of Luanda it is 10 miles distant.

Of the few boaters who pursue sailfish here, most troll only lures, or a combination of lures and ballyhoo. The latter are readily available and are caught in nets during the early morning hours; they can be purchased at dawn from local fishermen. Angling with live bait is not practiced here, as it is hard to come by. Schools of ballyhoo are rarely seen offshore, yet flying fish are sometimes plentiful. Although schools of baitfish are often observed offshore, it is rare to see sailfish feeding on them, and bird activity is virtually nonexistent. If the sea gets choppy in the afternoon, sailfish can often be seen tailing; these are usually hunting, and readily attack any offerings put in front of them.

Sailfish are not the only billfish lurking in Angolan waters. The first blue marlin taken here, a fish of about 400 pounds, was boated in December 1990. Since then more than 50 marlin have been caught off Luanda. This figure may seem low at first glance, but in reality it is quite respectable, given that there are few boats with fighting chairs, hardly anyone fishes for marlin, and what little effort is made is concentrated around Luanda, and that many marlin have been raised and lost.

Even more noteworthy is that there are few small marlin around. If small fish (100 to 200 pounds) existed in any quantity, they would have been caught by anglers trolling baits and lures for sailfish. In the late 1990s, the two smallest marlin weighed 175 and 253 pounds, the average was around 490, and the largest two weighed 815 and 943 pounds—the latter caught on 50-pound stand-up tackle in March 1998. Four others over 700 pounds were caught. It is only a matter of time before the first grander is caught.

Most marlin have been taken on lures, and analysis of the captures and sightings of blue marlin shows two definite peaks. The best time is March through May; in April, two to three strikes a day from 500-pounders can be expected. Marlin usually show up in mid-March, but in 1998 four marlin, three over 450 pounds, were caught in three days in late February. April and May peaks coincide with the highest abundance of weed clumps from the rivers and with the appearance of dorado that live under them. Dorado can be extremely plentiful at this time, though large specimens are rare and are sometimes a nuisance to anglers trolling baits for sailfish. They have repeatedly observed marlin attacking dorado and trying to eat hooked dorado.

In his book Tales of the Anglers, Zane Grey said, "All experience must be measured as much by what the angler brings to it as by what it gives."

The second marlin peak usually runs from October to December but varies from year to year. Marlin have been caught each month from September to June, so the season is theoretically very long. For marlin fishing, the calmer the sea the better, and the best time of day in Angolan waters has been between noon and three o'clock. Few marlin are raised on the rare days when the sea is rough.

The marlin sometimes come into very shallow water, and some have been hooked in water that is 60 meters deep. Blue water normally appears within a few miles of the coast, but sometimes green water appears and makes fishing virtually useless. The green water can last from a few days to many months, and during this time the sea appears devoid of life.

There is no structure on which to base a trolling pattern, so most boats concentrate on water between 100 and 150 meters deep, and on current and weedlines. Early and late in the season, offshore fishing becomes a marlin-or-nothing activity, when anglers may troll for days with not so much as a bite from other fish. When a strike finally comes, however, it's usually a big blue.

From December through April the only fish encountered offshore are dorado, sailfish, and marlin. Tuna are rare catches off Luanda, although yellowfins are reputedly abundant farther south and are a favored target of the commercial fishery. Very few people have ever encountered wahoo off Luanda, but a number of large basking swordfish have been spotted during the winter months (mid-May through August). Still, none had been hooked as of 1998.

Inshore fishing in Angola can be very good, although overharvesting by uncontrolled commercial fishing has taken its toll. The river mouths can provide excellent sport for tarpon, cubera snapper, threadfin, and jack crevalle. Two jack crevalle records—including the all-tackle 57-pound, 5-ounce fish—were set at the Kwanza River, which empties into the Atlantic near Luanda. The Mancha Branca, a shallow area south of Luanda, also produces huge barracuda—many of world-record proportions; a line-class 30.3-kilogram record barracuda was taken there in 1998. There are also cubera snapper to 50 kilograms, and threadfin to 50 kilograms.

The tarpon fishery in the Kwanza River was well developed pre-independence, but afterward—as with offshore fishing—many enthusiasts left the country. Unfortunately, netting has taken its toll in the river; tarpon and other species have decreased over the years. Tarpon to 100 kilograms were reportedly caught in the past.

Tarpon also appear along the coastline around Luanda, and the sportfishery in the Congo River to the north may well be fantastic and untapped. Mussulo Bay to the south of Luanda is a huge, beautiful bay that used to offer a variety of fishing, and has large areas of flats. Tarpon, bonefish, barracuda, and jacks were once available in Mussulo, but relentless local commercial netting has considerably depleted fish stocks. The coast to the far south has other species, including garrick, which reflects the colder waters there.

Unfortunately, the availability of charter boats is extremely limited, and as of 1998 there were no reliable boats for charter at the Kwanza River and only one boat was available for offshore fishing out of Luanda. With positive progress in implementing a peace accord, it is hoped that more boats will be available in time. As facilities improve, more anglers will visit Angola and more records are likely to be established, most likely for sailfish, jack crevalle, and barracuda.

Currently, no freshwater sportfishing exists, although evidently not for lack of fish. Civil strife has long made it extremely dangerous to venture into the bush, and the riverbanks are often mined. Perhaps someday there will be a freshwater fishery to explore. Tigerfish are believed to exist in some of Angola's rivers.

ANTIQUE FISHING TACKLE

Modern sportfishing is viewed by collectors in terms of two distinct periods: pre– and post–World War II. Since that defining event in history, fishing equipment, technique, interest, and knowledge have exploded, with each facet spurring on the other. Angling equipment, in particular, has evolved to advanced levels, a fact evident to even the casual observer and nonparticipant. With the plethora of tackle produced annually, each building technologically upon preceding equipment, it is only natural that some affinity with the tackle of the past was cultivated and that collecting these items became a more active and widely followed pursuit.

Antique tackle collecting was virtually unheard of prior to the 1950s, and even until the mid-1970s it was of minor interest. The few collectors who existed during that period labored in an uncharted field and knew little about each other. In 1976, however, three collectors formed the National Fishing Lure Collectors Club (NFLCC). An organization of more than 3,000 members at the end of the twentieth century, it boasts a continually growing membership.

Although the NFLCC was founded by lure collectors, it has since attracted people who collect all types of fishing tackle, and thus the name is today a bit misleading. Although lures, because of their sheer numbers and prominence in angling, are of foremost interest, all types of old fishing tackle have become popular. Collecting is now a natural extension of the hobby of sportfishing. There are few nonangling collectors of antique fishing tackle and related items.

Because the NFLCC has been promoting antique tackle collecting, the market has undergone some astounding changes both in numbers of collectors and in the prices of collectibles. Fortunately, for the most part, antique tackle has not gone the way of the extraordinary price increases seen in other collecting arenas, as in old hunting decoys, where six-figure prices are not unusual. The values of old fishing tackle remained fairly stable, with moderate growth, for the first 10 years of organized collecting but have realized considerable gains in the 1990s.

Nevertheless, prices have not gone so high in most areas of tackle collecting as to price the average collector out of the market. For example, in 1991 a 1922-vintage South Bend Pike Oreno plug was valued at about $10; today it is valued at $20 to $30. There are some famous aberrations, such as a small metal lure called the Haskell Minnow, which sold for $20,000 at auction, but extremes of this kind are exceedingly rare.

Some reels, on the other hand, are valued extraordinarily high. Early Kentucky reels can sell for $1,500 to $2,500, but there are hundreds of nice old reels available for $20 to $50. Many good contemporary reels will cost more than that at a tackle shop. Likewise, fine old fly rods will bring several hundred, some even thousands, of dollars, but great old casting rods can be found for less than $100, and many nice rods for even less.

Tackle collecting is not limited to lures, rods, and reels. Diverse angling-related collectibles, or ephemera, as some collectors call them, are plentiful. Included as ephemera are all the old manufacturers' catalogs. Some were works of art in themselves, and the market in these is very active. Even colorful old empty lure boxes are sought after; wooden versions are especially prized. Glass minnow traps and buckets, dipnets, calendars, fishing licenses and badges, advertising posters, manufacturer and tackle shop signs, promotional giveaways, metal and wooden tackle boxes, and ice fishing decoys and spears are also among the items collectors fancy.

Fishing tackle made in the United States and Canada from the 1800s into the 1960s is the predominant interest among collectors. Little fishing tackle was manufactured in North America prior to about 1880, other than a few fly rods. Before that, there was little interest in fishing for sport; the passion for angling at that time originated in Europe and most likely spread to the U.S. through European immigrants.

It is thought by some that the limited number of manufacturers over those eight decades resulted in a finite number of potentially available products. Although there is, of course, a finite number, that number is in the millions. Even the smallest lure companies, for example, made lures by the thousands or even tens of thousands. Larger companies, some in business for 50 years, produced millions of items. And many thousands of anglers added to the available collectibles by trying to invent a "better mousetrap" over all those years.

Most lure producers experimented with myriad designs in the continuing quest for the proverbial "secret weapon." There were thousands of these operations, from the one-person shop to the large manufacturer, that came and went during this time. The types of lures produced ranged from the sublime to the ridiculous, from the ineffective to the explosively successful. According to the advertisements of the day, just about every lure was the fabled supreme achievement. In a 1911 advertisement, for example, lure maker Anson (Ans) B. Decker boasted that he could catch more bass over 14 inches with his bait than the reader, and backed this up with a wager of "$1,000 against $500." Considering what a prodigious sum of money that was in 1911, this was a real challenge.

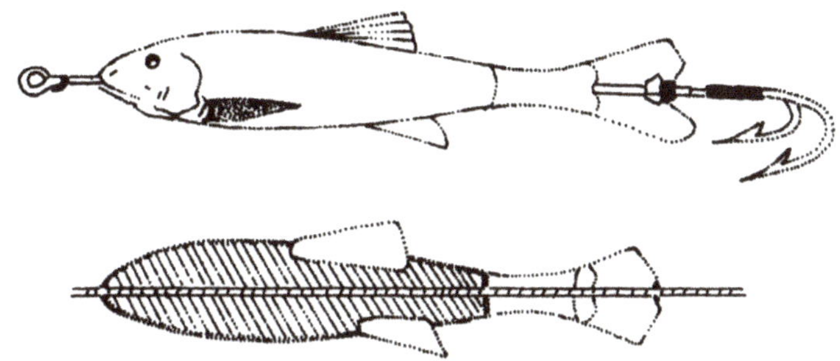

This rendition of the Haskell Minnow is derived from the original patent drawing.

Historical Perspectives

Fishing for food has occurred since prehistoric times, and fishing for recreation is in evidence since at least the late fifteenth century. Research suggests that reels were used by the Chinese as early as A.D. 300 to 400, but there are no clear indications whether this was for food or fun. The modern historical era for angling as recreation begins with a piece of English literature written in 1496. Titled *Treatyse of Fysshynge with an Angle,* it was an essay included in the second edition of *The Boke of Saint Albans.* Thought to have been written by Dame Juliana Berners—a claim since disputed by revisionist historians—it is the first known manual of sportfishing and the first published work espousing angling for recreation.

The development of fishing tackle has its roots in Europe from that point on. It included various methods of storing line on the rod; these setups were, in effect, predecessors of the reel. Single-action reels, whose purpose was primarily storing and secondarily retrieving line, evolved around this time and were used with natural baits or weightless artificial flies. The advancement of the modern fishhook in the seventeenth century (wood, stone, and bone hooks were used by primitive man, followed by copper, bronze, and iron) is credited to Englishman Charles Kirby, who also invented the Kirby Bend, a type of hook still in use today. By 1770, English rods had gained line guides and reel

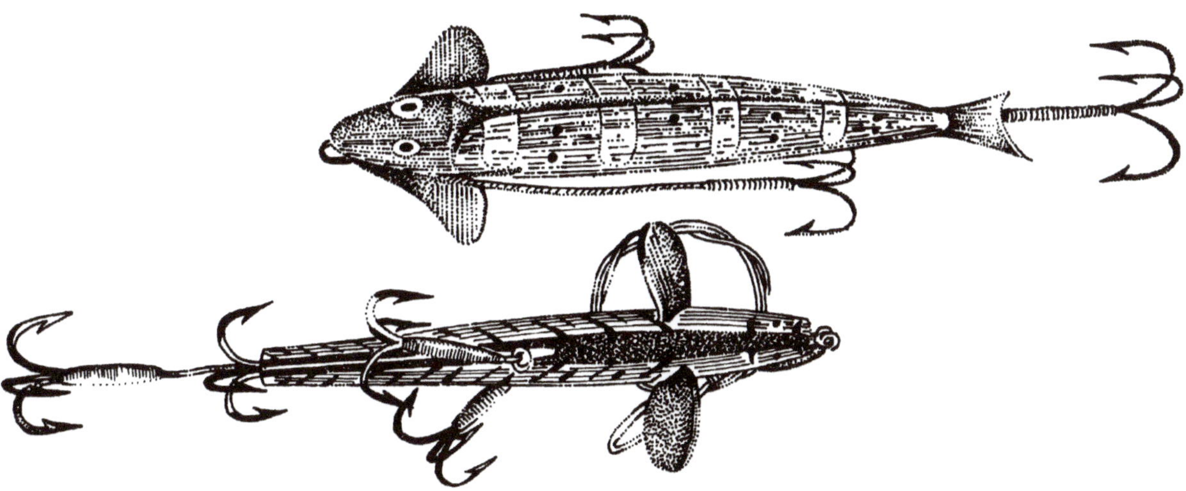

Shown are renditions of the Phantom Minnow (top) and Devon Minnow (bottom).

seats. Numerous artificial lures were developed and widely used in Europe, the most common of which were the Devon lures and Phantom Minnows. These were the primary lures imported and used by a relative few recreational anglers in America. For the most part these lures were made of a combination of hair, metal, and silk.

The modern baitcasting, or multiplier, reel had its origin in England in the latter half of the eighteenth century but did not catch on there. That product, however, was the model for the American craftsmen who fashioned the famous Kentucky reel. Notable among them were Kentucky watchmakers Jonathan Meek and George Snyder, who developed the first baitcasting reels in America around 1800 to 1810. It was at this time that North America joined in the development and manufacture of fishing tackle.

The roots of today's fine baitcasting rods are firmly planted in American soil. In the 1880s, James Henshall invented a new rod that was lighter and shorter than other rods of the time. By contemporary standards, his 8-foot rod was long, but compared to the 10- to 12-footers of the time it was much shorter. When anglers paired it with the Kentucky reel, the combination became extremely popular.

From that point until today, the U.S. has been a major developer, and the foremost consumer, of sportfishing tackle. As a result, the greatest interest in collecting antique fishing tackle revolves around American equipment, especially that produced from the early nineteenth century until about the middle of the twentieth century.

American Sportfishing and Tackle: A General Chronology

1800–10

1. First appearance of the Phantom Minnow in America. Artificial flies and natural baits were the only options heretofore.
2. George Snyder and Jonathan Meek credited with creating the first "Kentucky reels." These were multiple-action casting reels, developed at a time when a single-action revolving-spool reel was the only reel available for sportfishing, and anglers exclusively used natural baits or artificial flies. The single-action reel was primarily employed to store and retrieve line, and had no casting function.

1835–40 The Meeks brothers start the first commercial manufacture of "Kentucky reels."

1844–1925 Development of the "Henshall rod," beginning with Dr. James T. Henshall.

1848 Julio T. Buel begins commercial manufacture of the spoon lure. He actually invented the spoon lure around 1820 by accident, it is said, when a fish struck at a spoon (utensil) he inadvertently dropped from a boat.

1852 Julio T. Buel obtained the first U.S. patent on a spinner.

1859 Riley Haskell received the first known patent for a fishing lure that *mentions* wood as a possible material for the lure body. Haskell's lure was manufactured in metal, and a wooden version has never been found.

1874 First patent granted for an artificial bait that *specifies* the use of wood for the lure body. Patented May 26 by David Huard and Charles M. Dunbar; it is not known if the lure was ever manufactured.

1876 H. C. Brush granted patent for the Brush Floating Spinner on August 22. This is thought to be the first artificial bait actually manufactured that incorporated wood as a major component of the lure.

1880 First known U.S. patent granted for a lure utilizing glass for the body; it was issued to J. Irgens on September 7.

1883

1. Patent for "artificial bait" called the Flying Hellgrammite granted to Harry Comstock, Fulton, New York, on January 30.
2. First patent for the use of luminous paint on an artificial lure granted to Earnest F. Pflueger, founder of the Pflueger Bait Company.

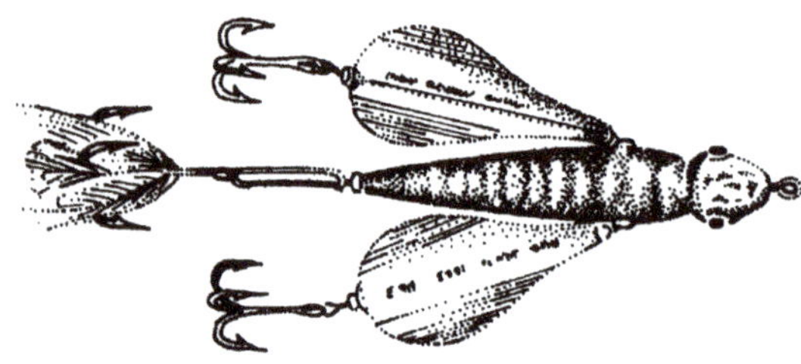

Depicted is a rendition of the 1883 Flying Hellgrammite.

1885 Development of the "Chicago rod," which was 3 feet shorter and more flexible than the 8-foot "Henshall rod." It took a mere five years for it to replace the Henshall product in popularity.

1890s The beginning of widespread baitcasting in North America. Although the reels had been invented 75 years earlier, it wasn't until this period that lures or plugs were born. James Heddon is generally given credit for inventing the first artificial wooden lure, which is known as the "plug" today. Lore has it that while waiting for a fishing friend, he was whittling on a chunk of wood. He threw it into the water, a bass exploded out of the water striking at it, and an idea was born (see related information later in this entry).

ca. 1900 Theodore Gordon created the first dry-fly patterns appropriate for New World waters around the turn of the twentieth century. Occurring on the Neversink River in the Catskill Mountains of New York, this invention started the American evolution of fly fishing.

1901–2 James Heddon's lure manufacturing company was founded.

1905 First development of the spinning reel. British caster Alfred Holden Illingworth designed and patented a mechanical means of retrieving line and rotating it around a handheld stationary spool. Anglers had previously hand-wound fishing line around stationary objects and used a weight to propel them. This device would not catch on in North America for three decades.

1907 First appearance of jointed wood lures—the "K and K Animated Minnows."

1910 The first widespread use of luminous paint on lure bodies.

ca. 1912 The first "water sonic" plugs appear. The 1912 Bignall and Schaaf "Diamond Wiggler" is thought to be the first of this type.

1913 William C. Boschen catches the first broadbill swordfish (358 pounds) ever taken on sporting rod and reel, using the first internal star drag reel, which he conceptualized and which was made for him by Brooklyn, New York, reel manufacturer Julius Vom Hofe.

ca. 1914 First appearance of fluted plugs. The first was probably the Lockhart "Wobbler Wizard," followed later by the Wilson "Fluted Wobbler" around 1917.

1914 The release of the "Detroit Glass Minnow Tube," thought to be the first commercially available glass lure.

1915 The first appearance of a self-illuminated lure using a battery and bulb—"Dr. Wasweyler's Marvelous Electric Glow Casting Minnow."

ca. 1917 Earliest known advertisement for a lure made of celluloid. This appeared in a May 1917 issue of *National Sportsman* for an Al Foss "Oriental Wiggler," a pork-rind minnow lure. Soon after, his ads began to say "Pyralin," a trade name for celluloid, instead of "celluloid." This may be the first plastic lure.

ca. 1922 The Vesco Bait Company of New York City began advertising artificial baits and spoons made of "DuPont Pyralin."

1932 The Heddon company introduced their "Fish Flesh" plastic lures. The first were the #9100 and #9500 series "Vamps." Soon after, their plastic lures were called "Spooks."

1938 The first spinning reel to be commercially distributed in the U.S., the French-made Luxor was introduced by New York importer Bache Brown. Like the reel developed by Alfred Holden Illingworth in 1905, and unlike other types of fishing reels of the day, it did not use a revolving spool for casting or retrieving line.

1939 The first introduction of nylon monofilament fishing line. Nylon monofilament, also referred to as mono, had a significant impact on rod and reel development, and sportfishing popularity. Synthetic superpolymers were discovered by DuPont research chemist Dr. Wallace H. Carothers in the mid-1930s; nylon was patented by DuPont in 1937. In 1939, leader material made from nylon was produced by DuPont, becoming the first nylon monofilament fishing line; that same year, nylon stockings were introduced at the New York and San Francisco world's fairs.

1944 Bache Brown designed a spinning reel based on the Luxor and built it in the U.S. Named Airex, it was the first spinning reel made in North America.

1947 R. D. Hull developed the closed-face spinning reel, better known as the spincasting reel. The first production reels, based on Hull's idea, were made in June, 1949, by the Oklahoma-based Zero Hour Bomb Company, later known as Zebco. This reel, which did not use a revolving spool for casting or line retrieval, was very easy to use and gained acceptance in the early 1950s at the same time the spinning reel became popular.

Like humans, whales and porpoises are warm-blooded and breathe with lungs, not gills like fish do; they may have lived on land at one point in time.

What to Collect

A collection of old fishing tackle can and often does get out of hand. Many collectors devote entire rooms or basements to housing or displaying their wide-ranging collections. Elaborate collections sometimes duplicate old-time bait and tackle shops. While these types of collections are fascinating and fun, most people don't have the resources or space to pursue such elaborate conglomerations. Sooner or later most collectors settle down to a more specialized collection. There are many possibilities.

Specializing in the products of one particular company is a popular concentration. Collecting just old reels is another; these can look like jewels in the right kind of display. An assemblage of all the colors, finishes, and variations that were available on a particular lure can be fascinating and a real challenge. A collection of all metal lures would be of interest. A collection of very old fly rods, fly reels, and flies could be beautiful and even have historical import. In fact, many individual collections have become important enough to tour museum circuits, and some have even become important parts of permanent museum collections. Whatever the area of interest, the hobby of collecting old fishing tackle is not one that is easily abandoned. Collecting becomes a sort of fever, and it is rare that a collector quits. Even those who have disposed of a collection through sale or gift to an institution frequently start anew.

Defining an eclectic collection, at least to a small degree, becomes necessary as it grows. For instance, one might wish to limit a collection to only those items in good to mint condition. This would be difficult, but challenging. However the collection is defined, most collectors, in order to add variety and interest, have a few items from other areas of collectible tackle. Hundreds of accessories are to be found, and many are illustrated in old catalogs and magazine advertisements. The old catalogs and magazines are fascinating and incredibly entertaining to read, not to mention valuable research tools in identifying old tackle.

An entry in a Marshall Field and Company catalog (ca. 1915) for a "Fishing Alarm Bell" costing five cents and described as "the sleepy fisherman's friend" is a good example of the entertaining aspect of some old catalogs. A 1919 catalog shows that for $1.35 the unlucky angler could obtain a "Line Releaser" complete with a leather carrying case. The copy states in part, "Ever have your fly in a tree? Got mad of course." and goes on to say that the device won't save your temper but will save your line, leader, lure, and possibly even the tip of your rod. It is placed on the tip of the rod, cuts the twig and " . . . down comes twig and your belongings." Where in modern times would one find such a quaint catalog entry?

How and Where to Collect

The four major categories of collectible fishing tackle are Lures, Rods, Reels, and Ephemera. Ephemera is defined as any related material such as tackle catalogs, store displays, pamphlets, and accessories. All share obvious common resources, but ephemera can be found just about anywhere.

Contrary to what some believe, plenty of collectible fishing tackle is yet to be found. The first resource is your own "backyard." Is there an elder in your family who used to fish? Chances are his tackle box is still around. How about your late great-grandfather's tackle box? Look for it. Ask friends and members of your family. Look in the attics, basements, garages, boat houses, well houses, barns, and workshops of not just old family structures, but also newer ones. Many people are loathe to throw out anything that was once treasured by a family member, even if they have no interest in it themselves. An old tackle box is the type of thing that might well have been placed in a dark corner years ago and forgotten.

There are still a few old general stores, hardware stores, and drugstores around; many of these carried tackle, especially lures. Try their storerooms and basements. Many treasures have turned up because someone felt around a dusty top shelf or in the corners of a storage room. Anywhere fishing tackle has been sold for 40 or more years is a good source, although such places are vanishing fast. It could be that present owners or employees may not even know that very old, unsold stock is stuck away somewhere.

Remember trading boards? Some tackle shops still have them. You pay 50 cents or a dollar, put your own lure on the board, and take another of your choice. You might find a collectible lure there. Many tackle shops and repair shops sell used rods and reels. A treasure or two might turn up there too.

Garage sales are particularly good hunting grounds if you're resourceful. Many anglers and most non-anglers don't think of old fishing tackle as particularly marketable and rarely include it in garage or tag sales. Ask if there's any old tackle around. You might be surprised.

Flea markets and junk shops are a source, but not a particularly good one. Dealers have learned that fishing tackle is collectible, and often the prices are way out of line. Most of the time, the tackle is common and/or badly damaged and is offered at grossly inflated prices. Don't ignore this source, however, because anything can happen.

Place a wanted notice on public bulletin boards. Many grocery stores provide them, as do some discount department stores and apartment complexes. Make up a want list with pictures or drawings and pass the list out to friends and relatives. You might even place this on the bulletin boards. Don't use names or numbers. You'll just confuse potential sources.

Don't forget estate sales and auctions. Fishing tackle is often overlooked as significant and just auctioned off as a lot or in a box with other goods not considered important. Sources are limited only by the imagination.

Collectors at an auction look over a variety of antique lures.

Identifying Old Reels

Many early craftsmen and manufacturers identified their products by engraving or stamping their names and/or patent dates and other information on them. Later, they used decals, hot stamps, transfers, and labels. Many others, however did not bother with any type of identification at all. Identification of these reels can defy even the most knowledgeable of collectors. In addition, many reelmakers furnished jobbers and retailers with their reels but marked them as these quantity buyers wished. This means you might find identical reels of the same vintage with entirely different markings.

The most scarce and valuable reels are those that were handcrafted from about 1800 to 1875. After that, modern mechanized production methods became prevalent. Those early reels were usually signed by the reelsmith and often had beautiful presentation engravings including the name of the craftsman, the recipient, and the date.

This British-made Ustonson brass winch multiplier reel from approximately the mid–nineteenth century sold for $9,500 at auction in 1998.

George Snyder, the man usually credited with the beginning of the Kentucky reels, made his earliest of brass. All his reels were quadruple multipliers (4:1 ratio). He incorporated jewel pivots and square, steel gears. A watchmaker, Snyder knew that jeweled movements were the most advanced state of pivots at the time. On these early reels, one end of the pillars was riveted to one base plate, and the other end was secured to the other plate by wire. Milam and Hardman improved this later, using screws to secure both ends of the pillars to the base plates. This allowed easier dismantling and reassembly, facilitating lubrication and repairs. The screws on Meek reels made after the period from around 1840 to 1845 were each numbered to match the number stamped at each screw hole. After the Civil War, the reels were made larger, and a double multiplier model was available for the saltwater angler. These early reels are exceedingly rare and valuable.

After mechanized manufacturing began, millions of reels of all shapes, types, and sizes were possible, and the reels found today in the collector market reflect this variety. Experience, a good reference book, and time are necessary for those interested in collecting reels. Start slowly and seek the help of experienced collectors. A good rule of thumb for beginners is if a reel looks good, everything works, and the cost is less than $15, it's probably a good buy.

Identifying Old Rods

Like early reels, most old handmade rods were signed by their makers. The signature is usually found engraved or stamped on the butt cap, but some craftsmen signed them on the shaft, just forward of the handle. If there are no markings at all, check the metal fittings. If the fittings are made of "German silver," the rod is probably an early handcrafted one. German silver (actually not silver at all but an alloy of nickel, copper, and zinc) typically tarnishes to a dull gray, sometimes tending toward green. There is occasionally a greenish corrosion in crevices or joints. Some of these early rods may also be found with nickel or brass fittings.

Early split cane rods had to be bound at short intervals along their entire length, since the glues and materials used prior to World War I were inferior. After the war, better glues and higher quality cane were used, and the number of wrappings needed was smaller. Often, the binding wrappings were necessary only at the ends of the rods.

The length of an early rod is a good clue to age. Most fly rods made prior to the early 1900s were 10 to 12 or more feet long, while those made afterward are more often found in 6- to 10-foot lengths. In general, baitcasting rods can be evaluated by the same length guidelines, but the collector should be aware that most baitcasting rods are shorter and stiffer than fly rods.

Another, less dependable, method of dating a rod is to examine the hardware, line guides, and handles. Most of the earliest baitcasting rods were made for two-handed gripping. The handles were made of wood and most were ribbed for a better grip. Cork became popular for handles around 1900. Both ribbed and smooth handles continued in wide use, and many were made for single-handed casting. Single-handled rods are often found with a triggerlike addition, which facilitates a more secure grip.

Early line or eye guides were sometimes made collapsible to protect them from damage during transport of the rod. Snake guides and soldered ring or eye guides were developed early on with the snake guide probably coming first. Trumpet-shaped eye guides are also an early development not found on modern rods. The ceramic-type eye guides are not a modern innovation. Many early tackle catalogs illustrate and offer agate eye guides. These are constructed in virtually the same way. The only difference is the use of agate rather than ceramic or some other synthetic material.

The earliest reel seats were simply a place to tie the reel to the rod handle with line. Slide-locking and screw-locking devices followed quickly.

Collectors should be aware that rebuilding rods, changing hardware, and other such replacements, are nothing new, and in the final analysis, identification of an old rod by maker is all but impossible in the absence of a brand name, signature, or other markings.

Identifying Old Lures

Identification of old fishing lures can be easy or very difficult. Identification primarily depends upon who made the plug and how the manufacturer chose to mark his products. Some companies marked them well, some vaguely, and others not at all.

There are some general guidelines for dating and identifying lures. The first thing to do is study the overall appearance of the lure. Most of the older

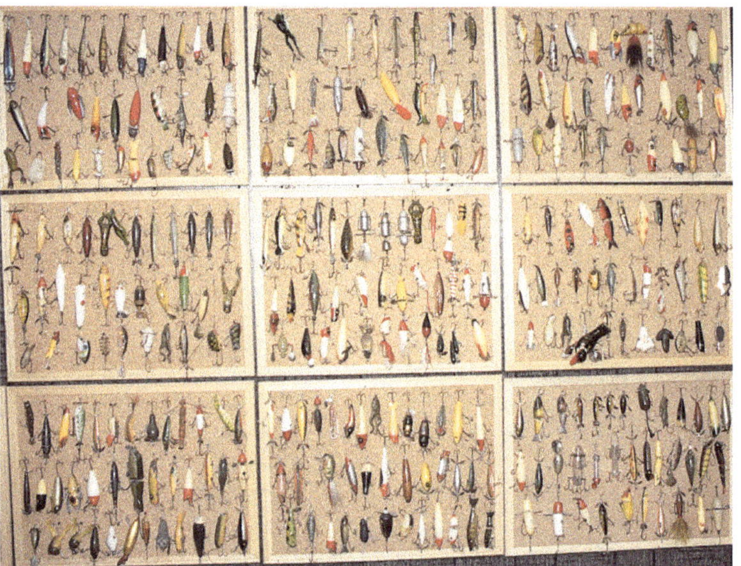

Some antique fishing lures, like those in this collection, are quite valuable.

bass plugs were made of wood and were marvels of craftsmanship, even many that were machine-made in the early days. Most received several coats of high-quality paint. Over time, this paint had a tendency to "check" or "craze," which is the appearance of hairline cracks in the finish. This is a fairly good indication of age; though not all paints on all old lures exhibit this characteristic, some fine finishes did check in just a few years. The collector should also realize that not all the old makers were conscious of quality and that none of them ever gave a thought to their products becoming highly sought collectibles. They most likely would have laughed at the mere mention of the possibility.

The metals used for lure hardware were brass, steel, nickel, and sometimes even gold plate and silver. The earliest hook fastener and line tie hardware was usually a wire passing longitudinally through the body (thru-body), twisted into loops at the front end for the line tie and at the rear end for the tail hook. This made the strongest system. The use of a simple screw eye was the alternative. There were many variations and methods but these two were the most common. The screw eye is the simplest and most common and continues in use today.

The first variation on the screw eye is attributed to the Heddon company circa 1902, when the screw hook was placed in a depression or hole in the body of the lure. This made changing fish hooks easier. Soon after that, Heddon and other companies began using flanges or rimmed metal liners in the screw eye/hook holes to protect the lure. These were soon given bottoms, making them rimmed metal cups. The liners and cups also improved hook presentation. The Creek Chub company used the cup hardware throughout the years they were in business. In 1915, the Heddon company filed a patent for a new hook hanger that collectors call the "L-rig."

Heddon lures have very specific hook hanger hardware progression changes and so are fairly easy to date. Other companies' hardware progressions are not necessarily so specific, but some have enough to be quite helpful in identification. Pflueger, as a case in point, patented a unique hook hanger called the "Neverfail" in 1911, which helps identify some of their lures.

The type of eye and eye detail is another characteristic helpful to identification. Most earlier plugs didn't have eyes on them at all. Then came a limited use of painted eyes. Glass eyes are common on early lures and a good indication of vintage. There was also the use of plain tacks and painted tacks for eye representation, but it is not possible to tell which came first, the tack eye or the glass eye. It is most likely that they were used concurrently. The tack eye survived long past the glass eye because it was cheaper. The painted eye outlasted the tack eye for the same reason.

The first type of glass eye was slightly rounded, with an opaque yellow iris and a black pupil. The second type was more rounded, with a clear outer section, a yellow tinted iris, and a larger black pupil. These yellow glass eyes vary in size, with the smallest generally being the oldest. The tack eye was one of the latest eye types to be employed before painted eyes became universal. It was a cone-shaped piece of plastic with a hole through the middle for a small tack or brad, which held it on and represented the pupil.

Because they may have been changed one or more times over the years as they were bent or broken in use, types of hooks are usually of no help to identification.

Early plastic lures are quite popular with collectors. In the early days some of the plastic compounds were inherently unstable and subject to self destruction. The earliest plastics were made up of compounds derived from animal and vegetable matter. Many collectors consider these "natural plastics" because of their composition. The first of this genre was created in 1869, when an American named John Hyatt patented a mixture of cellulose, nitrate, and camphor and gave it the trade name celluloid.

In 1910 a completely synthetic plastic was commercially produced. Leo Hendrik Baekelund, a Belgian-born American, invented a dark, thermosetting resin made of phenol and formaldehyde that was later trade named "Bakelite." Originally available only in a dark brown or reddish color, in 1928 a colorless version that could be tinted any color was invented. Unfortunately, this version was moisture-absorbent until it was refined in 1939. The original dark color was moisture resistant. The famous Al Foss Oriental Wigglers were first made of celluloid in 1917 and later of Bakelite.

Most lure companies didn't get on the plastics bandwagon until the Heddon company introduced their "Spook" series in 1932. This was the beginning of what would later become the widespread manufacture of plastic lures in the United States. Most companies continued with wooden lure production and were still a bit wary of this new material. Although they grasped the versatility of plastics, companies did not begin to widely produce plastic lures until the late 1940s and early 1950s. Many early plastic lures have been found disintegrated after years spent in the darkness of their original boxes. The mixing and ratio of the ingredients was apparently quite critical.

Pricing Collectibles

Pricing collectible tackle is a difficult endeavor. The old adage that "nothin' ain't worth nothin' until somebody wants it" certainly applies to tackle. A fair price could easily be described as what a willing buyer pays a willing seller. That can be quite different from one individual to the next. Price guides are available, but you should choose them with care. Many are written by collectors themselves, and the prices in the guide may or may not be influenced by what the collector/writer wants to buy or sell. Many serious collectors prefer to trade if they can. Members of the National Fishing Lure Collectors Club are able to contact other collectors for buying, selling, and trading through a membership directory. The club has an annual meeting where members display tackle collectibles for sale or trade. Some of these meetings produce over 600 tables. Regional shows may be more convenient in terms of size and geographical location. The meetings and shows are the best venues for the collector. The NFLCC has a very informative quarterly newsletter and a beautiful twice-yearly magazine. Many collectors send for-sale lists to the general membership. All of these publications can be very helpful in determining a value. The NFLCC also has a standard grading system that members use to describe condition and an ethical code for dealing.

Buying, Selling, and Trading Tips

- Knowledge is power. Get and study as much reliable printed data as you can find.
- Handle as much tackle as you can as often as you can. Intimate familiarity with the things you collect can help you avoid mistakes.
- Mutual cooperation builds better collections. Ask for help from knowledgeable collectors and, after you get smart, give an edge to those who helped you in the beginning.
- If you find you have a treasure, don't be greedy; be fair. If you don't deal fairly, you may find your sources drying up.
- If you find that you've made a bad deal, don't worry over it; learn from it. Turn lemons into lemonade by knowing better next time.
- Always make an offer. Nothing ventured, nothing gained. Remember that one person's trash is another person's treasure.
- Honest mistakes are made. If you build a good rapport with, and a good reputation among, collector friends, most mistakes can be rectified painlessly. Keep in mind, however, that it is not possible to make all deals mutually fair, only mutually acceptable. Don't squawk if you later find the deal wasn't so good after all. You can't win them all.

Tackle Collector Organizations

The National Fishing Lure Collectors Club (NFLCC); HCR #3, Box 4012; Reed Spring, MO 65737. The NFLCC is the premier organization of fishing tackle collectors. It publishes a quarterly newsletter, a full color magazine, and a directory of its over 3,000 members. No one interested in collecting old fishing tackle can do without a membership. The club has a large reference library service, a club shop, fishing tackle collection insurance, and other services.

Old Reel Collectors Association; 849 NE 70th Avenue; Portland, OR 97213. This very helpful organization for collectors of old fishing reels puts them in touch with each other through its newsletter.

Informative Books

Collecting antique fishing tackle is an extremely entertaining pastime, but reading about the history, development, and attendant lore and legend is fascinating, fun, and educational. The best way to master this hobby is to learn as much about it as possible. Dozens of books and publications cover this collecting discipline, and to buy them all represents a significant cash outlay. The following are fundamental references, some of which are periodically updated and revised in new editions.

Old Fishing Lures and Tackle—An Identification and Value Guide by Carl F. Luckey, Books Americana/Krause Publications, Iola, WI. The biggest and most comprehensive reference available on collecting fishing tackle. The main thrust is lures, but it has a fairly large section on reels and a discussion of rods. This book is a must for the lure collector.

Fishing Tackle Antiques and Collectibles by Karl T. White, Holli Enterprises, OK. An excellent and thorough research tool for the lure collector. It illustrates thousands of lures, rods, and reels in color and has value assessments.

Fishing Lure Collectibles by Dudley Murphy and Rick Edmisten, Collector Books, Paducah, KY. A very good full-color book dedicated to the most collectible antique fishing lures, and an excellent identification and value guide.

Antique and Collectible Fishing Reels by Harold Jellison and D. B. Homel, Forrest Park Publishers, Bellingham, WA. A comprehensive guide to the identification, valuation, and maintenance of all types of reels. It is profusely illustrated with

detailed photographs, color plates, and historic patent drawings. A must for the old-reel collector.

Lawson's Price Guide to Old Fishing Reels by Stu Lawson, Monterey Bay Publishing, Capitola, CA. The most comprehensive value guide for reels, with over 5,900 reel listings and 103 photo plates of numerous reels.

Antique & Collectible Fishing Rods by D. B. Homel, Forrest Park Publishers, Bellingham, WA. An excellent, authoritative guide to all sorts of rods, including wood, steel, fiberglass, and split bamboo versions. It includes important design patents and the history of rod materials, with close-up photos of ferrules, reel seats, and other distinguishing characteristics. Invaluable for the rod collector.

Fish-Bait: The First Plug

The introduction to Patent No. 696,433, issued on April 1, 1902 by the United States Patent Office to James Heddon, for an invention titled "Fish-Bait," reads as follows:

> *Be it known that I, James Heddon, a citizen of the United States, residing at the city of Dowagiac, in the county of Cass and State of Michigan, have invented certain new and useful Improvements in Fish-Baits, of which the following is a specification.*
>
> *This invention relates to improvements in fish-baits.*
>
> *The objects of the invention are to provide an improved casting or trolling bait which shall be conspicuous, and which shall be effective in presenting the hooks to the best advantage for catching the fish, and which is provided with means for keeping the same one side up, and which is provided with means for producing conspicuous agitation of the water, and which in view of the number of hooks which it carries is quite effective in avoiding weeds.*

Legend has it that one day James Heddon carved a piece of wood into the shape of a fish and tossed it into the water. A bass struck the "plug" of wood, and the idea for fishing plugs was born. That's an oft-repeated, perhaps somewhat accurate, yet hazy condensation of the actions of the man generally credited with devising the genre of lures we call plugs, one of the most historic developments in American angling history.

Heddon was no ordinary whittler. The 1902 patent was one of many he held. And the plug that he carved on the day in question may or may not have been his first. But it was definitely one of the first and a catalyst for millions to follow. The exact details of when and how his Fish-Bait invention came about are not completely clear.

The father of the casting plug was by trade a beekeeper. He was also a six-time patent holder and manufacturer of beekeeping equipment, book author, newspaper owner and publisher, and angler. He had been making lures out of wood since approximately 1890. Some accounts say that he gave them to friends and family and that around 1891 or 1892 he started making wooden frogs for bass fishing.

The exact date when Heddon whittled a fish shape and threw it into the water isn't known for certain. It may have been in the early 1890s. Some accounts have it happening in the early 1900s just prior to his 1902 patent. Many have reported that the incident took place on Dowagiac Creek near his apiary; some say it was on the creek pond near the dam that was built to run a nearby flour mill.

The most reliable of the five or more versions of this story may be anecdotal evidence from Larry Bowers, who rowed the boat for Heddon while he fished. In 1962, Bowers told Trig Lund, Dowagiac historical buff and Heddon company employee, that one day James Heddon was waiting by the pond for George Melvin, manager of the flour mill. While waiting he whittled a piece of wood and skipped it along the water. A bass hit it. A week or two later, Heddon made a plug from a corn cob and attached hooks to it. With Bowers rowing for him, Heddon caught seven bass on the corn cob lure. Eventually, though, the cob soaked up water, sunk, and didn't work. A few weeks later Heddon made his first slope-nosed plug from wood. This was the forerunner of the Fish-Bait that he patented in 1902.

At some point, perhaps later in 1902 after his lure was patented and a manufacturing company established, Heddon caught and kept 73 bass on his slope-nosed Fish-Bait, which would later be known as the Old Dowagiac Minnow. One account says the fish were caught in LaGrange Pond, 5 miles east of Dowagiac. The catch stirred up a lot of excitement. A published account states that he sent a photograph to a publication, but the editor replied " . . . if you had followed the usual method of fish hogs and stood beside the string, I should have been glad to print the picture in order that decent men might recognize you when they see you and shun you . . . ."

Another published attribution stated that Heddon's catch, which included a 6-pound largemouth black bass, had a total weight of 114 pounds and noted, "This wholesale slaughtering of bass has started an agitation which may result in presenting a petition to the legislature asking for passage of a law that will prohibit the use of more than one hook on a bait when angling for bass."

Time has blurred the boundary between fact and fiction in the circumstances surrounding the development of the first plug. It is known for

certain, however, that Heddon applied for his slope-nosed Fish-Bait patent on January 9, 1902. It was granted a few months later, on April Fool's Day.

James Heddon started the lure manufacturing company bearing his name sometime between 1900 and 1902. His son Will joined him in the business shortly thereafter. In 1903 the company was called James Heddon and Son. A few years later Son was changed to the plural when son Charles got into the business, and then later to James Heddon's Sons. Will and Charles are credited with much of the company's success. They were both accomplished anglers; Charles was a good businessman, and Will an ardent lure developer.

For a while the company was located and lures were manufactured in James Heddon's house. The plug manufacturing business moved to another building and then to a newly built factory. James Heddon died at his home in Dowagiac on December 7, 1911. That same year Will moved to Florida. Charles took over the tackle business, which would later include fishing rods; he successfully expanded the business, and ran the company until his death in Dowagiac in 1941. The company was later sold several times. It went from being one of the foremost tackle companies and lure manufacturing businesses in the world to an also-ran and then became almost nonexistent. In 1983, it was purchased by Pradco, a large tackle company, which continues to produce a few of Heddon's top lures of the past.

Lures are no longer manufactured in Dowagiac. There is a small historical display on the Heddon business at Southwestern Michigan College in Dowagiac, and a James Heddon Memorial Park at the old mill pond on the East Branch of Dowagiac Creek. It's a typical small lily pad pond with a variety of warmwater species, a lot of fishing pressure, and a sign that proclaims "first artificial fishing lure developed on this site in 1893."

Of course, Heddon did not create the first artificial fishing lure. He may have created the first fishing plug that you could cast and troll with its own built-in action. What he did above all was hook anglers forever.

See: Baitcasting Tackle; Conventional Tackle; Flycasting Tackle; Kentucky Reel; Line; Lure; Spincasting Tackle; Spinning Tackle.

ANTI-REVERSE

A switch that allows the handle and the gears of a reel to be put in reverse by turning it to the off position, or that keeps the reel automatically and constantly out of reverse by turning it to the on position. A reel with such a switch is said to have selective anti-reverse, meaning that the angler has a choice. A reel without such a switch cannot be turned backward, so there is no such choice.

When a reel is in the anti-reverse mode (or if it has nonselective anti-reverse), as the handle is turned forward to retrieve line and then stopped, or when a fish stops the retrieve by striking, the natural tendency is to pull up on the handle. In older-model reels, and in some lesser-quality current models, there is considerable play in the handle and rotor when the reel stops, and the handle may actually turn backward slightly before stopping. This tendency produces a feeling of sloppiness or instability; too much backward movement of the handle may adversely affect hooksetting and may allow a loop of slack line to appear on the spool in some retrieval motions, which may eventually impair casting. Ideally the reel should engage instantly and firmly, and better reels have features that allow this, which are usually called continuous anti-reverse or infinite anti-reverse. These should keep the drive gear from moving even the slightest bit backward, and most operate silently.

See: Baitcasting Tackle; Big-Game Tackle; Conventional Tackle; Flycasting Tackle; Spincasting Tackle; Spinning Tackle.

APOGEE

The point in the moon's orbit farthest from the earth, producing a lower tidal range.

See: Tides.

AQUACULTURE

The raising of fish or shellfish under some controls, usually for the purpose of commercial sale. Ponds, pens, tanks, or other containers may be used. Feed is often used. This term is applied generically to the raising of fish in either freshwater or saltwater, although it is usually more often associated with the latter because saltwater fish have more commercial interest. The word "fish farming" is often used to describe aquaculture operations, particularly in freshwater (resulting in the term "farm-raised" fish in restaurants), and "mariculture" refers strictly to the raising of marine species. A hatchery is also aquaculture, although hatcheries operated by government agencies usually release fish before commercial harvest size is reached, and usually raise them for the purpose of supplementing gamefish stocks. Private hatcheries may raise fish to be sold for private stocking efforts, or for commercial sale to food processors, fish markets, and restaurants.

As of the late 1990s, over 181 species of fish and shellfish were known to be raised through aquaculture, including trout, catfish, carp, tilapia, scallops, clams, and oysters, although shrimp and salmon dominate international markets.

See: Hatchery; Mariculture.

AQUATIC INSECTS

Aquatic insects spend all or part of their lives in water. They are very diverse and abundant in freshwater, especially in rivers and lakes, where fish feed on their immature and adult forms. So prominent

The Columbia River is not only the largest North American river entering the Pacific; but, together with its tributaries, it is the most important trout and salmon drainage in the world.

are aquatic insects in the diet of trout that they form the basis of most fly fishing activities for trout in rivers and streams, and are the object imitated by countless artificial flies.

The most abundant aquatic insects are mayflies, caddisflies, stoneflies, midges, dragonflies, and damselflies. They have varying life cycles, generally a year but ranging from two months to four years. That life cycle encompasses the egg to the immature nymph that emerges on the water's surface, where it hatches into a winged adult. Depending on species, life after hatching lasts only a few hours, days, or weeks; the adults mate, lay eggs on the water, and die. During each of these stages, they are consumed by fish, and artificial flies need to imitate the proper species and stage of the respective aquatic insects. Some anglers develop a great understanding of aquatic insects for both their fly tying and fly fishing endeavors.

See: Caddisflies; Dobsonflies, Fishflies, and Alderflies; Dragonflies and Damselflies; Mayflies; Midges; Stoneflies; Terrestrial Insects.

AQUATIC PLANTS

Most bodies of water support some type and quantity of plant life. Plants are important components of aquatic ecosystems because of their multiple functions. Plants act as a soil stabilizer, trapping sediments from erosion and causing these particles to settle out of the water near shore. In shallow water they protect shores from erosion caused by wave action. They provide nesting materials and sites for various species of birds and fish. They are important nursery areas for young fish, especially many gamefish species. They release oxygen to the water. And, most importantly, they provide food for many organisms that live in the water, as well as for some animals that do not.

Aquatic plants belong to two main groups: algae and flowering plants. Algae *(see)* are the most common and widely distributed of all aquatic plants and are found in both freshwater and saltwater; kelp *(see)* is a form of algae. Flowering plants, most of which are rooted to the bottom, are also found in both freshwater and saltwater, and are the most conspicuous aquatic plants.

Most anglers call them weeds, but aquatic plants are both good and bad for fish and for angling.

Flowering plants fall into three categories: emergents, submergents, and floaters. Emergents grow along the edges of water, with only short portions of their stems and roots submerged; they are sometimes called marsh plants. Common emergents include arrowhead, bulrush, burreed, cattail, pickerelweed, rushes, and sedges. Many of these have arrow- or spear-shaped leaves. Because of their very shallow or marshy existence, these plants are usually not direct influences on sportfish or on angling, except during high water periods.

Submergent plants grow in deeper water, are usually attached to the bottom, and gain most of their nutrients from sediments; many have a complete underwater existence, like the seagrasses *(see)* of shallow saltwater flats and estuaries, but others flower above the water surface. Common submergents in freshwater include elodea, coontail, milfoil, bladderwort, fanwort, naiad, eelgrass, watercress, hydrilla, and various pondweeds. These are significant aquatic plants for anglers, since many species are attracted to them for shelter and food, and much fishing is done in or around such vegetative forms.

Most floaters are rooted plants, with most of their plant structure, especially leaves, floating on the water surface; they absorb nutrients from the muddy bottom and their flowers are pollinated by insects. Floaters can also be unattached plants that obtain nutrients through small rootlets dangling in the water. These aquatic plants include duckweed, lotus, spatterdock, waterprimrose, watershield, white waterlily, waterlettuce, and waterhyacinth. Floaters also attract many fish species and are important for anglers.

In freshwater, fish rely on aquatic plants to varying degrees. Few actually eat the plants (carp, goldfish, and other cyprinids are exceptions), yet the plants provide food for many organisms that are consumed by fish. Many large and small fish also rely on plants for shelter from light, extreme warm temperatures, and predation; generally, plants with larger leaves provide the best cover and attract larger fish. Dense plant growths, however, can provide so much cover from predators that the prey may become stunted. While aquatic plants are also a vital source of oxygen in the water, they can also deplete oxygen when they decompose and are overly dense.

Aquatic plants are the subject of considerable debate and controversy among various water users. Anglers have seen that increased aquatic plant growth, especially in water bodies that had little or no such life before, has improved fish populations, especially for largemouth bass and sunfish. Yet other water users, and lakefront homeowners, may be disturbed by the thick wads of plants that grow. As a result, there are many chemical, biological, and mechanical control efforts enacted in water bodies to eliminate or reduce plant communities, and these efforts may have short-term or long-term impacts on the abundance and composition of fish species in the affected water.

Although most aquatic plants are native to their body of water or to the overall region in which they occur, some are not, and many plants have been inadvertently spread to places where they should not be by various means, including transportation on the hulls of boats and on the trailers that carry them. When exotic (nonnative) species of plants are introduced to new environments, they can have serious adverse impacts, and it's important to make sure that they do not get stuck on boats, motors, and trailers prior to leaving that waterway. Another common means of exotic plant introduction is through the dumping of aquarium water that contains nonnative aquarium plants; this should never be emptied into a water body.

Fishing. The majority of freshwater fishing occurring around aquatic plants is for largemouth bass, although some also occurs for walleye, northern pike, muskellunge, various sunfish, crappie, yellow perch, and bullhead. Anglers find that there are varying concentrations of aquatic plants—which most people simply lump under the umbrella of "weeds"—to contend with, and that the most dense are very hard to deal with. All of it can be fished, though you can't get your boat through the worst of it except by poling. Some types of plants extend through and cover the surface, as well as being submerged several feet, or they can be shallow or deep. You have to adjust to each situation, but certain patterns hold true for all conditions, and some lure types receive prominent usage. Pinpointing the location of the edges, which are called weedlines, is often a crucial element in determining boat position, lure presentation, and fishing technique. Sonar can be a big asset in this situation.

Before fishing in vegetation, it's a good idea to study things a bit to see where the water drops off and to find the plants, plant edges, and perhaps the bait and other fish. Finding plants, of course, is relatively simple, but studying them—determining conformations, edges, and depths—is a little more involved. The objective is to find the better places to spend fishing time.

Density is one element to look for; seek thick clumps as opposed to scattered plants, because the former offer more cover. Clumped plants are the easiest situation to fish. If they are not available, scattered plants become the second choice. Look to see if plants in a given locale grow in different stages or at different levels. Shorter plants in moderately deep water, for example, are often preferred by such fish as walleye over taller plants in the same depth. Look for the weedline and its depth. An excellent situation to find, though not one as readily fished, is where the plants are thick and the edge is close to a sharp bottom dropoff.

The most obvious, most often used, and most easily managed way to locate fish in vegetation is to work the edges. In large, fairly thick concentrations, for example, many species of gamefish stick close to the outside line, most likely because they can see and ambush prey there. This is especially true if this vegetation is so congested that you can't work any type of lure across the surface without it being fouled up. Milfoil beds are a prime example of this type of cover. Here, you may have to work the edges, with most strikes (from bass) occurring within a foot or two of the edge. Any irregularity in the weedline, such as a protrusion, pocket, and so on, may be an especially significant place to fish.

Frequently the key to unlocking the secrets of catching fish (especially largemouth bass) in sparse vegetation is to fish isolated clumps, small but thick patches that stand off from the main mass (they may be within the main body as well as outside). Take care to identify and fish every likely looking isolated patch. Usually there is a lot of ground to cover, and if you find a spot that is more worthwhile than others, work it thoroughly.

When the vegetation is sparse and partly submerged, you won't be able to find isolated patches such as these. However, if you're using sonar, you may be able to identify the thin and thick sections, as well as dropoffs or holes, by traveling across the area first. If either emergent or submerged plants are thick and you see visible holes, start casting. Clearings are prime fishing locations, and they are easier to fish than the thick spots.

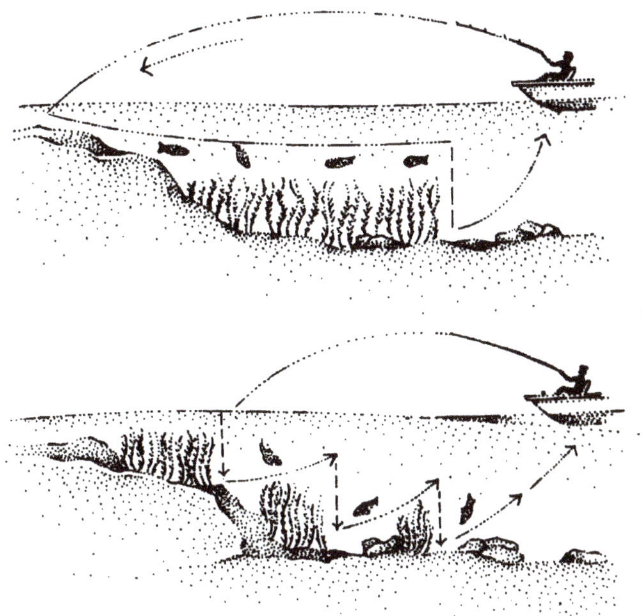
Methods of fishing in, along, and through submerged vegetation vary with type and conformation.

The key to the success and enjoyment of vegetation fishing is a weed-free, or so-called weedless, presentation, and your lure naturally plays the lead role. There are relative degrees of weedlessness in lures, just as there are relative degrees of manipulative retrieving skills, but there is no out-of-the-box, guaranteed-never-to-get-stuck fishing lure.

The plastic worm can be one of the most tangle-free lures, although it will hang up if the hook pulls through the plastic body or the sinker gets wedged. The key to using a slip sinker in vegetation is to fish the lightest one that you can toss and that will get the worm down adequately, and also to peg it with a toothpick. In grass or pad stems, or other vegetation, a free-sliding slip sinker pulls off the object, leaving the worm behind. You need to have the two working close together to achieve a proper, natural presentation.

Worms are primarily used for bass. These fish and others may prefer something that moves more enticingly, with a flash of metal. The weedless spoon and pork rind trailer has justifiably been a longtime favorite of bass, pickerel, and pike anglers. In moderately heavy cover, it is fairly tangle-free, and its action is reasonably good when drawn into open pockets from the clustered vegetation. Another popular combination incorporates an in-line spinner, a spoon, and a skirt. There are also good buzzbaits on the market, some of which incorporate a buzzing blade and shaft with a spoon, or spoonlike body; such lures work well over submerged vegetation. For good measure, you can also add a trailer hook to both of these arrangements. The trailer will mean more hooked fish per strike, though it also means more snagging on pad stems, grass clumps, and similar cover.

Spinnerbaits are a particularly effective lure when used near vegetation. When pads and grass are not too thick, as is usual in spring or early summer, a spinnerbait is the best lure for bass and one of the best for northern pike and chain pickerel. For thicker grass and pads, a spinnerbait can be effective when worked on the edges, either fishing parallel along them or fluttering it down vertically along the edges.

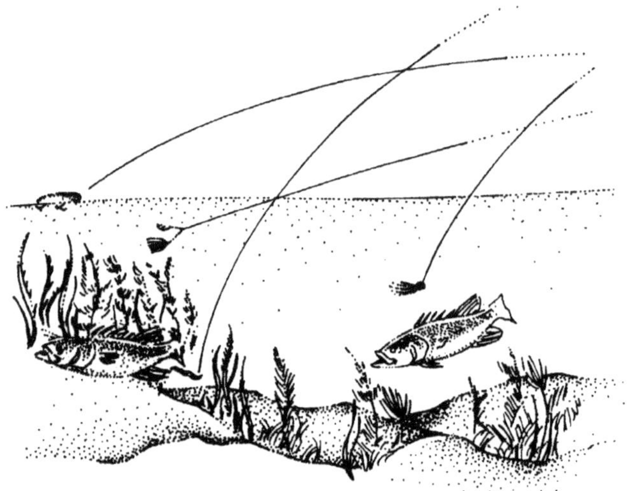

A surface lure, spinnerbait, plastic worm, and jig (left to right) are effective for catching bass around aquatic plants.

Some plugs have merit in and around vegetation, although they must be cast and retrieved judiciously. When fishing over the top of submerged grass, super-shallow-running floating/diving plugs, sonic vibrating plugs, and surface lures are effective. Surface lures will also work in areas that feature openings or channels through which they can be retrieved, and a few are capable of being slithered over the tops of even thick exposed vegetation. A crankbait might be worth using if the plants are not thick; crankbaits are very popular in walleye fishing, for example, but in weedy environs are mostly reserved for earlier in the season. A fine time to catch these fish on plugs is when the first green plants start to show. Jigs might also be worth a try, although they are not usually used in vegetation. A float-and-jig combo works well on windy days in the plants, and straight-lined jigs tipped with bait may also be used if you can maintain a good feel with them.

Bait is fished in and near grass, too. Shiners and worms are fished below bobbers in openings or just above submerged grass, as well as behind jigs and various bait rigs. Of course, attention must be paid to minimizing the fouling of these items. A float with a jig-leech/worm combo is a choice of walleye anglers. Fishing with large live shiners in vegetation is a specialty of many Florida guides, who use these baits in heavily matted saw grass, peppergrass, and hayfields, as well as around floating mats of hyacinths, where the bait can be freelined to swim well back and under this expansive cover.

When vegetation is so thick that you could almost walk across it, and the edges don't produce, you have to deal with fishing deep within, which poses obvious boating dilemmas and presentation troubles, and is primarily a need of largemouth bass anglers. Sometimes there are small holes in the mass that can be readily fished, but more often you wind up making your own hole and dunking in your lure (worm or jig). There is no casting here, just reaching over a hole, dunking the lure up and down, and moving on. You may even use your rod or an oar to poke the hole.

Vegetation fishing usually requires fairly stout tackle. This is not a place for real light line and limber rods, unless fishing for small species. Also, angling in vegetation often seems to be more productive in low-light situations than in bright daylight. Bright days tend to drive fish deeper and further into the vegetation, where they are harder to reach effectively. Dawn, dusk, and overcast days offer the best vegetation fishing conditions. Night is a good time as well.

Arapaima

ARAPAIMA *Arapaima gigas.*
Other names—piraruçu, giant arapaima, payshi, pirarocou, anatto, lou-lou, warapaima; Portuguese: *piraruçu;* Spanish: *paiche.*

The largest wholly freshwater fish, the arapaima reportedly grows up to 15 feet long. It is fished commercially and is a much-favored food fish in Brazil, usually available in public markets. The arapaima has gained minor familiarity with native anglers and with a few international traveling sportsmen, many of whom know it as piraruçu. Young arapaima are frequently displayed in public aquariums.

Identification. A large-scaled, big-eyed fish, the arapaima has pelvic fins well behind the base of its pectoral fins, most with scales but some with supra-branchial organs capable of breathing air; it also has a highly vascularized swim bladder that functions partially as a lung, and it can absorb oxygen from either water or air.

Size. The average length for arapaima is 6 feet, but it is known to grow up to 8 feet and 200 pounds. Some reports indicate the existence of specimens twice as large and heavy.

Distribution. Found in northern South America, the arapaima is common in the Amazon River and its branches in Brazil and Peru, as well as in freshwater lakes.

Habitat. Mostly inhabiting quiet waters, arapaima are usually spotted drifting or rolling in surface waters.

Life history/Behavior. The arapaima builds a nest about 2 feet in diameter in sandy bottoms among submerged plants. It spawns in April and May, laying about 47,000 eggs and guarding the young. Attracted by a pheromone secreted from glands in the skin of the parent's head, the young gather about the parent's head for protection.

Food and feeding habits. Little has been documented about the feeding habits of arapaima, although they are believed to be omnivorous.

Angling. Arapaima have been known to strike artificial lures, but they are an infrequent rod-and-reel catch. In Brazil they are speared and caught commercially in nets.

See: Brazil.

ARAWANA *Osteoglossum bicirrhosum.*
Other names—aruana, silver aruana; Portuguese: *aruanã;* Spanish: *arahuana.*

A fine food fish, the arawana is also a splendid gamefish as well as a popular aquarium fish in Asia.

Identification. The arawana has large scales, big eyes, and a head protected by a hard bone. Its elongated dorsal and anal fins are located very far back on the body and are barely separated from the tail. Like the arapaima, to which it is related, the arawana has a vascularized air bladder that acts as a lung. It also has two fleshy barbels on its lower jaw that are assumed to have a sensory function. A distinctive and identifying feature is its lower jaw, which slants sharply upward.

Size. The arawana grows to usually less than 2 feet in length, although it is believed to attain at least 3 feet in size. It can weigh as much as 11 pounds.

Distribution. Arawana primarily occur in central and northern South America, mostly in the Amazon drainage of Brazil and Peru.

Habitat. Arawana inhabit the same environs as arapaima *(see)*—mostly shallow, quiet backwaters. They live in marginal lagoons and small tributaries of large rivers during the dry season, and in flooded backwaters during the high-water season.

Life history/Behavior. Not much is known about the life history of this species. The arawana is believed to carry its eggs in its mouth until they have hatched, and to follow and protect its fry by holding them in its mouth.

Feeding habits. The arawana is said to be an opportunistic feeder, lurking on the bottom as well as feeding at middepths and near the surface. It is known to leap high out of the water to take fruit from overhanging branches, and it may be omnivorous. Some observers have reported that it can jump 6 feet out of the water to capture prey.

Angling. The arawana is a popular although unpredictable and infrequent catch for anglers. It is a strong fighter, takes artificial lures, and is usually caught in or near shallow areas in quiet backwaters, usually close to shore and in brushy habitat. Most anglers who encounter arawana do so when using large and noisy lures intended for peacock bass, and

Arawana

it is possible that more refined presentations could produce more of this species. Arawana are netted commercially in Brazil and are commonly found in fish markets there.

See: Brazil.

ARGENTINA

The second largest country in South America (after Brazil), Argentina has a surprisingly modest diversity of gamefish species, especially compared to Brazil, but it makes up for this by offering some of the finest trout fishing in the world, especially in the coldwater rivers of Patagonia and Tierra del Fuego. Saltwater fishing along the lengthy Atlantic coast has little to offer the visiting angler, although sea-run trout in the southern rivers are highly commendable, and dorado fishing in the north is spotty but exciting when at its best. Ironically, Argentina's salmonids are all imports, resulting from fortuitous stockings early in the twentieth century. A good food base and appropriate coldwater lakes and rivers have contributed to a healthy fishery.

This 2,070-mile-long country encompasses more than 2.8 million square miles of land, and its thousands of miles of rivers—some of which contain above-average-size trout—are well spread out. Many of these waters are on the eastern fringe of the Andes, which form a boundary on the west with Chile, and especially in the Patagonian Andes, which seldom exceed 12,000-foot elevations.

Argentina's topography is varied, including mountains, upland areas, and plains. The northwestern mountains boast peaks above 21,000 feet, the highest of which is Aconcagua. At 22,834 feet, it is higher than all other peaks in the world, excluding those in central Asia. The region east of the Andes is largely a flat or lightly rolling plain that slopes gradually from about 2,000 feet to sea level. In the north, these plains are the southern component of South America's Gran Chaco, and are succeeded for nearly 1,000 miles by the pampas—treeless plains that contain Argentina's major agricultural lands. South of the pampas, and roughly below the Rio Colorado, the terrain consists largely of arid, desert plateaus known as Patagonia. This southern region of Argentina covers about 300,000 square miles and includes the eastern, or Argentine, part of Tierra del Fuego, an archipelago off the southern tip of South America.

Northern Region

The dorado is northern Argentina's main claim to piscatorial fame. This exotic and powerful species has been locally revered, especially along the Paraná River, a mighty flow that courses through the north-central region. The Paraná originates in Brazil, forms the border of Paraguay and Brazil and of Paraguay and Argentina, is joined by the Paraguay River north of the Argentine city of Corrientes, and then heads south and southeast through Argentina and eventually to the Atlantic Ocean at Rio de la Plata. The Paraná and other rivers in this region have been dammed in places, which has ruined some of the best dorado fishing areas and also greatly reduced the likelihood of catching the monsters (50- to 70-pounders) previously taken here.

Today the majority of dorado fishing is concentrated in the northeastern region of Argentina, in an area of Corrientes province roughly enclosed by a border running from Esquina to Corrientes to Posadas to Mercedes and back to Esquina. The Paraná, above its merger with the Paraguay River to south of Posadas, and a large swampy backwater region to the south of this known as Esteros del Ibera, offer prime dorado fishing.

Ibera is a 20,000-square-kilometer region of swamps and grassland with a maze of channels, lagoons, bays, and streams. This region provides water to the Rio Corrientes, which in turn joins the Paraná. Most importantly, it is a clear-water system, which is important for catching the aggressive sight-feeding dorado, and it has a steady flow of water with abundant forage.

In 1996, a lodge was completed on the banks of the Esteros, and anglers explore the region by boat from there. Known for wildlife viewing, the area also hosts surubim catfish, piranhas, pacu, and other Amazonian species. Anglers have success with spinning, baitcasting, and flycasting tackle. The largest dorado caught by angling (larger ones have been speared by natives) in recent years was reportedly a 42-pounder, but the average fish weighs between 3 and 12 pounds. The dorado in this slow- or stillwater region are good fighters, but not as demanding as those found in fast river currents. The area is accessed from Corrientes or Mercedes, and the best season is reportedly summer, from September through March.

On the Paraná, the town of Paso de la Patria, about a half-hour ride from Corrientes, is the main jumping-off point for big-river fishing. Site of an acclaimed annual dorado festival, Paso de la Patria is a small village with a few hotels and restaurants, mostly geared toward a summer influx of tourists.

The Paraná's strong current and a chance to catch dorado from 30 to 45 pounds dictate big-water tackle and tactics. Sturdy baitcasting reels with long-handled rods and 14- to 25-pound line are the primary tackle. Favored fishing methods include trolling with deep-diving plugs, casting plugs to the shoreline, and drifting with live bait. Cleaner nearby tributaries provide other opportunities, though generally for smaller fish, and other species are available as well. Accommodations exist in Corrientes and Paso de la Patria.

Here, the summer fishing season runs from October through April. Unfortunately, the Paraná, as well as other big area rivers, are subject to fluctuating water levels due to rainfall, and high muddy water does not bode well for big-river fishing.

Patagonia

The northern portion of this region contains the lake region of the Patagonian Andes, and rivers that flow either east toward the Atlantic or west toward the Pacific through Chile. Nahuel Huapi National Park contains the famous lake of the same name, which is an Argentine favorite and certainly a tourist attraction, but not a fishery that attracts many visiting anglers. Visitors are more inclined to cast in the rivers than to troll and fish deep in the lake (something that North Americans can do less expensively, although perhaps in less delightful surroundings, in numerous homeland lakes).

Nahuel Huapi covers 557 square kilometers, with large islands and many peninsulas and deep arms. It is fed by several rivers, including the Espejo, Correntoso, Gallardo, Moreno, Gutierrez, and Frias, and its outlet is the Limay River, which flows eastward. The lake reportedly has depths to 454 meters and contains a variety of species, including introduced brown trout, rainbow trout, and landlocked Atlantic salmon. It has produced huge brown and rainbow trout in the past, and is next to the alpine village of San Carlos de Bariloche, making it readily accessible for even a short visit by anglers headed to the rivers north and south, who might want to try for big browns ascending the tributaries to spawn in the fall. Other lakes of note in the region include Traful, which had the first stocking of landlocked salmon, Correntoso, Espejo, and Gutierrez, but there are many smaller ones as well.

As mentioned, visiting anglers focus their attention on the rivers of this region. Bariloche is the hub of upper-Patagonia trout fishing, and it has many guides. The casual tourist interested in a day or two of angling while traveling in the region can find assistance here, with or without speaking Spanish. Many visitors, however, use outfitters and established camps and lodges with access to specific waters, many of which are on ranches in remote areas and offer less pressured and more private resources. Argentine law permits public access to all streams, provided that such access originates from a public point inside a streambed, which effectively eliminates a lot of areas that are simply too far from public spots to be fished without using the services of lodges *(hosterias)* that exist on working ranches that range from modest to enormous in size. Some waters are set aside for catch-and-release fishing, and fly fishing is the norm, especially on private sections of rivers.

The Traful River is one of those privately accessed waters. Not far from Bariloche, it is known for big brown and rainbow trout, and landlocked salmon, especially early and late in the season. This is one of Argentina's most hallowed trout waters, and landlocked salmon, which were first imported from Sebago Lake in Maine, migrate up from Lake Traful in March and April to spawn.

North of Bariloche are the rivers and lakes of the San Martin and Junin de Carlos region; these include the Chimehuin, Malleo, Limay, Alumine, Collon-Cura, and Caleufu Rivers, among others. Brown trout and rainbow trout are the mainstays, with some brook trout, and the fish commonly range from 1 to 4 pounds, although much larger trout—including browns to 10 pounds—are possible, especially at the mouths of rivers *(bocas)*. The Alumine, Collon-Cura, and Limay are floatable.

The Limay is a large and well-known trout stream but one that has received much angling pressure for large browns and rainbows in the past. The Chimehuin is a renowned trophy rainbow and

A trout fishing scene on the Carrileufu River of southern Patagonia.

brown river that flows for 60 kilometers from its origin at Lake Huechulafquen to its merger with the Collon-Cura River. Similar to the Chimehuin as classic fly fishing water is the Malleo, which is north of Junin de Los Andes and in the shadow of the Lanin volcano.

South of Bariloche there is excellent trout fishing in various waters within the Esquel region of southern Patagonia. This is the remote and beautiful area visited by Butch Cassidy and the Sundance Kid when they sought refuge in South America. Here, the Arrayanes, Frey, Menendez, Chubut, Carrileufu, and Rivadavia Rivers are all notable brown and rainbow trout fisheries, as is Arroyo Pescado, the region's best spring creek flow. The Rio Grande, accessible by auto and a tailwater fishery from Lake Futaleufu, is noted for its rainbows, and there's good lake fishing, especially in Lago Bueno and Lago Menendez.

Although the largemouth bass is the most popular single fish in the United States, only four states have designated this species as their state fish.

Trout season in Patagonia opens in mid-November and extends into April. The Southern Hemisphere's spring months of November and December are very good; high water and light fishing pressure are the norm. The water levels have dropped considerably by the onset of fall in March, and some may not be floatable, but late season has the advantage of fewer anglers again and some fishing for larger spawning-run fish. Peak angling activity occurs in the summer months of January and February. Varied water types and conditions present a smorgasbord of situations and gear requirements, though streamers and nymphs are effective on most waters throughout the season. The fish feed heavily on crabs *(pancoras),* and fish from 4 to 7 pounds will likely be encountered, although much larger fish are rare.

Opportunities for sea-run brown trout fishing in the southern Patagonia mainland exist, although established outfitters here are slim. Several lengthy river systems flow here. The Rio Gallegos, for example, which is the southernmost Argentine mainland river, has a run of sea trout from October through March, with good average-size trout and big-fish potential.

Tierra del Fuego

Tierra del Fuego, named "Land of Fire" by the explorer Magellan, is an archipelago at the southern tip of South America, separated from the mainland by the Strait of Magellan and jointly part of Chile (west) and Argentina (east). This archipelago consists of the main island of Tierra del Fuego and many smaller islands, with Cape Horn at the southern extremity and bordering the Atlantic, Antarctic, and Pacific Oceans. The northern part of this island is like flat prairie—a desolate, harsh, windswept land of rolling hills with few trees and millions of sheep—while the southern part has densely wooded hills. The eastern, or Argentinian, portion of the main island is an extension of the Patagonian plateau, and contains the Rio Grande and a number of tributaries, which collectively offer what is arguably the world's best fishing for sea-run brown trout.

Brown trout were introduced to the Rio Grande in 1934 and established a resident population, and then an evolved sea-run strain that has continued to improve. Today, large (over 20 pounds) sea-run browns are more common than at any previous time. In some rivers or sections of rivers, 7- to 10-pound fish are the average catch, with smaller fish rare, and specimens from 12 to 20 pounds a real possibility. These are well-fed fish, too, with stocky bodies. Under the best conditions, an experienced angler may catch quite a few trout in a day, and this is a handful of angling, considering that sea-run brown are leaping, thrashing, exciting fish.

Although there are numerous rivers on the main island, the Rio Grande is the most significant and, with its tributaries, receives the lion's share of angling attention. The Rio Grande courses 60 miles from its source in the Chilean Andes of western Tierra del Fuego to the Atlantic Ocean. The middle portions have an average width of 80 feet, and the lower area closer to the estuary widens, although it maintains an average of just over 100 feet. Seventy-foot casts are the norm, especially along the lower reaches, and these are often necessary with a double haul into the wind. Although this does not appeal to some people, it should be noted that some portions of the river are less troubled by wind than others. The wind typically blows from midmorning until evening, and often reaches gale force; it is customary to fish from early morning to midday, then return to camp for an early dinner, returning in the evening to fish (with light available till nearly 11 P.M. in midsummer). Rain occurs frequently, even in summer months, so warm clothes and rain gear are a must.

The Rio Grande has a smooth gravel bed that provides easy wading, and large pools merge into long, wide runs. The water is milky, and seldom permits sighting fish from a bank vantage. Several days of hard rain can make the river unfishable, at least for a day. Water levels generally remain constant during the November through March fishing period, perhaps because of consistent rain on western slopes that face the wind. On the lower Rio Grande, anglers encounter nickel-bright fresh sea-run fish *(plateados),* and these are powerhouses. Some anglers use two-handed rods in this larger water.

Several rivers flow into the middle portion of the Rio Grande; these include the Menendez, Mac Lennan, and Herminita, with the Menendez regarded most favorably. It has the same quality and quantity of sea-run trout as the Rio Grande but is a smaller tributary; 40-foot casts are the norm and easy wading exists.

Sea-run brown move into the rivers in September but they move through in small schools on a staggered basis throughout the season. They do not feed while on their spawning run. January and February—the summer period—is favored by many visitors, but the season runs from November through March. All of the fishing here is controlled by private access through established fishing operations run by various ranches, which own large tracts of land. Most rivers or privately controlled sections are restricted to fly fishing and catch-and-release. Most accommodate only a few people at a time.

Rainbow and brown trout are also caught, in addition to sea-run browns, and other opportunities exist outside the Rio Grande and its tributaries. South of the Rio Grande in the heart of Tierra del Fuego is Lake Fagnano, which has a total length of 115 kilometers (the western tip is in Chile) and various important tributaries. Fagnano is connected to the Pacific Ocean through its outlet in Chile, and it draws in sea-run browns; it also has resident brook trout, brown trout, rainbows, and landlocked salmon. All tackle types are used here, which makes it a good alternative for those unable to wade and flycast in rivers but who still wish to enjoy Tierra del Fuego's angling. The *bocas* here can produce trophy trout, and are especially attractive in late season.

Another southern river, west of Lake Fagnano and some 160 kilometers south of the city of Rio Grande, is the Yrigoyen. This has both sea-run and resident browns, is fly fishing and catch-and-release only, and has a mountain-river character in its upper reaches and a plains character in its lower reaches. Notable tributaries include the Udaeta and Malenguena, the latter reportedly as good as the main river.

See also: Chile.

ARIZONA

Fish and fishing are usually the last images that come to mind when contemplating the state of Arizona, primarily because tourism officials and advertising campaigns have created a finely crafted image of Arizona as "the desert state." When vacationers and newcomers visit or move to the Grand Canyon State, they generally bring their sinuses and their golf clubs. They marvel at the scenery, rejoice in the uniqueness of the desert, exclaim about the warm winters, and can't believe Las Vegas is only six hours away. Fishing rods are at most an afterthought. After all, with respect to fishing, Arizona is never mentioned in the same breath as, say, Florida or Minnesota.

But nearly 600,000 adults annually, plus another 100,000 or so unlicensed youngsters, believe Arizona's sportfish are worthy of pursuit. They do so because fish are in fact as abundant and varied in Arizona as in most states in the country, and thanks to a milder climate, these fish can be pursued pretty much year-round. In fact, as human beings came to depend on fish more for sport than food, the face of Arizona angling changed drastically. Stocking fish became a common practice; the fish, like many of Arizona human residents, originally come from somewhere else.

The ubiquitous largemouth bass, found in deep, clear reclamation reservoirs across the state's Sonoran Desert midsection and in the giant lakes of the Colorado River, tops the piscatorial menu. Rainbow trout, a put-and-take proposition due to the state's arid personality, are the resident angler's favorite and live mostly in the waters of the pine tree–studded mountains of the north and east. In addition, a variety of other trout, as well as smallmouth bass, striped bass, walleye, northern pike, catfish, crappie, bluegills, and numerous other species are available.

Within the state are distinct zones where certain species predominate. Which fish thrive where is dictated by climate, resulting in equally distinct warmwater fisheries and coldwater fisheries. But there are crossovers.

Catching hefty bass, along with rainbow trout, in a small pond in the 8,000-foot-high White Mountains seems a bit ludicrous. But no more than casting for trout in a desert stream 40 minutes east of the Phoenix metroplex, or trolling for walleye in a saguaro-framed reservoir on the Salt River.

For some anglers, soaking an anchovy for saltwater-transplanted striped bass in one of several Colorado River reservoirs is what it's all about. Others would rather cast flies for storied lunker rainbows in a classic tailrace fishery below Glen Canyon Dam, just before the Colorado River begins its 300-mile journey through the Grand Canyon.

Arizona's sportfishery may not be as plentiful as that of some states, but its uniqueness keeps anglers coming back.

White Mountains

Located in extreme eastern Arizona along the New Mexico border, the White Mountains offer an alpine setting for heat-weary refugees from central Arizona, New Mexico, and Texas during the summer. But anglers view it as a great place to fish for trout, and so they should. This mountainous region held the state's only two native trout species, the Gila and the Apache, discovered when Anglo-Americans began frequenting the 6,500- to 10,000-foot elevations in the early 1800s. Due to pressure from early settlers, both species became nearly extinct around the turn of the twentieth century.

Later, fisheries biologists decided that the Apache—easily recognized by its distinctive overall golden hue mixed with olive on the upper portions, and its unmistakable orange to yellow-orange cutthroat mark—belonged to Arizona while the Gila variety was assigned to New Mexico. A massive recovery program brought the Apache, also known as the Arizona trout, back; currently this unique salmonid is honored as the official state fish.

Apache trout thrive in the West Fork of the Black River and in a few other small impoundments

such as Lee Valley Lake, where it shares the water with Montana grayling. But the largest populations of Apache trout are found on the 1.4 million-acre Fort Apache Indian Reservation, where state fishing licenses aren't needed but special Apache permits are.

Fly and ultralight spinning anglers seek Apache trout up to 5 pounds on Scenic Christmas Tree Lake on the Fort Apache Indian Reservation. This special-fee lake is available to anglers only from the end of May through October, but the results make it worth the effort.

Rainbow, brook, cutthroat, and brown trout, as well as grayling—all of which were imported to the state between 1900 and 1940—reside in the 30-plus man-made lakes dotting the White Mountains. Big Lake, at 9,000-feet in the Apache-Sitgreaves National Forest, is a 450-acre fish factory and gets most of its attention from Arizona Game and Fish Department hatchery trucks, not to mention anglers. Eight- to 9-inch-long rainbow and brook trout are primarily caught here, but carry-over fish are plentiful, making the chances of hooking into a trout up to 20 inches extremely good.

Although flies, lures, and bait work well all year, anglers crowd the shoreline in the fall when brookies are attempting to spawn. Artificial salmon eggs will do the trick, as will the roe stripped from females that have been caught. A hefty brook trout and the changing leaves in the surrounding forest make for an unforgettable autumn outing.

Numerous fishable streams course through the White Mountains, but the Little Colorado River, which eventually joins the main Colorado in the Grand Canyon a half-state away, is the one to visit. It is accessible in the scenic mountain hamlet of Greer, among other places.

And a stop in Greer is a must. In addition to the Little Colorado, anglers have a choice of fishing River, Tunnel, and Bunch Reservoirs, where hefty rainbows have been taken.

North-Central Region

A scant two-hour drive due north of Phoenix is an area that offers perhaps the greatest variety of species and fishing in Arizona. Among other popular waters, it is home to Oak Creek, where the best wild brown trout in the state can be found.

Lakes and streams range in elevation from 7,000 feet in the Flagstaff area, south to 2,500 feet at Camp Verde along the Verde River. Everything from stocked rainbow trout in a variety of small coldwater lakes to largemouth bass, catfish, and other warmwater species are available to anglers who don't mind driving a distance to fish them.

Sharing the billing with the trout are a few species usually associated with similar colder climates at more northerly latitudes. Northern pike and walleye are staples in upper and lower Lake Mary. These two lakes, on the eastern outskirts of Flagstaff, produce excellent fishing when snow and rain are ample enough to keep them full.

Pike and another upper Midwest species, the yellow perch, make a good combination in Stoneman Lake, southeast of Flagstaff. Considered the only "natural" lake in the state, the tule-ringed 170-acre pond offers a respite from more popular fisheries. Successful anglers present soaked meal worms impaled on the hook of a small jig from a rowboat or canoe. Shore fishing is seldom attempted due to widespread aquatic growth; those anglers who do best position their crafts along the outer edge of the cattails.

Although the perch are small, there is good reason to keep a tight hold of the rod; it's not uncommon for northern pike, some weighing into the teens, to cruise by and take a whack at the offering.

Many trout anglers find their favored catch at Whitehorse Lake, west of Flagstaff and south of the small town of Williams. This 35-acre fishery also supports bass and catfish. Two no-bait waters offering rainbow trout are nearby as well: Perkins Tank and J. D. Dam Lake.

Large fishable streams are at a premium in Arizona, but the Verde River and Oak Creek serve up a diverse fish menu. While wild brown trout inhabit the upper portions of heavily wooded Oak Creek and its West Fork; the larger Verde contains largemouth and smallmouth bass, two kinds of catfish, and a population of smaller fish—from an elevation of 5,500 feet to Horseshoe and Bartlett Lakes just outside Phoenix.

Mogollon Rim

A sharp escarpment that can be traced in varying degrees from New Mexico northwest across Arizona, the 7,000-foot Mogollon Rim is at its most majestic approximately 110 miles northeast of Phoenix, where its rocky face rises above the thick mat of pine trees covering huge canyons and ridges that fall away to lower elevations.

Nowhere in the state is man's trout habitat handiwork more prevalent. Seven lakes, ranging from 200 down to 55 acres, are the result of a massive lake-building spree by the Arizona Game and Fish Department during the 1950s and 1960s. All are located in pine forests at 7,000 feet or higher.

The Mogollon Rim lakes serve as the second most popular destination for trout anglers, a fact not overlooked by state hatchery trucks. Regularly stocked from April through September, the lakes serve up mostly rainbow trout. Anglers looking for something a little heavier seek out Chevelon Canyon Lake for browns, primarily early and late in the season.

Anglers are limited to artificial lures and flies at Chevelon, and must trek three-quarters of a mile to reach their goal. That may not seem far, but the trail is steep and hiking out is more difficult than walking in. This a good spot for an inflatable boat or a float tube.

At 55 acres, Woods Canyon Lake is the smallest of the Rim lakes, but it is the easiest to access, at just 4 miles off the highway along a paved road. Close-by Forest Service campgrounds, a store, boat rentals, and plentiful trout make Woods Canyon an area favorite.

Several local streams are worthy of attention, including Canyon, Chevelon, and Christopher Creeks. Christopher sports a good family campground and stocked trout, and is just off the highway as you head up to the top of the rim. Chevelon is reachable by trail only, and can provide an excellent deep-canyon experience for big fish. Canyon Creek is tucked just under the top of the rim to the south and sports no-kill regulations for fly anglers chasing rainbows and browns.

Central Region

Seven deep, clear reservoirs are within an easy drive of Phoenix and the Valley of the Sun, where the majority of Arizona's largemouth bass fishing is done. Four lakes are on the Salt River, which drains the White Mountains to the east; and two are on the Verde River, which gathers up the watershed runoff from the north-central region.

On the Salt, the chain begins a bit over 100 miles away with Roosevelt, a 13,000-acre lake that was the first water reclamation project in the West when it was constructed in the early 1900s. Formed by the Salt River and Tonto Creek, which pours off the Mogollon Rim, Roosevelt provides excellent year-round fishing for smallmouth and largemouth bass and also attracts crappie hunters by the hundreds in the spring.

Moving west toward Phoenix along the Salt are Apache, Canyon, and Saguaro Lakes. All are under 2,500 acres and not only collect and hold water for the thirsty valley but produce power as well. Each serves up a variety of warmwater species, although with a few surprises. Apache, for example, also contains an excellent walleye fishery, and Canyon harbors decent trout in winter.

Below Saguaro—the last lake in the chain—what's left of the Salt River (before it joins the Verde and is channeled into canals) turns into a top fishery for stocked trout, primarily during the winter months. And it is not unusual to catch fish in 65°F water when the air temperature hits 100°F in the shade.

Bartlett and Horseshoe Lakes on the Verde are less developed than those on the Salt, but they still offer excellent angling opportunities. Bartlett is the best of the two for bass, crappie, and large catfish. The sections of the Verde between the two lakes and below Bartlett produce top bass and catfish action.

On the valley's northwest side is Lake Pleasant, part of the giant Maricopa County regional park system. When full, the 110,000-acre lake serves as a storage facility for water pumped across the desert from the Colorado River. The level fluctuates as much as 100 feet a year, but the up-and-down action gives the fishery a shot in the arm each season. The lake boasts excellent largemouth fishing, and offers white bass and crappie as well.

Although not in the Phoenix area, San Carlos Lake still qualifies as a central Arizona fishery. Located on the Gila River 100 or so miles southeast of Phoenix, San Carlos is on the San Carlos Apache Indian Reservation and, along with Roosevelt, Apache, and Pleasant, rates as one of the top bass fisheries in the state.

State licenses are not applicable at San Carlos, so anglers must purchase a tribal permit to fish this reservoir, which can swell to 17,000 acres after a couple of good rainfall years. Because of its ability to turn out big bass and its easy-to-access shoreline, San Carlos is a favorite of bass clubs during their weekend outings.

Southeast Region

Although not as water-rich as the central, eastern, and northern parts of the state, the southeast offers a milder version of the Sonoran Desert climate. The elevation climbs somewhat and the terrain changes from catclaw, cholla, and saguaro cactus to rolling grasslands.

A collection of small, man-made lakes offering both warmwater and coldwater species keep many southern Arizona anglers happy. Like the rest of the state, this part of Arizona is full of contradictions. Whereas most of the available fisheries are at an elevation of 3,000 to 4,000 feet, Rigg's Flat and Rose Canyon Lakes are nestled atop the region's two highest peaks.

Rose Canyon rests 7,000 feet atop Mount Lemon, just outside Tucson. It is very small and offers catchable trout in summer to Tucson residents looking to cool off. Rigg's Flat, on the 9,000-foot summit of Mount Graham, near Safford, is the region's highest lake and also offers trout if the hatchery trucks can bust through the snow.

Other area lakes are worth a look. Offering a combination of trout, bass, catfish, and panfish is Patagonia Lake, in a state park located between Patagonia and Nogales. Parker Canyon Lake near Sierra Vista, where travelers will find a small motel, rental boats, and other convenient features, has essentially the same species lineup as Patagonia.

The first known artificial fish structure was made in the late 1700s of weighted bamboo frames sunk in 20 fathoms of water by Japanese commercial fishermen.

Colorado River and Lakes

It's ironic that a state as arid as Arizona features a substantial river as its western boundary. And unlike most rivers in Arizona, which are generally disguised as dry streambeds, the Colorado River is wet all the way.

To say the mighty Colorado has been tamed, however, is an understatement. Not only is it tame, it has been beaten into submission via a variety of dams, both large and small. It seems everyone in the West has a claim to the lifeblood; today, the once giant tributary is a near trickle when it ultimately reaches the Mexican border below Yuma.

Fishing opportunities abound in numerous canyons of Lake Powell.

Lake Powell. Backed by Glen Canyon Dam a few miles southwest of the Utah border, the Colorado begins its life in Arizona as Lake Powell, a huge impoundment formed in the 1960s that backs up for 186 miles, most of it in Utah. It is here that Arizona's most varied sportfishing menu begins with a scenic red rock backdrop. Five marinas serve the public, and houseboats towing fishing boats abound.

Huge schools of striped bass, an introduced species that can be found throughout the system, inhabit the lake, along with largemouth and smallmouth bass, walleye, catfish, and crappie. Although Powell is deep and clear, several hundred canyons, some many miles long, give anglers ample opportunity to fish structure.

Striped bass have become the hallmark of this lake, and they are indeed bountiful. They cluster near Glen Canyon Dam to spawn in the spring, and can be found en masse there again in the fall, offering a chance to cast for surface-busting schools as they chase bait.

Powell—one of the largest man-made lakes in North America—can be intimidating, and it is subject to water level fluctuations; but it is a phenomenal place to fish, cruise, and enjoy beautiful canyon country.

The Colorado flows out of the bottom of Glen Canyon Dam at 50 degrees and transforms the next 14 miles of the river into one of the finest tailwater trout fisheries in the country. Rainbow trout weighing 8 and 9 pounds, plus a smattering of cutthroat trout, are common, with some catches weighing in the teens. Special regulations are in effect, and keeping fish is limited. Techniques include drifting lures from a boat and casting flies into the current while wading sandbars.

From here the Colorado roars into the Grand Canyon and, except for river runners and macho hikers, the next 300 miles doesn't see very much fishing action. Big trout exist. Check the regulations carefully.

Lakes Mead and Mohave. Lake Mead, formed in 1935 by the construction of Hoover Dam, is the next reservoir downstream, and it forms a partial boundary between Arizona and Nevada. Not as large as Powell, but still imposing, Mead is 110 miles long and covers some 162,000 acres.

Lake Mead has been a largemouth bass fishing staple for over a half-century. Bass from 4 to 8 pounds are taken here, in addition to smaller specimens. Las Vegas Bay produces good-size bass because of the available nutrients and forage fish.

Recently, striped bass populations have proliferated, and many people now fish the lake primarily for stripers. Stripers average 2 pounds, but fish in the 20- to 30-pound range have been caught, more commonly in the fall and usually on shad imitations. Beginning in July and continuing through much of the rest of the year, anglers can take striped bass using a variety of topwater lures, often by fishing early and scouting for surface activity.

The best areas to fish for all species in Lake Mead are in Las Vegas Bay, Calville Bay, and the upper Overton; feeder streams and washes at these sites add nutrients to the lake and enhance the production of forage fish. The Overton Arm is a top spot to fish for black crappie, some of which range up to 3 pounds.

Trout return to the menu directly below Hoover Dam. Anglers can catch stocked trout in the Willow Beach area, or below Davis Dam where there's good access for shore fishing.

The water spreads out after this to form 67-mile-long Lake Mohave, which was formed by the creation of Davis Dam in 1951. The upper 15 miles of the reservoir, where trout are stocked, regularly provide the best fishing for striped bass. Most of the stripers in Mohave are small, but a few can weigh from 40 to 60 pounds. The best time is at night or on a slightly breezy day in September through November. Cut anchovies, squid, and large shad-imitating lures work well here.

Largemouth bass up to 9 pounds are present in most Mohave coves that have weedbeds, except the cold upper 15 miles, in the spring. When water levels decline in the fall and weedbeds are exposed, fishing becomes productive again.

Channel catfish up to 15 or 20 pounds are caught throughout the summer on cut bait or stinkbait fished on the bottom. Bluegills are typically caught below the upper 15 miles of the lake.

Below Davis Dam, which backs up Mohave, anglers gamble for more than fish at casinos bordering the west side of the river at Laughlin, Nevada. The river here is essentially a channel. Again, stocked trout as well as stripers, which migrate upriver from Lake Havasu and may reach 20 to 30 pounds, are offered.

Lake Havasu. The river fans out into Topock Marsh and a gorge before it widens at Havasu, impounded by Parker Dam. Topock is a shallow backwater, averaging approximately 15 feet in depth. It harbors largemouth bass, catfish, crappie, and a variety of sunfish; however, anglers are more likely to see canoe campers than fishing boats in this area. At an elevation of 500 feet, Topock is inhospitable in summer due to the intense heat.

It was at Lake Havasu that striped bass were first introduced to the Colorado River in the 1960s, and stripers and largemouth bass have been the main attractions, although the lake also has crappie, channel catfish, bluegills, and rainbow trout. Havasu is 45 miles long and covers 25,000 acres, making it smaller than the upstream reservoirs; however, 450 miles of shoreline provide countless nooks and crannies for angling exploration.

One of the largest freshwater fisheries enhancement programs in North America was instituted here in the early 1990s, and it has resulted in nearly 900 acres of artificial habitat, placed strategically around the lake.

Due east of Lake Havasu on the Bill Williams River is Alamo Lake, another classic desert lake that features an excellent largemouth fishery. Here, Alamo State Park also contains a campground, a store, boat rentals, and other amenities.

Back on the river, California now shares the waterway with Arizona all the way to Mexico, and backwaters proliferate from Imperial Dam south to Yuma. In many places the river looks much as it did before the area was settled.

Large catfish, both in the river and in the backwaters, are popular with the locals. Largemouth bass up to 15 pounds are not uncommon in such backwater lakes as Mittry and Martinez.

Remnants of endangered species—those with such curious names as humpback chub, bonytail chub, razorback sucker, and the Colorado River squawfish—are the subject of recovery programs in the Colorado. It was the taming of this once silty, roaring river that primarily did these species the most harm.

ARKANSAS

Arkansas anglers enjoy exceptional freshwater opportunities and some of the best angling for such prominent species as largemouth bass, striped bass, and brown trout that can be found anywhere. Scattered throughout the "Natural State" are more than 9,000 miles of streams; 600,000 acres of lakes; and numerous bayous, farm ponds, creeks, and sloughs tailor-made for angling enjoyment.

Plug for largemouths on a huge reservoir, or jig for crappie on a cypress-shrouded oxbow. Sit under a shade tree for some lakeside catfishing, or relax on a fishing pier and dunk worms for bluegills. Cast for schooling stripers in the midst of a timber-laden impoundment, or troll the upper tributaries of a lake for walleye. Float and fish for trout or smallmouth bass on a cool, clear stream in the Ozark or Ouachita Mountains, or adventure down the Mississippi River while fishing for 100-pound catfish and alligator gar.

Mix all this opportunity with great scenery, and you have a state that draws anglers from near and far.

Game and Fish Commission Lakes

The Arkansas Game and Fish Commission owns and operates 35 man-made public fishing lakes covering more than 20,000 acres. It also owns more than 30 natural lakes open to public fishing in wildlife management areas and other locations throughout Arkansas.

At 6,700 acres, Lake Conway is the largest lake ever constructed by a state wildlife agency. Because of its size, central location, and excellent fishing, it has been one of the state's favored angling spots since completion in 1948.

Conway is best known for its seemingly endless supply of bluegills and redear sunfish. Creel surveys indicate these species, known as bream, are not only the most popular fish, they also account for the most poundage taken by anglers. Bass and crappie fans also flock to Conway, hoping to catch the lake's lunker largemouths or big slab crappie. Giant blue and channel catfish are abundant, and Conway is a hotbed for monster flatheads. An east-side nursery pond permits stocking millions of crappie, largemouth bass, and catfish directly into the lake.

White Oak Lake has a well-deserved reputation for producing big fish. This 2,676-acre site produces many 20-pound-class channel cats, numerous 10-pound-plus largemouths, abundant crappie up to 3 pounds, and bream to $1^1/_2$ pounds. The impoundment is actually two lakes in one; Arkansas Highway 387 separates the upper and lower lakes. White Oak's plentiful cover and structure are attractive to fish, and anglers do well probing around dead timber, cypress trees, riprap, lily pad beds, points, islands, and the White Oak creek channel running south to north across the lakebed. Combined with adjacent White Oak Lake State Park and Poison Springs Wildlife Management Area, the lake offers a full complement of outdoor recreation opportunities.

Cane Creek Lake, at 1,700 acres, is a cooperative project of the Game and Fish Commission, the Soil Conservation Service, and the Department of Parks and Tourism. The main merrymakers here are largemouth bass, channel catfish, bluegills,

crappie, and redear sunfish. The fishing for all these species is outstanding here, especially in cover along the inundated creek channel and the sloping west-south shoreline. Anglers also catch many rod-bending channel cats. Cane Creek is 3 miles east of Star City in Lincoln County.

Harris Brake Lake in eastern Perry County has cover and structure galore: shoreline brush, sunken timber, cypress trees, underwater islands, creek channel dropoffs, old docks, and more. Visiting anglers land plenty of big bluegills, redear sunfish, crappie, channel catfish, and largemouth bass. Hybrid stripers are also caught here, and when schools are chasing shad, anglers find fast action in open water. The 1,300-acre lake also harbors a host of neglected species like bowfin, bullhead, pickerel, carp, drum, and longear sunfish, which provide exciting sport when other fish have lockjaw.

Lake Overcup, north of Morrilton, is one of central Arkansas' premier angling sites. The bream and crappie are extraordinary, and lunker largemouths frequently round out the catch. This 1,025-acre lake has forged a place in the hearts of catfish anglers as well, doling out fast-paced action for channel, blue, and flathead catfish. Other popular sportfish inhabiting this fertile lake include hybrid stripers, white bass, chain pickerel, and warmouth. Boat lanes crisscross timbered waters to provide easy access to brushy, stump-laden fish habitat offshore, while those who prefer bank fishing can relax on the lake's fishing piers or earthen jetty or try for lunkers along the mile-long dam.

Located in the Ouachita Mountains 12 miles west of Waldron, Lake Hinkle offers some of the most diverse fishing opportunities of any Game and Fish Commission lake. In addition to the standard fare of largemouth bass, bluegills, channel catfish, and crappie, this 960-acre impoundment supports white bass, flathead catfish, spotted bass, redear sunfish, saugeye, and other popular sportfish. A south-side nursery pond provides regular stockings of hybrid stripers, crappie, and bass, and a caged fish-rearing operation is a source of catchable-size catfish.

The habit of spinning to tear apart their food is common to eels, whose 6 to 14 spins per second under water is greater than the 5 spins per second achieved on ice by the best skaters.

Meandering through the heart of the 16,542-acre Sulphur River Wildlife Management Area, Mercer Bayou is more like a stream than a lake. Indeed, before levees were built on the north and south ends of the lake to maintain the water level, Mercer Bayou was actually an offshoot of the Sulphur River. Although the lake covers only 800 surface acres, it winds 14 miles through the southwest Arkansas bottoms. Largemouth bass, crappie, channel catfish, bluegills, and redear sunfish are the main attractions, but the lake also provides good action for chain pickerel, warmouth, and flathead catfish.

Lake Atkins, which sits in the fertile Arkansas River Valley just south of its namesake town, is best known for crackerjack bream fishing. The water teems with huge bluegills and redear sunfish. Visiting anglers also find top-notch fishing for big crappie, largemouth bass, channel catfish, and flathead catfish. Many anglers consider this 752-acre lake the best small-lake fishery in western Arkansas.

Lake Charles, in the Ozark Mountain foothills of Lawrence County, offers a mixed bag of opportunities. Angling for jumbo largemouth bass, crappie, bluegills, channel catfish, and flathead catfish is excellent, and unlike most Game and Fish Commission lakes, 650-acre Charles also harbors good populations of hybrid stripers and white bass. Open water is prevalent, a condition conducive to good hybrid and white bass fishing, but one that makes it difficult to find concentrations of largemouths, panfish, and catfish. The Flat Creek channel winding through the heart of the lake is a good area to fish, and anglers also do well fishing points, coves, and the area around the dam.

Lake Bois d'Arc, 6 miles south of Hope in southwest Arkansas, is part of Bois d'Arc Wildlife Management Area. Excellent crappie, bluegills, and redear fishing are the main draws for this 650-acre lake, but angling for jumbo largemouth bass and channel catfish is also good. Boaters have ready access to many acres of good timber fishing, and shore anglers can pick a spot along $4\frac{1}{2}$ miles of riprap levee on the north, west, and south sides. There's also a man-made peninsula near the lower boat ramp built especially for bank fishing.

Nestled in forested hills atop Crowley's Ridge, 600-acre Lake Poinsett was the first Game and Fish Commission lake built in northeast Arkansas. Fishing is excellent here. Good catches of fat crappie are taken year after year, and fish population sampling has turned up state-record-class channel catfish. Redear sunfish, bluegills, and largemouth bass are also found in good numbers and good sizes. During much of the year, anglers concentrate their efforts around the stick-ups and submerged treetops covering the lake's numerous small coves. But the old Distress Creek channel and deeper water around the dam are also productive.

Game and Fish lakes of 500 acres or less include Ashbaugh, Barnett, Bentonville, Bob Kidd, Burnt Cane, Cargile, Cox Creek, Cox Cypress, Crystal, Des Arc, Elmdale, Frierson, Greenlee, Gurdon, Hindsville, Hogue, Horsehead, Kingfisher, Mallard, Pine Bluff, Pullen Pond, Sugarloaf, Tommy Sproles, Tri County, Wilhemina, and Wright.

Corps of Engineers Reservoirs

Sixteen large Arkansas lakes are under control of the U.S. Army Corps of Engineers. These reservoirs, which cover nearly a quarter million acres, provide the angler opportunities to pursue a wide variety of sportfish.

Four of these impoundments—Beaver (28,220 acres), Bull Shoals (45,440 acres), Table Rock (43,100 acres), and Norfork (22,000 acres)—are deep, rocky lakes in the upper White River basin

of the Ozark Mountains; Bull Shoals and Table Rock lie partly in Missouri. All offer superb fishing for largemouth and spotted bass, crappie, bluegills, redear sunfish, white bass, and catfish. Walleye reach huge sizes in Bull Shoals and Norfork, and healthy populations of smallmouth bass and stripers thrive in all the lakes except Table Rock. Excellent hybrid striper fisheries exist in Beaver and Norfork.

Greers Ferry Lake is hallowed water for walleye anglers. Few if any lakes have produced as many 20-pound-plus walleye. Large numbers of those monsters have been caught in late winter or early spring in the upper tributaries, although it takes a dedicated angler to have success. This 31,500-acre impoundment on the Little Red River is also one of the country's finest hybrid striper hotspots, having produced a number of record specimens. Other noteworthy angling opportunities exist for bream, catfish, crappie, black bass (including smallmouths), and white bass.

West-central Arkansas encompasses four Corps lakes. Lake Dardanelle (34,300 acres) and Ozark Lake (10,600 acres) are established pools in the McClellan-Kerr Arkansas River Navigation System. Both offer an abundant variety of sportfish, but Dardanelle is best known for producing extraordinary numbers of trophy-class largemouth bass, crappie, and catfish. Ozark is a winter hotspot for sauger. Blue Mountain Lake on the Petit Jean River near Waveland tends to be muddy, but this 2,910-acre reservoir is loaded with big crappie and blue, channel, and flathead catfish. Nimrod Lake, a 3,550-acre impoundment on the Fourche la Fave River, is rightfully recognized as one of Arkansas' top lakes for 2- to 3-pound crappie.

Two of the state's most popular lakes are 40,000-acre Ouachita and 13,400-acre DeGray, both in the Hot Springs area. Lake Ouachita is the largest lake entirely within Arkansas. Trophy striped bass and largemouth bass are common pursuits at Ouachita, but this is also one of the state's top producers of big bream, heavyweight catfish, jumbo white and spotted bass, slab-size crappie, and outsize walleye. DeGray lacks Ouachita's striped bass and walleye, but trophy-size hybrid stripers are common and frequently taken near the dam and midlake islands.

Arkansas' smallest Corps of Engineers lakes—Dierks, Gillham, and DeQueen (1,350 to 1,680 acres)—are grouped at the north end of Sevier County in the state's southwest corner. None offers extraordinary angling opportunities, but all are popular with local anglers seeking largemouth bass, crappie, catfish, and bream. Lake Greeson, a 2,500-acre lake just a few miles east in Pike County, offers similar fishing opportunities, plus a good fishery for 20- to 30-pound striped bass.

Millwood Lake (29,200 acres) near the Arkansas-Texas-Louisiana borders attracts numerous out-of-state anglers. Many consider this shallow, timber-filled impoundment among the South's best reservoirs for trophy largemouths, crappie, and catfish. Panfish anglers work woody cover for abundant bluegills, redear sunfish, and warmouth, and there's fair angling for hybrid stripers and white bass.

State Park Lakes

Scattered throughout the state, Arkansas' 49 state parks offer profuse scenic, recreational, and educational experiences, including excellent fishing opportunities. Several parks are on Corps of Engineers reservoirs and Game and Fish Commission lakes. Seven others provide outstanding public fishing on small lakes within park boundaries.

Lakes Dunn and Austell in Village Creek State Park near Wynne are tiny by most standards (68 and 64 acres respectively), but these two Crowley's Ridge impoundments are among Arkansas' top producers of 10- to 15-pound largemouth bass. Giant blue and channel catfish are also favored here, along with abundant crappie and bluegills. Walcott Lake (31 acres) lacks blue cats but otherwise offers equally good fishing opportunities in Crowley's Ridge State Park north of Jonesboro.

Petit Jean State Park near Morrilton has two lakes: 64-acre Bailey and 11-acre Roosevelt. Visiting anglers enjoy superb bank fishing for largemouths, crappie, bream, and channel cats. Three- to 11-acre lakes in Woolly Hollow, Logoly, and Old Davidsonville State Parks attract campers and other park visitors seeking the same quarry. An 8-acre lake in Devil's Den State Park is the only state park lake where anglers have the opportunity to catch smallmouth bass.

U.S. Forest Service Lakes

The Forest Service owns 18 public fishing lakes within Arkansas' three national forests, all of which cover less than 700 acres each. Anglers can nevertheless expect good fishing for bluegills, catfish, bream, largemouth bass, and other species.

Bear Creek and Storm Creek Lakes are the largest Forest Service lakes, at 625 and 420 acres respectively. Located in St. Francis National Forest near Marianna and Helena, they are among eastern Arkansas' most popular fishing lakes. Many anglers consider Bear Creek Arkansas' top lake for big redear sunfish (shellcrackers), with $1^1/_2$- to 2-pounders common. Storm Creek is the smallest Arkansas lake stocked with hybrid stripers, and frequently produces 10- to 15-pounders.

Six Forest Service lakes lie within the Ouachita National Forest in west-central Arkansas' Perry County. These are Cove Creek, Dry Fork, Little Bear, Rocky Branch, Site 8, and Sylvia. To the southwest, also within Ouachita National Forest, are Shady and Fenwood Lakes in Polk and Montgomery Counties. Public fishing lakes in the Ozark National Forest include Wedington (Washington County), Shores (Franklin County),

Cove (Logan County), Spring (Yell County), Lower Brock Creek (Conway County), and Driver Creek and Upper Brock Creek (Van Buren County). These waters range from 14 to 160 acres, but most cover less than 50 acres.

The Forest Service constructed these lakes for flood control, but each has been stocked with bluegills, channel cats, largemouth bass, and, in most cases, crappie and redear sunfish. Fishing opportunities are superb, but few of the lakes offer a launch ramp suitable for large boats. Lightweight jonboats or canoes that can be carried to the water are preferable.

Mirror Lake in the Blanchard Springs Recreation Area of the Ozark National Forest is the only cold-water lake in the bunch. Fed by clear, frigid waters from Blanchard Caverns, this 7-acre gem is popular for its rainbow trout, with the possibility of an occasional smallmouth bass.

City, County, and Corporate Lakes

Many Arkansas cities, counties, and major corporations own fishing lakes open to the public. Most are small, a few hundred acres at most, but a few are among the largest and most popular in the state.

The largest of these is 8,900-acre Lake Maumelle, owned and operated by Little Rock Waterworks. Just 8 miles west of Little Rock, this water-supply impoundment offers fantastic fishing for largemouths, spotted bass, stripers, white bass, the three major species of catfish, and a wide variety of panfish, including bluegills, redear sunfish, and crappie. Nearly all the timber on the lakebed was cut during the 1957 impoundment, so anglers can't rely much on visible cover like dead snags and brush when trying to pinpoint fish. Sonar is an invaluable aid for locating underwater structure that concentrates schools of fish.

Because it supplies water, Maumelle is governed by many unique regulations. For example, there's a no-fishing zone marked with buoys near the east end of the lake. Anglers should check with the Little Rock Municipal Water Works for details.

Lake Erling, near the Louisiana border in Lafayette County, is owned by International Paper Company. About 85 percent of this 7,000-acre lake's surface is covered with stumps and logs. It offers excellent bream and crappie fishing, but big largemouths steal the limelight. Hundreds of thousands of Florida-strain largemouths have been stocked in Erling, with many growing over 10 pounds. Good fishing areas include dead timber cover; the old Bodcau Creek channel; and shallow flats filled with lily pads, cypress trees, and other thick cover.

Lakes Catherine and Hamilton, two Ouachita River hydroelectric projects owned by the Arkansas Power and Light Company, helped transform the area around Hot Springs National Park into one of mid-America's favorite vacation/retirement areas. Both lakes are adjacent to the city of Hot Springs, providing local citizens superb nearby fishing.

Lake Catherine, 11 miles long and covering 1,940 acres, harbors a surprisingly diverse fishery for such a small body of water. It contains healthy populations of crappie, bluegills, redear sunfish, flathead catfish, channel catfish, blue catfish, striped bass, hybrid stripers, white bass, and even walleye and rainbow trout. Black bass, however, are the main draw for many visiting anglers.

At 7,200 acres, 18½-mile-long Lake Hamilton is much larger than its sister lake, but offers equally good angling for the same diverse sportfish. Black bass and crappie attract most anglers, but Hamilton is also well known for giant striped bass, including two state records over 53 pounds.

For relaxed fishing on less-pressured waters, anglers can investigate scores of smaller city-owned lakes scattered from border to border, including those in Bald Knob, Benton, Booneville, Camden, Charleston, Clarksville, Conway, Dierks, Eureka Springs, Fayetteville, Ft. Smith, Jonesboro, Mena, Nashville, Newark, Newport, Ola, Paris, Pottsville, Prairie Grove, Rogers, Siloam Springs, Van Buren, Waldron, and many other communities.

Oxbows and Other Natural Lakes

Hundreds of oxbows and other natural lakes are open to public fishing in Arkansas, particularly along the Mississippi, White, Arkansas, and Ouachita Rivers, and Bayou Bartholomew in eastern and southern portions of the state.

If fishing for bluegills, channel catfish, crappie, and largemouth bass tickles your fancy, check out Lake Chicot at Lake Village. This 5,300-acre Mississippi River oxbow is said to be the largest in the world. Action for these species is red-hot, and it starts earlier in the year than on most large Arkansas lakes, thanks to Chicot's extreme southern location. The best fishing is around cypress trees, willows, buckbrush, dead timber, and private docks along the shore, unless you're seeking hybrid stripers. Another of Chicot's prized sportfish, these hard fighters are most often taken in open water, where they feed on schools of shad.

Other top-notch Mississippi River oxbow lakes include Horseshoe (2,500 acres), Wapanocca (1,800 acres), Dacus (1,000 acres), and Island 40 Chute (350 acres) in Crittenden County; Midway (1,000 acres) and Whitehall (250 acres) in Lee County; Mellwood (1,000 acres) and Old Town (900 acres) in Phillips County; and Grand (900 acres) in Chicot County. All have a well-deserved reputation for large quantities of big crappie, largemouth bass, bream, and catfish.

More than 200 small (most less than 100 acres) oxbow lakes, are seasonally open to fishing in White River National Wildlife Refuge in southeast Arkansas. Dozens more are in Cache River and Holla Bend National Wildlife Refuges. Several wildlife management areas owned by the Game and Fish Commission also offer excellent oxbow fishing opportunities. These include Henry Gray/Hurricane Lake near Bald Knob, Shirey Bay–Rainey Brake in Lawrence County, and Dagmar near Brinkley.

Along Bayou Bartholomew in Drew and Ashley Counties are four even more popular oxbow fishing hotspots: Lakes Wallace, Grampus, and Enterprise (350 acres each), and Wilson Brake (150 acres). Another natural lake favored by east Arkansas anglers is Big Lake in Big Lake National Wildlife Refuge near Manila. Formed by the New Madrid Earthquake of 1812, this shallow 6,500-acre lake hosts bluegills, channel catfish, crappie, largemouth bass, redear sunfish, warmouth, and white bass.

Coolwater Streams

Scattered throughout the mountain regions of Arkansas are dozens of coolwater streams, where anglers can catch smallmouth and spotted bass as well as various other species that prefer cool water temperatures.

The best known of these is the scenic Buffalo River in the Ozarks. America's first national river, it runs for roughly 150 miles with 95,000 acres of public land along its corridor. The Buffalo is a model smallmouth bass stream with fast, clear, oxygen-rich water, a gravel bottom, and numerous boulder beds. It also harbors plentiful channel catfish, green and longear sunfish, rock bass, and spotted bass.

Another established Ozark stream is Crooked Creek, often described as "the South's best smallmouth fishery." Most recreational use occurs in the lower 50 miles, from Pyatt to the White River, where anglers catch not only smallmouth bass but also several varieties of sunfish, largemouth bass, spotted bass, and channel cats.

The Eleven-Point River is fed by numerous springs, making it an ideal destination for floaters year-round. Rising in the Ozarks of Missouri, this smallmouth haven flows 44 miles through Arkansas to its confluence with the Spring River. The number of smallmouths in these waters is phenomenal; hauling in a pair on a single crankbait isn't unheard of. Anglers also find good action for channel and flathead catfish, spotted bass, and longear sunfish.

Other popular Ozark float-fishing streams include Big Piney Creek, Cadron Creek, Illinois Bayou, Mulberry River, Spring River, Strawberry River, and White River.

The Ouachita Mountains encompass several blue-ribbon smallmouth bass streams. Among the best is the Caddo River, a 40-mile-long stretch of peaceful water that is ideal for family fishing. The most productive smallmouth angling begins near Caddo Gap and ends below Amity. Numerous sunfish are caught in this stretch as well. During spring spawning runs, walleye, white bass, and hybrid stripers ascend the Caddo from DeGray Lake, providing fast-paced fishing for savvy anglers.

The upper Ouachita River above Lake Ouachita offers another 70 miles of smallmouth and spotted bass fishing. The upper reaches are fast and narrow, suitable primarily for wading. But from Oden to the lake, canoeists find lazy pools and sparkling shoals where one can slow the pace and fish the river's rocky bottom thoroughly. In addition to plentiful smallmouths and spotted bass, catches include rock bass, catfish, bluegills, largemouths, and occasional walleye. In the lower reaches just above Lake Ouachita, the spawning runs of white bass attract crowds of springtime anglers.

The meeting of warm air and cold water causes fog to greet early-morning anglers on the White River.

Many other Ouachita Mountain streams serve up excellent float fishing. These include the Little Missouri River, Mountain Fork River, and the three forks of the upper Saline River.

Trout Waters

To the trout angler, there's just one word that adequately describes Arkansas: Paradise. Since 1945, the Arkansas Game and Fish Commission, through an aggressive stocking program and innovative, intensive management, has developed some of the world's finest trout fisheries. The state features 153 miles of tailwater trout streams.

The upper White River is the state's most famous trout fishery. Some consider it America's best trout river with respect to both size and number of. The most popular section is the Bull Shoals tailwater, a 92-mile stretch from Bull Shoals Dam to Guion. Big brown trout are the main attraction, with 3- to 5-pounders common and 30-pound-plus fish always a possibility. Rainbows are the river's bread-and-butter trout, and at times nearly every cast will produce a 9- to 16-inch fish. Cutthroats and brook trout are also present, thanks to stepped-up stocking efforts.

The Beaver Dam tailwater—another stretch of the White River—also has a reputation for high-quality trout fishing. This 8-mile-long section is stocked throughout the year with rainbow, brown, cutthroat, and brook trout. Rainbows are the predominant species, while browns offer trophy opportunities. The best fishing is in the upper 4 to 5 miles.

The Norfork tailwater, which constitutes 5 miles of the North Fork River, from Norfork Dam to the White River, has produced thousands of 10-pound-plus brown trout, including a 34-pounder and a 38-pound, 9-ounce former world record. Several state-record brook trout came from the North Fork as well, and a significant part of the catch is comprised of rainbows and cutthroats. Anglers fishing here have an excellent chance to catch a grand slam—at least one trout of each species 16 inches or longer.

The Little Red River serves up 29 miles of extraordinary trout fishing below Greers Ferry Dam at Heber Springs. Like the White River, this trout stream is touted as one of the finest in the world. That's partially because it produces big trout, like the mammoth 40-pound, 4-ounce all-tackle world-record brown landed by a local angler in May 1992 (on 4-pound line no less). Rainbow trout are usually just 9 to 12 inches long, but they're abundant enough to satisfy the fishing itch in most anglers. Brook and cutthroat trout are also stocked and commonly reach 13 to 16 inches.

Spring River near Mammoth Spring is unique among Arkansas trout streams. Its cold water comes naturally from a spring rather than artificially from deep within a man-made lake. The river stays cold enough to support a good trout population for 10 miles downstream. One to 3-pound rainbows are fairly common. Brown trout provide a trophy facet to the river's fishing profile. Cutthroat and brook trout are most numerous above Cold Springs.

Although they are limited in size and big-fish potential, short stretches of both the Ouachita and the Little Missouri Rivers provide excellent seasonal fishing for rainbow trout. On the Ouachita, coldwater releases from Blakely Mountain Dam (Lake Ouachita) and Carpenter Dam (Lake Hamilton) allow cool-season fishing for put-and-take rainbows for short stretches below each dam. On the Little Missouri, trout are stocked below Narrows Dam on Lake Greeson, and upstream from Lake Greeson in the Ouachita National Forest near Albert Pike Recreation Area. Stocking begins in late fall and continues through April. Persistent anglers will catch a few trout in summer, particularly below Carpenter Dam.

Warmwater Streams and Rivers

While fast-flowing, cold mountain streams are more popular with visitors, warmwater streams and rivers snaking their way across the delta and coastal plain regions of eastern and southern Arkansas should not be overlooked by serious anglers. These sluggish, flatland waters team with bass, crappie, catfish, bluegills, and a wide variety of other warmwater sportfish. In some areas, bank fishing is popular, while in others a boat is necessary for access to better fishing spots.

The Mississippi River, which runs almost the entire length of Arkansas' eastern boundary, is known nationwide as a phenomenal fishery for warmwater species. One of the state's most popular trophy catfishing areas, Ol' Muddy has produced some of the largest blue cats on record, including a $116^1/_2$-pounder caught in 1997 near Dermott. Backwater areas and adjacent oxbows give up enormous crappie, bluegills, and bass. Giant alligator gar still turn up occasionally, and it is not uncommon to catch freshwater drum topping 20 pounds, common carp over 30 pounds, and a huge assortment of other rough fish. The Mississippi is also a mother lode of hefty striped and white bass.

The Arkansas River spans the breadth of the Natural State, from Ft. Smith in the west to its juncture with the Mississippi River in the east, some 310 miles in all. In 1971, the U.S. Army Corps of Engineers completed the McClellan-Kerr Arkansas River Navigation Project, which included construction of 12 dams in Arkansas, turning the once untamed river into a series of comparatively tranquil reservoirs. The project not only improved navigation on the river, but the fishing as well.

Largemouth bass brought fame to the Arkansas River among hard-core bass aficionados, partly due to a series of national bass tournaments that produced record weigh-ins. Spotted bass, white bass, and stripers draw the attention of many visiting anglers, too, but these species are just a small part of the overall angling picture. Giant catfish are commonly taken in dam tailwaters, including blues up to 100 pounds, flatheads up to 140 pounds, and channel cats up to 25 pounds. Sauger attract winter fishing fanatics during their January and February spawning runs, and there are plenty of jumbo bream and crappie in river backwaters.

Arkansas has more than a dozen other large bottom-land rivers that offer superb fishing for a wide variety of popular gamefish. Among these are the Black, Cache, Fourche la Fave, St. Francis, lower White, lower Ouachita, lower Saline, L'Anguille, Little, lower Little Missouri, Petit Jean, and Red Rivers, as well as Champagnolle Creek, Bayou Meto, Bayou de View, and Bayou Bartholomew.

ARTIFICIAL FLY

An imitation of a natural aquatic or terrestrial insect, especially one consumed by fish. Because natural flies are rarely used by anglers, imitations are employed and usually referred to simply as flies rather than artificial flies (and fishing with these is simply called fly fishing); in the broadest sense, this is a form of lure.

See: Fly; Fly Fishing; Lure.

ARTIFICIAL LURE

An antiquated term for any nonnatural object with a hook that is used to catch fish.

See: Lure.

ARTIFICIAL REEF

A man-made artificial structure that provides habitat for many kinds of fish. Used in freshwater and saltwater, predominantly the latter, artificial reefs are constructed or placed in structure-less bottom areas to create new and diverse aquatic communities. They provide food, shelter, protection, and spawning areas for fish, and concentrate fish on or close to the structures.

Artificial reefs are made from rock, concrete, ships that are deliberately sunk, auto bodies, railroad flatbed cars, rubber tires, and wood, among many items. Decommissioned oil rigs, cut off well below the water level, have become artificial reefs, and the United States military has a program to recycle old military equipment like tanks, staff vehicles, and heavy equipment, even training their explosives experts to sink these objects.

Newly created artificial reefs are placed at various depths, sometimes to attract specific fish. Many are built as a community effort, with the technical assistance of government agencies, and placed on smooth bottom areas where they won't interfere with navigation and commercial fishing activities and are in relative proximity to launch ramps and marinas. Artificial reefs exist around the world, and are perhaps most used in Japanese waters, where reef development has been a priority of the government for commercial fishing enhancement.

See: Reef

ASP *Aspius aspius.*

Other names—French: *aspe;* German: *rapfen.*

This strong-fighting European fish is unknown to many anglers and, like its carp and barbel relatives, is a member of the Cyprinidae family.

Identification. Much like barbel *(see)* in general shape, asp are streamlined and thick-bodied for river and feeding adaptation. They are different from that species, however, in possessing a straight snout without barbels, a lengthier and tapered anal fin, and lighter coloration. They are dark on the back, silvery on the sides, and often have a reddish tint in the fins.

Size. The all-tackle world record for asp is a Swedish fish that weighed 12 pounds, 7 ounces and was caught in 1993 in Lake Vanern. This species has been reported at twice that weight, however.

Distribution. Asp are native to northern Europe and have been introduced to the Netherlands. They range from the eastern Netherlands throughout northern and central Europe to the Caspian Sea.

Habitat. These fish are primarily residents of the lower reaches of rivers, but they also dwell in lakes and their tributaries. They are particularly fond of pools and may locate around such cover as weirs and bridge pilings. They often occupy midwater sections of pools; in areas where they overlap with barbel, they may frequent similar waters.

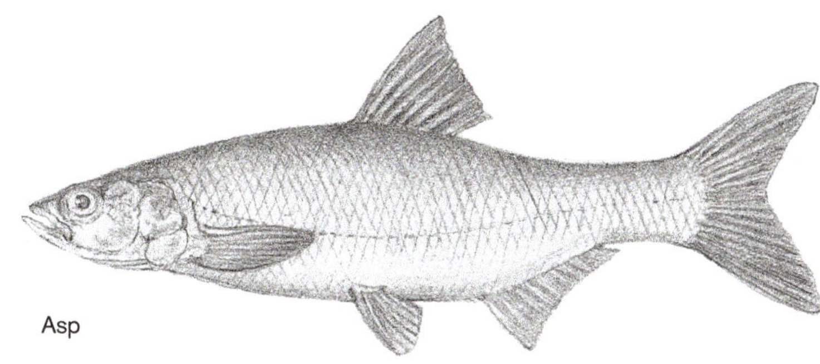

Asp

Food. Asp differ from most cyprinids in their food preference, which, rather than being benthic organisms, is small prey fish.

Angling. Asp are caught on live and dead fish, as well as on some lures, including spoons. Anglers catch them by casting, stillfishing, or trolling. This is a strong-fighting fish.

ASTERN

The direction toward the stern of a boat or beyond the stern of a boat; also the backward movement of a boat.

ATTRACTOR

(1) A type of trolling accessory that uses vibration or visual stimuli to get the attention of fish, especially in midwater to deep water, and draws them to a trailing lure. In freshwater, attractors are usually situated on a fishing line ahead of the lure, and do not themselves have a hook. In saltwater, attractors may be used on the surface in big-game fishing *(see: big-game tackle)* to create noise and motion; they are also called teasers. Here they are used without a hook, as a lure with a hook, or in front of a lure.

See: Cowbells; Dodger/Flasher; Trolling Lures, Saltwater.

(2) Cover, objects, or structures placed in the water that serve to attract prey and predatory fish, and which provide angling opportunities. Brushpiles, artificial reefs, and sunken vessels may all be some form of attractor.

See: FAD; Fish Attractor.

AUGER

A type of drill for boring holes in ice. Augers may be manual or automatic, the latter powered by gasoline. The diameter of the blade determines the size of the hole, usually from 7 to 9 inches in width. (Larger holes are necessary in situations

A

where larger-bodied fish might be caught.) The cutting edge of the blade should be sharp, uniform, and rust-free,

See: Ice Fishing.

AUSTRALIA

Lying between the Pacific and Indian Oceans in the Southern Hemisphere, Australia is the largest island and the smallest continent in the world, yet it is one big country. It has a land area of 7,682,300 square kilometers, and a coastline of 36,735 kilometers. Thirty-nine percent of the total area lies within the Tropical Zone. Made up of six states and two territories, Australia has a population of more than 18 million people, heavily concentrated in its larger cities. From the accessible city of Sydney to the remote city of Perth, and from the state of Tasmania to the "Top End," Australia is virtually equal in size to the continental United States.

Accordingly, Australia offers some of the most diverse fishing imaginable, and angling opportunities galore. No less a figure than the pioneering angler and world-famous author Zane Grey, in his book *An American Angler in Australia,* said that Australia has "fish and fishing which will dwarf all the rest known in the world." Grey based this on his experiences with black marlin and great white sharks, and, though written in 1937, it is quite true even today.

Many of Australia's waters are hard to access, however, and are still lightly explored. While the international saltwater community knows full well about Australia's remarkable billfishing, it actually recognizes only the east coast, especially the Cairns–Lizard Island region. New discoveries of big game are still being made in Australia, but many remain unpublicized. Others that are somewhat known are not even marginally exploited.

Some Presidents who were known to enjoy fishing: Herbert Hoover, Grover Cleveland, Jimmy Carter, Chester Arthur, Franklin Roosevelt, George Bush, and Dwight Eisenhower.

Western Australia, which falls into the latter category, has a good but vastly untapped billfishery. Only since the middle of the 1980s have a few anglers sampled blue, black, and striped marlin action off Exmount, some 800 miles north of Perth, and off Dampier, still farther north.

Nationally, some 19 species of freshwater fish are targeted regularly by anglers, the most popular being brown and rainbow trout and barramundi. Trout are not indigenous, having been introduced from England and the United States. They are ample in all states except the Northern Territory and Queensland. Barramundi are a native species, largely confined within the Tropical Zone of Western Australia, the Northern Territory, and Queensland.

Common marine species targeted by anglers number over 30 genera; the most popular gamefish are tuna, marlin, sailfish, sharks, trevally, yellowtail kingfish, cobia, dolphin, and mackerel. Superb saltwater fishing can be experienced from such bases as Cairns and Brisbane (Queensland), Port Stephens and Bermagui (New South Wales), Port Lincoln and Streaky Bay (South Australia), Albany and Broome (Western Australia), and Darwin (Northern Territory). Fishing safaris are popular and are available nationwide. The best opportunities in most areas come in the summer months. Anglers visiting from the Northern Hemisphere need to remember that the seasons are reversed down under. Although the warmer weather commences in September, summer starts in earnest in November and lasts through March.

The discipline of catch-and-release has become widely adopted throughout Australia, with most large angling organizations involved in concerted tag-and-release efforts for scientific research

Queensland

Cairns billfishing. Sensational gamefishing can be experienced in North Queensland waters, and the most famous area fishing resort is the city of Cairns, the renowned departure point for the best black marlin fishing in the world. Most big-game anglers think of Cairns as the modern-day mecca for black marlin, the Holy Grail for granders, and home of the Great Barrier Reef, which has often been described as the eighth wonder of the world. There is no finer place anywhere to catch black marlin—and unequivocally no greater place to have a chance at catching a 1,000-pounder—than the northwest coast of Australia, along the Great Barrier Reef from Cairns to Lizard Island. In fact, they record granders here by the score—and then some—each season. Among the more sensational occurrences in the past has been the capture of two granders in one boat by different anglers in a single day, and two granders by the same angler in one day.

This region has produced numerous line-class world-record black marlin, including two fish weighing more than 1,300 pounds each—the largest of the two being the 80-pound line-class record holder, a 1,347-pounder taken in 1979.

Black marlin records have been set and surpassed in nearly all categories off the Great Barrier Reef for more than 20 years. Still bigger fish—including the largest specimen recorded by the Gamefishing Association of Australia, a 654-kilogram (1,438 pounds) specimen taken off Cairns—have been reported, and the talk is often about whether a 2,000-pound black might swim in these waters. As with most marlin grounds, there are those who claim to have hooked and lost fish of similar gargantuan proportions off northwest Queensland.

The Great Barrier Reef, of course, is largely responsible for the presence of these billfish as well as so many other species. The seaward side of the reef takes the brunt of ocean swells and currents, and not much farther offshore the bottom slopes quickly into very deep water. Currents and upwelling here serve to push up bait, and marlin have been seen and caught in shallow water not far from the reef.

Cairns has been the jumping-off point for most of this fabulous marlin fishing, with anglers venturing both to the north and south. Because much of the fishing occurs so far from Cairns, however, mother ship operations have evolved to increase fishing time; formerly, runs of 60 miles or more were made in a day. Some anglers pursue the fish for several days at a stretch, overnighting on the same large boat they use for fishing, or staying at a mother ship and using a sportfishing boat for daily trolling.

Exploration north of Cairns has been gradual, resulting in catches around Linden Bank, the Ribbon Reefs, Agincourt Bank, and other shoals, reefs, and passages up to Lizard Island. Lizard is about 150 miles north of Cairns and some 17 miles off the Queensland shore.

Black marlin are fished in various ways, including lure trolling, dead-bait trolling, and live-bait fishing. Live bait is likely to be used on calm-sea days. Dead-bait trolling, using kawakawa, scad, skipjack, rainbow runner, and other baits, is very popular. Some baits weigh 7 or more kilograms, which is more than the weight of an ordinary catch on light tackle when fishing inshore in almost any locale.

The black marlin are here all year long, but the best action, and the biggest fish, occur from September through November and sometimes into December, which is the spring and early summer in the Southern Hemisphere. Smaller fish are reliably caught from August through January; the early and late months are best suited to lighter equipment, although 80- and 130-pound tackle is the equipment of choice at any time. Females (the males are smaller) are targeted in the blue waters close to the Great Barrier Reef. Approximately 90 percent of the marlin caught today are tagged and released.

Striped marlin are among the offshore catch, although they do not show up as frequently as blacks. Sailfish are part of the action, too, although not in the volume experienced farther south, off Cape Bowling Green. Blue marlin primarily remain farther south along the eastern coast, too, but a few monster fish that were tagged and released in Queensland waters and were originally believed to be black marlin were later suspected to have been very large blues. The first blue marlin caught in these waters was a 315-pounder taken off No. 10 Ribbon Reef in late 1988.

The catch-and-release ethic in all of Australia is exemplary. Local anglers were tagging and releasing black marlin long before it was fashionable to do so for pelagic species, and granders as well as near-granders and smaller fish have been tagged and released for many years.

Some anglers have had the good fortune to recapture fish previously tagged on their boats. One fish tagged off Queensland was recaptured almost 4,500 miles away. Obviously, science—not to mention the fish population—has benefited from this practice. In Australia, and in New Zealand, keeping a marlin is frowned on by local club members, unless it is a potential record.

Incidentally, offshore trollers from Cairns to Lizard Island do catch some other species as well, although outside this area one seldom hears much about this. Trollers take smaller marlin and sailfish, plus dolphin, bonito, wahoo, yellowfin tuna, dogtooth tuna, cobia, sharks, and mackerel.

Facilities for general tourism, accommodations, and charter boat fishing are excellent out of Cairns. The charter boats are superbly equipped and skippered by highly qualified, experienced anglers. Sportfishing tackle within all International Gamefish Association (IGFA) line classes is available for hire.

Great Barrier Reef fishing. The Great Barrier Reef is just 27 kilometers (14 nautical miles) from Cairns. Extending almost 2,300 kilometers (1,240 nautical miles) along the northeast coast of Australia, it is the longest coral reef system in the world, and the richest in biological diversity. Indeed, it is a coral jungle amidst a cobalt blue sea of striking beauty and remarkable clarity.

Important as the reef may be to big-game anglers, the black marlin is just one of more than 1,400 species of fish found in and around the Great Barrier Reef, many of which are coral denizens with amazing physical characteristics and intriguing behavior patterns. Continually growing and regenerating itself, the reef parallels the Coral Sea's continental shelf for much of its length. Not far from the reef, the ocean bottom drops away from 100 to 1,000 fathoms. Shoals rise and drop here, providing feeding sites for many species.

Anglers use handlines, and rod-and-reel outfits from light sport (to 10 kilograms) to heavy game (to 60 kilograms), and they have an extraordinary variety of fish species—more than 50—to choose from, including marlin, sailfish, giant trevally, barracouta, tuna, wahoo, sharks, queenfish, coral trout, red emperor, cobia, and Spanish mackerel.

Reef fishing methods, as opposed to those for gamefishing, are very ecumenical; no single angling methodology rules. Although 30- to 40-kilogram handlines are still used, however, the major assault is backed by short rods (to 2 meters), fine-tuned revolving-spool reels, lines to 15 kilograms, and leaders to 25 kilograms. Hook sizes vary from 6/0 to 10/0.

Charter boats will take visiting anglers out to productive areas of the reef, but small to medium-size boats, which allow freedom of movement, are preferred by the majority of sportfishing enthusiasts. Australian reef anglers have a great liking for aluminum boats (or "tinnies," as they are called) from 5 to 6 meters long, and they refer casually to offshore fishing trips of 20 to 30 kilometers out to the reef. Sonar is popular for locating fish and identifying the underwater topography.

Tactics atop the reef vary from bottom fishing (known here as bottom bouncing) to lure casting to

trolling. Fly fishing is increasing in popularity. Reef anglers have one aversion: sharks, which number in the thousands; they're cursed because of their propensity for attacking hooked fish and leaving only the head. The frustrated angler can only wonder about the size of the whole fish.

Bottom bouncers either catch their own bait, or use frozen pilchards sold by tackle shops. Heavy lead sinkers are essential to counter the current. Two species prized as superb table fish are the red emperor and the coral trout. Lure anglers, using baitcasting or spinning outfits and minnow-imitating lures, work both inside the reef and outside along its edge. Trollers fish the waters around the hundreds of islands and cays, or travel the outer edge of the reef, where they stand a chance of catching mackerel, tuna, black marlin, and other large species.

The best time of the year to fish these waters is from October through December.

Cape Bowling Green. Cape Bowling Green is in northeastern Australia's Queensland district, and south of Cairns. Accessed from Townsville, it lies along the Great Barrier Reef. Because the reef and continental shelf extend so much farther offshore here than at Cairns, offshore fishing opportunities are seldom sought after, although big marlin no doubt cruise the outer waters. Anglers are typically discouraged by the distance to be covered, often in heavy seas.

The richness of the bay, a mixture of currents, and abundant inshore reefs and shoals attract baitfish and small billfish to Cape Bowling Green. The reefs and shoals along this great coral bed lie in shallow blue-green water (20 to 40 fathoms). Watching for schools of bait and bird activity is a common element of this fishery. Anglers interested in variety, as well as lighter-tackle fishing for billfish (heavy tackle is the norm at Cairns because of the many opportunities for big fish), find the Cape Bowling Green area near Townsville among the finest angling sites in the world.

Sailfishing here has been phenomenal at times, with reported sightings of big schools of these billfish. Fortunately for local anglers and charter boat skippers, really good action can be had here from March through September; thus, they can pass the winter months (June, July, and August) pursuing light action but spend the end of the year farther north, geared up for granders.

Although marlin of several hundred pounds have been caught in this area, as mentioned earlier the fish run much smaller on average (27 kilograms or so—lighter early in the season and heavier later), and the tackle is scaled down to 10 kilograms and less, with 4- and 6-kilogram tackle most popular. Fly-rod tippet records for black marlin have been established off Cape Bowling Green, incidentally, as well as ultralight line-class records. It stands to reason that ample opportunity makes these record catches possible. With the exception of potentially record fish, virtually all billfish caught here are tagged and released.

Some 125 kilometers east-northeast of Townsville is Myrmidon Reef, a small reef on the edge of an enormous dropoff. It is seldom fished at what is believed to be peak time, in November and December, because of all the big-fish action at Cairns and the problem of accessibility previously mentioned. Blacks over 1,000 pounds have been lost here during the few forays that have been made, and a 989-pounder reportedly was once weighed-in.

Brisbane/Cape Moreton. In southeastern Queensland the coastal waters are home to more than 30 species of sportfish, including black, blue, and striped marlin; the occasional sailfish; sharks; mackerel; amberjack; yellowtail kingfish; and tuna. Some species appear seasonally, with the warmer summer months (September through March) bringing fish from more tropical waters. Charter boats are available, and should be used wherever possible; entry to offshore waters involves crossing bars, a hazardous procedure best undertaken by experienced boat skippers with local knowledge.

Back in the days of the Tangalooma (Moreton Bay) Whaling Station, Brisbane was the shark fishing capital of the universe. Even today, the eastern coast of Australia—including the waters off Brisbane as well as to the south in New South Wales—ranks among the best. Great whites, blues, makos, hammerheads, and tiger sharks of proportions that would make even Crocodile Dundee blanch have been captured in these waters. The record books are replete with line-class and all-tackle entries from this vast region.

Cape Moreton in particular has achieved fame with its great white sharks, but these days the international angling community's interest leans more toward the billfish, and the waters off Brisbane and Cape Moreton hold all the species. And although the Australian billfishery is generally synonymous with black marlin, Cape Moreton offers perhaps the best chance on this continent of catching blues, and big ones at that, including fish over 800 pounds and possibly to a thousand.

Most of the blue marlin action is for smaller fish, and at times the catch can be extremely good. Reports of double and triple strikes, and even a remarkable tagged-and-released triple-header, have been made, with many fish in the 300- to 400-pound class.

Blues notwithstanding, black marlin, stripers, and sailfish also frequent these waters, sometimes within relatively short range of shore when the east Australian current moves inward. The striped marlin and blacks are small but make good targets for light-tackle fishing efforts. These marlin average 65 to 90 pounds.

The season commences in summer, from October or November through March, with the striped marlin and blacks early and the blues

available from January through June. Seasons can vary, as this fishery is still developing. Sailfish, meanwhile, are extremely popular from February on, and other available species include various tuna and dolphin.

The good fishing around Brisbane/Cape Moreton is not far from the Gold Coast, a popular tourist locale. Although it is not as out-of-the-way as some destinations, as much as a two-hour run separates anglers from the big marlin grounds.

Inshore there is much to be had as well, with cobia, trevally, kawakawa, and the like. Between here and the neighboring waters in New South Wales, almost all of the IGFA kawakawa records have been set.

Fraser Island, north of the capital city of Brisbane, is the largest sand island in the world. It is noted for its beach fishing, especially for bluefish (known as "tailor" in Australia) from July through October. Estuarine waters hold species similar to those in northern Queensland, the barramundi being an exception.

Many inland impoundments and streams in this part of Queensland are stocked with golden perch, Murray cod, Australian bass, silver perch, and saratoga. Both spinning and baitcasting methods are favored for these species. Trout are nonexistent due to high water temperatures.

Other Queensland locations. Estuary fishing is popular along Queensland, and hard-fighting species like the mangrove jack, barramundi, threadfin salmon, sharks, trevally (various species), mulloway, queenfish, and long-toms, can provide exciting angling. The mangrove estuaries in the Townsville area are famous for mangrove jack and barramundi. Spinning and plugcasting with lures, fishing with bait, and trolling are practiced, and fly fishing is also an established sport.

Freshwater angling in tropical streams on either side of the Cape York Peninsula is excellent. Access is generally difficult, however, and four-wheel-drive vehicles and trailer boats are a necessity. Excellent guided fishing tours catering to both lure and fly anglers are popular. Species such as jungle perch, sooty grunter, tarpon, barramundi, mangrove jack, freshwater long-tom, fork-tailed catfish, and saratoga are favorites. A world-record 28.65-kilogram barramundi was taken from the Norman River near Karumba on the west coast of Cape York Peninsula. Some impoundments have been stocked with barramundi, and Lake Tinaroo on the Atherton Tableland is well known for its barramundi and sooty grunter fishery.

Precautions. There are dangers to be aware of when fishing Queensland waters. At the start of a fishing trip, especially to the Great Barrier Reef, visitors should take time to check which species are likely to be poisonous. (This applies to all states, in fact.) For example, the chinaman fish (and a number of other reef fish) of Queensland waters is inedible because its flesh contains a poison that can sometimes cause an incapacitating (and sometimes fatal) condition known as ciguatera *(see)*. The effects of this poison can recur years after ingestion.

Perhaps the most infamous venomous creatures in North Queensland waters are the sea wasp (box jellyfish) and the stonefish, each of which can cause excruciating pain and death. The estuarine crocodile is an ever-present threat to careless humans. The largest reptile in the world, it frequents tropical estuaries, billabongs (backwater areas of rivers), and swamps across the top of Australia.

Sensible precautions such as heeding warning signs (crocodiles), donning long trousers (box jellyfish), and wearing strong footwear (stone fish), are mandatory when wading any waters, or when walking the reef. Anyone interested in the study of mollusks must be extremely careful when handling cone shells, which can inflict a fatal bite. Sea snakes are common, but it is rare for an angler to be bitten. First aid is the same as that for ordinary snakebite. Sand flies and mosquitoes are prevalent.

Regulations. It is important for visiting anglers to check the angling and boating regulations for both saltwater and freshwater fishing, lest they exceed bag limits for various species, take protected species, or trespass in restricted areas. Details are covered in publications available from most tackle shops. Some areas of the Great Barrier Reef have fishing restrictions; maps of the affected zones can be obtained from the many offices of the Great Barrier Reef Marine Park Authority. Generally, best fishing times are from November through March.

The Great Lakes contain about 6 quadrillion gallons of water, enough to cover the lower 48 United States 10 feet deep.

New South Wales

The waters off New South Wales can be fished for more than 30 species of fish, including blue, black, and striped marlin, swordfish, tuna, yellowtail kingfish, albacore, greater amberjack, cobia, dolphin, mackerel, bluefish, sharks, trevally, and snapper.

The gamefishing bases of Sydney, Port Stephens, and Bermagui are world famous for their excellent facilities, while sport anglers of every persuasion can find something to interest them in bay, estuary, beach, rock, and inland fishing. Along the north coast are many outlets to coastal fishing, but only experienced boaters should attempt to cross the bars.

Rock and beach fishing opportunities are excellent; land-based sportfishing was pioneered in this state. Records include a 34.4-kilogram yellowtail kingfish, a 110-kilogram black marlin, a 26.2-kilogram cobia, and a 77-kilogram yellowfin tuna—all taken from the ocean rocks. Tackle consists of two-handed rods, 3 to 4 meters long, fitted with sidecast, surf-spinning, or surf-casting reels, and lines appropriate to the species sought. Surf-caught species include mulloway, bluefish, Australian salmon (kahawai), and sharks. Captures of marlin, yellowtail kingfish, and big tuna from the rocks are common, although conditions can be hazardous when seas are high.

A

Visitors should be accompanied by an experienced rock angler. Angel rings (life buoys), thrown to anglers washed into the sea, have been placed at angling black spots along the coast, and have saved a number of lives.

Estuary, bay, and coastal lake fishing from small boats, jetties, and shore, using light spinning and plugcasting tackle, is excellent for smaller species such as bream, flathead, whiting, bluefish, and mulloway. Access points are plentiful, as are boat ramps, and boats can be hired in most places. Sydney Harbour and Botany Bay are two of the better-known estuarine waters.

An offshore location worth noting is that of Lord Howe Island, which is southeast of Brisbane and some 435 miles northeast of Sydney. The waters in the vicinity of Lord Howe feature rocky pinnacles, immense depths, and sheer dropoffs. There has been almost no fishing pressure here until the late 1980s, but impressive catches of blue marlin, sailfish, wahoo, yellowfin tuna, and yellowtail have been registered, and some monstrous blues have been sighted. Many more species are available.

The freshwater fishery in New South Wales is superb, with brown and rainbow trout being the most targeted species. Large Lake Eucumbene and its smaller neighbor, Lake Jindabyne, in the Snowy Mountains region of the Eastern Highlands, are the prominent trout waters on the mainland; specimens in excess of 4 kilograms are not uncommon. Bait, lure, and fly fishing from shore or boat are accepted techniques, and captures of trophy fish are not uncommon, whichever method is adopted. Lake fishing is permitted year-round, but the warmer months from September to March, when the insect life is more active, are the most popular.

According to The Guinness Book of Records, the longest survival at sea was achieved by two Kiribati men, who spent 177 days adrift in their 13-foot open fishing dinghy in 1991–92.

There are many excellent trout streams in New South Wales, the majority of which are suitable for spinning and fly fishing. Other fine trout fisheries are found in the New England and Hunter regions, and the Central Highlands, with both rainbow and brown trout averaging 1 to 2 kilograms.

The Australian bass, which can grow in excess of 5 kilograms, is the second most popular freshwater species in New South Wales. It can be found in most streams that flow into the Pacific Ocean from southern Queensland to Victoria, and large numbers have been stocked in several big impoundments throughout the state. Bass plugs are the best lures to use in impoundments, while fly fishing with Muddlers, hair bugs, and streamers, is a favorite stream tactic. Redfin to 2 kilograms are prevalent in many of the inland dams and lakes, and they will respond to spinners and bass plugs. West of the Great Divide, in streams and lakes, there is an important recreational fishery that includes golden perch, Murray cod, silver perch, redfin, and catfish. European carp exist here, too, but are considered a pest and efforts are made to eradicate them.

The summer months, which last from November to March, are the best for most angling activities. During this time the main danger is snakes, the deadliest ones being the tiger snake and the brown snake. Encounters stream-side are not uncommon. Access to many streams can be difficult, but a considerate approach to landholders will rarely meet with a refusal.

Saltwater and freshwater angling and boating regulations exist, and visitors can approach fishing tackle shops for applicable printed material.

Victoria

While lacking the publicity given to the northern states, Victoria offers some excellent sportfishing in ocean waters off its eastern coast, from the New South Wales border to Port Phillip Bay. Southern bluefin tuna, yellowtail kingfish, marlin, striped tuna (skipjack), albacore, and sharks can be taken. Surf fishing from superb beaches, such as Ninety Mile Beach, will produce sharks, Australian salmon, mulloway, and bluefish. Tackle consists of surf rods to 4 meters in length, fitted with sidecast, surf, or spinning reels spooled with nylon line to 10-kilogram-strength nylon line. Baitfishing is the most popular angling method here.

Estuary fishing in the southeastern region is extensive, with a chain of lakes and bays holding smaller species such as bream, flathead, mulloway, garfish, and whiting. Light spinning and plugcasting tackle is appropriate. Hire boats (unguided rentals) are available in most areas, but extreme caution should be exercised if approaching dangerous entrances to the open ocean.

Port Phillip Bay is heavily fished for snapper, flathead, and whiting, and the entrance is famous for its large yellowtail kingfish. To the west of Port Phillip Bay, the coastline is less accessible, but surf and rock fishing can still be pursued, and there is some offshore fishing for tuna and sharks.

Victoria has a wealth of inland streams and large waterways that contain a surprising variety of fish species, the most notable being trout—both brown (to 4.6 kilograms) and rainbow (to 5.27 kilograms). Renowned fishing waters are found in the central region, where major lakes—such as Lake Eildon—and rivers provide excellent angling for trout, Murray cod, redfin, and golden perch. Some lakes have been stocked with chinook salmon, the largest of which registered 6.6 kilograms. The eastern and western regions also fish well for trout, golden perch, and redfin. Australian bass can be found in some of the eastern streams that flow into the Tasman Sea.

Angling methods include spinning, plugcasting, trolling, and fly fishing, and general angling services are available in all areas. Fly anglers can rely on nymphs and dry flies, and spinners and plugs can usually be cast or trolled successfully. Access to most waters is by car, although it may be necessary to ask landholders for permission to enter their properties.

There are some protected species and waterways; details on this are covered in regulations and boating rules available from tackle shops, and the offices of the Department of Conservation and Natural Resources throughout the state. The best fishing months are November through March.

Tasmania

This largely mountainous island state, situated at the most southerly part of the Australian continental shelf and bordered by the Indian, Southern, and Pacific Oceans, has an international reputation for providing some of the finest trout fishing in the world, and a less-widely known, big-game fishery along its east coast. The warm East Australian Current flows its length, and this brings within reach such larger saltwater species as southern bluefin tuna (the world record of 106.5 kilograms was caught here), skipjack, albacore, yellowtail kingfish, sharks, and striped marlin.

Coastal fishing includes offshore, estuary, rock, and beach fishing, and the preferred waters are those along the north and east coasts. Two Bass Strait islands, King to the west and Flinders to the east, offer excellent bay, beach, and rock fishing for Australian salmon, flathead, yellowtail kingfish, sharks, trevally, tuna, and snapper. Charter boats for offshore fishing are available.

Most of these species can be found along the north coast of Tasmania where boat, rock, and beach fishing are popular. Angling in offshore waters fronting Bass Strait should be attempted only in charter boats with experienced skippers, as the conditions are often windy and stormy. Estuarine waters are safe, and rental boats can be hired to fish for many species, including snapper, bluefish, trevally, flathead, whiting, and Australian salmon. These species, plus barracouta, are also taken by rock and beach anglers using rods to 4 meters in length and sidecast, spinning, or surf reels spooled with lines to 10-kilogram breaking strength.

The inland fishery is chiefly for trout, although redfin inhabit some waterways. Brown trout were introduced in 1864 from England, with a later introduction of rainbow and brook trout from the United States. The famous Salmon Ponds hatchery on the Plenty River now raises thousands of trout each year.

The central highlands region is most renowned for its trout fishing, with a number of major waterways, especially Great Lake, Little Pine Lagoon, Arthurs Lake, and Lake Sorell, acclaimed for their superbly conditioned brown and rainbow trout. The region is accessible by car, with ample lodging available. Both lure and fly fishing are popular, and boats can also be hired. Nearby, is the "Land of 3,000 Lakes," where thousands of smaller stream-fed lakes hold wild brown trout and a lesser number of rainbows. Access can be difficult, however, and visitors should be prepared to walk to most waters. Care should be exercised to avoid tiger snakes, which are common in many of these areas.

In the west coast region of Tasmania, Lakes Pedder, Burbury, and Gordon are the most popular. Easily accessible by car, they fish well for brown trout. A record brown trout of 8.25 kilograms has been recorded from Lake Pedder. To the north, the Leven, Henty, and Mersey Rivers have a reputation for good stream fishing, with sea trout also being taken in their lower reaches. In northeast Tasmania, the famous Brumby's Creek fishes well, and the Esk system of rivers is acclaimed for its excellent stream fishing. The southern region has a number of streams and lakes that hold both trout and redfin. Most are within a couple of hours drive from the capital city of Hobart.

Fishing with spinning tackle and lures like the locally made Tasmanian Devil, or bladed spinners, is permissible in most waters, although some, like Little Pine Lagoon, is a fly-fishing-only water. Fly anglers can stock up with both wet and dry flies, but local advice should be sought as to patterns. Mudeyes, the larvae of the dragonfly, are a deadly bait; they can be found under submerged rocks and logs, or bought from some tackle shops. However, some waters are closed to bait use.

Regional regulations and boating rules exist. Details are obtainable from the Marine Resources Division of the Department of Primary Industry, tackle shops, and all tourist centers.

South Australia

Situated between Western Australia and Victoria, South Australia's main angling claim to fame is its fishing for shark, southern bluefin (with a world record of 33.5 kilograms), Australian salmon, and snapper. There's a lesser trout fishery for brown and rainbow trout, while other freshwater species present include redfin, Murray cod, and golden perch.

Kangaroo Island, lying off the tip of Cape Jervis, allows rock, beach, and bay fishing for a variety of species, including Australian salmon, snapper, flathead, King George whiting, barracouta, and yellowtail kingfish. Charter boats operating offshore will take anglers out to where they can catch sharks, southern bluefin tuna, and yellowtail kingfish. The winter months—May to October—are best for southern bluefin tuna.

Spencer Gulf and Gulf St. Vincent waters provide some excellent fishing for both shore-based and boat anglers. Big snapper, King George whiting, sharks, Australian salmon, flathead, mulloway, and bream are some of the available species. Charter boats can also be hired within these areas, and pier fishing for bream, salmon, and King George whiting, with light tackle, is popular throughout the year. It was in these waters that famous gamefisherman Alf Dean landed a then-world record white shark of 1,208.38 kilograms in 1959.

The southeast region of South Australia extends from Victor Harbour to the Victorian border. It's here that the beaches of the Koorong, a chain of salt lagoons that run for more than 140 kilometers

behind the ocean shoreline, provide some of the best beach fishing on the continent for Australian salmon, flathead, bream, sharks, and mulloway. Huge mulloway to 40 kilograms have been taken from the mouth of the Murray River; fishing is best after dark. Beach rods to 4 meters; sidecast, spinning, and surf reels; and lines of 10 to 15 kilograms are used. Access is by four-wheel-drive vehicles.

The inland fishery in South Australia is small because it is the driest of the states, there's an absence of large rivers, and many of the streams dry to a series of pools during the summer months. Both the Onkaparinga River and the Broughton River rely on stocking for their brown and rainbow trout fishery, and golden perch and redfin are present in the Onkaparinga River. Spinning and fly fishing are practiced here. The freshwater reaches of the Murray River, which cuts across the southeastern corner of the state, hold Murray cod, golden perch, redfin, and catfish.

For angling and boating regulations, look for detailed information at tackle shops and Fisheries offices throughout the state. The best fishing is during the summer months, from November through March.

Western Australia

The largest of Australia's states, with an area of more than 2.5 million square kilometers (975,100 square miles), Western Australia includes some of the best rock, beach, offshore, estuary, and bay fishing in the world. Indeed, in its northern waters it surpasses North Queensland for abundance of angling species. Unfortunately, access to its remote angling areas is usually difficult, requiring large or small boats and four-wheel-drive vehicles driven by experienced anglers with a sound knowledge of the terrain and the climate. In addition, temperatures in excess of 40°C are not uncommon in the north during the summer months.

In the Albany region to the south and southeast of the capital city of Perth (said to be the most remote city in the world), there is excellent beach and rockfishing for Australian salmon, big bluefish, groper (grouper), sharks, large silver trevally, snapper, mulloway, Westralian jewfish, and samson fish *(Seriola hippos).* Rods to 4 meters, and sidecast, spinning, or surf reels equipped with lines of 10- to 15-kilogram breaking strength are used here. Also present in these waters are big yellowfin tuna.

Estuary and bay fishing for bluefish, mulloway, flathead, and King George whiting is very popular. Tackle consists of light to medium spinning and plugcasting outfits. Generally, both access and facilities are good, but some four-wheel-drive vehicles are needed to reach a number of good fishing spots.

In the Perth/Fremantle region lies the Swan River estuary, where Australian salmon, mulloway, flathead, bluefish, bream, and trevally are commonly taken. Anglers fish the beaches and rocks immediately north and south of Perth, with conventional beach/rock tackle, target bluefish, mulloway, Australian salmon, silver trevally, and snapper. The reefs surrounding Rottnest Island to the west are favorite fishing grounds for Spanish mackerel, yellowfin tuna, dolphin, and yellowtail kingfish, while still farther west is the Rottnest Trench, which is fished for blue marlin.

To the north, from Shark Bay to the Northern Territory border, exists fishing that most anglers only dream about. This is the Kimberley region, where high temperatures, rugged country, big seas, saltwater crocodiles, and cyclones can challenge even the most adventurous. Species to excite any angler thrive here, and include sailfish (a world record 77.95-kilogram Pacific sailfish has been taken here), amberjack, barramundi, cobia, dolphin, Spanish mackerel, black marlin, queenfish (including a 10.5-kilogram world record specimen), mulloway, samson fish, sharks, snapper, bluefish, giant trevally (a 39.5-kilogram world record fish came from these waters), yellowfin tuna, wahoo, and yellowtail kingfish.

Land-based angling in the area is famous among anglers nationwide, and cannot be bettered anywhere in the world. Because of the area's remoteness, however, it is strongly recommended that guided fishing tours (from Broome and Kununurra) be undertaken by those attempting this sport for the first time.

Offshore fishing is superb, and boats to work the waters for sailfish, wahoo, mackerel, and tuna can be chartered from Denham (Shark Bay), Exmouth, Port Hedland, and Broome. Gamefishing tackle in appropriate line classes is recommended, even for land-based fishing where rock fishing tackle may be considered unsuitable. This area is also famous for its excellent saltwater fly fishing, especially for sailfish, which abound. Smaller species can be fished with spinning or plugcasting tackle, and small-boat skippers will find wonderful angling in the complex of waterways for snapper, mulloway, flathead, bream, and whiting. The wet season (December through March) renders most of the Kimberley area inaccessible, but the dry season (June through September) is not only cooler, it opens up the country.

Inland fishing is confined largely to the Perth/Albany region in the south, and to freshwater sections of rivers like the Fitzroy and impoundments such as Lakes Argyle and Kununurra in the north. In the south, redfin are plentiful, and streams and dams are stocked with brown and rainbow trout, which are usually pursued with spinning, plugcasting, and fly fishing methods. The northern waters are renowned for their barramundi and sooty grunter fishery. These species are taken on both spinning and plugcasting tackle using lures. Lines from 7 to 10 kilograms are favored.

Regulations and boating rules exist for most areas, and copies can be obtained from Fisheries offices and most tackle shops. Potential dangers, mainly in the north, include saltwater crocodiles, cyclones, and big seas, plus heat that can be oppressive in the extreme. Sand flies can also be a nuisance.

Northern Territory

Constituting one-sixth of the landmass of Australia and located in the Tropics at the "Top End" of Australia, the Northern Territory is sparsely populated and replete with world-class sportfishing potential. Tourism here is rapidly growing, and it seems like more of that potential will be enjoyed by visiting anglers in the near future, for a variety of opportunities.

The upper end of the Northern Territory abuts the Timor Sea on the northwest, the Arafur Sea on the north, and the Gulf of Carpentaria on the east. Nhulunbuy is an aboriginal preserve that sports a bauxite mine, and provides a jumping-off point for fishing north of the Gove Peninsula, around its barren and desertlike islands. Bathurst Island is accessed by plane from Darwin, with fishing primarily concentrated on barramundi in the creeks and lagoons. Many of the rivers, estuaries, and lagoons to the east and west of Darwin have notable barramundi fishing as well, and there is a growing offshore fishery.

The capital city of Darwin is the base for guided fishing tours to all worthwhile parts of the hinterland, and to some exciting offshore gamefishing for black marlin, sailfish, Spanish mackerel, sharks, giant trevally, northern bluefin tuna, queenfish, and barracouta. Small-boat anglers have a wonderful playground to explore in the many bays and estuaries, which are within easy reach. In these waters they can catch barramundi, black jewfish, trevally, mangrove jack, threadfin salmon, queenfish, and many other species. A camera or camcorder is well worth carrying, to record what are almost certain to be memorable fishing moments in an unusual part of this continent.

Inland fishing in the Northern Territory is mainly for barramundi, sooty grunter, and saratoga, with mangrove jack, threadfin salmon, and fingermark bream being taken from the brackish waters that can extend for many miles upstream. Spinning, plugcasting, and flycasting are widely used.

Outside Australia, the Top End is most known for barramundi; specimens in excess of 27 kilograms have been recorded, not to mention various line-class world records. This cover-streaking hard-fighting leaper is caught in the estuaries and rivers that abound throughout the Northern Territory, and although these fish exist in various parts of Australia, they are nowhere as abundant as here.

Unquestionably, barramundi fishing in the Northern Territory is a true angling adventure, offering opportunities that are rare today. For one thing, this is the land of Crocodile Dundee fame—sparsely populated, wild, and sometimes dangerous.

Fishing takes place in remote areas in junglelike habitat. Mangrove-lined rivers and tropical lagoons and estuaries are the angling grounds, and casters fish amidst heavy cover, including vegetation and mangrove roots. The struggle to keep larger barramundi from reaching sanctuary once hooked is formidable. A lot of tackle gets tested to the maximum by these fish, and many a lure is lost. The fishing, to say the least, is challenging.

Perhaps as challenging is the fact that good barramundi fishing waters are frequented by saltwater crocodiles, which are aggressive, known maneaters and highly respected by anglers. Signs warn against swimming, and boaters do not venture close enough to risk an encounter.

Barramundi fishing demands an ability to play the tides, which can fluctuate severely here. The best fishing time is during low tide because it draws barramundi out of the mangroves in creeks, lagoons, and other spots and concentrates them in holes, channels, and the like, making them more accessible. Trolling and casting are both popular, using diving and rattling plugs on baitcasting tackle. Fishing is primarily done from small skiffs, 12 to 15 feet long.

Bathurst Island has some excellent fishing for relatively large barramundi, but the bulk of angling for this species takes place around Darwin, in jungle rivers and mangrove-lined lagoons. The Daly River to the southwest of Darwin, and the Mary River to the east, are among the top locations.

Both Bathurst and Melville Islands to the north are controlled by the Aboriginal Land Trust, and permission to travel on them must be obtained. They are well known for their good bay, beach, creek, and estuary fishing, with some excellent offshore angling for larger species. Some other areas on the mainland are designated aboriginal areas, and permission must also be obtained to enter and fish them.

The remote northern region of the Northern Territory has billfishing in two distinctly different

Anglers try to extricate a hooked barramundi from a snag on the Daly River.

The coast of the Northern Territory along the Sea of Arafura has lightly explored angling opportunities.

locales, neither of which received more than an occasional visit by ardent billfish anglers before the late 1980s. The easternmost of these locales is some 50 miles north of Darwin in the waters around Bathurst Island, and some remarkable catches of sailfish and black marlin have been made here.

The other billfish possibility exists off Gove Peninsula, more than 350 miles to the east. There, black marlin have been caught off Truant Islands and the English Company's Islands, reportedly in sizes over 500 pounds, as well as many sailfish. A few charter boats have worked this area from Nhulunbuy, and reports are that light-tackle fishing starts in March, with plenty of sailfish action at that time, and that larger blacks show up in October and November.

Both of these locales sport opportunities for other fish, either around island reefs or while trolling the offshore environs. The islands off the Gove Peninsula are especially a potpourri of opportunities for light-tackle angling for willing, aggressive fish. In the Gove region along the east coast of Arnhem Land, the fishing is largely untouched. Besides black marlin, other species include giant trevally, golden trevally, queenfish, mackerel, cobia, barracouta, Spanish mackerel, and northern bluefin tuna. Access is by plane to the remote mining town of Nhulunbuy, and facilities range from elaborate to austere.

Most of the coast of the Northern Territory bordering the Arafura Sea from Gove Peninsula east has seen little if any sportfishing ventures, and there are many bays, lagoons, reefs, and islands that could provide virgin fishing if there were access and if the fishing wasn't as good elsewhere. There is little motivation to explore this region. In any event, these are aboriginal lands, and access permits are required.

Guided tours for anglers visiting the Northern Territory are strongly recommended, especially in the wet season (October to April), when most roads are impassable. The fishing range is extended during the dry season (May to September), when many places can be accessed by four-wheel-drive vehicles. The best fishing for barramundi is during the months of April and May, which is the crossover period between the wet and the dry seasons.

The chief danger to anglers is the big saltwater crocodile that can move well up into the freshwater reaches of most waterways. Fishing from shore is inadvisable, as is fishing from a canoe. Wading could be a suicidal pastime! Heed all warning signs; they are empirically based. Sand flies and mosquitoes also exist, and can be an annoyance.

The tidal range is exceptional in Northern Territory waters, sometimes exceeding 7 meters. Anglers who hire their own boats for self-guiding will find that tide charts are essential; they can generally be obtained from tackle shops or the Darwin Port Authority. Regulations and boating rules exist, and copies of the "Northern Territory Fishing and Boating Guide" are available from tackle shops and the Department of Primary Industry and Fisheries.

AUSTRIA

With most of its 83,859 square kilometers of land in the eastern Alps, Austria is a central European country noted for stunning scenery and clear, clean waters that originate in the high peaks, offering good trout and grayling fishing before flowing into larger waters and coursing through broad valleys. Austria's high-quality mountain waters offer fishing as good or better than that found in most other European countries, particularly for salmonid species.

Roughly the size of the state of Maine, this predominantly mountainous country, with an average elevation of 3,000 feet, contains portions of the Danube, Europe's second largest river, and such prominent tributaries to the Danube as the Rivers Inn, Traun, Enns, and Ybbs. The high country is studded with small rivers and streams, as well as assorted lakes and reservoirs of varying size, plus a pair of large border lakes. Among the latter are the Bodensee, which forms the western border with Liechtenstein and Switzerland *(see);* also known as Lake Konstanz, it is part of the Rhine River, covering 544 square kilometers, reaching depths of more than 250 meters, and serving as an important commercial fishery for whitefish and pike. The largest lake entirely within the country's borders is the Attersee east of Salzburg, which is a major all-around recreation site for Austrians.

The cool rivers and streams and associated smaller lakes are really where the fishing action is for the majority of resident and visiting anglers. European grayling and brown trout, both native species, are abundant and vie for the distinction of most popular species, and are also found in the lakes. The largest brown trout are caught in lakes; a lake-resident brown trout here is known as a *seeforelle,* whereas a river- or stream-resident brown trout is known as a *bachforelle.*

Confusion over terminology exists when referring to brown trout in rivers versus those in lakes. In Europe, the Western term "lake trout" actually refers to a *seeforelle;* though published literature may indicate that lake trout exist in various waters, the species referenced is actually *seeforelle.* The species that Westerners refer to as "lake trout" *(Salvelinus namaycush)* is actually in the charr family, and the type of fish referred to in central European nations as "lake char." This is important to understand, because some of the largest brown trout in the world have come from European lakes, but they are still considerably smaller than the largest *Salvelinus namaycush* caught in North America. Few traveling anglers from the West would visit Europe to fish for *Salvelinus namaycush,* but they might try to catch a trophy *seeforelle* in its native environment (brown trout in the West are an introduced species).

Other salmonids are also found in many of the cool flowages and lakes in Austria. These include brook (speckled) trout, rainbow trout, lake charr, huchen, and whitefish.

Some of the deeper lakes contain two-story fisheries for various salmonids, usually brown and rainbow trout, plus warmer-water denizens like native pike and zander (pike-perch), as well as assorted coarse species. The latter can be found in many of the shallower and warmer ponds, lakes, canals, and rivers. Large specimens of wels catfish are in a few waters, and a number of lakes are reported to contain black r bass.

The River Traun, which flows northerly to the Danube, is one of the premier trout and grayling flows in the country. Other notable and larger rivers for these species include the Enns, Erlauf, Lammer, Salza, Traisen, and Ybbs.

Most fishery resources are privately managed and controlled. A system of fishing private waters (rivers, streams, ponds, lakes, and canals) exists through packages offered by a great many resorts and lodges, many of whom cater to angling visitors, some of them offering fly fishing schools.

Nearly all trout streams and rivers are restricted to fly fishing only, and without the use of shot or added weight. Barbless hook requirements exist at many prime sites as well. Lure fishing with spinning tackle is generally permitted in large waters; live bait is mainly prohibited, but some forms of bait are allowed for coarse fishing.

Selected Venues

This brief review of opportunities at some venues reflects a diversity in species and water types, and is generally representative of the broad array of fishing found at hotels and vacation sites throughout Austria. Many fishing sites are easily reached by auto, although those close to dense population centers are heavily pressured. The more distant and reserved waters tend to offer the best fishing overall, and most are managed via regulation and annual restocking.

Southern region. The southernmost portion of Austria contains the whole gamut of Austrian fishing experiences. Most of the rivers contain brown trout, rainbow trout, and grayling.

In the southernmost Carinthia district near the Slovenia border, the River Drau (Drava) is known for monster wels. This river is a mountain torrent in its upper reaches, then moderates on its way to the Danube, with the region near Völkermarkt being a place to do battle with big catfish. Large huchen, incidentally, have come from the Drau; 32- and 34-kilogram world records were caught in the Drau in the early 1980s.

Nearby Drau Reservoir is a narrow 25-kilometer-long impoundment of the Drau River that contains pike, zander, and catfish that may only be caught on artificial lures. The Gösselsdorfer See in the vicinity is a small lake with pike, carp, and tench, and area rivers possess brown and rainbow trout, which are governed by a barbless-hook fly fishing requirement. There are other small impoundments on this long river, some containing trout.

Farther west, and to the southeast of Villach, is the Faaker See, perhaps Austria's preeminent whitefish lake. One of the country's southernmost lakes, and a deep one at the foot of the Karawanken Mountains, it not only contains large and plentiful whitefish (which prompts an international whitefish competition each September), but counts brown trout, pike, and carp among its prominent species, and also contains lake charr, rainbow trout, zander, and black bass. Live bait is prohibited here, but all types of fishing methods are allowed.

Still farther west, and closer to the East Tyrol region of Austria, is Carinthia's highest altitude lake, the Weissensee. Outboard motors are prohibited on this premier lake nestled between mountains northwest of Villach, but various angling methods are allowed, and species include brown trout, rainbow trout, lake charr, zander, pike, whitefish, and coarse species. Pike to 16 kilograms have been caught here in the 1990s, and the lake has produced a former European record 21-kilogram *seeforelle.*

To the north of Villach, another mountain lake, Ossiacher See, is the third largest lake in this region. At more than 2,700 acres it has wels catfish, zander, pike, numerous coarse species, and black bass. Various fishing methods are allowed, but live bait and sonar are prohibited.

Central and northern regions. This central mountain region of Austria features some of the finest river trout fishing in the country as well as in Europe. The headwaters of the Traun system originate here in the Salzkammergut district, and such flowages as the Altausseer, Grundlseer, Kainischer, Koppentraun, and countless small streams and tributaries in the upper watershed provide oppor-

tunity for brown trout, rainbow trout, speckled trout, and grayling. There are countless small lakes and ponds in the region as well, many with brown trout, lake charr, and rainbow trout, and some with pike, zander, coarse species, and also bass.

Some of the finest river fishing for trout and grayling exists in the Traun below Traunsee Lake, from the town of Gmunden downstream. Rainbow and brown trout from 1 to 2.5 kilograms are abundant here, and specimens of both species exceed 4.5 kilograms annually. The Traun is considered one of the top trout rivers in Europe; it provides relatively easy wading and is restricted to barbless hooks and fly fishing. A number of fishing-oriented hotels are located here.

South of this area to the east and west is the River Enns and many tributaries to that long flow. Brown and rainbow trout and grayling are the mainstays, with the area from Gröbming to Radstadt of special note and with various hotels catering to anglers. Some of the streams here also have speckled trout and charr, and the lakes have most of the same species as noted elsewhere in Styria. A few have large *seeforelle* as well as large pike; some, like 655-acre Fuschlsee near Halbach, produce pike to 14 kilograms.

In the western Salzburg Province, Hohe Tauern National Park near Mittersill features more than 100 kilometers of trout and grayling streams, in a barbless-hook fly-fishing-only area that was formerly a haunt of the Austrian aristocracy a century ago. The Hohe Tauern is noted for the Grossglockner, the highest peak in Austria at 3,797 meters, and one of Europe's largest glaciers, the Pasterze.

Permits

Anglers need two types of permits to fish in Austria. One is the *amtliche Fischerkarte,* an Official Fishing License issued by the respective local government office (in Upper Austria and Vienna by the local fishing authority; in Tyrol and Vorarlberg by the owner of the fishing rights). This is a document with a photograph valid for one to three years throughout the province concerned. In all provinces except Upper Austria and Vienna, a temporary fishing authorization, *kurzfristige Fischergastkarte,* valid only for a specific fishing preserve, is issued by the owner of the fishing rights (in Burgenland only by the local government office). In some federal provinces, one-day tickets are issued.

The other necessary permit is the *private Fischereierlaubnis,* a Private Fishing Permit of the local owner. This is in addition to the Official License, and obtainable from the fishing water's lessee or proprietor for a fixed sum. A limited number of Private Fishing Permits may be issued for certain fishing preserves, as some waters are rationed as to the number of anglers who can access them at a given time. Permits for private waters are issued for varying periods of time, and are usually accompanied by regulations regarding catch limits, size limits, catch-and-release, angling methods, baits and lures, and so on.

AUTOMATIC REEL

A type of flycasting reel that retrieves line automatically.

See: Flycasting Tackle.

AUTOPILOT

A hands-free navigational instrument used for steering large boats on a preselected bearing. It is occasionally used by trollers.

See: Steering Device, Remote.

AXILLARY PROCESS

A fleshy flap, which is usually narrow and extends to the rear, situated just above the pectoral or pelvic fins on some fish.

See: Fish.

AYU *Plecoglossus altivelis altivelis.*

Other names—sweetfish, ayu sweetfish; Japanese: *ayu, koayu.*

The only member of the Plecoglossidae family, the ayu—more commonly known in English as sweetfish—is a prized species in Japan and a unique salmonid of economic importance. Fishing for ayu is very specialized.

Identification. The ayu has an olive brown body with a pale-yellow blotch on its side. Its fins, including the expanded dorsal fin, are reddish. There are 10 to 12 rays on the dorsal fin, 9 to 17 rays on the anal fin, 5 or 6 branchiostegal rays, and usually 59 to 64 vertebrae. When the ayu spawns, its fin colors are enhanced (the fish is then known as *sabi,* meaning "rusty"), and both sexes are covered with tubercles. The male does not develop a kype, but its upper jaw shortens; the female's anal fin expands during this time.

Size. The ayu attains a maximum size of roughly 12 inches.

Distribution. An anadromous species, ayu occur in the western North Pacific, from western Hokkaido in Japan southward to the Korean Peninsula, Taiwan, and China.

Ayu

Habitat/Life history. Adult ayu inhabit the upper reaches of rivers, where they mature before migrating downstream to spawn. Spawning occurs in the lower reaches, and most ayu die after spawning. Breeding occurs in the fall, and the fish begin to show their spawning colors during summer. The adhesive eggs hatch in three weeks, and the larvae move out of the river and into the sea when they are about 1 inch long. They overwinter in the sea and return in spring, when they are about 3 inches long, migrating upstream in huge numbers.

Food and feeding habits. Ayu have a peculiar but highly evolved mouth and dentition. When reentering freshwater, they develop a series of comblike teeth that lie outside the mouth; these replace the conical teeth they used to catch small crustaceans at sea. In freshwater, these fish feed on algae. The tip of each jaw features a bony pointed process that fits into a corresponding recess on the opposite jaw when the mouth is closed. It is believed that adult ayu eat algae from rocks by grazing, using their snout and teeth to scrape off the algae.

AZORE ISLANDS

See: Portugal.

B

BACK BOUNCING

See: Backtrolling.

BACK CAST

The backward motion of the rod and line in flycasting.

See: Flycasting Tackle.

BACKING

Reserve line that is connected to the main line on the spool of a reel for situations when greater line lengths are necessary. Backing is normally of a different type or strength than the main line and is most commonly used on flycasting reels, where it is attached to the fly line, since it is practical to cast only a certain amount of fly line. Backing may be employed with other forms of tackle, although in these it is most common to use a continuous length of the same line to fill the spool.

See: Flycasting Tackle.

BACKING DOWN

A boat manipulation tactic primarily used in offshore fishing *(see)* to help an angler gain line when hooked up to a large and strong fish. The boat is driven in reverse, with its stern facing in the direction of the fish and the line. The angler winds line on the reel while the boat backs (often swiftly) toward the fish. The boat captain backs down instead of turning and heading toward the fish so he can see the line and the position of the fish. This prevents the boat from interfering with the fish and also prevents slack from developing in the line.

This fish-fighting strategy may be necessary when a fish has taken an exceptional amount of line and the angler is in danger of losing all the line on the reel. It may also be used where significant boat traffic or obstructions could enable a fish to break the line. Because anglers have more control over a fish on a short length of line than a long one, backing down will narrow the distance to the fish and possibly help prevent its loss. This tactic may be put to use unfairly by anglers employing light tackle in open water (often when fishing during a contest or for the sake of establishing a light-line record). By lessening the effect of a long length of line on light tackle and reel drag, the angler can bring a fish to capture more quickly than would have been possible otherwise.

See: Playing Fish.

BACKLASH

The tangle of line that develops on the spool of a revolving spool reel as a result of the differential between the speed of the line moving through the rod guides and the amount of line being made available to follow the lure by the spin imparted to the reel spool. In essence, the spool moves faster than the line can depart, causing the spool to overrun the line and pile up line on the spool. The causes and preventions for this are discussed in other entries *(see: baitcasting tackle; conventional tackle).*

One way to attempt to remove a backlash in a revolving spool reel is to put the reel in gear, tighten the drag so it doesn't slip, press the thumbnail of your rod-holding hand on the snarl to flatten and relax the coils, take two or three turns of the reel handle, put the reel in gear, and pull out the line. This does not tighten the coils and should allow you to get all but the worst backlashes out in a few seconds. Make sure you reset the drag.

Many people pick at the backlashed loops of line with their fingers. To do this, put the reel in freespool with your thumb on the spool. Carefully pick away at the leading loops to remove tightening overwraps until you get to the loop that is dug in the worst; then pull it out. Get all snarled line segments out before rewinding the line on the spool, and do not wind over any loops.

See: Casting.

BACK-REEL

The activity of turning the handle on a reel backward. This is possible on reels with direct drive, and also on baitcasting, spincasting, and spinning reels that have a selective anti-reverse, in which the user can elect to turn the anti-reverse mechanism off, thus allowing the drive gear to move either forward or backward, as well as the handle of the reel to turn forward or backward.

In the past, when reel drags were poor and often unreliable, anglers felt more comfortable when playing a strong fish if they could reel backward to let line out to play the fish. Many were accustomed to doing this with baitcasting, or levelwind, reels, which initially had direct drive and had to be back-reeled, or wound backward, when a strong fish put a lot of pressure on the reel.

The trouble with back-reeling is that rarely can you reel backward quickly enough to keep up with a rapidly turning handle when a strong fish speeds off; therefore, you have to let go of the handle,

B

which usually spins wildly and may cause a snarl, backlash, or overrun upon completion of the swift back-reeling. When you try to grab the rapidly turning handle, it often smacks your fingers, a result that caused the old reels to be called knucklebusters.

Another problem is that you have to gauge the action of the fish in order to reel quickly to keep up with it. Although it is possible to back-reel small fish, like 2-pound bass, as long as the drag is a good one and properly set; it is better to keep the anti-reverse engaged, especially for stronger and harder-fighting fish.

Today, reel drags are quite reliable and efficient, especially when properly set; and there is no reason to back-wind, even if a reel has the ability to do so. Today's baitcasting, spincasting, and spinning reels do not really need selective anti-reverse, but most of them have it to give anglers—especially competitive bass anglers who insist on cranking the drag tension up high—the option of using it. Probably the only time that the average angler uses this feature is when line is accidentally wound around inner or outer parts of the reel and needs to be worked free. See: Baitcasting Tackle; Spincasting Tackle; Spinning Tackle; Playing Fish.

BACKTROLLING

"Backtrolling" refers to two freshwater fishing techniques primarily used by walleye, steelhead, and salmon anglers. In both methods, the angler uses a small boat and precise boat-handling methods to manipulate the boat while presenting a lure or bait behind the boat in a systematic way, making a thorough, slow, and careful presentation. A backtroller can maintain position along specific depths, nearly hover over selected spots, and maneuver the boat using wind direction to ensure that the following bait remains in the proper place. This is especially vital when a school of fish is packed into one small spot.

In one form of backtrolling, the angler runs a small boat stern first, and the boat is typically outfitted with transom-mounted splash guards to keep wave action from dumping water into the boat. Using a tiller-steered outboard motor in reverse, or a transom-mounted electric motor (with the lower unit turned so that the stern goes backward when the motor is technically in a forward position), the angler maneuvers the boat very slowly to maintain precise position around points, reefs, weedlines, sandbars, and along dropoffs. Favored by walleye anglers, this was once an extremely popular technique but has become less so.

A more common method of maintaining precise boat control and efficient lure or bait placement—one that is often used in rivers—is achieved by floating, drifting, or trolling slowly backward downcurrent. In some places this is called backtrolling or back bouncing, but in others it is called hotshotting (a derivative of the West Coast technique of using a tight-wiggling, deep-diving trolling plug) for river steelhead and salmon, or pulling plugs. In still other places, it is called slipping. In Europe, it is called harling *(see)*.

Whatever you call it, the idea is to have the bow of your boat pointed upstream, using the motor or oars to control the downstream progression of the boat. The boat moves very slowly—it actually drifts—downstream and at times remains stationary in the current (some boaters anchor in the spot where they catch a fish) as lures are fished at varied distances (from a few feet to 75 feet) behind the boat. The benefit of this technique is that the lures essentially dangle in front of fish that the boat has not yet passed over; in upstream trolling, the boat passes over the fish and alerts them to your presence and probably spooks them. Additionally, lures that are backtrolled downstream approach the head of fish instead of coming from behind and swimming past their head. Anglers usually fish these lures in the channels and deep pools where bigger fish lie, and the lures waver in front of the fish much longer than they would if cast and retrieved or if trolled upstream and away from the fish. Overall, this technique is highly effective in river fishing because the presentation is more natural (resembling, for example, a small fish struggling against the current and being slowly swept downward toward the fish) and because the fish are less likely to be disturbed by the lures before they see them.

In most downstream backtrolling, the angler uses diving plugs for fish that take them. Some fish, such as shad, don't take plugs; in that case, the preferred offerings are a shad dart (a type of jig) or tiny spoons fished behind a torpedo shaped beadchain sinker. Others respond well to bait; winter-run steelhead, for example, are caught with pencil lead-weighted spawn sacks, single-hook salmon eggs, or worms. Many different attractions, including plugs, spoons, spinners, flies, and baits, are used as conditions and location dictate. Plugs are most often flatlined with or without a sinker, and some form of sinker is always used with baits. If a plug is to be effective, it must run straight and dive to the bottom; if it doesn't, then it has to be tuned *(see: tuning lures)* to run properly.

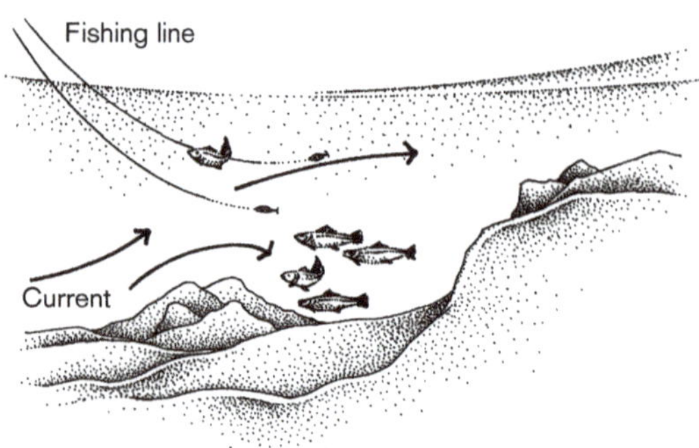

Depicted is the tail of a river pool and two lures that are being backtrolled downstream to approach fish facing upstream.

When backtrolling, skilled boat maneuvering is a prerequisite to precise lure positioning. The location and depth of the offering is critical to successful river fishing. The lure must be on or close to the bottom, and only the appropriate amount of weight or lure design will achieve this.

Pools and deep runs are the areas in which backtrolling is most favored. Often, the boat must be positioned far enough upriver so the lure works slowly from the head of a pool, or runs down through the tail of it; it's not sufficient to maneuver downstream to a spot and then hold position, as the fish you seek may be at the head of that location. When working from side to side across the river, realize that it takes awhile for a trailing lure to catch up to the boat's position. When you sweep close to a bank, for instance, hold that position momentarily, allowing time for the lure to work its way over too. If you sweep in and out quickly, the lure won't get as far to either side as you might like.

Be sure to troll backward in a slow, controlled fashion. When you stop rowing or throttle back the motor, a floating plug rises, a spinner doesn't spin, weights sink, and so forth. This is caused by the sudden lack of pressure against those objects. Slow, controlled backward movement keeps lures working best and draws more strikes. Boat control is maintained with oars, especially in rafts, jonboats, and river drift boats (McKenzie River–style dories), or with a small tiller-steered outboard motor. The bow of the boat is headed upstream and always above the area to be fished. It is important to row or run the motor just fast enough to hold even with the current.

Once in position and keeping pace with the current, if fishing a plug you should freespool or strip out line until the plug is the appropriate distance behind the boat; many plugs are fished 50 feet back. If you use several lures or several plugs, they should all be set out the same distance to avoid tangling and to thoroughly work the area downstream. The lure will dive when line movement stops; the stronger the current (and the lighter the line), the deeper the lure will dive, so keep constant pressure on it. After a few minutes, the boat operator can slowly decrease forward momentum so that the boat always runs downstream at a slower pace than the river's natural speed.

Under these conditions, the fish can see the plug, or bait, or other lure coming and can anticipate its arrival. Bear in mind that fish view these objects, especially lures, as territorial invaders; consequently, they may move away, move downstream, or stay and strike them. When they do strike, it is usually suddenly and aggressively. If an object is fished too quickly, however, fish will view it with less alarm and usually ignore it, or they will decide that it is moving too quickly to waste effort chasing it. By drifting slower than the natural current, the slowly moving object is available longer and is more threatening and provocative, or simply an easier meal.

Oregon anglers backtroll through a river pool for salmon.

If necessary, in order to get lures into the right spots and to fish a hole without moving the boat over the entire run, anglers use a tactic called back bouncing. To do this, slowly lift the rod tip upward and feel the lure working, then drop it down till it hits bottom. Then either reel up a bit or lift and bounce back the plug or bait with the current flow as you drift. As it is alternately dropped back to hit the bottom and then lifted, the offering is always worked back toward the fish.

It can be hard to get the hang of backtrolling and back bouncing, but anglers must remember to maintain contact with the bottom and constantly watch their rod tips for a strike and for the proper working action of a lure. Many anglers know how fast to run their boat by watching the action of their rod tips, especially when using hard-pulling plugs. A constantly pulsating rod tip, incidentally, indicates that a lure is working properly. In deeper holes, the fish will not come up much for a lure, so it must be kept on or near the bottom. In shallower water, fish will rise to the lure. Some fish are caught almost under the boat, so they do not fear it. This is not the case when a river is low and very clear.

See: Flatlining.

BACKWATER

A quiet, still pool, lagoon, or pondlike body of water on the side of a stream channel or river. Backwaters are often stagnant, shallow, and heavily vegetated or filled with such cover as stumps and timber; in large river systems they are often created or greatly enlarged during periods of high water.

See: Oxbow.

BACTERIA

Unicellular organisms that lack a distinct cell nucleus. They are different from plants and animals, and are important as the bottom rung of the food chain *(see)* in most aquatic systems.

BAG LIMIT

Synonymous with creel limit, bag limit means the quantity or number of fish of a species or group of species that may be taken, caught, or killed during a specified period. That period is usually one day, from 12:01 A.M. to midnight, and it may be identified as a "daily bag limit" or simply "daily limit." Bag limits may apply universally to many waters or may be site-specific. A bag limit is a legal game regulation established by the fisheries agency that has jurisdiction over the location being fished, and is enforced by fish and wildlife conservation officers.

See: Fisheries Management; Regulations.

B

In 1995, a South African angler donated a collection of nearly 300 sinkers of different shapes and materials to Knysna Angling Museum; he collected these over 40 years while diving.

BAHAMAS

When it comes to sportfishing, the 700-island Bahamas chain pretty much has it all, from the drama of Atlantic blue marlin and bluefin tuna to the singular thrill of silvery bonefish and the line-stretching adventure of grouper, snapper, and other reef dwellers.

Located as close as 50 miles from the continental United States, the Bahamas have been one of the world's most popular sportfishing destinations since the mid-twentieth century. Each year, tens of thousands of anglers travel to the Bahamas in search of 10-pound bonefish, 20-pound permit, 30- to 100-pound tarpon, 200- to 1,000-pound blue marlin, 20- to 60-pound dolphin, 40- to 120-pound wahoo, 300- to 1,000-pound giant bluefin tuna, 100-pound yellowfin tuna, and myriad bottom fish.

The Bahamas offer a potpourri of tropical angling opportunities but are especially known for big-game fishing—blue marlin in particular—and flats fishing, especially for bonefish. Bonefish range throughout the Bahamas, and some of the world's largest have been recorded at Bimini. Excellent flats guides and good boats are available at all the better-known resorts. Just about anyone who lives in the Bahamas can point you to a good flat where you can pursue bonefish and possibly other flats denizens as well.

Unlike many nations, the Bahamas has become a strong advocate of marine conservation. In the mid-1980s, the government established daily bag limits for recreational anglers and commercial fishermen. In an effort to conserve and preserve breeding stocks, it passed laws limiting overly effective commercial gear, including longlines. Pressure also was brought on tournament organizers to promote tag-and-release. The Bahamas is a popular site for big-game tournaments, and most of these now employ a combination of tag-and-release and limited killing of fish; minimum weights of 300 to 400 pounds for big-game fish to be brought to dock have been established. Inshore species such as bonefish have always been released. These efforts and more continue to make the Bahamas a popular, affordable, easy-to-reach, year-round destination for anglers in search of quality flats and big-game fishing.

Anglers are blessed with many choices in the Bahamas. In addition to hiring offshore charter boats and guides with flats boats, they can hire professional local guides at an economical price to accompany them on their boat, or they can use published charts and sportfishing guides to explore and fish the Bahamas on their own. Either way, the Bahamas is an angling oasis.

Bimini

Often called the birthplace of Atlantic big-game fishing, Bimini is among the world's most famous sportfishing destinations.

It was here off Alice Town that author Ernest Hemingway developed the aggressive fishing style that enables anglers to catch giant bluefin tuna before plentiful sharks can maul them. The first lever-drag big-game reel, a Fin-Nor, was tested off Bimini. Sitting around the docks at night, mates and captains developed important components of offshore fishing—like the Haywire Twist, ballyhoo rigs, and the Bimini Twist knot—that are widely used by big-game anglers to fish Bimini's waters.

Geologically, Bimini is a series of coral atolls. The two largest are the safety-pin-shaped North Bimini, where the main settlement of Alice Town is located, and the sparsely inhabited island of South Bimini. North Bimini is only 7 miles long by 150 yards wide, but it has the area's only road, the single-lane King's Highway. The rectangular-shaped South Bimini lies roughly east to west and is just 3 miles long; it has a 5,000-foot paved airstrip and a 281-foot radio tower. Cat Cay lies 10 miles south; the landmark Great Isaac Lighthouse is 19 miles north.

Bimini's ultimate appeal is due largely to the ambiance created by the friendly native population and to its close proximity to the United States; Bimini ranks as the easternmost of the 700 Bahamian islands. It lies 47 miles east of Miami along a deep-water drop in the Florida Straits, a migratory highway for bluefin tuna, blue marlin, and other big-game species. In this same area lies a 300-foot rectangle of large hand-hewn rocks that many experts believe is the lost city of Atlantis. Radioactive tests suggest these rocks were indeed situated above the water about 5,000 years ago. Scientists have theorized that the stones could be remnants of a highway system, built by a highly advanced culture.

Bimini is very accessible. By seaplane, it is only a 25-minute flight from Miami, and it doesn't take much longer to get there by boat. In calm weather, powerboats can make the trip in two to three hours. Fishing for snapper and grouper is a year-round sport off Bimini. The island also enjoys seasonal runs of giant bluefin and yellowfin tuna, monstrous wahoo, king mackerel, blue and white marlin, and sailfish.

Big-game fishing. The Bahamas' only 1,000-pound blue marlin was taken off Bimini. Although blue marlin are caught here year-round, the peak run is from late March through early May—when the fish are migrating north from their spawning grounds in the Caribbean and Gulf of Mexico through the Florida Current (Gulf Stream), which brushes against the western edge of the Bahama Banks. This is the eastern edge of the Gulf Stream, an area where depths go from 60 to 600 feet in a matter of yards. This 100-fathom curve runs 2 miles offshore of Bimini, between nearby Ocean Cay and Great Isaac Lighthouse, then turns sharply north into the Northwest Providence Channel.

In addition to marlin fishing, Bimini enjoys an excellent run of large wahoo from September through December. The action centers west of Bimini in 10 to 25 fathoms, just inside the 100-fathom line, from Great Isaac to North Pines Beach. Early in the season wahoo average 30 to 40 pounds. It often takes little effort to catch 8 to 10 a day. The fish get bigger as the season peaks in late November and December. Wahoo fishing is best on the outgoing tide, when bait delivery runs from the grassflats and inshore reefs to deeper water. A north or northwest wind is most favorable for wahoo here. Locals fish for them using barracuda strips, rigged mullet, and ballyhoo, as well as chrome-headed offshore lures with a green or black-and-red skirt.

At one time Bimini enjoyed a tremendous influx of giant bluefin tuna migrating along the offshore edge of the Bahama Banks between mid-April and May. Those fish still come, but in far fewer numbers and over a much less dependable period of time. Instead of hundreds of dark football shapes, you might see a dozen fish in a matter of weeks. The best tuna fishing at Bimini these days is not for bluefins as in the past, but for yellowfin tuna, which migrate by here between late February and April. Most fish are caught by trolling medium-speed blue-water trolling lures, or rigged baits with green-and-yellow skirts, across the edge of the Gulf Stream to the bank.

Spring delivers the best dolphin action. Bigger 50- to 70-pounders are caught in April and May, but as summer wears on, 10- to 20-pounders predominate. Schoolies are thick in August. Fall and winter are the seasons for mackerel on spoons and white feather jigs. Grouper and snapper are consistent year-round, with hogfish, lane and gray snapper, and good-eating margates plentiful everywhere along the dropoff of the continental shelf and among the numerous shipwrecks along the reef between Bimini and Great Isaac. Larger fish are found in 90 or more feet of water. At 30 to 80 feet, 8- to 15-pounders are consistently available in the fall and winter months.

Light-tackle fishing. When it comes to fishing for bonefish, tarpon, and permit, Bimini has produced its share of records, among them a 15-pound bonefish for golfing legend Sam Snead in February 1953. That was beaten a few years later by a 16-pounder that also came off the flats at Bimini.

Bonefish are caught year-round off Bimini's shallow east shoreline, and in the harbor in the fall, late spring, and early summer. Spring brings the biggest schools. Fall is when reel-stripping 8- to 12-pounders attract serious fly anglers. Bonefish are bottom feeders that hunt shrimp and crabs on the marl flats around Bimini. The fish bite best on the morning and evening incoming tides. You can also find them on the grass flats lying directly opposite the harbor and along the offshore edge of the islands dotting South Bimini.

The top areas for permit are along the tip and elbow of North Bimini in 12 feet of water. They are also caught on the bonefish flats.

Live shrimp is the best bait for bonefish, followed by small live crabs (which are best for permit) and fresh-cut conch. Fly anglers do best on shrimplike flies in pink, brown, and white.

A popular nighttime attraction at Bimini is the tarpon that appear each summer in the harbor. Although this is not a predictable fishery, 60- to 100-pound fish are sometimes taken by drifting live bait around the docks.

Walker's Cay/North Abacos

Located roughly due east of Vero Beach, Florida, and 150 miles northeast of Fort Lauderdale, Walker's Cay is a lush 100-acre outpost situated at the top of the Abacos Wall. A one-time anti-submarine base, Walker's Cay is a pure fishing resort—one often labeled as idyllic, peaceful, and secluded—and a frequent inclusion in listings of top-10 angling getaway destinations.

Walker's has as diverse a fishery as one could expect in the Bahamas, and has been the location for notable catches (including various world records), with its offshore fishing and reef bottom fishing most acclaimed.

Big-game fishing. Walker's is considered one of the best blue marlin areas in the Bahamas because of the island's northernmost location at the end of the Abaco Wall as well as its proximity to the Florida Current. Prodigious numbers of blue marlin are caught here year-round.

Blue-water fishing is so consistent here because off Walker's is not only the 100-fathom line but also a 1,000-fathom curve 12 miles offshore to the northeast. In addition, Walker's lies on the northeast point of the barrier reef that is the Abaco Wall. Deep water begins less than a half-mile offshore, plummeting from 60 to 90 feet and then from 200 to 600 feet. Just north of the 1,000-fathom curve, the bottom becomes even more irregular over a series of canyons dropping to 2,500 feet in places.

These seamounts, in concert with the ever-present easterly current, combine to create upwellings that force bottom water to the surface. The upwellings provide nutrients for small organisms that become prey to baitfish that in turn attract such pelagic species as blue marlin, white marlin, sailfish, giant bluefin tuna, hordes of yellowfin tuna, huge 100-pound-class wahoo, and scads of dolphin.

B

B

Weather permitting—and it usually does thanks to the protection offered by the Bahama Banks to the west of the island—good blue-water action for some of these species is available 12 months out of the year. Winter and spring, however, deliver the best blue-water fishing, when giant wahoo and white marlin are present, followed by blue marlin at their most active.

White marlin show up from January through March and roam the same 1,000-fathom drop where blues are found. Most whites weigh 50 to 75 pounds, but fish as large as 125 pounds have been caught here. The best offshore months overall are March through May, when yellowfin tuna and dolphin are most abundant. The dolphin can be big; an existing line-class record 80-pounder was taken here. With an advantageous north-northeast wind, it's not unusual for anglers to raise two or three blue marlin a day.

Reef and flats fishing. Walker's Cay is least heralded for flats fishing for bonefish, but depending on who you consult, it's either good here or just so-so. The latter description is typical of a bonefish fanatic looking for miles of flats, lots of opportunities, and big fish, especially for shallow-water tailing fish. But since most folks don't fit that category, they'll find the bonefishing pretty good here, and an interesting diversion from reef and offshore angling.

Flats are not extensive at Walker's, but bonefish are available year-round, mainly just past the marina by the airstrip, and over at Grand Cay and Double Breasted Cay. The flats also produce barracuda and sharks.

Although most anglers come to Walker's Cay for offshore fishing, there is also fast and furious bottom action here. When it comes to reef fishing, there's no better site in the Bahamas. The coral edges nearby and offshore in the deep-water reefs are the favored spots.

On the ocean side of Walker's the coral quickly drops off into 40 feet of water , and this provides action for both small red grouper and red hind (strawberry grouper), as well as Nassau, yellowfin, and black grouper. These species are present all the way out to depths of 150 feet or more, and although light-tackle fun can be had in shallow water, the larger fish frequent the deeper water, with 130 to 200 feet the range usually fished by deep jiggers. The fish they look to tempt in the deeper reef waters include the aforementioned species, plus the occasional African pompano, shark, amberjack, barracuda, and wahoo, among others.

Stout tackle is preferred because these fish can reach heavyweight sizes, and make vigorous efforts to escape by powering back into the rocky habitat. Twenty-pound grouper, especially Nassau and yellowfin, are common, and 40- to 50-pounders are possible. Red grouper may hit the 15-pound mark, and black grouper can be in the 40- to 60-pound class or larger; some over 100 pounds have been caught here.

Reef fishing is productive all year long at Walker's. Jigs tipped with curly soft plastics or with bait are the hot ticket, especially on a moving tide. Anglers usually work close to the bottom for grouper and up the water column to attract other species.

Generally, the northern Bahamas possess many varieties of snapper and grouper. The most common grouper are the red, Nassau, and black varieties, plus a fish Bahamians call yelloweye. Deep-water fish with small heads and big bodies, yelloweye taste a little like a yellowtail snapper. Most are caught on wire lines and electric reels in depths of 300 feet or more.

Of the three most common snapper species—mutton, mangrove, and yellowtail—mutton are the most prized catch because they are the biggest and wariest. Thus the most effective way to fish for snapper here and elsewhere in the Bahamas is to lure the fish in by chumming. The choicest chum are scraps left over from commercial conch fishing ventures, which often operate from major marinas throughout the Bahamas. Lacking a conch fisherman, you can easily catch or buy fresh conch to use for bottom bait and combine that with frozen blocks of pilchard, frozen glass minnows, menhaden, or leftover fish scraps.

When fishing for mutton snapper, fresh pilchards can be used both as chum and chunk baits to take quality 20- to 30-pound fish. Pilchards are easily gotten via cast nets tossed around marina docks early in the morning or late in the afternoon, when the light is low.

In the northern Abacos, the best snapper fishing is found in areas where there is grass around coral heads.

After you've set up a good chum line, patience becomes the order of the day. Mutton snapper are curious animals; they may not bite on the first go-around but will usually come back for a second look. Normally it takes 20 to 30 minutes of chumming for the fish to bite. The bite begins with 2- to

Light-tackle anglers revel in the expansive flats of the Bahamas.

5-pounders, which are soon replaced by 10- to 20-pounders. Don't strike a fish as soon as you feel it pick up the bait. Count to 5 before setting the hook.

When fishing for yellowtail snapper, always use small pieces or strips of bait, and bury the hook in the bait. Good choices include shrimp, conch, and pilchards. For yellowtail, drift the bait back into the chum line with no leader and little or no weight, to spook the fish. Bahamian yellowtail average several pounds, and 5-pounders are sometimes caught here.

With so few landmarks and the water looking pretty much the same throughout the Bahamas, it can be difficult to pick a good spot to bottom-fish. Charts and a color fathometer can be helpful. Dive charts are better yet because they contain all the wrecks and ledges.

Berry Islands/Chub Cay

Chub Cay is part of the Berry Islands, a bank of small cays that is 20 miles long and situated at the northern end of the Tongue of the Ocean. A short distance from Andros and Nassau, it is 90 miles east of Bimini.

Chub Cay is one of the most prolific big-game fishing areas in the Bahamas. The term "grand slam" for capture of a sailfish, white marlin, and blue marlin in one day was coined at Chub, which remains one of the few places in the world where grand and even double grand slams are regularly caught. Although most blue marlin here are relatively small (75 to 250 pounds), there are plenty of them. Three-fish days are almost routine at Chub during the peak months of May and June. These are also the months most likely to produce a slam. The billfish season runs from March through August, with white marlin usually more abundant in the spring and blues more abundant afterward. June has produced blue marlin in the 700-pound range and is considered a prime month.

The unique features of this area of the Bahamas is evident when looking at a navigational chart. A dogleg-like alley of water comes from the Atlantic Ocean and runs south of Little Bahama Bank, through the Northeast Providence Channel. It turns southeasterly below Chub Cay and parallels Andros Island, running up onto Great Bahama Bank. This strip is called the Tongue of the Ocean.

An area known simply as "the pocket"—a V-shaped notch where the Tongue of the Ocean and the Northwest Channel converge—is Chub's billfishing mecca. The best action is along the contour, from Joulter Cay on the south to Rum Cay on the north end of the edge. To the south, Morgan's Bluff can be good for big fish. "Yellow bar," between the lighthouse at Chub Point and Number Cay, produces some of the island's biggest fish. This is understandable because the water drops off precipitously into a virtual abyss a few yards from the reef.

Southeast breezes, which blow the bait into the pocket—where it gets trapped in the corner—are best for blue marlin. West, southwest, and northwest winds bringing dirty water are not conducive to good fishing.

Most anglers troll high-speed lures and rigged natural baits like 10-inch mullet, ballyhoo, or Spanish mackerel. They work from deep to shallow, back and forth across the edge, looking for color edges, weeds, and current eddies. The top of the outgoing tide, when the water is coming off the banks, brings small food that flyingfish and little tunny feed on. This is the ideal time for marlin here and elsewhere in the Bahamas. Fish also tend to bite best on the dark of the moon and up to four days before and after.

Some large dolphin are taken from April through June as well, although smaller specimens are readily caught in the winter months. The smaller dolphin hit trolled baits well, but they offer great sport on lighter casting tackle. Chub Cay produced some former line-class world-record dolphin, including a 76-pounder. Wahoo, sharks, barracuda, and other species round out the lineup, plus assorted reef species.

With most attention focused on big-game angling, the area's excellent flats fishing remains relatively unheeded. Bonefish are the mainstay, but permit are here as well. Although the majority of bonefish are small, some 8- to 10-pounders grace these waters, and larger specimens have been sighted. Ambergris Cay and the flats north of Chub are the prime locales, but it is often worth the trip over to Joulter, north of Andros, where large bonefish are a possibility.

Andros

Andros is the largest island (2,300 square miles) in the Bahamas, yet it is lightly populated and has only a few fishing camps. The eastern edge fronts extremely deep water, whereas the western edge fronts the shallows of the Great Bahama Bank. Andros is bisected, offering good angling in the middle reaches around the North and Middle Bights, along extensive flats and mangrove-lined swamps. Tidal passes or creeks, plus flats, exist on the east and west shores, and offer various species. At Andros the fishing is good no matter what kind of wind develops.

Among the large variety of fish available at Andros are small tarpon, ladyfish, barracuda, permit, various snapper and grouper, and blacktip sharks. The east-shore flats are more likely to harbor permit, probably because they edge deep water, although this species is also found elsewhere. The tidal passes on the east shore are best for tarpon, and the catch can be in the 60- to 70-pound range. These locales, referred to as "creeks," possess diverse opportunities on both shores, and light spinning tackle or flycasting tackle produces equally well.

Bonefish are the main quarry here, however, and they are both plentiful and large, sometimes traveling in vast schools. The best area for these fish is in the bights—the mangrove-studded cays and shores in the island's midsection—but good opportunities exist on the east and west sides as well. Bonefish at Andros average from 3 to 5 pounds, with larger fish to 10 pounds a common catch. Some 14- and 15-pounders have reportedly been caught, and still bigger fish have been seen. One of the known spots for big fish is Cabbage Creek, on the western edge and above the North Bight.

Middle Abacos/Treasure Cay/Boat Harbour

As a group of islands, the Bahamas are certainly well known and well visited. Certain islands are heavily trafficked by tourists and equally heavily publicized for their fishing opportunities. It stands to reason that a few less-publicized and/or out-of-the-way laces exist, including those that offer good but not heavily pressured fishing. Several such locales are in the northern Bahamas, in the central Abacos, and near Grand Bahama.

One such locale is Deep Water Cay, at the eastern end of Grand Bahama Island and separated from it by Rummer Creek. Found on few maps, this 2-mile-long island is reportedly home base for some 200 square miles of flats replete with various typical, finny creatures, but most especially bonefish and permit. The bonefish here average 5 pounds, but fish weighing up to 10 pounds are seen fairly often. Specimens of up to 14 pounds have been caught and are present year-round. Permit, too, roam the local waters, in sizes ranging from a few pounds to 25 pounds, and some up to 20 pounds heftier still. Burroughs Cay, a one-hour run, is a particularly good permit locale. Fly fishing is especially productive here.

Another destination situated in excellent bonefish country is Green Turtle Cay, midway along the ocean side of Great Abaco. Fish here are not large, but they are plentiful year-round, with good-size schools of bonefish spotted by wading or boating anglers. Poling in search of cruising fish, and stalking tailing feeders, are possible along flats devoid of people. A run up north to Little Abaco Island may be worthwhile (also from Deep Water Cay), where larger bonefish are sometimes found in the vicinity of Cooperstown and Fox Town.

Three miles across Abaco Bay from Green Turtle is another locale worthy of note, although not without regular patronage—mainly from the big-game crowd. This is Treasure Cay, which has a lot of small bonefish. The angler looking for a respite from the big water or hoping to get that first bonefish will find the skinny water near this island worth investigating.

All of these locales boast other flats species of note, as most Bahamian waters do, including barracuda, lemon sharks, blacktip sharks, and mutton snapper, as well as the usual assortment of bottom fish on the reefs adjacent to the flats.

Treasure Cay is the only one in this area, however, that has significant blue-water fishing. This part of the Abacos has the bottom structure and deep water necessary for great marlin fishing. The barrier reef just offshore drops quickly; only a few hundred yards east is the 100-fathom edge, and just beyond that, depths quickly reach 300 fathoms.

Local captains regard the week following or preceding the full moon to be best for marlin. While dark, clean blue water, current edges, and working birds are good signs, what you really want to look for when fishing for marlin here is bait down deep on sonar. Off Treasure Cay, that bait is likely to hold the small tuna that are the preferred forage of big blue marlin.

At Elbow Cay the island-hugging current makes its sweep offshore, a condition that contributes to tide boils and an ever-present bait supply. The depth at the tip of the point is 300 fathoms, but within a few feet it drops to more than 2,000 fathoms. A north current and wind are the most favorable conditions for targeting marlin and yellowfin tuna during the peak runs from April through June.

Boat Harbour routinely produces some of the largest blue marlin caught in the Bahamas. While blue and even white marlin action is consistent from spring to early fall, Boat Harbour is a good spot for dolphin, wahoo, and yellowfin tuna. Like Treasure Cay, deep water lies just offshore of the area's three natural inlets: Tillhoo Cut, North Bar Channel, and Man of War.

The best time to fish for marlin is when yellowfin tuna and dolphin are abundant, from March through June. A north-northeast wind is advantageous. Early in the season, marlin fishing is best in 300 to 900 feet of water; from spring through summer it's best in 1,000 to 6,000 feet.

Sportfishing boats sit ready in their berths at a yacht club in the Abacos.

Other Areas

Certainly, notable fishing opportunities exist in the southerly cays and islands of the Bahamas archipelago on the Atlantic side of the Great Bahama Bank, including Exuma, Long Island, Crooked Island, and Eleuthera. This is predominantly flats country fishing, although in some places good reef- and/or offshore fishing are available.

Eleuthera is farthest north and closest to Providence and is one of the southerly Out Islands known for big game. The northern end of this 100-mile-long island abuts the deep water of Northeast Providence Channel and is on the pathway of migrating billfish and tuna, so it merits attention from the trolling enthusiast. At the southern tip of Eleuthera, a ridge between that island and Cat Island to the south also provides trolling action.

Bottom fishing is particularly good for grouper here, and bonefishing is fair to good, depending on where one looks. Perhaps the most notable location for bones are the flats around Harbour Island, at the northeastern tip—where 5- to 7-pounders are possible and fair-size schools may be encountered—and St. George's Cay at the northwestern tip.

Moving south, Great Exuma has miles of small cays and flats that provide exciting bonefishing. According to local lore, the Exumas represent God's calendar: The 90-mile-long chain numbers exactly 365 islands, one for each day of the year. The Exumas are also green-water country—in other words, shallow. Thus, many people consider the Exumas to be the center of the bonefish universe. And at the heart of this shallow-water fishing mecca is the charming hamlet of George Town. Originally a sponge market, George Town has become the "in" spot for serious fly anglers the world over who come to stalk the gray ghost.

Overall, the Bahamas quite likely rank as the world's greatest bonefish habitat. In truth, all it takes to catch these fish is a shallow flat, which accurately describes the greatest part of the Exumas. Just about anywhere in the Bahamas there is superb bonefishing to be had from skiffs or by wading. In many places you won't see just a few tailing and rooting fish but, as in the case of the Exumas, schools upon schools of silvery shadows that keep coming in a seemingly endless parade. Some large bones are periodically encountered, but for the most part 3- to 5-pounders are the catch. Should bonefishing get too monotonous here, the reefs offer good deep jigging opportunities.

East-southeast of the Exumas, Long Island is one of the prettiest of the Bahamian Out Islands and a locale that has abundant bonefish and an opportunity for varied adventures. Narrow and 60 miles in length, Long Island can provide lee fishing when necessary. Bonefish, mostly small, range along the entire coast, and in large schools on 15 miles of easy-to-wade flats. Some bones up to 10 pounds cruise the shallows, and permit are a possibility. Long Island also offers good reef jigging for assorted species.

Still farther to the southeast, Crooked Island has seldom-explored bonefish flats, with the bonus of small tarpon. The latter are found up to 50 pounds, and the bonefish are on the small side but abundant. The flats in all of these areas also sport snapper, sharks, barracuda, the occasional permit, and the ever-present chance of spotting a huge school of silver streakers.

BAIL

An arm on a spinning reel, also known as a pickup bail, that gathers line for winding onto the spool. The bail must be opened to release line for casting, and is closed automatically or manually for line pickup and retrieval.

See: Spinning Tackle.

BAIT

(1) In the most strict, narrow, and accurate sense as used by anglers, the term bait refers to any natural or processed food that is used to catch fish; this is distinguished from a lure, which, through popular usage, has come to mean any man-made object that represents or imitates food.

Natural bait *(see)* is any live or dead organism that occurs in nature; examples include worms, crickets, assorted fish, shrimp, eels, leeches, frogs, fish eggs, squid, crabs, and clams. A review of this occurs separately.

Processed bait is food that does not occur naturally in aquatic environments; examples include bread, dough, cheese, cubed meat, seeds, and vegetables. Processed bait is often used when angling for coarse fish *(see),* and in association with chumming *(see),* and is reviewed in more detail in those entries and elsewhere *(see: float).*

Generally, food that is normally eaten by a particular fish is preferred by anglers as hooked bait for that fish, but on some occasions natural bait may include organisms that are rarely part of the diet of fish. A field mouse or a lemming, for example, is not an everyday food item for predatory freshwater fish, but these do occasionally occur in the water and are consumed by some species. These would represent an uncommon natural bait and one that, when in the water, attracts fish because of its movement. In a much different vein, a piece of chicken liver, which falls under the category of processed baits, is often an effective bait for catfish, which are attracted to it through their senses of smell and touch.

(2) In a broad sense, the term "bait" is used with reference to any object—natural, processed, and artificial—that is used to catch fish. In a confusing twist of language, the application of the word "bait" to lures (which in essence are "artificial baits") is primarily a U.S. phenomenon, where many types of lures are widely used in freshwater. Thus, the terms crankbait, spinnerbait, jerkbait, and so forth have become standards for very specific types of lures, and many anglers (especially those who fish for bass) refer to a lure as a "bait" even though it is strictly artificial. Lures *(see)* are reviewed elsewhere.

B

B

BAIT-AND-SWITCH

A saltwater angling tactic in which a trolled hookless teaser (usually an offshore lure or daisy chain) that has attracted a fish (usually a billfish) is quickly removed from the water while a hooked lure, bait, or fly is simultaneously presented. The substitute offering is usually one that—either because of its size or because of the light tackle being employed—could not be trolled at high speeds or would not create enough attraction to bring the fish in. The teaser does the work of bringing the fish close to the real lure. Bait-and-switch is used in particular with very light tackle, and for casting a lure or fly to a big-game fish.

See: Big-Game Tackle; Trolling Lures, Saltwater.

BAIT BUCKET

A round container to hold live bait; also, in saltwater, a term for a milk crate or chum pot *(see)* used for holding chum *(see)* in the water alongside the boat. Bait buckets may hold fish, frogs, crickets, eels, crayfish, or other items; large buckets used for containing baitfish may be equipped with portable aerators for oxygenating the water. For baitfish, common buckets are made of steel or plastic and have a perforated insert pail that contains the bait and can be easily removed to facilitate water changing; another common version is a floating plastic bucket with a spring-loaded door, which is kept in the water when the boat is at rest or when it is slowly trolled.

See: Bait Container.

BAITCASTING TACKLE

Baitcasting tackle is a type of light- to medium-light multipurpose fishing equipment characterized by a reel with a revolving spool that turns to dispense and retrieve line. The spool rotates like sewing thread, with the line moving perpendicular to the spool axis.

This equipment is related in general characteristics to conventional tackle *(see)*, which sports a larger revolving spool reel, has a greater ability to deal with strong fish, and holds more line. It is distinctive from spinning tackle *(see)* and spincasting tackle *(see)*, which both feature a stationary spool around which line is wound.

Baitcasting tackle ranks first in sales revenue in North America, where it is widely used, and third in sales volume (behind spincasting and spinning tackle), but it is not commonplace outside North America. Baitcasting reels are sometimes called levelwinds because all such reels have a feature that automatically distributes the line evenly across the spool as it is retrieved.

This tackle is not relegated to use with natural bait *(see)*, as its name implies; it can be used with natural bait and for trolling, but it is most likely to be employed in casting artificial lures. It can be used for light saltwater activity but is principally a freshwater fishing tool. It is especially popular in angling for largemouth bass and is widely used for most of the major species when fishing with heavier lures and terminal rigs.

Baitcasting reels predate spinning and spincasting reels. They were once notorious for being difficult to learn to use without incurring a backlash, or spool overrun, in which a bird's nest of line had to be painstakingly untangled. As a result, anglers flocked to the easier to use stationary spool products when they were introduced in the 1940s and 50s. Modern reels have greatly reduced this backlash problem. Meanwhile, the advantages of baitcasting tackle continue to be accurate lure placement in casting, superior cranking power, and control over strong-fighting fish.

Today, this equipment is vastly different, more angler-friendly, and compatible with diverse fishing methods. Appropriate baitcasting tackle may be used for virtually all fishing methods, including casting, trolling, and fishing with bait.

Reels

As a revolving spool product, the baitcasting reel has the same origins as the conventional revolving spool reel. The development of both has been intertwined since the nineteenth century. Baitcasting reels originated in Kentucky between 1800 and 1810, when a single-action revolving-spool reel (essentially a fly reel) was the only reel available for sportfishing, and anglers used only natural bait or artificial flies. The single-action reel was used to store and retrieve line and had no casting function. To present natural baits at any distance, anglers stripped an appropriate length of line off a single-action reel and either looped the line and laid it aside or coiled it in the noncasting hand. Using a wooden rod, they made a sideways motion to propel the bait and carry the stripped-off line. This was done because the bait and any weights used could not overcome the inertia of the single-action spool.

Between 1800 and 1810, George Snyder, a Kentucky watchmaker, and reputedly president of the Bourbon Angling Club, invented a reel with a delicate spool that would pay out line during the cast and that revolved several times for each turn of the crank handle. Thus was born the multiple-action reel, to be called the multiplier or multiplying reel, as well as a spool capable of dispensing line during a cast. The line of that day was raw silk, and there were no lures; for decades multiplying reels were small and because they were exclusively used for tossing natural baits, they were called baitcasting reels.

For most of the nineteenth century, such reels were made by hand. Various modifications and improvements were made, including the addition of a mechanism to distribute line evenly on the spool (called levelwind), better gears, and the addition of external drag. What had developed as a tool for freshwater fishing, primarily for bass, became available in large sizes for situations where greater line capacity and mechanical strength was needed.

These reels were soon used for really powerful fish in saltwater. The lack of an internal drag mechanism, however, meant the fish didn't have to work for the line it took off. To offset this, anglers applied pressure to the reel spool with their thumbs (which was ineffective for large fish and sometimes painful to the angler) or with a leather thumb pad attached to the reel frame.

William C. Boschen, a member of the legendary Catalina Tuna Club of California, is credited with originating the concept of the first internal star drag on revolving spool reels, a handy threaded knob adjustment that internally regulated spool pressure. A prototype of a reel with such a device was reportedly made for Boschen by Brooklyn, New York, reel manufacturer Julius Vom Hofe. Boschen used it to catch the first broadbill swordfish (358 pounds) ever taken on sporting rod and reel. That catch was made in the summer of 1913 off Catalina Island Later versions of this reel were named B-Ocean.

This product was the predecessor of modern revolving-spool reels. The star drag mechanism provided an internal friction adjustment mechanism, or brake, that provided greater resistance against strong fish and slowed the rate of line being pulled off the reel. This mechanism was incorporated in all types and sizes of revolving-spool reels in later years. Today all conventional or baitcasting reels feature a star drag. A baitcasting reel is essentially a small revolving-spool reel with a levelwind line-guiding mechanism and star-spoked wheel drag adjustment.

The largest baitcasting reel is about the size of the smallest conventional reel. Most modern baitcasting reels are used primarily for cast-and-retrieve angling (with lures rather than natural bait) and are likely to be fished with heavier lures and weights than spinning or spincasting reels. They're all suitable for casting, but the larger models are not comfortable for continuous casting. Some light models, however, are used with very light lines and lures, some heavier and large-capacity models are used in very demanding situations, and trolling and baitfishing are eminently feasible in addition to casting.

Gears, cast control, and drag are the most critical components of baitcasting reels. The cast control and gears are especially important because they significantly affect casting and retrieving functions. The main problem with a baitcasting reel is that, when casting, it is tough for the user to control the movement of the spool making it difficult to avoid a backlash. When control is mastered, however, the angler can be extremely accurate when casting with this equipment. Gears are of special concern when it comes to line recovery and cranking power. Many baitcasting reel users seldom use the drag feature; others, use it only occasionally, but when they do use it, it is important to them. Drag tension is not easily or readily adjustable to known levels, how-ever, during the fight of an especially strong fish, a weakness that is seldom a problem for anglers who know how to use their tackle well.

General Operation

Baitcasting tackle basically works like all tackle except flycasting: A weighted object at the end of the line pulls line from the spool. The spool of a baitcasting reel revolves as line pays out during the cast and as it is retrieved when the handle is turned. When the gears are disengaged and line is dispensed from the reel, a backlash, or spool overrun, can occur when the revolving spool turns faster than the line is leaving the spool. Applying light pressure to the spool can prevent this.

The baitcasting reel has a spool release clutch in the form of a button or bar that activates or deactivates the gears; this takes the reel into or out of freespool. With the reel on top of the rod handle and facing toward the angler, the rod-holding hand's thumb is placed on the spool to keep the line in check, and the free hand is used to depress the spool release, which disengages the gears and puts the reel in freespool. When thumb pressure is relaxed, line flows off the spool and out through the rod guides, carried by the weight of the object at the end of the line.

A few baitcasting reels (wide-spool versions) feature a click ratchet that signals when line is being taken off the reel; this can be used when a reel is not handheld or when it is left unattended. To retrieve line, the gears are engaged by turning the handle forward, which winds line onto the reel. A levelwind mechanism automatically distributes it back and forth across the spool.

Every baitcasting reel has an adjustable drag mechanism, which is activated by turning a star wheel on the drive gear. This is located on the sideplate under the handle. The drag tension is set

The components of a Daiwa baitcasting reel and their interrelationship are evident in this composite image.

to the desirable level at the beginning of each day's fishing and relaxed at the end of the day.

These are the basic elements of operating a baitcasting reel. Some models have cast control and anti-reverse features; the size of the spool, the materials used, and the designed application of each product are also relevant.

Casting/Line Release Features

Controlling the flow of line off the spool is an important and basic element of use in all baitcasting reels and in all means of fishing.

Freespool. Disengaging the gears of a revolving spool reel so that its spool can freely turn backward and dispense line is known as putting the reel into freespool. When using a baitcasting reel, the angler simply depresses the line release clutch, which is also known as the freespool switch and is in the form of a button or bar. When the clutch is depressed, the pinion gear is disengaged from the spindle, which it drives. The reel is then in freespool; the gears are still intact but not the drive mechanism.

To permit quick, one-handed operation, the clutch is conveniently placed on the front (facing the angler) of most reels. This may be a contoured bar over the spool that bridges the sidewalls, or a switch that is recessed in the sidewall and permits the thumb to slide onto the spool. On some new reels and many older ones, the clutch is a button that is located away from the spool; you hold the reel in one hand and use your noncasting hand to depress the button.

A clutch bar (also called a thumb bar) is generally more convenient than a recessed switch. A bar gives you constant control of the spool because the tip of your thumb is on the spool while the heel of your thumb pushes the bar down. As long as the bar is properly situated, you only have a slight chance of accidentally hitting it and inadvertently putting the reel into freespool, which could result in disaster while playing a hard-fighting fish. (Incidentally, baitcasting reel manufacturers report that premature engagement of the clutch while the spool is still rotating at high speed during a cast is the single most damaging action to these reels.) A large-capacity reel that might be used for big fish and for trolling more often than for casting, and one where you might apply thumb pressure as extra drag, is better suited, however, to a side button.

When you depress the clutch of some reels, the levelwind line guide moves back and forth as line goes out. Others have a curtain line guide made of two bars that separate; this is no longer common, as it is prone to malfunction. The line guide of most reels remains in position until the handle is turned.

Spool revolution. When putting the reel into freespool, you must apply finger pressure to the spool to prevent line from paying out prematurely or haphazardly. Without this pressure, and assuming that a lure or weighted bait is tied to the end of the line, the weight at the end of the line would cause the spool to turn the moment the reel was placed into the freespool position, which could cause an instant backlash on the spool.

It is therefore necessary to place the thumb of the rod-holding hand on the spool so the spool can't turn; this is done instantaneously when the reel has a thumb bar or recessed switch because the thumb of the casting hand contacts the spool as it depresses this clutch. You must use both hands if the reel has a clutch button, keeping the thumb of the non-casting hand on the spool while you press the button with your other hand. The line can then be released by easing the tension or, in some instances, by casting.

Spool braking/control. When releasing line without casting, thumb pressure is lessened on the spool to pay line out at a controlled rate; the objective is to let out the desired amount of line at a rate that doesn't make the spool turn so fast that it causes a backlash. This is important because a revolving spool can gather speed quickly and an uncontrolled spool can lead to a serious backlash in an instant. The backlash not only impedes immediate fishing effort because of the time required to undo it, but can also cause damage to the line.

This situation becomes even more acute when you use the reel for casting because the activity of casting builds up greater spool speed (spool speed in casting has been measured as high as 20,000 rpms). Casting requires very precise control of the revolving spool. In either application, it is necessary to brake the spool to slow its speed. The three means of controlling the spool when line is flowing off the reel during casting are mechanical, magnetic, and manual.

Manual spool braking is done by applying thumb pressure to the moving spool when casting. This is an action learned through trial and error and perfected with experience; it requires the application of different degrees of braking tension, depending on the weights on the line, distances being cast, and types of rods and reels being used. Although you can learn to use a baitcasting reel without applying thumb pressure, you cannot fish without some manual control all the time and with all reels, so it is something you must learn.

Mechanical spool braking is done by using centrifugal brakes (also called weights) to apply pressure to the moving spool. Reels with centrifugal brakes have blocks that must be engaged to effect spool braking. These blocks are usually found on the left side of the reel. They are accessed on some reels by removing the entire sideplate and on others by unlocking a quick-release bayonet cover. On the spindle of the spool is a cross pin with a centrifugal brake block on either side (some reels have a wheel-spoke system with four to six brake blocks). To be employed, these brake blocks must be moved out toward the spool flange and snapped into a notch. In this position they rub against the flange and apply centrifugal pressure to slow the spool and help avoid a backlash. The harder you cast (greater spool rpms), the harder the brakes work.

The centrifugal braking system varies with different products and manufacturers. Accessing this area is easy with most reels. Read the instructions that come with the product because some are supplied new with the brakes in the off position and some with the brakes in the on position.

These centrifugal brakes are used in conjunction with operating the spool tension knob. This device is a knurled knob or bearing cap on the sideplate where the handle is located, and it is adjusted by hand. Tightening this device puts tension on the spindle of the spool, but it is not purely a spool-braking device, as many people think. Its purpose is to control excessive end play, or sideways movement, of the spool, and its value in controlling spool braking is limited.

If the spool tension on a reel is too loose, there will be too much movement in the spool, and line could get behind it. If the engineering mechanics of a reel are correct, line should not get behind the spool; you should be able to loosen the spool tension knob completely and, although there will be excessive end play, you will not be able to pull the flange of the spool out of the centering ring of the sideplate.

As the spool tension knob on baitcasting reels is tightened, an interior wear plate rubs against the spool spindle. Tightening is usually accomplished in a clockwise motion, and the knob should be adjusted so that there is barely any perceptible sideways motion of the spool. Place your thumb on the middle of the spool and move it back and forth to see if you can move the spool. For general use, adjust the spool tension to a tight but not immovable tolerance.

The sideplate of this Marado baitcasting reel shows the spool tension control knob and the switch for a click ratchet, the latter being found on only a minority of such reels.

Spool tension needs to be adjusted according to the weight of the object being cast; in theory, if you switch frequently to lures of different weights, you should reset the tension each time. To do this when the reel is on the rod with line attached to a lure, hold the rod out and dangle a lure from the tip, place your thumb on the spool, and put the reel into freespool. Decrease thumb pressure and allow the lure to fall. Adjust the spool tension knob so the lure slowly descends to the ground when thumb pressure is relaxed. The spool should stop revolving at the instant the lure hits the ground. For continued long-distance casting, you may want to decrease spool tension and (if your thumb is well educated) put the centrifugal brake blocks in the off position.

Experienced casters tighten or loosen the adjustment knob, and employ this level of control in conjunction with an educated thumb. Newcomers to a baitcasting reel should start with a tighter adjustment at the outset to provide some assistance with spool braking, or they will be picking backlashes out with every cast. This tension can be gradually lightened as you become more proficient with thumb control.

Magnetic spool braking is a completely different system. It is common on the majority of reels from many manufacturers. Magnetic spool braking systems use a magnetic field to place variable degrees of force on the spool. A series of small disklike magnets are located in the interior of the sideplate opposite the handle. When an exterior magnetic control knob is turned, it changes the distance of the magnets from the metal spool; when the magnets are closer, more force is applied, and when they are more distant, less force is applied. Lower settings enable longer distance casts; higher settings help prevent backlash under adverse conditions, such as when casting into the wind.

While these systems are touted as "eliminating backlash," they are not foolproof, and if magnetic spool braking reels aren't used correctly, they will still backlash. They are, however, excellent for those who are learning to cast with this equipment when the proper settings are selected. Beginners should use a higher tension setting when they start; this will cut down on the distance achieved, but it is better to cast a shorter distance at first than to be frustrated by backlashes. With a little practice you can ease off on the tension and keep learning until you become comfortable with less tension.

Some of the newest magnetic spool control systems are very sophisticated and have the ability to alter magnetic force according to the speed of the spool during the cast. This is different from most systems and is significant because spool speeds vary from extremely high rpms at the outset to lower rpms near the end of the cast. Variable-force mag-

B

Removing the sideplate of this Zebco Quantum baitcasting reel allows spool changing and reveals the spool control magnets.

netic systems automatically apply pressure according to the speed of the spool, which is essentially what an educated thumb is supposed to do. This type of system actually allows a spool to maintain its speed longer, meaning that it will result in longer casts. While a longer cast sounds good, the best benefit of this system is avoiding backlash without sacrificing accuracy. Thus, with some practice and experience, and with proper setting of the magnetic spool control on better reels with a variable magnetic control system, it is possible, strictly by using the magnetic control, to cast without having a backlash.

It should be noted, however, that no matter how sophisticated these magnetic anti-backlash systems are, many expert anglers are very comfortable with, and continue to use, baitcasting reels without this feature. The late 1990s saw a resurgence in high-end premium baitcasting reels, very few of which had a magnetic spool control feature. If you only use a baitcasting reel for noncasting activities, you don't need magnetic spool braking; most saltwater anglers who use baitcasting tackle do not use reels with magnetic controls because of the likelihood of corrosion.

Incidentally, baitcasting reels usually do not have both centrifugal and magnetic cast control systems. It's one or the other. In both systems, however, you still use the spool tension adjustment in conjunction with the centrifugal or magnetic spool braking.

To set up a reel with magnetic spool control for casting, begin by adjusting the spool tension knob as previously detailed, starting with the magnetic control at the lowest setting. Once the mechanical tension knob is adjusted, turn the magnetic setting from zero to an appropriate level, make a few medium-intensity casts, and adjust the magnetic control up or down as necessary before you start serious casting. Slight thumb pressure on the spool is advisable when starting with low magnetic control, but you can apply less pressure than you would if using only mechanical braking. Complete beginners should set the magnets at maximum level until they get proficient at releasing the lure and applying thumb pressure.

A more detailed explanation of the entire backlash issue, especially the phenomenon that causes it, is contained later in this entry.

Flipping feature. Many baitcasting reels have a selectable switch that automatically engages the pinion. This is known as the flipping switch because it is primarily used in this method of bass fishing, which requires specialized short-distance casts *(see: flipping)*. It can also be employed, however, by anglers who use bait and need to let a fish run when it takes the bait offering.

With this switch on, the reel is out of gear only when the thumb is kept on the freespool bar. When you release thumb pressure, the reel is instantly in gear. The advantage is that you don't have to turn the handle to put the reel in gear. Because the reel is already in gear when a fish takes or when the line tightens, no time is wasted setting the hook. The kind of fishing and the techniques you use really determine whether this feature is necessary.

Retrieving/Line Recovery Features

Line pickup. To be in a position to set the hook and to return line to the spool, some drag tension must be established and the gears must be engaged. Line is retrieved by rotating the handle, which drops the pinion gear onto the spindle and engages the drive mechanism. As long as there is some drag tension in effect, turning the handle will revolve the spool, bringing line onto it.

Left/right retrieve. The great majority of baitcasting reels are set up only for right-handed retrieve and are not convertible. Although right- and left-handed anglers have been using this system for many decades, it favors the minority of people who are left-handed. A few reels are available with left-handed retrieve, but these are not nearly as accepted in the marketplace as right-retrieve reels.

Despite the fact that right-handed anglers have become accustomed to fishing backward with baitcasting reels, it is theoretically beneficial for people who are right-handed to reel with their left hand and for lefties to reel with their right hand, so that the dominant hand is the one that holds the rod and is used to play the fish or direct the retrieve. This is especially significant when frequent casting is involved, as is usually the case with baitcasting tackle. The dominant hand is used to cast the rod, so there is no need after casting to take further action to start using the reel; the other hand is immediately placed on the reel handle grip and turns the handle. This lack of time delay is important in some fishing situations.

Making a well-executed cast and getting the lure precisely on target, for example, is often not the end of the casting action. When angling in some places and using lures that sink, you have to be able to start fishing them the instant they hit the water, or they'll get tangled or snagged on objects in the water. A spinnerbait worked very shallow is an example of a lure that should "hit the ground running."

Left-handed baitcasters who retrieve with their right hand and right-handed baitcasters who retrieve with their left hand will have little trouble if they thumb the spool properly and get cranking the instant the lure touches down. Such anglers are in the minority, though; most users both cast with their right hand and retrieve with their right hand, meaning that they switch the rod and reel from right to left hand at some point.

Most good casters become adept at making this transfer while the lure is in flight, taking their right thumb off the spool just as the lure touches the water and then quickly grabbing the reel handle and cranking before the lure has a chance to get deep. This takes fine timing and is an oft-overlooked aspect of baitcasting technique. You must master this (or learn to cast with your other hand) in order to effect the best possible retrieve under certain circumstances.

As mentioned, there are some left-retrieve baitcasting reels. Most of these are flip-flopped copies of right-retrieve reels, although at least one company has recently produced a distinctive left-retrieve reel that has a rearward handle (instead of forward on all other reels) and a top-mounted line release that are meant to reduce the awkwardness of right-handed casting and left-handed reeling.

If you are new to baitcasting and are right-handed, you should consider getting a left-retrieve reel because you don't have old habits to break. If you're already accustomed to casting a spinning outfit with your right hand and reeling with the left, this is the same principle. Many new right-handed baitcasters have found it worthwhile to start out with a left-retrieve reel and continue with it (left-handed anglers can simply use the many standard right-retrieve reels).

Many experienced right-handed baitcasting users, who are already used to reeling right-handed, have found it difficult to make the transition to left-retrieve reels, however, especially when fishing with various outfits during a day. From a practical usage standpoint, owning both right- and left-retrieve baitcasting reels becomes more gear-intensive than most people like or can afford. The obvious answer is a convertible reel, but none are presently available.

Line winding/levelwind. Line is wound directly onto the spool of a baitcasting reel, but it is not necessary to manually level or disperse that line across the spool. All baitcasting reels have a mechanism known as a levelwind that automatically disperses line evenly across the spool. The levelwind may be gear-driven by the spool or by the main gear; it turns whenever the spool revolves, both forward and backward. It is located in a carriage that spans both sides of the reel. Inside is a nylon idler gear that turns a worm gear and catches a pawl that moves the line guide back and forth across the spool to distribute the line evenly, which helps eliminate line buildup.

Most winding lays line on the spool evenly in side-by-side wraps, but some reels use a cross-wrapping wind. The cross wrap helps with some lines, especially slick thin-diameter microfilaments, which have a tendency to dig deep into side-by-side wraps when subjected to severe tension.

Virtually all mass-produced baitcasting reels have featured a levelwind mechanism for many years. Only competitive tournament casters are likely to have a small revolving-spool reel without a levelwind, and that for distance events.

This brings up an interesting issue. The levelwind line guide contacts the line when it is cast and when it is recovered. Although a levelwind has great merit for constant cast-and-retrieve fishing, it has some drawbacks that most people do not realize. One of these is that it reduces casting distance. The reduction may be slight for the average angler, and is compensated for by the use of less resisting materials on the line guide. Levelwind line guides are made from many different materials. Some, and especially the old standards and large-spool models, have a long open metal guide; in others, the guide opening is narrow and made of ceramic, titanium, or aluminum oxide.

Line speeding off the spool on a cast contacts the spool by one of several methods. On a few baitcasting reels, the levelwind guide moves freely back and forth in its carriage when the line is outgoing (high friction); this is preferable to others where it does not move at all when line is outgoing or moves to a center position and stays there (both of which cause more friction when line comes off the edges of the spool).

The other drawback is that the carriage is prone to getting grit, dirt, and sand in it, which can hamper smooth use or cause the carriage to malfunction. Many saltwater anglers are skeptical of the levelwind and view it as a likely problem, if not because of sand then because of corrosion. Proper care and washdown of a reel should minimize this problem in good quality reels.

Gears. The most basic part of the operation of every reel is the gear set. In baitcasting reels, this is generally stronger and more efficient than that of a stationary or fixed-spool reel because the gear set operates on a parallel axis.

In a baitcasting reel, a large gear, the main or drive gear, engages a smaller gear, the pinion. The drive gear is linked to the reel handle, and the pinion gear connects to the spool. This system provides the multiplying gear ratio for ample line retrieval rates with a small spool and still delivers substantial cranking power. It also allows for the use of heavy lines.

Most baitcasting reels have pinion and main gears that are made from the same material, such as a hard brass. Some of the better quality baitcasting reels have dissimilar materials, such as a bronze pinion and a brass main gear. Very few have a stainless steel pinion gear and a bronze main gear (which is

In March of 1882, an estimated 1.4 billion tilefish were found dead on the Atlantic Ocean surface, covering an area 25 miles wide and 170 miles long.

B

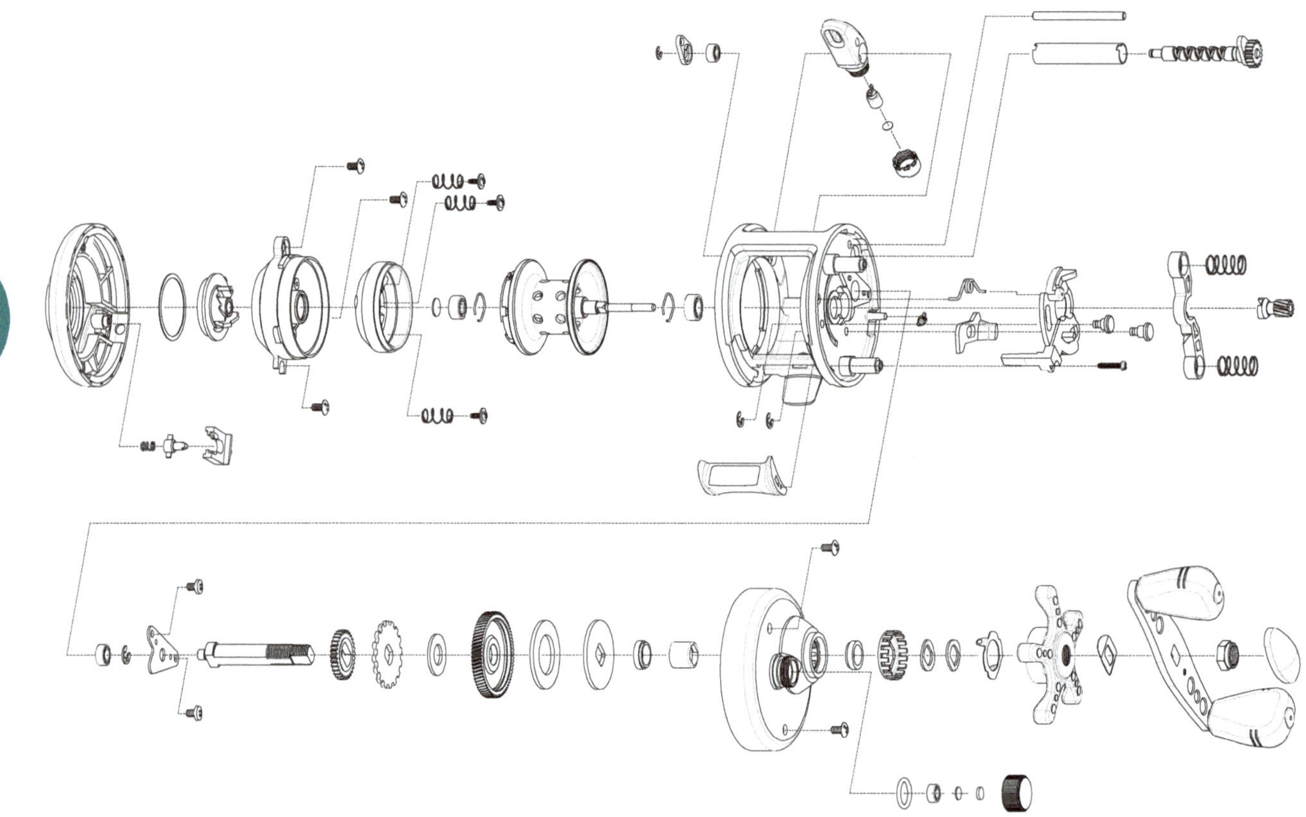

Shown are all the parts of a Quantum baitcasting reel, which includes a one-piece aluminum frame, centrifugal brake, three ball bearings, and continuous anti-reverse.

common on conventional reels). Unless one gear is slightly softer than the other, problems can arise.

In almost any simple gear set, one gear material should be different from the other. Use of the same materials tends to cold weld, or "gall" together; dissimilar metals nearly always offer the lowest coefficient of friction. The presence of an oil film helps to reduce friction. Use of dissimilar metals and an oil film ensures that gears run smoothly for a longer period of time.

The best situation is for the main drive gear material to be slightly softer than the pinion gear for wear characteristics, especially in reels that are used often for demanding applications, and where the gear ratio is high. In a multiplier reel (such as a baitcasting or conventional reel), one tooth of the pinion gear contacts its mating teeth on the main gear the same number of times as the gear ratio. That is, in a 5:1 ratio reel, each tooth on the pinion gear is activated five times more often than its counterpart on the main gear. Therefore, it is subject to five times the wear and needs to be harder simply to survive. Use of harder materials on the pinion gears produces a hardness differential that favors the smaller diameter pinion gear and provides longer life.

Gears are made to work in a given way with respect to each other, so there must be a certain distance between the two to match up; otherwise the gears will feel tight. Naturally, the gear teeth must be machined as precisely as possible to assure smooth operation and long life. Some reels, especially those with a higher gear ratio, have helically milled gears. This means that each gear tooth is spiral or curved, rather than straight, on the gear circumference. Helical milling results in increased contact area, greater strength, a thicker cross section, and a high degree of inherent smoothness, particularly for smaller gear teeth. The major benefit is that, unlike straight-milled gears where only a single gear tooth is fully engaged at one time, helical gears allow at least partial engagement of several gear teeth at all times, spreading the load and potential wear. This is mainly an issue where the gear teeth are small, as is found on higher ratio models, and there is less surface to make contact.

The high-stress cranking that is experienced when using baitcasting reels with some methods of fishing (such as using hard-pulling lures and landing strong fish), requires a rigid support system, so that under great duress there is no flex to affect the inner workings of the reel. The use of heavy line, and cranking large fish in extreme conditions, can put tremendous stress on all components. Both the material and construction of the frame and shaft supports are what keep the gears precisely located and delivering long life.

Gear ratio. Because the drive gear is linked to the reel handle and the pinion gear is engaged with the spool, the basic numerical ratio of the drive and pinion gears in a baitcasting reel merely establishes the number of revolutions made by the spool per turn of the handle. That number is determined by counting the gear teeth on the larger drive gear and dividing that by the tooth count of the smaller pinion gear. In a gear set consisting of a 53-tooth drive gear and a 10-tooth pinion gear, the ratio is calculated at 5.3:1, because the pinion will turn 5.3 times for each full rotation of the drive gear.

Gear ratios are generally categorized as high (fast) or low (slow), but this is relative to the type of reel and application. Furthermore, the size of the spool may be such that a low gear ratio reel actually recovers more line per full turn of the handle than a high ratio reel with a smaller spool. Typical low gear ratios for a baitcasting reel are about 3.8:1, and typical high gear ratios are from 6:1 to 7:1; most high gear ratio baitcasting reels are between 6:1 and 6.3:1. If numerical ratio were the only factor of comparison, what is low or somewhat low for many baitcasting reels would be high for nearly all conventional reels. In a baitcasting reel, a high gear ratio may be preferable for cast-and-retrieve fishing with lures that do not pull hard, but a low (or at least lower) gear ratio reel is preferable for hard-pulling lures. What is gained in retrieve speed is lost in cranking power.

The higher the ratio, the greater the potential for stripping gears under severe strain. On a high gear ratio reel, the individual teeth become narrower because more teeth are fitted into a given area and they are weaker. An inexperienced angler is more likely to do damage on a high gear ratio reel when he puts the smaller gear teeth under a heavy load. Fishing with a high gear ratio reel requires using the rod a lot, pulling it back and then winding line onto the spool quickly on the downstroke. This is necessary because, with high gear ratio reels, the smaller tooth configuration does not have sufficient cranking strength. This is a factor in all reels but obviously of more concern with reels that get a heavy load.

Cranking power. Gear ratio and cranking power are inextricably linked in all reels, and most affect how easy or difficult it is to retrieve a heavy weight or an object that offers a lot of resistance. Reels that can easily handle a heavy load are said to have a lot of cranking power. There are various factors that affect this.

The length of the handle has a bearing because length is a factor in the amount of leverage you can put on the handle. The longer the handle, the more leverage, and the easier it is to retrieve a set load. If you make a handle longer, you reduce the force at the knob. It is essentially the same principle as having a long-handled wrench; it's easier to loosen nuts with a long-handled wrench than with a short-handled one. So a longer handle equates to greater power (although your hand and arm must describe a larger circle to operate the reel).

The gear set itself is also a big factor with regard to cranking power. If you have a baitcasting reel with a gear ratio of 3.8:1, then it's easier to retrieve a load because this is a low gear ratio. If you have a baitcasting reel with a gear ratio of 6.2:1, which is high, it's much more difficult to retrieve a load, although you get more speed. If you're retrieving something that offers very little resistance, the high gear ratio is okay. You need a lower gear ratio, however, for something that offers more resistance. Thus, the lowest gear ratio reels have the greatest cranking power, and the highest gear ratio reels have the least cranking power.

Naturally, there are times when you want the best of both extremes. Some baitcasting reels have two-speed operation: in essence, the ability to switch between a higher and a lower gear ratio. In these two-speed baitcasting reels, gears are changed by moving a knob or lever. Most people who use these wind up doing nearly all of their fishing with the high-speed mode (6:1) because the low speed (3.5:1) is just too slow for retrieving most lures.

Regardless of the gear ratio, the evaluation of a reel's ability to retrieve line should boil down to something engineers call Inches Per Turn of the handle, or IPT. This is the amount of line recovered per turn of the handle or, simply, line recovery, which is a better measurement of retrieval ability than gear ratio. Line recovery is determined by spool diameter, which is a key dimension for any reel and which sets the circumference of the line level on the spool and the amount of line wound onto the spool with each turn of the reel handle.

When the level of line on a spool is low, as it might be when a strong fish takes a lot of line, less line is recovered per turn of the handle than it would be when all of the line is on the spool. Similarly, the amount of line recovered per turn of the handle of a fully spooled 4:1 ratio reel that has a small spool is less than the amount of line recovered per turn of the handle of a fully spooled 4:1 ratio reel that has a large spool.

Thus, the amount of line recovered is the measurement an angler should be most interested in. Yet anglers cannot quickly determine line recovery when evaluating a reel they might purchase because specifications on the circumference of the spool are seldom provided on the reel or in the packaging materials. You may know, for example, that in a 4:1 ratio reel one revolution of the handle puts four wraps of line on the spool, but if you don't know how much line is gained with each complete wrap, you don't know the actual recovery. (In a reel that you own, of course, this can be determined by marking the line and then measuring it.)

For a greater discussion of this subject, *(see: gear ratio)*. Although most people have a notion that gear ratio is of primary importance in retrieval and some think that the higher the ratio the better, other factors are involved, and line recovery is a major one. Remember, however, that reels with

Wild freshwater fish with low levels of fat and calories include yellow perch, walleye, pickerel, and crappie; high levels belong to chinook salmon, rainbow trout, and lake trout.

a low gear ratio do better under heavier loads, whether those loads are due to the size of the fish or the type of equipment being used (heavy weights, deep-diving lures, and so on).

This issue is most critical in baitcasting reels that are used in hard or heavy duty applications. Chances are, the bigger the reel the more likely it is that a heavy load will be placed on it. The larger the reel, the more noticeable the effect of a high gear ratio, so you'll feel that load a lot more.

Handle. The length of the handle affects cranking power, so the distance from the center of the gear stud to which the handle is attached to the handle knob is a key element in retrieval. A long handle equals power, yet many people have the misconception that a long handle also equals speed— that the longer the handle, the faster it can travel. The opposite is true. The longer the handle, the greater distance the cranking hand must travel with each turn. The shorter the handle, the quicker it can be turned, but there's less power, so there's a trade-off either way. You can't get power and speed simultaneously. All baitcasting reels have dual-grip handles, which provide a counterbalancing effect and easy grabbing of the handle without having to look at it. A baitcasting reel grip or knob is mainly grasped with the fingertips and operated by wrist motion, and is not affected by the presence of a second handle knob. There are various styles of grips. Most have a contoured, textured, paddlelike surface with grooves, which is quite comfortable; many are round, which is traditional. The size of the knobs and the handle is often a problem for many people who have long fingers and large hands. The smaller baitcasting reels seem designed for small hands and are not comfortable in a large hand when used for a considerable period of time.

Ball bearings/bushings. Bearings and bushings provide a way to minimize friction on rotating shafts. Bushings don't spin as freely as ball or roller bearings, which are typically viewed as durable and reliable and a way to add rotational freeness to the retrieval system. A bushing can deliver as smooth a retrieve as a ball bearing under low load conditions, but under heavy loads, ball bearings are vastly smoother and more durable.

One to four stainless steel ball bearings are used on many baitcasting reels, primarily on both ends of the spool shaft and on the crankshaft. Some reels have only one ball bearing and a bushing on the end of the spool shaft. It is possible to have up to 11 ball bearings in a reel, including one on the cap area of the shaft, one on each end of the worm gear, and two on each handle knob. They are unnecessary in most of these places, however, and drive the cost of the reel up; the most that baitcasting reels have is six or seven ball bearings. The most noticeable value of ball bearings is the smooth operation of the spool. Ball bearings are, or should be, of the highest grade to provide the most benefits. For a more detailed review of ball bearings and bushings, *see:*

Six stainless steel ball and roller bearings from a premium baitcasting reel.

Reel, Fishing.

Warning click. Known simply as a click or clicker, this is a ratchet device that is primarily intended to let an angler know that line is going out. It is only found on a small number of baitcasting reels, usually the larger wide-spooled models.

The warning click is generally used when a rod and reel have been placed in a rod holder (for instance, when trolling or baitfishing) and is not handheld. In some situations, as when fishing with bait, the reel is placed in freespool with the warning click on so that, if a fish picks up the bait, the line is free to move with minimal resistance yet without risking a spool overrun. In other situations, such as when trolling, the gears are engaged and the warning click is employed so that it instantly alerts an angler (or mate or boat captain) to a strike and to the fact that a fish is on and taking line off the reel.

The click itself features a spring-loaded tongue that moves back and forth against ratchet teeth to make this sound. It is activated by moving a small off-center button on the sideplate (usually the left sideplate). The click is intended for part-time rather than full-time use, and the click button should be disengaged when retrieving. Continued use of the click causes premature ratchet wear. Some people view leaving it on as a sign of an inexperienced angler, although some charter captains like it to be left on because the sound lets them know what a customer's fish is doing; when the clicking sound speeds up, for example, the fish is taking line. Some captains have even asked manufacturers for different types of sounds in the click. (This is especially prevalent in the Great Lakes, where the clicks are always used for trolling.)

Drag Features

The purpose of the drag function on any reel is to let line slip from the reel at varying pressures when force is applied to the line. It serves as a sort of clutch, or shock absorber, and is especially important when using light line, when playing large and strong species, and when fish make strong and sudden surges while being landed. If an angler never catches large fish, only uses heavy strength line, and is content to wind fish in, then it is conceivable that the drag will never be used.

Many people who use baitcasting tackle do not use the drag very often. Many bass anglers, who are major users of this tackle, seldom use the drag, or they tighten it down so that they cannot use it. This is not a good idea, however, as it defeats the purpose of this feature altogether. Those who do use the drag on baitcasting reels are anglers who generally fish with lighter strength line; those who catch big steelhead, salmon, catfish, pike, muskies, and stripers; and those who use baitcasting tackle for various saltwater species.

Catching large fish, which weigh more than the actual breaking strength of the line or that can apply extreme pressure on the tackle, requires some finesse rather than sheer strength. This means that the drag will come into play because if it doesn't, the force will exceed the strength of the line and the line will break.

When the drag comes into play, it allows the fish to continue applying force but at a pressure that is less than the breaking strength of the line. When the force reaches a certain level (usually a specific percentage of the line's breaking strength), a properly set drag mechanism turns the spool and allows line to slip from the reel under tension. In essence, this means that a fish can run instead of engage in a tug of war. The fish must work for the line it takes off the reel, however, which tires the fish and helps the angler subdue it.

Many people mistakenly think that they need to set the drag very tight for effective hook setting. When you have 20 yards of line out, and you have rod flex, line stretch, and the dampening effect of the water to contend with, you don't need very much drag force at the reel. You cannot exert the maximum pressure when you set the hook. When you set the drag pressure at or near maximum force, once the fish is close to the boat and less contribution is made by line stretch, rod flex, and water, having the drag locked down may mean that the line cannot absorb the sudden shock of a quick run, even from a fish whose weight is less than the breaking strength of the line. People are often amazed that a 15-pound fish can break 20-pound line, but that doesn't happen if the drag is set properly and the washers are allowed to slip freely when necessary.

In typical fishing with baitcasting reels, anglers set the drag at 25 to 30 percent of the breaking strength of their line. Some people measure this with a short length of line on a straight pull off the reel. Others measure it with line running through the rod guides and the rod flexed as it would be in fishing circumstances. Most people use the "feels good" method of establishing drag tension by pulling line off the reel and adjusting the star wheel until the tension feels right. The most precise way to measure drag tension is by using a reliable scale and attaching it to the line. No matter what method is used, the objective is to adjust the drag so that the line will not slip until the appropriate amount of tension is applied. Understanding how to use and set drag is one of the most important aspects of sportfishing; it is thoroughly reviewed in detail elsewhere *(see: conventional tackle; drag)*, so that information will not be repeated here.

It should be noted, however, that on baitcasting reels the drag is located on the main gear and is usually a multi-element system with washers that are keyed together to increase the working surface area.

This drag stack from a top-quality baitcasting reel has three friction washers interspersed between three metal washers, the latter keyed into the main gear and gear stud.

Different materials are used in the friction washers; a popular one in some better reels now is graphite-impregnated Teflon. Drag tension is increased or decreased by turning a drag star (radial-arm star wheel), which is located under the handle on the sideplate. The drag star threads onto the gear stud or drive gear, which is connected to the handle, so it rotates concurrently with the handle without affecting the setting.

Turning the drag star clockwise or forward increases tension; turning it counterclockwise or backward decreases tension. When spool friction exceeds the tension on the line, the reel handle turns the main gear and the spool, and allows line to be recovered. When tension on the line exceeds friction on the spool, the spool revolves against handle pressure, and line can be pulled off the spool. The handle is prevented from turning backward by a dog and ratchet, which is known as an anti-reverse.

This system eliminates the possibility of line twist due to turning the handle when line is flowing off the spool, which is a major contributor to severe line twist in fixed-spool reels. On a bait-casting reel, twist isn't possible if you're cranking the reel handle and the drag is slipping at the same time. There is no line twist unless it comes from the lure use or you put it on when the spool is filled.

The range of drag tension adjustment is somewhat more limited on baitcasting reels than spinning reels, although it looks like more because of the star wheel knob. With these products, it is often the case that a smooth drag and the ability to fully lock down the reel (so the spool cannot turn backward) are not compatible, although better baitcasting reels do have good drag systems with a wide range of adjustment.

Anti-Reverse Features

The anti-reverse component of reels is an element that restricts backward movement of the handle. In most baitcasting reels a dog and ratchet mechanism provides a variable amount of backward handle movement; this is a multi-stop anti-reverse. The amount of this movement is decided by the number of ratchets for the dog to catch. In some reels it is a one-way roller bearing that allows no backward movement and which is called continuous or infinite anti-reverse.

This feature is especially relevant to cast-and-retrieve applications and to some styles of bait-fishing, primarily because it is relative to how the reel operates when the forward-turning motion is stopped. There is a natural tendency to pull up on the handle when not reeling, whether to set the hook or to momentarily stop while retrieving. If there is considerable play in the handle and drive gear when the reel stops, the handle may actually turn backward slightly. This produces a feeling of sloppiness or instability, and too much backward movement of the handle may adversely affect hooksetting. Ideally, a reel used for casting should engage instantly and firmly. Many of the better baitcasting reels have a continuous anti-reverse that keeps the handle and drive gear from moving even the slightest bit backward.

The number of ratchets in the system is one factor that governs how quickly the drive gear engages in a reel with multi-stop anti-reverse. The ratchets are little stops for a dog; as you turn the handle, this part slides over a ramp, and when the dog stops moving, it slides backward and engages a ratchet. The greater the number of ratchets, the quicker it engages; 10 ratchets, for example, mean 10 stops per turn of the handle. More ratchets also mean finer teeth, which are easier to break or clog.

In theory, more ratchet stops could pose a strength problem because you're depending on more ratchets with less material backing to stop the force of the hookset. This seems as if it could be a problem when using low-stretch lines and when using line that is overmatched by strength for the reel. Fewer ratchet stops, however, may be worse because that provides perhaps an extra 4 or 5 inches of rod tip movement when you set the hook before you take up the slack and engage the dog. With a hard hookset using strong low-stretch line and a tight drag, you can develop a lot of force and strip the dog and ratchet system when there is this much rod tip movement.

In a trolling application, where baits or lures are always set out under a fair load, when you have a strike you are already in a position to respond without any backward movement of the handle regardless of the number of ratchets. So in this application there is no relevance. In a casting application, where it is undesirable to have backward travel of the handle when you set the hook, more ratchet stops are advantageous for quick hooksets. A one-way roller bearing, which provides continuous anti-reverse, however, is most desirable. Some baitcasting reels have an optional anti-reverse feature, which means that the anti-reverse can be disengaged so the handle and the spool can be turned either forward or backward. This is accomplished by moving a small spring-loaded lever on the sideplate (usually the right sideplate or handle sideplate). This may be referred to as a direct drive feature, although it is actually a mechanism for disengaging the anti-reverse.

This feature is often preferred for specific fishing applications when anglers want a direct feel of the line for strike detection, for instance, when they are drift fishing and putting the reel in and out of gear frequently, or when they are live-lining bait and want to let line out frequently to follow the movement of the bait. After casting, engage the gear by turning the handle, then disengage the anti-reverse. When a fish takes and runs off, flip the anti-reverse lever into the on position and set the hook. If you leave the anti-reverse disengaged, the reel handle will be free to move wildly backward as line comes off the spool, which could cause trouble. Make sure to keep your hand on the handle if you have the anti-reverse disengaged, or you'll have a runaway handle.

Other Features

Spool. Many people believe that narrower baitcasting spools are easier to cast and to attain distance with than wider ones, but this is a function of many reel elements and not an absolute determination. It is reasonable to believe that there is less friction on the line from the levelwind line guide during a cast because the line comes from less of a side angle when it's at the ends of the narrow spool. Narrow spools are smaller and also lighter, requiring less effort to get them moving, and they are very suitable for lightweight lures. Narrow spools also have less capacity, however, and when there is a lot of line out, it takes more work to recover line when the handle is turned. Wider spools also tend to be used with heavier lures, which provide more momentum in a cast, thus allowing for good distance, all other things being equal.

For a time there was a trend toward narrow V-shaped spools in baitcasting reels; very few of these are still produced because they tend to bunch the line, which impeded smooth outward line flow. Nearly all spools today are level from edge to edge, and capacity is determined by the width as well as the depth.

Many anglers do not need significant line capacity on a baitcasting reel, and most have more line capacity than the average caster needs, even with a thicker diameter line. Some hold just 100 yards of 10-pound test, but most hold about 150 yards of 12-pound line, and some large models hold more than 200 yards of 20-pound line. Naturally, this is relative to line diameter, which means a reel that holds 100 yards of conventional-diameter 10-pound line might also hold 100 yards of 17-pound line that has the diameter of a conventional 10-pound line *(see: line)*. Although not all reels have this feature, line capacity information, provided on the sideplate of many reels, is very helpful.

Incidentally, baitcasting reels are primarily used with 10- to 20-pound strength line. Some high-quality light models are suitable for use with 8-pound line and possibly with 6; some sturdier models are used with 25- to 40-pound line for special situations.

A recent trend is toward a shallower arbor on a wide baitcasting spool. The smaller depth means that the reel holds less line overall, but because these have less mass in the core region, they are lighter; this means it takes less effort to move the reel on a cast, so they cast very well. For use with light lures and special short-casting situations (bass anglers like this for pitching, *see*), this can be beneficial. Some spools are also perforated to decrease their weight. This also helps because, in general, a lighter spool requires less momentum to start turning, plus it doesn't have the inertia to keep it going, so it's easier to handle, especially for casting light lures.

Spools are primarily made of aluminum. Some of the best and higher priced reels have aircraft grade aluminum, and some of the lower end reels have graphite spools. Though lightweight, graphite spools are of dubious value for hard-core fishing with baitcasting reels. They are uncommon in conventional reels, which take much more punishment than the average baitcasting reel because they are frequently broken when subjected to extreme tension and the use of heavy line. A greater discussion about revolving-spool materials and properties is contained with the entry on conventional tackle *(see)*.

One other thing worth noting is that the spools of modern baitcasting reels are very easy to access for changing or to adjust the centrifugal brake shoes. Many reels now feature bayonet-style access to the spool; this is flush to the exterior sideplate that is opposite to the handle, and hands-down the quickest system for spool changing. Such a design is one of the best creations of manufacturers and eliminates the protruding finger-grip screw heads that exist on other reels. Actually, the majority of reels still feature relatively quick access via two or three screw heads that are located on the handle sideplate and which, when completely loosened, detach the entire opposite sideplate or (most commonly) the handle sideplate to provide spool access.

Because spool changing is not that common, most people never use this feature, although they may need it for easy access to the spool for adjusting the centrifugal brake. Rather than changing spools to use their outfit with different strength line (which means derigging and rerigging the same outfit), most anglers simply have multiple baitcasting outfits.

Frame. The weight, material, and construction of the frame can make a difference after many hours of use, and especially depending upon the severity of use in casting, retrieving, and playing fish.

The materials used in the frame and sideplates vary widely. They include one-piece forged aluminum spools on premium reels, as well as one-piece die-cast or machined aluminum and one-piece graphite models. One-piece frames provide superior strength and precision alignment of the spool and other components. One-piece aluminum frames are especially favored for heavy-duty applications; baitcasting reels used for lighter applications may have a multi-piece frame.

Multi-piece frames are also made of aluminum, graphite, and even plastic. Plastic frames are not durable enough for serious use. Graphite frames are generally adequate for most casting activities; graphite has weight and corrosion advantages over aluminum, but even the latest grades of graphite

A one-piece aluminum frame on baitcasting reels has strength and torque-free advantages, and provides the best possible gear alignment.

do not yet have the strength of properly manufactured aluminum, so it is not quite as resistant to torque or flexing. Thus, subjecting a graphite reel to a great deal of pressure could result in deterioration in the gears. This is why some reels have a graphite sideplate and an aluminum frame and spool; the weight of a reel with a multi-piece frame can be reduced if the sideplates are graphite, and these do not have much effect on overall strength. Only one sideplate on a reel has a one-piece frame; this is the handle sideplate and it is made of the same material as the frame.

All frames have a reel foot attached to them; this component sits in the reel seat of a rod and may be integral to the frame or riveted on. Riveting is less preferable because rivets can get loose and can't be tightened.

Ergonomics. The shape and weight of baitcasting reels is especially important because these products are either frequently or exclusively used for casting by many anglers. Baitcasting reels were once entirely round in design, but they are now ergonomic, with low profile and teardrop designs very common in addition to round models. Teardrop reels are especially favored by anglers who tend to palm the reel, so a smooth sideplate that cups neatly into the palm of the rod-holding hand is quite popular.

Although weight is a major concern of manufacturers, this is (or should be) subordinate to having strength and durability. The majority of baitcasting reels weigh between 9 and 12 ounces. Some are between 7 and 9 ounces and mini versions with plastic bodies may weigh less, while large-spool versions may weigh up to 21 ounces. Light weight can make a difference after many hours of use, but so can comfortable styling. A comfortable shape may be more important than overall weight, especially if just fractions of an ounce are involved. If you do not palm the reel when holding it, however, lower weight is probably preferable to shape.

Manufacturers would like to make lighter baitcasting reels, but have not completely figured out how to do it without making disadvantageous sacrifices and compromises. Furthermore, light and ultralight versions of these products have not caught on as well as larger versions, which dominate the market.

Cosmetics, or appearance, has nothing to do with function and doesn't have practical use implications. Handles do have a bearing on comfort and ease of use. Some people like bigger handles than are supplied by the manufacturers and some prefer smaller, and these can be changed. The other aspects of handles relative to speed and power were discussed previously.

Lastly, an overlooked item of convenience, or in many cases inconvenience, is that of threading line from the spool out the line guide or spooling it onto the reel for the first time. It's difficult to put line on many modern baitcasting reels because of the number of bars, narrowness of the spool area, and presence of a reel hood. Many hoods pop up to provide access to the spool for putting line on or for picking out a backlash, but these hoods are more of a nuisance than a help. Round reels with an open metal line guide and medium-width spool are the easiest to handle when putting line on, getting it through the line guide, and picking out a backlash.

Rods

As with most types of rods other than spinning and flycasting, baitcasting rods have guides that mount over the axis of the rod and are placed on top of it, with the reel sitting on top of the handle rather than under it. This arrangement, which is necessary because of the nature of baitcasting reels, is especially well suited to fighting and controlling a fish, as well as for retrieving lures. In a general sense, fighting fish is what this tackle does particularly well; therefore, since the load of a gamefish on the line applies both a crushing downward force on the guide ring and frame, and a simultaneous tendency to torque or twist the rod, guides have to be of top quality and properly spaced and placed.

The rings on baitcasting rod guides are smaller than they are on most other tackle because they don't have to accommodate large spirals of line coming from the reel when casting (as in spinning), the line is fairly close to the rod blank when it leaves the reel, and the line is not prone to twisting and coiling on baitcasting reels. Guides may be single- or double-foot versions, with the latter more likely to be used along the entire blank on heavy-action rods or just in the position of the first guide or guides (closest to the reel), and the former generally preferred because it improves rod action and slightly lessens the weight.

Guide rings on baitcasting rods have a smaller diameter than those on spinning rods; this is a double-foot guide.

Reels mount close to the handle in the reel seat, which makes it fairly comfortable to palm the reel and rod. They are secured in the seat with a locking foregrip that screws down on the reel foot or by a locking ring that screws up on the reel foot.

Baitcasting rod handles are straight or have a pistol grip design, the latter usually found on smaller models. All baitcasting rods that are used for casting have a trigger grip on the underside of the rod, opposite and at the lower end of the reel seat. When you hold the rod, this trigger grip rests under either the middle or ring finger. Rods designed for trolling, which have a long handle, usually do not have a trigger grip so they can fit onto rod holders.

Handle length and overall rod length vary widely according to application, ranging from $5^1/_2$-foot models to 9-footers for steelhead and salmon fishing. Most rods used for casting are in the 6- to $7^1/_2$-foot range.

Baitcasting rods are available in one- and two-piece models. Most of the better rods up to $7^1/_2$ feet long are one piece, although longer models may have a telescoping butt in which the upper section slides into the lower for storage. There are very few travel or pack models among baitcasting rods, but a few excellent ones exist in two-piece versions with a telescoping butt section.

Action, taper, and material construction vary considerably. Baitcasting rods are commonly made of graphite and a mix of graphite and other materials, and many models are specifically tailored to special uses and styles of fishing.

Unlike reels, many of the issues pertaining to baitcasting rods—functions, materials, and components—are similar to those of other rods; these are more fully detailed elsewhere *(see: rod, fishing).*

Using Baitcasting Tackle

Line. As mentioned, 10- through 20-pound line strengths are most commonly used with baitcast-

These G. Loomis rods exhibit typical baitcasting rod handles and cork grips.

ing tackle. Fishing line is not prespooled onto baitcasting reels, although when a reel is purchased from some tackle retailers, it may be spooled by the dealer with the brand and strength of line you desire using a line winding machine. Most people fill the reel with line themselves, primarily with nylon monofilament, but also with braided or fused microfilament lines. Line coiling is not much of an issue on revolving-spool reels, so suppleness may not be much of a factor in line selection. Most baitcasting reel users are especially concerned with abrasion resistance in their line, and in line diameter, especially since diameter affects the working of many lures.

Filling/refilling the spool. The various aspects of properly filling a reel spool are detailed elsewhere *(see: line)*. Putting line on a baitcasting reel spool is not complicated, but it should be done under tension. In brief, the spooling process entails mounting the reel on the rod and running line from a service spool through the rod guides beginning at the top of the rod, and then through the levelwind line guide of the reel. Tie the line to the arbor of the spool, snip off the tag end excess, and reel the line on under tension. It is important to avoid or at least minimize twisting of the line during the spooling process, as detailed elsewhere *(see: line)*. Fill the spool to within no more than $^{3}/_{16}$ inch of the lip.

Line twist. Line twist is not an inherent problem in baitcasting reels. With other types of tackle, twist is often caused when the angler turns the handle against a slipping drag. Twist isn't possible on a baitcasting reel if the handle is turning and the spool is simultaneously slipping. When the drag mechanism is activated on such a reel, the spool rotates and line unwinds in an untwisted manner. There is no line twist unless it comes from lure use or it is incurred through improper filling of the reel spool.

Matching and selecting. As with any type of fishing tackle, the issue of pairing the right reel to the right rod is an important one, but today it is a relatively easy one. Some baitcasting reels and rods are packaged in combination, but tackle retailers can match rods and reels for you. Usually, a reel is purchased separately from a rod. Matching these up used to be referred to as balancing, and properly paired outfits were referred to as "balanced tackle." This simply meant that the rod and reel felt right when used together; the outfit was not overly butt heavy due to a large reel paired with a lightweight rod, or tip heavy due to a small reel paired to a medium or heavy action rod.

Fishing rods are virtually all labeled by line classifications and by weight of objects to be used, which practically assures that you don't put a light-duty reel, for example, on a medium-heavy rod.

Baitcasting reels are occasionally classified according to specific use, or species of fish, but this is no absolute matter. Reels might be classified as high speed or heavy duty, but the exact definition of such categorizations can differ from one manufacturer to the next and, in any event, is determined by the line capacity, features, and components.

When selecting baitcasting tackle, as well as matching a rod and reel, you must take into consideration the applications for it. A beginning angler may be unsure what to select without any prior fishing experience. Guidance from a knowledgeable salesperson is very helpful; such a person is more likely to be found in a specialized store (a sporting goods dealer or bait and tackle shop); a knowledgeable salesperson will not be found with a mail-order supplier and seldom in a mass merchandise mart. Lacking such a person, or in addition, you might seek guidance from an acquaintance or relative who has experience with this type of equipment and some knowledge of the fishing that a beginner is likely to do.

In a general sense, selecting baitcasting tackle starts with a determination of the size of fish that you will likely catch and evaluating the conditions under which you'll be fishing. The larger and stronger the fish, the stronger the tackle necessary for beginners, until you get the experience to use lighter gear. Fishing where there are a lot of obstructions usually requires medium or heavy grades of this type of tackle. Most selection starts with a determination of the line strength necessary for the conditions, and having the rod and reel appropriate for this. You should also pay attention to line capacity so that you have an appropriate amount of line on the reel for the application (this is especially relevant where trolling is done).

Holding the rod and reel. This issue was detailed previously when reviewing the right- and left-retrieve features of baitcasting reels. When casting, anglers must keep their thumb on the reel spool and control the spool revolutions; their casting hand is positioned around the handle so that the index or middle finger simultaneously grabs the finger knob at the back of the handle. The palm may or may not cradle the sideplate of the reel depending upon user preference.

When retrieving, the same grip is made with the rod-holding hand (which may be the noncasting hand). Some people cast with two hands, in which case the hand that does not operate the reel is wrapped around the lower butt of the rod and used for leverage.

Many baitcasting outfits are held by palming the reel, with the fingers wrapped around the trigger grip underneath the rod handle. Another method is to move the hand slightly toward the butt, with most of it cradling the rod handle, although still with fingers wrapped around the trigger grip.

Casting technique. How to cast with baitcasting tackle is described in detail in a separate entry *(see: casting),* but it's worth reviewing a few key points here.

Before you cast, you must make sure that the drag control has been properly set, that the spool tension knob has been adjusted, and that the centrifugal or mechanical spool control has been set as applicable.

Many anglers attempt to use baitcasting gear without realizing that you don't cast it with the reel facing you as it rests atop the rod handle. Instead, do this: Depress the freespool button or bar and, with casting thumb on the spool, turn the reel sideways so the sideplate is facing you. Your wrist will be in the same position as if you were writing with a pen or tossing a dart. It stays this way throughout the cast. Release thumb pressure on the spool as the rod arcs forward, and you're in business.

If you lob or toss a lure with baitcasting gear, you're not really casting and you are inviting backlash trouble, although a lob can be desirable when casting some forms of bait so it doesn't tear off the hook. You can make this soft type of presentation more readily with a spinning reel, but in baitcasting with lures, you really want to make the rod do what it was designed to do, and employ its arc and power in both backward and forward cast motions. You can only do that if you're confident about your ability to control backlashes.

Although perhaps half a dozen casts are employed in baitcasting, the basic overhead style is by far most common. Here, the wrist and forearm do the work. The cast should begin with the rod low and pointed toward the target. Bring the rod up crisply to a point slightly beyond vertical position, where flex in the rod tip will carry it back; then, without hesitating, start the forward motion sharply, releasing the lure roughly halfway between the rod's vertical and horizontal positions.

The entire casting action should be a smooth, flowing motion; you are doing more than just hauling back and heaving. Remember that your thumb takes over with delicate spool feathering the instant the lure is released, and that the thumb clamps down on the spool to stop spool rotation the moment the lure reaches its target. Realize, too, that casting technique may vary a bit depending on numerous factors, including length and action of rod, weight of lure, distance to be achieved, and nature of cover, and that some modifications and adjustments may be necessary accordingly.

Although the majority of people cast with one hand most of the time, some people use two hands, especially when learning and where large or heavy lures are used, wind is encountered, or long distances are necessary. Some people cast two-handed with all kinds of baitcasting equipment the majority of the time, except for short distances. The result is crisp low-trajectory casts, improved distance, and increased accuracy.

Maintenance and repair. Many people do very little, if anything, to maintain their baitcasting reels. This may be alright if the reel is only used occasionally. Common sense dictates that if the reel has any loose part (most likely a sideplate screw) it should be tightened as soon as you notice it, and that you should rinse any reel that has encountered sand, dirt, mud, or saltwater. Clean the reel as soon after use as possible, using a fine spray of freshwater rather than a hard stream. There is nothing wrong with dipping a reel in freshwater if you must cleanse it of dirt or sand; after all, it is likely to be exposed to wet and rainy conditions while fishing. Just don't make a habit of it, give the reel a chance to dry out completely, and keep it lubricated.

Details on reel maintenance are discussed elsewhere *(see: tackle—care/maintenance/repair).* Manufacturers recommend that infrequently used reels be cleaned and relubricated annually, and that reels that are used several times a week be attended to monthly. Periodic maintenance means lightly oiling and greasing accessible parts. Check with the manufacturer's literature on the specific lubricant to use because this differs with certain parts and among manufacturers. Some reel manufacturers, for example, do not recommend lubricating their drag washers. Some reels come with small oil or grease tubes, and these can be purchased from tackle suppliers or obtained from the manufacturer. A thorough cleaning requires disassembling most of the reel, scrubbing or rinsing most of the gunk from the parts, drying, and then relubricating and regreasing. Do not apply excessive grease or oil.

Backlash Demystified

A backlash on a baitcasting reel is the tangle of line that develops on a spool during an imperfectly executed cast. Backlashes range from minor tangles that are easily undone to major bird's nests that require a lot of time to unravel, if indeed they can be unraveled. The tendency of baitcasting reels to develop backlashes has intimidated anglers for many decades. The fact that a backlash often occurs at inopportune times, such as when the fish are turned on and are willing to hit any bait presented to them, makes their occurrence all the more troublesome.

Cause. In designing and developing fishing reels and their mechanisms, manufacturers have made detailed studies of the effect of, and, more importantly, the physical cause of, this phenomenon, which is sometimes referred to, either politely or scornfully, as a "professional overrun."

Through many years of research and the creation of a variety of mechanisms specifically intended to control backlashes, some reel manufacturers employed a variety of means to observe the birth and evolution of backlashes during a cast. A great deal of empirical research has been conducted to learn how to deal with this unique phenomenon.

One manufacturer of modern high-performance reels used stroboscopic-flash photography to attempt to track the way a backlash starts in order to design a foolproof means of eliminating it completely. Through this study, the researchers discovered that the precursor to even the slightest backlash was that the top loops of line on the rotating spool would rise up above the line level before traveling through the levelwind and rod guides. Depending on numerous other factors, the line could relax back down to the spool for a problem-free cast or progressively snarl into a tangled mess.

Another manufacturer employed high-speed motion photography to create a super-detailed, slow-motion examination of every stage in the development of some of the worst backlashes ever observed. This film record provided a motion analysis showing that several causes contribute to a backlash, with each offering its own possible design solution. The slow-motion film proved that one form of backlash, usually the worst, occurs almost instantly at the start of the cast.

Basically a backlash results from a differential between the speed of the line moving through the rod guides behind the cast lure and the amount of line being made available to follow the lure by the spin imparted to the reel spool.

Although the end result may be the same— a backlash—there is more than one kind and more than one cause. Backlashes usually occur at the beginning or at the end of the cast and are respectively called an overrun or an overflow. Overrun backlashes have many causes: a jerky casting technique; lures with a great deal of air resistance, which begin to slow down right from the start of the cast; a rod that is too stiff to properly load with the lure weight being cast; casting directly into the wind, which slows down the lure; a line with a high percent of stretch; multiple thumb contact with the spool during the cast; and overly heavy line. Fewer causes contribute to overflow backlashes, but they include: late spool release by the thumb, which produces a short downward cast and a fast lure impact; striking an object such as a tree branch or dock before the lure has reached it target; and, most commonly, allowing the lure to hit the water without thumb control to stop the spool.

In order to help avoid or solve each of these problems, you should know what constitutes a proper cast. Technically, the perfect cast consists of a dynamic blend of optimum energy management. With the reel in freespool and the thumb holding the spool stationary, energy is transmitted from the casters' arm muscles and wrist flex to the rod, causing the rod to move forward in the direction of the cast. This movement creates an inertial lag in the rod and lure that causes the rod to bend or load, thus storing the transmitted energy to cast the lure. At a point in the forward movement, thumb pressure on the spool is relaxed and arm movement is stopped, unloading the energy stored in the rod and allowing the lure to travel in an arc through the air to its target. When the spool is released, the built-up kinetic and centrifugal energy in the rod and lure is translated to rotational energy in the spool, which suddenly begins to spin as a result of the fast initial lure movement. Spool spin releases the line, which travels through the line guides and follows the flight of the lure.

This spool spin is the critical factor in causing or preventing a backlash. Under ideal conditions, the spin imparted presents just enough line from the spool to follow the lure without creating any drag as it travels. It is almost as if a "zero gravity" effect is created; the line on the spool neither pushes nor drags the lure but merely appears behind it as a link to the reel. This lack of drag on the lure is the reason baitcasting and conventional reels can outcast all other designs. Casters have long recognized that their lures travel farthest when the line breaks and there is absolutely no line drag to stop their lure from heading to the horizon.

It is only when the spin rate of the spool, the speed of the line, and the travel of the lure through the air are all in balance that the cast is faultless.

Controls. Reel manufacturers have created several reliable designs to control or eliminate backlash. One of the earliest, and still most commonly used, is the mechanical spool control. This is usually a screw-down-cap device on the handle side of the reel that applies pressure to the ends of the spool axle. The resulting friction slows the spin of the spool. As described earlier, this mechanism is typically adjusted to control spool tension for the weight of the lure in use at any given time. Because it is friction-controlled, it is wear- and lubricant-sensitive. By over-controlling (tightening too much)

Caught by relatively few anglers, the colorful Arctic charr has the most northerly distribution of any freshwater fish; it is also one of the hardest fighting and finest eating species.

the spool with this mechanism alone, all overrun backlashes can be eliminated, as well as most overflow backlashes. However, all casts made at such an adjustment require much more energy input from the caster in order to achieve distance, and it can cause the mechanism to wear prematurely.

The centrifugal brake system was another of the early backlash control designs; it was first introduced by Garcia in 1953. That it was successful is attested to by recent modifications to improve its versatility and its inclusion on some of the most expensive high-performance reels now made. In this mechanism, multiple friction weights are freely suspended on radial shafts attached to the spool. The free ends of the weights are allowed to run against the inside surface of a highly polished circular drum or raceway. Depending on the size, number, and the material of the brake weights, a varying amount of friction is created between the weight and drum as the spool spins during the cast. High spool speed creates greater centrifugal force and, therefore, greater friction and braking action. Although the highest spool speed and braking takes place at the start of the cast, the centrifugal brake mechanism has some effect at all but the slowest spool speeds.

Centrifugal brakes have been designed to allow as many as six individual weights to contact the drum at once. Braking force can be fine-tuned by eliminating some or all of the weights from the system. In some large-weight designs, it is possible to exercise fine control by shaping the free end of the brake weight to change the amount of contact surface each weight presents to the brake drum. Finally, the performance and life of the brake weights can be extended by placing a thin coating of light machine oil on the raceway contact surface.

At one time, some reel manufacturers used a unique spool design—the V-shaped spool—to attempt to control both forms of backlash. This shape was created on the theory that, as the cast progresses, the line level drops deeper into the V-shaped spool arbor making less line available. With less line available to backlash, there was, theoretically, less likelihood of a backlash occurring. This was not one of the most popular or successful control attempts because not only was less line available for backlashing but also for extreme-distance casting, general fishing applications, and battling far-running gamefish. Additionally, as the line level on the spool was reduced, the spool spin rate had to increase as the cast progressed. This caused increased line drag on the lure, shortening casts or requiring much more energy input from the caster to achieve sufficient distance.

The genealogy of fishing line includes the use of vines in pre-history, horsehair in the Middle Ages, silk in freshwater around 1900, and linen in saltwater around 1900.

Magnetic spool controls were popularly introduced by several manufacturers in a variety of designs in the early 1980s, and first introduced by Daiwa in 1981. These designs offered an easily adjustable, nonwearing, friction-free spool control that would have an effect throughout the entire cast. The physics of this control are based on electromagnetism or, more specifically, eddy current braking. When a metal object is passed through a magnetic field, it creates an electromagnetically induced current, which causes resistance to the movement of the metal through the magnetic field, slowing its passage. This is known as eddy current braking.

This is used to control backlash in baitcasting reels by mounting a series of small but powerful rare earth magnets to the body of the reel with their magnetic fields aimed at the reel spool or at a drum attached to the spool flange. The magnets are mounted with alternating poles facing the spool: North-South-North, etc. The alternating poles reinforce the magnetic field of the adjacent magnet, intensifying the total magnetic coercive force and focusing the fields more closely to the magnet surfaces. This allows the resulting shallower, more powerful field to be adjusted, usually through a dial mechanism, by bringing the magnets closer or moving them away from the metal spool or drum. At the farthest setting, typically represented by a zero on the adjustment dial, the magnetic fields are theoretically far enough away from the metal that there is no resistance applied and no drag on the spool.

For use in baitcasting reels, the strength and life expectancy of these magnets are permanent. Because no parts come in contact in this control, there are no wear or lubrication concerns. Proper adjustment in use should allow for minimal spool control to a strong eddy current resistance.

Physical laws state that, for any of the available magnetic control adjustments, the eddy current resistance increases as the speed of the metal (spool) passing through the magnetic field increases. A spool spinning at high speed at setting X encounters greater resistance than when spinning more slowly at the same X setting. In this way the magnetic design "self adjusts" during the cast to control overrun at the start of the cast as the spool spins fastest and as the spool slows throughout the remainder of the cast.

Perhaps the most important and effective anti-backlash control is the caster's thumb. In the decades before the advent of the mechanical devices just described, it was only the "educated thumb" that stood between the caster and disaster. It is still the best and most reliable option available. Once trained to do its job, the thumb can deliver all of the necessary control inputs throughout the entire cast to eliminate both overrun and overflow backlashes.

The only way to train your thumb to control the spool is through practice, preferably away from water. Trying to learn to cast and to fish at the same time results only in frustration. A good idea is to go into the backyard or to a local park or ballfield and practice casting using a $^1/_2$-ounce practice plug.

Over-control the reel at the start by tightening the mechanical control, using all of the centrifugal brake weights, or dialing the magnetic spool control to its maximum setting. This helps minimize any tendency for the reel to backlash during a properly executed cast. Over-control with the thumb is also in order, by keeping a slight but constant drag on the line level of the spool, throughout each cast. Distance is not yet the goal. Timing of thumb release and line control is important at this point. As the rod moves forward, release the thumb pressure on the spool to allow the plug to be cast at an upward and outward angle. Monitor the spool spin with slight thumb pressure through the cast, and stop the plug before it lands on the water. This combination will provide full control of overrun and overflow backlashes.

Repetition teaches the thumb how to react, and sensory feedback from the thumb allows the brain to learn just how much control to input at any time. After some confidence-building practice, the reel can be de-controlled by reducing the various adjustable settings to allow a more freely spinning spool. This permits longer distances on the cast without requiring greater energy input. Eventually, the level of casting proficiency achieved permits use of the reel at minimal control settings for effortless casting. Adjustments are needed only when using very air-resistant lures, heavy lines, and when deliberately casting into the wind.

Clearing a backlash. To clear a backlash, put the reel in gear, tighten the drag so it doesn't slip, press the thumbnail of your rod-holding hand on the snarl to flatten and relax the coils, take two or three turns of the reel handle, put the reel in gear, and pull out the line. This does not tighten the coils and should allow you to get all but the worst backlashes out in a few seconds. Make sure to reset the drag.

Many people pick at the backlashed loops of line with their fingers. To do this, put the reel in freespool with your thumb on the spool. Carefully pick away at the leading loops to remove tightening overwraps until you get to the loop that is dug in the worst; then pull it out. Get all snarled line segments out before rewinding the line on the spool, and don't wind over any loops.

Other issues. Baitcasting gear is remarkably free of the line twisting troubles that are associated with spinning and spincasting tackle, so in a sense, it is more trouble-free. You can minimize casting problems and potential backlashes by soaking your line before casting. This is particularly beneficial when old line is on a reel or where the line is of high strength and heavily coiled. Dip the reel in freshwater or pour water on the spool before first use, or soak the spool in lukewarm water after putting new line on.

One source of much baitcasting trouble, via backlashes, comes from anglers trying to cast great distances. Anglers equipped with long rods with two-handed grips, thin-diameter lines, and deep-diving plugs that can cover a lot of territory, are often inclined to "air it out." The extra power required to send an ordinary lure an extraordinary distance with baitcasting tackle often overwhelms calculated thumb pressure, and the result is trouble.

Any time you get a little line overlapped on the spool or sense impending backlash trouble, make a medium-force cast in a nonfishing direction (downwind is best) to clear the spool, and then wind the line back on under pressure. It may help at such times to put your nonwinding hand on the rod shaft ahead of the reel and run the line through thumb and index finger as you quickly spool it back on. You should do this anyway when filling the reel with line.

Wind is the bane of many baitcasting tackle users, more so than spinning gear because of a heightened chance of backlash when casting into the wind. When casting with the wind, everyone looks like a champ. When you have to cast into the wind with baitcasting tackle, you should try low trajectories (use a low sidearm cast, if possible, and/or release the lure a little later than you ordinarily do), increase magnetic spool control and/or thumb pressure, and use more aerodynamic lures. You will probably have to use more force to achieve normal distance in a strong wind, so greater thumb pressure, in addition to increased magnetic force, will likely be necessary.

See: Conventional Tackle; Reel, Fishing; Rod, Fishing; Spincasting Tackle; Spinning Tackle.

BAIT CONTAINER

Devices to hold bait take many forms and rank fairly high on the list of accessories used by anglers who fish with bait. For baitfish, some form of steel or plastic bucket, including some with a perforated insert pail, which contains the bait and which can be easily removed to facilitate water changing, or floating plastic buckets with a spring-loaded door, are the primary models. The latter can be kept in the water and are especially useful for slow trolling. Both can be used for other bait, such as leeches, crayfish, or salamanders. Worms, however, are usually kept in small plastic or fiber containers, or simply in the Styrofoam container that small quantities are sold in. Larger bait, especially that used in saltwater, is kept in boat livewells *(see: livewell)* or large storage containers. For some species, particularly shad, alewives, and herring, the containers must be round; rectangular containers pile such fish up in the corners and they die quickly.

BAIT DROPPER

A device lowered on a rope or fishing line to drop bait on the bottom of a water body. These are tube-like with a flap that opens when the device contacts the bottom; the speed and force of the descent keeps the flap closed on the drop.

See: Chumming.

BAITFISH

A generic term used by anglers for any fish species that are forage for predators, although it often specifically pertains to smaller fish; this term also references fish that are used in live bait angling.

B

BAITHOLDER HOOK

A hook with mini-barbs on the shank.

See: Hook.

BAIT RIG

Technically, an arrangement of any type of natural bait with other terminal tackle for fishing, the term bait rig has become synonymous with methods of fixing whole fish, partial fish, and strips of fish for saltwater trolling activities. Three of the most important basic such rigs are detailed here.

Rigging a strip bait. Strip baits are about the easiest trolling bait to rig and are very effective. Strip baits are made from various fish, with such species as bonito, small tuna, and dolphin preferred for their durability.

To fashion a strip bait, cut an appropriate length from a fish's belly (a) and trim it as illustrated (b). With wire leader partially rigged to the hook, leave a long tag end that faces the barb (b) and insert that leader end into the bait close to the forward section; then insert the hook in the middle of the tail section (c). The strip should be flat, not pinched or curled, to skip properly without being destroyed in short order. Wrap the end of the wire around the leader several times (d). Cut off excess but leave enough tag end available to rerig when it's time to change baits.

Rigging a balao. To rig a balao, which is one of the most popular baits for sailfish and white marlin, start with a hook that has been prepared with wire leader using a Haywire Twist (1), and wrap in a length of light copper wire at the base of the pin. Keep about an inch of tag end protruding from the wire pin as shown, making sure it is in the opposite direction of the bend of the hook. Insert the hook by lifting a gill plate and sliding the hook point into the cavity (2), working it through by moving the hook and bending the bait (it may need to be softened first for this). Guide the point of the hook around and out the bait (3), and then slide the hook eye under the gill plate and push the protruding tag end of wire up

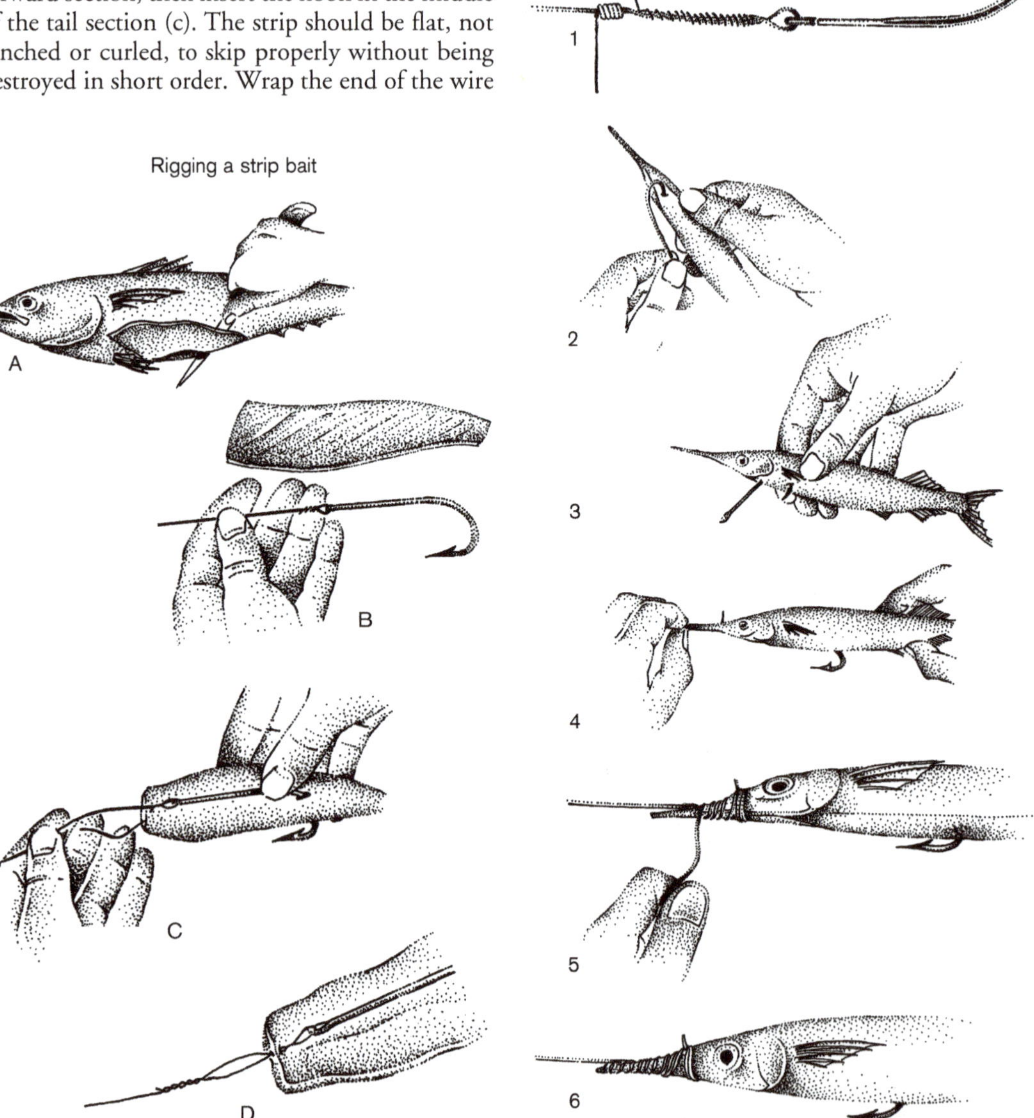

Rigging a strip bait

Rigging a balao

through both of the jaws (4). The hook should align with the bait; if the bait is curved or hooked, it will spin and not troll properly. Hold the leader wire firm under the balao and wrap the copper wire twice around the head behind the pin (5). Then loop the remaining wire around the head in front of the pin and halfway down the bill; snap the bill off close to the jaw (6).

Rigging mackerel. Follow these procedures to rig a mackerel for offshore trolling.

Begin by slitting the belly of the fish, gutting it, and removing the anal fin. Taking care to locate the dead center of the nose, use a pick to punch a hole through the nose just forward of the eyes, then cut a small hole dead center under the mouth. Measure the belly length for a double-hook rig; then prepare the rig and place it in the fish coming from the cavity. Push the wire leader through the head and lead hook eye, and make a loop that does not bind; then form a Haywire Twist to finish the leader. Using waxed thread or dental floss and a heavy duty needle, sew the bait's mouth closed, then the gill flap and body cavity, ending just beyond the rear hook.

See: Natural Bait.

BAIT TRAP

See: Trap.

BAITWELL

A containment device for keeping bait alive.

See: Livewell.

BALAO

See: Halfbeaks and Balao.

BALLAST

Additional weight placed low in a boat to improve stability.

BALLOON

Using small balloons when fishing with live bait is a crafty but little-used idea, though one that can be employed by freshwater and saltwater anglers alike. Instead of fishing live bait under a float *(see)*, it is fished below a colorful 4- to 5-inch-diameter balloon. The balloons are inflated and tied around the fishing line, take up no space before and after use, can readily be popped off a fishing line, and are easily moved up and down the line to change the distance to the bait swimming below. They are also easily observed when fished 40 to 60 feet away from the angler.

Balloons can be employed when drifting, at anchor, and when slowly trolling (the latter is popular with freshwater striped bass anglers in the fall). Generally reserved for use with large baitfish (a big shiner, shad, or herring), balloons not only keep the bait from finding a place to hide, but also indicate a possible strike as it reflects the agitated bait below.

BALLYHOO

"Ballyhoo" is a common name for balao, which are

Rigging mackerel

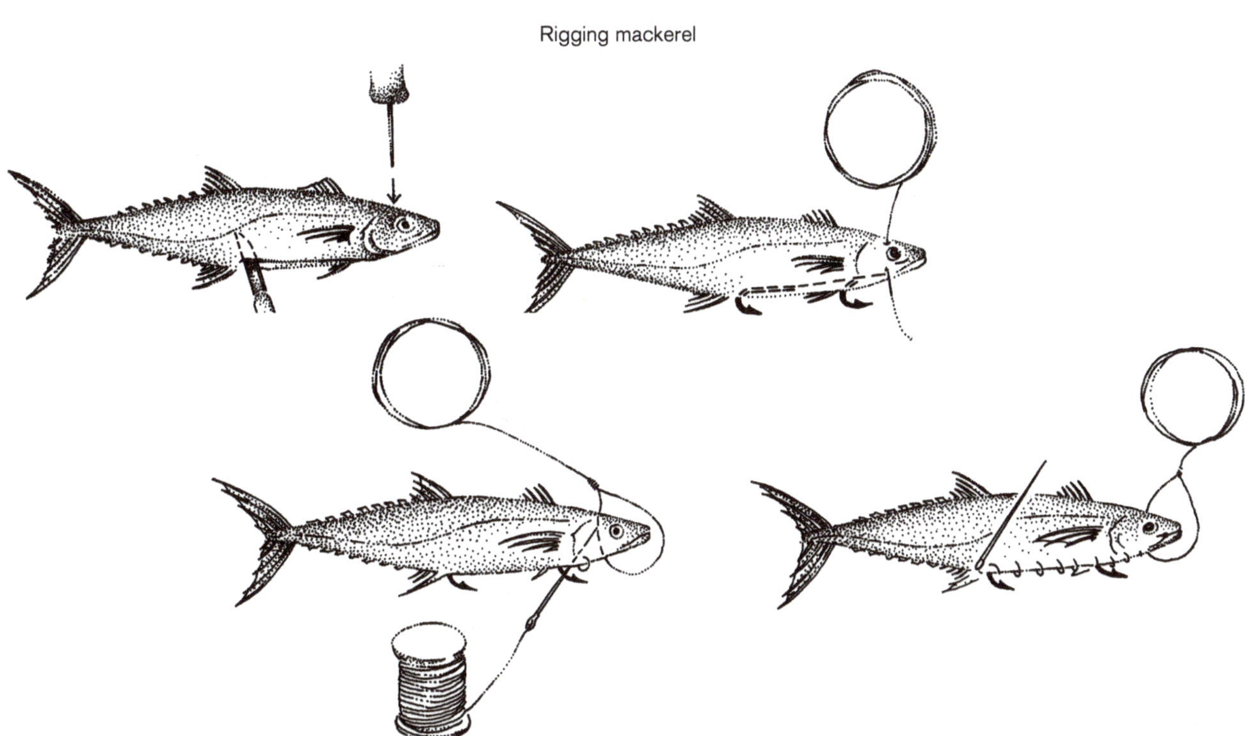

B

widely used as trolling baits in big-game fishing.
See: Halfbeaks and Balao.

BAMBOO ROD

A fishing rod made of split and glued strips of bamboo, mounted with a handle, reel seat, and guides. Split-cane bamboo rods were favored for fly fishing and baitcasting prior to the development of synthetic rod materials, particularly fiberglass, and the perfection of rods manufactured from those materials.

Once a primary rod construction material, bamboo is today in extremely minor use for rod construction, limited to custom rod builders and relatively light-duty freshwater fly fishing application. Some older bamboo rods, created in certain periods and by some well-known makers, are collectibles.

Long bamboo poles with attached fixed-length line may be used for stillfishing, primarily for panfish species. These are simply long bamboo stalks unaccompanied by reels or rod components, and are used for making short-distance (the length of the pole, which is 10 to 15 feet) presentations, primarily of bait; they are not cast.
See: Antique Fishing Tackle; Pole; Rod, Fishing.

BANK

(1) A shallow elevation of the bottom of a body of water, often in a river or estuary *(see),* that has shifting composition and may be hazardous to navigation, such as a sandbank or gravelbank. It is also known as a bar *(see).*

(2) An elevation of the sea on a continental or island shelf. Depths may range from 60 feet near an island to perhaps 600 feet on a continental shelf *(see),* such as George's Bank in the North Atlantic, Hurricane Bank in the Pacific off Mexico, or Hannibal Bank off Panama.

(3) The land abutting either side of a river or stream; also the shore of a lake. In freshwater, land alongside flowing water is called the bank while land alongside a lake or pond is called the shore, but increasingly the word "bank" is associated with lakes and ponds as well, and used interchangeably with "shore."

Rivers have a left bank and a right bank, which is determined by facing in the direction in which the water is flowing.

BAR

A shoal of sand, mud, rocks, oyster shells, or other debris. Bars are commonly located at the mouths of rivers and at harbor entrances but may also be found on the bends of rivers, in impoundments, and in natural lakes. Bars may be impediments to navigation, especially at low tide or during periods of low water, and may cause boaters to run aground. Often they are desirable angling locations, especially the edges that drop off to deep water. Fish that cruise shallows may be attracted to the flat areas atop a bar.

BARB

The sharp projection behind the point of a hook that impedes the hook's backward movement.
See: Hook.

BARBADOS

See: Lesser Antilles.

BARBEL

(1) A whiskerlike feeler on the snout of somefish that contains taste buds and is used for touching and tasting food before ingesting it. One or more barbels may be present on either side of the mouth of fish that are primarily bottom feeders and attracted by food odor. Catfish *(see),* carp *(see),* and sturgeon *(see)* are among the species with such appendages.

(2) *Barbus barbus.*
Other names—French: *barbeau fluviatile;* German: *barbe;* Italian: *barbo;* Spanish: *barboderio.*

This is a popular European river fish unknown to most North Americans and, like carp, a member of the Cyprinidae family.

Identification. This fish derives its name from a signature characteristic of four barbels (also called *barbules* by the British), two on each side like carp, that are intrinsic to its bottom-feeding behavior. It has a downturned mouth and fleshy lips that also make it especially efficient at scrounging for food.

Otherwise well adapted to swift waters, the barbel has a long and rather streamlined body with a flattened belly; it is much more sleek and trim than its fellow cyprinids, especially carp. Its coloration is a brownish gray on top, and brown to bronze on the sides, tapering to a whitish or light-gray belly. It often has a reddish cast, particularly on the fins. Juveniles may have speckled flanks and an olive green tint.

Size. Barbel are commonly caught up to 5 pounds; 16- and 17-pounders have been recorded, and 20 pounds is believed to be the maximum weight.

Distribution. This fish ranges throughout western and central Europe, excluding the Italian, Greek, and Iberian Peninsulas.

Habitat. A denizen of the upper reaches of clean and relatively swift-flowing rivers, barbel mainly live in the deeper parts of pools but will move into shallower waters, sometimes at night in heavily fished locations, and sometimes to slack waters. They may also feed at the surface among weeds on summer nights but are rarely caught at such times. In pools, they may hold behind objects that offer feeding advantages.

Spawning behavior. Barbel spawn in late spring or early summer after migrating upriver, the female laying eggs over rocky gravel and the male fertilizing them. The eggs are broadcast, not deposited in a nest; they adhere to the bottom and are poisonous to humans.

Food and feeding habits. Barbel are bottom feeders that eat a wide range of invertebrates, as well as algae, nymphs, worms, crustaceans, and eels. They root along the bottom, using their mouths like sucking tools, and are able to suck organisms off stones and from under rocks. They are extremely effective at vacuuming whatever they are after from the bottom and digging out their food. Their four mouth barbels have taste and touch cells that are important to feeding, allowing the fish to inspect probable food.

Angling. Because barbel run larger on average than many other commonly pursued European species (most referred to as "coarse fish"), and are a strong fish, they are a popular catch. Their fight, although not showy, is determined, and their perseverance has been favorably compared to that of carp and salmon.

Barbel fishing principally requires bottom presentations (called "legering" in Europe) with an assortment of prepared, processed, and natural baits, often in conjunction with groundbait *(see)* chumming. Maggots, corn, worms, cheese, bread, grubs, seeds, meat cubes, pastes, and other items are used, especially those commodities that have been employed in prebaiting or chumming if the fish have been conditioned to that food. Hooked baits may be fished with a float and drifted, but drifting with a hand-held tight line to sense light strikes is especially favored.

Anglers try to observe the fish and their movements if possible. In order to make an appropriate presentation fast to the bottom, anglers must be familiar with the bottom terrain. Barbel sometimes take a bait and head directly downstream, resulting in an unmistakable and forceful strike. Often, however, they just pick up the bait without moving, or move slightly upstream with it. British anglers use up to 12-foot rods, 6- to 10-pound-test line, and No. 8 to 12 bait hooks.

The depth of the pool and the severity of current will dictate fishing choices, although sometimes these fish move shallower, especially if the river is high and muddy. Daytime and nighttime locations often vary, and some areas produce best in low-daylight or overcast conditions.

BARBLESS HOOK

A hook that is manufactured without a barb behind the point, or whose barb has been pinched or filed down to render it inoperative.

See: Catch-and-Release; Hook.

Barbel

BARNACLE

A barnacle is a saltwater crustacean sometimes thought to be a mollusk because of its "shell." Although some species of barnacles are enclosed in calcareous plates, other species lack this modification. There are over 800 species of barnacles; some are parasites, but others are commensal or independent organisms, living in communities attached to marine animals. Barnacles feed by using their feathery cirri (slender feet) to strain food from the water and beat it into their stomachs. Most have both male and female reproductive organisms, and they grow in large colonies in marine environments. They are responsible for extensive damage done to ships, piers, and offshore structures.

BARRACUDA, GREAT *Sphyraena barracuda.*

Other names—'cuda, sea pike, giant sea pike; French: *barracuda, brochet de mer;* Hawaiian: *kaku, kupala;* Japanese: *onikamasu;* Portuguese: *barracuda, bicuda;* Spanish: *barracuda, picuda.*

A ferocious fighter and an excellent gamefish, the great barracuda is considered potentially dangerous because of its tendency to strike at flashing objects (which it mistakes for fish) and its ability to inflict serious harm, in or out of water, through its prodigious teeth. The great barracuda has been known to attack waders, swimmers, and divers, but such incidents are uncommon. It is also a dangerous fish to eat because it leads a list of marine fishes that cause ciguatera *(see)* when eaten, although small fish are apparently not poisonous. Not every barracuda causes ciguatera, but there is no safe or reliable way of recognizing toxic fish.

Identification. The great barracuda is long and slender with a large, pointed head, resembling a freshwater pike in body shape. It also has large eyes. The dorsal fins are widely separated, and the first dorsal fin has five spines, whereas the second has 10 soft rays. In a large underslung jaw, the great barracuda has large, pointed canine teeth. It also possesses a bluish gray or greenish gray body coloration above the lateral line and a silvery white belly. A few irregular black blotches are usually scattered on the sides of the body, especially toward the tail; it is the only species of barracuda that has these blotches. The young have a dark stripe down the side, which mutates to become the blotches as the fish grows. The great barracuda also occasionally has 18 to 22 diagonal dark bars above the lateral line. It grows

Great Barracuda

much larger, in general, than its relative the Pacific barracuda.

Size. Known to reach a weight of 106 pounds and a length of $6^1/_2$ feet, the great barracuda averages 5 to 20 pounds in weight; larger specimens are rare. The all-tackle world record is an 85-pounder.

Distribution. Great barracuda occur in all tropical seas except the East Pacific and range in the United States from Massachusetts to Brazil, although not in abundance from the Carolinas northward. They are caught mainly around Florida, in the Florida Keys, the Bahamas, and throughout the West Indies.

Habitat. Young barracuda live in inshore seagrass beds, whereas adults range from inshore channels to the open ocean. They are also found in bays, inlets, lagoons, and the shallows of mangrove islands, as well as around reefs, wrecks, piers, sandy or grassy flats, and coastal rivers where saltwater and freshwater mingle. They prefer shallow areas and appear to move inshore in summer, and offshore in fall and winter.

Life history/Behavior. Spawning behavior is triggered by a rise in water temperature; mating takes place between late spring and September, when the water temperature rises above 70°F. Young barracuda under 3 pounds usually inhabit shallow waters, such as harbors and coastal lagoons, until they become adults and live farther offshore, sometimes far out to sea. Smaller barracuda will occasionally school, but the large ones are typically solitary. Curiosity is a trait of all barracuda, and they will follow waders or divers as a result.

Food and feeding habits. The great barracuda eats whatever is available in its habitat, and needlefish, small jacks, and mullet are among the mainstays. They are attracted by shininess or flashes and movement, feeding by sight rather than by smell.

Angling. Barracuda often won't be around when an angler wants to catch one, but they can be a nuisance when he's looking for something else. On the other hand, many a blue-water troller has ventured a little too shallow inshore and been rewarded with a barracuda when seeking other game. Nonetheless, barracuda are able battlers that often strike savagely, and they frequently jump out of the water when hooked. The barracuda remains an underrated saltwater gamefish despite these qualities.

When holding in shallow waters close to shore, barracuda linger around such locales as mangrove edges, bridges, and jetties. When far from shore, they favor reefs, wrecks, oil rigs, coral heads, and the edges of dropoffs.

For a fish with a ferocious reputation, barracuda can actually be shy. They are alert to the presence of anglers and boats, even though they have been known to closely approach divers. They will follow a lure for quite a distance, but they'll scoot off as the lure nears a boat. For this reason, fairly distant casts, beyond the fish, are recommended. This gives it a chance to follow and strike the lure without being alarmed.

Barracuda are best caught on flashy, erratically worked items such as plugs, spoons, and surgical-tube lures. Fly anglers take them on big streamers. Flies and surface plugs, or shallow-running minnow plugs, are sometimes the best offerings, as they do not grab in the grass that is prevalent on so many shallow flats. A quick retrieve is favored, however, regardless of lure. Barracuda often follow a lure that is worked at a slow or moderate speed but refuse to strike it, or will ignore a lure that stops altogether, whereas an increase in speed, even if it means working it fast and then faster, can be provocative.

Casters often ply the shallows and flats looking for barracuda, most of which lie motionless, waiting to pounce on unsuspecting prey; they can be difficult to spot when still, despite their length. Light- to medium-action spinning, baitcasting, or flycasting tackle provides the best sport. Many anglers troll for these fish, too, although usually with heavier tackle and while simultaneously pursuing other fish. Their arsenal includes plugs, spoons, trolling feathers, and rigged baits.

Barracuda have a prodigious array of teeth and should be handled with care; it's best to use wire leaders with lures.

See: Barracuda, Pacific; Flats Fishing.

BARRACUDA, PACIFIC *Sphyraena argentea.*

Other names—California barracuda, barry, snake, scoots, scooter; French: *bécune argentée.*

The Pacific barracuda is the best known of the four types of barracuda found in Pacific waters. It has always been one of California's most prized resources, both commercially and to sportsmen, and it continues to be an important market fish and sportfish.

Identification. The Pacific barracuda is slim-bodied, has a tapered head, a long thin snout, and large canine teeth in a lower jaw that projects beyond the upper jaw. It also has a forked tail, large eyes, and short, widely separated dorsal fins with five dorsal spines and 10 dorsal rays. The anal fins have two spines followed usually by nine rays. Grayish black on the back with a blue tinge, shading to silvery white on the sides and belly, it has a yellowish tail that lacks the black blotches on the sides of the body that are characteristic of other barracuda. Large females have a charcoal black edge on the pelvic and anal fins, whereas the male fins are edged in yellow or olive.

Size/Age. The Pacific barracuda is shorter than the great barracuda *(see: barracuda, great).* It reportedly can grow to 5 feet but has been recorded only to 4 feet; it rarely weighs more than 10 pounds, and although specimens of about 12 pounds have been captured, most of the fish caught by anglers are much smaller. They live for at least 11 years, and the females grow larger than the males; most fish over 8 pounds and all fish over 11 pounds are female. The growth rate is similar in both sexes until the fourth year of life, when the females begin to grow a bit faster.

Distribution. Pacific barracuda occur along the Pacific coast of North America from Alaska to Magdalena Bay, Baja California, although their common range is between Point Conception, California, and Magdalena Bay. The Pacific barracuda is the only barracuda found along the Pacific coast of North America.

Habitat. Pacific barracuda prefer warmer water. Only caught off California during the spring and summer, they are caught in Mexican waters throughout the year, reflecting a northerly spring migration and a southerly fall migration.

Life history/Behavior. Spawning takes place off outer Baja California in the open ocean, peaking in June but extending from April through September. The eggs are pelagic, and once they hatch, the young come inshore and stay in the shallow, quiet bays and coastal waters while they grow. By July, fry spawned in early spring grow to 4 inches and average roughly 16 inches in length a year later. A few males spawn in their first year, and all do so by their second year, whereas most females spawn in their second year and all have spawned by their third year. When small, they travel in schools, although adults are normally solitary. They are naturally curious and attracted to shiny objects.

Food and feeding habits. The Pacific barracuda feeds by sight rather than smell, and eats small anchovies, smelt, squid, and other small, schooling fish.

Angling. Pacific barracuda, one of the most popular of the small gamefish in Southern California, are most abundant during the spring and summer, from close to shore to about 7 to 8 miles out. They are caught by anglers trolling or casting with $^1/_4$- to 1-ounce feather jigs, strip bait, or live bait.

The primary means of taking Pacific barracuda is with a live bait such as a sardine, queenfish, or anchovy fished at or near the surface. Many anglers simply tie their line directly to a nickel or silver hook and freeline it with or without a small bit of split shot for weight. Be sure to set the hook a few seconds after the strike so the fish doesn't swallow the bait and cut the line.

Larger Pacific barracuda have a greater tendency to attack lures than do smaller specimens, and they also have a tendency to hold in deeper water. Thus, a jig is a good lure for larger fish. Jigs can be cast and retrieved in a stop-start fashion, but sometimes it's necessary to fish it deeper and work it vertically.

BARRAMUNDI *Lates calcarifer.*

Other names—silver barramundi, giant perch, cock-up, barra, anama, barramundi perch, Asian sea bass, giant sea perch; French: *perche barramundi;* Japanese: *akame;* Spanish: *perca gigante.*

Excellent eating, the barramundi draws high prices in markets as a gourmet-quality fish. It should not be confused with an Australian species by the same name but of the genus *Scleropages,* which is a strictly freshwater species; nor should it be confused with a saltwater fish of the genus *Cromileptes* called "barramundi cod." It is one of Australia's most important and highly prized gamefish, and perhaps the one fish most synonymous

Pacific Barracuda

B

Barramundi

with freshwater angling on that continent.

Identification. The body of the barramundi is more or less elongated, and the head is relatively long and flattened on top, which accounts for a noticeable resemblance to its relative the snook *(Centropomus undecimalis; see: snook).* It is also closely related to the huge Nile perch *(Lates niloticus; see: perch, Nile).* The forehead is concave and the back is rounded; the maxillae of the huge mouth extend back beyond the eyes. The smooth tongue distinguishes it from the much smaller but closely related sand bass *(Psammoperca waigiensis),* which is often confused with the juvenile barramundi.

The gill flaps are particularly sharp-edged and will readily slice through fishing line and nets. The two dorsal fins are set close together. The tail is more or less rounded (convex), in contrast to the snook's forked tail, and the lateral line is highly developed. The sides of the body are silvery, and the back has a greenish gray tint. Startling pinkish red eyes, which glow brilliantly at night and even reflect in sunlight, are a striking characteristic of the barramundi.

Size. Fish of about 120 pounds and 5 feet in length are the largest officially recorded, although unverified accounts of barramundi up to 595 pounds exist. In Australian waters, barramundi of 50 pounds or more are considered unusually large; the average size caught by most anglers is in the 11- to 22-pound range. Barramundi weighing 20 pounds or less are preferred for eating. The all-tackle world record is 63 pounds, 2 ounces.

Distribution. Barramundi occur from Queensland, Australia, and southern Papua New Guinea to the Philippines, in southern Japan and southern China, and around the coasts of eastern India to the eastern edge of the Arabian Gulf.

Habitat. Found in marine, brackish, and freshwater environments, barramundi are catadromous fish, maturing in freshwater and moving downstream at the beginning of the summer monsoon season in October to spawn in the mouths of estuaries and on mud flats in water of about 2 to 3 percent salinity. As a result, they commonly stay close to shore, lingering in clear to turbid water, and prefer temperatures between 26° to 29°C.

Life history/Behavior. Barramundi are hermaphrodites, starting their lives as males and then becoming females around their second year when they weigh about 11 pounds.

Only fish that have access to the sea can initially spawn, although flooding during monsoons allows previously landlocked fish to spawn, accounting for a second spawning peak. Although spawning ordinarily ends in November, larvae have been found as late as January, and in one case, February. Each female can produce more than a half million eggs.

Newly hatched larvae are initially distributed by the flow of the tide but soon search out sheltered habitats in lagoons, swamps, and saltwater mangrove creeks. The young begin migrating back upstream after about six to eight months and enter freshwater streams by the end of their first year. They spread throughout rivers and estuaries during their second year.

With the return of the monsoon rains, most barramundi go downstream with the help of the tidal flow, and mature fish will spawn. A few barramundi may act contrary to this general pattern and swim upstream against the tidal flow, whereas others may remain in salt- or brackish water year-round. Though it was once believed that fish seen swimming upstream would eventually spawn, barramundi will not spawn in freshwater.

Food and feeding habits. The barramundi prefers live mullet, minnows, barra frogs, and prawns. It is not an open-water feeder; instead, this fish waits under cover along the banks, swiftly ambushing prey as it comes within range, inhaling it into a huge mouth before swallowing.

Angling. As a sportfish, the barramundi is somewhat like a snook, somewhat like a largemouth bass, and somewhat like tarpon, embodying several of the best characteristics of these premier gamefish. Australians, who possess the most known barramundi fishing, have become increasingly enamored with this species, and many international anglers have been eager to seek it out as well because it grows large, jumps madly, swims with the fearsome saltwater crocodiles, and tests the tackle and techniques of light-tackle anglers.

In Australia, barramundi, or "barra" as they are frequently called, are primarily caught along the Northern Territory coast, in scenic and rugged areas subject to extreme tidal fluctuations and in locales that vary from flood-plain rivers to rain forest creeks. Although some anglers pursue these fish in pure saltwater, most angling for barramundi occurs in brackish water or freshwater, much of it in billabongs—lakes and ponds that feed creeks and rivers but become landlocked some time after the rainy season ends. Depending on tides, and creek and river flows, barra water runs from brackish to completely salt-free.

Some anglers fish for barra from shore, but most chase their quarry from boats, as mobility is of great importance. This fishery occurs mostly where smaller flows converge with other creeks or with major rivers. Barra fishing is heavily influenced by seasonal weather. The wet season begins in October in northern Australia and extends through March. The dry season starts in April. The wet season sends great volumes of water out of the billabongs, allowing fish that have been trapped in still, fresh waters and swamps since the previous dry season to escape. It also concentrates small fish and baits (prawns and mullet). In coastal creeks the same thing occurs, although the tidal influences send saltwater up small creeks (called gutters) and pull it out on a falling tide. These changes attract barra to such spots.

The barramundi can be an elusive and difficult fish to catch, in part because it is a strong fighter and in part because it favors habitat that is challenging to anglers. Most of these places are in thick cover, which Australians call snags. Fishing in and near these snags is an important element of the barramundi chase. Tides play an critical part in barra location and fishing technique. Barramundi enthusiasts must do a great deal of casting around mangroves in coastal waters and around fallen trees in rivers, especially near gutters an hour before and after a low tide. Neap tides are particularly desirable periods. High tidal fluctuations, which can be up to 7 meters in the extreme, are harder to fish. When the tides are up, certain rivers and creeks experience the rush of a wall of water that quickly changes the flow direction of the river and repositions the fish. A fair number of anglers troll for barramundi, concentrating on water from 3 to 4 meters deep.

A barramundi from Australia's Daly River.

Whether trolling or casting, anglers primarily use baitcasting or spinning tackle and 2- to 6-kilogram lines, including sections of double lines and up to 50-pound-test leaders. Some anglers use heavier tackle, but sport-minded Australian anglers prefer the challenge of light gear. This is indeed light tackle, as the fish frequent extremely snag-infested locations, put up a vigorous extended fight, and can range to 40 and 50 pounds. Excellent results are possible with fly tackle, particular on streamers, and sometimes this can be more productive than tossing the standard offering of a swimming plug or a jig.

Although some fish are caught by casters, in large rivers and where there is considerable flow, the predominant activity is trolling with large mid- to deep-diving plugs. Anglers flatline these at varying distances behind the boat. Shallow runners are preferred by anglers casting with plugs in the backwaters. Surface plugs are extremely popular, especially because in the often turbid water, the fish zero in on the disturbance.

See: Australia.

BASIN

(1) A depression of the sea floor of an ocean (North Atlantic Basin); the bottom of a large inland lake (Western Basin of Lake Erie); part of a continent (Mississippi River Basin) of usually considerable extent.

B

(2) A series of watersheds *(see)* that drain into a large body of water; also known as a drainage basin.

BASS

Many species of fish, in both freshwater and saltwater, are referred to as "bass." Some are truly bass and some are not, but all have a physique and profile that is generally similar. Three of the most prominent freshwater sportfish with this name include the largemouth bass *(see: bass, largemouth)* and smallmouth bass *(see: bass, smallmouth)*, both of which are actually sunfish *(see)*, and the peacock bass *(see: bass, peacock)*, which is actually a cichlid.

True bass are members of the Serranidae family of sea bass *(see)*, which in freshwater includes the white bass *(see: bass, white)* and yellow bass *(see: bass, yellow)*, and in saltwater includes the black sea bass *(see: sea bass, black)*, striped bass *(see: bass, striped)*, giant sea bass *(see: sea bass, giant)*, kelp bass *(see: bass, kelp)*, and many other species that do not carry the name "bass."

BASS, AUSTRALIAN

Macquaria novemaculeata.

Rated as one of the three most popular freshwater sportfish in Australia (alongside trout and barramundi), the Australian bass is a member of the Percichthyidae family of temperate bass and an indigenous species to that continent. Although the fish has an excellent flavor, it is sought more for its tough fighting tactics and explosive surface strikes than for its culinary appeal. It should not be confused with the American smallmouth or largemouth bass, to which it is not related.

Identification. The Australian bass is sometimes mistaken for the estuary perch *(Macquaria colonorum)*, which is rarely found in freshwater. However, the more rounded and streamlined head-and-body profile of the bass, and the whitish leading edge and tips of its anal and pelvic fins, readily distinguish it from the perch. The back and sides of the bass are dark green, whereas the perch is silvery and has a slight hump on the head just behind the eye.

The tail is forked, and the deeply notched dorsal fin almost forms two separate dorsal fins. The edges of the gill cover are very sharp and should be avoided, and the opercular, anal, and ventral spines can inflict a painful wound that may be sensitive for several hours. It has large eyes and a big mouth, the maxillae extending to about the center of the eye.

Size. Unverified reports of bass to 8 kilograms exist, although it is rare to catch specimens exceeding 4 kilograms. They're commonly taken at 1 kilogram, and specimens of 100 to 200 grams are abound in nuisance numbers. Australian bass stocked in impoundments grow bigger than their counterparts in streams; captures of 2-kilogram fish are unremarkable.

Distribution. Wild Australian bass inhabit nearly all streams that flow into the ocean along the eastern seaboard, from southern Queensland to the Gippsland region of southeast Victoria. Hatchery-reared fish have been stocked in a number of large inland impoundments in both New South Wales and Queensland.

Habitat. In its home waterway, which may be a river, feeder creek, or lagoon open to a nearby stream with access to the sea, the Australian bass usually lies concealed under sunken logs, in submerged tree branches and roots, in and on the edges of weedbeds and reed gardens, under rock ledges and undercut banks, or in clefts in the shoreline. Its ideal temperature range is 18° to 20°C, and the pH should lie between 6.5 (acid) and 8.5 (alkaline). A euryhaline fish, it can tolerate fluctuations in salinity from freshwater to seawater. In impoundments, it seeks out the mouths of creeks, patches of dead trees, rocky shores, submerged weedbeds, and other

Australian Bass

underwater structure, where it lies in wait for food to enter its feeding zone.

Life history/Behavior. The Australian bass is crepuscular, becoming more active during twilight hours and from just before dawn to a couple of hours afterward. A catadromous fish, it moves into brackish water and saltwater to spawn during the winter months (June through September). In dry winters, bass range from the mid- to lower reaches of the estuary; when significant flooding occurs, they move down to the mouth of the estuary to seek out the correct salinity. Eggs are fertilized immediately after release, and the egg's shell becomes tough and rigid. They float on the surface of the seawater, or become neutrally buoyant, as determined by the water's salinity. Fecundity is high; a bass weighing 1 kilogram can spawn a half million eggs about 1 millimeter in diameter.

When the eggs hatch, the larvae are at the mercy of the elements and predators. In spring and summer, the survivors move into freshwater beyond tidal influence and take up residence in streams and lagoons, where they remain until the urge to procreate takes them back to the brackish water or saltwater in which they were born.

Bass that become landlocked or exist in an impoundment never spawn. Females can be full of roe, but the eggs are never shed and are converted into body fat. Successful artificial breeding of the Australian bass has been achieved at the Australian Bass Hatchery at Lower Mangrove in New South Wales.

Food and feeding habits. Australian bass will feed on anything small enough to eat, and any type of insect, fish, crustacean, or animal that falls into the water. Cicadas, fish, crayfish, lizards, baby birds, and other prey are readily taken. These fish are gluttons and will stuff themselves until their prey is literally hanging from their mouths. Small wonder, then, that they will attack a lure regardless of its size. During daylight hours, they lie in ambush, attacking prey that comes within their feeding zone, and by night they roam farther afield.

Angling. Anglers land Australian bass in streams, lagoons, and impoundments, using baitcasting, spinning, and flycasting tackle; casting, trolling, and baitfishing are preferred techniques. Ninety percent of them work from small to medium-size boats on large waterways, and from canoes and punts on lagoons and small feeder streams. Shore fishing is rare because access to most areas is difficult. Many craft use electric motors to control fishing position. The favored technique is to slowly drift within casting distance of home-based structures while casting lures as close as possible to the bass's strike zone.

Bass anglers pay careful attention to weather changes and plan their trips around the barometer, preferring the period prior to summer thunderstorms. The summer months provide the best fishing, especially after dark. Warm evenings, which induce active insect life, stimulate feeding, and bass embrace the cover of darkness to feed. Mid- and deep-diving lures are preferred during daylight hours, and surface poppers (also popular during the twilight and very early morning hours), are pivotal to successful fishing after dark. Floating/diving lures are favorites.

During the winter months, when bass have moved into the estuaries to spawn, some anglers troll using baitcasting and spinning tackle with mid- to deep-diving lures and concentrate on weedbeds and rocky shorelines. Most anglers prefer to toss lures in these situations, however, using deep-diving plugs that can cover the deeper water. Specimens taken in estuary environments are usually breeding adults weighing up to 2 kilograms. Most anglers voluntarily practice catch-and-release or do so to comply with legal requirements, as these fish are subject to catch limits.

Fly fishing is a well-established method, and No. 6 or 7 floating and sinking lines with 1X through 3X tippets are favored. All white or all black Muddler Minnows and Matukas take fish, but better results are gained with poppers, or clipped deer-hair frogs and bass bugs. Although small trout flies will take bass, they also attract 10- to 15-centimeter-long freshwater herring, so preferred hook sizes are Nos. 2 to 6.

Impoundment bass tend to grow faster and heavier than do wild bass, and they are eagerly sought. Anglers target patches of drowned trees, rocky shorelines, and the mouths of small creeks or streams. Many anglers use sonar to locate fish and identify underwater structures. Baitcasting and spinning with heavier lines (to 7 kilograms, to cope with cover-seeking fish) and deep-diving plugs are favored methods, but baitfishing with worms, crayfish, and crickets is frequently adopted.

BASS, BLACK

"Black bass" is a common name for all species and subspecies of the genus *Micropterus,* which belong to the Centrarchidae family of sunfish *(see).* These include largemouth bass *(see: bass, largemouth),* smallmouth bass *(see: bass, smallmouth),* redeye bass *(see: bass, redeye),* spotted bass *(see: bass, spotted),* Suwannee bass *(see: bass, Suwannee),* and Guadalupe bass *(see: bass, Guadalupe).* Black bass are strictly freshwater species, and they are more elongated and generally larger than their family relatives.

The term should not be confused with the various sea bass *(see)* that are members of the Serranidae family of saltwater fish, some of which have a physique similar to that of species in the genus *Micropterus.*

BASS BOAT

The term "bass boat" has evolved through common usage to refer to a type of boat that is popular for largemouth and smallmouth bass angling, but which is simply a good fishing boat that is particularly functional where a lot of casting is required and where presentation and boat positioning are especially important. So-called bass boats are also used for fishing for many other species, primarily in freshwater or in brackish bays and rivers.

Bass boats have evolved over several decades from narrow flat-bottom craft with raised seats to comfortable glittery high-performance machines. The most common example of a bass boat today is a craft that averages 17 feet in length, is made of fiberglass (though many are aluminum) and sports a six-cylinder outboard powerhouse, high-speed bow-mounted electric motor, console and bow sonar devices, livewells, rod locker, platform decks with pedestal seating, plus other accessories, and is usually stored on a trailer for transport to and from the water. These boats, or scaled-down versions, have become standard vehicles for freshwater fishing situations where casting is the primary, if not exclusive, technique, where the majority of fishing requires the use of an electric motor for maneuvering, where it is often necessary to travel a good distance from one place to another, and where the water conditions encountered are generally mild to moderate (although the better and deeper-hulled bass boats are used in huge waters that can get very rough, even though they may not provide comfortable fishing under extreme conditions).

Almost any boat can be used for bass fishing, though some suit particular situations better than others. In general terms, the most popular types of boats used for bass fishing are fiberglass V- or semi-V-hulls, aluminum V-hulls, flat-bottom rowboats (jonboats), and canoes.

Fiberglass or aluminum bass boats are well-outfitted, comfortable vessels with lots of room. A V-hulled, fiberglass version is especially suitable for large lakes, ponds, and rivers, where rough water dictates sturdy craft and where a big boat with a lot of engine muscle can help cover a lot of distance quickly. Aluminum bass boats can also be used under these conditions, but the flat-bottomed models do not handle rough water well. V-hulled aluminum boats take rough water better, but still not as well as a fiberglass boat. They sit up higher in the water, and because they are lighter are more susceptible to being blown around in the wind, making electric motor control a little more difficult.

The larger fiberglass and aluminum boats are generally preferred by people who do a lot of bass fishing and who need room in their boats for an abundance of gear (no one beats a bass angler for owning equipment). Storage is an important factor, as is room to move about within the boat (especially important if three people will fish in it). Dual consoles, once touted for all-around use as bass boats, are unacceptable to hardcore bass anglers because they cramp occupants and gear.

The larger bass boats may be 20 feet in length and propelled by outboard motors with between 200 and 250 horses of power. This seems extraordinary for freshwater fishing applications, but such craft are used in guiding applications and big-water fishing, especially in huge western reservoirs, as well as by

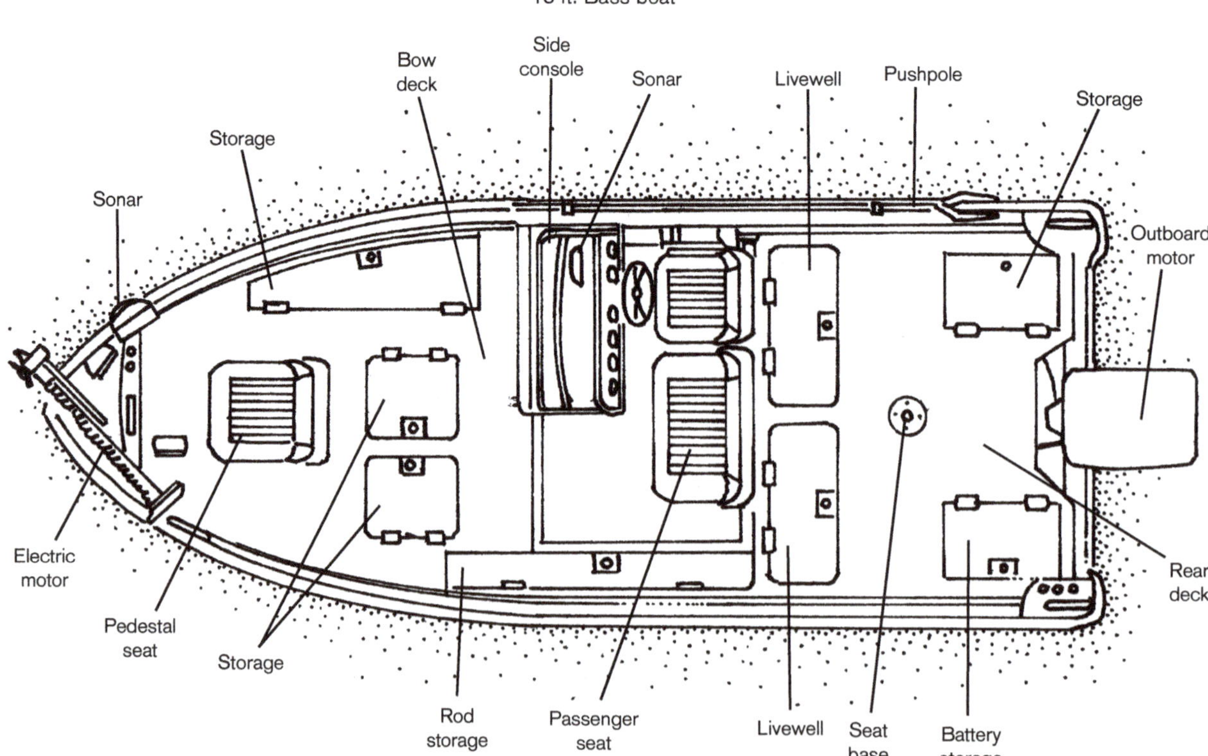

A bass boat provides a stable, comfortable platform for anglers who do a lot of casting.

tournament anglers for whom maximum speed and gear storage are big concerns. This notwithstanding, a 17- or 18-foot fiberglass boat equipped with a 150 hp motor is a common bass fishing tool on medium to large lakes and big river systems.

A smaller aluminum or flat-bottom bass boat is very functional for fishing on small lakes, rivers, and ponds, where it isn't necessary to cover a huge territory and where adverse conditions are seldom present. Many anglers use jonboats on small bodies of water where either outboard motors are not allowed or the sight of big boats might create ill feelings with local residents. Small aluminum V-hulled boats can be used in the same manner, except that they are less suitable for small river fishing than a jonboat and more suitable to moderate-size lakes, owing to their deeper draft design (meaning that they draw more water, which makes them less suitable for shallow, rocky water, such as rivers, but more suitable to small lakes).

Canoes are used primarily by bass anglers in small bodies of water, and on shallow rivers. As a vehicle for bass fishing, where constant casting and positioning are required, they are generally deemed too unsteady and too difficult to position. Canoes are influenced by current, the force of wind, or even the working of some lures, and if two people are fishing, one must be regularly paddling to position the canoe for the other. Canoes become moderately useful for bass fishing when used with an electric motor. They have the virtue of silent operation, however, as well as extreme shallow-water maneuverability.

Safety is the most important consideration in buying and using a bass boat, especially a highperformance model, many of which can fly in excess of 60 (even 70+) miles per hour. Speed is important primarily to tournament anglers and race jockeys, and is of less importance to the recreational angler. High performance bass boats are some of the fastest and most powerful vessels on the water, however, and they must be properly maintained (steering, propeller, etc.), and should be driven sensibly. Accidents involving bass boat operators have resulted from excessive speed, and speed limits have been enacted on some waterways for all boaters. If you have a modern bass boat, make certain that the now-mandatory ignition safety cutoff switch is always attached to the operator when the boat is under outboard power, and that life preservers are worn during high-speed operation.

Newcomers to bass boating face an array of choices and need to carefully evaluate the types of places they will be fishing and determine what they really need. They should also consider the type and quality of access facilities; bigger heavier boats are not as easy to launch in shallow and unimproved access spots. First-time purchasers should also consider the weight of the boat and rig and the ability of their vehicle not only to tow it, but to pull it out of a (sometimes steep) launch ramp.

A bass boat provides a stable, comfortable platform for anglers who do a lot of casting.

Much of the dissatisfaction that people have with their bass boats stems from anglers themselves as a result of their not knowing what they really needed when they first purchased and equipped their boat. Like other boaters, many bass boat owners started small and worked their way up to more sophisticated and more costly equipment through several trade-ins and purchases, when they needed the latter all along. If they had correctly judged their needs in the first place, they would have saved money and time by selecting properly initially. The converse is also true. Many bass anglers have far more boat and engine than is practical for their needs.

See: Boat; Motor, Electric; Motor, Trolling; Sonar; Trailer.

BASS BUG

A type of floating fly, or bug, tied with deer hair and primarily used in bass fishing.

See: Fly.

BASS BUG TAPER

A specially designed type of weight-forward fly line for casting large flies, deer hair bass bugs, and fly-rod poppers.

See: Flycasting Tackle.

B

BASS, CHEROKEE

"Cherokee bass" is a term for hybrid striped bass.

See: Bass, Striped; Hybrid.

BASS, EUROPEAN *Morone labrax.*

Other names—scientific: *Dicentrarchus labrax;* simply called "bass" in Europe, also white salmon, sea bass, European sea bass or seabass; Danish: *bars;* Dutch: *zeebars;* French: *bar européen;* Gaelic: *doingean;* Italian: *perchia;* Norwegian: *havaborre;* Portuguese: *robalo.*

The European bass is regarded by many European saltwater anglers, especially British anglers, as their best gamefish. It is a prominent species for commercial as well as recreational fishermen, and has been subject to overexploitation and varied abundance. It is sold both fresh and smoked in markets.

Identification. The European bass has a broad, extended body that is bluish gray on its back, silver on the sides, and a silvery white on the belly. On each gill cover there is a black mark, and other dark markings emphasize the lateral line. The fins are dark gray and deepen in color each year, whereas the anal fins remain tinged with white. A young bass, or "school bass," is usually lighter with a bit of olive or spotted coloring on its back, but older fish may be slightly brown or yellow. It has a large mouth that holds many teeth—including teeth on the roof of the mouth and the tongue—soft and spiny rays on its fins, and dorsal fins that are completely separated.

The European bass bears a resemblance to the striped bass *(Morone saxatilis);* although it lacks stripes, it has a similar body shape, leading some scientists to believe that it should be classified in the same family (Percichthyidae) as the striped bass instead of in the Serranidae family.

Size/Age. Although it can grow to more than 30 pounds, the common weight of a European bass is between 2 and 9 pounds. It can live up to 15 years in the wild and 30 years in captivity.

Distribution. European bass are an eastern Atlantic species restricted to the European coast, ranging from Norway to Morocco and northern Africa, the Canary Islands, Senegal, the Mediterranean Sea, and the Black Sea.

Habitat. Found in fresh, brackish, and saltwater, European bass prefer warm and temperate marine environs. They usually favor the strong surf of inshore waters in the intertidal zone, often lingering in less than a foot of water. They are also common in estuaries, lagoons, and sometimes rivers. Like the striped bass, they can live in freshwater, but they prefer turbulent and well-oxygenated habitat. When the surf cools, European bass move offshore, preferring waters that remain between 8° and 24°C. They are often nocturnal in shallow waters.

Life history/Behavior. When the inshore waters begin to cool in late October and November, European bass migrate out to sea to spawn in groups. They then return sometime between February and May, when the inshore waters warm again. Some schooling bass, particularly those in river estuaries, do not leave the inshore waters to spawn; those bass that do leave tend to be the first to return in the spring.

Evidence shows that even though European bass don't spawn inshore, the eggs are not shed during a fixed spawning time; instead, they may be shed over the period of time spent in the offshore waters to which the fish migrate. This pattern has been observed in mackerel as well. European bass eggs are buoyant, smooth, and round.

Food and feeding habits. A well-known voracious predator, the European bass will eat a wide variety of creatures, including mollusks, crabs, prawns, shrimp, razor clams, squid, and other small fish. Schooling bass feed on smaller crustaceans or fish fry.

Angling. Most angling for European bass occurs from shore; surf fishing on protected and unprotected beaches is particularly popular. Bass are found in the surf, in the troughs near beaches, on rocky shoals, and in channels. Most anglers offer them some type of bait, primarily worms, crabs, squid, clams, shrimp, and fish. These fish are also caught by boaters drifting with baits under floats, casting with spools and plastic eels, and trolling.

See: England.

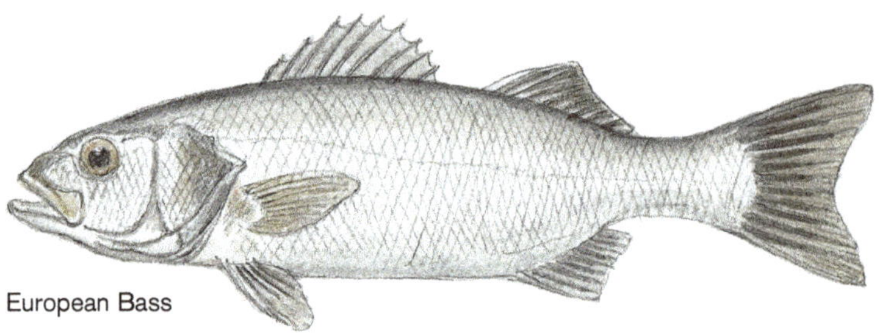
European Bass

BASS, FLORIDA LARGEMOUTH *Micropterus salmoides floridanus.*

The Florida largemouth bass, also known as Florida bass, is a subspecies of the largemouth bass *(see: bass, largemouth),* which in turn is often called a northern largemouth. This fish occurs naturally in Florida. Mixtures of it and northern largemouth are called intergrades, as they are neither pure Florida nor pure northern strains. These fish occur from northern Florida to Maryland.

Florida bass grow to trophy size more readily than do northern largemouth bass. They have been stocked in many states, including California, which has produced near world record 22-pounders from transplanted stocks, and in Texas, which has completely transformed its big-bass potential by stocking this fish.

B

Florida Bass

BASS, GUADALUPE *Micropterus punctulatus.* The Guadalupe bass is a member of the Centrarchidae family and is similar to spotted bass *(see: bass, spotted)* in appearance. It has 10 to 12 dark bars along its sides, which are less distinct in older fish; it usually has 16 pectoral rays and 26 to 27 scales around the caudal peduncle. It can grow to almost 16 inches and usually weighs less than a pound. The all-tackle world record is a 3-pound, 11-ounce Texas fish taken in 1983.

In North America, Guadalupe bass are restricted to the Edwards Plateau in the Brazos, Colorado, Guadalupe, San Antonio, and upper Nueces (where introduced) River drainages in southern Texas. It occurs in gravel riffles, runs, and flowing pools of creeks, as well as in small to medium rivers.

See: Bass, Black.

BASS, KELP (Calico) *Paralabrax clathratus.* **Other names**—calico bass, California kelp bass, rock bass, rock sea bass, sand bass, bull bass, kelp salmon, cabrilla; Spanish: *cabrilla alguera.*

One of a large number of sea bass found in the eastern Pacific, the kelp bass is one of the most popular sportfish in Southern California as a mainstay of party boat trips to the northern Baja. Because it is a powerful fighter and an excellent food fish, it is highly sought by anglers. Its popularity and nonmigratory status put kelp bass populations at risk from overfishing.

Identification. A hardy fish with the characteristic elongate and compressed bass shape, the kelp bass has a notch between its spiny and dorsal fins. The longest spines in the first dorsal fin are longer than any of the rays in the second dorsal fin. It is brown to olive green, with pale blotches on the back and lighter coloring on the belly.

Kelp bass are easily distinguishable from various sand bass by their third, fourth, and fifth dorsal spines, which are about the same length; sand bass have a third dorsal spine that is much longer than the fourth and fifth dorsal spines. Kelp bass also superficially resemble freshwater black bass, except that their dorsal spines are longer and much heavier, and their overall appearance is rougher.

Size/Age. Kelp bass grow slowly, taking 5 to 6 years to reach a length of 12 inches, when they are capable of spawning. Fish weighing 8 to 10 pounds may be 15 to 20 years old. The largest kelp bass are said to exceed 15 pounds, although the largest fish caught was only 14 pounds, 7 ounces. They can grow to $1^1/_2$ feet in length.

Guadalupe Bass

Kelp Bass

B

Distribution. Primarily found along the central and southern California coast and northeastern Baja, kelp bass range from the Columbia River in Washington to Magdalena Bay in Baja California.

Habitat. Kelp bass typically linger in or near kelp beds, over reefs, and around rock jetties and breakwaters or structures in shallow water; larger fish hold in deeper water, to roughly 150 feet.

Life history/Behavior. Spawning occurs from May through September and peaks in July. Kelp bass do not migrate and instead tend to be territorial.

Food and feeding habits. An omnivorous feeder, kelp bass favor assorted fish and small shrimplike crustaceans when young. Adults consume anchovies, small surfperch, and other small fish.

Angling. Kelp bass are a popular light-tackle fish caught from breakwaters in bays, or around kelp beds by anglers trolling, drifting, or stillfishing from anchored boats. Live baits such as anchovies, sardines, queenfish, and mackerel squid are popular, as are a variety of artificial lures, particularly a metal jig and whole squid, as well as streamer flies fished on a sinking shooting-head line. Chumming is often done in combination with baiting and jigging, and larger calicos are often caught at small patches of kelp away from the larger kelp beds. The best fishing is summer to fall, although kelp bass are caught year-round in some areas.

BASS, LARGEMOUTH

Micropterus salmoides.

Other names—black bass, largemouth, bigmouth, linesides, Oswego bass, green bass, green trout, Florida bass, Florida largemouth, southern largemouth, northern largemouth; French: *achigan à grande bouche;* German: *forellenbarsch;* Italian: *persico trota;* Japanese: *okuchibasu;* Portuguese: *achiga.*

The largemouth bass is the biggest and most renowned member of the Centrarchidae family of sunfish and its subgroup known as black bass *(see: bass, black).* As the result of widespread introductions throughout North America, it has become available to more anglers than any other species of fish. Its adoption of varied environments and its penchant for aggressive behavior have helped make it the most popular sportfishing target in North America.

Classified as a warmwater species, the largemouth bass thrives in relatively fertile bodies of water, primarily inhabiting reservoirs, lakes, ponds, and large slow rivers with quiet backwaters. In all of these environments, it is one of the top predators. It has a wide-ranging diet and seeks numerous forms of weed, rock, or wooden cover, which it uses to ambush prey. These characteristics make it suitable for a plethora of fishing techniques, thus also endearing it to manufacturers of fishing equipment. A species tailor-made for casting, it has probably spawned more artificial lures—and variation upon variation of lures—than all other freshwater sportfish combined. And its short-lived but action-packed fight, replete with aerial maneuvers and explosive bursts for cover, keep anglers coming back.

The largemouth bass is not actually a bass, as are the various members of the temperate bass family of fish, which include striped bass and white bass. It is a large sunfish, related to such other popular sunfish as the bluegill *(see)* and crappie *(see: crappie, black; crappie, white),* as well as to fellow members of the *Micropterus* genus. The word "bass" derives from the Middle English *basse,* which is either a corruption of the Old English *baers,* meaning bristly or spiny, or of the Dutch word for perch, *barse.*

Whether appropriately or inappropriately named, the largemouth is the one species that people in North America think of when they hear the word "bass," and this generic term has also come to be used in reference to boats, rods, reels, lures, and other gear specifically employed in pursuit of these fish.

Although largemouths are popular throughout their range, they are not as popular with some people as their close relative, the smallmouth bass *(see: bass, smallmouth),* even though the largemouth grows considerably larger on average. This is because smallmouths have an even friskier disposition when hooked and are more likely to be repeat acrobats. Smallmouths alternately jump and bear down for the depths, whereas largemouths head for the jungle, looking to break the angler's line on the nearest obstruction. The largemouth is more the kick boxer than the pugilist.

Largemouth bass have not always been atop the popularity chart in North America, although they have always been widely appreciated. The rise of levelwind tackle in the mid- to late 1800s, and the development of early lures, spinners, spoons, and plugs, helped move all forms of North American fishing from the cane-pole-and-bait approach, or the fly rod, into a different element that was perfect for bass.

Bass fishing arguably got its biggest boost in the mid-twentieth century when scores of dams were erected on rivers, creating large reservoirs that allowed populations of baitfish and predators to explode. With these changes came fast fishing and an explosion of opportunity.

Largemouth Bass

Today bass fishing is an entrenched activity in North America, and largemouths (and their black bass relatives) are the only species that see a widespread and high level of club activity and competition. They have benefited from intensive fisheries management and special regulations, and there is no commercial fishing for or sale of these species in the United States or Canada (although there is some in Mexico). Some populations have declined due to environmental and fishing pressures, however, and habitat alterations have played a part in the changing nature of some fisheries as well.

The bass fishing culture is such today that most avid bass anglers release every bass they catch, including trophy specimens. Many have a replica taxidermy mount prepared instead of keeping the fish. Largemouth bass are of fairly good table quality, especially the smaller specimens and those from clear-water environments; their white, flaky, and non-oily flesh is generally mild and not unlike larger specimens of other sunfish. Those taken from more turbid and weedy waters tend to be less flavorful.

The largemouth bass is sometimes confused with the smallmouth in places where both species occur, and also with the spotted bass *(see: bass, spotted)*. One subspecies, the Florida largemouth bass *(see: bass, Florida largemouth)*, *M. salmoides floridanus*, is capable of attaining large sizes in appropriate waters but is otherwise similar.

Identification. The largemouth bass has an elongate and robust shape compared to other members of the sunfish family; this shape has come to define species that are called bass, whether they be true bass *(see: bass)*, true black bass *(see: bass, black)*, or merely look-alikes. It has a distinctively large mouth compared with other family members, as the end of its maxillary (jaw) falls below or beyond the rear margin of the eye; the dorsal fin has a deep notch separating the spiny and soft rays; and the tail is broad and slightly forked.

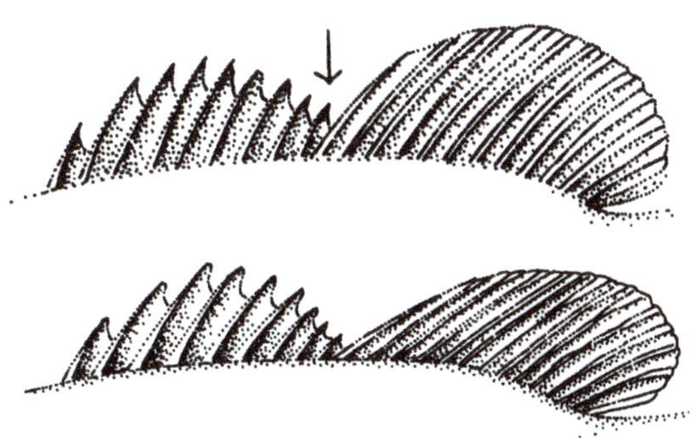
The separation between first and second dorsal fins is less in smallmouth bass (top) than in largemouth bass (bottom), a difference that aids in differentiating these species.

Although coloration varies greatly and is especially dependent on biological factors and host environments, the largemouth bass generally has a light green to light brown hue on the back and upper sides, white lower sides and belly, and a broad stripe of diamond-shaped blotches along the midline of the body. This stripe particularly distinguishes it from its close relative the smallmouth bass, as does the upper jaw, which in the smallmouth does not extend past the eye.

There are patches of dark scales above and below the lateral stripe, three dark bars on the sides of the head, and a complete lateral line. There are no scales on the base portion of the soft-rayed second dorsal fin of the largemouth bass, a characteristic unlike those of other black bass. The largemouth lacks a tooth patch on the tongue, which helps distinguish it from the spotted bass. Coloration can range from pale green or nearly silvery to extremely dark and near black on the upper sides and back. The lateral line, stripe, and other markings may be indistinct—all are dependent on the clarity and color of the water. The most distinctively marked fish tend to come from the clearest waters.

Size/Age. Although the largemouth bass can live up to 15 years, the average life varies; these fish seldom live more than 10 years. Throughout their

B

range, largemouth bass encountered by anglers average 1 to $1^1/_2$ pounds (10 to 13 inches) but are commonly caught up to 5 pounds and less commonly from 7 to 10 pounds. In northernmost waters, a largemouth bass over 5 pounds is uncommon, due to slow growing seasons. Fish exceeding 5 pounds are common in good lakes in southern regions, where fish can grow faster and enjoy a longer growing season. A 10-pounder is a trophy anywhere, and, with few exceptions, is harder to come by in modern times.

The maximum size attainable for largemouth bass may be 25 pounds, but this has not been proven, and only about a dozen bass in the 20-pound class are known to have been caught. The largest specimen is the all-tackle world record of 22 pounds, 4 ounces, caught from Montgomery Lake, Georgia, in 1932. This is one of the longest-standing freshwater records and certainly the most coveted of all sportfishing records. Although Florida once had the best chances of producing record-threatening largemouth bass, that distinction has moved west with transplanted fish (Florida strain) to California. Texas also boasts many large specimens today, and Cuba is another candidate for producing the biggest largemouths.

Distribution. The largemouth bass is endemic only to North America, and its native range was generally the eastern half of the U.S. and southernmost Ontario and Quebec in Canada. It occurred roughly from Iowa south to Texas and northeastern Mexico, and east to the South Atlantic coast and to western New York and western Pennsylvania; it was absent from most of the Appalachian and Ozark Ranges, most of the northeastern U.S. from Maryland to Maine, and easternmost Canada.

Since the late 1800s, its range has been expanded to include major or minor portions of every state in the U.S. except Alaska, and most of the southern fringes of Canada, as well as numerous countries in Europe, Asia, Africa, South America, Central America, and the Caribbean.

Habitat. In capsule summary, the largemouth bass is typically described as a fish that frequents the weedy sections of ponds and lakes. In reality, the largemouth is highly adaptable to many environments and to many places within various types of water. They inhabit creeks, ditches, sloughs, canals, and many little potholes that have the right cover and forage, but they live principally in reservoirs, lakes, ponds, and medium to large rivers, and not always in the weedy sections.

More specifically, however, they orient toward cover in those environments and find most of their food in or near some form of cover, whether it is visible in relatively shallow water or existing beneath the surface out of sight. Favored haunts include logs, stumps, lily pads, brush, weed- and grassbeds, bushes, docks, fencerows, standing timber, bridge pilings, rocky shores, boulders, points, weedline edges, stone walls, creekbeds, roadbeds, ledgelike dropoffs, humps, shoals, and islands. Although much bass cover is nearshore, some bass do spend time away from shore, especially in unvegetated lakes.

Largemouth bass are most active in waters ranging from 65° to 85°F; the lower 70s is likely optimum. Yet they do well in temperatures much higher and lower, including waters that touch the 90°F mark as well as frozen lakes that dip to the mid-30s. They can and do thrive in waters that are clear, as well as in those that are highly turbid.

Life history/Behavior. Largemouth bass spawn from late winter to late spring; the timing depends on latitude and temperature. Southern populations spawn earliest, and most northern populations latest. They begin to spawn about the time the water temperature reaches 60°F. Fish of about 10 to 12 inches are mature enough to reproduce for the first time. Males select and prepare the nest site, a circular bed usually in 1 to 4 feet of water, often positioned near or including some type of object along the shoreline. The female is nudged to the nest site by the male, deposits her eggs, and leaves; the male guards the eggs, which hatch in a few days, and then guards the young fry for a short period.

Largemouth bass do not undertake extensive migrations and are essentially cover-oriented homebodies. The pattern of their lives is fairly simple: hide, ambush, eat, and eat some more. This is oversimplified, but bass do have "home areas" that they seldom range far from unless environmental changes require it. The larger the fish, the larger its home area; the more vegetation, the smaller the home area. They are susceptible to changes in water levels and temperature, and may change behavior based on food abundance or availability. They usually favor shallow-water living (1 to 20 feet), but when temperature, falling water, abundance of deep baitfish, or other conditions dictate, they may move to deeper water.

Growth rates for largemouth bass are extremely variable, influenced as they are by broad geographical location (north versus south), the specific body of water they inhabit within a particular region, and individual differences even within the same population. Despite these influences, bass are capable of growing quickly under the right circumstances.

Food and feeding habits. Adult bass predominantly eat other fish, including gizzard shad, threadfin shad, golden shiners, bluegills and other sunfish, small catfish, and many other small species, plus crayfish. They are extremely opportunistic, however, which explains why anglers like them so much, and they may consume snakes, frogs, salamanders, mice, and other creatures. They swallow their food whole instead of biting off pieces, which limits the size of the prey they can consume. Any prey having a body depth less than the diameter of the largemouth bass's mouth may be consumed, usually headfirst.

As aggressive predators, bass primarily are ambush feeders, but they may pursue fish in open water, where there are no ambush opportunities. In normally warm waters, digestion occurs fairly quickly; however, at extreme warm or cold temperatures digestion actually slows, causing the bass to feed less frequently and making them less susceptible to anglers.

Bass are well known for their ability to locate prey in turbid water and at night. Although they are primarily sight feeders when water clarity permits, they otherwise use their highly developed lateral line to detect vibrations and locate prey. They can also detect odors, but their senses of smell and taste are poorly understood by scientists, and evidently used less for feeding than sight or hearing.

Angling. A particular charm of angling for largemouth bass is that bass lures needn't closely imitate specific forage. As a result, there is probably no other freshwater gamefish for which there is such a wide range of lure types, sizes, colors, and actions.

Spring is the most popular time to pursue these fish in most areas (a few states have seasons on bass and there is little or no spring fishing), as the bass are spawning and hold relatively shallow and close to shore. Water temperature, which varies according to geographical location, is a big factor in fish activity in the spring. Small lakes and ponds are best for early-season bass fishing because they warm up quickly. On large lakes, the shallow flats, coves, feeder creeks, and tributary areas are generally warmer than the rest of the lake in the early season and thus hold more fish.

Various lures are effective on spring bass, but few are more consistently effective than spinnerbaits and crankbaits. Of the latter, the best type to use depends on a number of variables. If the water is very cold, a lure that gets down 5 to 10 feet and is worked around points, steeply sloping banks, and shores with a breakline (a distinct dropoff into deeper water) may be best. In shallow lakes with many stumps, flats with cover (preferably vegetation that just starts to emerge), and the like, a shallow- or intermediate-running crankbait is best. As the water warms and the cover—which may be grass, milfoil, hydrilla, or cabbage weeds—begins to grow higher, an angler can use the same crankbaits to skim the edges and tops of that cover, perhaps varying only the speed of retrieval. Crankbaits are especially productive in places with a lot of deep water and where submerged creek or river channels meet the shore.

Spinnerbaits are generally fished close to the surface and within sight in the spring. Relatively snag- and weed-free, they work particularly well around moss, lilies, milfoil, and other forms of vegetation, and around stumps, standing timber, fallen trees, and docks.

Bass are generally harder to catch in the summer than in the spring, in part because anglers as a whole are not as persistent, and in part because bass become less accessible, going deeper or becoming more ensconced in thick cover that is difficult to fish.

A plastic worm lured this hefty largemouth bass from a Florida phosphate pit.

Generally, such surface lures as plugs or buzzbaits work best early and late in the day in the shallows. Plastic worms are the preferred offering otherwise, and jigging spoons or weedless spoons are also of value.

On lakes with ample cover, focus on the heaviest cover that a bass could hide in. The water probably won't be especially deep, but the cover provides bass with security, comfort, and many opportunities to ambush unsuspecting prey. With heavy cover, an angler often has to get into the midst of it to be successful, plodding along, working spots deliberately, and probing carefully.

The most obvious, most frequently employed, and most easily managed method of catching summer bass is working the edges of vegetation. In large, fairly thick concentrations of vegetation, the easiest fish to catch are those close to the edges, especially where the perimeter is readily observed. Pinpointing the edges of submerged weedlines, however, is not as easily done. Nevertheless, this can be a critical area, especially in clear northern waters, as much vegetation does not grow above the surface. A plastic worm, rigged with a slip sinker, is the main vegetation lure. Sometimes a lure that moves more enticingly, such as a weedless spoon with a plastic skirt or pork chunk, or a weedless surface product, is a better bet.

On big bodies of water with little vegetation, the midsummer trick is to locate deep water (15 feet or more) that holds largemouths, fish the edges of those areas, and present lures in a precise way. Look for submerged humps, long points, and old roadbeds well away from shore.

Bass are often found in flooded timber in the summer, and here, plastic worms, jig-and-pork combinations, and occasionally deep-diving crankbaits are the ticket. The junction of two old channels, the outside bend of a channel, clumps of timber, and timber adjacent to boat lanes where there is a depth change are all good locales. If bass suspend in the midsection limbs, a jigging spoon, worked vertically, is the lure of choice.

Don't overlook fishing at night during the summer, which may be especially beneficial on clear-water lakes that get copious daytime traffic. Surface plugs, spinnerbaits, and plastic worms are good nighttime lures.

In fall, bass are coming off their summer behavior and gradually moving shallower as the water cools. Temperature and habitat conditions vary greatly by geographic area, and far southern bass waters experience favorable conditions for a longer period of time than northern ones. Ponds and small lakes are especially worth fishing, although they cool off quickly after a succession of cold fall nights. Shallow and nearshore environs become worthy of greater attention in the fall, but anglers should not be averse to working deeper water if shallow prospecting fails to bring dividends. Spinnerbaits, crankbaits, jigs, and surface lures have merit at this time.

Because pinpoint presentations are more important in largemouth bass angling than in many other forms of freshwater fishing, and as boats equipped with an electric motor are in wide use among bass anglers, it is important to position the boat in ways conducive to accurate casting and proper presentation. The first cast to a likely bass hole is often the most important one, so it pays to make each cast count. Make casts to all sides of likely cover, and learn to feather your casts so that lures don't crash into the water like a bomb.

Serious bass fishing involves a range of angling conditions, lure styles and sizes, and fishing methods. Most anglers, however, are partial to baitcasting rods, particularly when using crankbaits and worms, fishing in heavy cover, and fishing for very large bass. Baitcasting tackle offers good casting control and favors big lures. Ten- or 12-pound-test line is the standard, although lighter or heavier line is used when appropriate.

Some anglers use spinning gear for largemouth bass, but they opt for lighter line and generally don't seek out areas with heavy cover where lures and fish are likely to get hung up. Fly tackle is also of merit at times, especially when fishing with deer-hair bugs and poppers for shallow fish.

See: Bass, Black.

BASS, NEOSHO SMALLMOUTH

See: Bass, Smallmouth.

BASS, NIUGINI *Lutjanus goldiei.*

Other names—Papuan black bass, Papuan black snapper; French: *vivaneau de Papua;* Malay: *ilkan merah;* Spanish: *pargo de Papua.*

Popularly nicknamed the Niugini bass and Papuan black bass, this species is actually a snapper that inhabits freshwater and brackish water. Known only to Papua New Guinea, it is a member of the Lutjanidae family of snappers and one of the world's toughest yet least-known fish found in freshwater.

Identification. The Niugini bass is a stocky fish with a deep, compressed body; it looks somewhat like a cross between a mangrove snapper and a largemouth bass, with large fanlike pectoral and pelvic fins. The first dorsal fin is spiny rayed and separated from the soft-rayed second dorsal fin. The body is silvery to steely gray, darker on top and lightening on the belly, and has large scales. Larger fish are darker. It has two canine teeth on the upper jaw, and smaller teeth on the lower jaw.

Size. The maximum size attainable is uncertain, although it can reportedly grow to at least

Neosho Smallmouth Bass

Niugini Bass

B

40 inches in length. Average weights are from 10 to 20 pounds, but fish weighing up to 30 pounds are common. Despite its great sporting virtues, the Niugini bass is not currently listed with the International Game Fish Association (IGFA), and no world-record weights have been established.

Distribution. The Niugini bass is known only in southern Papua New Guinea between the Port Moresby district and the Fly River. It may occur in rivers in Irian Jaya (the western half of the island of New Guinea).

Habitat. This fish inhabits large freshwater jungle streams and tributaries. It has not been reliably reported from marine habitats, but it may occur in estuaries. Little is known about the life history of this species; angler experiences suggest the fish favors cover, usually holding tight to the thickest snags and deadfall cover along riverbanks, where it waits to ambush prey. Deforestation and changes in jungle river environments may threaten sizes and populations.

Angling. The Niugini bass is a heavyweight jungle brawler, caught in locations full of snags and presenting extreme challenges for casting and for landing fish. Casting with surface plugs, and shallow- and medium-running plugs, is the primary practice, with emphasis on accurate lure placement very close to cover. Some plug trolling is done in main channels, where Niugini bass, as well as other species, may be encountered.

Owing to the fierce close-quarters battle of these fish, and the snag-infested nature of the jungle environs in which they are found, heavy baitcasting tackle is mandatory. Australians who have fished a good deal for this species use a minimum of 30-pound line, prefer 40, and will use 50-pound line. They use short, powerful rods and favor reels with top-quality drags. Like largemouth bass, Niugini bass are heavyweight short-term brawlers, and the key to catching them is stopping their freight-train-like bursts for cover.

Niugini bass are tough on tackle, and only lures with saltwater-quality hooks and the strongest connections will do; scarred and crushed lures and bent hooks are standard occurrences, and many fish are lost due to cover or when the angler is outmuscled. Very few anglers have encountered this excellent gamefish.

See: Papua New Guinea.

BASS, PEACOCK

Peacock bass are among the world's hardest fighting freshwater fish, and species that perform much the same as largemouth bass and can be caught using similar methods. Native to South American jungle or rain forest rivers and reservoirs, peacock bass have become popular with anglers as fishing opportunities in South America have increased and as these fish have been introduced in appropriate North American waters through stocking efforts, most notably in canal systems in southern Florida and warmwater reservoirs in Texas. They are valued in their native range as table fare, but their willingness to take lures, strike hard, and provide a strong and exciting fight make them primarily of interest to anglers.

The Name Game

The term "peacock bass" is a misnomer in nearly all respects, but it is a name that has good marketing value and one that has stuck in the English-speaking world. Species that are called peacock bass in English are formally known as *pavón* in Spanish-speaking South American countries and as *tucunaré* in Brazil.

The actual number of species that masquerade under the name "peacock bass" is unclear, as extensive scientific and taxonomic evaluations and reports have been lacking, especially in the English language and in the native range of these species. Because peacock bass are broadly referenced in

B

A dark, male peacock bass (note the humped back) from Guri Lake, Venezuela.

scant literature as fish of "the Orinoco and Amazon River basins"—which make up two of the world's greatest watersheds, thousands of tributaries, six or more relatively undeveloped countries, and probably half of an entire continent (much of it roadless)—it is not hard to understand that the exact number of different species and their ranges and life histories is barely known. In fact, more has been learned about one or two species due to their introduction to nonnative waters (as in Hawaii and Florida). It is known, however, that the biggest species and specimens have been caught in lakes and rivers in Brazil, Venezuela, and Colombia.

Like many other fish that are called bass, peacock bass are not true bass. Their body shape is generally basslike, however. All known species of peacock bass have a prominent black eyespot, surrounded by a gold ring (ocellus), on their tail fin. At some time North Americans saw the physical similarity between this fish and the largemouth bass, observed that it was readily taken on similar fishing tackle and techniques as largemouth bass, noticed that the eyespot was like that of the eyelike spot on the plumage of a peacock, and dubbed it a "peacock bass." This unofficial nickname turned into a fortunate stroke of public relations genius, and as more became known about the sporting attributes of this species, it kindled interest. Ironically, there are other species of South American fish that are also admirable but little known because of their less-familiar names and less-extensive range. These include payara *(see)*, bicuda *(see)*, matrincha *(see)*, trahira *(see)*, and arawana *(see)*.

Peacock bass probably would have become a star attraction under any name, and deserve their great reputation. They are stronger, harder fighting, jump more and higher, and are generally much meaner than a largemouth bass or most anything else that swims in freshwater. Some species of peacock bass grow much larger, or are found on average in larger sizes, than largemouth bass. They also hit surface lures like no other fish, and destroy lures, line, equipment, and the thumbs of anyone foolish enough to lip-lock them.

Species

As noted, the number of peacock bass species is unknown and most, including the more prominent ones, have not been thoroughly identified and described. Brazilian biologists at the Instituto Nacional de Pesquisa Amazonia in Manaus, reported in 1996 that there were "eight, maybe more" species of *tucunaré*.

Whatever the actual number of species, they are all cichlids, members of the Cichlidae family. Well known to aquarium hobbyists, this family includes the popularly collected oscar *(Astronotus ocellatus)* and angelfish *(Pterophyllum scalare)*, as well as the important food fish tilapia *(see)*. Cichlids are the third or fourth largest family of bony fishes, numbering approximately 1,300 species (with 105 genera), and are widely distributed in Africa, Central and South America, Syria, southern India, Sri Lanka, Madagascar, and Iran. Many cichlids are colorful species, which is a main reason for their popularity with aquarium hobbyists. Most have bodies that are moderately deep and compressed; this is especially so for peacock bass, which, although similar in shape to largemouth bass, are more sleek and appear more muscular, without the sagging belly that big largemouths develop.

It is estimated that 300 cichlid species are native to South America, primarily in rivers; the various peacock bass species are among the largest and most predatory of these. As with piranha *(see)*, many terms have been used to name the different peacock bass species, and the term "peacock bass " (also *pavón* and *tucunaré*) is often used by anglers and nonscientists generically to refer to any of these fish, regardless of their particular characteristics, appearance, or species.

In addition to being superb gamefish, peacock bass are excellent table fare, and larger species and individuals are important commercially. All known peacock bass have a similar shape and a particularly distinguished coloration; some are especially brilliant, and, individually or as a group, peacock bass are among the most colorful of all sportfish in freshwater or saltwater.

The three species currently recognized by the International Game Fish Association (IGFA) for record-keeping purposes are the speckled peacock, butterfly peacock, and blackstripe peacock.

Blackstripe Peacock Bass

Blackstripe peacock bass *(Cichla intermedia).* The blackstripe peacock is also known as royal pavon, royal peacock bass, *pavón real.* It is limited to the Orinoco watershed in Venezuela south of San Fernando, making it a less frequent encounter for anglers.

The blackstripe peacock bass has an irregular black stripe that runs laterally along the full length of the midsection of the fish and is crossed intermittently by a series of six to eight fainter black oval bars. This is the only species of peacock bass that has more than three black vertical bars. It rarely weighs more than 10 pounds, although 12-pound specimens have been caught. Some consider it the toughest species pound for pound.

Butterfly peacock bass *(Cichla ocellaris).* The butterfly peacock is also known as peacock cichlid, tucunare, tuc; in Spanish as *pavón mariposa, pavón amarillo, pavón tres estrellas, marichapa;* in Portuguese as *tucunaré-acu;* and in Hawaiian as *lukanani.* The full extent of its range in tropical South America is undescribed scientifically, although it occurs in the Orinoco and Amazon drainages and in the upper reaches of these systems in several countries *(see: Brazil).* It was introduced in Hawaii (where it is primarily known as tucunare) from British Guyana in 1957, and in Florida in 1984 and 1986; it has also been stocked in Puerto Rico, Panama, Guam, and the Dominican Republic.

Butterfly peacock bass possess great variation in color. They are generally yellowish green overall, with three dark, yellow-tinged blotches along the lateral midsection; these blotches intersect with faint bars, which typically fade in fish weighing more than 3 to 4 pounds. The iris of the eye is frequently deep red. A conspicuous hump exists on top of the head in breeding males, and spawning fish have an intensified yellow coloration. They are distinguished by the absence of black markings on the opercula and are believed to attain a maximum size of 11 to 12 pounds; the all-tackle world record is a $10^1/_2$-pound individual from Río Branco in Brazil.

Speckled peacock bass *(Cichla temensis).* The speckled peacock bass is also known as speckled pavon, painted pavon, striped tucunare; in Spanish as *pavón cinchado, pavón pintado, pavón trucha,* and *pavón venado*; in Portuguese as *tucunaré-pacu.* As with the butterfly peacock bass, the full extent of this species' range in tropical South America is undescribed scientifically, although it occurs widely in the Orinoco and Amazon basins. It was introduced to Florida in 1985 and has reportedly been stocked in other countries.

Butterfly Peacock Bass

Speckled Peacock Bass

Speckled peacock bass have dark blotches on the opercula and three distinctive vertical black bars on the body; these may become more pronounced with age, although this does not appear to be absolute. There are light or faint spots on the dorsal and caudal fins, and a conspicuous hump exists on top of the head in breeding males. Some individuals (described as another color phase) may have four to six horizontal rows of light-colored dashes or spots along the sides and speckling over the rest of the body and fins; these fish are called "spotted peacock bass" by many anglers and were previously thought to be a distinct species.

It is the only peacock bass that has broken longitudinal lines and spots on the head, opercula, and caudal and dorsal fin regions, resulting in a speckled appearance. Many speckled peacock bass, however, especially the largest specimens, do not exhibit this speckling along their flanks.

Speckled peacock bass exhibit many color variations, the adults being lighter than the juveniles. Generally, they are dark green to black along the back, golden to yellow or light green along the flanks, and lighter on the belly. The pelvic, anal, and lower half of the caudal fins are often reddish in color, sometimes yellowish green. These colors are general conformities, however, and significant variations exist, especially in intensity (some have an orange or bronze tinge), which may or may not be due to season or habitat.

This species attains the greatest size of all the peacock bass. The current all-tackle world record is a 27-pound speckled peacock bass from the Río Negro in Brazil, but fish of 30 pounds and better reportedly have been speared, netted, or handlined. Speckled peacock bass up to 10 pounds are the norm in many waters; however, specimens exceeding 10 pounds are common in some places, and fish over 15 pounds are considered trophies. Some waters consistently produce individuals from 18 pounds to more than 20 pounds.

Due to its size, the speckled peacock bass is an important commercial species, especially in the larger rivers of the Amazon and near population centers. Overall, owing to its wide distribution and large size, it is the most important species to visiting anglers, and the main object of angling interest throughout the Amazon and Orinoco watersheds.

Angling

Like other fish of the rain forest regions of South America, peacock bass are primarily river fish,

Spotted Peacock Bass

although they are sought by anglers in the flooded backwaters and in the still areas of lagoons. They are seldom found in swift current but have adapted to impoundments. Anglers often land them among flooded timber or along the edges of timber, and they occasionally take them in open water.

Peacock bass are categorically described as schooling species, and they are often encountered in schools; catching many fish from a school, however, is not a likely possibility, and it is not uncommon to catch single fish from various locations. Although they may become active as a school and chase baitfish, there are only occasional opportunities to spot a feeding school and to fish for them. When an active school is present, however, one strategy for keeping them around involves one angler catching a fish and letting it swim along, hooked near the boat, while a companion casts to following fish. Peacock bass will often follow a hooked companion to the boat, just as in some places hooked peacock bass will be attacked by a school of piranhas.

The life history and food preferences of peacock bass are not fully understood, although it is clear from their behavior that they are voracious predators and aggressive fish. They obviously consume other fish, although their favorite prey, if any, are unknown in their various native environments. The sizes of lures successful in taking these fish indicate that both small and large fish are their targets. In Hawaii, butterfly peacock bass are known to consume threadfin shad, tilapia, bluegills, and mosquitofish. Spawning is believed to occur in 80°F waters, and before the flood season; these fish build shallow nests and guard their young.

The chief concern for visiting South American anglers in catching either numbers or sizes of peacock bass is being in the types of waters that contain large fish and being present in the appropriate season *(See: Brazil)*. Because the rainy season greatly raises water levels and floods the rain forest, it disperses all fish populations and makes the job of locating peacock bass prohibitively difficult. The dry season usually results in receding waters, which concentrates fish in backwater regions (lakelike areas off main rivers or tributaries, also called lagoons). These seasons vary in different areas of South America, and, in some years, unusual weather patterns disrupt the norm.

Anglers in Brazil typically catch peacock bass by casting and trolling. Natural baits are almost never employed by visiting anglers, and live baitfish are generally unavailable or cannot be maintained in most jungle fishing situations. Casting is preferred over trolling, although in periods of slack activity, especially in the heat of midday, or when high water makes locating fish difficult, trolling can be effective. Peacock bass are often more active in shallower water early and late in the day, evidently moving deeper in midday.

A brilliantly colored peacock bass from the São Francisco River, Brazil.

Peacock bass strike a variety of flashy diving, shallow-running, and surface plugs, as well as jigs and large streamer flies and fly-rod poppers. They nearly always strike hard, and their explosive strike on surface plugs is savage if not heart-surging, especially if the fish is large.

Shallow-running floating/diving plugs are excellent lures in backwater cover and catch peacock bass and other species; blue-and-silver, chartreuse, and green-and-white work well. Lipless rattling crankbaits are favored by many anglers, especially in open-water fishing. Blue-and-silver is highly recommended, but a host of flashy colors will do. Shallow-and mid-diving crankbaits that have good action and noise will do the job in open water as well. Surface lures include large walking, popping, and buzzing models. Large plugs with fore-and-aft propellers, which make a lot of commotion, are good for big fish, and can be effectively trolled as well as cast; the former being a rather unique method of freshwater fishing but one that points up the value of making noise to attract fish.

Spinnerbaits produce some strikes but are greatly outfished by plugs, and they do not hold up to abuse. Weedless spoons are good in cover, and heavier nonweedless spoons are good in open water. A 4- or 5-inch heavy-body spoon in a five-of-diamonds pattern is especially effective when trolled.

Be prepared to have lures mangled, crushed, and stripped of their paint if the action is hot; standard freshwater lures for bass or walleye withstand abuse from peacock bass (and other ruffians in the same waters). These fish, and the angling circumstances, are tough on equipment. Heavy-duty hooks and connections are necessary on lures, as lightweight hooks will be bent and crushed. Replace treble hooks with sturdy singles for lures that will work as well in this manner. It's smart to fish with barbless hooks, as there are dangerous moments in close-quarters jungle fishing, with its shallow water, close-to-boat strikes, and thrashing fish. Lures often fly back at you, and the potential for being impaled is high.

Peacock bass jump often, make repeated powerful short runs, do not give up at the sight of the boat, and try to run for the security of heavy cover. In tight quarters and heavily obstructed areas, it takes a lot to stop them. Baitcasting gear loaded with 17- and 20-pound-test line is considered the minimum for dedicated peacock bass anglers, and some use 20- to 40-pound gear, including low-stretch microfilament lines. Spinning gear will do if it is heavy-duty, and lures can be cast very accurately with it. Lighter tackle may be appropriate in some situations, usually in open areas and where there are smaller fish. Casting accurately among heavy cover is often necessary, and this is much harder to do with spinning tackle than with baitcasting gear. Good-quality line and reels with an excellent drag are important, although line capacity is not critical. Short wire leaders of at least 20- to 30-pound strength are very useful for these and other species, and they don't seem to hinder the fish in most of their habitats.

BASS, REDEYE *Micropterus coosae.*

Other names—black bass, coosa bass, shoal bass, Flint River smallmouth.

There are two widely recognized forms of this member of the black bass group of the Centrarchidae family: the Apalachicola, which is called a shoal bass, and the Alabama, which is generally referred to as the redeye bass or the true redeye. The shoal bass has yet to be described fully or given a distinct scientific name, and there is some confusion over the two. A scrappy fighter, the redeye bass often jumps when hooked and is hard to catch. Its white, flaky meat is of good table quality, similar to that of other black bass.

Identification. As its name indicates, the redeye bass is characterized by the considerable amount of red in its eyes. It is bronze olive above with brownish to greenish sides and yellow-white to blue below, usually with dark vertical bars on the flanks. The bars on the caudal peduncle are diamond shaped with light centers. There is a prominent dark spot on the gill cover, and rows of dark spots on the lower sides, as well as white upper and lower outer edges on the orange-tinged tail. The upper jaw of its large mouth extends to the rear portion of the eye but not beyond, and there is usually a patch of teeth on the tongue. The redeye has redder fins than do other black bass; the first and second dorsal fins are connected, and the second dorsal and caudal fins and the front of the anal fin are brick red on young fish. There is a dusky spot on the base of the tail, which is darkest also on young fish. There are 12 dorsal rays and 10 anal rays.

The shoal bass can normally be distinguished from the redeye bass by a prominent spot immediately before the tail and another on the edge of the gill cover, which is generally indistinct on the redeye. The shoal bass also lacks white outer edges on the tail, has smaller scales, and lacks the patch of teeth on the tongue. It has 12 to 13 dorsal rays and 10 to 11 anal rays.

Size/Age. The redeye bass grows to $18^1/_2$ inches and about 3 pounds, although some reach more than 8 pounds and live as long as 10 years. The shoal form grows faster, although it generally reaches about 15 inches in length. The all-tackle world record is an 8-pound, 12-ounce fish taken in Florida in 1995.

Distribution. Redeye bass are found in North America in the Alabama, Savannah, Coosa, Chattahoochee, and Warrior River systems in Georgia and Alabama, and in southeastern Tennessee (Conasauga drainage). It has been

Redeye Bass

introduced to a limited degree in California, Puerto Rico, and Kentucky's upper Cumberland River drainage, as well as into other river systems near its native range.

Shoal bass occur in the Apalachicola River system in Florida and in the Chattahoochee, Chestatee, and Flint Rivers in Georgia.

Habitat. Inhabiting the rocky runs and pools of creeks and small to medium rivers, redeye bass prefer the cold headwaters of small streams. They seldom exist in natural lakes, ponds, or reservoirs, and they prefer water temperatures in the mid-60s. Shoal bass are most likely to thrive in main-channel habitats.

Spawning. Spawning occurs in spring, when water temperatures are between 60° and 70°F, usually over coarse gravel at the head of a pool. Males build the nest and guard the eggs and fry.

Food. Redeye feed primarily on terrestrial and larval insects, crayfish, and small fish.

Angling. Due to their limited range and small size, redeye bass are not known to many American anglers. There is little concerted angling effort targeting them.

Fishing tactics are similar to those for black bass, especially smallmouths in rivers.

See: Bass, Black.

BASS, ROANOKE *Ambloplites cavifrons.*

The Roanoke bass is a sunfish and a member of the Centrarchidae family, similar in body shape to a rock bass *(see: bass, rock)* or warmouth *(see)*. It can be identified by its unscaled or partly scaled cheek and the several iridescent gold to white spots on its upper side and head. It is olive to tan above, has a dark and light marbling on the side, and often sports rows of black spots and a white to bronze breast and belly. It is also distinguished by the 39 to 49 lateral scales, 11 anal rays, and 27 to 35 scale rows across its breast between the pectoral fins. The all-tackle world record is a 1-pound, 5-ounce fish taken in Virginia in 1991.

Growing to a maximum of $14^1/_2$ inches, the Roanoke bass occurs in North America in the Chowan, Roanoke, Tar, and Neuse River drainages in Virginia and North Carolina. It inhabits the rocky and sandy pools of creeks and small to medium clear rivers.

See: Sunfish.

Roanoke Bass

Rock Bass

BASS, ROCK *Ambloplites rupestris.*

Other names—black perch, goggle-eye, red eye, rock sunfish, goggle-eye perch: French: *crapet de roche.*

The rock bass is actually a member of the sunfish family and is not a true bass. Rock bass are fun to catch because they can be caught on many types of baits and lures and they put up a decent fight on ultralight tackle. Its meat is white and firm and makes good eating. Because rock bass prefer protected waters, however, they can have a muddy flavor or host numerous parasites. Rock bass are known to overpopulate small lakes, making population control measures necessary.

Identification. Although it looks like a cross between a bluegill and a black bass, the rock bass is actually a large and robust sunfish with a deep body; it is less compressed than most sunfish and is more similar to a black bass in shape. The back is raised, and the large head is narrow, rounded, and deep. The mouth of the rock bass is also large, especially in comparison to other sunfish; the upper jaw reaches beyond the beginning of the eye but not to the back of the eye. It has two connected dorsal fins, five to six anal fin spines, and large eyes.

The rock bass is olive brown or bronze on the back and sides, with faint lines of tiny dark marks; the centers of the scales below the lateral line also have dark markings that form 11 or more rows and give the fish a striped appearance. In some rock bass, the coloring is lighter but consistent underneath, whereas others are silver, gray, or white on the belly. The vertical fins have pale circular spots, and all fins are usually darker at their margins, although the edges of the anal spines are white, the tips of the pectoral fins are clear, and the pelvic fins sometimes have a white edge. A distinguishing characteristic is the bluish black blotch found on the tip of the gill covers. The young and breeding adults have a striking "checkerboard" pattern of squarish blotches; during spawning, some males become almost black. Rock bass can develop an overall bluish tinge in some waters.

Rock bass are frequently confused with the warmouth *(Lepomis gulosus; see: warmouth).* Warmouth have teeth on their tongue, whereas rock bass do not. There are also six spines in front of the anal fin of a rock bass as opposed to the three spines in the

B

A large rock bass from Balsam Lake, Ontario.

warmouth. Rock bass may also resemble the mud sunfish *(see: sunfish, mud);* rock bass have a forked tail and rough scales, whereas mud sunfish have a rounded tail and smooth scales.

Size/Age. The most common size for rock bass is about 8 ounces, although they have been known to reach 3 pounds. Often rock bass in a particular lake will weigh around a pound, with a few fish exceeding 2 pounds. As with most sunfish, however, size is extremely variable, and rock bass living in streams are often stunted. The International Game Fish Association (IGFA) all-tackle record is a 3-pound Canadian fish. Rock bass can reach a length of 12 to 14 inches but are usually less than 8 inches long. Although aquarium fish have lived for 18 years, those in the wild live 10 to 12 years on average.

Distribution. Native to the northeastern United States and southeastern Canada, rock bass range from southern Manitoba east to Ontario and Quebec, and southward through the Great Lakes region and the Mississippi Valley to the Gulf of Mexico as far as northern Alabama and northern Georgia. They have been introduced into other states including some in the western U.S.

Habitat. Rock bass prefer small to moderate streams with cool and clear water, abundant shelter, and considerable current; they are plentiful in shallow, weedy lakes and the outer edges of larger lakes, as well as in thousands of smaller lakes and ponds. Rock bass almost always hold over rocky bottoms (resulting in the name "rock" bass) where there is no silt. Young rock bass are frequently found in vegetation. Rock bass tend to frequent the same habitats as do smallmouth bass.

Life history/Behavior. Rock bass are able to reproduce once they are two years old or 3 to 5 inches long; spawning occurs from midspring to early summer, when water temperatures range from 60° to 70°F. Males move into the shallows three to four days prior to the females arrival, to establish territories. They begin building round nests in gravelly or sandy areas near weedbeds or other protection such as submerged tree trunks, using their pectoral, anal, and caudal fins to fan the gravel for the nest.

Spawning occurs during the day, usually in the morning. The females spawn at least twice, moving from nest to nest and laying from 3,000 to 11,000 eggs in total. The adhesive eggs are released and fertilized in short intervals over a period of about one hour; they hatch in three to four days at temperatures between 69° and 70°F. The males guard the nest until the eggs hatch and the young swim away, and many males nest a second or even a third time. After spawning, the adults leave the nesting area for more protected habitat.

Rock bass are a schooling fish and often cluster with other sunfish and smallmouth bass.

Food and feeding habits. Young rock bass feed on minute aquatic life when young, then on insects and crustaceans as they grow. Adults eat mostly crayfish, as well as minnows, insects, mollusks, and small fish. This diet varies with season and location. They can consume relatively large specimens because of their large mouths. Some evidence shows that they feed during the day and that feeding peaks in late afternoon; other evidence supports the claim that they feed both day and night. Rock bass generally feed on the bottom but may occasionally feed near the surface.

Angling. Rock bass are scrappy fighters, but they tire quickly. There is no need to use anything but light or ultralight tackle for these fish. Because they often travel in schools, anglers frequently catch several or many from the same location. Sunken logs or tree stumps are prime places to find these fish, as are deep-water rocky ledges, quiet, still pools along riverbanks where large rocks are present, deep-water gravel beds where a large weed structure begins, and beneath overhanging willows along a river or lake shoreline.

Traditionally, rock bass have been caught by cane-pole anglers using live baits. Many are still caught by live-bait anglers using garden worms, nightcrawlers, small crayfish, and small minnows. The most common tactic is placing a small worm on a short-shanked No. 4 hook with a few small split shot above it and stillfishing with a float or bobber, allowing the bait to sit about 6 inches above the bottom. Among artificials, small crankbaits, spinners, and spoons may work, as will fly-rod poppers or bugs. Light grub or curl-tail jigs and very light spinnerbaits are perhaps even more effective. These should all be retrieved very slowly. Fishing techniques for rock bass are similar to those for sunfish, especially bluegills.

See: Bluegill; Sunfish.

BASS, SHOAL

See: Bass, Redeye.

BASS, SMALLMOUTH *Micropterus dolomieui.*

Other names—black bass, smallmouth, bronzeback, brown bass, brownie, smallie, redeye; French: *achigan à petite bouche;* German: *schwarzbarsch;* Japanese: *kokuchibasu.*

The smallmouth bass is the second largest member of the Centrarchidae family of sunfish and a North American original. To anglers it is one of the most impressive of all freshwater fish and is coveted for its fighting ability. This is the fish to which the famous Dr. James Henshall quote, "inch for inch and pound for pound the gamest fish that swims," of the 1800s is ascribed. Henshall was probably not acquainted with some saltwater fish, or he might have restricted this praise to freshwater species, but it is certainly true that the smallmouth has spunky fighting habits and an appreciated willingness to take a variety of lures and baits.

It is less tolerant of very warm environs and is not as widely distributed as its close relative, the largemouth bass *(see: bass, largemouth).* Because most of the smallmouth's abundance occurs in the northern states and southern Canadian provinces, many avid freshwater bass anglers, especially in extreme southern U.S. states, have not made this fish's acquaintance.

The smallmouth is not actually a bass but a sunfish, and its mouth is only small in comparison to that of some other black bass relatives. It is naturally a fish of both clear rivers and lakes, and has been widely introduced to other waters outside its original range. Smallmouths that reside in small to intermediate streams do not grow as large, on average, as those from lakes or reservoirs, although fish from big rivers, and especially those with tailwater fisheries, can attain large sizes. River smallmouth are even spunkier than their lake-dwelling brethren, however, and tend to be more streamlined and to lack a drooping belly.

Although smallmouths have been popular with most anglers throughout their range, they were not well appreciated in the northeastern region of North America, where Atlantic salmon and brook trout were esteemed and bass were trash fish, until the early 1980s. There was once even a commercial fishery for smallmouths early in the twentieth century, although they are strictly a gamefish today wherever they are found, and are usually subject to careful management and regulations.

Unlike some members of the sunfish family, which are coveted for their tasty flesh, smallmouths are not sought for food by most people, and there's a high degree of catch-and-release fishing for them. This has not always been the case but has evolved in the latter decades of the twentieth century, as their value for recreation has become more important to avid anglers. Smallmouth bass are good to eat, however, particularly specimens from cool waters; their white flesh is similar in taste to that of other sunfish, and better than that of the largemouth bass but not as tasty as the walleye *(see),* both of which sometimes inhabit the same waters as the smallmouth.

The smallmouth bass is occasionally confused with the largemouth where they both occur, and also with the spotted bass *(see: bass, spotted)* and redeye bass *(see: bass, redeye).* They have been known to hybridize with spotted bass. Two subspecies are often recognized: the northern smallmouth, *M. d. dolomieui,* and the Neosho smallmouth, *M. d. velox.*

Identification. The smallmouth bass has a robust, slightly laterally compressed and elongate body, a protruding lower jaw, red eyes, and a broad and slightly forked tail. Its pelvic fins sit forward on the body below the pectoral fins; a single spine is found on each pelvic fin and on the front of the anal fin. The two dorsal fins are joined or notched; the front one is spiny and the second one has one

Northern Smallmouth Bass

spine followed by soft rays. Its color varies from brown, golden brown, and olive to green on the back, becoming lighter to golden on the sides and white on the belly. Young fish have more distinct vertical bars or rows of spots on their sides, and the caudal, or tail, fin is orange at the base followed by black and then white outer edges.

The smallmouth is easily distinguished from the largemouth by its clearly connected dorsal fins, the scales on the base portion of the soft-rayed second dorsal fin, and the upper jaw bone, which extends only to about the middle of the eye. The coloration is also distinctive, being usually more brownish in the smallmouth and more greenish in the largemouth. The smallmouth has faint bars on the body (prominent in the young), whereas the largemouth has a fairly wide streak of oval or diamond-shaped markings or blotches down the midline of the sides. In either species, the colors may vary, and the markings may be inconspicuous or absent in individuals based on time of year and various biological factors. Generally, the smallmouth has bars radiating back from the eyes, and although similar bars may be present in individuals of other species, including the largemouth, they seem to be more prominent and more consistently present in the smallmouth.

Size/Age. The average life span of the smallmouth bass is 5 to 6 years, although it can live for 15 years. Most smallmouths encountered by anglers weigh between 1 and $1^1/_2$ pounds and are from 9 to 13 inches long; fish exceeding 3 pounds are considered fairly large but not uncommon. Most anglers have caught few, if any, smallmouth bass over 5 pounds, although some waters do produce 5- to 8-pound specimens annually. The largest smallmouth known, and the presumed maximum weight, is the Tennessee state record, a fish that weighed 11 pounds, 15 ounces when caught from Dale Hollow Lake in 1955. It measured 27 inches in length and 21.7 inches in girth. The Canadian record was caught in Ontario in 1954 and weighed 9.84 pounds.

The Neosho subspecies, which is more slender than the smallmouth, occurs in the Neosho River and tributaries of the Arkansas River in Missouri, Kansas, Arkansas, and Oklahoma.

Distribution. The smallmouth bass is endemic only to North America, and its original range was from the Great Lakes and St. Lawrence River drainages in Canada south to northern Georgia, west to eastern Oklahoma, and north to Minnesota. It has since been widely spread within and beyond that range, across southern Canada west to British Columbia and east to the Maritimes, west to the Pacific coast states, and into the southwestern United States. It has also been introduced to Hawaii, Asia, Europe, and Africa. Although it has been nearly as widely dispersed as the largemouth bass, it has more specific habitat requirements, and within this broad range it is not as widely abundant or distributed as the largemouth bass. The biggest smallmouth populations occur in cool northern waters, but a greater number of big smallmouth are caught in the southern portion of their range.

Habitat. Smallmouth bass prefer clear, quiet waters with gravel, rubble, or rocky bottoms. They live in midsize, gentle streams that have deep pools and abundant shade, or in fairly deep, clear lakes and reservoirs with rocky shoals. Although they are fairly adaptable, they are seldom found in murky water and avoid swift current.

In the typical river, smallmouth bass predominate in the cool middle section where there are large pools between riffles, whereas trout occupy the swifter and colder upper section. In stillwaters, smallmouth bass may occupy lakes, reservoirs, or ponds if these waters are large and deep enough to have thermal stratification, and they are usually located deeper than largemouth bass once the surface layer warms in spring or early summer.

Life history/Behavior. Smallmouth bass spawn in the spring (or early summer in most northern waters), when the water temperature is between 60° and 65°F. The male builds a nest in water that ranges from 1 to 12 feet deep depending on the environment. The nest site is often over a gravel or rock bottom but may be over a sandy bottom in lakes, and it is usually near the protection of a log or boulder. In waters cohabited by both smallmouth and largemouth, the largemouth bass will spawn a little earlier, as their shallower nesting sites, chosen in protected areas with emergent vegetation, warm to the optimum temperature sooner than the deeper, rockier sites chosen by the smallmouths.

Females usually produce 5,000 to 14,000 eggs, depending on their size. They stick to stones in the bottom of the nest. The young are about 5.8 millimeters long when they hatch in 4 to 10 days, depending on the temperature. Hatching success can vary a lot. Sudden changes in temperature or water level can cause the eggs to die from shock, or they can cause the male to abandon the nest, leaving it open for predators. The male protects the young as they absorb their yolk sac and continues to guard them for three to four weeks until they begin to leave the nest. Young fish tend to stay in quiet, shallow areas with rocks and vegetation.

Older bass prefer rocky, shallow areas of lakes and rivers and retreat to deeper areas when water temperatures are high. They tend to seek cover and avoid the light, and generally do not inhabit the same types of dense, weedy, or wooded cover that largemouth bass prefer. They hide in deep water, behind rocks and boulders, and around underwater debris and crevices, preferring water temperatures between 66° and 72°F. Most bass do not travel great distances, and those in streams spend all season in the same pool. As temperatures fall, they become less active and seek cover in dark, rocky areas. In the winter, they cease feeding, remain inactive on the bottom, and stay near warm springs when possible. Smallmouth bass generally mature when they are about 10 to 11 inches long. Males usually mature a year earlier than females.

Food. These highly carnivorous and predatory fish will eat whatever is available, but they have a clear preference for crayfish and small fish. In lakes, this includes small bass, panfish, perch, and assorted fingerling-size minnows in lakes. In rivers, it includes minnows, crayfish, hellgrammites, nymph larvae, and leeches. Juveniles begin feeding on plankton and switch to larger prey like water insects, amphibians, crayfish, and other fish as they grow.

Angling. In lakes, ponds, and reservoirs, smallmouths prefer a rocky bottom, cool water, and crayfish. Crayfish make up an important part of their diet wherever these creatures are found. In lakes, smallmouths are mainly located around rocky points; craggy, clifflike shores; rocky islands and reefs; and riprap banks, preferring small rocks but also favoring boulders. In flowing water, smallmouth bass concentrate around boulders, smaller rocks, gravel, stone, shale, and various obstructions (fallen trees, bridge pilings, and the like) that offer holding and feeding benefits.

In rivers, anglers primarily tend to fish below structures or objects, which is fine in spring and during high water flowage. Later in the season, areas above these places are also productive. Anglers should work with the current to imitate the natural movement of fish in a river. This doesn't mean always retrieving downstream, however, except when fly fishing on the surface. Most casts should be made upriver at a 45° angle, and offerings should be retrieved across and down. In smaller flowages with less midriver structure, working the undercut banks, sunken logs, stumps, and rock walls is best.

Fishing for smallmouths with live crayfish, especially the soft-shelled variety, is particularly popular among bait anglers. Another good natural bait is a nightcrawler. Live crayfish and worms can be worked behind various bottom-bouncing rigs in flowing water, and on floats in stillwater.

Crayfish-imitating crankbaits are a popular river and lake lure for smallmouths. These look and act a bit like a crayfish, and can be productive all season if smallmouths aren't too deep; they are especially worthwhile in the spring. Bottom scratching is critical most of the time with these. Another good smallmouth lure is a floating/diving plug, worked by twitching it on the surface or by a stop-and-go underwater retrieve.

Surface lures have most merit in the springtime, and early and late in the day in the summer. Poppers, wobblers, and the aforementioned plugs are of most merit, and fly fishing with bugs and poppers is also effective when the fish are fairly shallow. Streamer flies and dry flies may also work in flowing water.

Perhaps the best all-around smallmouth bass lure, however, is a jig. Hair-bodied, soft-plastic, and rubber-legged jigs are tantalizing and very effective in the hands of a good angler. Rocky banks and sharply sloping shorelines are suitable for jig fishing, although it is critical to get the jig down and working along the bottom. Dark jig colors, such as black and brown, are good, but many anglers have success with yellow and white jigs with soft-plastic curl-tail bodies.

A scrappy battler, the smallmouth bass has to be tired out before it can be hand-landed.

In many lakes and reservoirs, smallmouth bass are fairly deep in summer when the water warms up. Fishing vertically with jigs or jigging spoons is necessary, and in some environs trolling with deep-diving plugs or with assorted lures run behind downriggers or off planer boards is the favored method.

Spinners are a good flowing-water lure for smallmouths at times, incidentally, especially in the spring. They may also be effective when fished on a slow-and-deep retrieve in the spring on lakes along rocky shores where bass are staging prior to spawning. Spinnerbaits can sometimes produce good smallmouth action as well, although they are not universally appealing. When bass are shallow and aggressive, especially early in the season, spinnerbaits are extremely effective (and better than a multihooked plug for releasing fish unharmed), but later, as these fish move deeper and become warier, spinnerbaits don't produce unless you want to spend time fluttering single-blade models off deep ledges.

Light- and medium-duty spinning gear will handle the majority of smallmouth bass fishing situations. Light (6- and 8-pound) and ultralight (2- and 4-pound) lines are practical, even desirable, because smallmouths are residents of open water for the most part; when hooked, they do not have to be muscled from obstacles other than the bottom, as is common with largemouth bass.

In many places, smallmouths inhabit relatively clear, deep lakes and are wary, so delicate presentations involving light, thin-diameter line, small lures, and corresponding rod and reel combinations make light and ultralight tackle a fundamental part of smallmouth fishing success. Using heavier gear, including baitcasting tackle, is usually overkill, although some plugs and large jigs are worked a little better on these outfits.

See: Bass, Black.

BASS, SPOTTED *Micropterus punctulatus.*

Other names—Alabama spotted bass, black bass, Kentucky bass, Kentucky spotted bass, lineside, northern spotted bass, redeye, spot, Wichita spotted bass.

Often mistaken by anglers for largemouth bass *(see: bass, largemouth),* the spotted bass is a lesser-known member of the black bass group of the Centrarchidae family than either the largemouth or smallmouth *(see: bass, largemouth; bass, smallmouth),* but this is a spunky and distinguished-looking species that no angler is unhappy about catching, even if the majority are encountered by accident.

The general term "spotted bass" really incorporates three recognized subspecies: the northern spotted bass *(M. p. punctulatus),* the Alabama spotted bass *(M. p. henshalli),* and the Wichita spotted bass *(M. p. wichitae);* the last was previously thought to be extinct and is still rarely encountered.

Spotted bass are scrappy fish whose fight is often compared to that of the smallmouth, although they jump less frequently. Their average and maximum sizes are smaller than those of the largemouth, and they are seldom encountered over 4 pounds. They are more likely to utilize and suspend in deep water, even moving about in deep water in loose groups rather than schools. Spotted bass have white, flaky meat with a good flavor, similar to that of other black bass. Most are released by anglers.

Identification. Spotted bass have a moderately compressed elongate body with coloration and markings that are similar to those of the largemouth bass; both have a light green to light brown hue on the back and upper sides, white lower sides and belly, and a broad stripe of diamond-shaped blotches along the midline of the body. Like all black bass except the largemouth, the spotted bass has scales on the base portion of the second dorsal fin, its first and second dorsal fin are clearly connected, and its upper jawbone does not extend back to or beyond the rear edge of the eyes. Spotted bass have a distinct patch of teeth on the tongue, which largemouth do not, and there is a large spot on the point of the gill cover.

The spotted bass differs from the smallmouth bass in that it lacks the vertical bars that are present on the sides of the body in the smallmouth. It also has small black spots in alternate rows below the lateral line (the rear edges of certain scales are black), unlike either the largemouth or the smallmouth. Reportedly, spotted bass and smallmouth bass have hybridized in nature, which could make identification of some specimens where both species are known to occur even more difficult. Juvenile spotted bass resemble juvenile smallmouths in having a broad band of orange at the base of the tail, followed by a broad black band and white edge.

The Alabama spotted bass has a dark spot at the base of the tail and on the rear of the gill cover, and 68 to 75 scales along the lateral line. The northern spotted bass also has a spot on the tail, but the spot on the gill cover is not as distinct, and there are only 60 to 68 scales along the lateral line.

Size/Age. Spotted bass seldom exceed 4 to 5 pounds and are rarely encountered up to 8 pounds. The all-tackle world record is a 9-pound, 7-ounce fish taken in California in 1994 (it was transplanted from Alabama spotted bass stock), which may or may not be the largest attainable size. Because of the difficulty in recognizing the species, it is probable that larger record-size specimens of spotted bass have gone unnoticed. The life span of about seven years is much shorter than that of the smallmouth or largemouth, and the growth rate is intermediate between the two.

Distribution. Spotted bass were once primarily found in the lower to central Mississippi River

Spotted Bass

drainages of North America, but their range has expanded greatly. They are now found throughout the central and lower Mississippi basin, from southern Ohio and West Virginia to southeastern Kansas and south to the Gulf of Mexico (from Texas to the Florida Panhandle), including the Chattahoochee drainage in Georgia, Alabama, Tennessee, Kentucky, and other nearby states where it occurs naturally or has been introduced. Spotted bass have been introduced as far west as California, where some of the larger specimens are now found, and outside North America, including South Africa, where the species has become established in several bodies of water.

The infrequently encountered Wichita spotted bass appears to be limited to West Cache Creek, Oklahoma. The Alabama spotted bass is native to Alabama, Mississippi, and Georgia.

Habitat. The natural habitat of spotted bass is clear, gravelly, flowing pools and runs of creeks and small to medium rivers; and they also tolerate the slower, warmer, and more turbid sections that are unlikely to host smallmouth bass. They are seldom found in natural lakes but have adapted well to deep impoundments, which were created by damming some of their natural rivers and streams. In reservoirs they prefer water temperatures in the mid-70s and are especially suited to deep, clear impoundments. Typical habitat is similar to that of the largemouth bass, although the spotted bass prefers rocky areas and is much more likely to inhabit and suspend in open waters; it may hold in great depths (between 60 and more than 100 feet) in some waters. Rocky bluffs, deep rockpiles, and submerged humps are among its haunts.

Life history/Behavior. Spotted bass spawn in spring at water temperatures of about 63° to 68°F. Males sweep away silt from a gravel or rock bottom to make the nest, generally near brush, logs, or other heavy cover. The males guard the eggs, and then guard the fry after they leave the nest. Fry are extremely active, much more than either the largemouth or smallmouth.

These fish tend to school more than any other member of the black bass family and are often encountered chasing shad in open water.

Food and feeding habits. Juveniles feed on small crustaceans and midge larvae, whereas adults eat insects, larger crustaceans, minnows, frogs, worms, grubs, and small fish. Crayfish are usually the most important item in the diet, followed by small fish, and larval and adult insects.

Angling. Most catches of spotted bass are incidental to attempts for other black bass. Fishing tactics in rivers are similar to those for smallmouth bass, and in impoundments to those for large- and smallmouth bass. They are likely to be found in groups, so more than one can be caught in specific places. Lures that imitate crayfish, as well as small jigs with grub or other soft-plastic bodies, are especially productive. In summer, deep fishing over planted brush piles, especially near a major creek or river channel, can be especially effective.

See: Bass, Black.

BASS, STRIPED *Morone saxatilis.*

Other names—striper, rock, rockfish, striped sea bass, striper bass, linesider, squid hound, and greenhead; French: *Bar rayé;* Spanish: *Lubina estriada.*

An excellent sportfish that attains large sizes, the striped bass is a member of the temperate bass family (often erroneously placed with the sea bass family). It has been considered one of the most valuable and popular fish in North America since the early 1600s, originally for its commercial importance and culinary quality, and in more recent times for its recreational significance. Striped bass have been successfully transplanted to landlocked freshwater environments and crossbred with related species. Both sea-run and landlocked stripers provide important angling opportunity in North America, and are among the most valued and prized species.

There have been great fluctuations in abundance of stripers in modern times, particularly in saltwater and on the East Coast, and many disputes among commercial and recreational interests. In California, the striped bass has been designated solely a gamefish since 1936, meaning that it cannot be harvested commercially from the wild, although it may be farmed. Gamefish designation has been sporadic and resisted on the East Coast, however, where stripers have historically been a mainstay of commercial fishing and where abundance has been threatened by overfishing, pollution, and other factors.

Since the late 1980s, due to restrictive measures and environmental cleanup along the East Coast, striped bass numbers, which are primarily dependent on the Chesapeake Bay and secondarily the Hudson River, rebounded from a near-endangered status to exceptional abundance. The sportfishing catch has been estimated as several times that of the commercial catch, although federal statistics indicate that up to 90 percent of the sport-caught stripers are being released alive, by choice or edict.

The striper's pleasant and almost-sweet white flesh has made it desirable table fare, and striped bass were long one of the most important market fishes along the East Coast. That market shrank to virtually nothing when Atlantic populations crashed and is still only a fraction of what it once was. Many of the striped bass presented in restaurants today, in fact, are farmed, but anglers are able to harvest enough fish to provide fine dining.

Identification. A large fish with a large mouth, the striped bass is more streamlined than its close relative, the white bass. It has a long body and long head, a somewhat laterally compressed body form, and a protruding lower jaw. Of the two noticeably separate dorsal fins, the first one has 7 to 12 stiff spines, usually 9, which make this fin quite a bit

higher than the second; the second dorsal fin has one sharp spine and 8 to 14, ordinarily 12, soft rays. The striped bass also has a forked tail and small eyes.

These fish are mostly bluish black or dark green above, fading into silver on the sides and white on the belly. On each side of its body, there are seven or eight prominent black horizontal stripes that run along the scale rows that are the distinctive markings of the striped bass; one of the stripes runs along the lateral line, and the rest are equally divided above and below it. The stripe highest up on the side is usually the most noticeable, although on some fish, one or more of the stripes is interrupted. Most of the fins are a dusky silver, with the exception of the white pelvic fins. The young of less than 4 inches long as well as the breeding adults have 8 to 10 dark vertical bars that are more apparent than the horizontal stripes. The vertical bars disappear as the fish mature.

In freshwater, the striped bass has been crossed with the white bass to create a hybrid called the whiterock bass *(see: bass, whiterock)* or sunshine bass *(see: bass, sunshine)*. Striped bass differ from hybrids in the regularity of their stripes, whereas the hybrid usually has interrupted stripes. The narrow body of the striped bass also distinguishes it from the white bass.

Size/Age. Growing rapidly in early life, striped bass average 5 to 10 pounds, although they often reach weights in the 30- to 50-pound range. The maximum size that a freshwater striped bass can achieve is unknown, although the largest sport-caught freshwater striper weighed 59 pounds, 12 ounces. The all-tackle record for the species—78 pounds 8, ounces—belongs to a saltwater fish, although larger ones have been reportedly taken commercially. Striped bass normally live 10 to 12 years, although most fish more than 11 years old and more than 39 inches long are female. The largest striped bass ever reported was a 125-pounder believed to be between 29 and 31 years old.

Distribution. On the Atlantic coast of the United States, the striped bass commonly occurs from the St. Lawrence River south to the St. Johns River in northern Florida. It has also ranged along the coasts of Florida, Louisiana, Alabama, and Mississippi in the Gulf of Mexico. Some fish migrate north from North Carolina, Virginia, or Maryland during the summer and return during the fall. Others living in estuarine river systems such as the St. Lawrence, the Santee-Cooper, or the Savannah are nonmigratory.

Striped bass were introduced to San Francisco Bay in 1879 and 1882; today, along the Pacific coast, they are abundant in the bay area and extend from Washington to California; some California fish migrate north to Oregon and are occasionally found off the west coast of Vancouver Island.

Striped bass need rivers with long stretches of freshwater and brackish water for spawning. Only a few places meet that criteria; the Hudson River in New York and the Chesapeake Bay in Maryland are the most prominent spawning grounds and are inexorably linked to the abundance, distribution, and future of saltwater stripers.

Habitat. Striped bass inhabit saltwater, freshwater, and brackish water, although they are most abundant in saltwater. They are anadromous and migrate in saltwater along coastal inshore environs and tidal tributaries. They are often found around piers, jetties, surf troughs, rips, flats, and rocks. A common regional name for stripers is "rockfish," and indeed their scientific name, *saxatilis,* means "rock dweller," although they do not necessarily

Striped Bass

spend most of their lives in association with rocks. They run far upstream during spawning runs and are also found in channels of medium to large rivers at that time. The striped bass is entirely a coastal species off the coast of the Carolinas and southward, never ranging more than a few miles offshore; along the entire Atlantic coast, they are rarely caught more than a short distance from shore except during migration.

Most striped bass along the Atlantic coast are involved in two types of migrations: an upriver spawning migration from late winter to early spring, and coastal migrations that are apparently not associated with spawning activity. Coastal migrations can be quite extensive; striped bass tagged in the Chesapeake Bay have been recaptured in the Bay of Fundy. Coastal migratory behavior appears to be limited to stocks north of Cape Hatteras and is related to sex and age.

Striped bass were introduced into freshwater lakes and impoundments with successful results. In some freshwater populations, striped bass were not introduced but landlocked, due to man-made barriers that blocked their return to the sea. In freshwater, stripers are commonly found in open-water environs, or in the tailrace below dams. They are seldom found near shore or docks or piers, except when chasing schools of baitfish.

Life history/Behavior. Striped bass males are sexually mature by their second or third year, whereas females are sexually mature sometime between their eighth and ninth years; males measuring at least 7 inches, and females as small as 34 inches, are known to spawn. Spawning occurs in fresh or slightly brackish waters from mid-February in Florida to late June or July in Canada, and from mid-March to late July in California, when the water temperature is between 10° to 23°C; peak spawning activity is observed between 15° and 20°C. They prefer the mouths of freshwater tributary streams, where the current is strong enough to keep the eggs suspended.

Females can carry 180,000 to 4.5 million eggs, depending on their size. When mating, each female is accompanied by several smaller males. The spawning fish swim near the surface of the water, turning on their side and rolling and splashing; this display is sometimes called a "rock fight." The semibuoyant eggs are released and drift with the current until they hatch two to three days later, depending on the water temperature.

The young move downstream to the estuarine portions of rivers in the late summer or early fall. As young and as adults, striped bass move in schools, except for larger fish, which either travel alone or with a few others of similar size. Most striped bass along the Atlantic coast are involved in two types of migrations: an upriver spawning migration from late winter to early spring, and coastal migrations that are apparently not associated with spawning activity. Coastal migrations can be quite extensive; striped bass tagged in the Chesapeake Bay have been recaptured in the Bay of Fundy. Coastal migratory behavior in the Atlantic appears to be limited to stocks north of Cape Hatteras and is related to sex and age.

Food and feeding habits. A voracious, carnivorous, and opportunistic predator, the striped bass feeds heavily on small fishes, including large quantities of herring, menhaden, flounder, alewives, silversides, eels, and smelt, as well as invertebrates such as worms, squid, and crabs. Young striped bass feed on zooplankton and quickly graduate to freshwater shrimp and midge larvae. Freshwater striped bass prefer shad, herring, minnows, amphipods, and mayflies. There has been controversy over the effect of freshwater stripers on other gamefish, most notably largemouth bass, but bass and other popular sportfish do not appear to be important components in the diet of freshwater stripers.

Feeding times vary, although many anglers believe that stripers are more active nocturnal feeders and that they are more effective at catching them in low-light conditions and after dark. Stripers are unlike some anadromous fish during their spawning run in that they will feed while migrating to their spawning grounds, although they reportedly cease feeding shortly before spawning.

Angling in saltwater. Striped bass are omnivorous feeders; in other words, they will eat almost anything in their environment that swims, crawls, wiggles, or slithers, and even some things that don't. They also have another unique feeding characteristic: They will usually feed on only one kind of food at a time when they are in an eating mood. Scientists still haven't determined how striped bass are able to communicate their menu of the day to other striped bass in a river or bay, but when they elect to feed on sandworms, they refuse such dependable baitfish as eels or bunker (menhaden) until the next dinner call. It's anyone's guess as to what will be on the new menu.

It is these two characteristics that often makes it difficult for both novice and experienced anglers to catch striped bass whenever they wish. But the feature that separates a pro from a novice is that he knows what striped bass like to eat and will begin trying all their favorite foods until he finds what they will take. In reality, it is not as difficult to determine what striped bass will feed on in saltwater because the choices can be narrowed down to three or four favorites.

Unlike other species of marine fishes that are most often caught using just one, two, or three fishing techniques, striped bass are caught by all the fishing tactics known to anglers. They can troll live baits, rigged baits, spoons, plugs, tube lures, and just plain hardware. Or they can use spinning, baitcasting, or conventional equipment to cast plugs and spoons, or live, rigged, or cut baits. These fish can be taken from an anchored boat by anglers using casting equipment or conventional equipment to fish on or near the bottom or at different levels in the water column, with or without chum attraction. They can be taken from boats drifting with the tide or pushed by the wind as anglers bounce bucktail jigs off the bottom, drag live eels or bunker near the bottom, or even use chunks of cut baits. Striped bass succumb to the fly rod, on streamers or artificial replicas of real baitfish, in every environment in which they swim.

Those environments are particularly varied in saltwater. Stripers linger off open beaches; in rips where tidal streams flow into bays or open water; off rock jetties or concrete walls; under docks, piers and bridges; or around pilings where baitfish naturally congregate. In other words, where there is something to be eaten, striped bass will at some time be there to feed upon it. The only time striped bass might be found in waters lacking food is when they migrate north in spring along outside beaches to their summering grounds, in fall when they move south to their wintering grounds, or in early spring when en route to their spawning grounds. But even at these times, they often migrate when their foods are also on the move, so baitfish are never really far away.

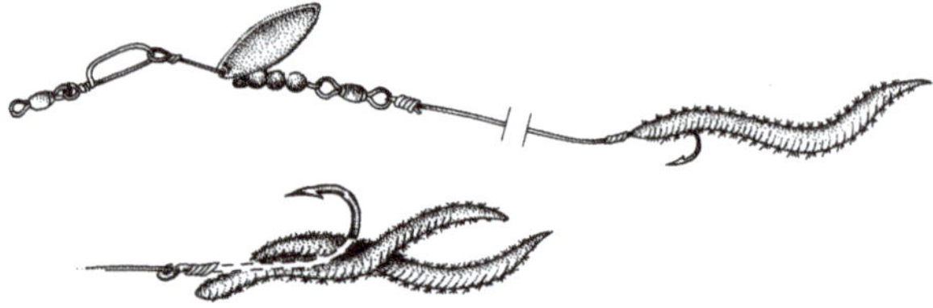

A shallow-water sandworm rig is productive in slow-trolling for stripers.

One of the most enjoyable ways to catch striped bass is from the beach. On the East Coast, surf casting for this fish has developed a devoted following, a highly social camaraderie of anglers who are in the suds both day and night. Long, one-piece rods are in order here, and plugs—either surface swimmers, poppers, or shallow divers—are the favorite enticements. The only drawback to surf casting is that too often the fish work surface waters just out of reach of an angler's longest cast.

The most effective way to fish for striped bass is from a boat, and another dedicated cadre of bass anglers takes bass only by plugging from a drifting boat. Many of these anglers work just outside the surf, and outside the range of surf casters, and plug toward the beach to pull bass from the surf.

The deadliest method for taking striped bass is by drifting live eels from a moving boat. Eels are the favorite food of striped bass, ahead of either bunker or mackerel. Here, the eels are hooked through both jaws and attached to a three-way rig. The hook is attached to a length of monofilament, which in turn is tied to one eye of a three-way swivel. The main line is attached to another of the swivel eyes. And the other eye sports a foot-long piece of lighter monofilament attached to a sinker. The sinker keeps the eel on the bottom; if it hangs up, the weaker leader breaks before the eel and hook are lost.

In many fishing ports, the favorite striped bass lure of charter boat skippers is the umbrella rig. This trolling setup does resemble the metal skeleton of an umbrella, and often four to six cross arms are used with small tube lures that contain hooks on the outer arms. The rig was designed to look like a small school of baitfish, and although it certainly fools the fish and can produce lots of them, many anglers scorn these rigs because they can snare more than one fish at a time and because the cumbersome umbrella rig must be used with very stout tackle.

Large single tube lures, often more than an inch in diameter and up to 18 inches long, are popular among trollers for trophy striped bass. These lures are mounted on leadheads that impart a swimming action to the lure, which is designed to duplicate a swimming eel. Because the tubes are so large, small fish are discouraged from striking them.

Fly fishing for striped bass in saltwater is not a new sport, as it has been practiced for more than a century. It has undergone a rapid expansion in the last decade, however. Historically, anglers who took their fly rods to saltwater looking for striped bass usually carried big, heavy, cumbersome tackle intended for salmon. The development of better rods from stronger materials, and the evolution of reels capable of handling 40- and 50-pound bass, have made fly fishing for striped bass in saltwater not only possible but efficient.

Flies have distinct advantages over plugs and baits when stripers are in shallow water. For example, it is otherwise impossible to avoid spooking a school of stripers when casting a plug into 2 to 3 feet of water along a clear, sandy beach at high noon. With a fly rod, the splash of a small streamer or other artificial is no more than that of a small spearing or silverside jumping out of the water to avoid a predator. This experience can be closely akin to bonefishing on tropical flats. When fishing in deep water, or when it is necessary to cover a lot of ground, however, anglers opt for other forms of fishing.

One of the hottest fishing techniques for striped bass, trolling with sandworms, is also one of the oldest. The lowly sandworm has made a great comeback as a striped-bass producer and the manner in which it is being fished—trolled as slowly as possible behind a small boat in shallow water—is one of the more pleasant ways to fish.

Although the sandworm is a natural bass food, over the years it has fallen from favor as a bass-producer, overtaken by a constant array of new plugs, spoons, tubes, and soft-plastic eels and worms that have flowed from the minds of innovative anglers. Although the new products work at times, they've clouded the picture for those new anglers and even old-timers who have abandoned marine worms.

Those who still favor the sandworm use the following productive technique: two or three long sandworms (the longer the better; see below) are skewered through their heads onto a hook and then trotted a hundred or so feet behind a boat, in shallow water close to shore. The ideal boat is a small aluminum or "tin" version pushed by about a 15-horsepower outboard. The aluminum craft easily bounces off whatever boulders it might strike, causing little or no damage. This low-horsepower motor is ideal because it can push the boat at a snail's pace but move out at a hurried dash when traveling to and from the fishing area.

Big, long worms are vital. Most sandworms bought at a bait station range from 6 to 12 inches. If you can convince the bait dealer to save his "bass worms,"—those on the longer side of the spectrum—for you, the better your chances of catching a big striper. Although the size of the worm is an important factor, the key to the rig's success is the terminal tackle that accompanies it. The proper rig first appeared in the angling literature in the early 1930s, when striped bass were making a reappearance in waters along the northeast coast of the U.S. after a hiatus of more than 50 years. Outboard engines were rare then, and a pair of oars and strong arms provided the power, pulling the rig slowly through the water.

A good shallow-water sandworm rig starts with a 5/0 or 6/0 hook, heavily dressed with either natural white or dyed red bucktail hairs. The worm is impaled on the hook, which is then tied to a 12- to 14-inch piece of 30-pound-test monofilament line. Ahead of the hook as an attractor is a Cape Cod spinner (a willowleaf-like blade), three or four 8-millimeter round red beads, then a size 6 hammered Colorado or Indiana spinner blade mounted on a size 4 folded clevis. Ahead of this clevis are three more red beads, then a size 5 blade of the same style, also on a clevis. To the end of the rig is added a 75-pound-test black barrel swivel. This terminal setup is connected via the barrel swivel to the main line by a snap swivel. A $^3/_8$-ounce in-line beaded lead drail is added 2 feet ahead of the rig on the main fishing line. To avoid twisting, which can occur with spinners, use the smallest available ball-bearing snap swivel, which is 60-pound test. When bluefish are mixed with schools of bass, substitute 30-pound-test black nylon-coated stranded (braided) wire leader for the monofilament.

Enthusiasts troll this rig along the beaches, working the shallows. It is most effective where large numbers of glacial boulders dot the shore, even at high tide. These are ideal places for striped bass to feed. The best time to fish such areas is during the last hour of the flood and throughout the ebb, or until you run out of water. The best winds are those that create a lee for your boat. Most of this kind of fishing occurs in 5 to 10 feet of water. With the worms well astern of the boat, engine noise doesn't seem to bother the fish. The biggest problem you'll encounter in catching striped bass by this method is locating exceptionally big sandworms.

Naturally, tides play a role in all striper fishing methods and locations. Many anglers hold fast to beliefs in specific tides, some preferring the ebb, others the flood. More than likely, however, there is no single best tide during which to fish for striped bass. Actually, it is the fish itself that determines which tide it prefers. Striped bass are drift feeders, preferring to lie in wait and let the tidal currents bring food to them rather than exert energy in searching for it. This is especially true of larger bass, fish exceeding 15 to 18 pounds, which are less prone to schooling than are smaller bass.

In certain places and at certain times, however, striped bass do show a preference for feeding on one or the other tide. When an ebbing tide drains a bay, tidal estuary, or river, emptying water from the area, baitfish become wary of being stranded. They

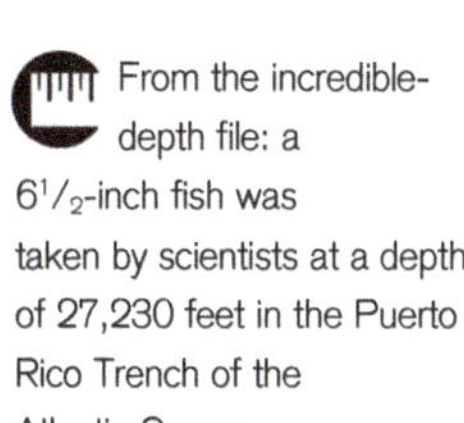
From the incredible-depth file: a $6^1/_2$-inch fish was taken by scientists at a depth of 27,230 feet in the Puerto Rico Trench of the Atlantic Ocean.

B

therefore exit with the flow of the ebb. So, if any one state of the tide is in fact better, it is most likely the ebb. As a result, many anglers who consistently catch bass will begin fishing during the last hour of the flood and then fish through the first two to three hours of the ebb.

Striped bass feed most often when the ambient water temperature is to their liking, that is, between 57° and 68°F. When it is colder, they become lethargic and don't feed for days, remaining in a semidormant state. In summer, when water temperatures rise above 70°F, striped bass stop feeding and search out cooler waters. Water temperatures that exceed 70°F for anything but a short period are lethal to striped bass. Because of these temperature preferences, the best seasons for catching striped bass are in late spring and mid- to late fall along the Atlantic coast.

Spring feeding is spurred by a return to an active life after the winter hiatus. Spawning also occurs at this time, but unlike most fish species, striped bass do not quit feeding during their spawning run, except for a day or two while the act takes place. In fall, striped bass feed with a renewed frenzy after the August doldrums. Striped bass along the northeast coast of the U.S., anticipating the long migration ahead, feed ravenously to prepare for the southward journey that may require long passages through areas where baitfish can be difficult to find.

To most bass anglers along the northeast coast of the U.S., the two best periods to catch striped bass are during and around the months of June and October. Farther south, the better periods are April and May, then November. On the Pacific coast, because the relatively narrow continental shelf and deep, cold water are always near, the best months are July and August. Along the Gulf of Mexico coast, the winter months offer the best fishing.

Angling in freshwater. Stripers are predominantly nomads in freshwater, so locating these fish is sometimes a more formidable task than catching them. They are vigorous predators, however, just as in saltwater, and their habitats are usually blessed with abundant forage populations, primarily gizzard and threadfin shad. Because they do a lot of eating, they are a good target for various angling techniques.

The methods of catching freshwater stripers include using live baits, jigging, casting, and trolling. Casting is done to schools of fish that are ravaging large pods of baitfish near the surface (observed by watching for bird activity), and to fish in the tailrace waters below a dam. Live baits are stillfished while the boat is at anchor or slowly adrift, using a fair amount of weight to keep the bait at the proper depth and immediately below the spot where you have positioned it. Cut bait, in the form of chunks or strips, is sometimes effective, but fresh, lively baitfish are usually preferred. Jigging is primarily done when stripers are holding in deep water in a defined area, using 1/2- to 2-ounce bucktail jigs and jigging spoons. Trolling may be practiced the most, either flatlining or downrigging, using plugs in a range of sizes and colors.

Long rods, in the 8 1/2- and 9-foot categories, are popular for casting, trolling, and bait fishing, especially if large fish might be encountered. Baitcasting reels with large line capacity, a solid drag, and a freespool clicker are popular. Most anglers prefer 17- or 20-pound line, although lighter line and other light tackle, including fly rods, are used in appropriate circumstances.

Stripers migrate up tributaries (if they exist) in the spring to spawn, usually when the water temperature is around 55°F. Fishing on channel bends is popular during the spring. After spawning, stripers scatter, migrating back to the lake and often following the path of channels and streambeds into deep water. They may locate over old creek beds and channels, near sunken islands, along ridges with quick dropoffs, at the deep end of points, near bridges and adjacent causeways, and near any natural funneling point for baitfish. In the fall, they move into shallow, flat areas and chase schools of baitfish. In winter, they stay deep and favor many of the same places they prefer in summer, although they travel less.

For freshwater striper fishing it is generally important to have some type of sonar to find the places that attract stripers, to locate catchable fish, or to determine the depth at which stripers are located so you can place your lures or baits at the right level.

Because stripers wander a good deal and exist in open-water environs on lakes, many anglers spend a lot of time trolling, flatlining a diving plug or using assorted lures behind downrigger weights. When stripers are within 25 feet of the surface, most trollers flatline by tradition; plugs, spoons, flies, and jigs can be used for shallow fishing, but only plugs have merit from 10 to 25 feet, unless sinkers or weighted lines are used.

Fishing with live baits is also extremely popular, especially in the spring and fall. The primary baitfish used are gizzard and threadfin shad, herring, bluegills (where it is legal to do so), alewives, shiners, and assorted minnows. Which one is preferable depends on which species is present naturally and whether it is available. Live baits are stillfished while the boat is at anchor or slowly adrift. Depending on the depth to be fished, the size of the bait, and whether there is current or wind, you'll need from 1 1/2 to 4 ounces of lead in the form of a bead-chain weight to keep the bait at the proper depth and right below the spot where you have positioned it. The weight should be about 2 feet ahead of the bait. Use a 2/0 or 3/0 hook for small baitfish like threadfin shad, and 4/0 to 6/0 hooks for larger baits. Hook them through the top of the back so they can swim freely if they are large, or through the top of

A bucktail jig with soft trailer is a top striper lure.

the nose if they are smaller (while using smaller hooks). Sometimes it is best to keep the weight just off the bottom, but when you already know where the stripers are, keep it slightly above the depth at which you've pinpointed them. Keeping baits fresh and lively is extremely important; this is difficult with alewives, herring, and threadfin shad. Circular livewells are used for those. Cut baits are also effective in some places.

Although casting lures for open-water stripers is seldom done, except when the fish are schooling, a fair amount of jigging takes place, usually once you have located stripers holding in deep water in a defined area, or when fishing submerged humps or mounds visited by feeding stripers. Metal and slab-sided jigging spoons are almost exclusively used for this, and both standard and speed jigging techniques are employed.

In many locales in the summer and fall, striped bass, hybrid stripers, and white bass chase and consume pods of baitfish (usually threadfin or gizzard shad) and roam over a wide area as they keep up with the baitfish and maraud them. Often this phenomenon is best observed in early and late daylight hours. With stripers it may happen anywhere, and the key to finding it is observation. The popular tactic is to race to the site of the commotion, glide to the outer edge of it, cut the motor, and cast into the melee with jigs, spoons, surface plugs, or flies, trying not to force the fish into the depths and trying not to lose which direction they're moving in.

BASS, SUNSHINE *Morone saxatilis x Morone chrysops.*

Other names—whiterock bass, wiper, hybrid striped bass, hybrid striper, hybrid bass, striper.

A hybrid striped bass resulting from the breeding of a male pure-strain striped bass and a female white bass, and a term used primarily in Florida.

See: Bass, Whiterock.

BASS, SUWANNEE *Micropterus notius.*

The Suwannee bass is similar in bodily appearance to the smallmouth bass *(see: bass, smallmouth)* and in markings to the redeye bass *(see: bass, redeye),* except that it is generally brown overall, and the cheeks, breasts, and bellies of large males are bright turquoise. It, too, has a large mouth, with the upper jaw extending under the eye, and possesses a patch of teeth on the tongue, a spot at the base of the tail, and blotches on the sides. It is further identified by its 59 to 64 lateral scales, 16 pectoral fin rays, 12 to 13 dorsal fin rays, and 10 to 11 anal fin rays.

Growing to just over 14 inches and weighing generally less than a pound, the Suwannee bass is a small species. The all-tackle world record is a 3-pound, 14-ounce fish taken in Florida in 1985. A member of the Centrarchidae family, it has the smallest range of any black bass *(see: bass, black),* occurring in North America, commonly in the Suwannee River drainage in Florida and less commonly in the Ochlockonee River drainage in northern Florida and Georgia. Limited range and small size make this species of minor angling interest, but it is an aggressive species found in rocky riffles, runs, and pools and is typically caught around rocky structure and along steep banks.

Suwannee Bass

B

BASS, WHITE *Morone chrysops.*
Other names—white lightning, barfish, striped bass, silver bass, striper, stripe, sandbass, and sandy; French: *Bar blanc.*

A member of the temperate bass family, the white bass is a freshwater fish known for its spunky fighting ability and its prolificacy, as well as its merits as an excellent eating fish. White bass are a popular, important gamefish in many regions of North America, particularly south of the Mason-Dixon line and in large river systems. Because of its small size, it is often considered as a panfish *(see).* White bass usually travel in schools and can provide a lot of action, making them highly desirable among light-tackle enthusiasts and for fishing with family and youths. Generous bag limits and fine-tasting flesh encourage large take-home catches where the fish are abundant.

Identification. The white bass has a moderately deep and compressed body which is raised behind the small head and large mouth, deepest between the two dorsal fins. It also has 11 to 13 rays on the anal fin and one to two patches of teeth at the back of the tongue. The coloration is mostly silvery with a dark grayish green on the back, and anywhere from 4 to 10 dark horizontal stripes running along the sides. It also has a yellow eye, clear to dusky dorsal and caudal fins, and clear to white pectoral and pelvic fins.

White bass are sometimes confused with other members of the temperate bass family. It resembles the striped bass *(M. saxatilis)* by possessing the same silver sides and black stripes; it is shorter, though, than the striped bass and has a smaller head, a deeper body, a humped back, and dorsal fins that are closer together. White bass are also similar in appearance to yellow bass *(M. mississippiensis)* but are more silvery in color and have unbroken stripes as well as a projecting lower jaw (in yellow bass, the jaws are about even); the white bass has separate spiny and soft portions of the dorsal fins, whereas those of the yellow bass are joined at the base. These two species sometimes occur in the same waters and are similarly colored.

The white bass also thrives in some waters inhabited by white perch *(M. americana),* particularly in the Great Lakes and tributaries. Due to similar size and coloration, these fish are often confused, although these species are members of different families. The white bass can be distinguished from the white perch by the lack of distinct stripes on the sides of the body of the white perch, although stripes are occasionally found on the young of that species. Closer examination reveals other distinguishing characteristics, especially with regard to fins, as noted in the accompanying illustration.

Size/Age. White bass average between $^1/_2$ pound and 2 pounds but may weigh as much as 3 to 4 pounds; the all-tackle world-record white bass is 6 pounds, 13 ounces. They can grow up to $17^3/_4$ inches long, averaging 10 to 12 inches, and can live at least 10 years, but few make it past age 4. Females grow faster and probably live longer than males. Cold water and a lack of shad in the north, and warm water and abundant gizzard and threadfin shad populations in the south, account for regional growth differences.

Distribution. White bass have a wide distribution extending throughout river systems in the Mississippi Valley (including Texas, northwest Florida, and Louisiana), the Ohio Valley, and the Great Lakes. Native in the east from the St. Lawrence River, in the north from Lake Winnipeg, and in the west from the Río Grande, white bass are found from Canada to the Gulf of Mexico. They have been stocked within and outside their natural

White Bass

range and transplanted into various states, including California.

Habitat. The white bass is most abundant in clear, cool lakes, reservoirs, ponds, and pools of small to large rivers. White bass prefer lakes exceeding 300 acres and with considerable stretches of water at least 10 feet deep.

Life history/Behavior. White bass are potadromous, which means they migrate within freshwater rivers to spawn, specifically 40 miles or less. Two-year-old sexually mature males reach the spawning grounds about a month before the females, moving into the same spawning grounds every year; they arrive sometime between February and June, depending on when the water temperature rises above 45°F. As with the striped bass, several white bass males gather around a female in 6 to 7 feet of water and push her to the surface, where she releases between 62,000 and 1 million eggs that are quickly fertilized. Settling on rocks and vegetation in shallow water, the tiny, adhesive eggs hatch in 45 hours at 60°F. The adult fish do not protect the eggs or the young, and as a result, very few fish survive their first year. Adults move to deeper water once they have spawned, where they swim in compact schools, often close to the surface. By the end of their first summer, young white bass have grown rapidly to reach 4 to 5 inches in length, and then they follow the adults into open water.

Food and feeding habits. White bass feed on shad, silversides, crustaceans, yellow perch, sunfish, insects, crayfish, and their own young. Although they stay mostly in deep waters, they usually come to the surface to feed on schools of small shad or other minnows and often make a great commotion that is noted by observant anglers; this normally occurs early or late in the day, or on overcast days.

Angling. Because white bass are a schooling fish, it is common to catch quite a few in one location. This ample action is one of the things that makes these small fish a popular species. This can be a misleading phenomenon, however, as white bass are often very fickle. Even when they are abundant in large schools, they may not be aggressive.

Light tackle is highly suitable for these fish, which are aggressive, tugging fighters. Spinning or spincasting rods loaded with 4- to 8-pound line are ideal, although a fly rod can be used at times as well.

White bass feed primarily on small shad, smelt, alewives, or minnows. Lures that correspond to the size and likeness of these baitfish are best. This includes small crankbaits, bucktail or marabou jigs, silver jigging spoons, spinners, sinking lures, and tailspinners, but also small stickbaits and buzzbaits. Some anglers troll for these fish, and in northern environs where anglers use plugs off planer boards for walleye, they accidentally catch a slew of white bass. Jigging, casting, and live baits account for the most success, however.

White bass from Norfolk Lake, Arkansas.

In the spring, white bass run up tributaries to spawn and provide a lot of action. Spring white bass runs are renowned on many large lakes and river systems, and this movement seems to generally take place once the water temperature in the tributaries exceeds 55°F. Late in the summer and into fall, anglers enjoy exciting angling for schools of white bass that feed near the surface on shad. There are many fish in such schools, and they are literally frenzied while tearing into the baitfish. Many boats follow these schools and enjoy fast jump fishing, similar to that experienced for striped bass. Often when one is hooked, another, or others, will follow along as it is played in, and angling companions can catch the followers. In the fall shallow, windblown, gravelly points are also a prime white bass locale. In rivers, look to those areas where streams enter, where bridge pilings disrupt current flow, above wing dams, along riprap, downstream from lock-and-dam structures, and on rocky points.

Because white bass are on the move so much, an angler who relies on one spot may be disappointed. In lakes and reservoirs, it is wise to pick out a dozen or so areas where white bass have been caught before and return to each one when you are pursuing these fish specifically (many anglers catch whites while fishing for other species, such as largemouth bass or stripers). At other times, look for riprap on shorelines, rocky points, reefs off islands, old river channels, sandbars, sudden dropoffs, and stony flats where the depths hold constant at a level between 10 and 16 feet.

White, yellow, or chartreuse marabou jigs are favored among casters, who usually swim them just off the bottom. Crankbaits can also be good for fish suspended in open water, however, especially if they are near humps. Some anglers use a small minnow for baitfishing, often with a popping cork ahead of it to make a surface commotion via twitching; the cork gets a fish's attention, and the nervous minnow several feet below draws the strike.

For surface lure action a small propellered floating plug twitched like a wounded baitfish is favored, especially when white bass are schooled and chasing small baits. Virtually overlooked, however, is the effectiveness of a $^1/_8$-ounce white or chartreuse buzzbait with a plastic blade; this is a killer off rocky points in the fall. Windblown points and adjacent shorelines are the best spots then, as they often have schools of baitfish, which in turn attract the whites.

Anglers should remember that except for the spawning period, white bass in a reservoir or river are constantly on the move. They often seem to prefer deep, open water but venture near the surface when vigorously pursuing baitfish. A school of white bass may slash into minnows or shad one minute, then vanish, traveling anywhere from a hundred yards to a mile before reappearing, in the process of plundering baitfish again. They may not reappear at all, or they may resurface out of sight.

This tendency leads to jump fishing, which is the activity that most white bass anglers, especially in big lakes and reservoirs, associate with this species. In those waters, anglers watch the horizon for circling, feeding sea gulls, which are attracted to surface-busting white bass because they often get an opportunity to snatch baits or pieces of fish from the melee. When you spot working birds, rush toward them, throttle the motor back upwind, shut the motor off, and drift to the school of surfacing fish, casting surface or shallow-running lures in their midst. This can go on for hours under the best of circumstances, although most schooling/feeding eruptions last only a few minutes, followed by a period of inactivity, and then a recurrence of action.

Jump fishing action is often a late-in-the-day or early-morning proposition, especially in late summer and in the fall. This activity can occur with striped bass or hybrid stripers, and occasionally the species will mix. When a striper takes, it becomes apparent very quickly, as they are usually larger and peel more line off the reel.

See: Jump Fishing.

BASS, WHITEROCK *Morone saxatilis x Morone chrysops.*

Hybrid striped bass have become one of the most popular introduced fish in freshwater. Hybrid stripers are the progeny of one pure-strain striped bass parent and one pure-strain white bass parent. When the cross is between the female striper and the male white bass, the result is primarily known as a whiterock bass; in some places it is referred to as a wiper, and in some simply as a hybrid striped bass. When the cross is between the male striper and the female white bass, it is called a sunshine bass (primarily in Florida), or simply a hybrid striped bass.

Hybrid Striped Bass

These fish, which usually look like stockier versions of pure-strain stripers, are an aggressive and hard-fighting fish that provide great sport. The fact that they are so strong and grow fairly large rather quickly endears them to anglers, not to mention that they can be a more ambitious lure and bait consumer than pure stripers.

Hybrid stripers do not occur in saltwater; they are strictly a freshwater phenomenon. In freshwater, whiterock or sunshine bass may crossbreed naturally in the wild, although this is not the norm. Most hybrid stripers existing in freshwater lakes and rivers are the result of state fish-stocking programs.

The first stocking of hybrid stripers was in Tennessee's Cherokee Lake in 1965, and they have since been widely distributed by fisheries managers, not only to provide additional angling opportunity but also to take advantage of abundant baitfish populations. In southern states this is essentially threadfin and gizzard shad, and in northern states it may include alewives as well as shad. In many waters these hybrids fill an ecological niche. They do not relate to nearshore structure, as so many popular warmwater gamefish do, and because they forage in open water for nomadic baitfish, they can help keep predator-prey balances in check, especially in waters where the balance of the biomass is composed of nonsport forage fish. Additionally, hybrid stripers, when they achieve certain sizes, are also a predator for large baitfish, particularly gizzard shad, which would be underutilized by other species.

Although very popular with the general angling public, whiterock and sunshine bass have been criticized by ardent largemouth bass anglers who fear that competition for forage or possible consumption by the more aggressive striper will adversely impact the universally appealing largemouth bass. This has not proven to be the case, however; hybrid striped bass (as well as their parents) tend to roam open water for bait schools and stay away from shallow cover, so they do not threaten largemouth populations.

Like both of its parents, the whiterock or sunshine bass is good table fare, and its flesh is virtually indistinguishable from that of the parent fish.

Identification. This fish looks like a stockier version of striped bass, usually having a shorter length and greater girth, but with very similar coloration. The primary means of distinguishing the whiterock or sunshine bass is by the less-distinct and interrupted or broken lines along its sides. The lateral lines of the parent fish are unbroken. Hybrid stripers (and pure-strain stripers) can be distinguished from white bass by the tooth patterns on their tongues. The white bass has a single broad U-pattern while the striper has two distinctive elongated tooth patches.

The accompanying illustration shows the distinguishing characteristics. It is important to learn the differences between these fish when angling in waters that may contain all three species, as regulations regarding them may differ.

Size/Age. Whiterock and sunshine bass have an extremely fast growth rate in their early stages. Specimens that have been stocked as inch-long fish have grown to 4 inches in just one month, and 15 inches by their second summer, so they quickly attain sizes of angling interest. When 18 inches long, a hybrid striper will weigh at least 3 pounds and possibly as much as 5 pounds.

Their maximum attainable size is uncertain, although they grow much larger than a white bass and are much smaller than a pure-strain striped bass. The all-tackle world-record hybrid striped bass is a 25-pound, 15-ounce Alabama fish.

Distribution. Hybrid striped bass distribution is limited to freshwater and to places with a good population of baitfish, principally members of the herring family. Nevertheless, stocking programs have resulted in plantings of these fish in lakes and reservoirs in more than 30 states, from California to New York and from Nebraska to Florida. The greatest concentration is throughout the southern half of the country, and the most fishing opportunity is in the southeast.

Habitat. Whiterock and sunshine bass inhabit the same freshwater habitats as their parents, primarily large lakes and reservoirs, but they also thrive in midsize to large rivers and occasionally in small lakes or ponds. They are largely nomadic in those environments and are found in the same places as their parents, sometimes commingling with them, mostly in open-water environs or in the tailrace below dams. They are seldom found near shore or docks or piers, except when chasing schools of baitfish.

Life history/Behavior. These elements are essentially the same as for the parent species, including spring spawning runs, open-water migrations, schooling, and baitfish-pillaging tendencies. One difference with whiterock and sunshine bass is that when planted in lakes with no other related species with which to interbreed, they can be controlled entirely through stocking programs. Unlike many hybrid fish, which are sterile, these specimens are fertile fish, but they can reproduce only if they cross with a pure-strain parent. But in lakes where neither pure-strain stripers nor white bass are present (usually in northern states), fisheries managers have stocked hybrid striped bass with the comfort of knowing that the fish wouldn't expand beyond the numbers stocked. Thus, if the fish proved detrimental to baitfish or other game species, they could be eradicated by discontinuing stocking.

Food and feeding habits. The food preferences and feeding habits of these fish are similar to those of freshwater striped bass and white bass.

Angling. Prodigious eating habits can mean that hybrids are vulnerable to angling, especially if stocked in sizable numbers. This is good news to anglers but does not guarantee success.

In general terms, the methods of fishing for whiterock and sunshine bass are akin to those for striped bass and for white bass. However, these fish often exist where there are no pure-strain striped bass, and sometimes in places where there are no white bass; thus, anglers may be unfamiliar with the other species.

The most popular season for whiterock and sunshine bass fishing is in the spring, although good success is possible in all seasons if one spends a lot of time on the water and can track the movements of these fish. In spring, hybrids attempt to spawn in tributaries when the water temperature reaches the mid- to upper 50s. They usually are right on the heels of white bass, and just before pure-strain stripers, although in many of the lakes where hybrids are stocked, one or both of the parents do not exist.

A hybrid striper from Boone Lake, Tennessee.

B

Hybrids travel in schools. When located, it's often possible to catch more than one or two. The most exciting fishing for them is the frenzied jump fishing that occurs early and late in the day from late summer through fall, when hybrids locate a school of baitfish, pin them against the bank, a sandbar, or the surface of the water and rip into them.

When jump fishing, casting with assorted lures (spoon, spinner, fly, jig, surface lure, and the like) is obviously effective. If surfacing schools are not apparent, trolling becomes the preferred method, both as a means of fishing and in order to locate the fish. Trollers will jig vertically for them once located, or in areas they are likely to visit.

Whiterock and sunshine bass are primarily sight feeders. Lures that work well for them are those that imitate small baitfish, especially if they have white, silver, chrome, and clear or translucent finishes. Live baits, of course, are also effective, particularly herring and threadfin shad.

Places to locate whiterock and sunshine bass include gravel and sandy bars, points, tailrace runs below dams, spillways, the mouths of rivers and creeks, between submerged or visible islands, along dropoffs, and above humps or levees. They are often found above humps, ledges, and points in the summer; and, in some really warm waters, hybrids will gather at roughly 20 to 22 feet—around the thermocline.

Hybrids congregate in the tailrace water below dams which provides shore and boat fishing opportunities. Near the dams, most action occurs on the side of the river that is opposite the locks, and low-light hours are prime.

See: Bass, Striped; Bass, White.

BASS, WIPER *Morone saxatilis x Morone chrysops.*

See: Bass, Whiterock.

BASS, YELLOW *Morone mississippiensis.*

Other names—barfish, brassy bass, stripe, striped bass, streaker, yellowjack, jack, streaks, gold bass.

A popular light-tackle quarry and usually lumped into the category of panfish *(see),* the yellow bass is a scrappy fighter and provides good sport on light tackle. With white, flaky flesh, it is also a good food fish, on a par with or exceeding white bass and compared by some to the yellow perch.

Yellow Bass

Many anglers are unfamiliar with this member of the temperate bass family because it is largely restricted to the middle portion of the United States and is smaller than its relatives; a true bass, the yellow is related to striped bass, white bass, and white perch. Those fishing with larger lures and baits for largemouth bass or stripers are likely to encounter only the occasional, and larger, yellow bass specimen, although they can be caught with great frequency where they are abundant and by anglers using light tackle.

Identification. The body shape of the yellow bass is very similar to that of the white bass: moderately long and stocky, with the deepest part between dorsal fins, as opposed to round and compressed. It has a small head, a large mouth, and connected dorsal fins. Its coloration is a brassy, silvery, or bright yellow, sometimes with a grayish olive on the back, and it has clear to blue gray fins that are particularly blue when the fish is in water. Five to eight distinctively dark horizontal stripes line the sides, and the lower stripes may be irregularly interrupted and offset above the anal fin; these markings are different on either side of the fish.

The yellow bass can be distinguished from the white bass by its golden coloring and broken stripes. Also, the second spine of the anal fin is longer and thicker than the third on the yellow bass; in the white bass it is noticeably shorter. The yellow bass has even jaws, whereas the white bass has a projecting lower jaw.

Size/Age. Yellow bass are smaller than the largest bluegills, and the usual size caught by anglers ranges from 4 to 12 ounces. They can grow to 2 pounds and 18 inches, although few are seen over a pound; the all-tackle world record is a 2-pound, 4-ounce Indiana fish caught in 1977. These fish grow slowly after becoming juveniles and rarely achieve the size of white bass, perhaps because they are extremely prolific and often become stunted. In some places, their small size and bait-stealing tendency brands them a nuisance. They have a short life expectancy of about four years on average, and may live to age 7.

Distribution. Yellow bass inhabit the Lake Michigan and Mississippi River basins from Minnesota, Wisconsin, and Michigan south to the Pearl River drainage in Louisiana, the Galveston Bay drainage in Texas, the lower Coosa and Mobile Bay drainages, east to western Indiana and eastern Tennessee, and west to western Iowa and eastern Oklahoma. Found mostly in the central Mississippi Valley area, they have been stocked only within their native range and transplanted to nearby states, and have been generally unsuccessful elsewhere. They are scattered within this range and vary in abundance from lake to lake.

Habitat. Yellow bass thrive in quiet pools, ponds, backwaters of large streams, small to large rivers, large lakes, clear to turbid waters below lakes, and reservoirs; they are somewhat tolerant of weedbeds, more so than white bass, and are fond of warm water.

Spawning. Yellow bass spawn in the spring and move into tributary streams when the water temperature reaches the upper 50s. They spawn on shoals and abandon their nesting site without protecting the young.

Food and feeding habits. Yellow bass feed on insects, minnows, small shad, and small sunfish. Insects and insect larvae constitute a good portion of their diet, especially in smaller sizes. Similar to white bass, they will maraud baitfish in schools, although with less of a tendency to do so on or near the surface. Yellow bass are more active in shallow and nearshore environs early and late in the day, and roam deeper open-water expanses during the day.

Angling. Yellow bass are one of those species that are ignored in favor of largemouth bass, crappies, bluegills, and other popular fish, but they are as sporting and spunky on rod and reel as any of these other fish, even though they are smaller. In some waters they are very abundant, and can provide day-long light-tackle fun. They may even be a secondary quarry when other species fail to cooperate. In the spring, when they are in large schools, fast action is possible.

Like white bass and other panfish, yellow bass are caught on various lures, including small jigs, spinners, spinnerbaits, and spoons, as well as streamer and wet flies. Minnows and worms, usually fished on a float and near the lake bottom, whether drifting or anchored, are common. Some anglers locate schools of yellow bass by trolling or when fishing for other species, then stop and set up for more deliberate action. Light and especially ultralight tackle in the 2- to 6-pound-test range, is just right for these frisky fish, which typically fight stubbornly enough to convince an angler that a much larger specimen has been hooked.

BATFISH

Members of the Ogcocephalidae family, batfish are mostly small fish comprising nearly 60 similar species. These peculiar-looking fish are closely related to anglerfish and employ the energy-saving tactic of luring instead of hunting for their food. This method is valuable in deep-sea environments, where food is scarce and thinly distributed.

Identification. The head and trunk of the batfish are broad and flattened, having either a disc or triangular shape, and its body is covered with broad spines. The long pectoral and rodlike pelvic fins enable batfish to "walk" on the sea bottom. There is a protuberance, the rostrum, on the front of the head between the eyes, which can be long or short. Under the rostrum hangs a small tentacle that acts like a lure. The mouth is small but capable of opening broadly. Batfish are usually heavily armored by bony tubercles and hairlike cirri, with the exception of the gill opening on the pectoral fin. Coloration varies among individual species; for example, pancake batfish *(Halieutichthys aculeatus)* are yellowish with a net design, whereas polka-dot batfish *(Ogcocephalus radiatus)* are yellowy white with small black dots. Most are camouflaged according to their surroundings.

Shortnose Batfish

Batfish can be distinguished from goosefish and frogfish by the reduced fins on their head.

Size/Age. Batfish can be between 2 and 20 inches long, but the average length is 7 inches.

Distribution. Most common in the Gulf of Mexico and southern Florida, batfish inhabit waters from North Carolina to Brazil. They are also found in Jamaica. In warm Atlantic and Caribbean waters, it is most common to see the longnose batfish *(Ogcocephalus vespertilio),* which is often camouflaged in the sand by its warty, brownish body.

Habitat. Most batfish are found along reefs, dwelling anywhere from the water's edge out as far as 1,500 feet. Some species prefer shallower water, but most batfish remain in deeper waters between 200 and 1,000 feet. Shallow-water species frequent clear water, mostly in rocky areas or around the bases of reefs; deep-water species prefer more open, muddy or clay bottoms.

Behavior. Batfish partly hide by covering themselves in sand or mud during the day, and swim at night.

Food and feeding habits. Mostly feeding on polychaete worms and crustaceans, batfish also eat other fish. Prey are attracted by the vibrations of the batfish's lure; if a smaller fish swims close enough, the batfish explodes from its hiding spot and engulfs the prey. Batfish reportedly produce scented secretions that entice prey with their odor. Batfish are capable of swallowing fish nearly as large as themselves by suddenly opening their mouth very wide, creating a suction effect.

Angling. Batfish have no angling value, but anglers occasionally observe them in shallow waters, and, infrequently, they may catch one.

B

B

BATTERIES

See: Motor, Electric.

BAY

A bay is an extensive area of a large lake or the ocean that extends into the land, being enclosed on three sides. Bays are prominent for inshore fishing *(see)* in saltwater and also for varied fishing activities in freshwater, in part because of their generally shallow nature, often the presence of current, and the fact that some (especially in saltwater) are part of estuary *(see)* systems. In small lakes an area that would otherwise be classified as a bay may be called a cove.

BEACH BUGGY

A term for any four-wheel-drive vehicle used by surf anglers for accessing coastal beaches.

See: Surf Fishing.

BEAD HEAD

A term for an artificial fly weighted with a bead head.

See: Fly.

BEAM

The width of a boat at its widest point.

BEAR

To move or point in a given direction. In nautical terms, when a boat bears toward an object, it is heading directly toward that object.

BEARING

The direction or position of an object relative to one's own position, usually related in degrees or points of a compass, and sometimes in relation to the hour hand of an imaginary clock (the bow being 12 o'clock).

BELGIUM

Belgium is a small country of just 30,519 square kilometers, but it has a little diversity in its fisheries thanks to distinctive coastal plain, central plateau, and highland regions. It borders the Netherlands (Holland) and the North Sea on the north, Germany and Luxemburg on the east, and France on the south, and has numerous canals, rivers, and streams with sportfishing opportunities, although this seldom attracts visiting anglers except for match competitions. About half of the Belgian population speaks French, the other half Vlamish/Dutch.

The coast is a low-lying area with fine sandy beaches and slight inclination, with polders (sections of land reclaimed from the sea and protected by dikes), behind which is flat pasture land drained by canals. Various flatfish species, as well as eels and cod, are the primary interests here.

Inland, the central plateau is slightly more elevated and features wide fertile valleys and many waterways, most of which are slow and warm, and productive for coarse and warmer-water species. The Ardennes highlands, a densely wooded and generally rocky region in southeastern Belgium, has numerous peaks ranging between 300 and 700 meters, and is popular with hikers, canoeists, campers, and anglers. Trout, found in many rivers and tributaries, are the mainstay of this region.

Freshwater

The freshwater resources of Belgium can be generally characterized according to major river watersheds, which in a broad sense host coldwater species in their cooler and swifter upper flows, and warmwater species in their warmer and slower middle and lower reaches. Trout and grayling are the primary coldwater catch; perch, eels, carp, roach, bream, and other coarse species are the primary warmwater attractions.

Pollution has taken a high toll in many of the public waters of Belgium. The numbers of fish are down compared with the same types of waters in Holland, for instance, and the size of the fish often leaves much to be desired as well. Water quality is improving, however, although slowly. Zander and pike are still rare in the rivers and canals of Belgium; to find these species, Belgian anglers usually go to Holland.

The major Belgian rivers are the Schelde and the Meuse, which originate in France and are essentially navigable throughout Belgium. The Schelde is Belgium's principal waterway, and hosts the ports of Antwerp, Brussels, and Ghent. Its primary tributaries are the Lys, Dendre, Senne, Dyle, Gette, Demer, Great Nèthe, Small Nèthe, and Rupel Rivers.

The Schelde basin is situated entirely in the lower and middle regions of Belgium. The main river and its tributaries possess various coarse species, as well as perch, eels, and smelt, in the lower tidal section; but heavy traffic, pollution, and muddy water have hurt the fishing. Many canals connecting to the Schelde have been formed in lower Belgium, particularly in the areas of Flanders, Campine, and Brabant-Hainault.

The Meuse River basin in Belgium is a more important system for fisheries, and its highland tributaries are trout and grayling water, while its slower reaches are home to chub, perch, eels, carp, and various coarse species. Most of the rainfall in the Ardennes is transported to the Meuse, the remainder toward the Rhine River.

The Sambre and Ourthe Rivers are the principal tributaries of the Meuse, but others include the Ton, Semois, Viroin, Hermeton, Lesse, Lomme,

Bocq, Molignée, Hoyoux, Amblève, Vesdre, Berwinne, Geer, Vierre, and Rulle. The Semois, Ourthe, Lesse, Lomme, and Amblève rivers are familiar to many European trout anglers.

Early in the season, when the water is cold and running high, the rivers and creeks of the Ardennes are fished with worms and baitfish for brown trout. Later, wet flies, nymphs, and dry flies are cast over the same water.

There are a few catch-and-release stretches on these rivers, mainly on the Ourthe, but for the most part anglers are allowed to keep their catch, and many do so, enjoying cooking it over a campfire. Because of this, once the fishing season is a few months old, the better part of the trout population on large stretches of the aforementioned rivers has disappeared. Those that remain are wary and respond only to very small nymphs and dry flies, fished on very fine tippets. The better fishing is likely to be in the least accessible locations.

During the day the traffic from passing canoeists can be a problem, but in early morning and late evening anglers have the water to themselves. Brown trout are the major angling interest here, but European grayling and chub come to a well-presented fly just as readily. Wading is not allowed on these waters until June 1 each year, a measure imposed to protect the eggs deposited by trout and grayling.

The Meuse, Schelde, and many other rivers and canals in Belgium are frequented by coarse anglers. The long pole is still the number one tool of the trade; Belgium has a long and rich tradition of fishing with this method—the tip of the float antennae rests just barely over the water surface. Where allowed, bloodworms are the finest bait for local pole anglers, with maggots, casters, and worms following in productivity.

More than 150 years of organized coarse fishing events, and the last 30 years of practicing catch-and-release for these species, has resulted in educating Belgium's most sought-after coarse species—roach and bream. This has made ultra finesse a necessary element of catching these fish consistently.

Anglers, especially those in match fishing competitions, thus use small, specialized floats carefully balanced so that all bites are detected. This method, involving a take-apart (multisection) pole from 2 to 12 meters long, was developed on the Belgium/France border around the city of Roubaix, and became known throughout Europe as *roubaisienne.* Belgians have won numerous world-match fishing titles, making them one of the leading countries for this style of fishing.

Other noteworthy angling opportunities in Belgium deserve mention here. In southeast Belgium, trout and grayling frequent the headwaters of the Süre and Our Rivers, which flow to the Rhine, and black bass are reportedly present in the Semois River. Private ponds abound in Belgium. These small lakes, owned mostly by fishing clubs, are regularly stocked with bream and roach, and they host fishing matches nearly every weekend. These matches typically impose a restriction on the length of the rod and line, and the float should be capable of carrying the weight used on the line. Here, fine and concentrated fishing is necessary to gather a good catch.

Many small ponds, called reservoirs, in Belgium are stocked with rainbow trout; a water the size of a backyard swimming pool may be a designated trout fishery. This practice continues to exist because trout waters are in great demand in Belgium. As a result, Belgian reservoir fly anglers are among the best competition anglers in Europe. There are a few first-class trout reservoirs in Belgium, and these are managed by fly fishing clubs. Here, because at least part of the catch is usually released again, a fly angler should be able to handle all techniques.

Licenses and permits. Fishing licenses are a complicated matter in Belgium. The state sells regional fishing licenses, obtainable at post offices. To fish in the Flemish and French districts, plus the area around Brussels, an angler needs three different regional licenses. Each of these is also sold as a license to fish from the bank, from a boat, while wading, etc.

For nonnavigable waters, especially in the French region, an extra license from the owner of the water or the local fishing club is also necessary. On many small ponds, all that is necessary is a license from the owner or the fishing club that rules over the water; regional licenses are not required here.

There are closed season and special regulations for different species as well.

Saltwater

Saltwater fishing has been developing along the Belgian coast over the past few decades. It largely consists of fishing for various flatfish, but other species are present as well.

The Belgian coast is only 60 kilometers long and has few obstructions or islands, making it different in this respect from neighboring Netherlands. This coast is protected by immense breakwaters sunk deep into the sea, especially from Zeebruges to the Dutch border. Fishing along the breakwaters produces eels and sea perch, and cod through the winter. The fine sandy beaches of the coast are primarily places for catching plaice, sole, flounder, and turbot. European bass, mackerel, and garfish are also among the catch, these species taking lures as well as bait.

In the east, the Zwyn Gulf is noted for surf fishing, and produces rays and various flatfish from the beach. The breakwaters from Lekkerbeek to Knock-le-Zoute are known for sole, eels, cod, and ray.

West of there, Zeebruges Harbor produces a host of species, and is noted for conger eels. There is a 1.5-kilometer-long pier here that is extremely

In early America, much of the economy revolved around the exportation of salted fish; 1 bushel of salt was required to cure 100 pounds of fish.

popular with shore anglers, and produces conger eels among its rocky footings. Farther west, various flatfish and cod are caught at the pier and jetty at Blankenberghe. The east jetty at Ostend is popular for sole and eels, and the same species, as well as cod, are caught in the estuary environs of Newport.

Although there's a good deal of shore-based fishing along the Belgian coast, small seaworthy boats are seen more frequently of late and some boaters cross the British Channel on calm days and fish wrecks near the UK for cod, pollack, coalfish (pollock), whiting, conger eel, and ling. Larger party boats leave for a day's fishing for either mackerel (summer) or cod (colder months) from all larger harbors along the coast.

In general, cod are prevalent from September through March, eels from May through September, whiting from October through January, plaice from October through June, and sole from May through October. Flounder are available year-round.

B

BELIZE

Place-names like Orange Walk, Pulltrouser Swamp, Monkey River, and Double Head Cabbage may not sound like inviting fishing locales, but the country that contains such sites has a name that no one can positively explain either: Belize.

It is speculated that *Belize* is a derivation of the Mayan word *belix,* which means muddy river. Belize definitely has muddy waters among its plentiful creeks and flooded mangroves, but it also offers beautifully clear water out on the reefs and around its various islands and keys (islets known locally as *cays*). Muddy or clear, the water of Belize hosts almost as diverse a fish population as its jungle rain forest does birds.

One of the least-known freshwater sportfish is the sheefish, or inconnu; these members of the whitefish clan are found in Alaska, the Northwest Territories, and Siberia.

That rain forest was part of the route of the Maya in pre-Columbian times, and it is virtually inconceivable that one hour from the Belize border, at Tikal in Guatemala, there was once a jungle community that was home to 55,000 people in the ninth century. One wonders what sort of fish they encountered.

The impact of the Mayan civilization can be seen even out on the water while fishing. Some of Belize's highly respected flats fishing takes place around a spit of land that should have been part of Mexico. Ambergris Cay was once connected to the mainland as a small peninsula on the Yucatan, but a thousand years ago the Maya built a canal there to circumvent the site's coral reef, making Ambergris an island and eventually part of what would become Belize.

Mexico's loss was Belize's gain because that location is one of many in this country that have earned Belize its sterling reputation for fine light-tackle angling for the fastest and toughest fish of inshore waters and shallow flats. This not only includes such obvious gamesters as bonefish, snook, tarpon, and permit, but also cubera snapper, jack crevalle, and mutton snapper.

Belize is situated between Guatemala and Mexico's Yucatan Peninsula, along the western Caribbean. The shoreline is relatively undeveloped; flats and inshore fishing predominate along the coast, in and around river mouths, and in the creeks, inlets, bays, and other environs. Mangrove-covered keys, islands, and shores are plentiful. An outstanding coral reef, which attracts many divers, extends along the coast, and reefs exist offshore as well. The Turneffe Islands and Ambergris Cay are a short distance from the Belize coast, and the former comprises numerous keys within a barrier reef. Sharp dropoffs to extremely deep water exist close to the inshore and offshore reefs.

The Belize coast is predominantly mangrove-lined. There are many creeks, rivers, canals, and overgrown backwaters that provide great habitat for snook, small tarpon, and snapper. The Belize and Sibun Rivers, in central Belize and not far from Belize City, and their many tributaries and backwater lagoons and sloughs, were especially notable in the past, with snook up to 20 pounds and numerous small to midrange tarpon. Most fishing for these species, however, now takes places along the coastline and at various river mouths.

Snook up to 20 pounds and small tarpon are prominent here, and most are caught along the mangrove shores and in the creeks and canals and inlets rather than on the plentiful flats, although some larger tarpon—from 50 to 100 pounds—are found cruising the flats in front of the Belize River, usually in small schools. Sight fishing is possible here when the water is calm and clear, which is most likely from April through July and sometimes even through summer until early October (March is often very windy). The coastal shores provide excellent opportunity when bad weather or heavy winds make the reefs and flats impossible.

Bonefish are plentiful on the various flats along the coast and around the keys. They run small as a rule, with the average catch being a few pounds. Some weigh up to 6 pounds (although few larger), which is typical of this region as a whole. Numerous flats along the coast host these fish, as well as permit, which are often sighted daily and in large numbers; flats near Dangrigia, Placentia, and the Monkey River—all in the south—are especially good for permit. Permit have become more abundant throughout Belize, making it one of the best places to catch this species on light tackle or a fly rod. Some are taken to 25 pounds.

Some of the finest flats fishing in Belize is at the Turneffe Islands, offshore and about 20 miles east of Belize City. Here a grand slam—taking a bonefish, a tarpon, and a permit on a single day—is very possible, and wading and sight fishing for schools of bonefish are run-of-the-mill experiences in the right conditions. Here, too, the fish average several pounds, although anglers occasionally encounter much larger specimens.

The palm-studded Turneffe Islands lie within a barrier reef that extends more than 30 miles and include many mangrove-covered keys. The bonefishing, for which these islands are most noted, as well as the permit fishing generally occur on the eastern shore. Out at Lighthouse Reef, some 12 miles to the east, anglers enjoy bonefishing, with particularly good angling around Long Cay. The reef is more than 20 miles long and offers shallow fishing for other species as well.

There is an abundance of reef opportunity off the Belize coast, in fact. A string of coral reefs, flats, and atolls is just offshore and extends all along the coast; it is part of the world's second longest barrier reef (which extends northward along the Yucatan Peninsula as well). The usual flats fish are found here, too, along with barracuda, grouper, and snapper.

Out at Turneffe, on the southwestern side of these islands, the water spills from a reef to very deep water, and this edge is a great place for jigging or trolling. The usual reef dwellers live here, plus king mackerel and wahoo. Anglers who have devoted serious efforts to jigging the reefs have landed jack crevalle, amberjack, Nassau grouper, cubera snapper, and a host of other species. Between these and the various flats species, at least two dozen types of fish can be hooked. Wahoo are said to be extremely abundant in these offshore waters from November through March, and they provide reef trollers with plenty of action, sometimes with several dozen in a day. Wahoo up to 70 pounds have been taken here, but 20-pounders are the norm.

Offshore fishing for billfish is still relatively ignored, although when conditions are right, the areas around Turneffe and Ambergris Cay are worth exploring. Tarpon and bonefish are the most sought after species at Ambergris. Flats that hold tarpon are found a short run from the island, and this species can be sight-fished here year-round. Bonefish are plentiful, and run small for the most part; they can be caught by wading or fishing from a skiff. Permit are also available here, especially on the northern outside flats; jack crevalle and barracuda are common flats catches; and other opportunities wait inside the reefs.

Although there is only offshore trolling here, it makes sense that pelagic species would be present, given the proximity to deep water and the Cayman Trench. Anglers pursue sailfish, tuna, dolphin, wahoo, and king mackerel , mostly in April and May. White and blue marlin have been caught here in the past; these were generally small, yet some of the latter ranged to 400 pounds. The marlin arrive a little earlier than the sailfish. The minimal effort expended for these fish—when compared to the deference accorded light-tackle flats action—implies that less is known about offshore opportunities. On a few occasions, however, local boats have experienced spurts of blue marlin activity. Good offshore sites are in the remote waters and atolls beyond the barrier reef, and around Glover Reef, Lighthouse Reef, and Turneffe Islands; the water around each of these drops off steeply.

Several lodges cater to anglers along northern Belize, with at least a pair at Turneffe and one at Ambergris. A lodge on the mainland not far from the airport runs a mother-ship operation that cruises the inner reef and keys and the coastline, towing fishing skiffs behind. There are also several fishing lodges in southern Belize, in the vicinity of Placentia. Good guiding services are also available.

B

BELL BUOY

An aid-to-navigation sound buoy with a bell that rings as the waves move it.

See: Buoys.

BELLY BOAT

A term for oval-shaped self-propelled float tubes.

See: Float Tubes.

BELT, FISHING

See: Rod Belt; Waders.

BENTHIC

The bottom layer of the marine environment and the fish or animals that live on or near the bottom.

BERLEY

Australian term for chum *(see)*.

BERMUDA

Rising off the floor of the Atlantic is the remains of a volcanic pedestal, which gives rise to two underwater pinnacles and one shallower platform on which rests the group of about 150 islands collectively known as Bermuda. Situated solitarily in the North Atlantic—at 32° north, 64° west—and some 600 miles from Cape Hatteras, North Carolina, Bermuda comprises a total landmass of about 21 square miles, surrounded by reefs and shallows.

Best known for beautiful pink sandy beaches and crystal clear waters, Bermuda also offers plenty of angling opportunities for both the casual angler and the most dedicated record hunter.

The Gulf Stream to the west of Bermuda serves as an effective temperature buffer for cold fronts coming off the North American continent. This moderating effect is most pronounced in the winter months and ensures that water temperatures seldom drop below 62°F, making Bermuda the site of the northernmost coral reefs in the world.

Although mild, the winter months are unfortunately unreliable from an angler's standpoint; blustery conditions often prevail. From about mid-April through November, however, the same climatic system provides conditions favorable to those inclined toward piscatorial pursuits.

Devoid of freshwater, Bermuda nonetheless offers both variety and quality in its fishing. The shoreline, sandy beaches, flats, the reef platform and dropoff, and the open sea offer some of the most challenging action to had anywhere. Perhaps unexpectedly, given Bermuda's proximity to the coast of North America, such popular game species as bluefish and striped bass are absent. The reason for this is that well over 90 percent of Bermuda's marine fauna is derived from the Caribbean region, making the Bermuda experience more tropical than temperate.

Bermuda fishing is usually classified by shore, reef, and offshore opportunities, although there are areas of overlap and certainly many of the fish don't recognize any such artificial boundaries.

Shore Fishing

The shore-bound angler will find that docks and jetties offer a surprising variety of fishing opportunities. Gray snapper, Bermuda chub, small yellowtail snapper, several species of grunts, and bream (an endemic member of the porgy family) are all commonly encountered. This sort of fishing is often best pursued in darkness, particularly if the preferred quarry is the super-smart gray snapper, but there is action virtually all day long. In spring, night fishing produces sennet, a small member of the barracuda family, readily taking both bait and lures.

Casting artificial lures from the beaches will entice palometa, a tough member of the pompano family that seldom exceeds 4 pounds but more than makes up for its lack of size with sheer determination to avoid the landing net. Barracuda cruise these same gin-clear waters during the summer, and although they offer absolutely no danger to swimmers, they will take a variety of lures, including spoons and tube lures. Streamer flies can also be productive. Fishing the bottom off the beaches will occasionally produce a bonefish, although bonefishing is of itself a bit of a specialty.

The Bermuda surf is worth prospecting for an assortment of species.

The sandy shallows and grassy areas harbor bonefish that are larger than in most places. The fish move inshore when the water warms up in April, and continue to be readily available well into October. Averaging better than 6 pounds, this species may be sought from shore, by wading through picturesque sandy coves, or from a boat on the grass flats farther offshore. Although their scarcity makes them seldom deliberately sought after, a few tarpon and the odd permit frequent waters favored by bonefish.

Spinning tackle with fresh bait or proven artificial lures has long been the preferred equipment for catching the gray ghost of the shallows in Bermuda, but more recently it has been demonstrated that a well-placed fly is also an effective tool. There are more than enough bonefish to ensure multiple opportunities for hookups. Best of all, the tendency toward catch-and-release means that many individuals of this relatively lightly fished species are significantly larger than average here, and there can be little doubt that some record candidates cruise Bermuda's shallows.

Reef Fishing

Leaving the coastline and moving offshore a few hundred yards provides the transition from shore fishing to reef fishing. The diversity of the reef environment makes for a number of different habitats, each of which offers its own particular type of fishing action.

In the shallower waters overlying muddier bottoms such as ship channels, the most commonly encountered species is the gray triggerfish (locally called turbot) and whitewater snapper (actually lane snapper). Although neither species attains more than a few pounds, both can occur in large schools, and it is not unusual to catch many of these after just a few hours of fishing.

Just about anywhere over the reef, anglers can expect action from Bermuda chub, a species of little food value but exceptionally game on light tackle—so much so that in years gone by lobster was used as the preferred bait. This species occurs inshore, but the largest schools are found in 12 to 20 fathoms of water.

Over coral areas, catches are likely to be far more varied, often including species that are more usually encountered in blue water. Chumming, which has been raised to a fine art form in Bermuda, will see false albacore rocketing through the slick at the surface, while amberjack, Almaco jack (locally "horse-eye bonita"), and yellowtail snapper can be lured off the bottom. The gwelly, a relatively poorly known species related to the jack family, is also common and is a powerful game fish well suited to light tackle. All of these species reach record proportions in Bermuda, and all are avidly sought game species.

Dropping a line down to the bottom will tempt

some of the smaller grouper species such as the coney, red hind, or barber (Creole fish). Porgy, wrasse, snapper, and triggerfish are all likely candidates as well. There are also seven other grouper species, ranging from the brightly hued 1-pound mutton hamlet to the hundred-plus-pound black grouper (rockfish), which is all but unstoppable on anything other than the heaviest gear.

Night fishing over the reefs during the summer offers the best chance for a haul of gray snapper and, as the season progresses, yellowtail snapper are more than willing to please in a big way at night. Deeper fishing produces red snapper and misty grouper along with other obscure species.

For the most part, reef-fishing tackle is conventional gear in the 16- to 30-pound-test range, with anchovy, cut fish, or squid as bait, although many anglers prefer to use spinning gear. The latter is generally used for bait fishing, although most standard lures can be productive.

Offshore Fishing

The offshore fishing scene draws the most angling attention and supplies the real glamour. The opportunities range from top-flight light-tackle action to working the abyss in search of a record-class heavyweight blue marlin. As Bermuda is surrounded by the reef platform, it is necessary to travel past the so-called inner bottom out to the dropoff, where it quickly becomes apparent that the island is anchored out in the middle of the open ocean.

Fishing from the eastern end of the island means the shortest run to the "Bermuda Edge" (the colloquial name for the 30-fathom curve), and there is plenty of potential along both the northern and southern fringes of the reef platform. It is the western end, however, that offers access to the greatest variety of fishing grounds. These include the famed Challenger Bank, which is 15 miles southwest of the island, and Argus Bank, which is a farther 10 miles offshore.

A normal daylong excursion will include fishing the southwestern edge before moving off to one or both offshore banks. In recent years, the very deep water between the Bermuda Edge and the banks has been exceptionally productive for blue marlin.

Trolling is the main means of offshore fishing. Although trolling produces year-round, the best sporting action starts in late April and runs through early June, and then picks up again in late August and continues into October.

The tackle aboard most charter boats tends to be 50-pound class or heavier, but, with few exceptions, lighter gear in the 20- or 30-pound classes is better suited to most Bermuda game fish. Virtually all local angling tournaments are restricted to line classes ranging from 8- through 30-pound-test, and most of the world records set in Bermuda waters have been on the lighter line classes. Opportunities for the ultralight line classes are plentiful as well—for those who are proficient enough.

Standard trolling baits are in common use, with garfish (ballyhoo) and flying fish the preferred naturals, whether used in combination with a skirt or other artificial. It is not unusual for a troller's spread to include artificials on the outriggers, and bait combinations on the downriggers.

Downriggers are an essential part of Bermuda fishing. It has been determined that speed is the key to catching fish in blue water, and it has the added advantage of allowing anglers to cover 100 or more miles of water during the course of the fishing day.

The wahoo is the most sought-after blue-water gamefish in Bermuda, and there can be no doubt that Bermuda is a premier destination for anglers seeking this particular challenge. With their lightning strike, high speed, and often erratic runs, these sleek, handsome fish are particularly challenging when an angler is trolling with light tackle.

The wahoo's speed, keen vision, and razor-sharp powerful jaws often enable it to cut off baits without giving any indication that they have done so. For this reason, trolling speeds in Bermuda are considerably faster than in most other places, even when rigged baits are being fished exclusively. Although wahoo are present year-round, the largest fish (to well over 100 pounds) tend to be caught outside the summer months, when schoolies in the 12- to 25-pound bracket are most common.

There is a minor run in the late spring/early summer and a major autumnal run that gets underway in late August or early September. This latter run often coincides with an influx of juvenile false albacore, which makes for some of the fastest, finest live-baiting to be had anywhere.

Trolling also catches yellowfin tuna, locally referred to as "Allison tuna." These never-give-up battlers range from just a few pounds to 200 pounds or more. Large tuna tend to be caught early and late in the season, with the middleweights dominating from June through early August. There are, however, plenty of exceptions to this rule.

Blackfin tuna, another very worthy opponent, commonly take trolled offerings, while barracuda, dolphin, false albacore, rainbow runner, and oceanic bonito (skipjack) are all likely to help round out a mixed bag from a day's trolling.

As the height of the summer approaches, attention shifts from trolling and focuses on chumming on the banks, or right on the dropoff at anywhere from 30 to 90 fathoms. During extremely calm weather, drifting is also an option; but either way, plenty of fast action can be expected. This is an extremely effective means of fishing and, although the primary target is yellowfin tuna, the chum slick can rustle up everything from an ocean robin (a live bait par excellence) to a blue marlin.

The chum can consist of anchovies, hogmouth fry, or other small baitfish that are ladled overboard with great precision. The action often starts almost immediately with false albacore and brightly hued rainbow runners flitting in and out. It has been recently discovered that blue marlin is the ultimate chum bait, with the tuna going berserk when diced chunks are tossed overboard. With the clarity of the water and this method of fishing, it is actually possible to select an individual fish to which to toss the bait and, if the bait is marlin, there is little doubt that the fish will inhale it. However, locals do not encourage killing marlin for bait.

Chumming is often combined with kite fishing using either dead, rigged flyingfish—which are especially effective on tuna—or live baits, usually robins or false albacore.

The school-size yellowfin tuna generally range from 20 to 60 pounds, although considerably larger fish have been taken while chumming. These fish offer optimum sport on light tackle, with 8- and 12-pound lines the choice of local anglers. This method of fishing also lends itself to the use of both spinning and fly tackle, with the tuna readily taking both flies and an assortment of artificial lures.

The blackfin tuna's fighting spirit more than makes up for its lack of size when compared to the yellowfin. Many a record blackfin tuna has been caught in Bermuda, and even an average fish in the 15- to 18-pound range gives an exceedingly good account of itself.

Catches of tuna are often exceptional, and there is an increasing tendency to tag and release fish. As a result of this conservation effort, it should be noted that tuna are sometimes recaptured here within days of having been released.

Most other blue-water species will invade a chum line. Wahoo commonly take up residence, and barracuda can become positive nuisances, often attacking smaller fish that are hooked. Dolphin, skipjack tuna, and even billfish have been drawn to within a few feet of the transom of a chumming boat, thereby providing the added excitement of a visual thrill prior to the hookup.

Working the waters nearer the bottom while chumming will not only produce a selection of fish similar to those found over the deeper coral reefs, but also invite the attention of large amberjack (to well over 100 pounds) and Almaco jack. Despite the latter's slightly smaller size, both these species offer a great challenge on suitable tackle.

The remnants of an offshore rig remain submerged on Argus Bank, and this wrecklike structure is a veritable fish bowl. Large barracuda and a tremendous variety of jack species can be lured to the surface in such numbers that the water actually becomes discolored—a splendid opportunity for fast action.

Although not highly regarded as gamefish by most local anglers, sharks provide plenty of sport. Commencing over the reef areas and extending out to the offshore banks, various shark species offer sporting action. The most common species is the Galapagos shark (closely related to the dusky), but tigers are numerous; the pelagic sharks thrive in good numbers out toward deeper water. Blue sharks are abundant but not sought after, and large hammerhead sharks are commonly encountered. During the early summer, mako sharks occasionally attack hooked wahoo and tuna, and each year sees a few makos brought to gaff. These range from fish less than 100 pounds to the full-size versions weighing in at 800 pounds or more.

White marlin are never truly abundant, although they occur pretty much year-round. They are most often raised during the early summer, when trolling is the preferred fishing method. In May or June there is frequently a period of two weeks or so when they are relatively common, before giving way to the prevalence of blue marlin.

The exception to light-tackle fishing in Bermuda is the blue marlin. Bermuda blues run big and, although seasonally available, the action is top class. Peak season for blues is from about mid-May through September. There seems to be a rough pattern to the blue marlin. Early-season fish tend to be females. Smaller fish, probably mostly males, predominate later in the season, when numbers also seem to be greater.

It is not unusual to raise several fish in a day, and as many as seven blue marlin have been caught in a single day. The average size of the fish is close to 300 pounds and, in recent years, the use of 130-pound tackle has revealed that granders are very real possibilities. Indeed, quite a few have been caught; the Island record is more than 1,300 pounds, with reports of huge fish every season.

It is noteworthy that, with few exceptions, most marlin are released, and there is heavy emphasis on tagging programs to help promote billfish research.

Sailfish and spearfish are also taken incidentally, usually when anglers are trolling for wahoo or tuna. Other rarely encountered species of interest are bigeye tuna, bluefin tuna, cobia, and kingfish.

Evidence of other undeveloped fisheries resources exists. Commercial longliners and exploratory sportfishing efforts have revealed the presence of both albacore and swordfish around Bermuda. Each year sees a few albacore taken, usually by trolling early in the morning or at dusk, and the extremely limited effort directed toward swordfish has been surprisingly successful. The application of different techniques in the future may well mean even more varied fishing opportunities.

BICUDA *Boulengerella ocellata.*

Other names—pike-characin; Spanish: *picudo, per lápiz.*

Although "bicuda" refers to the barracuda in Spanish and Portuguese, a number of fish that thrive in the tropical freshwater drainages of South America are known in English as bicudas. In Brazil, the species referred to as bicuda and shown in the accompanying photograph is extremely popular in those places where it is encountered. In shape, it looks somewhat like a barracuda and also somewhat like a North American pike.

Bicuda, in fact, are pike-characins and members of the family Ctenoluciidae. They belong to the American pike-characin branch of the family and are distant relatives of African pike-characins. They are freshwater fish of tropical origins; juvenile specimens are generally regarded as aquarium candidates. Other known species of bicuda include *B. lateristriga* (striped), *B. lucius* (golden), and *B. maculata* (spotted).

Information about the different bicuda and their behavior and life history is fairly slim, but the frisky behavior and energetic leaping ability of *B. ocellata* make it a welcome catch and an admirable sportfish.

Identification. Color patterns differ according to the species. The Brazilian bicuda encountered most by anglers are silvery gray, slightly darker on top and lighter on bottom, but may have tinges of yellow on the lower half of their body, particularly around the gills and fins, with yellow orange coloring on the tail. They have a dark spot at the base of the caudal fin.

Bicuda are slim and elongate with a long, pointed snout. The upper jaw extends beyond the lower, and the tip of the upper jaw is slightly rounded and bulbous. They possess a small adipose fin, and their dorsal and anal fins are situated along the posterior end of the body. The tail fin is broad and slightly rounded.

Size. The larger species of bicuda can reach up to approximately 40 inches in length and reportedly may weigh up to 13 pounds.

Distribution. Bicuda are found in tropical South America, primarily in the Amazon basin and adjacent areas.

Habitat. The primary habitat of bicuda is evidently flowing water, and they generally favor the moderate-flowing sections of rivers, especially in pools, and the mouths of lagoons and bays that empty into rivers.

Food and feeding habits. Bicuda are carnivorous and are usually present in small schools. They attack forage fish aggressively, although it is unknown which species, if any, they have a preference for.

Angling. Larger bicuda will attack assorted lures, leap out of the water frequently when hooked, and fight hard on light tackle. They are not endurance battlers, nor are they prone to streaking off with large amounts of line, unless caught on very light tackle. They are aggressive, however, and may repeatedly strike a lure. Most anglers who encounter bicuda do so by accident, usually while fishing for peacock bass and using fairly stout tackle, although bicuda do not inhabit the same cover-laden backwaters as peacock bass. They may be nearby, however, and sometimes are caught when anglers turn their attention from the shore and areas with cover to ply the more open reaches of water. Spoons, spinners, and an assortment of plugs—including large surface plugs that walk, pop, chug, and make a commotion—are effective on bicuda.

A bicuda from Brazil's São Francisco River.

See: Brazil.

BIG GAME

A general term that refers to large and strong saltwater sportfish that are customarily caught in offshore *(see)* waters and with medium- to heavy-duty conventional tackle *(see)* or big-game tackle *(see)*, even though some of these species, or smaller specimens, may be caught with other equipment. Historically they were pursued with heavy equipment, primarily by trolling or drifting, and the term has stuck.

The principal big-game species include all of the billfish (marlin, sailfish, and swordfish); most sharks; the larger tuna (bigeye, bluefin, dogtooth, and yellowfin); and wahoo. Dolphin do not grow as large on average as any of these fish, but they are caught in the same offshore waters and via the same methods, and are generally lumped into this designation as well. Tarpon are considered big game by some because of the heavy-duty tackle sometimes used for them, they are often caught as large (100 pounds) as many of the aforementioned species, and they are very active when hooked.

See: Offshore Fishing.

BIG-GAME FISHING

See: Big-Game Tackle; Offshore Fishing.

BIG-GAME LURES

See: Big-Game Fishing; Trolling Lures, Saltwater.

BIG-GAME TACKLE

Big-game tackle is a type of high-performance saltwater fishing equipment characterized by heavy-duty revolving-spool reels equipped with a lever drag mechanism. It is related in a general way to

B

conventional tackle *(see),* although the hallmark of big-game tackle is reels that feature superior drag performance and durability.

Big-game tackle may also be referred to as offshore tackle, trolling tackle, or lever drag tackle, and it is almost exclusively used in saltwater. Although some extremely large and stubborn freshwater fish might lend themselves to angling with small-size big-game equipment, 99 percent of big-game tackle usage is in marine environs, and the vast majority of that by big-water boaters. This tackle is most often associated with blue water trolling or bait-fishing for billfish, tuna, and sharks, but smaller models are suitable for some types of reef and inshore fishing, and some may also have limited casting application.

This tackle has evolved a lot in recent decades. With the advent of smaller reels, improved drag materials, reels with greater line capacity, and new rod designs, the uses for big-game tackle have expanded greatly. Though more expensive than similar purpose conventional tackle, big-game tackle has become very popular, especially among anglers likely to encounter the largest and most gear-punishing saltwater species, largely because of its ability to endure extreme pressures and to subdue tough fish quicker than would otherwise be possible. For this reason, line capacity, gears, and drag are the most critical components of big-game reels.

Appropriate versions of big-game tackle can be used in applications ranging from giant marlin trolling offshore to baiting tarpon in bays, and to such in-between uses as reef fishing for big groupers, live-baiting for cruising sailfish, and employing light thread for assorted large species at times when fish become "line shy." Appropriate models of big-game reels with corresponding rods—classified by the intended line strength—may be used for various tasks, although specific outfits are best suited to particular applications.

Smaller and lighter versions of this tackle, especially those with two-speed gears, have been popular for lighter-duty uses, displacing some conventional gear and being used in such diverse applications as fishing for large cobia and striped bass around bridge and buoy structures, school tuna in open water, and deep bottom-hugging halibut. These are likely to become increasingly popular and more widely used.

Big-game reels, such as this group, are premium products in price, features, and performance.

Lever Drag Reels

The origin of big-game tackle is intermingled with that of conventional tackle, and, indeed, the term "big-game tackle" was once used to refer solely to rods equipped with large-capacity revolving-spool reels that sported star drag mechanisms. The first revolving-spool reel with a star drag was used in 1913; prior to that time, reels did not have an internal drag mechanism. Pressure on the reel spool—to make a fish work for the line it took off—was applied by putting the thumb on the line (which was ineffective for large fish and sometimes painful to the angler) or by a leather thumb pad that was attached to the reel frame.

The star drag mechanism provided an internal slip clutch to help pressure strong fish and slow the rate of line being pulled off the reel. It was incorporated in all types and sizes of revolving-spool reels in later years. All products that are today categorized as conventional reels feature a star drag; this also includes baitcasting *(see)* reels.

The large-capacity star drag reel of the early twentieth century was a big advance for its time and has been greatly improved to this day. Arguably, the biggest improvement has been in the area of drag performance, due to advances in drag washer materials. Nevertheless, early conventional reels, and to some extent their modern counterparts, often provided insufficient drag performance when used to strike and fight large, powerful fish. It should be noted that large, powerful fish are not necessarily the biggest and toughest specimens; a 50-pound Atlantic sailfish caught on 12-pound-test line can do some furious greyhounding through the water, possibly overheating a reel in the process. Therefore, size and strength in a fish is relative to the class of tackle and strength of line employed.

The problem with conventional reels is that drag tension is not easily or readily adjustable to known levels. Turning the star wheel adjusts the drag tension, which is usually set to a predetermined level before fishing. If that wheel is deliberately or accidentally turned later, especially while playing a fish, drag tension is changed and may be too little or too great for the circumstances. Once the tension is changed, it cannot be recalibrated with absolute certainty while playing a fish. Furthermore, it may be desirable to deliberately increase or decrease drag tension while playing a fish (usually a very large and powerful one for the tackle), but doing so means making an adjustment to a "guesstimated" level of tension, and being unable to return to a known preset tension level later on.

Experienced anglers can make adjustments to the preset tension of a star drag reel and be reasonably close to the tension level necessary for the circumstances, but most anglers cannot do so, and may have a high degree of error when making adjustments by feel under difficult and pressured angling circumstances, which can have harmful results. This is most significant when fishing for the toughest species, when using light lines, and in circumstances where a lot of line is taken from the reel.

This drawback, which was originally of greatest significance to big-game anglers fishing with fairly unsophisticated conventional reels, lead to the development of the lever drag revolving-spool reel by Fin-Nor in the mid-1930s. For several decades, this product was available in limited supply in large-capacity heavy-line models that were very expensive and tailored to the elite offshore angler. In 1966, Penn Reels, a major conventional reel manufacturer, produced its first two models of lever drag reels; these were more affordable than existing products, and in ensuing decades, this entire genre of tackle improved exponentially. Lever drag reels came to be known as offshore reels because the first applications, with large models, were geared to billfish and tuna. It later became known as big-game tackle, although it should be noted that many heavy-duty, large-capacity conventional reels are used to catch big-game species.

In lever drag reels, the drag adjustment mechanism is separate from the reel handle and doesn't turn with the handle as the star wheel on a conventional reel does. This, plus the fact that the position of the drag lever is constantly visible, means less chance of inadvertently changing drag tension, and always being certain of the level of tension applied. Lever drag reels also have several (at least Strike- and Full-drag) tension settings, which permit preset tension at one level for setting the hook and at another level for bringing maximum pressure to bear on a stubborn fish. This is a significant difference from conventional reels, which can only be preset to one drag tension setting and whose tension adjustment cannot be reliably changed to precise levels during use. Lever drag reels also feature a device to limit the drag-setting range, and the drag is capable of being fine-tuned.

Essentially, a big-game reel today is one with lever drag operation. It does have overlapping features with conventional reels, and in some instances, the same rods can be used with either type of reel. Categorically, however, these reels are generally more expensive, more durable, and heavier than conventional reels that hold a comparable strength and amount of line. Models with two-speed gearing are wholly unlike conventional reels, and have special application for catching tough fish.

Big-game reels are rarely used for casting and are almost entirely used for trolling lures or bait and for fishing at various depths with sinking lures or bait, both of which call for paying line off the reel rather than casting. However, a growing interest in varied methods of fishing has caused some modern big-game reels to be used for casting either lures or natural bait, as well as for other types of fishing, despite their comparatively large size and greater weight.

A common characteristic of all big-game reels is that they do not possess a level line-winding mechanism. When using them, the angler must manually direct the placement of line on the spool to produce an even line lay. This can be a problem for inexperienced anglers or those who are unfamiliar with this action. When line is not wound evenly, it bunches and may prevent either retrieval or dispensing, as well as contributing to the binding of line wraps. Manual line leveling can seem even more burdensome when combined with the fact that big-game reels, which sit on top of the rod facing the angler, are heavy and, for some people, awkward to hold.

The two-speed gear components of a Fin-Nor Ahab big-game reel are evident in this composite image; quick one-step gear shifting is possible with this reel.

Being heavy is a double-edged sword, however. The weight is a result of the size necessary for adequate line capacity, and a result of the sturdy components necessary for the frame, spool, and gears, which, in addition to the drag, are the elements that make these reels capable of subduing fish that can instantly peel a lot of line off and need backbone to land.

General Operation

In the most basic sense, big-game tackle works much like all other tackle except flycasting in that a weighted object at the end of the line pulls line from the spool. The spool of a lever drag reel revolves when you turn the handle as line pays out and when line is retrieved. When the reel is placed in freespool and line is dispensed from the reel, a backlash *(see)* or spool overrun can occur if the revolving spool turns faster than the line is carried off that spool. Applying light pressure to the spool prevents this and may be accomplished in several ways.

The big-game reel has a lever that applies various amounts of drag tension on the spool; the greater the tension, the more force it takes to pull line from the spool. Completely releasing tension allows the spool to turn most freely (freespool). In use, the reel sits atop the rod and faces toward the angler; the rod-holding hand thumb is placed on the spool to keep the line in check, and the free hand is used to move the drag lever backward to minimum tension, which places the reel in freespool. When thumb pressure is relaxed, line flows off the spool and out through the rod guides, carried by the weight of the object at the terminal end of the line. Big-game reels feature a click ratchet, also called a warning click, used to signal that line is being taken off the reel; this may be employed when a reel is not held or left unattended.

To retrieve line, the drag lever is moved forward to apply some degree of tension on the spool, and the spool is turned by rotating the handle, which winds line onto the reel. When line is wound onto the spool, the user must level the line manually for even line distribution.

The adjustable drag mechanism is activated by moving a lever that is located on the same sideplate as the handle. Unlike other reels, this equipment has dual drag settings, usually referred to as Strike and Full, which are preset to the desirable level at the beginning of each day's fishing and relaxed when the day is concluded. These are the basic elements of operating a lever drag reel.

When recovering line on a big-game reel, it's necessary to guide the line evenly onto the spool with your thumb.

Line Release Features

The vast majority of lever drag reels, and most large models, are not used for casting, but primarily used for trolling or for drift fishing with bait, generally in situations where a modest amount of line is let out. Nevertheless, controlling the flow of line off the spool is an important element of usage.

Freespooling. Technically, there is no such thing as freespool on a lever drag reel, although the term is universally used and is a carryover from other types of revolving spool reels, where the gears are disengaged to achieve freespool. In lever drag reels, the gears are always engaged, and the drag mechanism drives the spool. To achieve freespool—in this case meaning a state where there is no tension on the spool and line can flow off without resistance—disengage the drag by moving the adjustment lever fully backward. This disengages the clutch parts while leaving the gears intact. Moving the drag lever forward applies tension to the spool and allows a return to a known, preset level, as will be explained shortly.

Spool revolution. Before putting the reel into freespool, you must apply finger pressure to the spool to prevent line from paying out prematurely or haphazardly. Without this pressure, and assuming that a lure or weighted bait was tied to the end of the line, the weight of either object would cause the spool to turn the moment the reel was placed into the freespool position, which could cause an instant backlash on the spool.

It is therefore necessary to place the thumb of the rod-holding hand on the spool so the spool can't turn, and then move the drag lever fully backward. Now the line can be released by easing the tension. Thumb pressure is lessened on the spool to pay line out at a controlled rate; the objective is to let a sufficient amount of line out for the fishing circumstances at a rate that doesn't cause the spool to turn so fast that it causes a backlash. This is important because a revolving spool can gather speed quickly and an uncontrolled spool can lead to a serious backlash in seconds. The backlash not only impedes immediate fishing effort because of the time required to undo it, but can also cause damage to the line.

Tension releasing. Line can also be released from lever drag reels under moderate tension. This is often done by anglers when lengthening the amount of line already out while trolling, or feeding more line to bait that is drifting with current. This is accomplished by turning the warning click on and backing the drag lever off to a point between the Strike setting and freespool, where line can be pulled off easily yet without causing an overrun. Line can then be paid out in intervals as necessary, generally by pulling it from the tip-top guide or directly from the reel. When enough line has been deployed, the drag lever is returned to its original setting (usually the Strike position).

Retrieving/Line Recovery Features

Most factors that affect line retrieval with lever drag reels are similar to those for other revolving-spool reels, although because of the applications of these products, some elements, particularly gears, are very significant.

Line pickup. To be in a position to set the hook and to return line to the spool, some drag tension has to be established. In the most basic sense, with the drag lever moved forward so that some level of drag tension is in effect, turning the handle revolves the spool, bringing line onto it. When there is sufficient resistance from a fish, the mere act of turning the handle, even with tension applied to the drag washer, may not place line on the spool, which causes other actions—increased drag tension, methods of playing the fish, boat manipulation, etc.—to be used to aid line recovery.

Left/right retrieve. Lever drag reels are manufactured in right-handed cranking versions and cannot be converted by the angler, as a spinning reel can, although some lever drag reels (as well as conventional reels) may be converted to or even originated in left retrieve by custom shop operators. The reason for this is that applications with big-game reels are very demanding, the outfits are generally heavy, and most people are right-handed, meaning that it is normal to want to use the dominant hand for the hard cranking work that is often an element of lever drag reel use. Lever drag reels are especially used for landing big fish, and it is common to attach these reels to a harness, which relieves the rod-holding arm. If a person is right-handed, all of the heavy-duty cranking of the reel is done with the stronger hand, which in theory is better for anyone who is right-handed, although not as desirable for a lefty.

Lefthanders complain about this to reel manufacturers, but the problem is basically economic on two levels. If there was enough demand, manufacturers would make left-handed lever drag reels. But there aren't enough left-handed anglers (or not enough of them have complained) to make it worthwhile for manufacturers to undertake the costs necessary to produce two versions of every lever drag reel. Furthermore, from a practical usage standpoint, owning both right- and left-handed retrieve models of expensive lever drag reels becomes more gear-intensive than most people would like or can afford. This is especially true for party boat operators, charter captains, or private boat owners, who take customers, friends, and family fishing. It is simply easier to have everything that works the same way (right-retrieve), especially since most people are right-handed.

Line winding. Line is wound directly onto the spool of lever drag reels, but they do not have a mechanism for leveling or dispersing that line across the spool (called a levelwind). This leveling must be done manually. The hand that holds the rod (usually the left hand) must be situated in such a way that the thumb can be used to direct the line back and forth onto the spool as it is retrieved. This means holding the rod at the foregrip ahead of the reel, and extending the thumb to the right to catch the line with both sides of the tip of the thumb, moving it to the left and right to disperse the line. (An alternate method when using a harness is to run and direct the line between the fingers while the rod hand is held over the reel.) This leveling has to be done whenever the handle of the reel is turned and line is recovered onto the spool.

With his thumb controlling spool speed, this angler lets line out on a big-game outfit; note the full set of roller guides on the rod.

Failing to disperse the line by hand results in bunching on the spool. If the line bunches severely enough, it may jam at the frame crossbars and prevent retrieval of additional line or inhibit outflow of line when the reel is placed in freespool. Bunching also causes wraps to bind among each other, impeding the free flow of line off the spool; and makes it more likely to incur a spool overrun; a horrific tangle that will have to be painstakingly picked apart.

The reason these reels have no levelwind mechanism (also the case on many conventional reels), is that really big, powerful fish can strip line extremely fast off a reel. The line guide cannot keep up with the swift back and forth movement of the departing line, necessarily putting friction and more tension on the line, which might cause the levelwind to fail or the line to break. Furthermore, the levelwind, which is always exposed to the elements, might break due to the corrosive effect of saltwater, even when carefully cleaned and maintained, or a really powerful fish might be lost due to friction on the line.

Gears. The most basic part of the operation of every reel, and one of its most significant attributes, is the gear set, which in a lever drag reel is as heavy duty as reel gears get.

In a lever drag reel, a large gear, the main or drive gear, engages a smaller gear, the pinion. The drive gear is linked to the reel handle, and the pinion gear connects to the spool. This system provides the multiplying gear ratio for ample line retrieval rates with a small spool and still delivers substantial cranking power. It also allows for the use of heavy lines.

Top quality lever drag reels have stainless steel main and pinion gears. In some products these are the same grade; in others one grade of stainless steel is slightly stronger than the other.

In almost any simple gear set, one gear material is normally different from the other. This is because use of the same materials would tend to cold weld, or "gall" together; dissimilar metals nearly always offer the lowest coefficient of friction. The presence of an oil film helps to reduce friction. The result of using dissimilar metals and an oil film is that gear runs smoothly for a longer period of time.

The best situation is for the main drive gear material to be slightly softer than the pinion gear for wear characteristics, especially in reels that are used often for demanding applications, and where the gear ratio is high. In a multiplier reel, one tooth of the pinion gear contacts its mating teeth on the main gear the same number of times as the gear ratio. That is, in a 5:1 ratio reel, each tooth on the pinion gear is activated five times more often than its counterpart on the main gear. Therefore, it is subject to five times the wear and needs to be harder simply to survive. Lever drag reels, however, generally have low gear ratios and a greater tooth configuration that doesn't produce such problems.

Gears are made to work in a given way with respect to each other, so there must be a certain distance between the two to match up; otherwise the gears will feel tight. Naturally, it is important that the gear teeth are machined as precisely as possible to assure smooth operation and long life. Due to the high-stress cranking that is experienced with lever drag reels, it is also important that they have a rigid support system, so that under great duress there is no flex to affect the inner workings of the reel. The use of heavy line, and cranking large fish in extreme conditions, can put tremendous stress on all components, and both the material and construction of the frame and shaft supports are what keep the gears precisely located and deliver a long life.

Gear ratio/single and dual speeds. Since the drive gear is linked to the reel handle and the pinion gear is engaged to the spool, the basic numerical ratio of the drive and pinion gears establishes the number of revolutions made by the spool per turn of the handle. That number is determined by counting the gear teeth on the larger drive gear and dividing that by the tooth count of the smaller pinion gear. In a gear set consisting of a 53-tooth drive gear and a 10-tooth pinion gear, the ratio would be calculated at 5.3:1 because the pinion will turn 5.3 times for each full rotation of the drive gear.

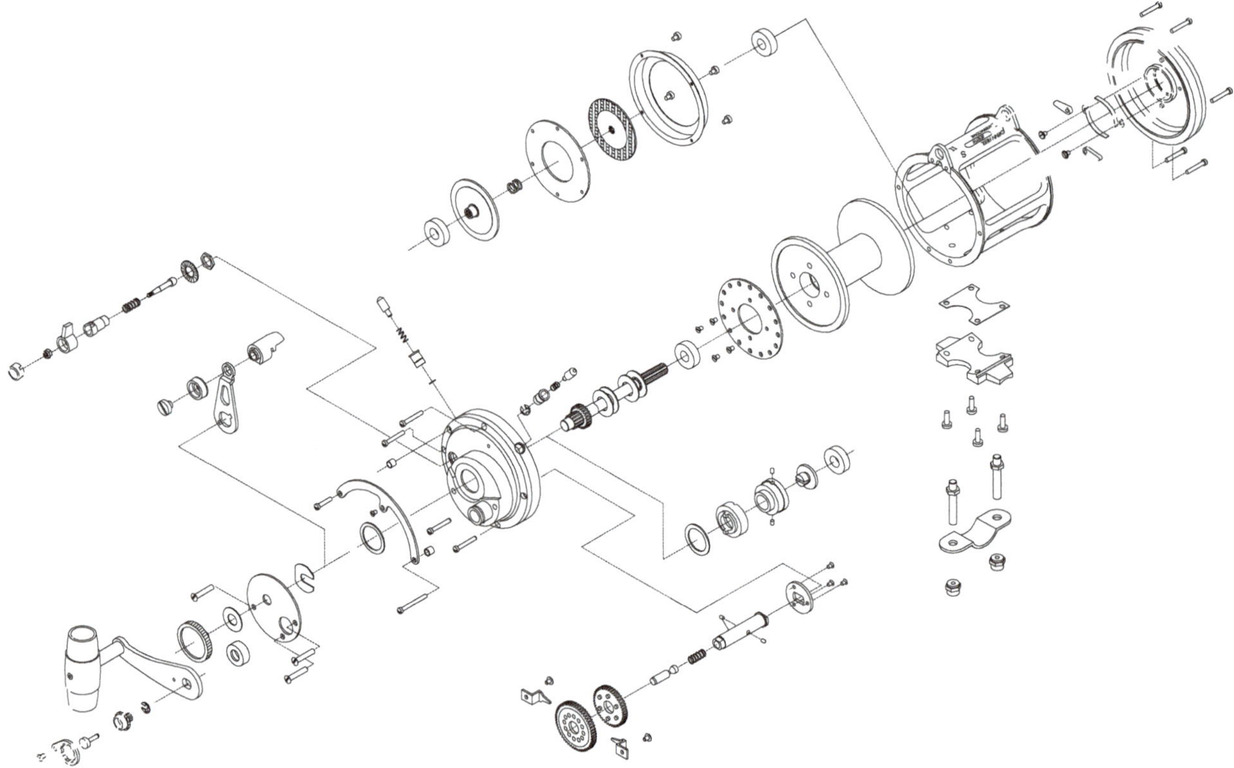

All of the parts of a Penn International II big-game lever drag reel are shown here; this product features quick-changing two-speed stainless steel gears, a carbon-fiber friction drag, and a machined one-piece frame.

Gear ratios are generally categorized as high (fast) or low (slow), but this is relative to the type of reel and application. Furthermore, the size of the spool may be such that a low gear ratio reel actually recovers more line per full turn of the handle than a high ratio reel with a smaller spool. If numerical ratio were the only factor of comparison, what is high for many lever drag reels would be low for other revolving-spool reels. Low gear ratios for lever drag reels range from 1.2:1 to 1.8:1 and high gear ratios range from 2.2:1 to 4.5:1

In general terms, the higher the ratio, the greater the potential for stripping gears under severe strain. On a high gear ratio reel, the individual teeth become narrower because more teeth are fitted into a given area, and they are weaker. An inexperienced angler is more likely to do damage on a high gear ratio reel when he puts the smaller gear teeth under a heavy load. Fishing with a high gear ratio reel requires using the rod a lot, pulling it back and then winding line onto the spool quickly on the downstroke. This is necessary because, with high gear ratio reels, the smaller tooth configuration does not have sufficient cranking strength. This is a factor in all reels, but obviously of more concern with reels that get a heavy load, such as conventional and lever drag reels.

In the past, most lever drag reels were single speed, meaning that they had one fixed gear ratio. Today, there are lever drag reels with dual-speed operation, meaning that they can operate at two gear ratios, one of which is classified high and the other low. Shifting from one gear to the other is simple, generally done by pressing a button on the handle. Although more expensive, two-speed lever drag reels have become very popular and may account for half of all lever drag reels sold (aftermarket conversions installed by reel technicians can convert some single-speed reels to dual-speed models).

There is a good reason for this popularity. Having two-speed operation permits shifting from high ratio, which would be used for most purposes, to low ratio for the extra cranking power necessary for demanding situations. Low is used for power, and high is used for speed. If you have to clear lines quickly, for example, you do this in high gear; there is little resistance, and you can crank away quickly. Being able to instantly shift from high to low speed provides benefits for various situations, including out-muscling a big fish that has sounded directly below you, or pulling a large grouper away from its craggy bottom hole.

When you're using high gear to fight a fish, and it gets to be a tough fight, you can switch to low gear and make the work easier. In principle, less line is recovered per turn of the handle in low gear, so you theoretically spend more time when using this gear. You'll find it easier, however, to get a strong fish's head, turn it, and be in control, when using low gear. If you were using a high gear ratio to battle a stubborn fish, it might actually take more time, since it is harder to turn the handle, and thus you actually have to work harder with the fish.

Having both gears provides opportunity to employ either one on the same fish as circumstances warrant. The greater power of the low-speed mode, when used in combination with high speed (gaining line quickly, for example, when a fish runs toward you) can have the benefits of reducing fighting time overall, which is clearly helpful for releasing fish in good health, as well as diminishing angler fatigue, which can otherwise lead to mistakes and prolonged battles.

High and low are relative terms when discussing gear ratio, and categorization is relative to the size and diameter of the reel. A 2.2:1 gear ratio might actually be a "high" gear ratio on a large line capacity lever drag reel (like a 130-class model), and would provide a lot of line recovery compared to a smaller diameter reel that had a numerically greater gear ratio.

Cranking power. Gear ratio and cranking power are inextricably linked in all reels, and most affect how easy or difficult it is to retrieve a heavy weight, or an object that offers a lot of resistance. Reels that can easily handle a heavy load are said to have a lot of cranking power. Various factors affect this.

The length of the handle has a bearing because length is a factor in the amount of leverage you can put on the handle. The longer the handle, the more leverage and the easier it is to retrieve a set load. If you make a handle longer, you reduce the force at the knob. It is essentially the same principle as having a long-handled wrench; it's easier to loosen nuts with a long-handled wrench than with a short-handled one. So a longer handle equals greater power (although your hand and arm must describe a larger circle to operate the reel).

The gear set itself is also a big factor with regard to cranking power. If you have a reel with a gear ratio of 2:1, it's easier to retrieve a load because this is a low gear ratio. If you have a reel with a gear ratio of 5:1, which is high, it's a lot more difficult to retrieve a load, although you get more speed. If you're retrieving something that offers very little resistance, the high gear ratio is okay. You need a lower gear ratio, however, for something that offers more resistance. Thus, the lowest gear ratio reels have the greatest cranking power, and the highest gear ratio reels have the least cranking power. Obviously, there is an advantage to having dual-ratio reels, so the best of both reels can be employed as necessary while angling.

No matter what the gear ratio is, the evaluation of a reel's ability to retrieve line should boil down to something engineers call Inches Per Turn of the handle, or IPT. This is the amount of line recovered per turn of the handle, or, simply, line recovery, which is a better measurement of retrieval ability than gear ratio. Line recovery is determined

The earliest written account of fishing reels appeared in England in 1651 in The Art of Angling by Thomas Barker; the earliest visual depiction of a reel appeared in a Chinese painting from the mid–twelfth century.

B

by spool diameter, which is a key dimension for any reel and which sets the circumference of the line level on the spool and the amount of line wound onto the spool with each turn of the reel handle.

When the level of line on a spool is low, as it might be when a strong fish takes a lot of line, less line is recovered per turn of the handle than would be when all of the line is on the spool. Similarly, the amount of line recovered per turn of the handle of a fully spooled 4:1 ratio reel that has a small spool would be less than the amount of line recovered per turn of the handle of a fully spooled 4:1 ratio reel that has a large spool.

Thus, the amount of line recovered is the measurement an angler should be most interested in. Yet anglers cannot quickly determine line recovery when evaluating a reel they might purchase because specifications on the circumference of the spool are seldom provided on the reel or in the packaging materials. You may know, for example, that in a 4:1 ratio reel one revolution of the handle puts four wraps of line on the spool, but if you don't know how much line is gained with each complete wrap, you don't know the actual recovery. (In a reel that you own, of course, this can be determined by marking the line and then measuring it.)

For a greater discussion of this subject, *(see: gear ratio)*. Although most consumers have a notion that gear ratio is of primary importance in retrieval, and some think that the higher the ratio the better, other factors are involved, and line recovery is a major one. Remember, however, that reels with a low gear ratio do better under heavier loads, whether those loads are due to the size of the fish or the equipment being used (heavy weights, deep-diving lures, and so on).

This issue is critical in lever drag reels because of their basic size, capacity, and applications, which often result in a heavy load being placed on them.

Handle. The length of the handle affects cranking power, so the distance from the center of the gear stud to which the handle is attached to the handle knob is a key element in retrieval. A long handle equals power, yet many people have the misconception that a long handle also equals speed, that the longer the handle, the faster it can travel. The opposite is true. The longer the handle, the greater distance the cranking hand must travel with each turn. The shorter the handle, the quicker it can be turned, but there's less power, so there's a trade-off either way. You can't get power and speed simultaneously. The handles supplied by manufacturers with lever drag reels are fairly similar and have a moderate length suitable for most tasks.

Lever drag reels have a single handle grip, or knob, which is what you hold to turn the handle. These are barrel- or torpedo-shaped, and tend to be grasped by the whole hand rather than by just the thumb and index finger.

Some users of lever drag reels, especially those with single speed versions, opt to replace their handles with aftermarket products, some of which may be adjustable so you can change the distance from the crankshaft connection to the handle knob and thus affect power and speed to best suit the physical build of the angler. Some aftermarket handles sport a grip that is angled farther outward than factory grips, which are said to be more ergonomic.

Ball bearings/bushings. Bearings and bushings provide a way to minimize friction on rotating shafts. Bushings don't spin as freely as ball or roller bearings, which are typically viewed as durable and reliable and a way to add rotational freeness to the retrieval system. Ball bearings, rather than bushings, are imperative on lever drag reels because they are vastly smoother and more durable under heavy loads, and most use sealed versions of the highest quality. The main ball bearings are placed on both sides of the spindle, and others are located on the drag stack and the gear stud. On the biggest lever drags reels, there are also two ball bearings on the handle. For a more detailed review of ball bearings and bushings, *(see: reel, fishing)*.

Warning click. Known mainly as a click or clicker by most anglers, this is a ratchet device intended to let an angler know that line is going out. All lever drag reels have this, and it is generally employed when a big-game outfit has been placed in a rod holder and is not handheld. In some situations, as when fishing with bait, the reel is placed in freespool with the warning click on so that if a fish picks up the bait, the line is free to move with minimal resistance, yet without risking a spool overrun. In other situations, such as when trolling, the drag is set to the Strike position and the warning click is employed so that it instantly alerts an angler (or mate or boat captain) to a strike and to the fact that a fish is on and taking line off the reel. On some lever drag reels, the click is adjustable so you can go from a soft to hard clicking sound. The soft click is preferred for drifting bait when minimal resistance is desired, while the hard click is preferred for trolling when you want a loud sound.

The click itself features a spring-loaded tongue that moves back and forth against ratchet teeth to make this sound. It is activated by moving a small off-center knob on the sideplate (usually the right sideplate). The click is intended for part-time rather than full-time use, and it should be disengaged when retrieving. Continued use of the click causes premature ratchet wear.

Drag Features

The hallmark of lever drag reels is their drag mechanism; how it is employed and how well it does its job are the elements that separate these reels from all others. Because drag function and performance are so essential to big-game fishing, it is important to review the basic principles of drag and the factors that are especially influential in big-game fishing.

Overview. The purpose of the drag function

on any reel is to let line slip from the reel at varying pressures when force is applied to the line. It serves as a sort of clutch, or shock absorber, and is especially important when using light line, when playing large and strong species, and when fish make strong and sudden surges while being landed. If an angler never catches large fish, only uses heavy strength line, and is content to wind fish in, then it is conceivable that his drag might never be used. This is not the case with lever drag reels and big-game tackle, which is expressly meant for catching large fish and dealing with tough conditions.

Nevertheless, catching large fish, which weigh more (usually far more) than the actual breaking strength of the line or which can apply extreme pressure on the tackle, requires some finesse rather than sheer strength. This means that you cannot simply winch a fish in when using sporting grades of line; the drag will come into play, because if it doesn't, the force will exceed the strength of the line and the line will break.

When the drag comes into play, it allows the fish to continue applying force, but at a pressure that is less than the breaking strength of the line because when the force reaches a certain level (usually a specific percentage of the line's breaking strength), a properly set drag mechanism allows line to slip from the reel under tension by turning the spool. In essence, it means that a fish can run instead of engage in a tug of war, but it has to work for the line that it takes off the reel, which is tiring to the fish and helps the angler subdue it.

In typical fishing with lever drag reels, anglers set the drag at 25 to 30 percent of the breaking strength of their line. This is measured by some people with a short length of line on a straight pull off the reel. It is measured by others with line running through the rod guides and the rod flexed as it would be in fishing circumstances. When using other types of tackle, many people use the "feels good" method of establishing drag tension by pulling line off the reel and adjusting the drag mechanism (the star wheel for other revolving spool reels) until the tension feels right. The most precise way to measure drag tension, however, is by using a reliable scale and attaching it to the line. No matter what method is used, the objective is to adjust the drag so that the line does not slip until the appropriate amount of tension is applied.

Understanding how to use and set drag is one of the most important aspects of sportfishing, and is also reviewed elsewhere *(see: drag),* but needs special consideration with lever drag reels due to the applications that these reels face. Because a lot of line is often taken from lever drag reels and because big-game fish have to be battled for sometimes long periods, the buildup of heat, and the dissipation of that heat, are critical issues, and it is essential that the drag pressure remain relatively stable. Furthermore, big-game fishing techniques, especially offshore trolling, benefit from having one preset drag tension for striking and playing fish and another for maximum pressure.

Big-game fishing issues. As noted, the drag system on a fishing reel is meant to allow line to slip smoothly from a reel before the line's breaking strength is surpassed by the load placed on it by a fish. The ideal drag system for big game is one that is fully adjustable and provides consistent performance over a wide range of tension settings. This is of most importance when fishing for large, strong fish, and when using light tackle. In big-game fishing the drag is of particular importance not only because of the size and strength of the fish, but because some of the lines used have very little stretch, which puts the full fighting load on the rod and reel drag. A line with sufficient stretch would act a bit like a shock absorber and be more forgiving, but only up to a point *(see: line).*

While it has always been the goal of reel designers to produce the ideal drag system, in the wide range of big-game reels available today, few drag systems actually meet this criteria and only a few have recently come close to meeting this criteria when new and fresh out of the box. Many anglers, especially big-game aficionados seeking large fish and record specimens on light line, have taken manufactured reels to specialists to overhaul, fine-tune, or improve the drags on their reels. This is especially true for reels using lever drag systems.

In big-game fishing, the lever drag reel is the main workhorse. With the latest generation of drag materials in use, the lever drag reel is capable of delivering the degree of drag performance that both light- and heavy-tackle anglers demand. A modern lever drag reel meters out line under precisely controlled resistance that forces a hooked fish to overcome that preset pressure before it can take line. The physical effort it takes to overcome drag resistance during the fight should quickly tire the fish and lead to its capture or release.

Whether they are on spinning, baitcasting, fly, conventional, or big-game reels, drag systems share a few common problems. One of the most significant of these is start-up inertia, which is the increased effort required to start a spool turning from a dead stop. Another is acceleration, or surge, which is the difference in effort required to turn the spool at various speeds. In big-game reels, the spool and line have significant mass, which is difficult to start in motion and, once moving, has to be controlled by the drag. Resistance can vary considerably between slow-speed and high-speed running drags, and thus have a big impact on fishing effectiveness.

The performance provided by any reel drag system is the end result of the composition and design of the system and the materials used, including the friction disc(s), metal drag disc(s), backing plates, heat sinks, and thrust mechanism; the surface finish, heat dissipation ability, and thermal stability of these items are especially significant. The primary

The Guinness Book of Records reports that more than 300 people were killed and eaten by piranhas in 1981 when an overloaded boat capsized and sank at the Brazilian port of Obidos.

B

factors that ultimately dictate the performance of any drag design are the amount of friction of the drag material; the amount of surface contact with suitable metal disc(s); and the amount of mechanical pressure or thrust applied to these components to determine the drag tension. Other variables that influence drag performance include heat buildup, conductivity, expansion, distortion, glazing, galling, and the amount of line on the spool at any given time during the fight of a fish. When the line level changes, it affects performance. Drag resistance increases as spool diameter is reduced, which is what happens when a fish takes line off a reel. The less line on the reel, the greater the drag pressure.

All of these factors add to the complexity of designing an efficient drag system. They may be unknown to the average angler, who is usually only concerned with determining the ideal static drag setting for the reel in relation to the breaking strength of the line. He then sets the drag and goes fishing. Understanding what actually happens to the drag when fishing is useful, however, for knowing what problems exist and understanding what the limitations of the reel are in order to adjust accordingly and ensure that there is not a tackle-induced loss of fish.

In part, Americans owe the tradition of bountiful harvests celebrated on Thanksgiving to menhaden, an abundant mid-Atlantic food fish that was liberally used as fertilizer in colonial times.

The principle behind a drag system is the conversion of mechanical energy into heat energy through friction This is accomplished by the discs and washers spinning against one another. How smoothly this friction can be controlled is the difference between an average drag and a really great drag. When a fish makes a long run against a substantial drag tension setting, a tremendous amount of heat is generated; in simulating this on machines to test their reel's components, some manufacturers have gotten reels so hot that water boils on top of them.

Heat buildup can drastically change the amount of friction between drag washers and discs, and can cause major problems if not efficiently conducted away from the drag washers. In general, heat expansion increases the amount of pressure between the parts of the drag, resulting in greater friction. To eliminate or reduce this pressure, heat must be transferred away from the drag washers and discs to other surrounding components of the reel. The components of the reel, including the main gear (which may act as a heat sink) and the frame, help to do this. If the pressure is long enough and intense enough, however, you reach the maximum ability of the components to dissipate heat, and the drag friction material has to handle the pressure.

One sign of a superior drag system is its ability to conduct heat away from friction-generating surfaces as quickly as possible through the washers, spool, spool shaft, and housing, where it is dissipated. If a drag washer's surface is damaged by extreme heat, it becomes unreliable and produces erratic performance, often with disastrous effects. If this heats builds up quickly and is not dissipated, or not dissipated fast enough, there is a major problem brewing—a reel seizing and the drag pressure becoming too great for the breaking strength of the line.

Clearly, the materials that are used in the drag system are critical to proper performance, more so with this type of tackle than with any other. Yet, because the friction coefficient of various materials is not constant—it also depends on whether the material is operating dry, lubricated, or partially lubricated—and because the friction washer is asked to do nearly opposite jobs—slip freely and also create a high amount of pressure—finding the perfect friction lining material has been difficult. Thus, the design of big-game fishing reel drag systems and the use of different materials has been a calculated compromise to meet varying applications.

Older drag-lining materials, made of asbestos and other elements, expand when hot and actually increase drag pressure. Because the expanding parts have nowhere to go, they're trapped and therefore exert greater force on each other; this continues to compound the tension problem, and when the pressure builds too much, the line breaks. Various older materials (including Teflon, which is slippery, and cork, which is jerky when it gets wet) were also employed and proved to be quite a challenge when used in long and hard battles with fish.

In the development of drag systems, titanium-impregnated washers evolved and helped greatly to counter the problem of heat buildup. They are still in use today but, unfortunately, are greatly affected by water intrusion or condensation, which produces acceleration problems. Some manufacturers of reels with titanium drag washers try to address this by offering alternative drag setting recommendations.

The use of modern materials, as well as continuing research and development, has been aimed at achieving the best possible drag performance, and utilizing materials with a coefficient of friction that is stable over a wide range of temperature changes. Today, the heat problem has been greatly reduced through the use of drag materials made of carbon fiber, which can withstand extreme heat without distortion, and through more efficient heat-conducting designs to cool the drag system.

Heat and thrust affect carbon-based washers differently than other materials used in the past. One of the physical properties of carbon fiber is that it has a natural slipperiness to it. Another is that drag friction decreases with heat; as it gets hot, the carbon fiber actually gets slicker. However, this can be a problem when the washer's drag coefficient decreases too much under heat, thus resulting in less drag tension than would theoretically be desirable (although you have to remember that other factors, like spool diameter and water resistance, are also at work and may compensate).

This may be better than having more tension, and is not the perfect answer, but it's the best one yet known (although some repair specialists who install drag washers that are made with a silicone-impregnated zinc and rubber compound rate this very highly). To deal with this aspect of carbon fiber washers, one manufacturer developed a self-compensating oil-filled expansion piston in the spool of their lever drag reels; this expanded with heat, theoretically compensating for drag drop-off by automatically applying additional thrust to maintain a stable setting. Reel designers continue to argue the pros and cons of such a system, but it illustrates the lengths to which they will go to create a drag system that is as consistent as possible.

In addition to heat buildup, there's the problem of controlling acceleration differences, a phenomenon known by anglers as "surging," and common in all of the myriad combinations of drag frictional materials and metal friction discs. This is exemplified by the varying speed at which line may be pulled from the reel, as occurs when fighting a powerful fish.

Acceleration differences are more clearly evident in some reels than in others, and anglers should check this. Some brands of reels have more problems with surging than others, and those that are seriously deficient should be modified by a skilled big-game reel technician; if not, it is necessary to make a careful tension setting to compensate for variations in drag performance at low and high running speeds.

You can illustrate this phenomenon yourself with the following test:

Take a lever drag reel fully loaded with line and mounted on a rod; tie a loop in the terminal end of the line and pass it through the guides. Using a good quality drag scale (or force gauge), hook it to the loop and have someone use the scale to pull line from the reel with the drag preset to 25 percent of the breaking strength of the line at the Strike position (i.e. 12.5 pounds for 50-pound-test line). This will simulate the drag temperature of a reel that may have been standing for some period in a rod holder. Do this at least 10 or 12 times before taking any readings to ensure that friction surfaces are mated correctly, slightly warm, and maintaining full surface contact.

Pull 10 or 15 feet of line from the reel by walking backwards at a reasonably slow rate. Do this at least six times, taking readings from the scale after each pull, and carefully rewinding the line. Add the scale readings together and divide by the number of pulls to obtain a mean average drag setting for all the test pulls. This should still be 25 percent of the breaking strength of the line.

Then, secure the rod and reel well and have someone pull line from the drag by taking a few steps at normal speed and then actually running for a short distance. Do this at least six times, then compute the mean average for the high-speed pulls and compare the two mean averages against each other. The differences in drag friction at the two speeds is probably quite different. If it is low, like 2 to 3 pounds, this is acceptable and should not pose a problem in actual fishing. That is often not the case, however, and there can be as much as a 50 percent increase in drag resistance between slow- and high-speed tests for some reels. These differences, and the range of speeds that are encountered under fishing circumstances, are what have to be offset with a properly functioning running drag.

If the difference is high, you should probably take the reel to a competent big-game reel technician to modify the reel and correct the problem. Correcting the problem is cheap insurance against the possibility of losing the fish of a lifetime because the reel malfunctions and the line breaks.

The acceleration problem is generally less troubling than the start up inertia problem, where a cool drag system must immediately go from idle to speeds in need of braking control. Difficulties here can be responsible for breaking off fish on the strike or at the very beginning of a fish's first hard run. Experiments to correct excessive start-up inertia or the so-called "sticky drag" have included treating carbon fiber drag washers with various forms of synthetic lubricants, a subject which is also debated by engineers.

The friction value of carbon fiber is low compared to other types of brake materials, and it requires running against suitable metal pressure plates. The choice of material, the flatness (as flat as possible is important), and the surface finish of such metal plates has a great effect on the overall performance. Some manufacturers have opted for carbon fiber materials treated with synthetic lubricants, running on highly polished stainless steel pressure plates. Others recommend no lubrication, and install their carbon fiber washers dry. While lubrication in general reduces start-up inertia problems, it also causes a reduction in the amount of desirable or necessary friction—which is needed to create drag resistance. This, in turn, requires much higher thrust pressure to attain the ideal drag performance of 25 percent of the line's breaking strength in the Strike position and 50 percent at the Full position.

When all is said and done, fine-tuning drag systems on big-game reels has become a cottage industry and a job that is more than the average reel repair technician can handle (most small tackle shop repair people cannot). Out of a need to service and correct drag problems in older big-game reel drags, a new breed of technicians with machine shops arose. Many of these are fine reel specialists, all trying to develop the ultimate drag either by reworking existing reels or by designing complete aftermarket systems.

Using a master big-game reel technician is also beneficial for addressing other issues with reels, and these specialists can fine-tune a reel for absolute maximum performance, particularly for the IGFA-class line that you may be using (especially important for record-setting efforts). Fine-tuning factory big-game reels is analogous to Grand Prix racing. There, many production cars prove very successful, although they have been rebuilt and modified to achieve winning results.

Nevertheless, by working with different mediums and approaches, today's manufacturers have come closer to solving the problems that exist in the high-tech world of big-game fishing reels. They will likely be improving these reels further by mating even better synthetic materials with improved surface finishes and exotic metals for drag discs.

Water resistance and line level. There are two very important factors affecting drag pressure that anglers must deal with when fighting big fish. The first is the effect of water resistance on line being dragged through the water by a running fish.

Not only does water resistance increase drag on a straight-away run, but many times the fish will turn, which forms a giant belly in the line and magnifies the problem greatly. Even when an angler does nothing more than just hold on, without pumping and reeling, a gamefish can break the line with nothing more than the pressure created by water resistance if the angler and captain allow a large belly to occur. This situation can only be overcome through angling skill and good boat handling. The person on the rod has to understand when to reduce drag settings to compensate for the problem that exists when a large belly develops. The captain has to work the boat to try to prevent a large belly from forming.

The second issue is increasing drag tension due to lower line levels. As previously noted, more line is recovered per turn of the reel handle when the diameter is greater than when it is smaller. So it is easier to retrieve line when the diameter of the spool is high. Where the drag is concerned, as line is pulled off the spool and the diameter decreases, the leverage that the line has on the spool diminishes, so it takes more effort to move the spool against the drag. So, drag tension increases as the level of line on the spool decreases; it starts out at one level when the spool is full of line, but increases when the diameter of the spool is smaller due to a fish having taken plenty of line. Depending on the diameter of the spool, when the line level is reduced to half capacity, the drag pressure usually increases by almost double the original setting. If the line level decreases further, the drag pressure could increase to triple the setting that was established when the spool was full.

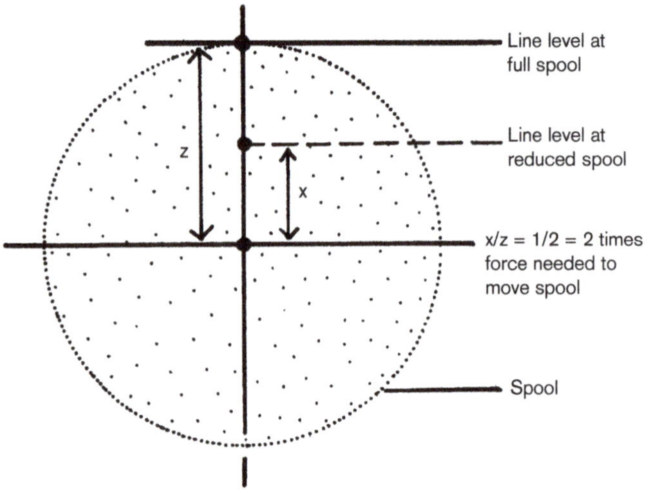

This is a matter of physics and an unchangeable one, but it's important for anglers to recognize. When spool diameter has decreased and drag tension increased, it is all the more important to have a smooth drag and a friction washer that maintains top performance. Because of the dynamics of carbon friction washers, drag tension remains on a more even level with heat buildup, rather than increasing as line is lost; these washers do not make it easier to pull line off when the level of line on a spool decreases, but it does make the drag tension more consistent, meaning that more even drag pressure is maintained.

Despite this, and especially for older reels that do not have carbon friction washers, the angler should be prepared to compensate when a fish runs a lot of line off the reel. He must know when to compensate for this mechanical increase in drag pressure during the fight by backing off on drag tension.

Drag system components. The drag mechanism on lever drag reels is comprised of an adjustment lever that is rotated in circular fashion and located near the handle and on the same sideplate of the reel as the handle (usually the right sideplate). The metal part that denotes drag lever position may be referred to as a quadrant, and may sport numerical markings correlated to tension settings. Moving the adjustment lever along this arc changes the tension settings.

Internally, most lever drag reels feature a large-diameter single friction washer that is affixed to a drive plate and driven by the spindle (some two-speed models have two washers that sandwich the metal disc). The adjustment lever is eccentric and keyed to cams so that more or less pressure is brought to bear on the spool by the friction washer. Moving the lever completely backward (toward the angler) totally removes spool pressure, resulting in a drag-free condition that is commonly called freespool. Moving the lever forward from this position gradually applies pressure to the spool over a varied range of tension settings. When spool friction exceeds the tension on the line, the reel handle turns the main gear and the spool, and allows line to be recovered. When tension on the line exceeds friction on the spool, the spool revolves against handle pressure, and line can be pulled off the spool. The handle is prevented from turning backward by a full-time nonselectable dog and ratchet,

Line level at full spool
Line level at reduced spool
z
x
x/z = 1/2 = 2 times force needed to move spool
Spool

As shown in this mathematical representation, when line on a reel spool is reduced to half of its full level, twice the amount of force is necessary to move the spool at the reduced level than at the full level. This has significant implications for reel drag performance if a large fish takes a great amount of line off a reel.

which is otherwise known as an anti-reverse.

Whereas other revolving-spool reels have multiple friction washers and multiple metal washers, lever drag reels have either single-plate or multiplate clutches. Many have just one friction washer, so there is low inertia start up, but the size and material of that washer is critical. As noted previously, the drag in any reel should ideally operate smoothly, without hesitation. In other words, it will start immediately when needed and maintain a constant rate of tension as line flows continuously off, as well as keep the same level of tension as is periodically called for during the time it takes to play and land a strong fish. The less variation there is in the performance of the drag, the better.

The friction washer is asked to do something very difficult—slip freely but also create a high amount of pressure. Thus, you're looking for two opposite attributes. Most modern lever drag reels have a woven carbon fiber friction washer, referred to by some as graphite, which does an excellent job of addressing these demands.

Positions. Although they may be labeled differently in some reels, the primary drag settings in lever drag reels are referred to as the Free, Strike, and Full positions. The Free position, as noted, is zero drag tension, or freespool. In some reels, it is obtained by moving the adjustment lever fully backward; in others, the adjustment lever is moved backward until it hits a stop button (to prevent accidentally achieving freespool), which is pushed in to allow the lever to be moved from a minimal drag tension to zero tension. This is used whenever line has to be paid out.

The Strike and Full settings, also known as Strike Drag and Full Drag, have to be preset to desired levels of tension that correspond to a percentage of the breaking strength of the line being used. The Strike and Full positions receive most attention by anglers, but the whole range of tension from just above Free to Full is available. Starting at the Free position and moving the adjustment lever forward gradually increases drag pressure until you are up at the preset Strike position (which is usually 25 to 30 percent of the breaking strength of the line); manually overriding the button brings you to the preset Full position.

The Strike position is the one used for most fish-fighting activity, and most anglers will fish or troll with the drag set at, or slightly below, the Strike position. When drifting with bait, where it may be necessary to let a fish take and run with the offering momentarily, anglers may place the drag in the Free position with the warning click on, or just barely over the Free position with the click on. There is a button at the Strike position that must be pressed to move the drag adjustment lever forward and apply more pressure, as well as to reach the Full position.

The Full position is designed so that once you get up close to a big fish (in big-game fishing that is likely to be when the double line comes onto the reel), you can apply a few extra pounds of pressure. The Full position does not signify a tension setting that is equal to the breaking strength of the line, nor does it signify lockup, in the sense that no line can be stripped from the reel; it signifies the maximum tension that has been preset, which is likely to be 50 percent of the breaking strength of the line, or some factor between 25 to 30 percent and 50 percent. It is not a good idea to use the Full setting for normal fighting of a fish because drag tension becomes that much greater as the line diameter of the spool decreases due to a large fish taking a lot of line.

Setting drag. Drag-setting procedure is a hotly debated subject among highly skilled anglers, and there are varying opinions on how to do this with a lever drag reel. The following recommended method is generally accepted as being applicable for most, if not all, fishing situations, particularly for lines under 80-pound class (37 kilograms). You can use it for 80- and 130-pound-class reels, although some anglers increase the Strike drag setting to 33 percent for these heavy line categories.

The base point of reference for all drag settings begins with a reel that is filled to capacity with line. As previously noted, drag pressure increases when the amount of line on a spool decreases, so the starting point for drag-setting considerations on any type of reel must be determined on a reel that is fully loaded.

To set the drag, mount the reel on a rod, tie a loop in the terminal end of the line and thread it from the reel spool through the rod guides and

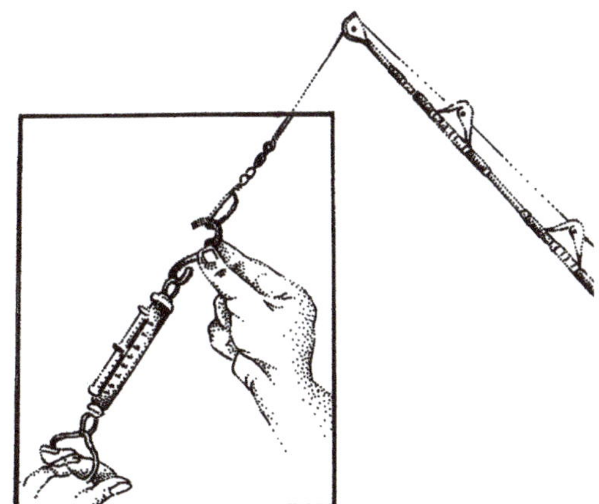

A top-quality spring scale, especially one with an easily read gauge (inset), can be used to accurately measure reel drag tension.

attach it to an accurate drag scale with calibrations suitable for the line class and drag setting. Brass barrel scales with a weight indicator for drag-setting purposes are in standard use for this purpose.

Pull the drag lever all the way back into the freespool position, which should allow the spool to turn with no resistance from the drag washers. If there is any drag on the spool in this position, adjust the preset knob to eliminate it. Push the drag lever to the Strike position. Most reels have a built-in safety stop that requires the angler to push a button to go past the Strike setting. Pull some line off the reel to seat the washers and warm them up before proceeding, or have someone hold the line and turn the reel handle with the lever at Strike for a minute to accomplish the same thing.

Have someone draw on the scale to pull line from the reel. There is some disagreement among anglers and manufacturers as to whether this is best done with the rod tip pointed directly at the scale, or with the rod angled up so that it applies tension on the line. The general principle of how to set the drag is the same, although the tension effects may differ.

The following describes how to set the drag without rod tension: With the rod tip pointed directly at the scale, read the drag resistance on the scale in pounds after each pull. If the setting is too light or too heavy, back off the lever to the free-spool position and increase or decrease the thrust pressure by turning the preset knob. Never adjust the preset knob with the drag engaged. Repeat this procedure until you reach the desired drag pressure in the Strike position. If the reel is in good operating condition and being used for the line rating it was designed for, it should offer a no-resistance freespool setting, a light running drag setting, a 25 percent Strike drag setting, and approximately a 50 percent Full drag setting.

If you do this with the rod tip pointed directly at the scale, you will obtain a completely static setting—the absolute minimum pressure possible.

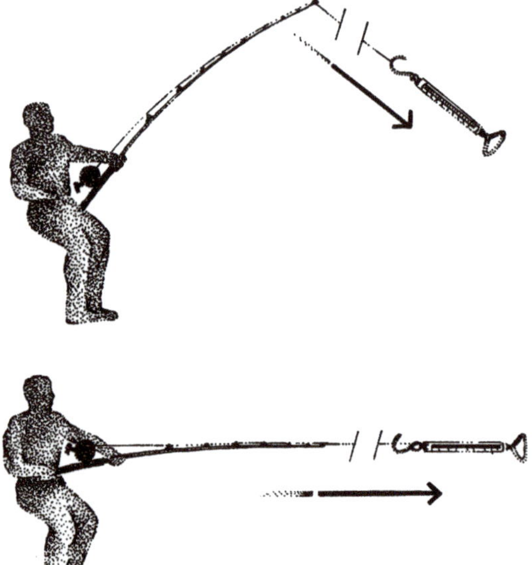

The most accurate way to measure reel drag tension is with a scale and by pulling line off a fully loaded rod from a greater distance than is shown in this compressed depiction. Measuring with the rod at a high angle (top) produces greater drag resistance due to friction from rod guides. Pointing a rod directly at a fish or at the scale (bottom) results in line being pulled straight off the reel, producing the least amount of drag tension.

When the setting is obtained this way, it eliminates any additional drag tension caused by the pressure of the loaded rod. Therefore, percentages of drag refer to a straight pull off the reel. When you measure drag on a loaded rod, with the line pressing on the rod guides, there can be variations in drag setting achieved because of variations in the amount of drag created due to many different rod-and-reel (and guide) designs, and because rods differ in their loading characteristics. In all line classes the 25 percent value compensates for these other variable and incalculable values, but it is still true that as rod arc increases, line tension multiplies. When you are always using a particular reel on the same rod, setting the drag on a loaded rod gives you an indication of what the pressure is when the rod is flexed, and many anglers like this method because they reason that the rod is always flexed when a fish is on. However, setting drag tension without rod flex gives you the lightest possible scenario. If your reel experiences significant variations in drag force when accelerating, and in light of the many factors that can affect drag performance, it is probably wise to err on the light side and measure it by taking line directly off the reel.

Strike drag. This is the basic fish-fighting drag pressure. Most people fish with the drag lever set at or slightly below the Strike position. This may depend on the method of fishing, however. When a rod is sitting in a holder and anglers are chumming *(see)* and/or chunking *(see),* anglers will often put the reel in freespool with the warning click on, or keep it just barely over freespool. For other fishing, especially trolling, the drag lever should be placed in the Strike position, and this should be calibrated to 25 percent of the breaking strength of the line. Thus, if the unknotted wet breaking strength *(see: line)* of a line is 50 pounds, a 25 percent Strike drag setting would produce a straight-pull drag resistance measuring 12.5 pounds.

Since the Strike drag is the most critical setting, it is important to get it right, so take your time and double-check the finished setting before you start fishing. If your drag system has been properly designed and calibrated for a specific IGFA line class, it should come very close to obtaining the other desirable settings (depicted in the accompanying graph) automatically when you set the Strike drag at 25 percent of the breaking strain.

Drag Quadrant in Straight Plane

0%	*R*	*25%*	*50% +/–*
Free Spool Position	Running Drag Position	Strike Drag Position	Full Drag

There is an exception to the 25 percent ratio that some anglers call into play with 80- and 130-

pound line classes. They prefer to increase the Strike drag setting to 33 percent with this gear. If you do this, remember that it reduces the margin of error when fighting big fish and that other variables, like spool diameter, become even more critical during the fight. Remember, you can always increase your drag setting above Strike if you need more pressure on a fish. That's why most people prefer to use the 25 percent ratio for Strike drags in almost all instances.

Running drag. With the Strike drag properly set, you should have a slight "Running" drag when the lever is initially engaged just above the freespool position to prevent backlash problems from occurring when an outfit is left in a rod holder. When a fish grabs a trolled offering, especially a live or rigged natural bait, the Running drag allows line to slip from the spool freely without backlashing the reel. Anglers can grab the rod, let the fish take the bait for a few moments, then move the lever to the Strike position and set the hook. A good Running drag will allow this to happen without backlashing line on the spool or causing tension on the fish that causes it to drop the bait.

Some reels have a hard time accomplishing the correct Strike drag setting while still maintaining a workable Running drag or even attaining full freespool capabilities. If this is the case, the reel is ready for some serious drag maintenance or refinement.

Full drag. The Full drag setting is not really full in the true sense of lockup. Full is the highest recommended setting above Strike for a specific strength of line. Full drag is the position of last resort in a battle. It is designed so that once you get the fish close to you and double line is on the reel, you can apply a few extra pounds of pressure. You could also use the Full setting to apply a few more pounds of pressure during the initial stage of a fish's run, then back it off, but this is a gamble that not many anglers want to take, especially with monster or record-class fish. It is also not advisable to keep the drag tension at the Full setting for fighting the fish, as this would be too much pressure when you take into account the effects of decreasing line on the spool.

The maximum or Full drag setting should be approximately 50 percent of the line's breaking strength. Rarely is this much drag used on any size reel, except in certain circumstances when 80- and 130-pound-class tackle is being used to fight very big fish from a chair. A bucket harness and curved butt rod are needed to capitalize on such a high drag setting.

A properly operating reel will offer a smooth transition from the Strike position on up through the Full position so that you can get more than Strike resistance but less than the maximum. Some savvy anglers will mark one or two additional drag positions on the reel housing with a marker or tape. This is used to apply more pressure to a fish while still maintaining control of the amount of drag pressure throughout the fight. If you do this, mark each additional setting so you know just how much pressure you're putting on the fish at any given time.

Other considerations. It's a smart idea to allow reels to reach the outside ambient temperature before setting the drag. Don't make the mistake of taking your reels straight from the storage area in an air-conditioned cabin or house and then setting the drags. Once you've done that, and the reels sit in the sun, the drag setting can increase due to heat expansion of the parts. In extremely hot climates, particularly with larger reels, it is advisable to check the drag settings several times during the day's fishing.

As mentioned, the drag should be "preheated" before the Strike drag setting is adjusted. This can be done by engaging the drag, holding the spool, and turning the reel handle to create friction, or by having someone pull line against the drag as you turn the reel handle. This process should be repeated at least 15 or 20 times, which ensures that everything is up to operating temperatures and that any lubricants have dispersed and thinned to a workable consistency on the drag surface.

Be aware that you run the risk of having problems with reels, especially with the gears and drag mechanism, when bumping up line strength over the manufacturer's rating. Putting 80-pound-test line on a 50-pound-class reel has obvious ramifications for line capacity (depending on diameter), but not-so-obvious ones for internal parts that may receive more punishment than they were designed to take.

Water intrusion in drag systems can also be a major problem. If you run the boat with your outfits in rod holders in the cockpit exposed to a lot of spray, it is of major importance that the drag systems be fully engaged to keep any water that may enter the reel from getting into the drag washers. Reel covers or even a plastic shower cap placed over your reels will help greatly. When cleaning reels after use, position the lever at Full drag and spray them using light water pressure. Only after a reel is completely dried off should it be put in the freespool position and the ratchet or clicker engaged to prevent line tangles in storage.

Water can cause many problems, even condensation, which can collect inside a reel when it is taken from an air-conditioned room to the outside. It can affect drag performance or your drag settings, which is another reason to use the drag warm-up procedure outlined previously.

When storing lever drag reels between uses, the golden rule is to back the drag lever to the freespool position. This removes any pressure and allows the washers to relax. This also ensures that the drag components won't fuse and become bonded to the pressure plate, resulting in a frozen drag. When doing this, back the drag completely off, turn the reel handle while holding the spool, and crank for

10 to 20 seconds. This ensures that the washers are all totally free and clear of each other.

The care and checking of your lever drag reels should be something that you do religiously. There is nothing as final as a line broken on a good fish; understanding and proper use of your reel's lever drag system will greatly reduce this problem.

No twist. Because of the revolving-spool nature of lever drag reels, no twist is imparted to the line when an angler reels at the same time that line slips off the spool via the drag. This is a common problem with spinning *(see)* and spincasting *(see)* reels. Twist isn't possible on a lever drag reel if the handle is turning and the spool is simultaneously slipping. When the drag mechanism is activated, the spool rotates and line unwinds in an untwisted manner. There is no line twist unless it comes from lure use or you put it on when the spool is filled.

Other Features

Frame/spool materials. Because lever drag reels are used in saltwater and susceptible to extreme stresses and fishing conditions, construction and materials must be of the highest caliber.

One-piece frames have been standard on better models for nearly two decades because they are more resistant to torque and twist, providing superior strength and precision alignment of the spool and other components. These frames, which also help dissipate heat, are usually made from the highest grade of extruded marine alloy aluminum, although some are made of graphite.

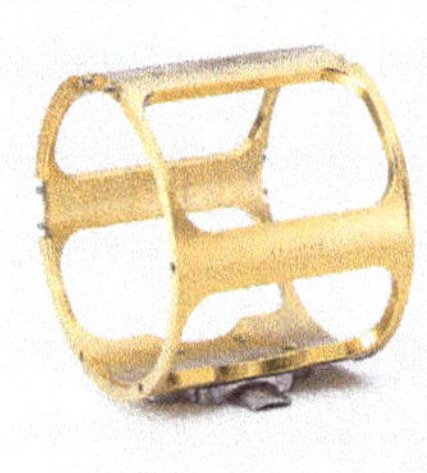

The one-piece frame (left) and lever drag system shown here are from a Penn International big-game reel.

The spools are aluminum, and may be extruded, machined, or forged, and sideplates are usually machined aluminum. The finish is anodized, an aesthetic and corrosion-inhibiting feature that doesn't affect performance. Other materials, incidentally, include aircraft quality stainless steel ball bearings.

Clamps/lugs/braces. Lever drag reels all have clamps to secure the reel to the rod, lugs for attachment to a fighting harness, and, on some versions, a brace for additional support.

Older reels used to have metal rod clamps, which were fastened around the rod with exposed wing nuts. These could get in the way of grabbing or lead to scratching. They've been replaced by molded synthetic clamps with recessed screws; there is no protrusion to get in the way, and they allow easier handling or even palming of smaller models.

The harness lugs are situated on the top of the reel because when fighting a large fish, the angler is likely to wear a shoulder or kidney harness *(see)*, which is attached to these lugs. Forward and rear braces on the largest models are used to provide torsional stability on rods.

Preset drag lock. Some large lever drag reels have a preset drag lock that is tamperproof and meant to keep the preset drag adjustment from being accidentally altered. You must purposely press a button to override the lock; this is mainly an advantage to charter captains out for big marlin and tuna, who don't want an itchy fingered client to accidentally turn the drag adjustment button and thereby cause the loss of a prized fish.

Reel designations. Lever drag reels are classified by the strength of line that they are designed for and the capacity they hold. Unlike conventional reels, which use an "O" (or ought) designation from decades ago, lever drag reels conform to well-established line classifications from 12- through 130-pound strengths, with corresponding capacity and drag system capability. These classifications are usually specified as being IGFA class, which means that they conform to established parameters of line breaking strength for world-record consideration. Thus, a 30-pound IGFA class lever drag reel is intended for line that will break according to IGFA record-testing specifications; in this case, that would be 15 kilograms, or 33 pounds *(see: line)*.

Naturally, the diameter of the line has a bearing on the capacity, and the reel can be spooled with line that is heavier or lighter than the rating. Many anglers do use a different strength of line with some models than what they are designated for. They might use a lighter line (say 20-pound on a designated 30-pound reel) to get more of that strength on a reel, or they might use heavier line (say 50-pound on a 30-pound reel) to get the benefits of heavier line with a smaller and lighter reel. Increasing the strength of line can have ramifications for the drag and freespool, however.

Some manufacturers have models with differing spool widths but meant for the same strength line, to allow for capacity concerns. Certain wide-spool models may hold up to 200 yards more line than a standard-spool reel, and the greater capacity provides an extra dose of confidence that you won't be spooled out. But even the wide-spool models have been fished with heavier lines than they were intended for (especially by long-range party boat anglers) to get greater capacity of heavier line.

The largest lever drag reels, the 80- and 130-pound class versions, are used for the biggest game, such as monster billfish and tuna. The 30- and 50-pound reels have been more popular for wide-ranging offshore applications, but greater interest in light-tackle and stand-up fishing *(see)* has increased the popularity of 12-, 16-, and 20-pound reels.

Line capacity is way up there, of course, for all of these products. The 80- and 130-pound-class reels hold about 1,000 yards of line; lighter models hold between 500 and 900 yards of line, but this varies with wide-spool versions and according to the diameter of the line used.

Ergonomics. Lever drag reels are large, generally cumbersome, and heavy. There are few points to be made about their ergonomic nature other than weight and rod clamps, which have been discussed, and handles. Cosmetics, or appearance, has nothing to do with function.

Some people like bigger handles and some smaller, owing to application and interest in power versus speed. Handles can be changed, and aftermarket accessories are available for this. The barrel shape is fairly uniform on handle grips; this is deemed necessary because it is easier to put an entire hand on such a grip, and the whole hand is needed to fight big fish with this equipment.

Rods

Big-game rods used with lever drag reels, also called offshore rods, tuna rods, billfish rods, and, less commonly, deep sea rods, have some overlap with rods used with heavy-duty star drag conventional reels, and are generally short, stiff, heavy-action products that have to be more solidly built than other rod types and extremely dependable. The stress and torque put on these products is extraordinary, which requires that components and construction processes be of the highest caliber.

At one time, big-game rods were all $6^1/_2$ to $7^1/_2$ feet in length, featuring detachable wooden, aluminum, or fiberglass butts and a long slow-curving tip section. New rod manufacturing technology and changing needs have shortened many big-game rods and resulted in one-piece products with shorter butts and lighter tips that bend into the foregrip, resulting in an ability to put a lot of pressure on a fish for quicker and easier landing, especially for stand-up fish fighting. Big-game rods today range from 5 to $7^1/_2$ feet in length, with the majority being $5^1/_2$ to $6^1/_2$ feet long, and the butts are largely aluminum or graphite composite.

These workhorse rods have long, beefy two-handed handles and heavy-duty reel seats that securely accommodate lever drag reels, and they have a cushioned foregrip large enough for two-handed use when fighting and lifting heavy-duty fish. The butt of all these rods has a gimbal for insertion into a gimbaled rod holder or kidney belt.

Heavy-duty roller guides are used on most big-game rods and all of the top line-class models. These are mounted (with two feet) on top of the rod like the reel. This is because these rods are mainly used for fish fighting (as opposed to casting, retrieving, or detecting strikes), and the load of a gamefish on the line applies both a crushing downward force on the guide ring and frame, and a simultaneous tendency to torque or twist the rod, so guides have to be of top quality and properly spaced and positioned. Most big-game rods feature a full complement of roller guides, and some have tip and butt-end (stripper) roller guides. Graphite, fiberglass, and composites of the two are used in their construction.

All big-game reels are designated according to line strength based upon the IGFA record classification; this ranges from 6- through 130-pound test and coordinates with both the reel and line strength that the product was designed to handle. However, there is some latitude in this, and anglers will go up or down (usually up) one line size, using a 50-pound IGFA class rod, for example, with a wide-spooled 50-pound lever drag reel filled with 80-pound line.

Unlike reels, many of the issues pertaining to rods used with big-game reels—functions, materials, components, etc.—are similar to those of other rods, and these are more fully detailed elsewhere *(see: rod, fishing)*.

Using Big-Game Tackle

Line. Although various line strengths from 12 through 130 pounds can be employed with the appropriate big-game or lever drag gear, 20- through 80-pound lines are the most commonly used strengths. Application dictates use, and one of the things that is frequently done by lever drag reel users is stepping up to a higher strength line, which may not be what the reel is designed for. As noted previously, often anglers use a wider spool version of a particular model to step up in line strength while maintaining capacity. Some may step down in line strength to get a greater amount of a lighter line on the reel (i.e. putting 12-pound test on a 20-pound reel).

Fishing line is not prespooled onto lever drag reels, although it may be spooled at some shops that cater to offshore anglers. Proper spooling of line—under tension and with proper manual leveling—is essential to this equipment and is covered in the following section.

Nylon monofilament is the primary choice of line type for lever drag reels; there is some use of microfilament line and braided Dacron lines. Since line coiling is not much of an issue on these large-spool reels, suppleness may not be much of a factor; abrasion resistance and stretch are high priorities in line for many lever drag reel users. Basic strength—the rated strength of the line when tested in a wet condition—is critical for many (if not most) lever drag reel users because of the possibility of catching a record fish, and because the reel drag is finely tuned and set to specific standards based on knowing the absolute breaking strength of the line. This is why IGFA class lines are the only type of line used by many lever drag reel users.

Obviously lever drag reels hold a lot of line. The range is from approximately 500 to 1,000 yards with conventional diameter nylon monofilament line, and this is often understated by

B

manufacturers. Using line that has the strength of conventional diameter nylon monofilament but a thinner diameter allows for greater capacity; in other words, a 20-pound-class lever drag reel holds more thin-diameter 20-pound class line than it will conventional diameter 20-pound-class line. Using a heavier strength line with conventional diameter results in less capacity; in other words, putting a conventional-diameter 30-pound line on a lever drag reel designed for 20-pound line results in less line being spooled on the reel. Using a lighter strength line with conventional diameter results in greater capacity; in other words, putting a conventional-diameter 12-pound line on a lever drag reel designed for 20-pound line results in a greater length of line being spooled on the reel.

Generally, it is best to keep within the recommended line strengths when filling a reel. For the most part, you can take a lever drag reel and not have a problem going 10 or 20 percent over the recommendations. Remember that when a manufacturer recommends using 30-pound line with a particular reel, that recommendation is based upon a standard 30-pound line with a conventional diameter. You can probably use conventional diameter 25- and 40-pound line as well, but it would not be worthwhile to use much heavier line. Not only is spool size and capacity an issue, but this reel may not be able to handle the greater stresses that might be generated with much heavier line, as noted previously. So, for example, putting 50-pound line on that reel could be problematic (although manufacturers and technicians do modify reels to cope with this).

However, and this is where things get tricky, there are 50-pound lines that have the diameter of a conventional 30-pound line, so you can get just as much of it on the spool. Nevertheless, it is still line with a 50-pound breaking strength (and may actually break much higher); this may be capable of overpowering the reel frame or spool. If the rod is up to handling a lot of stress, and the line is rated to break at a minimum of 50 (often more) pounds, and the reel is meant for up to 30-pound line, then the forces generated on the reel by maximum pressures could be harmful.

On the other hand, you might use a 30-pound line with a diameter of conventional 17-pound line, and achieve much greater line capacity on the reel at a line strength that the reel is rated for. Or, you could "cheat" a little bit and use 40-pound line that has a diameter of conventional 20-pound line, if that benefited your fishing situation *(see: line)*. This is a grossly misunderstood aspect of reel usage that has largely been brought about by the emergence of thin diameter lines (nylon monofilaments, braids, and microfilaments). However, most lever drag reel users, especially those who fish tournaments and who fish for records or who want to be certain of qualifying for a record if the circumstance arises, stay within the manufacturer's rated strength of the reel.

Filling. There is no form of fishing in which it is more important to fill a reel properly than big-game fishing; in a nutshell, the key here is packing new line on tightly. If you fish with a big-game reel that has been loosely packed with monofilament line, there's a good chance of losing a terrific fish.

When a truly big fish rips line from a reel on its initial sizzling run, there is enormous tension on the line. If the line is not tightly packed on the reel, it can bind into itself, hanging up deep in the line mass or even digging all the way down to the spool arbor. That's usually enough to cause it to break off at the reel. When the line breaks there, it does so with a sound as sharp as the crack of a rifle shot; the sudden realization of what has happened is enough to make an angler feel sick.

Most often, such binding happens when new line is spooled onto the reel under little or no tension. You may have seen anglers spooling new line on their reels from a filler-spool bouncing about the cockpit deck. It's the easy way, and it may be suitable for lighter tackle and less demanding species, but it can cost you the fish of your lifetime when a big tuna or billfish is using its power to stream away.

The solution is simply to spool new line by packing it tightly under tension. This should be done with the reel's drag set to the Strike position and a slight bend in the rod. Two people can do this with one seated in a fighting chair or on the floor at home with a shoulder harness snapped to the reel lugs and the rod butt nestled on a pillow on the floor. In either case the line should be run through all of the rod guides. The helper stands a short distance away, holding a dowel placed through the middle of a bulk filler spool (often one holding about 2,400 yards of line). The helper should wear heavy gloves and hold small towels against the ends of the filler spool to create enough friction to cause tension on the rod as the person holding the rod in a holder cranks line onto the reel. Keep the rod bent slightly while cranking so there is enough tension

An angler holds on as a fish takes line from a big-game stand-up outfit.

to lay the line on the spool tightly. As you put the line on, crisscross it every five or six turns to help prevent binding. Fill the spool to within $^1/_4$-inch of the edge of the spool flange.

Any similar method for creating tension on the line as it's spooled will do the trick. Although the job of cranking the reel is tough, it's well worth the effort when the first fish is on the new line. While it might be argued that a normal fight with a fish creates enough tension to pack the reel tightly, that is true only if the line doesn't bind and break in the process of playing that first fish. Playing a fish under tension does pack a reel tightly, but only if the line has been packed properly to start, so that the underlying line does not allow the respooled line to dig in. You have to get it right for the first fish.

Incidentally, the same binding and breaking problem that occurs when line is loosely spooled onto a reel can occur when line is allowed to mound in one place on the spool of the reel. Mounding occurs when the line is not properly leveled by hand when being retrieved. Obviously, whether the reel is packed tightly or not, line must be fed back and forth onto the spool as it's being packed.

When it comes to retrieving line under tension, as when fighting a fish, realize that the power of nylon monofilament under a heavy load (as is generated by hard-cranking the line under the great pressure of a big fish) has caused spools to break, popping the flange by spreading the spool. This has occurred with some of the best reels when a big fish has been fought for hours. When line with compounded stretch is retrieved onto the spool and then compacts, it can cause tremendous pressure. Be aware that a large amount of lighter strength monofilament can do more damage than a smaller amount of heavier monofilament. There are more layers of the lighter line and in total a greater stretch factor, so you can get more stretch out of lighter nylon monofilament lines. Manufacturers have turned to forged spools to help eliminate this problem, and spreading the line properly onto the spool helps as well.

De-spooling. When seeking trophy fish with big-game tackle, line must be changed regularly. Sometimes that means after every trip or after each protracted fight with a large fish, especially if the line has been stretched and dragged through the sea for great lengths of time, where debris can abrade it in the process. Sargassum weed can be very abrasive, as can the junk that often floats along in weedlines. Your next big fish should be fought with fresh line with no risk of cutoff due to damage from previous fishing activity.

When you're taking old line off a big-game reel it must be completely emptied from the reel and properly discarded. This is a lot of line to deal with, as these reels have great capacity. To de-spool, simply pull the line from the reel against minimal drag while holding the butt of the rod down with one foot. It's a tedious process, but it avoids littering the ocean with discarded tangles of line.

An easier method than pulling it off by hand is to employ an electric drill with a dowel inserted into the bit clamp. Wind the line over the dowel, turn the drill on, and empty the reel quickly. Although there are a number of battery-powered devices for pulling line from reels, most are engineered for lighter line and don't handle heavy offshore trolling sizes.

Refilling the spool. Line on a lever drag reel is often replaced because it's been used severely rather than because it gets low on the spool. Extreme pressures, as when fighting tough fish, put a lot of stress, especially stretch, on the line. Many anglers replace the entire spool of line, even though it is a lot of line and costly, rather than replace a portion of it.

With most other reels, when the line is suspect and needs replacement, or when the line gets low on the spool, you have the option of completely refilling the spool, or refilling only part of the spool. Although economically it seems to make sense to refill these large-capacity spools with just 120 or 180 yards of line rather than the full complement of 500 or 900 yards, that may not be a good practical decision.

When you partially refill the spool, you have to tie a line-to-line knot *(see: knots, fishing).* The weakest portion of a line is usually the knot, so this connection must be a good one to maintain the basic strength of the line, should that knotted section come under severe pressure. This is especially important when angling for large and strong fish. However, the problem with making a line-to-line knot for most lever drag reel filling is that the line used is fairly heavy with a thick diameter, and the line-to-line knot is bulky and obtrusive on the reel spool. Furthermore, it may get caught on a rod guide when departing under extreme pressure and cause a break off or spool overrun. This disadvantage is a deciding factor when it comes to refilling lever drag reels, and thus, most anglers do not tie line-to-line knots on the reel, but completely respool with new unknotted fresh line.

Matching and selecting. As with any type of fishing tackle, the issue of matching the right reel to the right rod is an important one, but in these times, it is a relatively easy one, as big-game rods are designed and classified for specific line strengths. Thus, a 30-pound IGFA-class rod is matched with a 30-pound lever drag reel.

When selecting big-game tackle, as well as matching a rod and reel, you must take into consideration the applications for it, and determine the size of fish that you will likely catch, and evaluate the conditions under which you'll be fishing. The larger and stronger the fish, the stronger the tackle necessary for beginners (which is why heavier gear is most often used on offshore charter boats), until

B

you get the experience to use lighter gear. Most selection starts with a determination of the line strength necessary for the conditions, and having the rod and reel appropriate for this. You should also give a lot of attention to line capacity so that you have an appropriate amount of line on the reel for the application.

Holding the rod and reel. Lever drag reels are too large for palming and not conducive for usage like a baitcasting reel, so they are usually held by putting the left hand on the rod foregrip. This is obviously the hold for placing the butt in a belt gimbal or into a harness. Holding the foregrip with the left hand also helps with guiding the line on the spool in a level manner.

Backing off the drag. Before any on-the-water use of a big-game reel, it is vital to set the drag to the proper amount of tension. Issues pertaining to setting drag were reviewed earlier in this section, and using and setting drag is covered in more detail elsewhere *(see: drag).*

At the end of each day of fishing, and after a reel has been washed and dried, it is a good idea to back the drag tension off to relieve pressure on the drag washers. This is not quite as important for lever drag reels with carbon fiber drag washers, as they resist compression better than washers made of other friction material; nevertheless, releasing tension is still a good idea. This is done by moving the drag lever back to the freespool position and making sure that the clicker is engaged so the spool does not spill loose line. It's a good practice to keep pressure off the washers, and it also allows internal parts to dry out if necessary.

Maintenance and repair. Maintenance is an ongoing issue for big-game tackle users. Rods and reels must be washed down every time they are taken on the water, even if not used, because they are likely to be exposed to salt spray. Use a fine but ample spray of freshwater, rather than a hard stream, to clean the reel and remove salt deposits, and do so as soon as possible after you return to the dock or launch site. Use soap and a scrub brush to remove any hardened matter. Warm water is best if available, and make sure not to use a hard stream, which could drive salt deposits into the internal mechanisms. Dry off excess freshwater on the reel and lubricate exposed areas, perhaps with a pressurized spray oil. A light coating of oil with a rag can also be applied to exposed metal parts. Give the reel a chance to dry out completely, and store it in a cool, dry place, not in a bag that is wet or which will promote condensation. Be sure to keep the drag tension set when washing to help keep unwanted moisture out of internal parts, especially the drag washers. Some reels have a special internal collar to help keep moisture and dirt out, but you should keep maximum drag tension on anyway until the reel has been wiped down and is ready for storage. Then back off the drag pressure completely.

Make sure to periodically examine screws and fittings. If the reel has any loose part, which is most likely to be a sideplate screw, it should be tightened as soon as you notice it. Do not excessively lubricate reels, which may cause harm if oil or grease get on parts that don't need, or shouldn't have, the lubrication. That includes carbon fiber drag washers. Using the wrong kind of lubrication is also a problem. Follow the manufacturer's recommendations for the type of lubrication to use, the locations, and the frequency, as this will vary with different brands.

If you are mechanically minded, you can carefully strip down and examine and clean the reel yourself. Pay special attention to the drag components and to the drag friction washers. If the drag has been underperforming, it may be due to (excessive) lubrication. You may be able to alleviate some of the problem by washing the friction washer in white spirit or dry cleaning fluid (do this in a well-ventilated area and wear a mask to avoid breathing fumes) until all traces of the lubrication have been removed. Allow it to dry thoroughly. You can relubricate the friction washer lightly if recommended by the manufacturer and only with the suggested lubricant, or, in the case of carbon fiber washers, do not lubricate it. Carefully reassemble the parts (you did save the manufacturer's manual with schematic diagram, didn't you?). Although some people try polishing the metal friction disk or drag pressure plates to improve performance, manufacturers say that polishing can cause an uneven surface, so they recommend replacement.

Details on general tackle maintenance are discussed elsewhere *(see: tackle—care/maintenance/repair).* Manufacturers recommend that lever drag reels be overhauled at least once a season, perhaps more if used vigorously. Periodically oil and grease moving parts, but don't overdo it, and only use the type of oil and grease recommended by the manufacturer. A thorough cleaning requires disassembling most of the reel, scrubbing or rinsing most of the gunk from the parts, drying, and then relubricating and regreasing. If you are unsure about doing this yourself, have a reel service and repair shop do it, or send it to the manufacturer for servicing.

Lever drag reels, as previously noted, are subject to maintenance and repair work by very specialized master technicians. These are the finest high-tech fishing instruments in the world, so it makes sense to have maintenance done in the off-season by professionals, as well as to have them look at fine-tuning operational features, especially the drag.

BIGHT

A bay formed by an indentation or curve in a coastline.

BILGE

(1) The lowest part of the interior of a boat.

(2) Rank water collected in the bottom of a boat.

BILHARZIA

See: First Aid.

BILLABONG

An Australian term for a backwater or pond connected to a river; it is derived from the aboriginal words "billa," meaning river, and "bong," meaning dead. Billabongs have vegetation and fallen or flooded trees (snags), and they drain during the dry season. During and after rainy periods, billabongs are usually flush with water and may host gamefish, especially barramundi, amidst profuse cover. During the dry season, billabongs may dry up, or they may develop into a stagnant pool cut off from the main stream, at which time they are likely to support only carp.

BILLFISH

The term "billfish" refers to members of two families of marine fish: Xiphidae, which has only one genus and one species, the swordfish; and Istiophoridae, which numbers 11 species in three genera and includes marlin, sailfish, and spearfish. Of the latter family, the term "marlin" is used for the larger species, "spearfish" for the smaller species, and "sailfish" for the species with a high dorsal fin. All are good sportfish, and some—especially swordfish, blue marlin, and black marlin—are among the largest and most coveted angling quarries.

Billfish are characterized by a long spearlike or swordlike upper jaw or beak that may be used to stun prey during feeding; although this bill has been employed in apparent aggression to spear objects, including boats, it is not deliberately used to spear prey. These species are pelagic, migratory, and found in all oceans. They are related to tuna *(see)* and mackerel *(see)* and, like those fish, are able to swim at great speeds; the sailfish is considered the fastest of all fish, having been clocked at 68 miles per hour over short distances. Billfish also have complex air (or swim) bladders that enable them to compensate rapidly for changes in depth and thus can move without difficulty from deep water to the surface.

Billfish grow fairly rapidly and feed on various pelagic species. When alive, they are generally ocean blue above and silvery below. They spawn in the open sea and are usually solitary or travel in pairs or small groups. Sportfishing interest in these big-game species is high, although due to their migratory and pelagic nature they are seldom accessible to large numbers of anglers, and rarely to those who fish from small boats and inshore. Fishing in offshore blue-water environments is the norm.

A Pacific sailfish from Huatulco, Mexico.

Most billfish, particularly swordfish, have good to excellent food value and are of significant commercial interest. As a whole, and especially in certain parts of their range, billfish stocks are overexploited and have seriously declined due to commercial longlines and gillnets. Sportfishing has not adversely impacted billfish stocks; only a small percentage of the world's billfish are caught by recreational anglers, and a still smaller percentage of those are killed. Angler tagging of released billfish has contributed significantly to scientific knowledge about this species. Nevertheless, worldwide, commercial fishermen kill millions of billfish annually. The Billfish Foundation, a research and conservation organization, reports that more than 500,000 billfish in the Atlantic Ocean alone were killed each year from the 1970s through 1990s by longlining. Furthermore, their data show that for every porpoise killed by commercial tuna fishermen, 10 tons of billfish were killed during the same period. Although efforts to save porpoises from commercial destruction have been widely reported and awareness has triggered some success, no organized international effort has emerged to prevent the commercial overharvesting and destruction of the world's billfish stocks.

See: Marlin, Black; Marlin, Blue; Marlin, Striped; Marlin, White; Sailfish; Spearfish; Swordfish.

B

BILLFISH ON FLY TACKLE

Although offshore fishing has long been the domain of big fish and beefy tackle, a surge has occurred in the number of people who pursue what some consider the ultimate light-tackle challenge: billfish on a fly rod. Although there are practical limits to what can be done with a fly rod—the real heavyweights are beyond its capabilities—the envelope of achievement in this arena has been steadily pushed forward for the last few decades.

In the early 1960s, attempting to catch sailfish or marlin on a fly rod would have been thought virtually impossible, or merely a stunt. A few pioneers were convinced it could be done even then and set about trying to prove it. Lee Cuddy caught the first record billfish on a fly—an Atlantic sailfish of 47 pounds, landed off Florida on June 4, 1964. Stu Apte caught the first Pacific sailfish of record on a fly (on 12-pound tippet) at Pinas Bay, Panama, on June 25, 1965. Lee Wulff landed a fly-caught striped marlin of 148 pounds at Salinas, Ecuador, in May 1967, and accomplished a record that still stands; but Floridian Doc Robinson caught a 145-pound striped marlin off Baja California in 1965, establishing him as the first to catch a marlin on a fly. After those feats, the pursuit of billfish on a fly became more serious, and people took it up for the general fun and achievement as well as in an attempt to establish records. South Carolina's Billy Pate was the first to set saltwater fly-rod records in all the marlin and sailfish categories except Pacific blue marlin. And by the 1990s, Jack Samson had become the first to catch both Atlantic and Pacific sailfish, as well as all five species of marlin, on a fly rod, achieving a "super grand slam" of billfish.

Since the late 1980s, catching large ocean fish on a saltwater fly rod has been an established niche game. Although bonefish, tarpon, bluefish, and striped bass are still the most popularly sought saltwater species among fly anglers, sailfish and marlin are now pursued by a growing legion of enthusiasts.

A fly-hooked sailfish clears the water close to the boat, forcing the angler to point his rod directly at it to minimize drag.

Fly-tackle dealers on all coasts are catering to neophyte fly-rod billfish anglers in search of the proper gear and more information on this growing sport. Thanks to more information, better equipment, and the accomplishments of earlier anglers, catching some of the ocean's most spectacular fish on a fly rod is a realistic goal, particularly for experienced anglers. For those who are less experienced, sailfish, white marlin, and striped marlin are reasonable targets, as these species do not attain the monster weights of their blue and black marlin brethren. Due to their size and availability, however, sailfish are the primary billfish for saltwater fly rodders.

Fish size is a bit of an issue, and a limitation, where fly rodding is concerned, especially for marlin. Unlike conventional big-game anglers, fly rodders are generally limited to billfish up to about 400 pounds. The largest fly-caught marlin record to date is a 260-pound Pacific blue marlin caught on 20-pound-class tippet. No one knows how many larger marlin have been caught by anglers who don't care about records and release their fish without fanfare, although it seems likely that extremely few have accomplished such a feat. It seems possible that larger fish can be caught, and perhaps some will. For an experienced angler, it is no problem holding billfish below 200 pounds. The biggest fly-caught sailfish in the record books weighed 136 pounds—caught in 1965 on a 12-pound tippet; but again, perhaps some bigger sailfish have been caught by fly rodders who prefer not to kill their quarry and instead turn it loose.

Today's billfish angler is limited mainly by skill and luck, mostly the latter. The rods, reels, lines, leaders, and flies exist to catch larger billfish. Some anglers who have specialized in this type of fishing, however, have been after bigger fish for many years and haven't landed them. So this particular sport is definitely not an easy one.

Technique

The technique used to take a big striper out of the surf won't work on a striped marlin, and the 7-weight rod and line used to catch big bonefish would be like a child's toy if used for sailfish. Furthermore, the game of stalking and casting for shallow-water and inshore species is nonexistent for pelagic species.

As many conventional big-game anglers know, sailfish and marlin generally are taken from a trolling boat underway. This is because the ocean is big, a lot of ground has to be covered, and the fish have to be attracted to your offering. This is all true in fly fishing for billfish, but the resemblance ends there. In general terms, an angler could theoretically troll a fly, but the chances of catching a billfish on a trolled fly are fairly slim, and this technique would not meet International Game Fish Association (IGFA) requirements for establishing a record, should the fish be large enough to qualify. Because it is never known when a record fish might be caught by offshore anglers (those using big-game tackle or flycasting tackle), most ardent anglers follow accepted procedures that guarantee they will be within record-setting guidelines whenever and wherever they are fly fishing.

IGFA world-record rules state that a fly can be cast to billfish only while a boat is out of gear (not trolling and moving forward). The original rules, set up by early saltwater fly rodders, make a lot of sense on closer examination. The boat is taken out of gear partly to ensure that an angler casts rather than drags a trolled fly, but it is primarily done to ensure precise presentation of a fly that will land close to a billfish searching for food. Billfish come up and strike baits, lures, and flies with their bills; they stun the object so they can turn and then take it. If the fly is moving at the same speed as the boat, and directly forward of a fish swimming immediately behind the boat, it is almost impossible to position the lightweight fly inside a billfish's mouth at a spot where you can set the hook.

Billfish must be attracted up behind the boat by trolling baits and teasers. Veteran billfish fly rodders generally agree that big, gaudy teasers run off outriggers or on flatlines behind the transom, and dead baits rigged without hooks and trolled 30 to 50 feet behind the boat, work best to attract billfish in an effort to present a fly to them. There is considerable leeway in this. Some veterans like to troll a daisy chain of squid as teasers, and others like trolling live baits without hooks. Most experts prefer trolling a rigged dead bait on a long, whippy teaser rod so they can retrieve it rapidly when a billfish appears or strikes it.

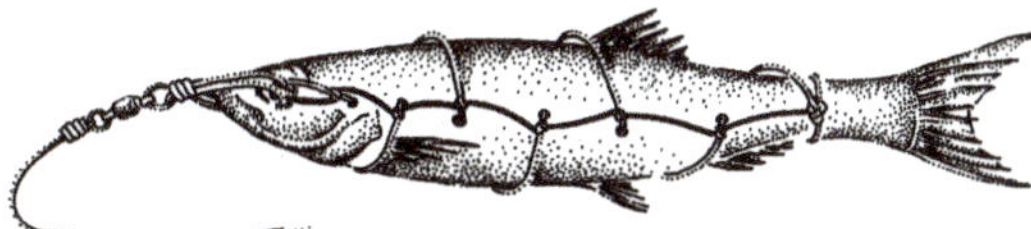

A durable sewn teaser bait is used for bringing billfish into casting range.

Whatever the choice of attractor, when a billfish comes up to eat it, it is imperative that the trolled offering be pulled rapidly toward the boat ahead of the searching billfish, until it is possible to cast a fly to it. At that time, the boat is taken out of gear, the bait is rapidly yanked from the water, the fly is cast, and the billfish is allowed to pursue the fly. The aim of this tactic, often referred to as bait-and-switch *(see)* is not only to get the billfish to take the fly, but for the angler to set the hook in the corner of the billfish's mouth as it makes a turn with the fly. Most successful billfish flies today are tied in tandem, one hook riding point up and another point down, in order to increase the chances of getting a hook into tough cartilage. It should be set either in the corner of the mouth or in the soft top of the mouth. If the hook is sharp enough, clamping down on the line with the thumb and forefinger should set the hook firmly, but yanking hard on the rod will certainly help set the hook better.

Once the billfish is hooked, it is important to make sure that the rest of the fly line, the running line, and the backing is free to run out through the rod guides as the big fish makes its first run. For that reason, when casting to billfish most anglers keep that line in a large plastic bucket at their feet. Snagging on the least obstruction in the cockpit, or stepping on the line, will cause a tippet to part.

More about teasing. Perhaps the most critical aspect of fly fishing for billfish is the act of attracting, or teasing, a fish and exciting it so much that it is willing to strike the fly. This activity requires teamwork from a crew, usually a minimum of three people, which includes the angler, captain, and mate.

The items used to attract billfish are hookless trolling lures *(see: trolling lures, saltwater)* and hookless rigged baits. These are all referred to as teasers because they are used to attract a fish and perhaps draw a strike but are not meant to be consumed or grabbed and held by the fish. They are usually skipped across the surface rather than fished below it. The number of people in the boat available to reel in lines when a fish appears determines the number of teasers used. The lures may be run off a line attached halfway up one outrigger, as well as on transom flatlines. Some anglers prefer to use lures on the outside and longer trolling lines, primarily those with a soft head that are easy to retrieve quickly. A lure or bait (usually the latter) is attached to a long sturdy rod (9 feet or longer) and trolled off the transom. The bait is a completely sewn mullet, mackerel, ballyhoo, or flyingfish, but it could be other items, as well as strips of bait if whole fish are unavailable; these are often adorned at the head with a colorful plastic skirt. The long rod is necessary to exert control over the teaser when it is close, and to quickly yank the teaser out of the water. If 9 feet of line, measured from the rod tip, is let out, and the rod holder stands flush against the transom, a 9-foot rod allows for placement of a teaser approximately 18 feet behind the boat, yet the teaser is still capable of being instantly lifted out of the water. The object is to get the fish just behind that close-range teaser and pursuing it excitedly.

When a fish comes into the spread, the captain reels in the outrigger teaser lure and then watches the fish while preparing to adjust speed. The mate(s) retrieves the other lures while maintaining the interest of the following fish. The billfish may switch from one teaser to another, but it is important to attract it to within 20 to 25 feet of the boat in pursuit of the teaser attached to a teaser rod. The person holding the teaser rod tries to maintain the interest of the fish without letting it firmly grab the teaser, generally trying to keep the fish a few feet behind the moving teaser. If the job is done well, the billfish will keep slashing at the teaser, trying to stun it and appearing to have missed it. This game is a bit different for some species than for others, or may differ by location, requiring faster or slower boat speeds, for example, to sustain the interest of the pursuing fish.

Assuming the fly angler is right-handed, the best casting scenario is for the angler to stand in the port transom corner of the boat, with excess fly line and backing in a tub or bucket at the feet. There should be no nearby obstructions that could snatch the line, and the port outrigger should be in a vertical position so the angler has plenty of room for a back cast. The person doing the teasing tries to keep the teaser lure or bait to the starboard side of the whitewater boat wake, and the angler gets the fly in the water and about 20 to 25 feet back. The fish is allowed to touch the teaser, and the captain is told to put the boat in neutral; with the boat in neutral, the angler picks up the fly line and casts behind and to the right of the billfish. The teaser is yanked away, the fly is stripped into view, and the fish turns toward the fly, putting itself into position for a good set should it immediately strike the fly. The same tactic is used if the angler is left-handed, except that the angler would stand in the starboard corner and the fish would be teased to the port side.

Generally, slower boat speeds make for better teasing, although this method may not raise or excite fish. Fish that are really excited and aggressive are most likely to take the fly. And if the fish doesn't take the fly after a careful effort and perhaps a second cast and retrieve, then it may be necessary to resume trolling with the teasers to re-attract the fish.

Fighting and Landing

After the billfish has made its initial runs, landing it is usually simply a matter of maintaining control until the fish is tired and can be brought to the boat. A fight with a billfish on fly tackle can last hours, depending on the class of leader tippet, the weight of the fish, and the experience of the angler.

It takes a sturdy rod and reel and well-tied knots to withstand the pressure of battling billfish on fly tackle.

Fighting big fish on a fly rod takes some physical strength, but not so much as to prevent women from enjoying the sport as much as men. Although you can power-fight a billfish, it takes considerable strength to tire a billfish in the first few minutes of a battle. It is better to let the parabolic curve of the big saltwater fly rod do its work, which it will certainly do in time.

When a billfish is making its first runs and jumps, it's best to almost freespool the big saltwater reel. In this way, the pressure of the shooting head passing rapidly through the water does not put undue strain on the class tippet. The sailfish or marlin will eventually tire and will settle down to a stubborn fight. At this point, the angler can increase the reel drag and begin to take up line while the skipper backs down slowly in the direction of the fish.

Some billfish elect to stay near or on the surface for the duration of the battle, which makes life easier for the angler, but others may head for the depths. This is where the size and construction of the fly rod becomes important. Many 12- and 13-weight fly rods are simply not constructed to lift big billfish from the depths; they either break or do not put sufficient pressure on the fish to budge it. Manufacturers have lately been making 14-weight rods to compensate, and the relatively new breed of "lifting" fly rods, which are strong 15- to 18-weight models, can bring up a stubborn billfish from the depths when no other fly rod would work.

As the billfish begins to close in on the transom for landing, the crew becomes all-important. These strong fish often make sudden thrashing moves at the last minute and can inflict injury. Billfish anglers must be able to anticipate violent moves by the fish and make sure to grasp it properly. It is not necessary to sink large gaffs into a billfish to get it alongside the boat. Many times the fish can be led alongside with a small bill gaff; now and then a tail rope may be slipped over the tail. A crewmember can grasp the bill with a gloved hand, and the fish can be released at the boat or brought in over the transom briefly for photographs before being released.

A beginning fly rodder can use any strength leader to take billfish, but if angling for records, IGFA stipulates seven leader tippet categories: 2, 4, 6, 8, 12, 16, and 20 pounds. For the novice, and for general fishing purposes, a 20-pound tippet makes the most sense. Because most billfish are released, using a heavier tippet usually ensures a shorter fight, which is generally better for the fish than one that is long and drawn out. If you have no concerns about records (although if you're fishing with established charter boat captains, they usually are very attentive to this), you could choose a tippet size that exceeds IGFA regulations but still ensures a good fight. With some experience under your belt, you can move down in tippet size.

The lightest tippets are very difficult to use for billfishing, however, and this is evident from existing fly-tackle world records. Several of the light-tippet categories for sailfish are still vacant, and for the five species of marlin, most of the categories under 12-pound tippet are vacant. The light-tippet categories for marlin are vacant because few anglers have hooked marlin on a fly, even on the heavier tippets. Although it's possible to land billfish on light tippets, years of experience are generally necessary before even the best of anglers can handle a billfish on such fragile leaders.

Fortunately, almost any size boat can be used to catch billfish on a fly. It is no longer necessary to use the big, expensive sportfishing boat common to conventional big-game angling. Today, small, fast, compact, and maneuverable boats are taking billfish off all North American coasts. They transport fly rodders out to the billfish grounds fast and are able to return home in a hurry. Although small boats provide a degree of angler maneuverability that big yachts may not, the distance offshore to the billfish grounds, the potential sea conditions, and the skill of the captain are all factors that impact boat selection.

The vast majority of those who use fly tackle for billfish do it for the thrill of the sport and release most if not all of the billfish caught *(see: catch-and-release)*. The exception might be for fish that are potential records, although anglers should make every effort to evaluate the size of their catch quickly *(see: measuring fish)* and determine if it's large enough to be a potential record. If there is any doubt, the fish should be quickly released. In most cases, a photograph of the fish, plus its measurements, should be enough to establish the record.

Tackle

Sailfish and marlin require a different set of tools than do other fish sought with flycasting tackle: strong fiberglass and graphite rods in the 12- to 16-weight class, reels capable of carrying 400 to 600 yards of line and backing, and sinking shooting-head lines in 12- to 16-weight categories. These fish also demand strong leader material and a set of knots that will not part under enormous strain; these are knots that most fly anglers have never had occasion to use.

Flies that imitate the many species of ocean baitfish need to be tied on hooks that will not break and will resist the constant effects of corrosion from exposure to saltwater. These hooks must be filed to points sharp enough to penetrate the tough mouth cartilage of billfish, which is no small task.

The beginner has plenty of excellent rods, reels, and lines to choose from, as the major line companies have spent a lot of time researching and developing lines that will stand up to rough treatment in saltwater. Leader material has come a long way in the past few decades, and many brands are available. Although one can have a custom rod made, first-class billfish fly rods are being manufactured today by various companies, primarily in

Large, bright streamer flies, some with popping-style heads, are standard for billfish.

10- to 14-weight models for smaller fish, and 14- to 16-weight for larger fish.

The most import aspects of a big-game fly reel are the line capacity and the drag. Today's big-game fly reels are machined from solid blocks of aircraft-quality aluminum and stainless steel bar stock. The drag systems use stainless steel bearings and multiple-disc surfaces of metal, Teflon, and cork; the spools are also machined from the same high-quality aluminum. These fast-spinning spools are counterbalanced to within a few grains of weight.

To handle strong and far-running billfish, a big, saltwater fly reel must have a capacity of at least 400 yards, preferably 600 or more yards, including 30-pound Micron or Dacron backing plus 100 feet of nylon monofilament running line (optional) and 25 to 30 feet of 15-weight sinking shooting-head fly line. A reel just for sailfish, particularly the big Pacific sailfish that run in excess of 100 pounds, should have a total capacity of 350 to 400 yards. For marlin, a fly reel should carry no less than 600 combined yards of fly line and 30-pound backing; many of the best have a capacity of 800 to 900 yards.

Although beginning fly rodders might use a floating fly line, it is better to have a sinking line. The floating line is easier to pick up off the water for casting (or recasting, as it were), but its bulkiness becomes a drag problem when a billfish has steamed off with a lot of line and then turns, creating a huge bow in the line, which increases drag. Experts use a 30-foot head of fast-sinking line and a short total fly-line length (under 60 feet) to reduce drag. The angler and captain need a brightly colored backing in order to see where the fish is and how far out it is, especially if it becomes necessary to follow the fish.

With big billfish-class fly rods, it isn't necessary for an angler to be in a casting class with the best distance flycasters—these rods are so heavy, it's difficult to heave line far, and very few casts per day are required in billfishing. Under ordinary circumstances, it's unnecessary to cast a big billfish fly any more than 30 to 40 feet.

Critical knots. It is absolutely essential that saltwater fly rodders, especially those intent on catching billfish, learn to tie knots well. Knots are the most important element of terminal tackle. The backing is fastened to the running line by back-to-back Nail Knots. The running line is connected to butt leader sections with Loop-to-Loop or Double Surgeon Knots. Leaders and tippet sections utilize Bimini Twist Knots or Spider Hitches, and leader sections are connected to 80- to 100-pound shock tippets by Albright Knots or modified Nail Knots. The shock tippet may be fastened to the fly by a three-turn Improved Clinch Knot *(see: knots, fishing)*. Most of these knots are difficult to learn and harder to tie, but they are absolutely necessary to hold fish in the 100- to 300-pound category when traveling at great speeds.

Some anglers aren't knot aficionados, and even though they may use such knots as the Albright, the Surgeon's Loop, and the Spider Hitch, they prefer metal connector sleeves when forming certain connections. These connector sleeves are used to fasten the fly to 100-pound-test shock leader and also to make loops in the ends of the shooting-head fly line, which are fastened to either butt leader or mono running line with loop-to-loop connections. These sleeves may not be as pretty as knots, but they are very strong and don't slip when used properly.

Some anglers use a Spider Hitch Knot rather than the hard-to-tie Bimini Twist. The Spider Hitch is simple to tie and is every bit as strong as the Bimini in lines below 30-pound test, which are applicable for nearly all saltwater fly fishing.

Where to Go

For the specialized game of fly rodding for billfish, knowing only where billfish will be at any time of the year is not sufficient. You also must know where the right size billfish will be. Thus, for practical reasons, anglers hoping to land billfish on a fly must seek these species in sizes that average from under 100 pounds up to 350 pounds, and this prerequisite somewhat limits the selection of locations.

There would be little sense, for example, in fishing with a fly rod off Cairns, Australia, in October or November for black marlin, when 1,000-pound blacks are cruising and the average black ranges from 500 to 600 pounds. On the other hand, if you wanted to catch a nice fly-rod black marlin, it would be wise to fish off Townsville, Australia, which is inside the Great Barrier Reef, in August or September. The blacks there average 50 to 100 pounds then. Though most fly rodders think the only place one can find small black marlin is off Australia, there are small black marlin off Panama in January, February, and March. Off the mouth of Pinas Bay they run in the 300- to 500-pound range during those months and are caught on a regular basis by conventional big-game and light-tackle anglers.

White marlin almost never grow much larger than 100 pounds, so during for most of the year you can fish for them almost anywhere. They are caught all up and down the Atlantic coast, from late spring until late summer. To find them in great numbers, however, serious anglers head for Venezuela in October and November. A month later, they appear in concentrated numbers off Brazil.

Places to catch small Atlantic blue marlin are few, but possibilities include Jamaica in February and March, St. Thomas later in the spring and summer, and Venezuela in October, November, and early December. The channel that runs between the island of Cozumel and the east coast of Mexico, close to Cancún, is a great spot to pursue Atlantic blue marlin from February through May.

Finding small Pacific blue marlin is a tough one to call. Unfortunately, there is really no one place in which one can be certain of finding smaller sizes of this fish in great numbers at any one time. Pacific blue marlin exist off Hawaii and a number of Pacific islands, but their size renders them impractical for a fly rodder. The best place to try for small Pacific blue marlin might be off Cabo San Lucas. El Niño notwithstanding, the best time to pursue them off Baja would be from late spring up through November. Although there is no guarantee that they would be the right size for fly anglers, the catch records indicate that more blue marlin in the 200- to 400-pound category are caught there than anywhere else. Some blues in the 60- to 70-pound class have been caught there, which indicates that they migrate past that port at a fairly early age.

Atlantic sailfish congregate off Florida's East Coast, particularly in the winter off such areas as Jupiter Inlet and Palm Beach. But they are usually also plentiful off the Florida Keys at that time and later in the spring. Cozumel in March is a fine spot for Atlantic sails, as well as white marlin and small Atlantic blue marlin through May.

Pacific sailfish range all the way up the west coast of Central and South America to Baja and the Sea of Cortez. The best place to catch Pacific sailfish at any one time might be Panama in April and May, particularly at Pinas Bay. Also worth considering are Bahia Pez Vela on the upper coast of Costa Rica and Flamingo in the spring. During the winter months, when the winds make fishing almost impossible in those northern areas, Golfito in extreme southern Costa Rica, and Quepos, where a barrier range of mountains keeps the winds down and the seas calm, are good candidates.

In Mexico, Mazatlán is the top Pacific sailfish location, especially from May through October. But that is on the mainland—off Baja there are plenty of sails in the late spring and summer months, from an area south of La Paz all the way up to Loreto and Mulege.

The acrobatic Pacific striped marlin is a natural for fly rodders. It seldom exceeds 150 pounds in weight, which is just right for most fly anglers. The East Cape of Baja, from about La Paz down to Cabo San Lucas, is prime striped marlin territory from May through October. Another excellent spot for striped marlin is off Ecuador in the spring out of the port of Salinas, although it is a difficult place to reach. Striped marlin are caught regularly off Panama and Costa Rica, but they don't seem to congregate in any one spot at any one time. Striped marlin are also found resting on the surface in small pods off Mazatlán from February through April.

Striped marlin in the 250-pound class are regularly taken in New Zealand, although not on a fly. Since the records for striped marlin in New Zealand on conventional tackle are impressive—from 271 pounds to nearly 500 pounds—this fishery seems to offer possibilities for fly rodders as well.

BILL-WRAPPED

The wrapping of the bill of a marlin or sailfish with the leader or fishing line. This occurs occasionally during the fight of a fish. It may cause the line to be chafed and cut or may inhibit the behavior and fight of the fish.

BIMINI TWIST

A double-line knot primarily associated with saltwater fishing, especially the use of heavy leaders and big-game angling.

See: Knots, Fishing.

BIOLUMINESCENCE

The emission of visible nonthermal light by chemical reaction in living organisms. Bioluminescence is a highly developed characteristic of species in the deepest parts of the ocean, and a less highly developed characteristic of many near-surface ocean creatures, including species of bacteria, phytoplankton, metazoans, marine invertebrates, and fish. It occurs when luciferin, a compound found naturally in the luminescing organism, combines with oxygen and the enzyme luciferase to form oxyluciferin, water, and energy. Thus, chemical energy is transformed into light energy, and the resulting light is often used to attract prey. Some species have daily light cycles; others have seasonal ones. Individual luminescing organisms are difficult to see, but a large population of organisms glowing together becomes visible in darkness.

Saltwater anglers who fish at night, and boaters traveling at night, sometimes observe an eerie glow in the water caused by luminescent organisms being displaced by the movement of the boat.

BIOMASS

The total weight or volume of a stock or of a component of a stock. Also referred to as standing stock. Spawning stock biomass is the total weight of all fish in a stock that are old enough to spawn.

BIRDS

Birds are a good indicator of fish in saltwater, although less so in freshwater. In freshwater environments, anglers are likely to see such fish-eating birds as herons, kingfishers, loons, mergansers, and cormorants, as well as seagulls. Herons are shorebirds usually found where there are many small fish in shallow water. Mergansers and most other diving ducks are seldom of much assistance to anglers, although actively feeding loons and cormorants may indicate the nearby presence of baitfish schools. Seagulls are seldom of much fish-locating value, except when they are actively following schools of surface-feeding striped bass in impoundments.

The situation in saltwater is quite different, however, because there are more birds and more surface food to attract birds. In the marine environment, noticing birds, learning to recognize them, and following them, can help find gamefish. Knowing which ones to follow and when is a skill that comes from experience. When to follow them is usually dependent on whether they are searching, actively feeding, or flying by. When birds are searching, their flight path is straight, graceful, and relaxed. Once they spot a food source, they speed up; their turns become sharp, and eventually they begin swooping down to the water. An increased level of excitement is obvious from loud chattering, which is meant to attract other birds. Take particular notice of whether birds seem afraid to sit on the surface. If so, bluefish are probably present, and the birds have good reason to fear having their feet bit-

When diving to pluck baitfish, seagulls and terns often indicate the presence of feeding gamefish.

ten off. Pelicans, though, will actually dive into the water and feast on smaller bluefish.

The number of birds that you see is not necessarily an indication of the number of fish below them. A single large billfish might push up a large ball of bait and attract many birds, yet only a few birds may be observed at a site where there is a school of other gamefish. And not all birds are reliable fish indicators; examples in saltwater include cormorants and albatrosses. Here is a synopsis of birds commonly observed at sea, and their general significance.

Terns. Terns are a wide-ranging bird, with long, slender wings, straight beaks, and forked tails. Smaller than seagulls and known for their flitting, dive-bombing activity, terns are good indicators of fish location. Within a few miles of shore, they are great indicators of baitfish—information that is helpful when you're catching bait. Offshore, they often provide an excellent clue that schools of baitfish are being worked over just beneath the surface. If terns are swooping but not touching the water, they may be positioned over patches of algae—and often big dolphin. If terns are tightly bunched, the fish are probably small. If the flock is moving quickly from one spot to another, the baitfish are likely being run by schools of king mackerel, tuna, or bonito. In inshore waters, they can be indicators of mackerel, bluefish, tarpon, snook, and kingfish.

Frigate birds. The most reliable offshore fish-finders are frigate birds, also known as man-o'-war birds. They're easily recognized from a distance by their wide wings and long, deeply forked tails. High-flying frigates are known for helping anglers find big blue-water gamefish (and floating objects), including bull dolphin, marlin, and sailfish, by shadowing their movements from above. They'll follow large, solitary predator fish in anticipation of diving quickly to the surface to grab fleeing baitfish. Closer to shore they may be found in groups of two dozen or more but are more solitary farther offshore.

Shearwaters. These pelagic seabirds are similar in appearance to gulls. They often beat their wings several times, then glide low to the water. Shearwaters will swim underwater to catch bait, at times feeding so heavily they struggle to fly. Offshore, look for them on top of kelp paddies; their presence helps you spot paddies from long distances, and their movements tip you off to the direction in which the fish are headed. They are often associated with tuna and less commonly with billfish.

Boobies/gannets/pelicans/jaegers. Boobies can be found in huge groups numbering in the hundreds and can be visual aids for leading anglers to baitfish and gamefish. Gannets are high-diving birds that plummet into the water for food and are noticeable from a long distance. Pelicans are sometimes an indicator that such offshore gamefish as billfish and sharks are feeding, and may be present where mackerel and anchovies are balled up. Jaegers look like dark-colored seagulls with erratic, flared-tail flight, but their sharply bent wings and long central tail feathers distinguish them from gulls. These food thieves tend to follow other birds that have found fish.

Seagulls/petrels. Some saltwater anglers do not find seagulls very useful, although others do. Inshore, seagulls can be terrific indicators of fish activity along the beach, especially for mackerel, bluefish, tarpon, snook, and kingfish. They do not dive but pick up scraps off the surface, as well as wounded baitfish on the surface, which could be an indication of feeding gamefish in the area. Offshore, seagulls are perhaps the least reliable seabird because they have a tendency to get excited about picking at floating garbage. Many anglers do not find petrels useful, but others find them helpful for locating tuna.

See: Finding Fish; Sight Fishing.

BIRD, TROLLING

A common term for a bird- or airplane-shaped teaser used in offshore fishing, especially for marlin and tuna.

See: Trolling Lures, Saltwater.

BITE

(1) The strike of a fish, especially common to natural bait usage.

(2) An expression for hot sportfish activity, as in, "There was a good walleye bite on spinners yesterday."

(3) A point of measurement on a hook *(see).*

BITE INDICATOR

Any small object, usually one that floats, which is used to indicate a bite, or strike, by a fish on some form of bait. All floats *(see)* and bobbers *(see)* are types of bite indicators, although not actually called bite indicators. In Europe, the term bite indicator is used for a small object that may be attached to the rod tip or to the line when fishing groundbait *(see)* without a float. Bite indicators are more sensitive than rod tips.

See: Float; Legering; Strike Indicator.

BIVISIBLE

A highly visible, high-floating, and generally light-colored type of dry fly *(see).*

BLACKFISH

"Blackfish" is the common or regional name for black sea bass *(see: sea bass, black),* bowfin *(see),* luderick *(see),* tautog *(see),* and tripletail *(see).*

BLACK SALMON

A term for kelt *(see),* or overwintering sea-run Atlantic salmon.

See: Salmon, Atlantic.

BLACKMOUTH

A term used in the Pacific Northwest for immature, resident chinook salmon *(see),* derived from a black gum line that helps distinguish them from other salmon species.

BLADE BAIT

A lipless sinking lure with a thin metal body.

See: Spoon.

BLANK

The shaft of a fishing rod. This refers both to the newly fabricated product unadorned with components (guides, wrapping, handle, and reel seat), and to the shaft of a completed rod. The exterior of most rod blanks is fitted with guides to assist in dispensing and retrieving line; however, line passes through the interior of some completely hollow blanks. The material of the blank is most commonly fiberglass, graphite, or a composite of these materials.

See: Rod, Fishing.

BLIND CASTING

Fishing in circumstances in which the fish cannot be seen, and lures or flies are presented without firm knowledge that the quarry is present.

This term is most often applied to stalking saltwater species (including tarpon, permit, and bonefish) in shallow water and in circumstances in which the fish are casually observed and cast to even though the water conditions (depth or turbidity) prevent visual sighting and exact presentation. In all but clear-water conditions, however, or when fish are actively feeding in an observable manner, most casting in fresh- and saltwater is done in a "blind" manner, that is, the angler relies on knowledge of the water and the quarry to make a presentation in the right place and in the right manner.

See: Finding Fish.

BLOOD KNOT

A fishing knot for line-to-line connections.

See: Knots, Fishing.

BLUE DUN

A gray blue color of hackle preferred for fly tying, and also called iron blue dun.

BLUEFISH *Pomatomus saltatrix.*

Other names—blue, tailor, elf, chopper, marine piranha, rock salmon, snapper blue, snapper, Hatteras blue, skipjack (Australia), shad (South Africa); French: *tassergal;* Japanese: *amikiri;* Portuguese: *anchova, enchova;* Spanish: *anjova, anchova de banco.*

The only member of the Pomatomidae family, the bluefish is an extremely voracious and cannibalistic saltwater fish. A fierce opponent, it has gained a reputation among marine anglers as the hardest fighter per pound. These fish put up a long battle, even though they are typically caught in the 5- to 12-pound range. True to their scientific name (*saltatrix* means "leaper"), they will also jump if not caught on very heavy tackle. Schooling bluefish are particularly aggressive, often rampaging through a pod of baitfish. They have distinguished themselves as an occasional menace to bathers, and have attacked and lacerated bathers. They have also been known to run up on the beach when frenziedly chasing baits in the surf wash.

Bluefish are an important commercial fish, noted for a strong but delicious flavor; the flesh becomes soft if not eaten fresh and does not keep well if frozen for a long time.

Identification. The body shape of a bluefish is fairly long, stout, and compressed, with a flat-sided belly. The mouth is large and has extremely sharp, flattened, and triangular teeth. The first dorsal fin is low and short and consists of six to eight spines, whereas the second dorsal fin is long and has one spine and 23 to 28 soft rays; the anal fin has two

A bluefish caught on a party boat near Cape May, New Jersey.

B

Bluefish

B

spines and 25 to 27 soft rays. Both the second dorsal fin and the anal fin are covered with small, compact scales. The coloring is greenish or bluish on the back, and silvery on the sides; a distinguishing characteristic is a dark blotch at the base of the pectoral fins. The tail is dusky and deeply forked, and, with the exception of the whitish pelvic fins, most of the fins are dark.

The bluefish is distinguished from the greater amberjack *(Seriola dumerili)* by the spine in the second dorsal fin, the absence of markings on the head, and the lack of a space between the dorsal fins. The absence of finlets easily distinguishes bluefish from mackerel.

Size/Age. Bluefish can grow to about 45 inches in length and more than 44 pounds in weight. They average 1½ to 2 feet and 3 pounds, although it's not uncommon for a fish to weigh around 11 pounds. The rod-and-reel record is a 31-pound, 12-ounce fish. They live for about 12 years.

Distribution. Found worldwide in most temperate coastal regions, bluefish inhabit the eastern Atlantic from Portugal, Madeira, and the Canary Islands southward along the African coasts to South Africa, including the Mediterranean and Black Seas. They are also present in the western Atlantic from Nova Scotia and Canada to Bermuda and Argentina, as well as in the Indo-West Pacific, but are absent from the eastern and northwestern Pacific. They are also rare between southern Florida and northern South America.

Habitat. Favoring temperate to tropical waters, bluefish range along rocky coasts and in deep, troubled waters, although they are known to be sporadic, if not cyclical, in occurrence and location. The young are often found in bays and estuaries. Adults migrate along coastal areas and are caught from the beach by surf anglers, on shoals and rips inshore, or farther offshore.

Life history/behavior. Atlantic coast bluefish spawn mainly in the spring in the South Atlantic Bight and during summer in the Middle Atlantic Bight. Recent studies suggest that fish from the two spawning seasons mix extensively on the fishing and spawning grounds and probably constitute a single genetic stock. At breeding time, bluefish migrate out to open sea to spawn, anywhere from 2 miles offshore to the continental platform. The eggs are released and drift along with plankton in surface waters, hatching about 48 hours after fertilization. As adults, bluefish are commonly found in schools, especially when foraging on schools of baitfish—menhaden in particular. Along the U.S. Atlantic coast, bluefish migrate northward in the spring and southward in the fall.

Food and feeding habits. Insatiable predators, bluefish feed on a wide variety of fish and invertebrates but target schools of menhaden, mackerel, and herring. These fish have earned the nicknames "marine piranha" and "chopper" because they feed in large groups, viciously attacking schools of smaller fish. This feeding frenzy destroys everything in their path, including their own young. A bluefish may continue to attack its prey even when it is no longer hungry. These creatures are said to consume twice their weight in one day.

Anglers must use care when landing and handling these fish; even when a bluefish has been taken out of the water, an angler can lose a finger if not wary. Most bluefish enthusiasts use a dehooking tool to steer clear of the snapping dentures of this fish.

Angling. Historically, bluefishing has been a feast or famine pastime for East Coast anglers, and in recent years these fish have been overexploited, in part because bans on commercial fishing for striped bass set a higher priority on bluefish. Nevertheless, recreational anglers have been responsible for more than 80 percent of the catch in the past decade. Blues have long been a favorite among party boat ventures, and in the past party boat anglers have caught and kept copious (indeed excessive) numbers of this species when they encountered a lot of fish.

Availability and abundance are somewhat unpredictable, however. Bluefish roam widely, at times staying well offshore and at other times venturing up into the surf. They are sometimes caught in marshes, brackish rivers, and estuaries, although these are usually small fish, called snapper.

Birds working a slick are a dead giveaway to bluefish plundering schools of baitfish. Casting, jigging, and trolling on the perimeter of the slick are standard tactics. At other times, however, blues are a little harder to locate; they often favor deep water, tide rips, and unruly water, particularly inshore on a moving tide. Bluefish feed on a wide range of small fish, usually preferring whatever is most available, but they can be selective feeders and will also scrounge the bottom for sandworms and eels.

Bluefish succumb to a host of angling techniques and terminal tackle, in large part due to their aggressiveness. This is true for boat and shore anglers alike. Trolling may be the most employed boating technique, using diving plugs, thick-bodied spoons, and surgical tubes; a fast speed is preferred. Drifting and jigging are popular where bluefish are known to linger; metal jigging spoons and bucktails, sometimes tipped with a piece of meat, are preferred offerings. Live baits work better than dead baits, but some anglers chum for blues and successfully drift hooked pieces of cut bait amidst the chum. Casters use a variety of plugs, as well as streamer flies, when the fish are thick. Shore, surf, and pier anglers can stillfish with baits in current, or cast surface or diving plugs and squid-imitation spoons. There should always be movement to the offering, as still lures or baits go untouched. Some anglers, incidentally, "sniff out" bluefish by smell, searching for a fresh-cucumber odor where blues have been plundering baitfish.

Tackle varies widely, from heavy boat rods for trolling and deep jigging to light spinning tackle and fly rods. The reel drag should be of good quality, and anglers should use a gaff for fish that are to be kept. It bears repeating that bluefish have extremely sharp teeth; great care is a necessity when handling these fish. Many an angler has been scarred, or worse, when unhooking a lively blue.

BLUEGILL *Lepomis macrochirus.*

Other names—bream, brim, sun perch, blue perch, blue sunfish, copperbelly, blue bream, copperhead bream, red-breasted bream, bluegill sunfish, roach.

At times easily caught by novice and experienced anglers alike, bluegills are among the most popular panfish species in North America. This notoriety is the result of their vast distribution, spunky fight, and excellent taste. Commonly referred to as "bream," bluegills are the most widely distributed panfish and are found with, or in similar places as, such companion and related species as redbreast sunfish, green sunfish, pumpkinseeds, shellcrackers, and longear sunfish, all of which are similar in configuration but different in appearance.

Despite their abundance and popularity, bluegills are not heavily targeted in some waters and are thus underutilized. Bluegills are so prolific that their populations can grow beyond the carrying capacity of the water, and as a result many become stunted; these stunted fish are regarded as pests, and waters containing them must often be drained and restocked. There are three subspecies of bluegills in existence, although stocking has intermingled populations and subspecies.

Identification. The bluegill has a significantly compressed, oval or roundish body, a small mouth, and a small head, qualities typical of members of the sunfish family. The pectoral fins are pointed.

Its coloring varies greatly from lake to lake, ranging from olive, dark blue, or bluish purple to dappled yellow and green on the sides with an overall blue cast; some fish, particularly those found in quarry holes, may actually be clear and colorless. Ordinarily, there are six to eight vertical bars on the sides, and these may or may not be prominent. The gill cover extends to create a wide black flap, faint in color on the young, which is not surrounded by a lighter border as in other sunfish. Dark blue streaks are found on the lower cheeks between the chin and gill cover, and often there is a dark mark at the bottom of the anal fin. The breeding male is more vividly colored, possessing a blue head and back, a bright orange breast and belly, and black pelvic fins.

Size/Age. These fish range from 4 to 12 inches in length, averaging 8 inches and reaching a maximum length of $16^1/_4$ inches. The largest bluegill ever caught was a 4-pound, 12-ounce specimen taken in 1950. The growth of the bluegill varies so much that estimates of age as it relates to size are at best inexact. Bluegills are estimated to live for 10 years.

Distribution. Native to approximately the eastern half of the United States, the bluegill's range extends southward from the St. Lawrence River

A bluegill from a Georgia farm pond.

B

Bluegill

through the Great Lakes and the Mississippi River basin, eastward from New York to Minnesota and draining south from the Cape Fear River in Virginia to the Río Grande in Texas, including states as far east as Florida and as far west as New Mexico. Also found in a small portion of northeastern Mexico, the bluegill has been widely introduced elsewhere in North America as well as in Europe, South Africa, Asia, South America, and Oceania.

Habitat. Although mainly lake fish, bluegills inhabit sluggish streams and rivers, vegetated lakes and ponds, swamps, and pools of creeks. They prefer quiet waters and may hold in extremely shallow areas, especially early in the season and during spawning time, although when the surface and shallow water temperature is warm in summer, they may go as deep as 30 or more feet. They occupy the same habitat as their larger relative, the largemouth bass.

Life history/Behavior. The age of sexual maturity varies with environment and locale, although most bluegills reach spawning age when two or three years old. Spawning occurs between April and September, starting when water temperatures are around 70°F.

The males build shallow, round nests in water up to 6 feet deep over sandy or muddy bottoms. These nests occur in colonies of up to 500 along the shoreline, densely concentrated and easily spotted by anglers. Females may lay between 2,000 and 63,000 eggs, which hatch 30 to 35 hours after fertilization. It is common for fish to spawn many times, with a particular fish laying eggs in several nests and a single nest containing eggs from more than one female. Males guard the eggs throughout the incubation period and stay to protect the hatched young. Having reached lengths of $^1/_4$ to $^1/_3$ inch, the young leave their nests for deeper waters. Bluegills travel in small schools typically made up of similar-size individuals.

Food and feeding habits. A variety of small organisms serve as food for bluegills, including insects, crayfish, fish eggs, small minnows, snails, worms, and sometimes even plant material. The young feed mostly on crustaceans, insects, and worms. Adults will feed at different depths depending on temperature, so they obtain food on the bottom as well as on the surface. Active mostly at dusk and dawn, the larger bluegills move inshore in the morning and evening to feed, staying in deeper water during the day.

Angling. Bluegills are highly respected fighters even though they are diminutive fish. They are most commonly pursued in the spring and early summer while spawning in shallow water and where their round, clustered nests are readily visible along the shoreline of ponds and lakes. Vegetation is a prime place to seek bluegills, followed by stumps, logs, and fallen trees.

Many anglers pursue bluegills and other sunfish with live worms and bobbers in relatively shallow water, although the bigger fish are usually found deep. Because sunfish don't have large mouths, a long-shanked No. 8 or 10 hook is best, unweighted or with just a small split shot. Other baits include crickets, tiny minnows, and mealworms. Small jigs are a fine lure, and small spinners and spinnerbaits can be productive. A slow retrieve is best. Bluegills (and other sunfish) are popular in winter, too, taken on small jigs, flies, and mealworms.

The tackle used for these panfish needn't be stout. Light spinning or spincasting outfits are more than adequate; in many areas, anglers use long cane poles without reels to dabble baits into selected pockets for various sunfish species. Four- to 8-pound-test line is ample. Fly fishing is also an excellent way to pursue bluegills and other sunfish species, especially when they are in shallow water in the spring or during the summer when the surface is relatively calm. Floating and sinking flies, small streamers, and poppers are the terminal items.

See: Panfish

BLUE HOLE

Dark blue spots that are distinguished from surrounding bottom covered with sand or vegetation. Found in the Caribbean, these are submerged limestone caverns or sinkholes of ancient lineage, with powerful currents moving in and out.

BLUE RIBBON STREAM

A term used to describe highly rated or highly productive trout streams, especially in the western United States.

BLUE TANG *Acanthurus coeruleus.*

Other names—blue tang surgeon; French: *chirurgien bayolle;* Portuguese: *acaraúna-azul;* Spanish: *navajón azul.*

A member of the surgeonfish family that has distinctive coloration and is occasionally encountered by anglers, the blue tang is sometimes used as an aquarium fish and is also marketed fresh.

Identification. The oval, deep-bodied, and compressed blue tang is more circular than other surgeonfish. Its coloring is almost entirely blue, ranging from powdery to deep purple, and it has many dark or light blue horizontal stripes running down the sides and blending into the background. The dorsal and anal fins have a bright blue border, and there is a white or yellow spine on the base of the tail. Juvenile blue tang are colored bright yellow, whereas intermediate fish have blue heads and bodies and yellow tails. The yellow of the tail is the last to change to blue, and some fish are found with yellow tails. The change from juvenile to intermediate to adult coloration does not depend on size; some blue adults are smaller than yellow juveniles.

Size. Blue tang average 5 to 10 inches in length and may grow to 15 inches long.

Distribution. In the western Atlantic, the blue tang is most commonly found in Bermuda, and from Florida to the Gulf of Mexico and Brazil. In the eastern Atlantic, it inhabits the waters off Ascension Island.

Habitat. Blue tang favor inshore grassy and rocky areas, and shallows above coral reefs.

Blue Tang

Life history/Behavior. In the fry stage, the pelvic, second dorsal, and second anal spines of some fish are venomous and cause a painful sensation like a bee sting. This venomous quality is lost once they reach the juvenile stage. Blue tang form schools that may include surgeonfish and doctorfish.

Food and feeding habits. Blue tang feed entirely on algae, mostly during the day.

Angling. Blue tang are of little significance to anglers. Most are incidental catches by bottom anglers, although divers do take them with spears.

BLUE WATER

That portion of the open ocean that is blue in color and usually many miles from shore. Blue-water fishing is synonymous with offshore fishing *(see).*

The water in the open ocean appears deep blue in a manner similar to the blue color of the sky. Particulate matter in the open ocean is relatively scarce, and marine life has a low concentration in comparison with coastal waters, causing the water to appear blue due to the size of the water molecules and the fact that they disperse solar radiation in such a way as to mostly scatter wavelengths for blue light. Coastal waters are usually greenish in color, partly because of yellow-green microscopic marine algae in coastal waters but mostly because they have more large particulate matter, dispersing solar radiation so as to mostly scatter wavelengths for greenish or yellowish light.

BOAT

In simplest terms a boat is a floating object propelled by oar, sail, or motor. It is a vital accessory for anglers who want to be highly mobile and find fish that aren't accessible from the bank or surf or pier, or by wading. Without a boat, anglers are restricted to areas that can be accessed by walking,

Anglers take to the water in a variety of boats, as this fall salmon-fishing scene on New York's Black River attests.

and to covering only water that can be reached by the length of a cast.

Because many species of fish roam widely in their environments, and because much fish habitat is located away from shore or at great distances from the areas accessible by land, boats extend the range of anglers as well as pare the time necessary to reach desired locations. Boats also enable anglers to carry and store extra fishing equipment and accessory gear, and they provide for the storage and maintenance of fish and bait.

Each year a high percentage of people who purchase boats (and motors) list fishing as a primary or secondary intended use for that equipment. Some boats are designed purely for fishing, some are for specific angling situations, and some have general recreational use, including fishing.

Many factors influence the choice of a fishing boat. These include the size of the body of water; extreme conditions that might be encountered; distance to be traveled; type of fishing; equipment needed; number of anglers; preferred boat length, hull design, or method of propulsion; and funds available. In many cases, anglers go to places or boat in conditions that are seldom visited or experienced by nonfishing boaters.

Boats for saltwater fishing are larger because of the influence of tide, current, waves, weather, and the size of fish. Long, broad-beamed fiberglass sportfishing boats *(see),* also called offshore boats, are the pride of the angling fleet, used for distant big-game forays. Eighteen- to 25-foot fiberglass V-hulled boats fill the bill for most inshore saltwater anglers. Center console models are preferred in warm weather climes and where a variety of casting, jigging, and drift fishing by several anglers is done. For shallow water flats fishing, most aluminum or fiberglass shallow draft boats, many with bow casting and aft poling platforms, get the nod.

In freshwater, a V-hulled fiberglass boat is especially suitable for large lakes, ponds, and rivers, where rough water dictates sturdy craft and where a big boat with a lot of engine muscle can help cover great distances quickly. Aluminum boats can also be used under these conditions, although flat-bottomed models do not handle rough water well. The V-hulled aluminum boats take rough water a little better, but still not as well as fiberglass boats; they sit up higher in the water and, because they are lighter, are more susceptible to being blown around in the wind. Sixteen- to 25-foot boats, aluminum and fiberglass, are used in a wide range of freshwater fishing, with those over 20 feet generally reserved for the largest inland waters.

A smaller aluminum flat-bottom boat (jonboat) is very functional for fishing on small lakes, rivers, and ponds, where covering a lot of territory is not necessary and where adverse conditions are seldom present. Small aluminum V-hulled boats can be used in the same manner; their deeper draft makes them less suitable for small river fishing and more suitable to moderate size lakes. Canoes and canoelike craft are popular in small lakes and ponds and in flowing water, although they are unsteady vessels for the inexperienced and are highly susceptible to positioning problems.

This overview is necessarily generalized. Other types of craft are used for fishing, such as pontoon boats and inflatables, and some standard boat hulls are useful in both freshwater and saltwater, although the interior configurations are greatly different.

A fishing boat is a tool that gets you where the fish are. It must weather the best and the worst water conditions. It must be reasonably comfortable to allow you to put in long hours. It must be versatile enough to handle a variety of angling pursuits. It must be designed and/or modified to allow you to fight and land fish (especially big fish). And it should have readily available accessories.

Fishing boat designs and interior configurations have changed a great deal in the past few decades because of manufacturing advancements, changes in propulsion systems, and the evolving styles and interests of anglers. Virtually all of the changes in fishing boats, be they flats skiffs, walleye boats, bass boats, or offshore boats, have evolved to meet the particular needs of anglers in the places they fish and in the manner they fish. The more popular types of fishing boats are reviewed in more detail in their respective entries, as are methods of propulsion, but the following information generally applies to all fishing boats.

Types of Fishing Boats

Anglers use nearly anything that floats as a means of getting to and from desired fishing locations. Among smaller vessels, that includes such generally manually operated craft as canoes *(see)* and canoelike boats such as pirogues and kayaks *(see),* folding boats, inflatable boats *(see);* and float tubes *(see),* which are also known as belly boats and aren't really boats from a navigability standpoint. Fishing boats might include such "incidental" craft as sailboats or jet-propelled personal watercraft *(see),* and such specialty items as pontoon boats, houseboats, and one- or two-man cartoppers for ponds.

Among midsize craft, popular fishing boats include a jonboat *(see),* bass boat *(see),* flats boat *(see),* and walleye boat *(see),* and any number of aluminum and fiberglass vessels that have been designed for fishing but have not come to be associated with a species or style of fishing. Larger fishing boats include center console, cuddy, and walkaround versions of outboard- and inboard-powered offshore boats, which may be called sportfishermen or sportfishing boats *(see),* and inshore boats.

Hull Styles

Because a boat must not only float, but move through varying water conditions, hull configurations differ. Depending upon the size of the body of water you fish, the hull can be more important to an angler than the overall size or the interior layout of a boat. Categories of hulls are displacement and planing. Displacement hulls include canoes, jonboats, and flat-bottomed dories or skiffs, and are noted for slow speed; they push through the water rather than ride on top of it. Planing hulls include V-bottoms and are noted for faster speed and quicker steering response; speed is largely a function of engine power, and most of the hull is raised out of the water while running.

The standard types of these hulls on fishing boats include flat, semi-V, modified-V, deep-V, and cathedral. Some other hulls, such as tunnel, and catamaran also exist.

Flat-bottom hulls are probably the oldest hull style in existence and are of primary use in small streams, shallow rivers, ponds, and small lakes. They are easy to control by oar, paddle, or electric motor, but are unstable in lengths under 12 feet. Flat-bottom hulls are not advisable for heavy loads or for use in rough water unless they are large, broad-beamed, and properly powered. Anglers who like to cast from a standing position may find these boats a bit tippy, especially in the shorter lengths and narrower beams. Flat-bottom hulls are easy to row, paddle, or pole in shallow water and perform well with an electric motor; they tend to pound the water when underway, and the (lighter) bow may slap the water when it is choppy, which can be alarming to fish.

V-bottom boats can be primarily separated into deep-V, modified-V, or semi-V versions, with the latter sometimes described as round. Some type of V-hull is preferred over a flat-bottom in places where the water gets rough, so they are a very popular fishing hull. The difference between them is primarily in deadrise, which is the angle formed at the transom by the V and determined by the amount of the V that is carried from the bow through the transom. Boats with a transom deadrise over 19 degrees are considered deep-Vs, but this is a general rather than absolute indicator. Because deep-V-hulls carry their shape all the way to the transom, they ride better in rough water than modified-V-hulls; some deep-V boats handle poorly off-plane at slow speeds, but modifications to the chines and stern have changed this in more recent hulls. The greater the deadrise at the transom, the more water a V-hull draws, meaning that it is less suitable for shallow operation (how shallow depends on the size of boat and the depth of water). A deep-V-hull

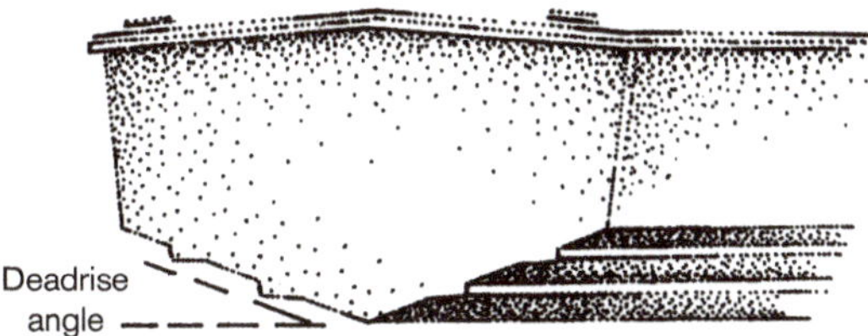

The angle between the dotted lines shown is the boat's deadrise.

B

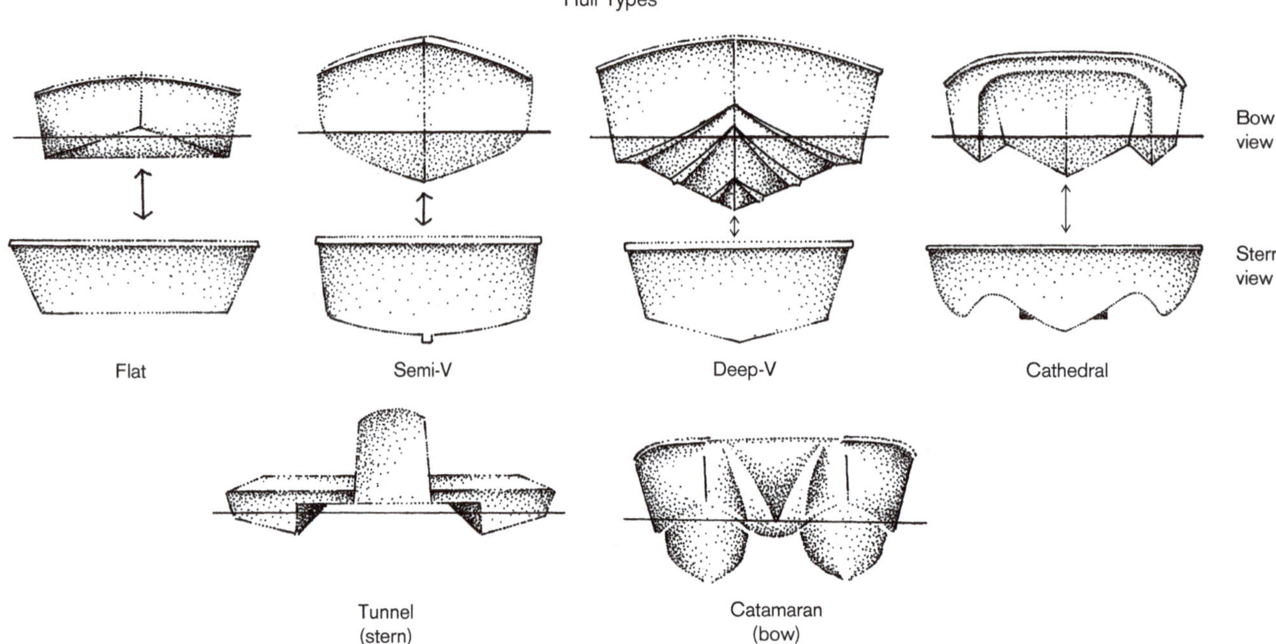

requires more horsepower to attain top and cruising speeds than hulls with less deadrise need. That means more expense in the cost of the engine(s), and greater gas consumption.

Some type of modified-V-hull is a favorite with many freshwater anglers in boats under 18 feet long, and with many inshore saltwater anglers. Recent versions of these, called variable-V or progressive-V-hulls, have a deadrise that is greater toward the bow and less at the stern. The original deep-V-hulls carried the same deadrise at the transom quite a bit forward (some as much as two-thirds the distance) before it began to increase significantly. The newer versions begin that increase ever so slightly in the beginning, from almost immediately forward of the transom. Thus, you can find a 20-foot boat, for example, whose deadrise progresses from 18 degrees at the transom to almost 40 degrees at the stem, and which has longitudinal bottom strakes that provide lift, eliminate the tendency to plow that would otherwise be typical of having so much deep-V forward, and still produce a fast (40 mph) speed with just a single outboard.

Within this category are also flat-bottom and V-bottom hybrids. For example, some high-performance bass boats have a modified-V-hull with a flat pad on the transom; this produces great speed in calm water or small waves, but a tooth-jarring ride in sloppy conditions and a spine-pounding ride in rough water.

The cathedral hull, also known as a tri-hull, has faded in popularity but had a following in small boats into the 1980s, especially in freshwater and for inshore saltwater use. Cathedral-hull boats are stable, roomy, wet, and slow. They ride poorly in rough water, but well in flat water or small waves. They do have the advantage of ample interior space, largely because of their essentially rectangular shape, but their general disadvantage is that they have the same basic horsepower requirements as a deep-V-hull because they run on more wetted surface.

The catamaran hull is one that is now contending with deep-V-hulls. These have been used with increasing popularity in the seas of Australia and South Africa, where the water is usually anything but gentle, and have been forging into the North American marketplace. Catamaran, or cat, hulls are faster than deep-V-hulls when weight and horsepower are the same. Nothing beats the catamaran's stability at rest in a nasty beam sea, which is a factor that anglers can easily appreciate when drift fishing. A steep deep-V-hull tends to snap roll miserably when drifting in a rough sea, and other boats usually can't take it at all.

The so-called tunnel hull is similar to a squashed down version of the catamaran hull. It is not intended for long stretches of very rough water, but it is faster for the same horsepower. Its big advantage to anglers is that the engine can be mounted far higher on the transom than normal, which allows the boat to jump quickly on plane in bare inches of water. It's a very popular design among the thin-water redfish and sea trout crowd along the Texas Gulf Coast, where it performs superbly.

These are the general characteristics of common fishing boat hulls, but evaluating a hull is not always simple. Many manufacturers use the same terms to mean different things (like calling a semi-V model a deep-V). Hybrid hulls and nuances to certain basic hull types, plus the use of other terms also confuse the situation.

Many prospective fishing boat buyers spend more time looking at the interior of a boat than they do evaluating the hull and determining whether it is the right type for their intended use. Clearly, an angler who spends a lot of time on the ocean, especially offshore, or on big lakes, and who needs to travel long distances with the likelihood of encountering rough water, requires a deep V-hull. Anglers who primarily spend their time in shallow areas, such as on flats or in moderately protected bays, can use a boat with little draft. If, however, they must cross water that is sometimes rough to get to those shallow places, a compromise may be necessary. The trick is to find a happy medium between riding comfort and hull efficiency.

Keep in mind that any boat's comfort and riding ability, as well as it's aptitude for certain water conditions, may have to be tempered with fishability. Big fish in skinny water, for example, like bonefish, permit, tarpon, redfish, striped bass, largemouth bass, and northern pike, are among the many gamefish sensitive to noise, and even if the draft of a boat is shallow enough to get you there, a hull that slaps or thumps in that environment is like a hunter wearing fluorescent orange in a duck blind while standing up and waving both arms. In some areas there's been a trend toward "stealth" hulls, with slightly rounded chines that may give up some dryness but don't telegraph the boat's presence before you're close enough for an easy cast.

To select the best hull shape for your type of fishing, analyze your goals and needs carefully, then go looking. Ask others who already do the type of fishing you want to do, and get out with someone who experiences that type of fishing. Spend a day or two aboard as many boats that fit your profile as possible, especially when conditions are less than favorable. Have a seller, including a new boat dealer, take you out for a serious test ride. And remember that all boats behave well when the seas are flat.

Picking the Right Boat

Usually, if you're a serious angler you already know how you intend to use a new boat, and this guides your choice. Inexperienced anglers and first-time boaters, however, often make the mistake of getting a boat that isn't right for their needs (especially for developing needs as they get into different types of fishing and wider-ranging activities). This means either replacing the boat or making some significant modifications to its interior. The old homily about not being able to make a silk purse out of a sow's ear was never more true than when applied to boat hulls. If the basic hull is unsuitable, there's nothing you can do to make it right, no matter how extensive the interior modifications. So, if you plan to do any serious angling from your boat, choose carefully.

Picking a fishing boat starts with knowing what kind of fishing you'll be doing—taking it everywhere, just to small lakes, or just on the ocean—and under what conditions you'll be doing it—only on fair weather days, whenever you have the chance, or any time they're hitting. Then come the other considerations, such as whether you will tow the boat and how much weight your vehicle can handle, how much space you'll need for stowing gear and carrying passengers, and whether the boat can accommodate all the accessories you need.

Consider carefully the size boat you need. You don't want to select "not enough" boat; being caught out in rough seas in a too small boat could get you in serious trouble. On the other hand, buying "too much" boat because you're unnecessarily worried about potentially rough seas could make the vessel almost completely unfishable. Every boat is a series of compromises, and choosing size is the first of many decisions you'll have to make.

If you don't have a solid idea regarding the boat you want, get friendly with someone who has a lot of experience in the type of fishing you have in mind. Get out on boats with others who have had experience, and learn as much as you can. Spend time prospecting various boats before you buy. That time will be repaid a hundredfold if you do your homework properly.

After you decide what type of boat (or actual brand and model) you want, it's a question of buying new or used. If you're considering buying a used boat from its current owner, take someone with you who has experience with that particular model (and also the engine, if possible). Such a person might help you avoid some pitfalls. You should have an experienced mechanic take a look at the engine of any used boat and, if possible, run it in the water. Put the entire boat in the water and run it for awhile as well. Once you buy a used boat—and there are plenty available—you're stuck with it, so make sure you cover all bases, just as you would if you bought a used automobile from a private party.

If you're planning to buy a new rig, try to select a good dealer. Sometimes you can't choose the dealer unless you're willing to do a lot of traveling because many dealers of the same brand boats are (deliberately) not close to each other. Don't sign anything or put any money down, until you've had a test ride in the exact model, with the same horsepower engine you plan to use. Be almost as careful about selecting the dealer as you are in selecting the boat. Ask around before you sign any purchase contracts. Check with reliable boating friends and perhaps the local Better Business Bureau, and don't be pushed into buying extra equipment that you don't need.

Unfortunately, no one ideal boat suits all fishing needs and interests, no hull type handles all conditions, and no interior configuration meets every angler's desires. Some boats have multi-species or multi-water applications and suit varied angling; anglers who do only one type of fishing, however, prefer a boat that is especially suited to that activity, like a flats boat *(see)* or a bass boat *(see)*.

Be especially careful about trying to get a boat that will serve many needs other than fishing. While it seems good to have a boat that the family can use for general boating, cruising, and skiing, multi-purpose boats seldom make serious anglers

B

happy. Runabouts—boats that are primarily meant for general boating—are seldom suitable for serious fishing, although many people in freshwater and saltwater go fishing in them.

When you've selected the hull you feel is best suited for your angling interests, the next step is to choose the proper power for it. In some cases you won't have much choice among the types of power due to the model or design of boat or because the entire rig is assembled at the manufacturer's plant. If you have time to wait for a custom-ordered boat, a dealer can order some models with different types of power. If it's simply a matter of changing the existing outboard motor to one with a different horsepower, they can usually do that without a long wait. For more information on power and selection, see the appropriate motor entries.

In small and midsize boats, a major selection issue is the material used in constructing the boat. Fiberglass is the most widely used material for boats over 16 feet long because it is strong, easy to work with, and cost effective in construction. Aluminum is still the lightest material, though used more often on smaller boats, and Kevlar (an aramid fiber used for radial tire cords and bulletproof vests) is close behind in weight, though stronger. Wood is still being used to build simple craft, but it is barely a factor in the new powerboat field, and some plastics are being used for specialty lightweight boats, but not in fishing boats.

Aluminum boats are most common in freshwater and for fishing on rivers, where there may be obstructions, and on smaller bodies of water. Aluminum is lightest and fiberglass heaviest. Aluminum boats are easier to tow, which is a big consideration for many freshwater anglers, but fiberglass generally tracks better and, without rivets to pop loose, is less likely to need maintenance. Aluminum, however, is more forgiving for regular contact with the bottom, like scraping over rocks and beaching. Aluminum is ideal for boats under 16 feet long because it produces a light and easily portable boat, and is cost effective for both builder and buyer. It's major drawback is that it is noisy, but that can be improved upon with interior modifications, such as platforms and carpeting. It is not used as much for boats over 16 feet, although it can be and there are some large aluminum boats. Generally, as boat length increases, and the size of the water fished grows, most anglers choose fiberglass.

Some choose Kevlar as an alternative to fiberglass. Kevlar is more expensive than fiberglass but stronger and lighter. That lightness can translate into significant fuel economy when a Kevlar boat is powered, for example, by a 75-horsepower engine and gets better performance than an identical fiberglass boat with a 115-horsepower engine. It can also translate into greater top-end speed when the same boats with identical engines are compared. The material is far more resistant to impact damage and to flexural fatigue (which is the reason why most fiberglass hulls fail).

When choosing a larger boat (either trailerable or permanently moored), after you reach a decision on hull type and overall boat size, the most important item of consideration is usually the amount of usable deck and cockpit space. This is of much greater concern to anglers than it is to people who ski, cruise, or enjoy general boating. Anyone who has been cramped into the tight quarters of a boat primarily meant for cruising or skiing understands

25 ft. Saltwater Sportfishing Boat

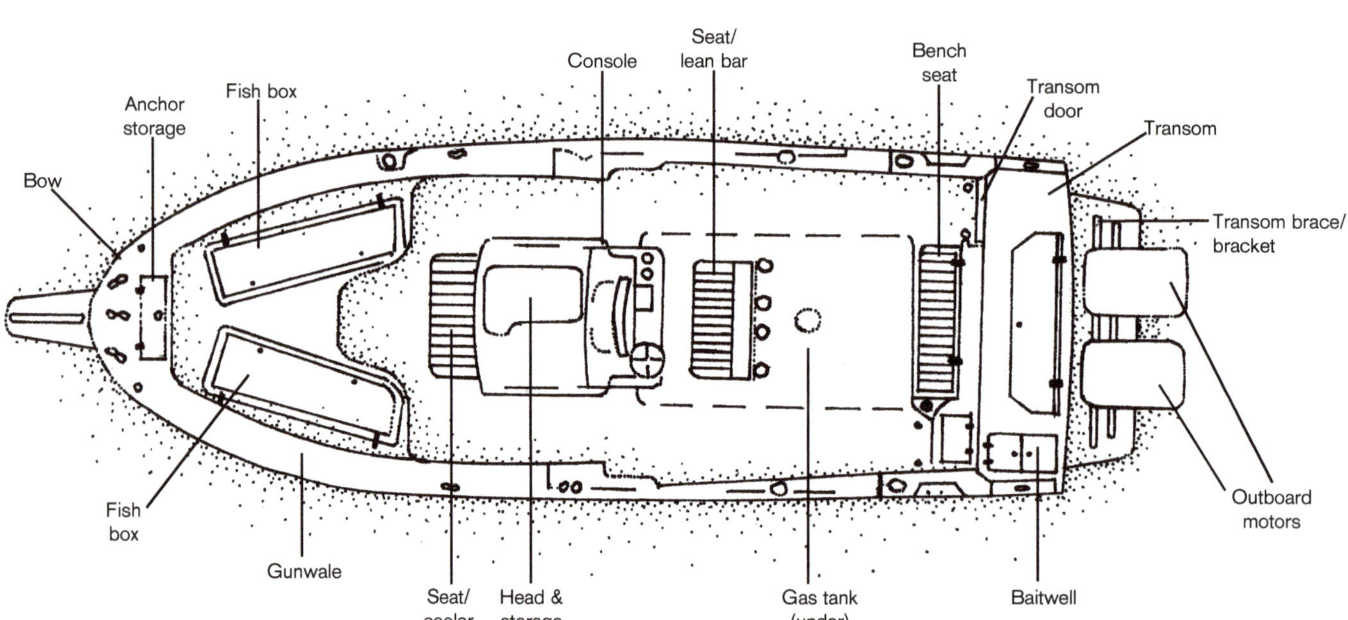

how unacceptable these craft are for storing gear, using accessories, fighting fish, and getting out of the way of fellow anglers. It is surprising how many people try to adapt a runabout or ski boat to serious fishing, although the usable space for gear and mobility within such boats is seriously lacking. Space in a fishing boat, whether for moving around to fight a big fish, or being able to keep myriad gear out from underfoot, is a big concern. Check the layout of the boats you review for uncluttered and usable inside space. Remember that you might want to add some accessories, such as downriggers, to the boat, and will need appropriate and accessible places to do so.

As a general rule, a boat that is to be used primarily for casting needs to have open space on raised decks or platforms, definitely in the bow and preferably both bow and stern. The boat should provide enough room to stand or to sit, and storage space beneath the anglers. For fly fishing, a clean deck with nothing to catch loose fly line, and possibly a thigh-high bow brace or rail, are special considerations.

In bigger boats, which are used for big-water fishing, storage space should be in a cabin, under or alongside a console, or below decks, and in large boats, it is a combination of these. The bigger the boat, the more fishing action that takes place from amidship to transom, so this area has to be clutter-free. It is important to make sure consoles have ample space for mounting all electronic devices.

Storage is one of the most important items to consider. You need both tackle storage and incidental storage, and while some boats look great, they suffer from a lack of proper storage area when in use, especially if the boat can accommodate three or four (or more) people. Anglers tend to quickly clutter a boat with fishing paraphernalia and accessory items, so pay attention to the storage that a boat has. Look for dry storage if you need to keep various things under cover.

As for tackle storage, first consider rods. Good rods are expensive and should not be left to bounce or tangle in a heap; be sure that they can be properly restrained when the boat is running on the water and when it is in tow. Check that rod storage areas will hold the length and style of rod that you use most often, or can at least be customized to adapt to your special needs. Make sure they are easy to access and, preferably, lockable. Rod holders, for storing rods while the boat is underway or when trolling or baitfishing, are also a common consideration.

As for tackle boxes, only you know what storage you need in this regard, though most avid anglers carry more than they need or can use. Tripping over tackle boxes, having them slide around, and not being able to get them out of the way for fishing action, are common troubles that can be avoided. Look for a boat that meets your needs in this area while fishing as well as running, and which provides storage while wasting a minimum of space.

In addition to tackle storage, remember that boats must be equipped with proper life preservers for every person onboard, so these must be kept somewhere accessible, and you need a place to store an anchor and rode. Add these, plus foul weather gear, spare parts, a first-aid kit, a fire extinguisher, and possibly an external cooler for food and beverages, and you can pile a lot into a boat.

Do you keep fish or bait alive while angling? If so, you'll need some type of livewell or baitwell. Long-term storage and boating great distances usually demand built-in systems, with adequate aeration. A system that brings water in from outside, rather than recirculating the same water, is infinitely better. Recirculation is especially undesirable when the water is warm. Systems that don't operate, or operate minimally, when the boat is traveling at high speed (because of poor water intake), may kill fish, so it is important to have a high circulation raw water system that pumps a constant flow of highly oxygenated water on the fish to keep them perky.

On larger boats, don't overlook the (possible) need for fishboxes or ice chests, a transom door for bringing big game into the cockpit, and fuel capacity.

In new trailerable boats, the consolidation of motor and boat manufacturers and the desire to market ready-to-go items have made packages the rule rather than the exception. The majority of these are targeted at anglers. Whether you're thinking new or used, prepackaged or mix-and-match, you should take a critical look at all aspects of the boat you buy for fishing, and not be swayed by appearance (although, chances are if you don't like the appearance, you won't buy it anyway).

In addition to appearance and interior appurtenances, the motor and the propeller are important considerations in the selection of a proper fishing rig. With the wrong items, and depending on boat and hull type, fuel efficiency can be drastically lowered. As a general rule, the motor on a boat should be no less than 80 percent of the boat's rated maximum horsepower. Underpowering a boat is a common problem. A boat that doesn't seem to run properly may actually have the wrong propeller. The wrong propeller causes a boat to labor to get on plane and to fail to reach proper rpm. Be careful also about putting excessive horsepower on a boat, especially if you're are buying a used boat and a motor from different sources. Every boat has a capacity plate that specifies its maximum horsepower rating. Exceeding this may be illegal, and may void your insurance if an accident occurs.

Lastly, many boats need a trailer that is suited to the specific hull type and length of boat *(see: trailer, boat).*

Minnow is a word applied to many small fish; in scientific terms the minnow family, with more than 1,600 species, is one of the largest in the world.

Rigging for Fishing

Many new boats come with most, if not all, of the accouterments that an angler needs for fishing, but others need modification to suit angling styles.

B

Many things can be done to rig a boat for fishing, or to make it more angler-friendly.

The hull usually gets little attention in this regard, although trim tabs can be added to improve rough water performance and splash guards can be added to the transom if you backtroll. Ditto for the motor, although on some outboards, boaters add a hydrofoil to improve planing ability, or a trolling plate to slow boat speed for trolling.

The interior of the boat is where most rigging attention is focused. Anglers address all of the following issues, and more: rod storage, fore and aft platforms, livewells, baitwells, tackle and dry gear storage, downriggers, trolling boards, outriggers, planer retrievers, rod holders, towers, Bimini or T-tops, electric motors, remote steering devices, seats, fighting chairs, and assorted electronic devices. In small boats, especially aluminum models, anglers commonly add carpeting to their boats to deaden noise, as well as nonskid paint or adhesive strips.

Self-rigging, especially of small and midsize fishing boats was a bigger issue in the past, but the advent of factory-rigged boats, sold as a package, has made it a bit less of an issue today. Some anglers, however, still make many modifications to their boats for fishing purposes. The selection and location of rigging items requires a lot of attention, as does the setup that has been predesigned by manufacturers.

When evaluating a boat that is already rigged for fishing, or when deciding how you will modify or rig a boat yourself, your foremost concern should be how it will improve your fishing. Sonar, for example, must be placed so that it can be viewed easily from wherever you'll be sitting or standing (in some cases both). Every item used for fishing and boating must be readily accessible, so some things that look nice (like a curved console that does not provide a sonar or GPS mounting surface) can be problematic.

Maintenance and Storage

Constructed primarily of aluminum or fiberglass, modern fishing boats need less care and maintenance than did the wooden boats of decades ago. Most maintenance needs arise from accidents, from being towed on poor-fitting trailers, or from striking underwater objects or running aground. A leak may be caused by a loose rivet, insufficient caulking around installations on the transom, or a crack. Clearly, it pays to inspect the hull periodically, especially after an unusual occurrence (nicking a rock or wedging atop a submerged piling, for instance). Small aluminum repairs can be made with an epoxy-based aluminum putty, or by melting an aluminum repair stick onto the affected area, but larger problems require heliarc welding. Larger problems with fiberglass boats require a dealer's attention, but gel coat repairs can be made easily enough with the proper paste and polish.

Accessories should be routinely checked. Boats that are used in big waters and run at high speeds can take a severe pounding, as can boats that are trailered often, and it is not unusual for fittings to loosen. Bolts and screws especially need periodic surveillance and tightening. If they are not of the highest marine quality, mechanical and electrical equipment are subject to malfunction when exposed to the elements. Some sonar and radio equipment can run underwater, but not all marine electronics are so blessed, and anglers should protect those items that need it, especially in a saltwater environment. Boats that are used in brackish water or saltwater should be rinsed with freshwater after

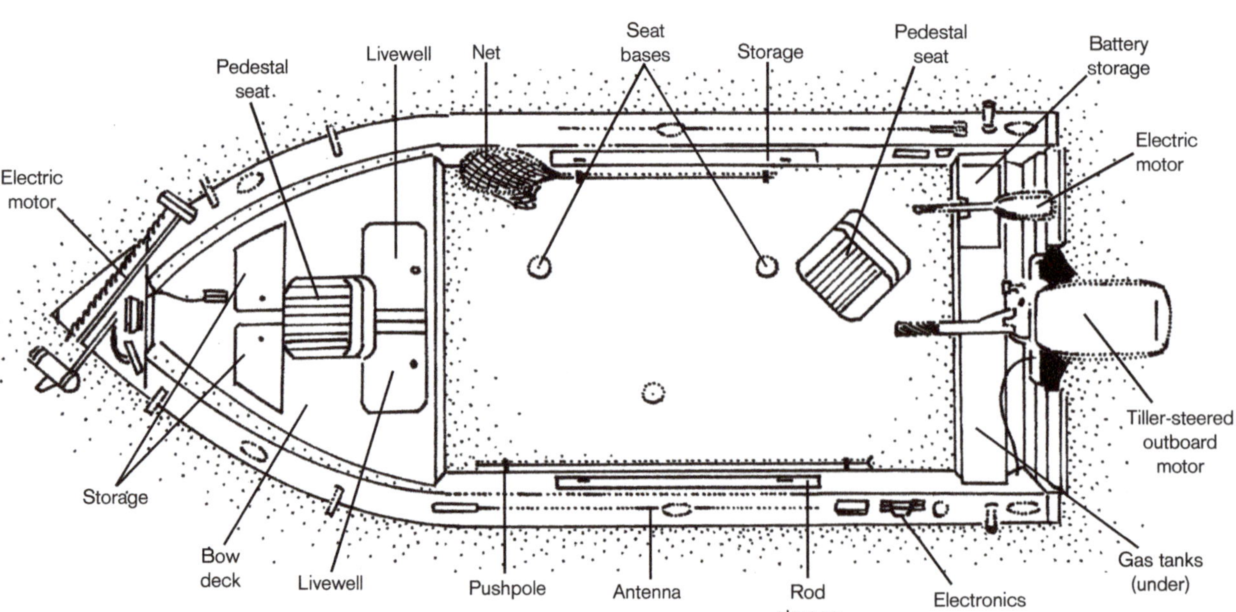

every use. A washdown is also necessary if a boat has gotten especially dirty, slimy, or bloody from fish or bait. Once slime, blood, bait parts, and the like get baked onto a boat from the sun, they are particularly hard to remove, so it can be good to make a preliminary washdown while on the water and a final scrub back at the dock or at home.

Boats can be stored in the water at a dock or a slip, on a trailer at a marina or at home, and on the ground or on supports in a yard. Storage at docks or boat slips requires sufficient bow and aft lines and a knowledge of proper knots for mooring to the dock, the use of boat fenders to keep the boat from rubbing against the dock or pilings, and consideration of the effect of waves, storms, and tidal fluctuations. Many a boat has been damaged or sunk at docks or boat slips because the boat operator did not take proper steps for its storage. Trailer storage requires the use of a trailer that is appropriate for the length and weight of the boat. Smaller boats and trailers may fit into a garage or under a carport. This is especially good as it keeps the boat and trailer protected from the elements and lessens trailer rust and boat fading. Boats on trailers do not have to be covered, but fitted covers or tarps do protect them from sun, rain, and snow, and from road grit while trailering; covers are especially useful for boats that are stored outdoors through the winter and for long periods without being used. Small boats that can be carried by one or two people generally are not covered, but are often turned over, either resting directly on the ground or preferably propped on supports.

In places where the water freezes, a boat is usually taken out of the water for the winter, although electric water bubblers can be used to move the water around a dock or slip and keep ice from forming. This is only useful if larger floes of ice cannot be pushed into the dock or slip when the wind shifts during spring. For winter storage, the drain plug should be removed and the boat propped up in the bow so that water and melting snow or ice drains to the stern. The bigger the boat, the more attention to winter preparation it needs, including cleaning the hull of algae, fungi, and barnacles, and thoroughly cleaning and drying all parts of the boat. Remember that some ventilation is important to evaporate condensation.

Boat Handling

General Issues. Handling a boat looks very simple to the inexperienced and to those who view that operation in open, unobstructed water. Although it is not generally difficult, some situations and factors make handling a boat very different from driving an automobile, and not all boats handle the same way due to hull design and/or propulsion system. Learning to handle a boat properly comes from on-the-water experience.

Speed and direction are the basic factors to be controlled in all boating, complicated by the fact that, unlike automobiles, a boat has no brakes to slow it down or stop it. Rowing, paddling, or using an electric motor are the simplest methods of moving a boat, and the least troublesome in most situations because only minor speed is attained. Boating under power, however, where significant speed is possible, and where boats of varying size are employed, is a different matter.

A boat that is overloaded in the front (top) will plow and may dig into an oncoming wave; one that is overloaded in the rear (middle) will be hard to steer and perilously low in the stern. One with passengers and gear well distributed (bottom) is safest and will handle best, since it is properly trimmed fore and aft.

Most power boats are directed by a steering wheel located on a console. Some midsize boats, and most small boats, are directed by a tiller handle on the motor. The throttle, or accelerator, is located on the handle of small outboard motors, and by the steering wheel in larger boats. Some boats, especially bass boats, are fitted with after-market foot-control throttles for high-speed boat operation with two hands on the steering wheel, but there are obvious drawbacks to this, and it is not a widely used option.

Because boats are pushed from the rear by a motor, they steer by the stern. When the motor is turned to the left, the thrust of the propeller drives the stern to the left and the bow to the right. This is of special significance in heavy traffic, when trying to run the boat over a specific bottom contour (as when trolling), when faced with current or wind, and when negotiating tight spaces such as a dock or boat slip in a marina. The motion of a boat is stopped when the engine is put into neutral and its natural drift ceases. This is often aided by placing the engine into opposite gear (reverse when the boat is moving forward), but only at slow speeds.

B

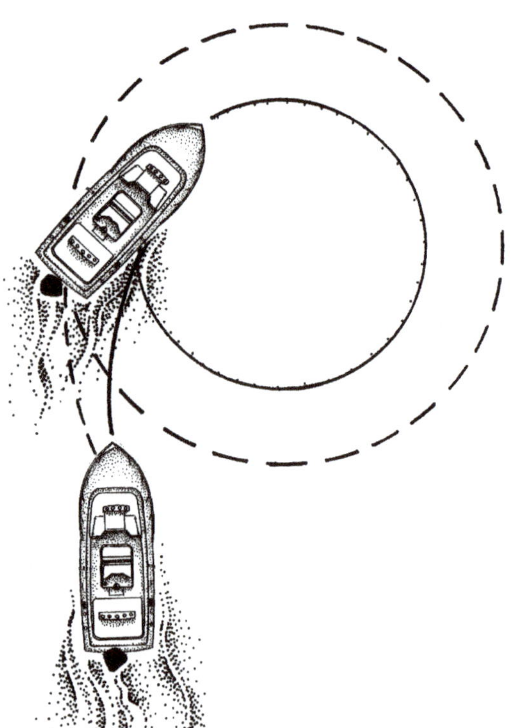

Steering a boat is not like steering a car. As this illustration shows, in a turn, the stern of a boat follows a different and larger path (dotted circle) than the bow (solid circle).

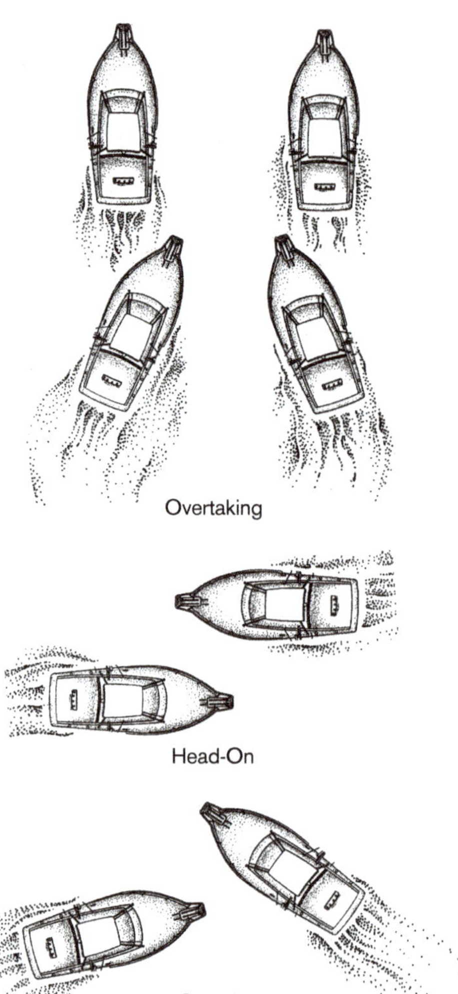

Depicted are three of the most common boat-to-boat encounters. When one boat is overtaking another from behind (top), it may pass on either side, but should slow down while passing. When boats approach head-on (middle), each should stay to the right. When paths cross (bottom), the boat that is coming from the starboard side of the other boat has the right of way.

All boaters are required to observe established rules of the road. These exist in freshwater as well as saltwater, although boaters in saltwater and on large navigable waterways are generally more cognizant and observant of these rules than their counterparts in freshwater. These rules cover most circumstances, including which vessels have the right of way when meeting, crossing, or overtaking one another; signals to be issued to declare intentions; actions to avoid collision; and so forth. The United States Coast Guard publishes navigation rules, which apply to navigable waterways. State and local regulations apply to landlocked bodies of water. Boat operators are legally responsible for knowing these rules and abiding by them, and may be liable for not adhering to them. Because waterways are more open than the roads traveled on land, and because there is less law enforcement presence on waterways, it is a fact that many boaters knowingly or unknowingly violate established rules of the road. This is particularly so in freshwater, and among nonfishing boat operators.

Some general rules that anglers should be aware of include:

- Boats under manual power (paddling or rowing), have the right of way over power boats.
- Sailboats, if propelled by sail and not auxiliary motor, have the right of way over power boats (including fishing boats that are slow trolling).
- Boats approaching each other head-on should stay to the right.
- A boat overtaking (passing) another boat can pass on either side but should slow down.
- In a crossing situation, a boat that is off the starboard of another boat, from a dead-ahead point to a position just aft of amidship, has the right of way.
- Boaters must undertake a safe speed at all times; safe speed varies with visibility, traffic, maneuverability, prevailing weather and water conditions, and other factors.
- Navigating in a no-wake zone means no wake; note: an off-plane speed, though slow, may still produce a wake.
- Give way to boats that are heading with the current, as in a river; boats with a following current have less maneuverability than boats headed into the current.
- From sunset to sunrise, boats are required

to use navigational lights in order to avoid collision. Commonly referred to as "running lights," these must include red and green sidelights on the bow centerline (red to port, green to starboard), and a single white sternlight visible over a 135-degree arc.

One of the most commonly violated rules or laws by all boaters regards the safe distance to be maintained from other boats, swimmers, waterskiers, docks, and shore. In most places that distance is 100 feet. Some precautions or unwritten rules are more an adherence to common sense than established laws. Anglers who are boating on a river, for example, should slow down and leave no wake when passing people who are wading, even if they are a safe or legal distance from those individuals. A power boat should always be operated slowly near people, docks, marinas, and the like, and should idle away from, or into, these situations in complete and safe control. Lastly, no boat should be operated under the influence of alcohol or drugs.

Rough water handling. Rough water and changing conditions are a fact of life for anglers virtually all year long. Anglers are often on the water in boats when conditions change, perhaps starting the day in calm seas and later facing big waves. They may get caught miles offshore or away from their launch site in a sudden squall, or they may simply need to cross a severely wind-blown section of lake to get to a back bay or creek. There are certainly times when a small boat does not go forth, and times when it is prudent for even a large boat to stay at the dock. But when you must venture into rough water—because the forecast is for improving conditions, or you know that it will be better at your ultimate fishing destination—or when conditions change and you have to face worse seas than you started out in, it is important for health and safety that you do so in the right manner.

Nothing can take the place of experience in handling rough water. You have to do it and be in it to fully learn how to handle a boat properly.

"Rough water" and "heavy seas" mean different things, of course, depending on the body of water and the boat. Five-foot waves are extremely rough and very dangerous on large lakes, but it can be a lot worse than that on the ocean. In a small boat, genuine two-footers are rough. Furthermore, "rough" is different depending on whether a boat is in shallow water or deep water. Large shallow lakes, for example, provide some treacherous boat operating conditions when powerful winds whip it up, since the waves are spaced closer together and the danger of running the boat or motor aground while in a trough also exists. On a deeper body of water, that same wind may create big waves with large swells, but be much easier to negotiate.

Before you commence running under difficult conditions, it is necessary to take certain precautions. All loose items in a boat should be put away. Anything that is not lashed down or properly stored could be washed overboard, bounced overboard, broken while banged around, or become an impediment to safety. Bilges should be pumped dry, not only because the extra weight affects boat operation, but also because spray and waves often bring water into the boat when it is rough, and you may need to work the bilge pumps often to discharge incoming water. Life preservers should be available for those in large boats, and worn by all occupants of smaller boats. In a large boat, where anchor rope may be laid on the foredeck, stow the rope away; if it gets washed overboard and grabs in the propeller, the boat will be dangerously impaired.

Wind direction, wind velocity, and current are key factors in how to handle rough water. Here are some general guidelines for operating under heavy seas:

- Plan your approach to minimize discomfort if possible. If you can run along a protected shoreline for a while, even if it takes you slightly out of your way or is longer than a straight-line approach, it may be advisable to do so to lessen rough-water running. Take a course across the troughs for a while, if that is easy running, before turning to run straight into the sea or directly with the sea.
- Match boat speed to the sea conditions. A lot of people take an unnecessary beating because they operate the boat too fast, so it pounds or slams down. Freshwater anglers have hurt a lot of backs this way. Slow down to a speed that allows you to make headway, holding the bow at a 45-degree angle to oncoming waves if possible. If you go too slow, however, the water controls the boat.

Quartering into a Head Sea

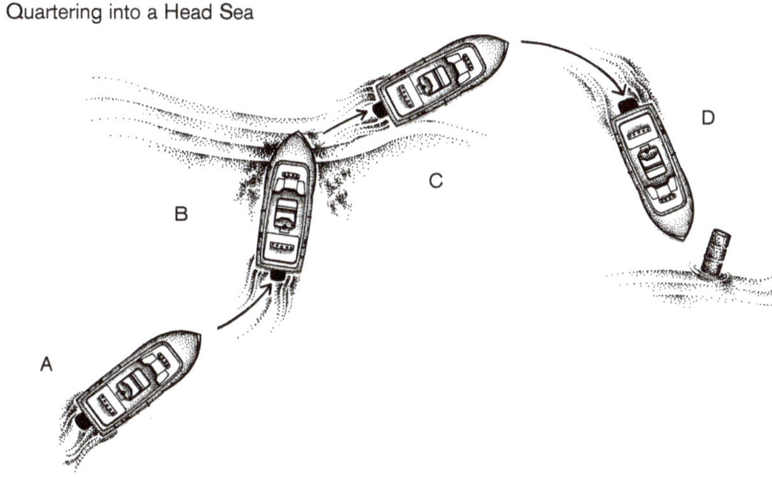

When you need to reach a position (the buoy here) that would require quartering into a head sea, which would be a rough, rolling ride, a safer and smoother-riding alternative is to (A) head directly into the oncoming waves (B) until you're upwind of the desired position (C), then turn and head directly downwind with the following sea to that position (D).

B

- Try tacking or quartering with the waves, much as a sailboat operates. Ride the edge of the waves and then head into the waves or with them, so that you are only briefly in the trough. Then ride at a 45-degree angle again for as long as you can, either zigzagging to stay straight ahead, or moving more in one direction according to destination.
- Adjust the trim on your motor, and, if necessary, adjust the weight distribution in your boat. When heading into waves, if the boat is not adjusted properly or has too much forward weight, the bow will stay down and may plow through a wave rather than ride over it. If you have too much weight aft, however, the boat will ride back with a wave. Generally, however, it is preferable to keep the bow up.
- Vary the speed to ride the waves, throttling up and down as necessary to time big swells or waves. This can be done by increasing speed to reach the crest of a wave, then throttling back at the peak to ride smoothly down the back of the wave and repeating this for the next wave. Small boats can do this just as well as large boats; however, small boats used in freshwater are more likely to encounter waves that are closer together, and not as easy to vary speed on.
- Head straight into a really large wave to minimize the possibility of it catching you sideways and broaching the boat.

When you are fishing in rough water, rather than running through it, you must handle a boat similarly, although the slow speed of fishing can lead to a boat being sideways to the waves often, which can be dangerous in some craft. In drifting, some motor positioning is required to keep the drift from being too rapid or to keep the boat in proper relation to oncoming waves. Landing a fish, especially a large one, can be a problem, especially if the boat operator has to abandon the wheel to assist. Essentially, the boat has to be steered into the waves when landing a fish (especially a large one); steering with the waves can cause the boat to be lifted up and crash down uncontrollably and may lead to capsizing (capsizing is the third most common reason for boating accidents). With three people, one holds the boat into the waves; with two people, the operator steers into the waves until the fish is right at the boat, then leaves for a quick assist, returning immediately to the wheel to maintain control.

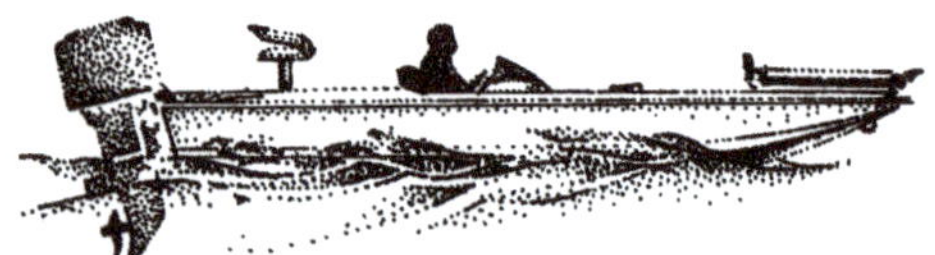

Motor in, bow low, boat plows

Motor out, bow high, boat pounds

Proper trim, smooth ride

How a motor is trimmed affects the planing action and the ride.

Safety

Proper handling of a boat means safe handling, of course, and boating anglers should bear in mind some safety concerns. Some of these are common to all boating, but anglers need to be extra careful because they handle hooks, knives, gaffs, and thrashing fish. Being careful with fish, especially large and toothy ones, is a safety issue, too. Some anglers have found themselves hooked to a lure that was in turn hooked to a powerful fish that was thrashing on the floor of their boat. A life-threatening medical emergency can arise in a moment.

Boat Operation Directly into a Head Sea

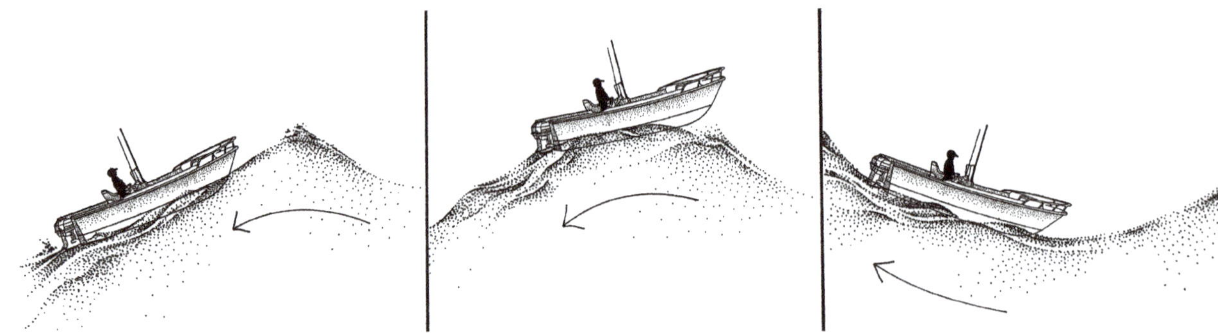

When running into a head (coming toward you) sea, trim the boat so the bow is up and doesn't dig into an oncoming wave. Increase speed to climb the face of the oncoming wave (left), decrease speed as you reach the top of the wave (middle), coast down the back of the wave (right), then speed up to climb the next wave.

Boat Operation with a Following Sea

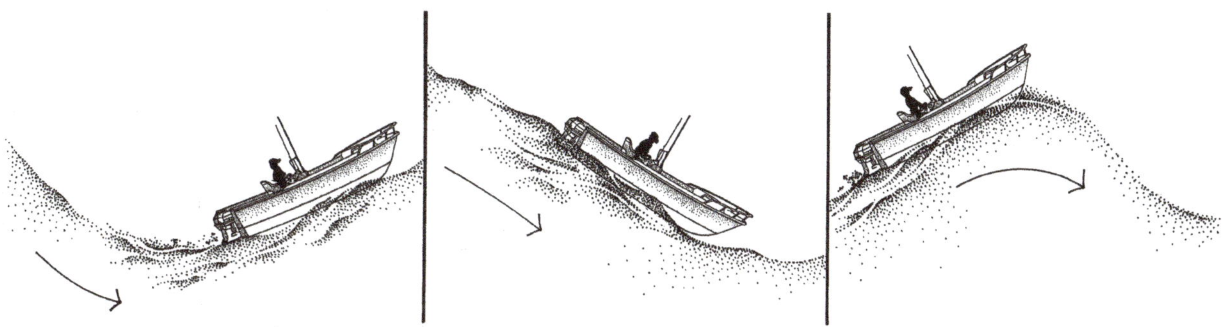

When running with a following sea, maintain position on or near the back of a wave (left) by constantly adjusting boat speed. When a following wave starts to overtake you (middle), increase boat speed to regain position on the back of the preceding wave.

Pre-trip. A pre-trip check should ensure that you have all legally required equipment as well as optional equipment. If a fishing license is required (it is not in some coastal waters), it must be with you on the boat. Although it is not a safety item, boats must be registered with appropriate authorities, and proof of either registration or documentation should be carried onboard; in some states it is not necessary to register a nonmotorized craft, like a canoe or rowboat. Carry proof of insurance as well.

Make sure that you have ample fuel. Be careful about fueling the boat, especially if it is done at a marine dock or if filling external tanks; make sure that no one smokes at the fuel pump. Because unforeseen events do occur on the water, it's advisable to top off your fuel tank, especially if you'll be ranging far and spending a long time on the water. Be attentive to the fuel level, not only to prevent running out of gas, but to avoid it happening at a critical time (heading toward swift water on a river, for example, or negotiating a rough inlet).

When boarding small boats, be careful to step into the middle of the boat and keep your body low and along the centerline, holding onto the gunwales to help steady the boat. Do not step on the gunwales or jump into the boat. Pass heavy objects in if there is another person onboard. Be seated when someone else is boarding, and keep the boat as steady as possible. If entering from a beach or shore, come in over the bow. Have a companion go to the rear to weight the stern of the boat to make it easier to push it away from the shoreline. Although few people actually fall out of a small boat while boarding, many lose their balance and fall inside the boat, sometimes hurting themselves or doing damage to fishing equipment.

In larger boats, entry is usually from a dock. Do not jump in, but step down. Wear proper footwear with soles that will not scuff the boat and which will grab the deck when it is wet and when you are bouncing in waves.

With large boats that will be traveling some distance, it is recommended that a float plan, detailing destination, route, and other information, be filed with a friend or family or marina in case of an emergency. This may not be a bad idea for anyone, even small boaters, especially if you're headed into some backcountry area. Make it as detailed as possible, including information on your trailer and tow vehicle, as well as expected launching site; this could help narrow the search for you considerably.

Before you depart, it's a good idea to check on the weather forecast so you can be aware of any predicted weather patterns that might adversely affect fishing and boating. This is especially important on large bodies of water, and for people who are traveling long distances to fish, with a lengthy return later in the day. The best forecasts for marine purposes are usually obtained from The National Weather Service. These forecasts are available on handheld marine radios as well as marine VHF radios; they should be checked occasionally during the day. Storms, lightning, water spouts, heavy rain, and fog are some obvious natural phenomena that deserve respect and attention on the water. These may or may not be forecast, but they do require evasion or special navigational consideration. If you can identify weather signs, you have a good chance of avoiding potential trouble. Give yourself plenty of time to avoid a thunderstorm or squall; many anglers have run into trouble by waiting too long to make their move. Be aware of the changes in wind speed and direction, and the changes in wave height. On small bodies of water, once whitecaps start appearing on the waves, you should be thinking of heading to port, especially if you're in a small boat.

Before departing, it is wise to check with passengers to determine their physical limitations and/or swimming proficiency so you are aware in case something unforeseen happens. You should also orient them to the boat and to the location of all safety and emergency equipment, including first-aid items.

Equipment and emergencies. Basic safety equipment should be carried on boats, and is required on most. These include personal flotation devices *(see)*, or life preservers, for each passenger, fire extinguisher, lights, horn or whistle, flares (for larger boats), paddle or oars, visual distress signals, and in some places a bilge pump or bailer. As a practical as well as a safety matter, the following items may also be carried: compass, boat hook, fenders or bumpers, EPIRB (Emergency Position Indicating Radio Beacon), flashlight or searchlight, anchor, sonar or lead sounding line, extra rope, tool kit and spare parts (especially fuses), and a VHF marine radio or handheld weather radio. Some other items that may come in handy include: a cellular phone, rain gear, warm clothing, an extra hat, flashlight, emergency signal mirror, binoculars, extra fishing pliers, emergency food rations, insect repellent, sunscreen, lip balm, extra eyeglasses or sunglasses, matches in a waterproof bag, seasickness remedy, and anti-diarrhea tablets.

From a survival standpoint—should your boat break down and you have to spend a night or more on the water—you should at least have raingear and warm clothing, perhaps a change of clothes as well; enough fresh water for at least 24 hours afloat; a little bit of food; some type of signaling device or flares; some means of electronic communication; a signal mirror; and a waterproof flashlight with good batteries.

Communicating when you need help. A VHF marine radiotelephone is standard for communicating on the water, but its range is limited. You might reach 40 miles over open water with a 25-watt unit and a good antenna under ideal conditions, but in wooded backcountry it could reach only 10 miles or less. Handheld VHFs rarely make it past 5 miles, but they can still help.

Cellular telephones can offer more help options if an antenna site is close enough. Sometimes you're in a fringe area where signals are there but hard to get. Try just a slight change of position in the boat, or move the boat just a little by whatever means available to get as far from trees or other tall vegetation as possible. Or get as high as you can. Sometimes just elevating that antenna by three or four feet is all it takes.

If these don't work and you have an EPIRB, this can save your bacon. Don't overlook flares. You are required by law to carry both day and night Coast Guard-approved visual distress signals if your boat is over 16 feet in length and you are operating on waters more than 2 miles wide. You must also have them aboard any size boat if you operate after dark. Only flares, hand/fuse type or aerial, meet both day and night requirements. Aerial flares can be seen at far greater distances, and their meaning is unmistakable. Aerial flares come in shells for a pistol, and hand-launched in self-contained tubes (you must carry at least 3 day/night signals). For small boats the hand-launched variety makes a lot of sense because they take up so little space and are easy to carry.

With a flashlight you can signal for help from dusk to dawn. The international distress signal is three short, three long, three short (Morse code for SOS). If you don't already know this, it should be committed to memory or permanently etched onto the flashlight. During daylight hours a small mirror can do the same job if the sun is bright enough to make a distinct shadow. To flash sunlight at a target, such as a passing boat or aircraft, hold the mirror under your master eye and extend your other arm with the thumb up, like the front sight on a rifle. Position your thumb just below the target, and flash the sunlight back and forth across its tip in the SOS sequence. Ready-made signal mirrors are unbreakable plastic, small, inexpensive, and have a built-in sight. They also come as part of many compact flare kits.

Overloading and overpowering. Overloading boats, especially small ones, is a common occurrence and a major cause of mishaps. Anglers should know the capacity of their boats. This information is displayed on a certification label affixed to the boat (for boats that must comply) by the manufacturer. It is illegal for anyone to remove or alter this certification label, which provides maximum capacity information as well as maximum horsepower rating.

Exceeding these ratings by overloading and overpowering can be dangerous and may draw citations from law enforcement authorities. Maximum capacity standards were developed for boats by the United States Coast Guard because most boats, especially small ones, can accommodate more people and gear than they can safely carry. Inexperienced boaters run the risk of overloading a boat. Overloading reduces the freeboard and makes the boat more likely to swamp in bad weather or from the wakes of other boats. Overloading can have adverse effects on the stability of a boat and make it hard to control, particularly if the weight is unevenly distributed or moves about suddenly.

Proper distribution of weight in a boat is important for personal safety as well as boat handling.

The capacity information on the label or plate is a guide and not an absolute. Two capacities are listed: the maximum persons capacity and the maximum weight capacity (which is the total weight-carrying capacity of the boat). The persons capacity is the most prominent information; persons capacity is referred to as "live load," which can move around the boat and affect stability. Generally, the persons capacity is less than the maximum weight capacity, except on very small boats where the persons capacity and maximum weight capacity may be the same.

The maximum persons capacity is shown on the label both in terms of the number of people and the total number of pounds. Total pounds is the controlling figure. The number of persons is a convenient and approximate guide. If you subtract the persons capacity from the maximum weight capacity, you get a figure that represents the total weight of portable gear (which on small boats could include an outboard engine, portable fuel tanks, and coolers) that can be brought aboard. If you want to bring aboard more portable gear than is allowed, you'll have to carry fewer people to compensate.

Bear in mind that the capacity of a boat, either in weight or number of people, is largely a measure for calm to moderate water conditions; heavy loading of a boat, even though it may still conform to the manufacturer's recommendations, may be dangerous in rough water.

As to overpowering, a boat with an engine that exceeds the certification label rating is dangerous. Too much power can make a boat difficult to control. As the power of an engine increases, so does the weight. Overpowering of an outboard boat can produce a stability problem due to excessive weight on the stern. This decreases freeboard at the stern and increases the chance of following seas or wakes coming over the transom, possibly swamping or capsizing the boat. In addition to being unsafe, overpowering may be illegal, and overpowered boats may not be covered by insurance policies or covered by the warranties of boat manufacturers.

Obviously, operating a boat at safe speeds—which vary with seas conditions, localities, and traffic—is of great importance. Do not operate a boat with a passenger in a bow pedestal seat, or sitting on the bow deck (legs dangling over the edge).

PFDs. Safety also applies to standing up in a boat, and being careful not to fall out. Most anglers prefer to stand up in a boat to aid casting, retrieving, fish playing, hook setting, and vision. This necessarily entails some problems, primarily in small boats, since standing changes the center of gravity. It has long been recommended that boat occupants wear PFDs, but the fact is that few do, unless they cannot swim and are afraid of the water, or unless they are young and are obligated by elders to wear them. Some people do wear PFDs while moving at higher speeds in a boat, and this has saved some lives. Striking a submerged object or losing control of a fast-moving boat has thrown small-boat operators and passengers out of their vessel; in such a situation, a careening boat makes a clockwise circle back toward its passengers due to the rotation of the propeller and literally can run the passengers over. Someone who falls out of a boat in this manner may need a good PFD to save them from drowning, especially if they are rendered unconscious by striking the boat. Some people who were not wearing a PFD when this happened were killed.

Anglers occasionally fall out of boats that are not under power, often by losing their balance from a raised platform. For many this has not been a problem, but if they fall on top of a submerged tree stump or rock or piling, they could receive serious injury. If they panic, struggle, and get tangled in vegetation, they could drown. In fact, some people drown this way every year, not necessarily as the result of falling, but more likely diving in to cool off. A common cause of drowning, not necessarily of anglers, is men who fall overboard while relieving themselves. Often this type of accident is alcohol related, but in any event, it is best to do this in a kneeling rather than standing position, or to use a bail bucket.

Even anglers who wear a PFD when a boat is underway usually take it off when the boat is at rest or when actually fishing, whether trolling, drifting, casting, or stillfishing. It is more comfortable to have the PFD off (unless it is the inflatable suspender type), and this is generally regarded as acceptable by most anglers. Common sense is the key here. If you can swim well, if the water is warm, if there are no objects nearby, and if the boat is not likely to run you over or be bounced on top of you, then you probably have little to worry about. Standing up is more likely to be a problem in small boats, in tipsy boats, in boats with raised casting platforms, in boats with slippery platforms or decks, and when the water is rough enough to bounce a boat around. It is less likely to be a problem in large boats, especially those with high gunwales and plenty of freeboard.

If you are ever in doubt about your own safety, concerned about existing conditions, or encounter troubles with your boat under adverse conditions, put on your PFD if you're not already wearing it, and have your passengers do the same. If your boat should swamp or capsize, stay with it unless your life is threatened. Rescuers will be better able to find you if you stay with the boat. Obviously, there are conditions that would mitigate this advice (such as if you are very close to shore), and in some cases, it may not be possible to stay with your boat (a capsized canoe in rough water is hard for several people to hang onto, or your boat might even have sunk).

Most outboard boats manufactured since August 1, 1978 (as well as manually propelled boats less than 20 feet long) are required by law to have level (also called upright) flotation to make it easier for people to stay with a boat that has been swamped or capsized. This requirement does not apply to canoes, kayaks, inflatable boats, and some other specialty craft.

B

Coast Guard accident statistics suggest that many drownings could be prevented after a capsizing or swamping accident if the occupants stayed with the boat rather than trying to swim to shore. Thus, the Level Flotation Standard, as it is called, requires the manufacturer to provide enough flotation material in a boat so that, if the boat is holed or swamped, the fully loaded boat will float the passenger carrying area at or just below the surface of the water, providing a survival platform for the occupants until help arrives. Even if the boat capsizes, the overturned hull must still float basically at the surface so the occupants can get out of the water by climbing onto the hull.

Most inboard and inboard-outboard boats manufactured since August 1, 1978 are required by law to have basic flotation. The Basic Flotation Standard has a lesser degree of flotation performance than the Level Flotation Standard because swamping and capsizing accidents are not as prevalent with inboard boats and because it would require large and costly amounts of flotation material to compensate for the heavy inboard engines. To satisfy this requirement, the manufacturer must provide enough flotation to keep any portion of the boat above the surface of the water after swamping or capsizing so that passengers can hang on until helps arrives. This requirement also does not apply to canoes, kayaks, inflatable boats, and some other specialty craft.

Alcohol and drugs. Operating a boat while under the influence of alcohol or drugs is no less a concern than it is for vehicular driving. Many boating related accidents are due to impaired judgment as a result of alcohol or drug use, especially the former. This applies not only to those who operate a boat, but also to those who are passengers. Accident statistics show that more than half of all the people who drown in boating accidents had consumed alcohol prior to their accident. Several hours of exposure to sun, glare, wind, boating, noise, fishing, and the various elements that make up a day on the water are in themselves fatiguing without introducing alcohol or drugs. Sometimes, just a couple of beers is enough to seriously impair the judgment of an angler or boat operator. People who are tipsy are more likely to fall overboard—an oft-cited government statistic is that many of the alcohol-influenced men who have drowned after falling out of a boat had the fly to their trousers unzipped. Alcohol reduces the body's ability to protect against cold water, so if you are under the influence and fall into cold water, you may have less time to call for help or swim to safety. And a drunk person can actually get disoriented in the water.

Furthermore, operating a vessel while intoxicated (Boating Under the Influence or BUI) has been a federal offense since 1988. Operating a boat under the influence of alcohol or drugs may be considered negligent operation subject to civil or criminal penalties, so, in addition to practical safety issues, there are civil and criminal issues associated with boat operation while under the influence.

This entire section can be summed up with the proviso: Always be careful, no matter where you go, no matter what the conditions are, and no matter what type of boat you go fishing in.

See: Bass Boat; Canoe; First Aid; Flats Boat; Jonboat; Navigation; Motor, Electric; Motor, Trolling; Outboard Boat; Personal Flotation Device; Sonar; Sportfisherman; Trailer; Walleye Boat; Weather.

BOATHOOK

A pole with a hook at the end, used for picking up or retrieving objects, especially rope, and for fending off or holding onto a dock or other boat.

BOAT LAUNCH

An access site, usually with a paved ramp, for getting boats off a trailer and into the water. Boat launches may be at parks, marinas, fishing camps, concession docks, and other places. They may be improved, with long paved ramps that extend far enough into the water to allow for water level fluctuations, or they may be unimproved, without pavement and possibly with gravel, sand, or mud that may impede access efforts. Usually a fee is charged to launch a trailered boat at privately owned ramps, and there may be a fee at publicly owned and maintained facilities, but some locations, such as those provided by the Corps of Engineers on inland waters, are free.

A boat launch is commonly referred to as a boat ramp, and most have ample parking nearby for trailer and tow vehicles. Boat launches are also used by anglers with smaller boats not carried on trailers, including cartop boats and inflatables.

See: Launching.

BOBBER

A North American term for a lightweight surface-floating device that is attached to fishing line and indicates the subsurface bite or strike by a fish. Sometimes referred to as a "dobber," this form of bite or strike indicator is more properly known as a float *(see),* and the types and fishing methods are discussed under that entry.

BOBBIN

A small tool that delivers the thread used to tie flies.

See: Fly Tying.

BOBBING

A term for ice fishing *(see),* commonly used in the Midwest where bobhouses *(see)* are utilized.

BOBHOUSE

Shack or shanty used for ice fishing *(see).*

BOCACCIO *Sebastes paucispinis.*

Other names—salmon grouper, mini-grouper (juveniles), red snapper, Pacific red snapper.

Abundant off the central and southern coast of California, the bocaccio is one of the most commercially important rockfish in that region. It is also a well-known gamefish in its range and a good eating fish with soft and juicy white meat. Anglers should be cautious when handling the bocaccio, because it has venomous first dorsal and anal spines.

Identification. Although its elongate and compressed body form is less bulky than that of most fish in the scorpionfish family, the bocaccio has a large mouth. The upper jaw extends farther back than the eye; the lower jaw extends past the upper one considerably. The first dorsal fin has spines and is deeply notched, and there are usually nine soft rays in the anal fin. Bocaccio are variably colored olive or brown on the back, reddish on the sides, and pink or white on the belly. Young fish are generally light bronze with speckling over the sides and back. As they mature, their color generally becomes darker and the speckling gradually disappears.

Size/Age. Bocaccio can grow up to 3 feet and 21 pounds and can live for 30 years.

Distribution. These fish inhabit waters from Punta Blanca, Baja California, to Kruzof Island and Kodiak Island, Alaska.

Habitat. Adults dwell in waters over rocky reefs but are also common in deeper water. Young bocaccio live in shallower water and form schools; they are caught more frequently than adults, especially in rocky areas.

Life history/Behavior. One- or two-year-old bocaccio travel in loose schools and move into shallow water where they may be captured in quantity. With increasing age, they seek deeper water and move from near the surface to near the bottom. Adults are commonly found in waters of 250 to 750 feet over a somewhat irregular, hard, or rubble bottom. They are known to dwell in depths as great as 1,050 feet.

Females start maturing when they are 17 inches long. As with all rockfish, fertilization is internal, and development of the embryos takes place within the ovaries of the female until they are ready to hatch. A 28-inch female was estimated to contain 1.5 million eggs. The main hatching period runs from December through April.

Food. Bocaccio feed mainly on fish, including other rockfish. Their diet comprises surfperch, mackerel, sablefish, anchovies, sardines, deep-sea lanternfish, and sanddabs, as well as squid, octopus, and crabs.

Angling. Almost any rocky or rubble bottom at depths of 250 to 750 feet will yield bocaccio. The usual rig is made up of three to six hooks above a sinker that is heavy enough to take the line to the bottom on a fairly straight course. Because of the extreme depths fished, a lot of weight and a lot of line are required to fish bocaccio. The bait should be sufficiently firm to stay on the hook while being chewed upon by bocaccio; for this reason, squid are a common bait choice.

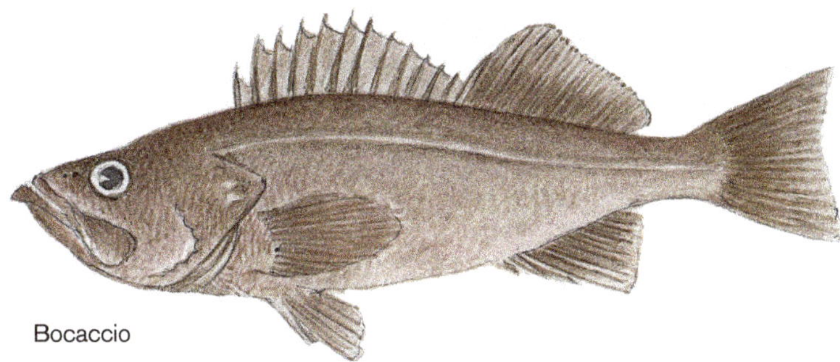
Bocaccio

See: Rockfish.

BOILIE

A small ball of processed protein bait made from assorted ingredients (milk and animal proteins, eggs, soy flour, wheat germ, coloring, and flavoring) that have been rolled together and boiled. It has a crusty shell that retards small fish pecking. This is a European term and innovation primarily used in carp fishing.

See: Carp.

BOLIVIA

One of only two South American countries without access to the sea, Bolivia is the fifth largest country of that continent, and strongly influenced by two ranges of the Andes Mountains. It contains a portion of Lake Titicaca, the largest lake in South America, which has no currently known sportfishing significance *(see: Peru),* and numerous rivers, most of which flow to the north through plains and rain forests and into Brazil, eventually meeting the Madeira River and flowing to the Amazon River. The many rivers and fishing opportunities here are described in the Amazon review under Brazil *(see).*

BOLT RIG

A European term for a shore-based baitfishing setup for carp utilizing a heavy sliding sinker, a rod and reel in a fixed holder, and a taut fishing line, which results in a fish hooking itself.

See: Carp.

BOMBORA

An Australian term for a rocky reef, usually found near shore, that is submerged at high tide and exposed at low tide. The reef may be obvious because of crashing waves, or it may be hidden to boaters, especially in calm midtide conditions. Bomboras attract certain fish species.

B

BONEFISH *Albula vulpes.*

Other names—banana fish, phantom, silver ghost, ladyfish, grubber, silver streak, tenny; French: *banane de mer, sorte de mulet;* Hawaiian: *o'io;* Japanese: *soto-iwashi;* Portuguese: *juruma;* Spanish: *macabí, zorro.*

Although the bonefish was previously thought to be the only member of the Albulidae family, there are now five recognized species. The bonefish is the only significant sportfish among them, however, and is one of the most coveted of all saltwater gamefish. In keeping with its scientific name, which means "white fox," it is indeed a wary, elusive creature, one that usually must be stalked with stealth and that bolts with startling speed when hooked or alarmed.

Although bonefish have little food value to anglers and virtually all are released, they are a subsistence food in some locations. It is generally believed that bonefish are not good table fare, but some gourmands maintain that bonefish flesh is firm and tasty and the roe a delicacy.

Identification. The bonefish has armor plates instead of scales on its conical head and is distinguished from the similar ladyfish by its suckerlike mouth and snout-shaped nose, which are adapted to its feeding habits. It also has a single dorsal fin and a deeply forked tail. The coloring is bright silver on the sides and belly with bronze or greenish blue tints on the back; there may also be yellow or dark coloring on parts of the fin and snout, and sometimes there are dusky markings on the sides. The young have bronze backs and nine narrow crossbands.

Size. Although the average bonefish weighs between 2 and 5 pounds, bonefish weighing up to 10 pounds are not uncommon. They can grow to 41 inches in length, averaging 1 to $2^1/_2$ feet long. The all-tackle world-record catch is a 19-pound fish.

Distribution. Bonefish are found worldwide in tropical and subtropical waters. Around North America, they are most bountiful in the Florida Keys, the Bahamas, and the Caribbean, more so in winter than in summer; they are also somewhat abundant in Belize, Panama, and other Central American countries.

Habitat. Occurring in warm coastal areas, bonefish inhabit the shallows of intertidal waters, including around mud and sand flats as well as mangrove lagoons. They are also found in waters up to 30 feet deep and are able to live in oxygen-poor water because they possess a lunglike bladder into which they can inhale air.

Life history/Behavior. The particulars of bonefish reproduction are not well known, although it is thought that bonefish spawn from late winter to late spring, depending on locale. With a small head and a long, transparent body, the young bonefish looks like an eel until it undergoes a leptocephalus larval stage. It grows to about $2^1/_2$ inches long during this period, then experiences a metamorphosis that shrinks the young bonefish to half that size. The fins begin to appear during the shrinking, and in 10 to 12 days it attains the adult bonefish body form, only in miniature size. This growth process is similar in tarpon and ladyfish development. The young migrate out to the open sea to live on plankton, returning as juveniles to live in the shallows.

Generally, bonefish are a schooling fish; smaller specimens are seen traveling in large numbers on the flats, whereas larger ones prefer smaller schools or groups of 5 to 10 fish.

Food and feeding habits. Bonefish feed on crabs, shrimp, clams, shellfish, sea worms, sea urchins, and small fish. They prefer feeding during a rising tide, often doing so near mangroves. They root in the sand with their snout for food and are often first detected while feeding with their body tilted in a head-down, tail-up manner, with all or part of the tail fin protruding from the surface. These are referred to as tailing fish. Bonefish also sometimes stir up the bottom when rooting along, which is called mudding; this can be a telltale indicator to the observant angler.

Angling. Although some bonefish are caught accidentally in deep water, the primary habitat

Bonefish

explored by anglers is shallow tidal flats and shoals. Bonefish feed on these flats, scouring the bottom for small clams, crabs, worms, and shrimp. The shallow flats, which range from less than a foot to as much as several feet deep, leave the fish most vulnerable, so bonefish have good reason to be skittish. Engine noise will send the fish scattering, so boaters prefer to pole silently along in search of fish, staking the boat and fishing from the boat or by foot when bonefish are spotted. Waders walk on hard bottoms and carefully approach feeding fish.

Bonefishing is primarily sight fishing, so this species, in effect, is stalked. Unless their tails are poking through the surface, the silvery form of a bonefish can be surprisingly difficult to see, even in the shallowest water. Polarized sunglasses aid through-the-water vision and are virtually a necessity. Calm water and bright sun help visibility as well. When bonefish are spotted, the angler maneuvers into position to intercept the fish with a judicious cast.

If the terminal tackle lands on top of the fish or a school, the fish will dart away. So the lure, fly, or bait should be cast 6 to 10 feet ahead of feeding or cruising fish.

At the strike and hookset there is an explosion in the water, and the bonefish instantaneously streaks across the flats toward the security of deep water. It is not uncommon for a bonefish to strip 80 to 100 yards of line off the reel in a scorching run, and the angler must have the drag set properly and keep the rod tip high so the line avoids mangrove roots, grass, and other flats objects that could cut the line or leader.

Bonefishing is primarily done with fly or light spinning tackle, using a 6- to 7-foot spinning rod or a 9-foot fly rod and a reel with adequate line capacity. Six-pound nylon monofilament line is just right for spinning gear.

Small streamers or a weighted fly pattern like the Crazy Charlie and epoxy flies work best in light browns and yellow; jigs are the primary artificials, in pink, white, and yellow; and shrimp, clams, and conch meat are popular baits. Shrimp is the best natural offering for bonefish. They are particularly attracted to the scent of fresh shrimp, so break off the tail and two of the four fans and thread the shrimp on the hook. A piece of conch or crab will also catch bonefish. Chum slicks are equally effective. Some bonefish anglers anchor or stake their boat and chum with crushed shrimp.

The end of an ebb tide and the beginning of a flood tide are usually best for the sake of spotting shallow fish (bonefish coming in over the flats on a rising tide are not half as wary when the tide starts to fall), but a slack flood tide can produce for anglers who fish waist-deep water by casting blindly with small jigs. Seldom do bonefish feed on shallow flats when the water temperature falls much below 70°F; they stay in deeper water then.

A bonefish is released near Islamorada, Florida.

The main secret to catching bonefish is in the presentation. Bonefish spend most of their time probing for food and tend to pounce on any tidbit that looks tasty. Thus, if you can get a fly, lure, or natural bait in front of the fish in a natural manner, you should get a strike.

Bonefish arrive on the flats with the incoming tide, working higher on the shoal as water depth increases. Receding water forces them to retreat to deep holes or channels until the tide returns. These eating machines are opportunistic feeders, constantly in search of crustaceans and small baitfish. With their hard nose, and eyes set high on the head, they are built to dig. In skinny water, you'll see them standing on their noses, their tails waving in the air as they ferret out dinner. Thus, the best way to catch a bonefish is to get the bait, lure, or fly down on the bottom.

Bonefish need to see, hear, or smell the bait, lure, or fly. Blessed with an incredible sense of smell, acute hearing, and terrific eyesight, they can do this easily. A bonefish can hear a fly or a shrimp "splat" on the water some distance away. To utilize their sense of smell, feeding bonefish work into or across the current. They expect their food to be carried by the tide, which means that it's best to make a presentation upcurrent from the fish. When fishing natural baits, this is critical if you expect your quarry to get a whiff of your offering.

Regardless of tackle, aim your cast so the lure lands in front, but not too close to the fish. If the bait goes astray, the fish won't see it; but drop even the tiniest fly too close and every fish in the school vanishes. Always position your offering in front of the fish and beyond its path of travel. If the cast is not perfect, retrieve it quickly until the lure lies directly in the path of the fish. Then, start a stripping retrieve. When fishing artificials, the idea is to "take" the lure away from the predator. The lure must be moving away from the fish, not toward it. With natural baits, cast upcurrent and let the bait lie on the bottom a short while, so the fish can get the scent.

There is little point in keeping a bonefish for eating or mounting. Replica taxidermy mounts are readily available, and the meat of a bonefish, although better than most anglers believe, is still not the equal of many other species. Bonefish can fight until so exhausted that it may be necessary to carefully revive them after capture.

See: Flats Fishing.

BONITO, ATLANTIC *Sarda sarda.*

Other names—common bonito, katonkel, belted bonito; French: ***bonito à dos rayé, boniton, conite, pélamide;*** Japanese: ***hagatsuo, kigungegatsuo;*** Portuguese: ***cerda, sarrajão, serra;*** Spanish: ***bonito del Atlántico, cabaña cariba, cerda.***

The Atlantic bonito, a relative of the tuna, has a reputation as a tough fighter and a tasty fish. This combination makes it highly popular among anglers. In the eastern Atlantic, this species has moderate commercial value, although it is of limited importance in the western Atlantic, specifically off southern Brazil, Argentina, Venezuela, Mexico, Martinique, and Grenada. The light-colored meat is served dried, salted, smoked, and canned.

Identification. The Atlantic bonito has a completely scaled body (some types of bonito have only a partially scaled body), a noticeably curved lateral line, and six to eight finlets on the back and belly between the anal fin and the tail. The caudal peduncle—the narrow muscular area connecting the body and the tail—has a lateral keel on either side with two smaller keels above and below the main keel. It also doesn't have a swim bladder or teeth on its tongue. The back is blue or blue green, fading to silvery on the lower sides and belly; a characteristic feature of the Atlantic bonito is the dark lines that extend from the back to just below the lateral line. It can be distinguished from the tuna by its slimmer body, a mouth full of teeth, and dark lines on its back rather than its belly.

Size. The Atlantic bonito averages 2 to 10 pounds, although it may attain a weight of 20 pounds and a length of 36 inches. Smaller fish are often used as trolling baits for big-game fish. An 18- pound, 4-ounce specimen holds the all-tackle world record.

Distribution. As implied by its name, the Atlantic bonito inhabits the Atlantic Ocean, from the tropical and temperate waters around Nova Scotia to Argentina in the western Atlantic, and from Norway to South Africa in the eastern Atlantic. In the United States, it is most abundant from southern New England to New Jersey. The Atlantic bonito is rare in the Caribbean and the Gulf of Mexico; it is absent in the West Indies, although it is frequently found in the Mediterranean and Black Seas. In the Pacific Ocean, other members of this family take the place of Atlantic bonito.

Habitat. Atlantic bonito occur in brackish water and saltwater, particularly in tropical and temperate coastal environs. Schooling and migratory, they often inhabit surface inshore waters.

Life history/Behavior. In coastal waters, spawning occurs from January through July, depending on locale (June and July in the western Atlantic). Bonito reach sexual maturity at about 16 inches in length. Spawning usually takes place close to shore, in warm coastal waters. By the end of the first year, females will sometimes spawn, although many wait until the end of their second year of life. They release 450,000 to 6 million eggs, depending on size. Growth is rapid.

Food and feeding habits. Living in open waters, the Atlantic bonito feeds primarily at or near the surface in schools that are often 15 to 20 miles offshore, but are also found close to shore. Adults prey on small schooling fish and will also eat squid,

Atlantic Bonito

mackerel, menhaden, alewives, anchovies, silversides, and shrimp; they also tend to be cannibalistic. Atlantic bonito larvae feed mostly on copepods but eat larvae of other fish as well, as do juveniles.

The Atlantic bonito is an athletic swimmer and a ferocious feeder, occasionally leaping out of the water in pursuit of its quarry. Young bonito develop this killer instinct as soon as they become able to feed. Adults and young alike feed during the day but are especially active at dawn and dusk.

Angling. Bonito are often caught by anglers trolling with baits or lures for larger quarry. When caught on the heavier tackle used for that sport, the fish are understandably overmatched. When caught on light tackle, however, they are a robust battler—diving, surging, running, and generally doing their best to stretch the fishing line. They typically streak away after a smashing strike, making tremendously swift runs, and then head deep, where they may stay until whipped.

Some anglers keep light tackle handy for use while trolling, in case they encounter a school of bonito (when bigger baits are retrieved and light rods—equipped with a jig, spoon, or plug—are used). They sometimes employ light tackle when drifting and live-bait fishing or when chumming and using live or cut baits. A light- to medium-action spinning rod, 7 to 8 feet long, with 10- to 15-pound line, is about right. Still lighter tackle will ensure more of a battle.

An Atlantic bonito caught near Montauk, New York.

When trolling deliberately for bonito (as well as skipjack and small tuna) a fast boat speed is usually best, as are trolling plugs and feather jigs. The fish are primarily caught near the surface and aren't put off by the wake of a boat or engine noise, so flatline length can be relatively short.

In some areas of the northeastern U.S., bonito are caught near shore and may be pursued deliberately by casters using various tackle and catching these fish on assorted lures and flies, either from boats or from beach and jetty. Metal jigs, long minnow plugs, and streamer flies that imitate sand eels and spearing are used; 12-pound line on spinning or baitcasting tackle provides great enjoyment, as do 9- or 10-weight fly outfits with a weight-forward or sink-tip line.

See: Bonito, Pacific.

BONITO, PACIFIC *Sarda chiliensis.*

Other names—California bonito, eastern Pacific bonito, bonehead, Laguna tuna, striped tuna, ocean bonito; French: *bonite du Pacifique;* Japanese: *hagatsuo;* Spanish: *bonito del Pacífico.*

The Pacific bonito is an important gamefish, often caught from party boats and from shore. It is valued more for sport than for food, as is the Atlantic bonito. The flesh is light colored and tasty; commercially caught fish are mostly canned and sometimes sold fresh or frozen. They are less valuable in the commercial market than are tuna family members and cannot be labeled as "tuna," even though they are related.

Identification. Similar in size and pigmentation to the Atlantic bonito, the Pacific bonito is distinguished from most other bonito by the lack of teeth on its tongue and the possession of a straight intestine without a fold in the middle. The Pacific bonito has 17 to 19 spines on its first dorsal fin and is the only tunalike fish on the California coast that has slanted dark stripes on its back. Like other bonito, its body is cigar shaped and somewhat compressed, with a pointed and conical head and a large mouth. It is dark blue above, and its dusky sides become silvery below.

Pacific Bonito

Size/Age. The Pacific bonito can grow to 25 pounds and 40 inches, although they are usually much smaller. The all-tackle world record is 14 pounds, 2 ounces. Fast-growing fish, bonito will be 6 to 10 inches long by the early part of their first summer, weighing 3 pounds by that fall and 6 to 7 pounds the following spring.

Distribution. Pacific bonito occur discontinuously from Chile to the Gulf of Alaska. Their greatest area of abundance occurs in the Northern Hemisphere in warm waters between Magdalena Bay, Baja California, and Point Conception, California.

Habitat. Bonitos live in surface to middle depths in the open sea and are migratory. Older fish usually range farther from the coast than juveniles. Bonito may arrive off the coast in the spring as ocean waters warm, but they may not show up at all if oceanic conditions produce colder than normal temperatures.

Life history/Behavior. Pacific bonito form schools by size; at two years old, they reach sexual maturity. Spawning occurs sometime between September and February. Although spawning is usually successful each year in the southern part of their range, it may not be successful each year farther north. The free-floating eggs require about three days to hatch at average spring water temperatures.

Food and feeding habits. Pacific bonito prey on smaller pelagic fish as well as on squid and shrimp, generally in surface waters. Anchovies and sardines appear to be their preferred foods.

Angling. Fishing methods for Pacific bonito are similar to those for Atlantic bonito. These include trolling at or near the surface, as well as casting, jigging, or live-bait fishing with small fish, squid, cut or strip baits, or with any of a variety of small artificial lures.

Pacific bonito are excellent fighters, and their hearty appetites make them willing to strike many lures and baits. Once a school is aroused, they will take almost any bait or lure anglers toss their way. Most Pacific bonito are taken by a combination of trolling and live-bait fishing. Anglers locate the schools by using trolling feathers, and live anchovies or squid pieces bait the fish once located. Most fishing for Pacific bonito takes place offshore over a bottom depth of 300 to 600 feet, but it can occur next to kelp beds when the fish are near shore.

Anglers usually catch 3- to 12-pound bonito. Activity tapers off in the fall as the water cools, but good fishing is still possible around warmwater outflows associated with power plants.

See: Bonito, Atlantic.

BONY FISH

Fish that have a bony skeleton and belong to the class Osteichthyes. Basically, this includes all fish except sharks, rays, skate, hagfish, and lampreys.

See: Fish.

BOOK COLLECTING (Rare/Out-of-Print Fishing Books)

The literature of angling, certainly in terms of quantity, and most probably in terms of quality, surpasses the literature of any other sport or pastime engaged in by civilized men and women.

The first English language book, *The Treatyse of Fysshynge Wyth an Angle,* was printed in 1496 and was reputedly authored by a nun, Dame Juliana Berners. Izaak Walton's *The Compleat Angler* (1653) is said to be the third most reprinted book in the English language after the Bible and *Pilgrim's Progress.*

Serious collectors and bibliographers were active as early as the late eighteenth century, their heyday in England being the nineteenth century. During the mid-nineteenth century, a new era of increased prosperity and leisure time began to develop in America, and the first American fishing books started to appear. Some of the important books were *Natural History of The Fishes of Massachusetts, Embracing a Practical Essay on Angling* by Jerome V. C. Smith (1833); *Schreiner's Sporting Manual* by William Schreiner (1841); *The American Angler's Book* by Thaddeus Norris (1845); *The American Angler's Guide* by John J. Brown (1845); *Fishing in American Waters* by Genio C. Scott (1869); *Favorite Flies and Their Histories* by Mary Orvis Marbury (1892); and the numerous works by Frank Forester (who used the pseudonym of Henry William Herbert).

Since the late nineteenth century, and particularly since the growth in sportfishing after World War II, the number of fishing books published—and the interest in collecting books about and related to sportfishing—has grown. Book collecting has become a small hobby for some, and a major one for others. Usually but not always, collectors are people who partake in the sport, their focus is rare and out-of-print works.

Starting a Collection

The most important consideration in building a quality fishing book library is to buy titles that appeal to your interests. Buy wisely, buy books in the best condition you can afford, and take good care of them. Try to buy first editions; if a book was originally published with a dust jacket, try to buy it with the dust jacket.

Study bibliographic material to learn the values of fishing books. Alfred B. Maclay, Henry A. Sherwin, Dean Sage, Daniel B. Fearing, and John Gerald Heckscher, among others, amassed some of the finest angling collections during the late 1800s. Most of these collections were sold in the mid 1900s, and their auction catalogs have become important references for some of the very rare books they owned. For more recent values, study the auction catalogs of Col. Henry A. Siegel, Harry and Elsie Darbee, Joseph D. Bates, Jr., Rudolphe Coigney, and Charles B. Woods III.

An important bibliography by Henry P. Bruns, *Angling Books of The Americas,* is still available from many out-of-print book dealers. Most sporting magazines carry ads of book dealers who specialize in fishing books; write and subscribe to their catalogs. Those with detailed bibliographic information will become valuable references.

Make friends with experienced collectors and pump them for all the information you can get. Once you have done all of this, don't worry when you still make a mistake. It happens to the best.

The Focus

Forming a library exclusively of American fishing books is no small achievement. Collecting the early American fishing books can be expensive and challenging. Since the mid-twentieth century, a veritable avalanche of fishing books has been published, making it a necessity (unless you have unlimited resources) to focus your collection on a particular area of personal interest.

One possible subject area is books on a particular species, such as tarpon, brook trout, black bass, striped bass, salmon, and muskie, to name a few popular ones. If you enjoy fly tying or tackle collecting, buy books on tying freshwater and/or saltwater flies, lure making, tackle, rods, and trade catalogs.

Many people collect all the books by their favorite author, such as Roderick Haig Brown, Zane Grey, Joseph Bates, or Charles Brooks, or a group of authors who all knew each other, like George LaBranche, Edward Ringwood Hewitt, Emlyn Gill, Preston Jennings, and Eugene V. Connett. Many collect fishing books published by a particular press, such as Derrydale Press, Knopf/Borzoi, Penn, or Van Nostrand; others collect every bibliographic book available.

Some people collect beautiful fine-leather bindings bound by famous binders of the period. Favorites among collectors are books signed by the author or signed presentation copies; the best of these, of course, is a book signed by the author to another well-known fishing writer or to a spouse.

You can have fun with children's fishing books or fishing humor. Fishing club histories and mysteries with fishing plots are two fascinating new areas for exploration. Collectors with a scientific bent buy ichthyology, fisheries, and conservation titles.

One popular area is books about a person's favorite type of fishing as practiced in a certain part of the country or world: surf casting, saltwater fly fishing, big-game fishing, carp on a fly (it exists!), trout fishing in Montana or Chile or South Africa, salmon fishing in Norway or Scotland or Canada, western steelhead fishing, etc. Another focus might be books covering a specific locale or river and maybe your home state, province, or country: the Catskills, the Rockies, the Florida Keys, Montana, Maine, Texas, British Columbia, Michigan, New Zealand . . . .. The list can be as endless as your imagination.

Valuations

Older fishing books have continued to hold their value very well. Fishing has become a popular sport, and the demand has increased greatly, especially with the classics. For example, a fine copy of the 1892 first edition of Mary Orvis Marbury's *Favorite Flies and Their Histories* sold for $300 in 1993; now, when one can be found, it will bring $500 or more.

An interesting trend over the past several years is the influx of younger collectors with an avid interest in the history and literature of angling. This influx has caused a surge in the reprint market. Many classic fishing titles are being reprinted at modest prices, and some of the reprinted books have started to climb in value if they are well cared for. For example, Haig Brown's *Fisherman's Winter,* first published in 1954, was reprinted in 1975 at $7.50; a fine reprint copy now sells for $40. Not a dramatic increase, but it sure beats bank interest rates.

Recently published books can produce some real bargains if you're astute and lucky enough to choose the right author. John Gierach's *Sex Death and Fly Fishing* was published at $19.95 in 1990 and now sells for $200. All of Dana Lamb's limited editions published by Barre Press in the 1960s were issued at $15 to $20, and all now sell for over $150. Art Lee's *Fishing Dry Flies for Trout on Rivers and Streams* was $19.95 in 1982 and now sells for $85. Norman Maclean's *A River Runs Through It* was $7.95 in 1976; now a pristine copy of the first printing sells for $1,000. What a movie can do for a book! Harry Middleton's untimely death increased the prices of his first printings tenfold. These books were all published by different publishers, and all had very small first printings. In some cases, when a paperback and hardcover are issued simultaneously, as was the case with the Gierach and Lee books noted, the hardcover printing will be quite small, sometimes as low as 1,000 copies. That's almost a limited edition, and the hardcover version becomes an instant collectible.

Where to Buy Books

There are many sources for collectible rare and out-of-print fishing books. The best sources are reputable booksellers specializing in out-of-print works, but they usually know the value of what they sell. You won't find too many bargains, but you can depend on them for quality. They may also be able to locate particular titles that you want to add to your collection.

Auction houses that specialize in selling books have some sales featuring out-of-print fishing books. Other, more chancy, sources are used bookshops, local library sales, tag or estate sales, and flea markets. When you start buying from these places, your own storehouse of knowledge is important. Many general bookshop owners grossly overprice very common books, and the condition of books at flea markets can be appalling. Keep digging and trying all sources; part of the fun of book collecting is the treasure hunt.

B

Care of the Collection

Ideally your books should be kept in a climate-controlled room. This can prove difficult. At best, the room should be air-conditioned in hot, humid weather. Store normal-size books upright on a bookshelf, never too tightly packed, but tight enough that all the books stand up straight. Make sure there is normal air flow around the books to prevent mildew. Place tall or heavy books flat on the shelf.

Did you know there was a right and left bank to every stream or river? It's determined by facing in the direction in which the water is flowing.

If you look closely at any book, you'll notice that the cloth covers are slightly larger than the printed book block. When you stand it on the shelf, the weight of the book block pulls against the binding. This may create broken hinges and loose bindings.

If possible, locate your bookshelves on a wall that does not get direct sunlight. Sunshine is the cause of many a faded spine. Once a year, take your books off the shelf and dust them. If the book has a dust jacket, take it off and wipe the book with a soft cloth. Dust collected along the top of the book will mix with the acids in the air and permanently darken it. Wrap the dust jackets in Mylar covers to prevent tearing or chipping. These can be purchased from any library supply house (like Brodart Office Supply, Williamsport, PA).

Did you see your favorite author's obituary in the newspaper? Don't put it into his book! Newsprint is the most acid paper there is and will leave a permanent brown spot. First, encase it in clear plastic wrap, then lay it in the book. Writing your name in pencil on the first blank page is acceptable, but never use an embossing stamp. Never store books in boxes in the basement or the attic. Boxed books don't receive the needed air flow; basements are often damp; and hot, airless attics can turn paper brown and brittle.

This sounds like a lot to do, but not when you've spent a lot of time and money collecting your books. Taking good care of them will only help to maintain their value. Most importantly, read and enjoy your books. If over the years your books increase in value, enjoy that too.

Selective Bibliography

Biscotti, M. L. *The Borzoi Books for Sportsmen.* Madison, OH: Sunrise, 1992. Lists all the books published by this high-quality publisher, and includes Penn Publishers.

Bruns, Henry P. *Angling Books of The Americas.* Atlanta: Privately printed, 1975. Over 18,000 annotated and cross-indexed entries with outdated price values. Available from many specialist dealers at $165.

Carter, John. *ABC for Book Collectors.* New York: Knopf. Seventh edition still available at $25. A valuable book to understand the bookman's language.

Coigney, Rudolphe L. *Izaak Walton: A New Bibliography 1653–1987.* New York: Cummins, 1989. The latest bibliography of all the editions. Covers in detail over 525 editions and their variations. Out of print but if your interest is Walton, worth the search for a copy.

Drury, Clyde E. *Books of the Black Bass, fourth edition.* Tacoma, WA: 1991. Privately printed. An exhaustive bibliography based on Drury's own collection and all other information he dug up.

Gingrich, Arnold. *The Fishing in Print.* New York: Winchester Press, 1974. Out of print but worth the hunt for a copy. It's not hard to find and usually sells for around $50.

Goodspeed, Charles E. *Angling in America.* Boston: Houghton Mifflin, 1939. Limited to 750 signed copies. Long out of print but copies do turn up in specialist's catalogs.

Heckscher, John Gerald. Merwin Clayton Auction House, New York, 1909. This is a listing from the auction house; Heckscher had one of the largest privately owned libraries to be auctioned at that time. It contained over 2,320 lots.

Oinonen Book Auctions. Sunderland, MA. Specializes in books and has held many angling auctions over the last 10 years (Darbee, Bates, Siegel, etc.).

Sage, Dean. Parke-Bernet Auction House, New York, 1942. This listing from the auction house is an excellent reference to American fishing books, as over 2,000 volumes collected by Sage were included in the auction.

Sherwin, Henry A. Parke-Bernet Auction House, New York, 1946. Sherwin's huge collection of over 5,000 volumes sold in two parts by this auction house.

Siegel, H. A. et al. *The Derrydale Press: A Bibliography.* Goshen, CT: Angler's and Shooter's, 1981. May still be available from the publisher.

Westwood, T. and Satchell, T. *Bibliotheca Piscatoria.* First published in England in 1883. Numerous reprints have added a supplement covering books published up to 1901. This is the best bibliography of older British fishing books. A reprint edition was published in New York in 1996.

Wetzel, Charles M. *American Fishing Books.* First published in 1950 and since reprinted. All reprints are out of print, but the most recent one, published by Meadow Run Press, still turns up.

Zack, Stanley S. *The Muskellunge: A Bibliography.* Rhinelander, WI: Fishing Hot Spots, 1986. Another based on the author's collection.

BOOT FOOT WADERS

See: Waders.

BOOTS, WADING

See: Waders.

BORON ROD

A rod that uses boron in conjunction with another material, usually graphite, in the construction of the blank. Though some rods may be labeled "boron" rods, they have a small percentage of boron fiber content, and the material of the rod is not solely boron. Boron fiber is stronger than graphite but also heavier.

See: Rod, Fishing.

BOTSWANA

Roughly the size of Kenya, this landlocked country in southern Africa has some of the last unspoiled wilderness in Africa, game reserves roamed by large herds of wild animals, spectacular wildlife and birdlife, and excellent angling for tigerfish in the world's largest inland delta.

The waterless Kalahari Desert, in the central and southwestern regions, constitutes two-thirds of Botswana. In the north lies one of Africa's prime fishing grounds and most pristine wildlife regions, the Okavango Delta, a vast marshland that covers 15,000 square kilometers of lush subtropical islands, waterways, and crystal-clear streams.

The headwaters of the delta begin more than 600 miles away in central Angola. Rainwater falling in this region flows slowly southward in the Okavango River, through varying geographical regions and into northwestern Botswana, until it finally reaches the Kalahari and transforms the desert into one of Africa's wildlife wonders. The Okavango's waters spread out through a labyrinth of channels and shallow basins; almost all of the water evaporates in the delta, where there is extensive aquatic vegetation. The volume of water fluctuates with the wet and dry seasons, the greatest amount arriving from upriver in March.

In the best fishing areas, the Okavango is clear and bilharzia-free. More than 75 species have been documented, but sportfishermen focus on tigerfish and bream (tilapia), the latter valued for table fare as well.

To fully appreciate the Okavango, anglers should experience its three geographical areas: the perennial waters comprised of fast-flowing rivers and large lagoons, the seasonally flooded plains, and the islands and woodlands, which also possess the best game viewing. The perennial waters offer the most sought-after fishing spots, but anglers must be willing to travel to fish for the biggest tigers. The northern Okavango and the Chobe River boast the largest of the species, which reach up to 15 pounds; the larger bream can reach 8 pounds.

Accommodations in the Okavango are generally best in the small tented lodges. Botswana doesn't feature many of the large, impersonal Kenya-style hotels. The tented lodges, which typically serve a maximum of 16 guests, offer the atmosphere and excitement of a camping trip with the comforts of a hotel, with activities tailored to the guests. There is an assortment of these that cater to tigerfishing. Each has standard fishing gear and boats.

The best fishing is generally from September through May, when the waters are at their warmest. The peak months are October and November. This is also when the famous "barbel run" takes place, as thousands of small catfish swim up the main rivers to their breeding areas. Predator species are attracted to these small fish, and one can actually see and hear the waters boil and bubble when the barbel run passes by.

Most fishing is done from 18-foot aluminum boats, but the more adventurous can also try fishing from *mekoros* (dugout canoes). All lodges supply fishing tackle and standard rods, except fly fishing equipment. Dedicated anglers should plan to bring their own gear. Most anglers use lures, with very few people using live bait. Both tilapia and tigers take lures quite readily.

Although lightly populated, Botswana has been prospering, in large part due to diamond mining. Tourism is geared to attract the discerning visitor, and mass tourism is discouraged. The emphasis is on quality; service and the personal touch are more in evidence here than in most African countries.

BOTTOM

(1) A common term used by anglers to refer to the floor underneath a body of water, although not necessarily the deepest part of that body of water. A bass angler in a lake retrieves his or her jig slowly over the "bottom," for example, in 15 feet of water, although the maximum depth of the lake is 65 feet. Describing fish as being "on the bottom" usually means that they are on, or quite close to, the lake, river, pond, or ocean floor.

Technically the bottom is the bed of a body of water, such as the lakebed, riverbed, or seabed; it is also known as the substrate *(see)*.

(2) That portion of a boat from the waterline to the lowest part of the hull.

BOTTOM BOUNCER

A bent wire-armed weighted bottom rig for trolling or drift fishing with bait or lures. The lower extension of a bottom bouncer features a wire arm with a cylindrical weight about midway along the arm; the extended wire minimizes hangups while the rig ticks along the bottom. The crook of the wire arm attaches to the fishing line, and the other wire extension features a snap swivel, to which a leader containing natural bait, a small floating/diving plug, or other lightweight lure, is attached. Worm spinner harnesses are especially popular with a bottom bouncer.

The rig is especially useful in rocky areas, which is why it is preferred for some walleye and smallmouth bass fishing efforts. Its jerky, stumbling motion can be helpful in imparting some realism to the action of the trailing bait or lure. It is important to set out just the right amount of line to reach bottom and keep the rig at a 45-degree angle. Fishing with a rig of the right weight (they vary from about $^1/_2$ ounce to 3 or 4 ounces) is essential, so you may have to change rigs until you get it right.

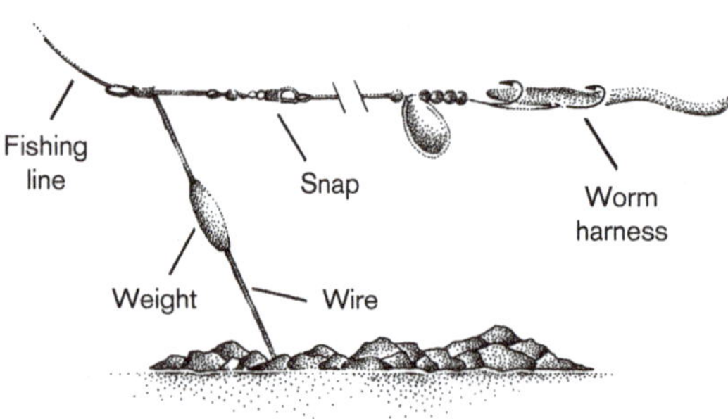

Depicted is a bottom bouncer rig, used to fish a nightcrawler on a spinner-worm harness along the bottom.

These rigs, in different weights, are homemade by some anglers, or purchased in tackle shops. Some similar bottom-walking rigs, incidentally, do not have the long wire arm, but are a keel-like weight at the end of a shorter wire arm. These are also used for some lighter current situations.

BOTTOM BOUNCING

The deliberate manipulation of bait or lures along the bottom of a body of water, aided by current or the movement of a boat. This practice is also called bottom bumping. Some form of weight is usually employed and must be heavy enough to keep in contact with the bottom, but not so heavy as to invite snagging or unnaturally slow the drift.

See: Back Bouncing.

BOTTOM FISHING

Fishing on the bottom of a body of water, usually with stationary baits presented on or just above the substrate, but also with baits that are drifted.

See: Chumming; Drift Fishing; Float; Inshore Fishing; Surf Fishing.

BOTTOM RIG

Any type of weighted terminal tackle configuration for fishing a bait, lure, or fly along the bed of a waterway. Most bottom fishing rigs are used with some type of live or dead natural bait *(see)* or a processed bait *(see);* they are especially used in freshwater for walleyes, catfish, and panfish in lakes and rivers, as well as coarse fish *(see),* and in saltwater for a variety of inshore and reef species.

See: Drift Fishing; Float; Inshore Fishing; Surf Fishing.

BOUNCE CAST

A cast made with spinning or baitcasting tackle in which a lure is made to bounce or skip over the surface to reach an object or area to be fished. This requires horizontal rod movement, usually with the rod or rod tip held low to the water; is mostly done with a soft lure like a plastic worm or grub; and is generally employed where there are overhanging objects (tree branches, dock, boathouse, and the like) that have to be avoided to reach a targeted area. A bounce cast is usually a short-distance cast and requires skill to avoid both hitting and hanging up on the overhead object, as well as creating a backlash or snarl on the reel.

See: Casting.

BOW

The forward part of a boat.

BOWFIN *Amia calva.*

Other names—dogfish, freshwater dogfish, blackfish, mudfish, western mudfish, mud pike, cabbage pike, shoepike, griddle, grindle, spottail grindle, grinnel, lawyer, scaled ling, speckled cat, cypress trout, cypress bass, cottonfish John A. Grindle; French: *choupiquel, poisson de marais.*

Described as a living fossil, the bowfin is the only existing member of the Amiidae family, a group of fish that originated in the Cretaceous period more than 100 million years ago. Of little commercial value because of their poor-tasting

Bowfin

B

flesh, they are excellent fighters and are caught by anglers wherever they are abundant, although mostly unintentionally. When not abundant, they are a rare catch, and many anglers are unfamiliar with them. Although it is sometimes considered a pest or a nuisance by anglers seeking other quarry, the bowfin is helpful in constraining otherwise large, stunted populations of smaller fish.

Identification. An ancient fish in design, and described by some as looking more like a serpent than a fish, the bowfin has a rounded tail and a considerable amount of cartilage in its skeletal system. Underneath its head is a large, bony gular plate, with several other bony plates protecting the skull. Distinctive qualities include a large flattened head with tubelike nostrils and long, sharp teeth, as well as a long, spineless dorsal fin that extends almost the entire length of the body. Another interesting feature of the bowfin's anatomy is a modified, lunglike air bladder, in addition to gills; as in the gar, which possesses a similar organ, the bowfin is able to breathe surface air and, consequently, live in water too polluted or stagnant for most fish.

Its long, thick, cylindrical body is covered with large olive-colored scales, although it occasionally has a brownish or gray cast that fades to white or cream underneath. The male has a dark spot on the upper tail with a yellowish orange rim around it, and the female has a less-conspicuous spot without a rim.

Size/Age. The bowfin can grow to up to 43 inches in length but averages 2 feet. The world-record bowfin weighed 21 pounds, 8 ounces, although the average weight is in the 2- to 5-pound range. The male is smaller than the female, and they survive up to 12 years in the wild and 30 years in captivity.

Distribution. Bowfin occur only in North America, from the St. Lawrence River and Lake Champlain drainage of Quebec and Vermont west across southern Ontario to the Mississippi drainage, from Minnesota south to Texas and Florida.

Habitat. Bowfin are generally a big-water fish and inhabit warm and swampy lakes with vegetation, as well as weedy rivers and streams. With a significant tolerance for high temperatures and a modified air bladder, the bowfin is able to live in stagnant areas by taking in surface air.

Life history/Behavior. When bowfin are three to five years old, they reach sexual maturity. They spawn between early April and June, when water temperatures are between 60° and 66°F. Males move into the weedy shallows after dark, before the females, and build bowl-shaped nests of plant material among tree roots or under fallen logs. A single male may try to mate with more than one female, and sometimes several pairs of bowfin will use the same nest.

The male is left to protect the eggs, which hatch in 8 to 10 days. The newly hatched bowfin use an adhesive organ on their snouts to attach themselves to the bottom of the nest as they grow to about 1/2 inch long. Once they reach this length, the fry school and follow the male, which guards them for several weeks against potential predators. Adult coloration appears when they are about 1 1/2 inches long, and the young begin to protect themselves at this stage. They stop schooling entirely when they reach 4 inches in length.

Bowfin swim slowly along the bottom, although they can move very quickly if disturbed or when in pursuit of prey.

Food and feeding habits. Bowfin can be extremely ravenous and eat a large variety of food, including crayfish, shrimp, adult insects and larvae, small fish, frogs, and large amounts of vegetation. Scent is as important as sight in obtaining food, and bowfin have the habit of gulping water to capture their prey. Although bowfin are always ready to feed, they are most active in the evening.

Angling. Although bowfin strike viciously and provide hardy action, they are generally considered a nuisance by anglers. They are seldom deliberately pursued, but a small minority of anglers will sight-fish for them in the shallows in the spring. At that time, they typically linger in very soft mud bottoms that can be impossible to wade. Bowfin are difficult to land and release, and anglers must be careful when unhooking them. They habitually snap their jaws and can do serious damage to fingers. Bass anglers are particularly likely to catch bowfin, especially when angling in shallow, murky backwaters, as these fish are susceptible to many bass lures. They are caught occasionally on surface lures, as well as on diving plugs, and assorted live or dead baits. Bowfin nibble bait rather than inhale it; thus they are harder to land on baits. They are also caught in southern locales on baited commercial trotlines.

B

BOWFISHING

Hunting for, and shooting, certain species of fish with archery equipment. Also called bow and arrow fishing, it is practiced by bowhunters who convert regular bows into fishing bows by attaching a reel directly in front of the grip. The reel is spooled with 70- to 100-pound line, tied to the head or the shaft of the arrow. The line spools off the reel after a shot, and the fish are pulled in by hand. Bowfishing arrowheads have large wire barbs that hold fish as they struggle to escape.

Some bowfishing enthusiasts wade into the water; others use shallow-running boats with raised platforms for shooting. Bowfishing boats also feature floodlights for finding fish at night, a time when many of the species sought are active.

The act of bowfishing is regulated by fisheries agencies; usually requires a fishing license; is subject to seasons; and is often practiced for rough or coarse species, primarily carp, gar, chub, buffalo fish, and suckers. Bowfishing is prohibited for designated gamefish species, and may or may not be permitted with a crossbow. It is popular with some archers and bowhunting enthusiasts but is not widely practiced. Where legal, it is considered a form of recreational fishing, but it is not treated as sportfishing by the general angling community. The topic is rarely addressed in sporting publications.

BOWING

Leaning forward, lowering a fishing rod to horizontal or near-horizontal position, and pointing the rod toward a tarpon to give it slack line when it jumps clear of the water. This is known as "bowing" or "bowing to the fish." It is mainly done so that the tarpon, which shakes its head violently when jumping, cannot use line tension to rip the hook from its mouth. The instant that the fish falls back to the water, the angler resumes high rod tension and a tight line.

BOWLINE KNOT

See: Knots, Boating.

BRACKISH WATER

Water that is somewhat salty, but its salinity is not as high as the sea; water that contains too much salt to be drinkable. Habitats characterized by a mixture of freshwater and saltwater—particularly marshes, estuaries, and wetlands—are said to be brackish, as is a certain portion of tidal rivers and streams.

See: Salinity.

BRAIDED LINE

See: Line.

BRAZIL

Occupying almost half of the South American continent, and the fifth largest country in the world, Brazil can boast of its overall stature among international and Brazilian anglers alike. With thousands of fish species in its freshwaters alone, and with incredible water resources in general, Brazil can rightly assert itself as one of sportfishing's superstars. Its reputation continues to grow despite its poorly developed infrastructure for angling tourism and both because and in spite of the fact that many of its top waters are remote and very difficult to access; it is subject to seasonal extremes in water levels; and its rivers and tributaries are incomprehensibly vast.

Of Brazil's waters, the Amazon River receives the most angling attention, and this is well deserved; the northerly Amazon basin encompasses more than a third of the country. Many parts of the tropical rain forest in this basin have been little explored, making any report on fishing opportunity a partial one at best. The Brazilian Highlands, which encompass most of the southeastern half of Brazil and are closer to its largest cities, are themselves comprised of extensive forested tracts and a network of lesser-known but commendable rivers and tributaries, especially the Plate and São Francisco systems.

Still less known, and hardly encountered by visiting anglers, is the saltwater opportunity along 4,650 miles of Atlantic Ocean coast.

Freshwater

With 3,286,488 square miles of terrain and seemingly countless rivers and tributaries, Brazil ostensibly has the largest hydrographic network in the world, which is a bit hard to describe in simple terms. Much is yet unknown about the full breadth of freshwater fishing opportunities, but much has happened since the late 1980s. As mentioned, interest in sportfishing has been growing rapidly within Brazil, and international visitors increase each year, although the majority head for the large peacock bass waters of Amazonia. To make an overview of Brazil's freshwater fishery comprehensible, one can look at the country's principal hydrographic basins, which are those of the Plate, the São Francisco, and the Amazon.

The Plate basin of southwestern Brazil is the second largest in the country and is predominantly made up of the Paraná and Paraguay Rivers, which flow into Paraguay, Argentina, and Uruguay. The main course of the Paraná has been impounded for hydroelectric purposes in several places, altering the composition and sizes of the native fish species.

The main rivers of this basin include the Paraibuna, Grande, Tietê, Paranapanema, Paraná, Paraguay, Iguaçu, Teles Pires, Cuibá, Taquari, and Coxim. The lower reaches flood during the rainy season, from November through April. Major fish species include peacock bass, payara, pacu, curimbata, traíra, corvina, piapora, piraputanga (a relative of matrinxã), dorado, and some catfish.

The São Francisco basin of southern and eastern Brazil consists of the primary São Francisco, Preto, Jequitinhonha, das Velhas, and Grande Rivers. It is the only basin that originates and stays within the country. In the highland headwaters these rivers are clear, but the main São Francisco eventually becomes sediment laden. There are a number of hydroelectric impoundments here, and the species vary according to rivers and impoundments, with prominent fish including matrinxã, curimbata, piapora, payara, traíra, piranhas, peacock bass, catfish, and dorado.

The Amazon basin is so vast, and includes so much water, that the best way to detail it is to include with it the Orinoco watershed of Venezuela, and consider both with respect to their species and fishing possibilities.

Falls and swift water on the São Francisco offer opportunity for payara.

Amazon and Orinoco Watersheds

Two great South American rivers, the Amazon and Orinoco, and their watersheds are the arteries of life for much of the South American continent. The region that these rivers encompass extends from the Andes Mountains to the west, the Guiana Highlands to the north, the Brazilian Highlands to the south, and the Atlantic Ocean to the east. This vast and essentially roadless area is equivalent in size to the western two-thirds of the United States. Most of this is comprised of the Amazon basin, referred to as Amazonia, and the entire region is one of the few places on earth that offers a combination of plentiful prized gamefish, few people, fewer anglers, and ample opportunity to enjoy fishing in remote, pristine waters surrounded by abundant and exotic wildlife.

The Amazon River is the world's largest by virtue of its watershed area, number of tributaries, and volume. It is second only to the Nile in length, flowing about 3,900 miles from its headwaters in the high Andes in Peru to the Atlantic Ocean in northeastern Brazil, where it forms a delta maze that is more than 150 miles wide. Half of the Amazon's 2.3-million-square-mile drainage area is in Brazil, the remainder being in Peru, Ecuador, Bolivia, and Venezuela.

The Amazonia watershed encompasses the largest and wettest tropical plain in the world. It experiences periods of heavy seasonal rainfall, which affects the width, speed, and volume of the entire system. Nevertheless, the Amazon proper is navigable for ocean freighters to Manaus, a distance of 1,000 miles, and for smaller ships to Iquitos, Peru, a distance of 2,300 miles. Small steamers and houseboats can navigate at least 100 of the larger tributary rivers. A dozen tributaries of the Amazon are larger than both the Mississippi and the Missouri Rivers in North America.

The Orinoco River flows for 1,590 miles from its source in the Guiana Highlands in southeastern Venezuela, on the border of Brazil, to the Atlantic Ocean in northeastern Venezuela, where it forms an enormous delta. An arm of the Orinoco becomes the Casiquiare River, which heads south for 180 miles and merges with the Río Negro, a prominent tributary of the Amazon River. The main river is joined by numerous tributaries as it winds through Venezuela and along its border with Colombia. The Guaviare, Meta, Apure, Caura, and Caroni Rivers are among the major tributaries; the main river is navigable for oceangoing vessels for 260 miles to Ciudad Bolívar; the delta begins about 120 miles from the ocean.

The thousand-plus tributaries of the Amazon and Orinoco watersheds make up the most biologically diverse region on earth. Freshwater gamefish abound here, as do thousands of plant, insect, and animal species. Categorizing the fish species and angling opportunities, however, is complicated by the size of the rivers and the extent of land area, the relatively unexplored nature of some parts of this landmass, the nature of the waters, and the significance of the wet and dry seasons.

Most of the region's fishing waters are in Brazil, but many waterways extend into Venezuela, Colombia, Ecuador, Peru, Bolivia, and Guyana. Political boundaries tend to be obscured in such remote areas; the population density ranks among that of the world's least inhabited lands. Some native tribes still have little or no contact with civilization. Major population centers along the Amazon are Iquitos in Peru, and Manaus and Belem in Brazil. Only these three Amazon cities have direct flights from North America. Caracas is the preferred city for travelers to and from Venezuela.

Seasons and water levels. The equatorial rain forests of South America have only two seasons: wet and dry. These seasons occur at different times of the year in three general regions of the Amazon and Orinoco basins. The wet season corresponds with high water levels, and the dry season with low water levels. Periods of low water and low rainfall are the prime sportfishing seasons. With high water and high rainfall, the rivers may rise as much as 40 feet, flooding all but the highest grounds in the rain forest and scattering fish over thousands of acres. Low water concentrates fish in rivers, lakes, and lagoons.

The rainy season in the southern third of this region generally starts in November in the Brazilian Highlands and the Andes, and the water levels rise and flow north to the main channel of the Amazon River. These rains usually end in April each year. Southern-tributary water levels rise greatly during this period, receding in April or May and continuing until the rains fall in November. The lowest water level and best fishing in this region is normally from June through October.

The rainy season in the northern third of this region, in the northern Andes and Guiana Highlands, generally begins sometime in April or May, with corresponding high water levels from May through October. By November, water levels are low enough to permit good fishing, with ideal conditions usually present, from Venezuela's state of Amazonas to the Río Negro and Río Branco region of Brazil, from December through March. The rainy season begins again around April.

The central third of this region is essentially the flood plain of the Amazon River. This huge area is impacted by rain and subsequent flooding from an enormous number of northern and southern tributaries. The only respite from this constant torrent of water usually occurs around August and lasts until late November. During this period, anglers will find low water levels and good sportfishing in waters just north and south of the Amazon River. The natural lakes here (mostly lagoons or oxbows) adjacent to the Amazon are extremely large, compared to other Amazon basin lakes. Some are more than 40 miles long and up to 10 or 12 miles wide. Constant flood waters along the main Amazon channel have resulted in lakes at the mouth of the Xingu and Tapajos Rivers that are nearly 100 miles long and more than 5 miles wide.

Sportfishing in this region usually takes place in the smaller tributaries of the major rivers, and in lakes and lagoons adjacent to these tributaries during the low water period. The larger rivers and lakes are fished by commercial fishermen for a variety of species. Anglers may fish the larger lakes, but most are inhabited by local villagers who may practice both subsistence and commercial fishing with gillnets and other devices.

Access. This is a very big region overall and access has been largely limited to using the rivers as highways. When rapids and falls are encountered, anglers portage around the obstacle if the boat can't navigate the hazard. Big boats can only go so far, which is partly why the native dugout canoe is still the vehicle of choice among natives. A shallow-draft aluminum fishing boat works well for the rest of us, but most anglers are in more of a hurry than the native with a dugout and a paddle. The Amazon native doesn't mind sleeping under the stars along the way. Nor does he mind a journey of a few days or weeks.

Small charter planes have improved accessibility to the interior of these watersheds. Flights can be expensive, however, and landing strips are few and far apart. The region does have a few floatplanes, but almost all are too small to carry more than two to three anglers with gear.

All of this, plus other factors, has limited sportfishing access to this region somewhat, but a great variety of facilities are nevertheless still available to the Amazon angler, including fixed lodge facilities, houseboat based operations, outpost camps, tent camps, floatels, and progressive float-trip operations with mobile tent camps. Sometimes it is necessary to give up creature comforts to access the most productive, remote fishing spots. Sometimes you can have comfort *and* great Amazon fishing. The possibility of being the first outsider to cast a lure to fish in a remote Amazon stream still exists.

Many parts of the Amazon have been set aside as national parks or reserve areas, or restricted to nonfishing and nonhunting refuges. Native Indian lands are often off-limits to all but the natives and a few government agencies. Many villages have established nearby waters as private fishing areas for personal use.

Commercial fishing in a large part of Amazonia is very common, and since this tends to center around populated areas and local communities, it usually diminishes fish populations nearby and often requires some travel from established areas by anglers to reach areas that are productive. Some remote areas are indeed accessible to those willing to make the effort.

Water types and colors. Understanding the complex nature of this region and tapping its great sportfishing potential require a knowledge of when and where to fish a number of distinct geographic zones for a variety of species. A knowledge of various water types and what each may provide in the way of species variety, numbers, and size is extremely important to the guide or outfitter in this part of the world, and helpful to the visitor. Waters and their sportfishing attributes can be classified according to their color and flow characteristics. There are white-, brown-, black-, and blue-water rivers in the region. All but whitewater occur throughout the Amazon and Orinoco watersheds, but each is predominant in one particular region.

Whitewater rivers. These are clear, swift-flowing waters in the higher elevations of the Brazilian Highlands, Guiana Highlands, and Andes Mountains. They are devoid of the warmwater gamefish that are especially prized and highly sought in the Amazon and Orinoco watersheds. Whitewater rivers are insignificant as a fishery for coldwater sportfish when compared with the great trout waters found in the more temperate climates of Patagonia and Tierra del Fuego. In the Andes region of the Amazon basin, these waters carry heavy sediment and nutrient loads into the basin, forming brown-water rivers.

Brown-water rivers. These coffee- and cream-colored waters of the upper Amazon basin are rich in sediments and nutrients washed from the high Andes. As these waters settle into the flood-plain basin of the upper Amazon, their flow is greatly slowed by a nearly flat topography with a level just above that of the Atlantic Ocean. Surprisingly, these are not great fishing waters for giant specimens of the most prized gamefish of the Amazon, like peacock bass and payara. Payara grow to giant proportions in other areas, but not in these slow, off-colored waters. Peacock bass are found primarily in black-water lakes and oxbow lagoons located adjacent to the rivers, or in the black-water creeks or channels that often connect the lakes and rivers.

Peacock bass do not grow to giant proportions in this upper watershed region, even though it is rich and fertile. They are found in abundance, however, and generally range in size from 3 to 6 pounds, with a maximum weight of about 13 pounds. Most anglers catch peacocks of 10 pounds or less, and smaller butterfly peacock bass predominate.

The major brown-water tributaries are the Napo in Ecuador and Peru, the Maranon and Ucayali in Peru, the Putumayo in Peru and Colombia, the Japura in Brazil (called the Caquetá in its upper reaches in Colombia), the Yavari in Peru (known as the Javari in Brazil), and the Jaruá and Purus in Brazil. The Madre de Dios, Beni, and Mamore rivers in Bolivia are also major brown waters, and they form the giant Madeira in its upper reaches in Brazil. The Madeira is the largest brown-water tributary of the Amazon. The Amazon itself, called the Solimões above the city of Manaus, is the largest brown-water river. The Mamore is called the Guapore in Brazil, and it is a blue-water river in its headwaters.

Blue-water rivers. The rivers of the southeast region of Amazonas flow down from the Brazilian Highlands into steep and beautiful lush green valleys in their upper reaches, creating topaz-colored rivers. These are lovely watersheds that abound with rapids, waterfalls, narrow gorges, boulder-strewn river bottoms, and beautiful white-sand beaches. The Brazilian Highlands are extremely old formations and carry a low sediment and nutrient load into these crystal-clear rivers as they snake their way through the verdant carpet of the rain forest.

A great variety of gamefish exists here, more so than in any other region of the Amazonas. It is common to catch nearly a dozen different species during a week's stay on one of these waters. In the swift, upper stretches of blue-water rivers, payara grow to 20 pounds or more, and in the lower parts of these basins, peacock bass can often grow to 15 pounds, although fish of less than 10 pounds are far more common. Black-water lagoons often occur here, along with larger lakes, but neither are as common here as in regions that exhibit flatter

Peacock bass are Brazil's major gamefish attraction; this colorful specimen was caught on the southerly Cururu River.

flood plains. Consequently, anglers are forced to spend more time fishing in the river channels and creeks, which results in catches of a greater variety of species. Anglers in these waters who concentrate on lakes and lagoons only for peacock bass will frequently catch just a few other species. If they make an effort to also fish the rivers using a variety of lures and lure sizes, they can catch a great many species.

The major blue-water tributaries are the Tapajos, Xingu, and Araguaia-Tocantins. A large hydroelectric dam and reservoir, the Tucurui, now exists on the lower Araguaia-Tocantins. This lake is more than 100 miles long and more than 12 miles wide. Terms like "large reservoir," "big lake," and "major tributary" are inadequate to describe an area in which everything seems to be monumentally huge, and where such "tributaries" are larger than the biggest rivers in North America.

Black-water rivers. For the most part, these rivers originate in the Guiana Highlands on the Venezuelan-Brazilian border, in the northernmost reaches of Amazonia. Several brown- and blue-water rivers are also found here, but black water is predominant. The Vaupes and Guiana Rivers originate in the Andes of southern Colombia, and both flow into the upper Rio Negro near the Colombian borders with Venezuela and Brazil. The lower part of Venezuela's mighty Orinoco is coffee and cream brown; it becomes stained by other rivers from the Colombian Andes, which flow through that country's Llanos region (comprised of plains or grasslands).

The most important fishing waters in this region are all black-water tributaries, and this area produces the very largest of the peacock bass and payara in Colombia, Brazil, and Venezuela. Natives call these rivers "starvation rivers" due to the absence of nutrients and biomass in the black waters. They are so acidic that mosquito larvae cannot survive and propagate. Population density is very low on these

A houseboat carrying anglers lies at rest on the Trombetas River, near its confluence with the Rio Negro.

rivers, which are all in remote areas with no roads, with poor soil for farming or grazing, and with little commercial fishing efforts or prospects. Why peacock bass grow to more than 25 pounds and payara to more than 35 pounds in these places remains a mystery. The color of the water is also a puzzle, but most believe that tannic acids leach out of the rain forest and into the flood waters during the six months each year when the forest is inundated by river waters.

The significant black-water rivers of this region all merge with the Orinoco or the Amazon. They include the Paru, Jari, Trombetas, Uatuma, Jatapu, Río Negro, and Río Branco in Brazil; Vaupes, Guaviare, Meta, and Vichada in Colombia; and the Cinaruco, Capanaparo, Ventuari, Casiquiare, Apure, Caura, Paragua, and Caroni in Venezuela.

The Casiquiare is a unique river because it diverts part of the upper Orinoco into the Guainia River on the Colombian border, forming the upper Río Negro, which flows south into the Amazon at Manaus, thus connecting the Orinoco with the Amazon.

The Caroni and Paragua Rivers are at the headwaters of Guri Reservoir and Dam in Venezuela. Guri is another 100-mile-long reservoir. The upper headwaters of the Caroni cascade from atop the mesa-like mountain Ayán Tupui, also known as the mile-high waterfall, Angel Falls. The tailwaters below Guri Dam, and three other dams on the Caroni, flow into the Orinoco at the city of Puerto Ordaz. Guri Lake, the Caroni River, and the Paragua River are important fishing waters for peacock bass and payara.

The Uatuma in Brazil was also dammed, creating Balbina Reservoir, but Balbina received heavy commercial fishing pressure from the time it was completed. Sportfishing in Balbina has been disappointing.

Gamefish species. The total number of fish species throughout the Amazon and Orinoco Basins is still unknown, but it numbers many hundreds, including aquarium species and some of the largest and most fearsome specimens in freshwater. Of these, relatively few fish species are the targets of anglers, and only a few others are caught incidentally.

The Amazon is generally thought to have an extreme abundance of fish, and although that may be true to some extent—especially in some waters—it is also a fact that much has changed since the 1960s, when there was almost no sportfishing by anyone and when local fishing was largely subsistence netting and spearing.

The growth of some cities and other population centers, the accompanying pollution, and a greater diversification in commercial fishing activities have led to diminished fisheries in accessible areas, as well as a reduction in the size of some of the larger species of fish. Recreational fishing by residents is growing rapidly in some South American countries, especially Brazil, but it is not a major factor in overall pressure on resources, except perhaps in a few isolated locations. Subsistence fishing in remote areas, and commercial fishing (especially gillnetting), are prominent activities.

Nevertheless, the Amazon and Orinoco watersheds region is one of the last great frontiers of sportfishing, boasting lots of fish and relatively few anglers. Peacock bass remain the single most highly pursued freshwater species, although many other fish have been only lightly—if at all—targeted by serious anglers. The size and remoteness of the watersheds have ensured a slow growth in sustained fishing tourism. There is virtually no tourism infrastructure in these countries, however, and that is unlikely to change in the near future, given the challenges posed by seasonal water levels, equipment, personnel, logistics, and myriad other matters. Thus, sportfishing development has largely been at the hands of individual entrepreneurs.

There are few lodges or camps relative to the size of this region, and most operators use houseboat-like river vessels (some fairly primitive) for accommodations and as a means of reaching distant waters, towing aluminum skiffs for fishing with them. Since the mid- to late 1980s, there has been a sharp growth in peacock bass fishing excursions—especially based out of Manaus, Brazil, and in the less risky areas of Venezuela such as at Guri Reservoir and its tributaries; only a small number of outfitters are conducting sportfishing operations, yet the places they visit are largely unexplored by nonfishing tourists. Virtually all fishing opportunities throughout these watersheds are managed by one of these operators, fishing in boats they provide and with local guides who are usually more navigator than guide. Self-guided fishing is impractical and a rarity, due in part to language barriers and in part to the lack of facilities and equipment.

Most Amazon fish can bite, slash, or sting, so it's best to let the guide handle and release fish, and to be very careful (use a gripping tool) if you do this yourself. Guides won't use nets for some species, such as payara, trairão, and piranha because they chomp through the net bottom. In this region, for most species, traveling anglers will need stronger rods, reels, lines, baits, hooks, split rings, knots, and other terminal tackle than they are likely accustomed to at home, as well as a strong heart for the topwater strikes of certain species. Surface strikes by peacock bass in particular are explosive.

Peacock bass. This fish is not a bass at all, but a cichlid. In Spanish it's called *pavón,* and in Portuguese (the language of Brazil) it is *tucunaré.* North Americans saw the similarity between this fish and the largemouth black bass and observed that it was readily taken on the same lures and stackle and by utilizing similar methods. Someone dubbed it a "peacock bass" due to the round spot on its tail. This nickname was a fortunate stroke of public relations genius; as word spread north, anglers flocked to South America in search of this new kind of "bass."

The peacock really did not need to be hyped because it has made and deserved its own great reputation. This one species has put the Amazon on the world's fishing map, and established itself on the most wanted list of many anglers. The peacock bass is bigger, stronger, harder fighting, jumps more and higher, and is generally much meaner than a largemouth bass or most anything else that swims in freshwater. It also hits surface lures like no other fish, and destroys lures, line, equipment, and the thumbs of anyone foolish enough to lip-lock it.

Although peacocks exist in a few places outside this region, all of the big specimens—and all of the world records—have been caught in lakes and rivers in Brazil, Venezuela, and Colombia.

Payara. This is the Spanish name for this so-called saber-toothed, silver salmon, which is also known as *cachorra* in Brazilian Portuguese. There is no English name for this toothy fish, and there is certainly nothing like it in North America. The payara is extremely strong and acrobatic, and found in rivers and reservoirs, especially in Brazil and Venezuela. In rivers, payara often frequent the swiftest water and hold near the largest boulders. In reservoirs they are a less predictable catch, sometimes caught by deep jigging. A specimen of more than 20 pounds will make several long runs and spectacular jumps. Its long canine teeth are very sharp and frequently puncture plastic and wooden lures. A strong steel leader and snap swivel, the stronger the better, are necessary for fishing. Large, tough, diving minnow plugs, lipless crankbaits, heavy spoons, and heavy-duty jigs are the lures of choice. Heavy-action rods, with baitcasting reels capable of holding 100 yards of 30-pound-test line, are commonly used. The current world record is 39 pounds.

Traíra/trairão. Known as *traíra* (trairão is a larger specimen) in Brazil, this species is called *imara* in Venezuela and *guabina* in Colombia. It resides in lakes and rivers, especially in shallow cover and in low-oxygen environs. It looks like a bowfin (mudfish). In the Amazon it grows to more than 40 pounds and strikes artificial lures, including topwater plugs. A trairão of 25 or 30 pounds may fight for more than 15 minutes before coming to the boat, after you've towed it around for awhile. This fish has a nasty set of teeth and is mean and ugly. The same tackle that is used for peacock bass and payara is useful for this fish.

Bicuda. This fish has a hard birdlike beak and a pikelike body. It hits a variety of baits, including topwater tackle. The bicuda runs like a barracuda and makes spectacular jumps. It may stay airborne for most of the battle. Bicuda seldom exceed 12 to 13 pounds, but such a fish will test heavy tackle. Pound for pound, it compares very favorably with a northern pike. Bicuda are always found in rivers.

Matrinxã. This species looks and fights like a hefty American shad and can grow to 11 to 12 pounds. A close cousin, the *jatuarana,* may weigh as much as 17 pounds and is usually caught in the Pantanal region, just south of the Amazon range of the matrinxã. Most matrinxã in the Amazonas run from 3 to 6 pounds. Small spoons, in-line spinners, and jigs are very productive, with lighter spinning tackle, 6- to 10-pound line, and steel leaders recommended. This fish is very acrobatic, and its silver-scaled sides flash through the water when it runs and in the sunlight when it jumps, which it does often. A matrinxã smoked on an open fire is as tasty as any salmon. It is a resident of clear-water rivers.

Piranhas. These notorious, toothy critters are found throughout the Amazon and Orinoco watersheds; specimens of 3 to 8 pounds are great sport. Piranhas, like almost all sportfish of this region, are great table fare, and close cousins of pacu and tambaqui, which can grow to more than 30 pounds. That's big enough and strong enough to make you think about cutting your line after a 10-minute battle and no sign of surrender (from the fish). The biting strength of all three can crush nuts, shells, and bones. Small spoons, jigs, and lipless crankbaits are effective for these species, with a steel leader advisable. There are dozens of species of piranhas (the morocotto variety of the Orinoco is a close relative of the tambaqui), and some are vegetarians. These are all river species, but they can adapt to lakes. Piranhas are commonly found in rivers, lakes, and lagoons in most watersheds.

Arawana. Called *aruanã* in Portuguese and *arahuana* in Spanish, and also known as the "monkey fish," this acrobatic performer with a snakelike body can leap many feet into the air to get food. The arawana grows to 11 pounds or more and leaps repeatedly when hooked, or thrashes its body on the surface. This fish also takes a variety of lures, including topwater plugs. It is most often caught in lakes and lagoons or in backwater areas of rivers.

Amazonas—Region by Fishing Season (Dry Season)

Sportfishing Regions of South America's Amazonas

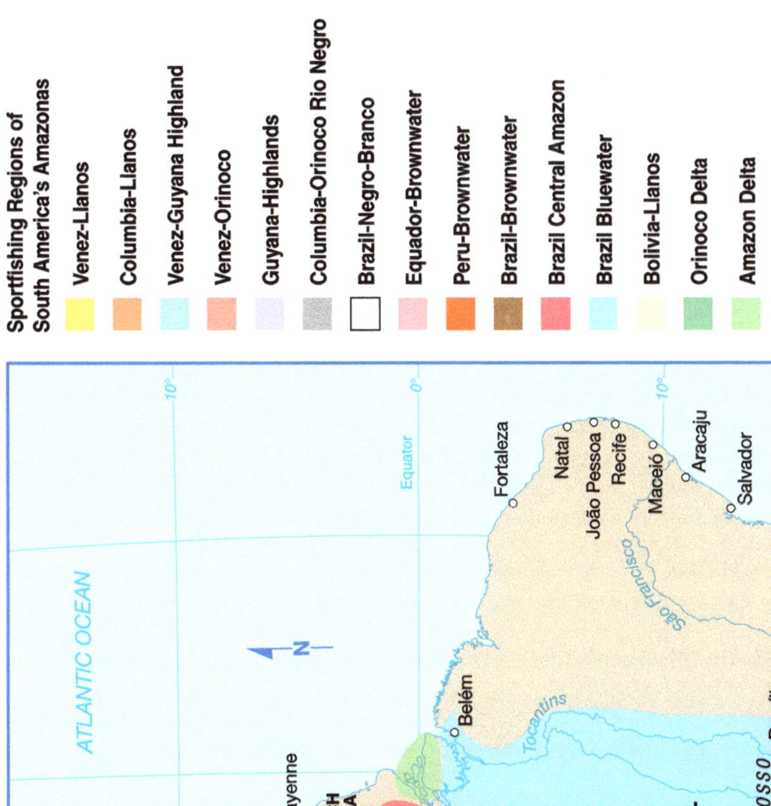

Regions by Predominant River Water Colors

B

Sardinata. Found in the Orinoco watershed of Venezuela and Colombia, this "leaping maniac of the Orinoco" looks like a small tarpon, grows to 15 pounds, and frequently fights more out of the water than in it when hooked. Small surface plugs, spoons, and lipless crankbaits are effective. The sardinata is frequently caught in lakes, lagoons, and river backwaters.

Pirarucu. This giant-scaled fish can grow to several hundred pounds and is occasionally hooked by an Amazon angler, resulting in Moby Dick–like tales. Natives shoot them with bow and spear, with a strong rope attached, and the fish tows the native's dugout canoe around for hours before giving in, or tries to sink the boat. A machete is at the ready to cut the rope. These fish frequently tail-walk across the surface in rivers, and the sight of this spectacle is awesome to behold. The huge scales from a large pirarucu are used as files or sandpaper. Pirarucu are at home in rivers and lakes.

Catfish. Sorubim and pintado are two shovel-nosed, tiger-striped, or spotted catfish that frequently strike spoons, crankbaits, diving plugs, and jigs. Both get very large (40- to 80-pound specimens are not uncommon), and they are great fighters. Most Amazon catfish are great table fare, and these two battlers are very tasty as well. Many visiting anglers consider these two species gamefish because they are often enticed into taking artificial baits and give a great account of themselves in battle. Both are more commonly caught in rivers but frequently cruise lakes and lagoons for food.

Jau, dourada, pirarara, piraiba, and other catfish may be encountered by anglers. Some catfish species in the Amazon, such as bagre, valenton, and dourada, grow to several hundred pounds and can be seen hanging like sides of beef in local fish markets. These catfish are usually caught by stillfishing with bait and heavy tackle. Big catfish are seldom found in the smaller lakes and lagoons of the Amazon but are frequently taken from rivers and from larger lakes, such as those adjacent to the main Amazon River channel.

Other species. Some other species are frequently encountered by anglers in the Amazonas region. One of these is apapa, a freshwater herringlike fish that is comparable in size, appearance, and fighting ability to white bass; a 6-pounder is very large. The pescada-do-piauí, or corvina, is a drum or croaker-like fish that can grow to 17 pounds; when schools of these are found, it's great fishing fun. The curimbatá is a silver-scaled, bottom feeder frequently caught on jigs and spoons, which fights very much like a white bass or hybrid striper; it can reach weights of nearly 17 pounds and is a double handful of trouble in swift waters. The jacunda could be compared to the rock bass of streams in the United States. The smaller peacock bass, like the butterfly and royal varieties, could be compared to smallmouth bass. Almost without exception, these South American counterparts of prized North American gamefish are bigger, stronger, and meaner.

Most all of the species found in the Amazon and Orinoco watersheds are also found in the swamplike Pantanal region and River Plate region, both located just south of the Amazon Basin in Brazil. It has been reported that the infamous golden dorado has also been taken in the Amazon Basin, but this is not substantiated and it would be a rare catch.

A great many more species, some very colorful and unusual looking, are taken occasionally on rod and reel, and certainly by locals using nets. The numbers, varieties, sizes, beauty, and fighting abilities of these species—combined with the natural, unspoiled beauty of their environs—certainly make this one of the world's premier sportfishing destinations.

When and where to fish. A seasonal approach is the right way to plan for a South American fishing adventure, and the best way to view the Amazon and Orinoco watersheds is to acknowledge their various distinctive fishing regions. Some of these are established by political boundaries, some by seasonal differences, and some by limitations to access due to physical boundaries. Most of these regions have a few knowledgeable and capable outfitters and guides. In others there is little or no infrastructure for sportfishing.

Southeast Brazil's blue-water region. By mid-April the rivers of this area have dropped to an acceptable level, and the dry season is well underway. Beginning in the upper reaches of the Araguaia, Xingu, or Tapajos, you could fish this region through the month of October, prospecting the lower end of these rivers later in the season. You can expect to catch a great variety of species here, but not huge peacock bass or trophy-size payara. Ten-pound peacocks are a realistic expectation, however, and there are some 20-pound payara with a rare larger specimen. In addition, you will surely catch a good many other species, including bicuda, pacu, matrinxã, trairão, piranhas, corvina, sorubim, pintado, curimbatá, and a variety of catfish. It is not uncommon to catch a dozen different species during a week's stay on one of the rivers here.

Local gateways to this region are Alta Floresta, São Felix do Araguaia, São Felix do Xingu, and Tucurui. International gateways are Belem and Brasilia. These rivers, all flowing out of the Brazilian Highlands, are among the most beautiful in all of Amazonia.

Many Amazonia references do not include the Araguaia-Tocantins watershed within their defined boundaries of the Amazon basin. This is only because this system empties into a subchannel of the Amazon south of huge Marajo Island, located in the deltaic mouth of the Amazon. The flow from the Araguaia-Tocantins passes Belem as it enters the Atlantic from this southern route. Hydrologists consider the Amazon channel to be the channel that is routed north of Marajo Island, entering the Atlantic Ocean at that point. If the southernmost channel were included in the full length of the

Amazon, then it would be not only the world's largest river by volume, but also the longest. Actually, the Araguaia is in every way a true Amazonas river, with a typical Amazon rain forest watershed.

The lower Araguaia-Tocantins has been dammed to provide hydroelectric power, forming huge Tucurui Lake. Like Guri Lake in Venezuela, it is an important fishery for peacock bass and even for payara in its upper reaches. Unlike Guri, there is a large, well-organized commercial fishing operation here on a year-round basis, which has severely impacted sportfishing results.

Due to the large number of rapids and waterfalls on the Tapajos and Xingu, and many of their tributaries, this remote and sparsely populated region remains cut off and isolated. There are also a number of Indian reserves here, with little or no acccss to these reserved lands and waters. There are a few outfitters in the region, however, and they have hosted a number of international anglers.

Brazil's central Amazon basin. The dishpan-like central Amazon flood plain has its gateway in Manaus at a crossroads where the largest tributaries of the Amazon come together. The Río Negro flows southward past Manaus, where it joins the muddy Solimões rolling down from the Andes of Peru. At this point, the mighty river is called the Amazon, and several miles east of Manaus that great brown-water river of southern Amazonia—the Madeira—joins the Amazon.

This central Amazon basin is impacted by seasonal runoff from huge tributaries on almost a continual basis, so the fishing season in this region is short. Water levels in the tributaries and lakes in this area are low enough to provide excellent fishing from about mid-August to mid- or late November. Although many of the larger rivers hold brown water, black-water tributaries like the Uatuma, Jatapu, Trombetas, Nhumanda, Marmelos, Tupana-Maderinha, Jari, and Paru provide excellent fishing for peacock bass, along with most other Amazon species.

Blue-water rivers also run here, and black-water tributaries of the Manicore, Aripuanã, Abacaxis, and Maués provide excellent fishing in season. Peacock bass can reach 20 pounds but are most frequently encountered in the teens. Good-size payara can be had in the upper reaches of those black-water rivers coming out of the Guiana Highlands from August through November, and from the lower Xingu and Tapajos Rivers during the fall fishing season. More and larger payara, however, come from areas north and south of this central flood plain. Arawana, piranhas, and many species of catfish are frequently caught in this region.

Manaus hosts a number of houseboat-based fishing operations that are highly mobile and may travel north, south, east, and west to reach good fishing waters in season in the Central Amazon basin. However, they can and do extend their season by moving up the Río Negro to the north, accessing those tributaries from November through April in the Río Negro's black waters near the equator.

Brazil's black-water region. From November through April, this area of northwest Brazil provides some of the greatest peacock bass fishing the Amazonas has to offer in tributaries of the Río Negro and Río Branco. The Vaupes, from Colombia, also enters the Río Negro here in Brazil, as does the Branco. The largest black-water river on earth, the Río Negro flows south to the Amazon. The Branco is actually tinged brown for most of the year, but like the Orinoco to the north in Venezuela, most of its tributaries are black-water rivers.

The current 27-pound world-record peacock bass was caught in a tributary of the Río Negro, and tributaries of the Branco have yielded a 26-pounder and numerous fish over 20 pounds in the late 1990s. The Vaupes in Colombia has a reputation for giant peacocks, too, as does the upper Río Negro and the Casiquiare. There is no question that this region is home to giant peacock bass.

This sparsely populated region is beautiful, remote, and contains more than a dozen species of the most sought after gamefish species. Payara grow large here, but sportfishing operations have concentrated on the big peacock while largely ignoring the swifter, boulder-strewn rapids of the region's rivers, where huge payara lurk. Local gateways here are Barcelos and Boa Vista, and international access is through Manaus. Boa Vista may also be reached through Caracas.

Venezuela's black-water region. The tributaries of the mighty Orinoco in Venezuela are predominantly black-water rivers. These are the Ventuari, Sipapo, Atabapo, Conorochito, Pasimoni, Pasiba, and the Casiquiare and its tributaries, all in the Venezuelan state of Amazonas. World-record-class peacock bass, payara, and many other species are routinely taken from these waters. The Pasimoni produced the largest peacock caught on a fly rod, a fish of $25^1/_2$ pounds. A 31-pound payara caught in the Orinoco near Puerto Ayacucho was the all-tackle world record for many years, and the Orinoco in that area continues to produce world-class payara.

The season here is from November through April, and these black waters are almost a mirror image of those in the Brazilian black-water region. They are located just south of the Guiana Highland mountain range, which separates the two countries, leaving similar terrain on either side of the range. The renowned and primitive Yanomami Indians consider the lands on both sides of the mountains and borders their homeland, and tribal families are located in both Venezuela and Brazil.

The Brazilian and Venezuelan black-water regions are connected by the Casiquiare, which runs from the Orinoco into the Guainia to form

A layer of natural barnacle cement $^3/_{10,000}$ inch thick over 1 square inch will support a weight of 7,000 pounds.

the headwaters of the Río Negro, which in turn flows into the Amazon at Manaus, connecting two giant watersheds. Puerto Ayacucho is the local gateway, and Caracas the international gateway. These waters are home to sardinata, morocotto, imara, piranhas, and numerous giant catfish, in addition to peacock bass and payara.

Colombia's black-water region. Here the Orinoco is fed by the Tomo, Vichada, Mataveni, Guaviare, Inirida, and Guainia Rivers on the Venezuela border (which is the Orinoco River) and the Vaupes eventually feeds the Río Negro in Brazil. These are the black-water rivers of Colombia, and they are full of trophy-size peacocks and payara and all of the other species common to the neighboring Venezuela-Orinoco tributaries.

This area in Colombia and Venezuela contains all the speckled, spotted, butterfly, and royal varieties of peacock bass in its rivers. The Mataveni produced a previous 26-pound world-record speckled peacock, and Colombia's side of the Orinoco produced the previous 31-pound record payara. This region, unfortunately, has had no sportfishing operations for international anglers for some time because of safety concerns due to illegal drug production and trafficking, and frequent kidnappings. This is truly a blow, because the remote, productive, lightly populated, and beautiful rivers, lakes, and lagoons here provide great fishing from November through April. Gateways are Puerto Correño locally, and Bogota for international access.

Venezuela and Colombia's llanos regions. Brown-water rivers flow toward the Orinoco basin from the Andes of northern Colombia and through the llanos of central Colombia and Venezuela. In Venezuela these rivers are the Apure, Arauca, Capanaparo, and Cinaruco. In Colombia they are the Meta and Bita. The smaller tributaries, lakes, and lagoons contain black water during the dry or fishing season (November to April), but for most of the year these rivers color the lower Orinoco a very brown hue. This llanos area has never produced the giant peacocks and payaras found just south in the black-water Amazonas, but great numbers of teen-size and smaller fish have been consistently found in rivers like the Cinaruco and Bita.

The earliest known success at facilitating anadromous fish passage in America was the 1882 construction of a pool-type fish ladder at Willamette Falls, Oregon.

Unfortunately, drug trafficking, kidnapping, and plane hijackings have taken their toll on this area, and sportfishing camps in Colombia have all closed. In Venezuela, they remain open with caution and extreme safety measures in force. Many roads, ranches, and private river camps are now located in this area. The fishing remains very good, but a very real threat to the safety of tourists in the area exists. Local gateways are Puerto Carreño in Colombia, and Puerto Ayacucho and San Fernando de Apure in Venezuela. International gateways are Bogota and Caracas.

Venezuela's Guiana Highlands. Angel Falls cascades from the mile-high top of Ayán Tupuy Mountain in east-central Venezuela, and the stream below cuts through the Guiana Highlands and Gran Sabana region of Venezuela to the Caroni River. The Caroni flows north toward the Orinoco River and is joined in this highland valley by the Paragua River. These are the headwaters of Guri Lake, a huge impoundment dammed for hydroelectric power production at Guri Dam and by three more dams near the boom towns of Puerto Ordaz and Ciudad Bolívar.

Huge Guri Lake has been an important sportfishing destination since the mid-1980s for peacock bass and payara. While 15- to 20-pound peacocks are still caught, and payara of 20 pounds are caught on occasion in the lake, the world-record-class payara in the Paragua River are now the main attraction in this area. The 39-pound all-tackle world-record payara, and most of the line-class records, were set on the Paragua and its falls in the upper river, above the lake. There are still a number of camps on the upper end of the lake near the two rivers. The season is from November through April. Access is via Caracas to Puerto Ordaz, or Ciudad Bolívar.

Brown-water regions (Peru, Brazil, Ecuador, and Colombia). By late May or early June, the rainy season has ended in the upper Amazon rivers flowing out of the Andes in Ecuador and Peru. These nutrient-rich and chocolate brown rivers include the Napo and Pastaza in Ecuador and Peru, the Maranon and Ucayali in Peru, the Putamayo and Caquetá in Colombia, the Yavari and Jupurá in Brazil, and several more that join to form the Solimões in Brazil. The Juruá, Purus, and Madeira also add to this great brown massive river, which then becomes the Amazon.

From June or July until the November rainy season, it is fishing time in the upper Amazon's brown-water tributaries. Anglers concentrate on the black-water tributaries, lakes, and oxbows off the large rivers. (It is worth noting that throughout the Amazon, commercial fishermen and native subsistence fishermen ply the area year-round, in all kinds of waters and at all water levels, for all kinds of fish. Keep that in mind when asking locals about the best times and places to catch fish.) In this region, many of the lakes become landlocked in the dry season, and it may be necessary to leave the river and portage into the lakes, where small boats or dugout canoes have been placed for the occasion. Thick vegetation at the mouths of lakes may also make access difficult. Vegetation growth on these sand and mud bottoms, as well as dead fall trees may be the keys to locating peacock bass and other species.

These are usually slow, sluggish rivers (the tributaries), and in the dry season the absence of swift current and rocks is accompanied by an absence of swift-water species like payara, morocotto, sardinata, and matrinxã. You may find sabalo, however, in moving black-water rivers and creeks. This species is related to the matrinxã.

These waters generally hold piranhas, payara, pirarucu, arawana, butterfly peacock bass, and many catfish species, including sorubim. Peacocks do not exceed 13 pounds, most won't reach 10 pounds, and the norm is 3- to 6-pounders. The number of peacocks can be very good in lakes that are not fished by locals or commercial fishermen, but finding those waters can be difficult.

Iquitos is the gateway to this region in Peru, and there are a couple of sportfishing outfitters in the area. Most operations cater to the ecotourist, which is seldom suitable for the avid angler. In Quito, Ecuador, you may find someone to organize a fishing expedition into Amazonas, but you should be prepared to rough it and do a lot of exploration. As in Peru, peacock bass are not big in Ecuador.

In Brazil, tour operators have largely ignored the brown-water region, becausc of the much smaller peacocks and the existence of many villages along most of the more productive fishing waters. It costs the same to fish for small peacocks as it does to fish for big ones, and the big ones are on more attractive and remote rivers. The access to these Brazilian brown-water rivers is through Manaus to Tabatinga, Coari, Tefe, or Fonte Boa. In Colombia you may try to find an outfitter in Leticia.

Another Peruvian sportfishing destination is the Manu National Rain Forest, near Puerto Maldonado in southern Peru. Nearby Cusco and Machu Picchu are popular tourist attractions. Rivers here are the Manu, Madre de Dios, Piedras, and Tambopata, with the latter boasting large payara. There may be an outfitter in Puerto Maldonado who will guide an exploratory float-fishing/camping trip in the area for peacocks, piranha, sabalo, and/or payara. Efforts at sport-fishing here have been a hit-or-miss proposition.

Guyana's highland rivers. The Rupunuini, Essequibo, and New Rivers in Guyana harbor plenty of peacocks, payara, piraracu, catfish, and piranhas, but there is no infrastructure for sport-fishing in the remote upper-watershed rivers. Finding someone in Georgetown, Guyana, who knows fishing in these rivers may be difficult, but that's the place to start. Presently there are no outfitters offering fishing expeditions into this region. An angler looking for a real adventure may want to take a chance in Guyana. The fish are certainly still there and waiting.

Bolivia's llanos region. The rivers in this region originate in the Bolivian and Peruvian Andes and flow through hundreds of miles of plains and grasslands before forming the headwaters of the Río Madeira in Brazil at Abuna. These tributaries are the Guapore, Mamore, Beni, Abuna, and Madre de Dios. Most are brown-water and some are black-water rivers.

This Llanos area is a huge, saucerlike depression with north-flowing rivers. The Madeira, strengthened by combined waters, cuts through the highland here as it rushes north to the Amazon. Some large lakes have formed in this vast and relatively flat topography, and many are full of small peacock bass. Payara thrive in some of the swifter streams, and also catfish and piranhas. During floods in the rainy season, these waters mix with those of the swampy Pantanal area, resulting in a common pool of many species.

The fishing season here is from May or June through October. Gateways in local areas are Vilhena, Porto Velho, and Guajara-Mirim in Brazil, and Cobija, Trinidad, and Riberalta in Bolivia. International flights into this region are through Santa Cruz and La Paz in Bolivia, and Manaus and Brasilia in Brazil.

Delta regions of Brazil and Venezuela. The delta regions of both the Orinoco and the Amazon contain peacock bass and other freshwater species, but very little is known about freshwater fishing in the many channels and lagoons in these two areas. Outfitters in both have tried to establish fishing operations for tarpon and other salt-/brackish-water species, but not for peacock bass. These two frontiers require further exploration.

Travel suggestions. The Amazon is not the hostile environment pictured in some B movies. You will not be eaten by snakes or jaguars, speared by natives, or caught up in a revolution (although there is some danger, as noted in and near Colombia). Deadly diseases are extremely rare among tourists here, and the cities and villages of these regions are more crime-free than most cities inhabited by North Americans.

Probably the biggest concerns will be protecting skin from intense equatorial sun and the bite of tiny insects. Immunization and preventative medication against yellow fever and malaria are recommended but not required. Sun dehydration is prevented by consuming lots of bottled water during the fishing day and with meals. Tourists visiting this region for the first time may experience an upset stomach and diarrhea.

Traveling here is really no different than traveling to any other part of the world, although more patience may be required at certain times and places. Those journeying to remote areas anywhere should be in reasonably good health, as medical facilities may be difficult to reach in a reasonable period of time during an emergency.

Saltwater

Brazil's saltwater sportfishing has been called a sleeping giant at least since the mid-1970s, and it seems to continue that way, despite an enormous coastline and a wide range of species. The main reason is that relatively few Brazilians (the majority of whom reside in just a few areas, mostly Río de Janeiro) have large sportfishing vessels, and charter operations have been almost nonexistent. That's not to say that there has been no fishing, as private boats have plied offshore waters for marlin and sailfish regularly; but it can still be said that the offshore environs of Brazil constitute a virgin or near-virgin big-game fishery, and that only minimal effort has been generated in just a few areas.

Given the size of the country, the amount of water to cover, and the lack of boats to cover it, this relative lack of interest is not difficult to understand. Nevertheless, efforts to increase the interest of serious anglers in the blue marlin, white marlin, and sailfish here—especially blues—has slowly boosted charter operations, and today it is possible to find commercial sportfishing ventures in a few locations.

Most of this activity occurs from Río de Janeiro north to Ilhéus, a distance of more than 600 miles, with activity concentrated out of Río, Victoria, and Comandatuba Island south of Ilhéus. Vitoria has produced at least seven world-record white marlin, including an all-tackle fish of 181 pounds, 14 ounces, and in 1992 it saw the capture of an all-tackle world-record blue marlin that weighed 1,402 pounds and 2 ounces. Nearby seamounts, a strong southerly current flow, and sharp dropoffs—especially near Vitoria—are key factors, but conditions may be even better farther north, from Salvador to Natal and beyond, and offshore from Natal to such structures as Atol das Rocas and the 21-island archipelago of Fernando de Noronha, a former penal colony that rises 13,000 feet from the ocean floor.

Wahoo, dolphin, yellowfin tuna, and king mackerel are also among the offshore seamount catch, and there were once many sightings of broadbill swordfish. The wahoo and dolphin can get large, and the sailfish average 60 to 65 pounds. The spring and summer seasons here—from October through February—are the primary time for billfish, with northern areas getting the early burst and southern areas the later one. Río de Janeiro, for example, sees its best sailfishing from November through February, usually peaking in December and January. Blue marlin arrive in mid-October, beginning some 60 to 70 miles south and west. White marlin are uncommon at Río but bountiful off Vitoria; sailfish, on the other hand, are rare off Vitoria.

A smorgasbord of other species is available along the coast and inshore, almost none pursued by visiting anglers. Tarpon, snook, jack crevalle, various snapper and grouper, bluefish, weakfish, mackerel, drum, pompano, amberjack, and many others frequent these waters. Large bays, estuaries, and various river deltas with lagoons and lakes exist, and inshore opportunities—sometimes well up tidal rivers—should be present, although boats and operators to exploit them may not be; recent information about these areas is lacking.

BREACHING

The free jumping of an unhooked fish in offshore waters.

BREAKAWAY LEADER

A light leader, branching from a heavier main line, that usually extends to a sinker or other weight and is intended to break free if it gets snagged. This is intended to save the lure, bait, and other terminal tackle on the main line.

BREAKERS

Waves reaching their highest point in shallow water; usually refers to waves that crest into foam on a beach.

BREAKING FISH

Fish that are chasing baitfish, usually in open water, and herding them to the surface while feeding, with the result that the bait and/or the pursuing fish erupt on the surface in such a manner as to be visible from a distance. This event is often accompanied by active birds who hover over the melee, trying to pick up stunned or injured baitfish.

BREAKING STRENGTH

The amount of pressure, expressed in pounds or kilograms, that must be applied to an unknotted line before the molecules part and the line breaks. This may also be expressed as breaking strain.

See: Line.

BREAKLINE

Where the sloping bottom of a body of water changes distinctly from one contour level to the next, as determined by observation of a sonar device or contours on a hydrographic map or chart. Most often used with regard to lakes, this term generally references a place where the bottom moves more sharply from one depth level to the next. Depending on depth, species, and presence or absence of other underwater features, the breakline may be a place to find fish, especially during warm weather.

See: Dropoff.

BREAKOFF

To end a fight with a fish by breaking the line. Occasionally this term refers to losing a fish because the hook pulls out, but the primary meaning is losing a fish through line breakage. An unintentional breakoff occurs when the line is cut or is stressed beyond its breaking point. An intentional breakoff occurs when an angler deliberately applies more tension to the line than it can stand in order to end a fight. This is usually done by increasing the drag on a reel, applying pressure to the line on a reel spool, pointing the rod directly at the fish, and holding tight when it surges away.

B

BREAKWATER

A man-made barrier to break the impact of waves and/or current at the mouth of a harbor or inlet, in front of a marina, or in front of a boat launch or other access site. A breakwater is usually detached from the shoreline, and may be parallel to the shore or at an angle to it. It is built up from the ocean or lake bottom and usually protrudes above the surface, at least to average wave height, except under extreme water conditions; it may or may not have navigational aids. A breakwater serves essentially the same function as a jetty *(see)*; when it extends directly from the shore, the terms are interchangeable.

A breakwater for a harbor is usually made of concrete or stone, and anglers may be able to fish directly from it. For those fish not accessible to anglers by foot, trolling, casting, or drifting nearby may be worthwhile.

Breakwaters may exist in noncoastal locations, such as in large inland lakes and reservoirs, where they are usually intended to diffuse wave action and protect marinas. They may be fashioned from various materials, including auto tires, and are seldom accessible or fished from.

See: Jetty Fishing; Surf Fishing.

BREAM

Many species of both freshwater and saltwater fish around the world are referred to as bream, particularly in Australia, the United Kingdom, and the United States. In the U.S., "bream" (pronounced "brim") is a colloquial expression for various freshwater panfish species, particularly sunfish *(see)* and especially bluegills *(see)*.

In Europe, the bream pursued by anglers are members of the Cyprinidae family and are relatives of carp *(see)*, barbel *(see)*, and tench *(see)*. These primarily small or midsize fish (less than 8 pounds) are bottom feeders and are widely distributed. They are also a popular coarse fish *(see)*. The primary quarry is the bronze bream *(see: bream, bronze)*, which is also known as the common bream or carp bream.

In saltwater, various members of the Sparidae family are known as sea bream, and are related to porgies *(see)*. Sea bream *(see: bream, sea)* occur in temperate and tropical waters worldwide.

BREAM, BRONZE *Abramis brama.*

Other names—bronze bream, common bream, carp bream, skimmer (small fish) bream; French: *brême;* German: *brachsen brasse;* Italian: *brama.*

This popular coarse fish *(see)* is a member of the Cyprinidae family and a relative of carp *(see)*, barbel *(see)*, and tench *(see)*. It is the largest-growing and most abundant member of the bream clan and is pursued for sport and food, having local commercial value in some parts of its range.

Identification. The bronze bream has a comparatively small head and a deep body that produces

Bronze Bream

a broad girth. The laterally compressed body is punctuated with a humplike appearance on the back, just ahead of the dorsal fin, and tapers sharply to the caudal peduncle and a deeply forked tail. The back is dark brown, and the sides are golden brown, fading to a grayish white on the belly. It has a long and tapered anal fin, and the fins may have a light reddish tint. The scales are small, and the body is covered with thick mucus.

Juveniles are lighter in coloration, being silvery with black fins; these young fish are confused with a similar-looking silver bream *(Blicca bjoerkna)*, which is found in many of the same waters but is much smaller at maximum weight (about 1 pound) and slender.

Bronze bream with light broad stripes inhabit parts of Ireland, where they are referred to as Irish bream, and can grow to 10 pounds. Bream may breed with roach *(see)* and produce a hybrid fish that is a bit lighter, slightly less humpbacked, and with a shorter anal fin. The anal fins are a distinguishing difference, with 14 to 19 rays in the hybrid and 23 to 29 in the parent bream.

Size. The all-tackle world record for bronze bream is a Swedish fish caught in 1993 in Lake Vanern that weighed 12 pounds, 7 ounces. Bream have been reported to twice that weight, however, and commonly weigh 3 to 7 pounds.

Distribution. Bronze bream range from Ireland eastward throughout most of Europe and into central Asia.

Habitat. Stillwaters and deep, slow-flowing rivers are the primary preferences of bronze bream. Their wide distribution includes lakes and canals, and they locate in places with rich bottom life, usually over a mud bottom.

Life history/Behavior. Bream spawn in late spring and early summer, usually in weedy shallows, broadcasting numerous adhesive eggs rather than constructing a nest; this activity is usually accompanied by an obvious splashing and rolling commotion. The fry stay in schools and gather in large congregations. Bream are one of the most intensive schooling of all cyprinid species, and they gather in large groups when smaller, tapering to small schools of a few of the oldest individuals. These schools (called shoals) generally consist of similar-size individuals.

B

Schools of bream wander and feed, often in habitual patterns or paths of travel. Their route is frequently discernible due to the roiling, muddying, or bubbling of the water caused when numbers of these fish feed by rooting among plants, sediment, and soft bottom. They also have a tendency to roll on the surface prior to or during feeding, another indicator of their presence.

Food and feeding habits. Bream eat insect larvae, worms, mollusks, crustaceans, algae, and other bottom organisms. They occasionally feed in midwater, perhaps when the school is thick and stirring up food, and less occasionally on the surface, but the bulk of activity occurs on the bottom. Bream assume a more angular, rather than horizontal, position when feeding on the bottom, and their tail is pointed up as the mouth, used like a sucking tool, is positioned to pick food off the bottom. They are extremely effective at vacuuming up what they are after, blowing on the bottom to wash out food and then sucking up what has been uncovered. By alternately sucking and blowing several times, they wash their food and remove sand from it.

Like tench, bream are low-light feeders and are more active at night, dawn, and dusk, and on dark days. They are active in temperatures up to 68°F and relatively inactive in water below 45°F. Because they are a schooling fish, when active they may sometimes be caught in good numbers in a given location.

Angling. Bream are tenacious although not spectacular fighters, but they are a popular fish for many Europeans, especially British anglers. Fishing for bream is similar to fishing for tench and other coarse fish, although more bream may be available in a given spot.

Bottom fishing with assorted baits is the favored technique for bream. This involves intensive prebaiting or chumming, using groundbait *(see)* and an assortment of prepared, processed, and natural baits. Baiting may be done for long periods in advance of fishing, and is considered necessary to acclimate a school to a location and to keep them there while angling. Sometimes a school of bream come through and stay only long enough to scour the bait before moving on.

As with other coarse fishing, maggots, corn, worms, cheese, bread, pastes, and other items are used, particularly those commodities employed in prebaiting or chumming (although in areas where fish have repeatedly been caught with the same bait, they become conditioned to avoid that item).

Hooked baits may be fished with a float or without one, but many bream anglers prefer a bolt rig *(see)* and a bottom feeder (a device for precise-location chumming). Anglers use rods from 11 to 14 feet in length, line from 4 to 10 pounds in strength, and No. 6 to 14 bait hooks.

Most bream anglers fish from the bank or from shore, and often at distances of more than 60 feet from the water's edge. Where possible, fishing from an anchored boat, with the ability to move to new locations, seems beneficial.

BREAM, SEA

Numerous members of the Sparidae family that are found in temperate and tropical waters are referred to as sea bream, or seabream. They are related to porgies *(see),* have moderate to important significance commercially (depending on abundance and geography), and are commonly caught by inshore anglers. These fish are tough, dogged fighters that are commendable on appropriate light tackle, and they rate as excellent table fare. The more commonly distributed and popular species are noted here.

The red seabream *(Pagellus bogaravero)* is an important food and recreational fish found in the eastern Atlantic Ocean, from Norway through the Strait of Gibraltar and into the western Mediterranean Sea, including Cape Blanc in Mauritania, Madeira, and the Canary Islands. It has red fins and a reddish tint on the back and sides, lightening to the belly, with a large dark spot above the pectoral fin and behind the gill cover. It is also known as the blackspotted seabream and common seabream. Other names include, in Danish: *blankensteen;* Dutch: *zeebrasem;* Finnish: *pikkupagelli;* French: *dorade rose;* German: *meerbrasse, seekarpfen;* Italian: *rovello;* Norwegian: *flekkpagell;* Portuguese: *besugo, esparidoes;* Spanish: *besugo, bogarrabella;* Swedish: *fläckpagell.*

The black seabream *(Spondyliosoma cantharus)* is an important food and recreational fish found in the eastern Atlantic Ocean from Scandinavia south to northern Namibia, including the Strait of Gibraltar, the Mediterranean Sea, and, rarely, in the Black Sea, as well as in Madeira and the Canary and Cape Verde Islands. It is a silvery gray color with a dark back and six or seven bars on the flanks. Other names include, in Danish: *lavrude;* Dutch: *zeekarpfen;* Finnish: *meriruutana;* French: *dorade grise, griset;* German: *seekarpfe, streffenbrassen;* Italian: *tanuta;* Norwegian: *havsruda;* Portuguese: *choupa;* Spanish: *chopa;* Swedish: *havsrusa;* Turkish: *sarigöz.*

The black bream *(Acanthopagrus butcheri)* is a popular recreational catch found in the western Pacific Ocean in Australia, from southern New South Wales to Victoria, Tasmania, South Australia, and as far north as Shark Bay in Western Australia; it is possibly found in New Zealand. The black bream's body color can vary with its habitat from a silver, bronze, or olive brown dorsally, to a whitish belly, and dusky gray to black fins. It is also known as sea bream, eastern black bream, and southern black bream.

The silver bream *(Acanthopagrus australis)* is also a popular recreational catch found in the western Pacific Ocean, occurring in Australia from southern New South Wales to northern Queensland, and also reported in Taiwan. The silver bream's body is silvery to olive green dorsally, shading to a whitish belly, and its ventral and anal fins are splashed with a bright to dull yellow. Its pectoral fin has tinges of yellow in it, and there is a dark spot at the base; the caudal fin is distinguished by a distinct black trailing edge. It is also known as yellowfin bream, sea bream, eastern black bream, southern bream, golden bream, and, in Japanese, as *ósutoraria-kichinu.*

The river bream *(Acanthopagrus berda)* is a prominent commercial and recreational catch that is wide ranging in the Indian and western Pacific Oceans, occurring from South Africa to Japan and northern Australia, and appearing in the lower Zambezi and Lucuara Rivers in Zimbabwe and South Africa respectively. It is also known as pikey bream (Australia), black bream, black porgy, black seabream, dark-finned porgy, sly bream. Other names include, in Arabic: *shaami;* Cantonese: *hak lap;* French: *pargo picnic;* Japanese: *nanyóchinu;* Malay: *bandan, kuku, kapas-kapas.*

The western yellowfin bream *(Acanthopagrus latus)* is a prominent commercial and recreational catch that is wide ranging in the Indian and western Pacific Oceans, occurring from the Persian Gulf through India to the Philippines, north to Japan and south to the northwest coast of Australia; it also appears in Djibouti.

The sea bream *(Archosargus rhomboidalis)* appears in the western Atlantic Ocean from the northeastern Gulf of Mexico to Argentina, including the Caribbean and West Indies. Its bluish back is streaked with gold, the belly is silvery, and there is a black spot on each side just above the pectoral fins.

Size. Most of these sea bream can reach a maximum weight of between 3.5 and 4.5 kilograms, but on average they weigh between 0.5 and 1 kilogram. The sea bream of the western Atlantic is rarely more than a foot long.

Habitat. Some sea bream are abundant in estuaries, and some are found in deeper, offshore waters. Some move up into brackish water but not into freshwater. The black bream, however, which rarely ventures beyond its estuary confines, ranges well upstream in freshwater. The silver bream can be found in estuaries and also in offshore waters, especially in the vicinity of reefs, in the corners of beaches, along surf beaches, and off rocky headlands. It also moves upstream into brackish water but seldom extends to the freshwater reaches. As adults, red and black seabream are found in deeper continental slope waters (the latter from 50 to 300 meters and the former from 400 to 700 meters). Coastal and offshore sea bream are found over a wide variety of bottoms. In the estuarine environment, bream frequent seagrass beds, underwater reefs and rocks, bridge pilings that grow mussels, and oyster beds.

Spawning behavior. Red seabream spawn from January to June depending on location, and black seabream spawn from March to May in their northern reaches. Both are hermaphroditic.

Sea Bream

Along the east coast of Australia, silver (yellowfin) bream spawn close to river entrances during February in southern New South Wales, and progressively later through to August the farther north they are found (in July and August in Queensland). Black bream start spawning from October through early December within estuaries in Victorian waters, from November through January in South Australia, and between July and November in Western Australia. Each species is thought to produce from 300,000 to 3 million eggs during the spawning season. The eggs of the silver bream are planktonic, as are the larvae that hatch after about two days. After a month, the larvae are carried into the estuaries by flood tides and settle into seagrass beds. The eggs of the black bream are pelagic and hatch after about two days, and the larvae also settle into and over seagrass beds.

Food. Bream are largely omnivorous and feed on crustaceans; crayfish; mollusks, including oysters and mussels; small fish; worms; and algae. Some will also eat bread, chicken gut, mullet gut, cheese, and meat, all of which are sometimes used for baits.

Angling. A spirited and determined fighter and an excellent table fish, the ubiquitous bream responds readily to many natural baits, as previously noted, plus pieces of pilchards, garfish, tuna, squid, and other baitfish. It will also take small plugs, spoons, soft plastics, spinners, and flies in prawn, shrimp, or streamer patterns.

Tackle varies with location; 5- to 7-kilogram lines are generally used, and 5- or 6-weight outfits are favored for fly fishing. Handlines to 7 kilograms are popular with estuary anglers. Hook sizes to 3/0 in the surf, and to 1/0 within estuarine waters, are best and, where practical, the lightest-weight sinker, or none at all, is recommended.

Depending on species, sea bream are taken from surf beaches, ocean rocks, and estuaries by shore anglers, and from estuaries, bays, and deeper offshore reefs from a boat. The best fishing gener-

B

ally occurs early in the morning and late in the afternoon and into the night. Baits should be kept moving across the bottom using a slow rate of retrieve. Strike timing is especially important. Close inspection of the bream's mouth reveals a series of tough, crushing molars that hooks are often unable to penetrate, so the bream must be allowed to swallow a bait before striking to set the hook. Chum and bait mixtures are extremely important, and usually consist of minced fish flesh, prawn scraps, soaked wheat, tuna oil, and bread.

Lure anglers wade over sand flats and cast to seagrass beds or deep channels during daylight hours. Sight fishing is sometimes possible but is more the exception than the rule. Bass plugs are popular in Australia for black bream, which are often taken by anglers plying freshwater and brackish-water reaches for Australian bass. Many anglers there make their own bream lures, often tying a bunch of yellow plastic hair to the shank of a No. 1 hook, and crimping a split shot over the binding just behind the hook eye; this rig is bounced across the bottom.

Very sensitive and timid, bream are easily frightened away from a bait by sudden noise or, at nighttime, by flashing lights.

BRIDGE FISHING

Bridges span many bodies of water, especially canals, marshes, and bays where there is either one-way current from upstream flows or two-way current from tidal action. In freshwater, bridges range from large structures that cross over large rivers to small-roadway bridges that pass water through a culvert. In saltwater, they range from bay bridges that are miles in length to small culverts to narrow passageways connecting sections of a marsh. Nearly all bridges offer some ready and accessible fishing opportunities that should not be overlooked by anglers, whether they fish on foot or from a boat.

Bridges provide current breaks and ambush opportunities for many varieties of opportunistic fish.

Smaller bridges obviously form a narrowing of water that slows the upstream section and then shoots it through the downstream section (this works both ways in tidal situations, which would be uptide or downtide). This action scours a hole on the downstream side and may cause full-blown eddies or minor countercurrents on the downstream edges, as well as slackwater pockets, if the situation is conducive. Similarly, culverts will have a deep hole where the greatest force of water emerges, and possibly a small backcurrent to the sides of this. All of these areas may hold fish, especially the bottom of the hole or edge areas where little or no current has to be overcome by the fish and where they can grab food as it drifts by. Eddies on the upstream side of a narrow bridge, along the shore and created by funneling, may also hold fish.

Larger bridges crossing bigger rivers have bridge pilings or pylons for support. Pilings are pillars, whereas pylons are larger and more islandlike support structures. Pilings create downstream pockets of holding water; pylons may do likewise, and may also create eddies or even a dead area directly ahead of the structure on the upstream side. Changing current or tide flows may alter the position of fish here, and in slow or slack water cause them to move about more. Larger bridge supports can be trolled, cast with leadhead jigs, or fished with live baits. When casting, the first step is to find a position that will enable proper presentation. The offering must sweep across the face of the bridge supports and swim toward them; one doesn't start at the supports and work away from them.

Fishing from above and sweeping, however, often sends the bait or lure down the middle of the current chute. To avoid this scenario, it may be necessary, especially in confined areas, to do some creative casting in addition to finding the right spot from which to cast. Bounce casts, short flips, lob casts, and casting to shore and then dragging your lure into the water may be necessary to achieve a productive effect.

Shade, which varies depending on the angle of the sun, and shadow lines created by overhead lights must also be factored into this type of fishing. Fish favor locations that take advantage of the dark/light interface.

Be aware of some problems inherent to bridge fishing. Fishing from the road-surface areas on bridges can be dangerous due to vehicular traffic; in some cases it may be illegal. Bridges that experience boat or canoe traffic can be difficult to fish, especially if you anchor and sit in the main channel. And the current funneling through some bridges is more powerful than inexperienced anglers or waders realize; it is possible for wading anglers to lose their footing and be swept into a swift current.

Bridge fishing is also discussed in pier fishing *(see)*.

BRIGHT FISH

A term for fresh, migratory anadromous fish that have recently entered and are ascending a tributary. Such fish are still silvery from their life at sea (or perhaps in large lakes), and do not yet exhibit their spawning coloration and markings. In the case of sea-run Atlantic salmon, a bright fishery is one for fresh-run specimens, as opposed to those that have overwintered, which are called kelts *(see)*.

See: Salmon, Atlantic.

BRILL *Scophthalmus rhombus.*

Other names—Danish: *slethvarre;* Dutch: *griet;* Finnish: *silokampela;* French: *barbue;* Italian: *rombo liscio;* Norwegian: *slettvar;* Portuguese: *rodovalho;* Spanish: *rémol;* Swedish: *slätvar.*

The brill is a left-eyed member of the Scophthalmidae family of flatfish *(see)* that has been commercially significant for European markets and is mainly caught by commercial trawlers. Like other flatfish, it undergoes a unique maturation from egg to adult in which the eyes migrate to one side of the head.

Identification. The body of the brill is oval; the eyed side is grayish to greenish brown with variable-color patches, and the blind side is white.

Size. This species grows to 30 inches and is reported to reach 16 pounds, but it is commonly 12 inches long.

Distribution. The brill occurs in the northeastern Atlantic along the coast, in the Mediterranean and Black seas, and from Morocco to about the 64° latitude.

Habitat. Brill are located over sandy and mixed bottoms in depths between 100 and 300 feet.

Spawning behavior. Spawning occurs from March through August; males reach maturity at 14 inches, and females at 13 inches.

Food. The diet of brill consists primarily of various fish and larger crustaceans.

Angling. Brill are primarily caught from party boats by anglers fishing with heavy weights and natural baits, or heavy metal jigs.

See: Drift Fishing, Flatfish, Inshore Fishing.

Brill

BRITISH COLUMBIA

Spectacular by nature is what some say of British Columbia. Beauty is its birthright say others. Indeed, this Pacific Northwest province can justifiably flaunt its inland and coastal attractions. There may well be no prettier place to wet a hook than the high mountain lakes and rivers of British Columbia's interior, or the tranquil coves along its northern coast, where there are enough inlets and straits and river mouths to explore that an entire summer could be spent delightfully cruising and fishing.

British Columbia's 1,600-mile-long coastline serves up a daily menu of salmon, halibut, lingcod, and some 14 species of rockfish. Almost every beach yields shellfish, Dungeness crab, king crab, and sometimes the prized box crab. There is plenty of drive-to angling in the lower portion of the province, but because so much of British Columbia's coast is remote, saltwater fishing adventures are enjoyed as packaged trips at more than 150 saltwater lodges and resorts. These provide guides, gear, and fish care. Almost every fly-in lodge is situated in a serene wilderness location, and each day's fishing is punctuated by encounters with such marine wildlife as orca, gray, and humpback whales, porpoises, sea lions, bald eagles, and, on a few occasions, black or grizzly bears.

Bald eagles, egrets, blue heron, assorted waterfowl, bears, wolves, cougars, moose, and goats live in almost every mountain watershed, where rivers run from snow-capped mountains to the Pacific Ocean. All contain sustaining runs of sea-run salmon, and many also have steelhead.

Several hundred campgrounds and a like number of lake lodges, many with outpost camps and licensed guides, exist within this 1.3 million-square-mile province. Provincial fisheries managers maintain a huge annual stocking program on thousands of lakes and hundreds of rivers, which supplements abundant native resources. The more northerly and interior of these see few if any anglers in a season, if not a lifetime.

Saltwater

Five species of salmon and multiple species of bottom-dwelling fish are indigenous to the coastal waters of British Columbia. Although there are some area and seasonal closures, chinook, coho, chum, pink, and sockeye salmon can all be taken from these waters. Of course, salmon are the prime drawing card for both visitors and residents. Considerable interest in other species exists as well, however, especially lingcod, yelloweye rockfish, and halibut.

The beautiful white fillets of the lingcod are favored by many anglers over all other fish. When properly filleted, yelloweye rockfish are equally praised. Lings are minty green when hooked from depths up to 150 feet, whereas a sharp blue cast covers the pearl white meat of a deep-caught fish.

B

There is no difference in taste, however. All of the really large lings (more than 15 pounds) are female; some can reach weights of 70 to 100 pounds.

A huge British Columbia population of halibut almost matches the quantity of salmon. This popular white-fleshed species of fish-and-chips fame can attain weights of more than 400 pounds and can be found in ocean depths to 3,000 feet. Most anglers are limited to catching "chicken"-size halibut in waters less than 200 feet deep, but the really large "barn-door" brutes move into these shallower depths at certain times of the year.

British Columbia's most productive halibut grounds are on the north coast and along the rises west of Vancouver Island. Halibut baits range from plain jigs to herring and octopus. Strong halibut rods must have full spools of 70- to 90-pound line, and anglers can count on an arm-tiring battle in bringing larger halibut to the boat.

The main angling quest is larger chinook, known by the native Indian word *tyee,* which refers to any specimen 30 pounds or better. Early-run fish are locally called "spring" salmon. Chinooks are distinguished from other salmon by their black mouth and gums, and from coho by virtue of the spots on both the top and bottom of the tail fin (the coho sports these on the top only).

Also highly sought in British Columbia waters is any size of the flashy, acrobatic coho, especially the aggressive late-season kype-nosed specimens called "northerns." In general, coho are also referred to as "silver" salmon. These sleek fish may not grow as large as chinooks, but they lack nothing in the way of excitement at the end of a fishing line. Known for repeated acrobatics, swift runs, and jolting strikes, coho are the darling of light-tackle enthusiasts. They commingle with chinooks and can be caught at the same time, but the angler who targets coho would do well to scale down offerings, use lighter tackle, and focus on later seasons when these fish are most abundant.

Both chinook and coho are anadromous fish, spending their lives in the ocean and returning to their rivers of birth to spawn, after which they die. In the ocean for several years, they wander great distances and feed prodigiously. Most of the salmon are caught relatively close to shore and in the nearshore vicinity of offshore islands, especially where there is deep water and the influence of currents.

Carp were imported by the U.S. Fish Commission in 1876 with high praise as gamefish; the value of carp decreased considerably as they began to take over American waters and crowd out other fish.

Most British Columbia anglers prefer to catch salmon by mooching *(see),* keeping the weighted line and rigged bait at a 45-degree angle by utilizing a slow boat speed. For spring salmon, the optimal depth to hold the rigged bait is 3 to 5 feet off the bottom. Coho are usually in the upper depths. Use of downriggers to troll either bait or plugs is on the increase.

By far the greatest saltwater lure for salmon is dead natural herring or anchovy. Herring are fished whole or cut plug style; anchovies are fished in a rig referred to as a baitholder. Both are sometimes accompanied by a dodger. Plugs are fished both with a dodger and by themselves.

In the Queen Charlotte Islands and along the west coast of Vancouver Island, anglers and salmon are not finicky about their bait hookups; anything works fairly well there. Along the midcoast, near Bella Coola, Hakai, and Rivers Inlet for example, success comes to anglers who can cut and rig their baits to present either a slow roll for chinooks or a fast roll or spin for cohos.

Downriggers and long, light rods are popular along the north coast and in the inside waters of the Strait of Georgia to achieve the depths of the returning salmon. Mooching with 6- to 12-ounce weights is the normal style at Rivers Inlet or along the western fiords of Vancouver Island. Plugs and hoochies behind a dodger, which are the main lure of commercial trollers, are also top producers for anglers all along the coast on certain runs at certain times. Many anglers have also achieved good success with jigging baits, spinning gear, herring strips, hoochies, and spoons.

Using a fly rod to quickly fish a lightly weighted bucktail in the wake of a boat is one of the most exciting techniques for catching northern coho in the fall. Tackle consists of an $8^1/_2$- or 9-foot fly rod for 6- or 8-weight line, with a long extension handle and a salmon fly reel that will hold 600 yards of 8-pound-test monofilament. A streamer fly (with or without a weight) is trolled on or just below the surface. When the fly is fished on top, watch for a big wake from a large charging fish.

Southern region. Most of the fishing emphasis in the southern region is along the mainland coast, between the mainland and the eastern perimeter of long Vancouver Island. The western part of Vancouver Island, however, has excellent fishing and less crowded conditions. From early May through late September, large numbers of migrating Canadian and American chinook salmon are available at such popular west coast destinations as Kyuquot Sound, Nootka, Clayoquote, Tofino, Ucluelet, Bamfield, and Sooke. A good run of northern cohos move down the coast in the fall, and the rivers provide trout and steelhead fishing, which supplements the ocean fishing and is especially enjoyed on those afternoons when conditions become uncomfortable. Halibut are also a common catch here, with larger fish caught on offshore banks. These sites are accessed direct by floatplane, or by road from locations on the island.

Campbell River, at the midpoint of Vancouver Island, has justifiable reason to proclaim itself Canada's Salmon Capital, as more than 50,000 anglers annually fish here for the hordes of salmon that return through the narrow tidal surges and rapids en route to their spawning rivers. The largest of these, the Fraser, has historically been one of the world's most important salmon rivers.

British Columbia is not a place one associates with crowds, yet when fish are plentiful, on any summer night hundreds of fishing boats are scattered throughout the Campbell River area. Moreover, when the action is particularly hot, several thousand boats—each with two to four anglers—will be within a few miles of that river, most tightly packed into two or three locations. As a result, in peak season, Campbell River is home to 500 guides, and a mecca for small-boat salmon fishing, especially using live bait or cut plugs.

This is due in large part to the salmon, of all sizes, that filter past Campbell River in prodigious numbers. The waters in the Discovery Passage between Vancouver Island and the mainland are like a funnel for Pacific salmon stocks. A high percentage of all salmon migrating to or by British Columbia go through the passage, some headed to Vancouver Island rivers, others farther south or north. The passage is to salmon as Times Square is to New Yorkers. En route this way and that, any fish coming inside Vancouver Island passes by.

Unlike most other prominent sportfishing destinations, which are of relatively recent discovery, the Campbell River area has more than 100 years of sportfishing tradition. In October 1896, British angler Sir Richard Musgrave wrote in *The Field* of his experiences fishing for tyee with an Indian guide out of a dugout canoe off the mouth of the Campbell River. His largest catch was a 70-pounder; a model of it, which was once proclaimed as the largest salmon ever taken on hook and line, is still on display in the Natural History Museum of South Kensington, London.

Musgrave attracted others, who attracted others, and in 1924 the now-famous Tyee Club—analogous to the Catalina Tuna Club—was founded, for the purpose of standardizing the sport of salmon fishing in British Columbia. The club formulated many sportfishing guidelines, most of which are in force for members to this day. These include fishing with only light tackle and artificial lures (spoons or plugs) with a single hook, trolling from a boat powered only by oars, and fishing with no help from the guide other than netting.

Nowadays, in the inky predawn blackness Tyee Club members tow their rowboats to the fishing grounds, anchor the towing vessel, and row off in fiberglass skiffs, hoping to tempt an early-morning salmon in either Tyee Pool or Frenchman's Pool. The "Tyee Angler of the Year" title is awarded each year to the angler with the largest catch. A ruby lapel button is awarded to those who land a tyee of 70 or more pounds, a diamond pin for a fish in the 60s, a gold pin for a fish in the 50s, silver for a fish in the 40s, and a bronze button for any fish over 30 pounds. Fewer than 100 members are inducted into the select club each season.

The rowers, of course, are vastly outnumbered by powerboaters, who are more mobile and more efficient; but sometimes sportfishing isn't about efficiency or success ratios.

Not that there isn't plenty of success for both chinook and coho salmon anglers in these rich waters. There is so much success, in fact, that people come from all over the world to try to pluck some bounty from the intricate tidal currents of Discovery Passage.

The premier salmon fishing spot, not only here but probably worldwide, is the gigantic back eddy in front of the lighthouse where the Strait of Georgia and Discovery Passage meet. It is here that 600 to 700 boats often fish at a given time, with thousands upon thousands of salmon annually falling to the hook. When the run is on, boats routinely have doubles and triples; all across the eddy, nets are waving and rods are bending.

Another extraordinary spot, although not as conducive to heavy traffic or to boaters with a weak heart, is Seymour Narrows. Here, when the tide is high the current can flow as fast as 16 knots, and there may be 50- to 60-foot-wide whirlpools. At 10 knots it is estimated that 1 million gallons of water move by per second; nonetheless, this dangerous water draws salmon.

And those salmon can be quite large. Several 60-plus-pounders are accounted for every season, although it isn't every day that fish of 40 pounds or more are garnered. Hereabouts the emphasis is on sportsmanship, especially with the larger lodges and their guides, so a good deal of fishing is done with relatively light tackle—swift waters notwithstanding.

This is especially true for coho salmon, which are abundant in this locale. When there is a good run of cohos on, 30 to 40 can be caught in a day. The sizes run smaller than they do farther north, but light line, long rods, and fly tackle are popular among anglers fishing for coho, so a scrappy bout is virtually ensured. An excellent spot for coho is Whilby Shoal on the extreme southern tip of Quadra Island. A substantial shoal bed of kelp runs from green to red buoy and from point to point, and it supports thousands of fish, especially coho, which feed on massive pods of tiny shrimp.

Although salmon are the main attraction, some river fishing for sea-run cutthroat trout and for steelhead occurs here. The latter enter the area in the fall and winter and provide good river fishing, although it doesn't get the attention that is directed toward king salmon.

Because of its protected location, this region is fishable year-round, no matter what direction the wind is from. This is another good reason for its popularity and makes it a good place to hold tournaments, of which there are many. Here anglers can book a trip well in advance and be assured of meeting fishable conditions.

Guides are numerous, not only because of the numerous lodges in the area, but also because these waters are tricky. Both boat handling and technique are complicated by these complex waters. For example, the tide is important here. When it

B

is low, fish don't move and are widely scattered, causing some places to produce better than others. The new and full moon phases produce higher tides and are better times to fish. The depth to work varies as well, although for tyee the lure or bait must generally be just off the bottom.

Mooching with herring is extremely popular for salmon; lighter tackle, smaller hooks, and smaller bait are used for coho. A fair number of anglers, however, fish with artificials and light outfits, and trolling and jigging are also practiced.

Campbell River is one hour from Vancouver and is accessed by floatplane (with water taxi service) or wheeled aircraft from the mainland. Anglers with boat in tow can ferry to Victoria and drive north.

August is prime tyee season, when the big fish, preparing to spawn, are around. The best time for bigger cohos is September and October. For pure numbers, June is tops, with May also a good bet because there are fewer grilse (2-year-old salmon) around. When the grilse are abundant, you can catch 50 in a morning. Other coho average 5 to 6 pounds, with bigger northern coho in the 6- to 12-pound range in the fall.

Midcoast. The midcoast region of British Columbia is inaccessible by road and thus available only to those who access seasonal lodges and camps, or to those who have a large boat capable of long-distance cruising and overnight voyaging. The latter are few, and the former are relatively few, at least when compared to areas to the south. The result is that there is a lot of water to fish but not many anglers to fish it. Channels, inlets, and islands abound in this large area, portions of which comprise part of the Inside Passage, a 1,600-kilometer waterway extending along the Pacific Northwest from Seattle to Skagway.

Shearwater and Bella Bella in the northern portion of this region are good fishing destinations. Anglers take salmon, halibut, red snapper, and lingcod in the remote waters of Seaforth, Spiller, and Return Channels; from Idol Point to Cape Swain; and in Milbanke Sound south to Cape Marks.

Big chinook salmon, like this one from Rivers Inlet, are British Columbia's main coastal draw.

Chinook over 40 pounds are caught in these areas, and barn-door halibut can be found in the offshore depths. Anglers have particular success with coho in Lama Pass, between Denny and the Campbell Islands.

South and east, Hakai Pass is a good place for big chinooks, as some world records have been established here, including an 85-pound line-class specimen. Forming the northern entrance to Fitz Hugh Sound, Hakai enjoys a clustering of fish as they funnel through coastal islands. Early runs of spring salmon occur here in March and April and compete at the same time with a flood of halibut. The first cohos appear by midsummer, with late July and August being tops for an abundance of northern coho. Larger chinook are available in late summer and early fall; popular spots include Odlum, The Gap, Kelpie Point, Bayley Point, and Spider Island.

Farther south, the most prominent area of the midcoast is Rivers Inlet, east of Fitz Hugh Sound and protected from the northwest by Calvert Island. Forty miles long and 7 miles wide at its entrance, Rivers Inlet is situated at the southeast corner of Queen Charlotte Sound, just north of Cape Caution. The cape is a funneling spot for large numbers of chinook and coho salmon. Fish migrating northward, having come from the Strait of Georgia between Vancouver Island and the mainland, land right at the doorstep of Rivers Inlet. Salmon migrating southward along the coast, having come from the Hecate Strait and Queen Charlotte Sound, swim right by as well. Some of these fish are not just passing through; they are returning to spawn in one of the four major rivers that empty into the inlet. The result is that from mid-June through September the action is continuous.

Chinook are the main attraction, and large specimens have been caught here in the past. An 82½-pound chinook, taken in 1951 at Rivers Inlet, stood as the all-tackle world record for three decades until surpassed by an Alaskan fish, and that was eclipsed locally by an 84-pound fish caught at Rivers Inlet in 1986. Other 80-pounders have been caught since. At some point years ago a chinook of 126 pounds was caught in a commercial net at the mouth of the inlet. While the monsters aren't always predictable, 50- and 60-pounders are sure to be caught every year. These are impressive-looking fish, deep-bodied and with thick girth.

King salmon aren't the only catch at Rivers Inlet. Silver salmon, some weighing up to 25 pounds, come into the Inlet in two different runs; and chum, sockeye, and pink salmon are seasonally available as well.

Salmon fishing at Rivers Inlet has actually been improving in general, due in part to a hatchery at the head of the inlet that was started in 1985 and is operated by the lodges in the area (40-pounders have already been produced from hatchery stock), and in part to less pressure. In the 1960s there were many canneries in Rivers Inlet, and lots of traffic. Virtually all of the canneries are now gone.

The salmon fishery starts in mid-June at Rivers Inlet, when there is an early run of big kings. July is the month for unadulterated action, when small coho show up as they follow baitfish schools. Coho get larger as the season progresses, with northern coho available in late August and September. September is generally the best time to catch a large coho.

Pink and chum salmon show up in mid- to late July. The run builds in late July and peaks in early August. Chinook salmon fishing is good from the beginning of the season through the end of August, with the biggest fish usually being caught in late July and the first three weeks of August.

One of the best locations for all salmon species at Rivers Inlet, especially for large chinook, is a spot known locally as "The Wall," west of Goose Bay along the southern shore. Here the water drops sharply by a cliff into 90 feet, and is 180 feet deep a short distance offshore; it then drops to 400 feet around 100 yards offshore. Fish congregate in this spot.

Early morning and late afternoon are preferred times for catching fish at The Wall, with some importance attached to having lines in the water at first light. Many a large salmon is hooked before the sun pokes over the mountains and filters through the fog that wafts up the valleys. It is cold then, without the sun; even in summer the water temperature is in the upper 40s. But salmon that have come into the inlet during the night are more agreeable before boat traffic increases and before the brighter light sends them deeper.

Rivers Inlet has plenty of deep water and many places worth fishing. The inlets of minor tributaries—back in secluded bays hemmed in by spruce and hemlock—are particularly appealing; at times one easily forgets that this is saltwater fishing, not angling in a pristine mountain lake or deep in a fiord. And at Drainey Narrows, on a good tide, water rushing out of Drainey Inlet produces a 6- to 8-foot waterfall. Out in open water, however, the sight of a breaching whale serves as a reminder that this is indeed saltwater.

Northern region. For a long time the waters of northern British Columbia, both along the main coast and on the offshore Queen Charlotte Islands, were simply too remote for all but a handful of people to access. And with good and closer fishing elsewhere in the province, this northern bounty went unrecognized. But that changed as salmon, halibut, and lingcod fishing declined in southern waters; now a half-dozen luxurious lodges exist around what have become the fabled waters of the Queen Charlottes, as well as a few at Portland Canal, practically a stone's throw from Alaska. Langara Island on the northwest corner of the Charlottes, and Dundas Island at Naden Harbour to the east, are now fished by many people from May through September. Anglers take barn-door halibut and massive tyees here every year, accessing the region via charter flights from the South Terminal at Vancouver Airport, and also via floatplane from Prince Rupert.

The Portland Channel can be excellent for chinook and halibut fishing, with little competition from other anglers, but the focal point of the northern region is the Queen Charlotte Islands. Roughly 150 islands make up the Queen Charlottes. Located between the 52nd and 54th latitudes, they form the western boundary of Hecate Strait north of Queen Charlotte Sound. The most noted fishing occurs at Langara Island, which is the northern-most point of the Queen Charlottes and is actually closer to the Alaska Panhandle than to mainland British Columbia, and near Rennell Sound on the western end of Graham Island.

Since the mid 1980s or so the Queen Charlottes, especially the northern tip in the Langara area, have become a coveted place for tyee. Taking a cue from the popularity of mainland floating resorts that moved from hotspot to hotspot, entrepreneurs at first devised a mother-ship approach for exploring the Queen Charlottes, using large boats that could be moved to accommodate changes in fish distribution and that could be secured in a protected moorage, complete with a fleet of small sportfishing craft. These continue, but now land-based lodges exist as well.

The Charlottes are truly 60-pound salmon country. It takes a 50-pounder to raise eyebrows, and 40-pounders are routine. In fact, these fish are so fat and chunky that newcomers routinely underestimate the size of their catch, later learning that the fish they thought was 35 pounds was nearly 50. Quite a few fish 70 pounds or better have been caught here, so there are obviously some real leviathans to be had.

As with other British Columbia salmon grounds, there are generally two times when the biggest salmon are more prevalent. One is early in the fishing season, which in the Queen Charlottes is from mid-May through June, and the other is through the month of August. It is uncertain whether this phenomena is due to two different runs of fish, and, in fact, big fish do appear throughout the summer. They are more prevalent in some years (although which years usually isn't predictable) than in others.

The Queen Charlottes experience some truly nasty weather, with rain and mist almost a surety in the course of a short visit. Westerly and northwesterly winds frequently pound the archipelago, and some days fishing is possible only in sheltered locales, if at all. Good foul-weather gear is a must here, to protect against both wind and rain, and is provided by outfitters.

When the weather is more hospitable, however,

anglers are able to get in long days of fishing, with first light coming as early as 4:30 in the month of June and lasting well past 9 in the evening. It is common for many anglers to fish the morning and evening periods and to rest during midday.

King salmon aren't the only fish here, although they certainly are the most coveted. Plenty of coho swim among the Queen Charlotte Islands. Cohos become increasingly abundant as the season advances. Small fish appear early, with 10- to 15-pounders becoming available through the summer; northerns of 20 pounds and more are present from late August into October.

Halibut are abundant in sections of the Queen Charlottes, and have been known to occasionally rise to take the trolled herring presentations of salmon anglers, which is unusual behavior for these bottom dwellers. Taking a 60-pound halibut and a 60-pound king salmon in the same day, let alone the same trip, is a possibility, and many over 100 pounds are landed. The larger halibut, however, are generally caught by anglers deliberately pursuing this species rather than catching them accidentally. Lingcod and snapper, incidentally, are also caught here.

Because of the difficulties in establishing a fishing operation, it isn't likely that the Queen Charlottes will get overrun with anglers. If commercial fishing operations and other influences don't decimate salmon stocks, and if anglers moderate their take of trophy kings, there will be outstanding tyee fishing in the Queen Charlottes for a long time.

Resource Issues

The future of salmon in British Columbia is a complicated one, and centers around the fish, federal regulators, 6,000 unionized commercial fishermen, native Indians, and more than 400,000 saltwater anglers. The federal Department of Fisheries and Oceans (DFO) administers the salmon resource, although there is also a provincial Fisheries Ministry. Commercial fisheries include unionized seiners, gillnetters, and trollers. Native Indians have been allocated rights to a number of fish from each run.

Overfishing by the commercial fleets, habitat loss, and pollution have taken their toll of the salmon resource in British Columbia. A prime example of this loss is on the Fraser River, which is still the world's greatest salmon producer and one of the three top salmon rivers (along with the Skeena and Nass) in the province.

For more than a century, sockeye salmon have been the economic basis of commercial salmon fleets and the salmon processors. Sockeye leave saltwater in the fall to head upriver to their spawning grounds. En route, they are targeted by in-river gillnetting and native harvest. In 1996, the Federal Fisheries Ministry introduced a reduction plan for the commercial fleet that cut 800 (of 6,000) licenses in the first year. However, 90 percent of the fisheries allocation management plan still goes to commercial fishermen, while natives and recreational anglers each take about 4 percent of the resource, with only the remaining 2 percent allowed to spawn and to repopulate. Not surprisingly, a limited number of British Columbia salmon farms are raising and selling more salmon each year than the total catch of the commercial fleets.

The net effect of the fleet cutbacks has been to reduce the number of seine and gillnet boats. But because of electronics and efficiency, the catch taken by commercial boats now equals the amount taken prior to the cutbacks. These same boats compete for herring stocks for the export of herring roe.

Urban growth and chemical discharges from the Lower Mainland and the Fraser Valley threaten the lower Fraser's tributaries below Hope, the area currently responsible for rearing 90 percent of the river's chum salmon, 80 percent of the chinook, and more than half of the pink and coho salmon stocks.

Biologists report that a third of the streams in the Fraser Basin were devoid of salmon in 1998. Since the early 1980s, sportfishing salmon limits have been reduced from 16 fish a day to only 4. Some runs, particularly the sockeye run on the Horsefly River, which was devastated in the early 1940s to less than 1,000 fish, have now responded with 10 million returning spawners. Anglers hope for similar success with enhancement projects on chinook and coho.

Freshwater

If wilderness in large doses, breathtaking scenery, solitude interrupted by the cry of a loon, and plenty of fish to catch are your requisites for trout fishing, then British Columbia has the goods. Rainbow trout and Kamloops trout are the dominant quarries for almost 400,000 anglers who fish British Columbia's rivers and lakes each year, yet in the north the province also offers opportunities to catch whitefish and charr, and in the southeast, bass. There's also brown trout, lake trout, and, of course, some of the finest steelhead rivers in North America.

Steelhead. In British Columbia, steelhead come in two sizes, big and bigger; and in two seasons, summer and winter. Although most large steelhead are historically found in the larger rivers (Nass, Skeena, and Fraser), there are dependable runs in smaller rivers in the Queen Charlottes, Vancouver Island, and most coastal fiords that lead to river systems. These bright fish are sought by a special breed of anglers who willingly endure wading in icy water.

In order to avoid crowding and overfishing a limited resource, a classification system is in effect on some of the top steelhead waters. This requires a nonresident to buy a special license, fish with a guide, and pay a premium price for each day's fishing. Two-thirds of these restricted waters are on tributaries of the Skeena River in northern British Columbia.

Summer-run steelhead are taken from June through October. Winter-run fish are more numerous and are caught from mid-November through March.

Major steelhead waters on Vancouver Island are the Big Qualicu, the Cowichan, Englishman, Campbell, Gold, Nanaimo, Oyster, Quinsam, Somass, Sproat, and Stamp Rivers. On the Lower Mainland, large numbers of steelheaders find success on the Vedder, Capilano, and Squamish Rivers. The greatest runs, size, and diversity of steelhead are found in the northern part of the province on the Bulkley, Kispiox, Morice, Kitimat, and Skeena Rivers. In the interior, the famous Thompson River is the only major steelhead water, whereas in the Cariboo Coast region, action is found on the Dean and the Bella Coola, the former being one of the more highly publicized fisheries.

The lower Dean affords first opportunity for strong, silvery fresh-run fish, although it is not an intimate experience because it's accessible to the public and has numerous campsites. The salmon run peters out on the Dean by late June, when the steelhead are just starting. Steelhead numbers are best here in summer and fall, when the water is low, but by late August the river is so crowded with pink salmon that it's hard to hook steelhead.

Southwest and Vancouver Island. There's a wide variety of lake and river fishing for trout, salmon, and steelhead within two hours of Vancouver. The Vedder and Capilano Rivers are located here, too, and provide steelhead and coho salmon fishing.

The Fraser River courses through this region as well and, in addition to salmon, harbors white sturgeon—one of the world's largest and oldest freshwater fish. There is no commercial fishery for Fraser sturgeon, and in the late 1990s the sportfishery was on a strict catch-and-release basis while biologists sought to find the cause of mysterious deaths by many large sturgeon in 1994 and 1995.

The lower Fraser River is wide, shallow, and slow moving. From Mission to Hope, the majority of sturgeon anglers fish for the giants, which spawn in the creeks and beaches of tributary rivers and lakes. Above Hope, the river narrows and plows through a narrow channel, foaming through white rapids. Between the rapids each sand-bottomed pool offers ideal sturgeon water. There is a good, active catch-and-release fishery for large sturgeon at Lillooet.

Hooking and playing sturgeon is a matter of practice and luck. Gear is usually strong 11-foot rods with conventional reels filled with 60- to 80-pound nylon monofilament. Sturgeon are bottom feeders, and they are attracted to odors. Eels soaked in garlic—plus shrimp, meat scraps, and fist-size worm balls—are all presented, along with fresh salmon roe. Fishing is either aboard stout river boats or from sandbars. When landed, each sturgeon is tagged and measured for report to fisheries managers. Most fish these days are between 18 inches and 10 feet. Few records were kept in the early glory days, but a mammoth specimen of 1,387 pounds was pictured hanging above railway cars in New Westminster in 1897.

Fishing in interior British Columbia offers great trout action among fabulous scenery.

On Vancouver Island, there are various species of fish, although rainbow and cutthroat trout take precedence. Brown trout, brook trout, kokanee, Dolly Varden, charr, and smallmouth bass are also present in some locales. The southern part of the island contains bass in Elk Lake, and brook trout in Spectacle Lake, but it experiences greater angling pressure than the other areas due to a higher population. The northern part of the island has the least fishing pressure.

Some brown trout grow to double-digit weights in the Cowichan River on Vancouver Island. This river is a terrific fishery in every respect, and also has coho salmon, steelhead, cutthroat trout, and rainbows. This is a short (two-day drift) river that flows from its headwaters lake to Georgia Strait; every pool is named, and each reach holds fish.

Okanagan, Kootenay, and Rockies. The Okanagan Valley has a different texture than other regions of the province, and its fisheries reflect that. Most opportunities are associated with various lakes and focus on trout, although bass exist in the region as well. The big Okanagan, Kalamalka, and Skaha Lakes are good spring and fall fisheries for large rainbow trout, plus lake trout and kokanee salmon (landlocked sockeyes). Wood Lake, at the southern end of Kalamalka, has produced exceptionally large kokanee in the past. Excellent Kamloops fishing is available in many high-elevation lakes on both sides of the valley; better-known ones include Tepee, Hatheume, Oyama, Postill, Swalwell, Beaver, Bolean, Pinaus, Spa, Arthur, and Aberdeen Lakes. These are easily accessible waters.

The Kootenay region boasts the unique Gerrard strain of huge rainbow trout, which can rival a tyee salmon in size and spirit. Guide boats on the large Kootenay lakes can lead anglers to these giants, which have been introduced to more than 30 lakes in central British Columbia. The largest sport-caught Gerrard came from Kootenay Lake and weighed $35^1/_2$ pounds.

The larger lakes of this region, incidentally, are also the best places to find burbot, a freshwater fish likened to saltwater lingcod, and gaining in winter fishing popularity. This includes places like Slocan Lake and Upper and Lower Arrow Lakes, which also have Dolly Varden and rainbow trout.

To the east, the lake-dotted Rocky Mountain Trench has good opportunities for cutthroat and rainbow trout in the upper lakes, plus whitefish and Dolly Varden in the valley lakes. There's a smattering of smallmouth bass in the lower lakes as well.

Central interior. The areas known as the Cariboo Chilcotin and High Country regions have tremendous resources of rainbow and Kamloops trout. Both regions boast of providing "a lake a day, as long as you stay." The city of Kamloops has excellent surrounding lakes with abundant weed-beds to provide forage for trout, and the result is terrific fly fishing opportunity. Kamloops trout have inspired multiple high-country lodges to band together under the "Rainbow Capital" banner. The lakes around Kamloops open early; three—Roche, Tunkwa, and Paul—were a past venue for the World Championship of Fly Fishing.

At the towns of Sicamous and Salmon Arm lies enormous Shuswap Lake, which has 1,000 miles of shoreline and is undeniably the houseboat capital of British Columbia. Trophy Kamloops, as well as Dolly Varden, kokanee salmon, and whitefish, are found in Shuswap.

In the southern Cariboo region, between 100 Mile House and Little Fort, Highway 24 travels through a lake-rich plateau known as The Interlakes. This is one of British Columbia's famous collections of very fishable high-altitude lakes.

In the northern Cariboo region, Williams Lake is the jumping off point for a great variety of opportunities for fly fishing, big-lake trolling, and salmon, steelhead, and trout fishing on the Dean, Atnarko, Bella Coola, and Blackwater Rivers. Likewise, the town of Anahim Lake provides interior access as well, especially to Moose Lake and its exceptional trout fishing on the Blackwater River.

Dapping, the practice of dancing a dry fly on the surface of the water, is the oldest form of fly fishing.

Moose Lake is near the Coast Mountains—which include the tallest peaks in the province—and on the eastern bush-country fringe of Tweedsmuir Park, the largest provincial park in British Columbia. The surrounding area is full of rugged wilderness terrain, from boggy meadows and glacial rock formations to unending forests and brim-full lakes whose shallows bear the crisscrossing tracks of moose.

It is just remote enough to have been spared from extensive logging and access roads, and probably not much changed since Alexander Mackenzie first explored this region 200 years ago. Having already traveled the great Arctic river that bears his name, Mackenzie struck westward from the Northwest Territories in 1793 searching for an overland route to the Pacific for the fur-trading North West Company. He ultimately found a low pass to the sea near Bella Coola. Today, parts of the Mackenzie Trail are accessed by horseback and floatplane from Moose Lake.

The Blackwater is one of the finest rainbow trout flowages in the province—and a small, swift, brush- and tree-lined gem. There are other flowages like this here, however, as well as a variety of remote turquoise lakes with easy trout pickings and no identification on the maps.

Northern region. In the northeastern sector of the province, the area known as the Peace River Alaska Highway region includes the cities of Dawson, Fort Nelson, and Chetwynd, and covers vast stretches of lightly fished wilderness. Charr, arctic grayling, whitefish, Dolly Varden, and rainbow trout are on the angling menu, and anglers can choose from hundreds of rivers to pursue these species. At least two dozen of these and a half-dozen lakes are easily accessible along the Alaska Highway.

The coastal northwest region has the steelhead and salmon runs previously noted, and also some interior lakes and remote small rivers that are often overlooked. Some of the coastal rivers are reached via helicopter, an exhilarating experience but a rather common one inland in northern British Columbia. The mountains here form a divide that separates Pacific and Arctic watersheds, so that rivers on one side flow northerly, and on the other side flow southwesterly through Alaska.

Inland, perhaps 40 miles from the town of Atlin and accessed only by floatplane, is one of the finest lakes in western Canada. This is Hall Lake, a narrow 12-mile-long body of water that features numerous rocky shoals and a fair number of islands. It has barely been fished but compares extremely favorably with its better-known neighbors—Atlin, Teslyn, and Gladys Lakes.

From early June until early September, the attraction is lake trout, including 15- to 20-pounders; pike up to 20 pounds; and a nonstop parade of grayling. Couple a visit here with a wild river salmon experience, and you simply have the best that the Pacific Northwest has to offer.

BROACHING

Also known as broach to, this nautical term refers to the unplanned, sudden turning of a boat so that it is broadside to the waves and wind and in danger of capsizing or swamping.

B

BRUSH

A collective term in freshwater for flooded bushes and small trees, the tops of large trees that have fallen into the water, and isolated piles of material that have been placed in the water to attract fish. The latter is called a brushpile *(see: fish attractor),* which is a small tree or group of small trees bundled together, weighted, and strategically placed on the bottom of a lake.

Brush can provide excellent fishing opportunity for largemouth bass, and sometimes other species, depending on the depth and location. Bushes are a common characteristic of many reservoirs, where they exist on flats, along tributaries, and in shallow locations subject to flooding during high water. It includes buckbrush, small willows, and assorted shrubs, most of which can thrive when flooded as well as when dry. Fallen treetops exist in all types of waters, but obviously near shore. This usually means that they are in shallow water, although in some places the bottom drops sharply away from a wooded shore and the water can be up to 20 feet deep where a treetop has fallen.

Where there is a lot of fishing pressure, as occurs on most lakes and reservoirs, it is important to develop a system for approaching these places and fishing them properly.

Brush and bass. Bushes or small trees showing in the water usually mean that the water level is high. High water causes more food in newly flooded areas for small fish—and thus more small fish for predators like bass. Bushes offer ambush cover to bass and draw food.

In natural lakes, bushes may grow along shorelines or around the shore of islands. Bushes along mainland shorelines usually indicate that there is a couple of feet of water near the shore, and perhaps an undercut bank. The bass are close to the edge here because these bushes don't extend very far into the water. Usually they are just temporarily flooded. When fishing shore-based bushes, you may be able to get close if the water is turbid; but when it is clear, you have to stay a reasonable casting distance away. If you can get close, it pays to pitch a jig or plastic worm to the cover. If you have to stay back because of water clarity, a surface lure, especially one with subtle motion that doesn't move too far too fast, is a good bet.

If the fish are not aggressive and/or the water is clear, try a slow-moving lure like a soft jerkbait or Texas-rigged worm. These should be cast parallel to the cover rather than perpendicular to it because it is unlikely that a bass will come far out of the cover to get it. Therefore, you need to work the lure as close to the cover as possible, for as long as possible; casting parallel accomplishes that.

Much of the same is true for bushes that are around an island or marshy hummock, although water may extend farther into this brush and thus bass may get back into this cover. Focus attention on the points of the island brush cover and on the pockets that indent the island. If the bass are not aggressive, perhaps because of cold water, a front, or angling pressure, they are likely to be deeper in this cover and tougher to coax into striking. Pinpoint presentations, and perhaps low-light approaches, may be necessary.

In reservoirs, bushes and small trees are usually found in patches near or away from the shoreline. High water often means a lot of bushes; the trick is figuring out which ones to fish. Bushes on points are an obviously important place to concentrate, and so are bushes along creek channels, in shallow bays, along flats, and in small coves or pockets. Isolated bushes are likely to have fish, as are bushes that stand out from others because they are on the points of a cluster or the edge of an opening; large bushes frequently harbor bigger bass.

Bushes may hold fish from springtime, when the water starts warming, through the fall. In midsummer, however, when the water is low and very warm in the shallows, the shallowest bushes are unlikely to be productive. On the other hand, shallow bushes may be very productive in the spring when the water is warming and bass are preparing to spawn. Thus, in spring, bushes in backwater areas are likely to be better than bushes along a mainland shoreline, but the reverse would be true later in the season. Bushes located along creeks would also be good in the summer.

Fallen treetops and bass. Fallen trees are a common bass cover, particularly on natural lakes and ponds, and in many places they remain as cover for a long time, regardless of water levels. They usually fall nearly perpendicular to the shoreline, or on enough of an angle from the shore to put all

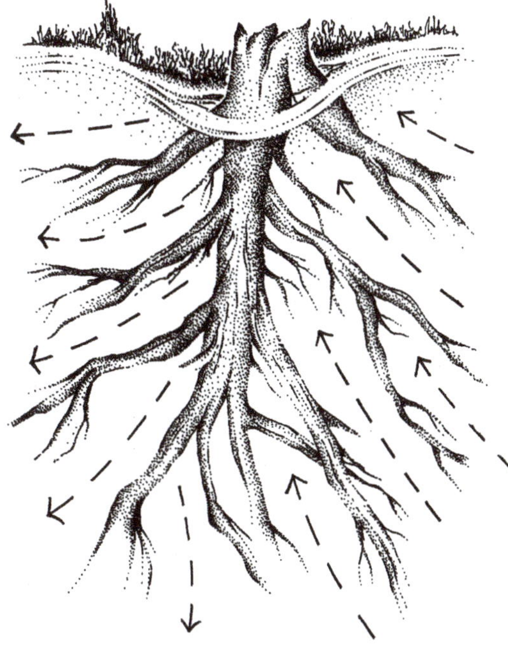

When fishing for bass among the snaggy cluster of a fallen tree, you must retrieve your soft worm, weedless jig, or spinnerbait through lanes and parallel to the limbs.

B

High water, common to reservoirs in spring, often floods brush; this is a scene at Lake Eufaula, Alabama.

the upper branches into the water. These branches, limbs, and trunks provide cover for bass to ambush prey; in time these objects collect organisms that attract small fish, which attract other fish, and soon a food chain has developed around the tree.

Fallen treetops are obvious spots to fish for largemouth bass, and they do see a lot of lures. Some trees attract numerous bass; others may hold just one or two. Those holding only one may hold the king of the pond. A fallen treetop on a point would be an exceptional place to find bass, but that seldom happens, although a tree close to the point or just around the corner can be just as attractive. Fallen treetops near a creek channel, in a location also having other cover (like lily pads or grass), in flooded backwater areas, and on rocky shorelines or banks with riprap, are especially worthwhile. If the water is extremely shallow, the tree is unlikely to hold bass, except in spring at spawning time and in late fall. With a few feet of depth or more, and preferably some shade, the tree could attract bass throughout the season.

Not all fallen treetops are alike; some are much thicker than others. Recently fallen ones may be full of leaves, which offer cover and shade. Bass may be suspended in the limbs, underneath them in the deeper water, or back up near the trunk in the thickest part of the tree.

Proper approach. Whenever you're fishing brush, you should approach it strategically for several reasons. First, the cover may hold a number of catchable fish. Second, you don't want to spook the fish. Third, heavy cover like bushes and small trees means a lot of limbs and roots that can snag a hook and around which a bass will charge once it has your lure. The fewer snags you incur the better, and if you're ready to muscle a fish away from cover, you've got a better chance of landing it.

The clarity of the water and the depth will influence how you approach brushy cover. Generally, bass are spooked if you bring your boat into very shallow water, especially if you make noise. Also, if the water is clear, you shouldn't bring your boat too close to the cover. A lot of bass waters, especially in the south and in reservoirs, are fairly turbid, especially in spring and early summer. Turbidity means you can get closer. Many waters in northern locations, and also natural lakes, are quite clear throughout the season. When the water is clear, you cannot get too close to fish or their cover without alarming them. Within reason, you can get closer if the brushy cover is thick and has depth to it. But if it is shallow and sparse, you cannot.

These are generalities, but the point is that conditions should dictate how you approach the cover; you can always change if you find things different from what you expected. For example, if bass are feeding heavily on minnows in the shallows, as they often do in the fall, then you might be able to get close to thick cover even in shallow, clear water because the fish are aggressive.

Fishing close to brush entails pitching and flipping jigs or worms, or short-casting spinnerbaits. Longer casts allow the use of these lures as well as surface or near-surface lures and sometimes crankbaits. Shorter casts and closer presentations are generally preferable because accuracy is better, less time is spent casting and retrieving, more presentations to the cover can be made, and you likely will fish deeper in the cover, which is often where the fish are. Longer presentations make it difficult to get lures to deeper cover and to work effectively in it.

Whether you're approaching brush from a distance or close by, first cast to the edges rather than to the heart of it. This may pick off a fish on the fringes, or it may bring a fish from the interior of the brush to the edge to strike your lure. Casting around the edges of brush may pick up aggressive fish without lessening your chances of drawing a strike from other fish in this cover. The reverse is not true; if you cast into the middle of the cover and catch a fish and then have to battle it out, chances are any other fish in that cover will be too disturbed to catch for a while.

Larger bass, however, are likely to occupy the thicker and deeper part of the cover. If you are specifically targeting larger fish, you may not want to fish the fringes of cover, but go right for the whole enchilada. Also, when the sun is out, target your approach to the shaded areas, keeping in mind that the thickest limbs or trunks provide the most shade.

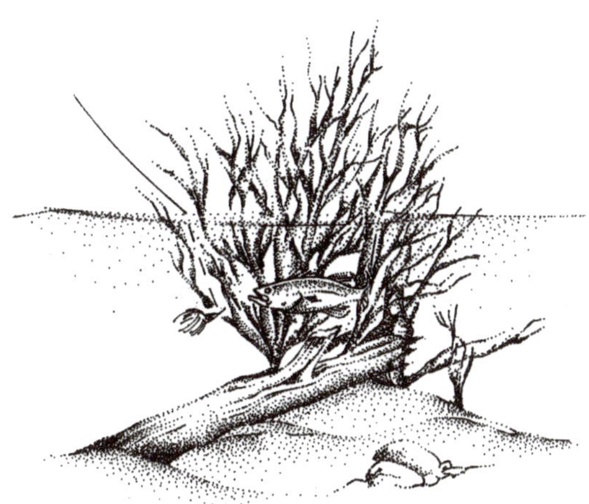

When fishing a jig for bass that are lurking in a bush, get the jig directly on the edges and in the midst of the bush.

Since you want to fish in, around, and through this type of cover, you must make accurate presentations and avoid getting hung up. Often, the first cast to a bush or fallen treetop is the one that gets rewarded with a strike, so if an errant first cast snags a limb in or out of the water and you have to jerk it free or go over to liberate it, you can usually kiss that cover goodbye.

It is also important to make strategic casts so that the path of retrieve goes with the flow, so to speak. You don't want to retrieve a lure crosswise to a series of limbs, but rather lengthwise with one limb. If you're going to dabble a jig into a fallen treetop, try to get over the top of it, or extend your rod tip over the top of it, so that the presentation is vertical in the brush and thus less likely to snag. Presenting the jig from a distance, where it has to crawl over a succession of limbs, is more likely to cause a snag.

So fish the edges first to draw out bass; then probe the inner sanctum with casts that fish the right places in the right direction.

Lures for bass in brush. Clearly it is beneficial to use weedless or relatively snag-free lures in bushes and treetops, especially if they are thick. You can certainly use lures with exposed hooks around the edges of this cover and over the top of the submerged portion.

A spinnerbait, which is a relatively snag-free lure even though it has an exposed hook, is a favorite for brush fishing. That hook is a single one, and it rides up rather than down, so it doesn't hang up that readily. Additionally, vibration, flash, and ability to be worked through cover make a spinnerbait dynamic for fishing bushes and fallen treetops. The flashes mimic the look of small baitfish in the water, and the vibration makes it detectable by fish, even when they cannot see it very well. This is a lure for drawing aggressive fish, however, and out of necessity it is fished on a steady retrieve. When fish are active, a spinnerbait can be fished fairly quickly; but if not, it has to be slowed down.

Large spinnerbaits cast well but are not always the ticket, especially if the local food comprises very small baitfish. You may not know what the food is, but if a large spinnerbait, say $^{5}/_{8}$-ounce, fails to produce, then you try dropping down in size, either to a $^{3}/_{8}$-ounce or perhaps even to a $^{1}/_{4}$-ounce. A spinnerbait with tandem blades, especially a rounded Colorado blade followed by a willowleaf, is a good bet for brush, but don't overlook using a lure with a single large round blade for extra vibration. Tandem blades stay up better in the water, and when it's necessary to fish slowly, these are a better choice. Both styles can be fished through the tops of brush on a steady retrieve, but they should be worked through lanes in this cover if any exist, and rolled over limbs as well as bumped into trunks, limbs, and the like before being rolled over or around them. This draws strikes from some fish that are close to the cover and not chasing.

To help make a spinnerbait more snag-free, do not put a trailer hook onto it, and bend the overhead arm closer to the lower body.

The primary lure for close-quarters flipping is a lead jig with a rubber skirt, weedguard-protected hook, and trailer. Most anglers use a pork trailer, but a plastic lizard, eel, or other adornment can be used, and the dressing on the shank can also be bucktail instead of rubber tentacles. These lures are very unobtrusive and are fished slowly, which makes them excellent for sluggish bass and bass deep in cover, not to mention larger-on-average fish.

Many anglers tend to fish a jig too fast in brush because there is a lot of it and they want to cover as much ground as possible. However, if the fish are not aggressive, then it may take a couple of presentations to a good-looking bush to draw a strike. It may be necessary to work the jig down through the limbs as well. Bass that are suspended will take a jig before it gets to the bottom, but those on the bottom usually do not come up into the brush for it. Pay attention to whether you catch fish up or down, so you can repeat this effort as you move from bush to bush. If bass are suspended in brush, then it might pay to use a light jig, which will not fall through the cover as quickly.

Worms can also be flipped, or cast from moderate distances. Rigged Texas style, and with the slip sinker pegged so that it doesn't slide, a worm will ride through limbs without snagging, although sinewy curl-tail worms tend to grab onto wood like an opossum. A jerkbait worm, however, which is rigged without a sinker and fished in a slow stop-and-go manner and through the cover, can be very effective. Sometimes fish will take these worms when they are cruised through the top of the cover, and other times when they settle down into the midsection.

Surface lures are always a candidate for fishing over and near cover, and their commotion, especially

B

if it can be generated with slow tantalizing retrieval, can draw explosive strikes. Surface lures present some problems around brush and fallen treetops, however. They are usually of necessity fished around the fringes, which means they have to appeal to an active or aggressive fish. Many anglers try this because it isn't too difficult, and the fish may wise up to this. Also, a multi-hooked surface lure can snag on the brush when a fish grabs it and dives for his inner sanctum, so the chances are greater of losing a fish that strikes such a lure because it gets into the cover, than they are with single-hook lures. Nevertheless, poppers, minnow-style stickbaits, walking stickbaits, and sometimes propellered plugs or a buzzbait, can produce around this cover.

It is also possible, incidentally, to use a crankbait near brush or over submerged brush. A suspending plug, for example, can be effectively worked through the tops of a bush or fallen tree limbs. Also, some buoyant diving lures can avoid snagging limbs with a stop-and-go retrieve, but they are usually best for brush in deeper water rather than for bushes and fallen treetops in shallow environs.

Panfish in brush. It is common to find panfish around brush. Shallow flooded bushes provide spawning habitat in the spring for crappies, and fallen treetops can be a place to catch crappie, bluegills, and other panfish, especially if the treetop is thick and there is 5 to 10 feet of water at the end of the tree. These species are seldom fished in the same manner as bass in bushes or treetops, although large panfish will occasionally strike a spinnerbait or plug. This is rare but may be indicative of the presence of fish of similar size.

If the water is turbid, panfish anglers can quietly get close to brush and sit near or on top of it. Small jigs fished plain or tipped with a piece of worm, or such live bait as minnows, crickets, and worms, are the top choices. Hooks should be light wire so that they can be straightened if they snag on the cover and freed (they can be rebent for continued use), and both jigs and bait can be fished beneath a small float or bobber. Fishing vertically is best to minimize snags, and if you can't get close enough to the cover to do this, it may be necessary to use a long (perhaps cane or telescoping) pole for precise presentation.

In deeper water, submerged brush is often a target of anglers who seek panfish, and a lot of hidden brush in lakes and reservoirs is planted by anglers specifically for this purpose. Similar tactics, as well as the use of vertically fished jigging spoons, work in these places.

See: Fish Attractor; Flipping.

BRUSHGUARD

Synonymous with weedguard, a piece of plastic, metal, or rubber that covers a fish hook to help prevent snagging in cover.

BRUSHPILE

A tree, treetop, or group of small trees bundled together, weighted, and strategically placed on the bottom of a lake to attract fish. Many brushpiles are made of cedar trees or various Christmas trees, and placed near private docks on large lakes and reservoirs for crappie and bass fishing.

See: Fish Attractor.

BUBBLE

See: Casting Bubble.

BUCK

A mature, male fish in spawning mode; this term is usually applied to anadromous *(see)* spawners.

BUCKTAIL

(1) A type of streamer fly, tied with hair or other fur.

See: Fly.

(2) A jig dressed with hair.

See: Jig.

(3) A large in-line spinner featuring a single or treble hook dressed with hair, used in casting for muskellunge and northern pike.

See: Spinner.

BUFFALO, BIGMOUTH *Ictiobus cyprinellus.*

Other names—buffalofish, common buffalo, lake buffalo, slough buffalo, blue buffalo, baldpate, bullnosed buffalo, brown buffalo, stubnose, pug.

A member of the Catostomidae family of suckers, the bigmouth buffalo is so called because of its humped back. Its body form resembles that of the carp. A fairly important commercial species, the bigmouth buffalo has white flesh of excellent quality. It is seldom caught by anglers, although it may be hooked by accident on occasion. These run-ins provoke high expectations by the angler, owing to the fish's size and pulling power.

Identification. The robust and deep-bodied bigmouth buffalo has a large head with a big, distinctively oblique, and toothless mouth. This terminal, thin-lipped cavity angles downward when closed, although the edge of the upper lip is practically on a level with the eyes. The sickle-shaped dorsal fin is characterized by a taller lobe at the middle of the back that tapers off into a shorter lobe; the whole fin extends to the caudal peduncle. A comparison between the bigmouth and smallmouth buffalo reveals that the smaller mouth of the smallmouth buffalo is nearly lateral when closed, and subterminal—angled downward—as is more typical of suckers. It is the only member

Bigmouth Buffalo

of the sucker family with its mouth directly in the front of the head.

The color of the bigmouth buffalo may be gray or coppery olive brown or slate blue on the back, and the sides are yellowish olive, fading to a white belly; all the fins are blackish in tint. Although the bigmouth buffalo resembles the carp, the latter can be recognized by its lone serrated spine at the front of the dorsal fin, whereas the former possesses only soft rays.

Size/Age. The largest of all the suckers, the bigmouth buffalo is said to grow to 80 pounds, although the all-tackle rod-and-reel record is a 70-pound, 5-ounce fish. It typically weighs between 3 and 12 pounds, and it has been known to grow as long as 40 inches. Most fish will live only six to eight years and grow to 20 pounds.

Distribution. Found only in North America, bigmouth buffalo occur in the Nelson River drainage of Hudson Bay, the lower Great Lakes, and the drainages of Lake Erie and the Ohio and Mississippi Rivers, from Ontario to Saskatchewan and Montana south to Louisiana and the Gulf of Mexico. They have also been introduced in Arizona, California, and Cuba with success.

Habitat. Bigmouth buffalo have a preference for pools and backwaters of small to large rivers and are found in lakes and impoundments.

Life history/Behavior. At about three years of age, adults spawn in April or May, waiting for water temperatures to reach the 60° to 65°F range. During their runs in the shallows, adults seek weedy areas in 2 to 3 feet of water to lay their eggs. The randomly scattered eggs stick to vegetation and hatch in 10 to 14 days without the protection of the adults. Young bigmouth buffalo stay in the shallows until the end of their first summer. They travel in schools throughout their lives and are capable of tolerating temperatures of up to 90°F in waters with little dissolved oxygen.

Food and feeding habits. Roughly 90 percent of the food a bigmouth buffalo eats is small crustaceans. It may feed on plant matter and algae as well, but insects, insect larvae, fish, and other bottom organisms are a very small part of its diet.

Angling. The bigmouth buffalo does not take ordinary baits or artificial lures and is seldom caught by anglers. There is virtually no dedicated fishing by anglers specifically in pursuit of this species. Most bigmouth buffalo are taken accidentally by anglers using some form of bait, especially a worm or doughball, or a small jig. Some are inadvertently snagged on the hook of an artificial lure. These large fish, which are often confused with carp, are strong and present a challenging fight, especially if hooked on light tackle. Like carp, they are overlooked for their sporting virtue, playing second fiddle to species that have historically received better press. Their rich flesh has made them an important commercial species, particularly along the Mississippi River.

See: Buffalo, Smallmouth; Suckers.

BUFFALO, SMALLMOUTH *Ictiobus bubalus.*

Other names—razorback buffalo, roachback, thick-lipped buffalo, channel buffalo, humpbacked buffalo, high-back buffalo, river buffalo.

The smallmouth buffalo is second only to the bigmouth in the sucker family in terms of size and commercial importance, although it has a better reputation as a food fish than its larger relative. The smallmouth buffalo, however, is less abundant and subsequently less commercially important. Limited abundance contributes to its lack of significance as a sportfish, caught only occasionally or accidentally by anglers.

Identification. A deep-bodied and compressed fish, the smallmouth buffalo has a small conical head, a high-arched back, and a long dorsal fin. It also has a small, thick-lipped mouth with distinct grooves on the upper lip; the upper jaw is considerably shorter than the snout. Usually lighter in coloration than other buffalo, it is gray, olive, or bronze on the back, black to olive yellow on the sides, white to yellow on the belly, and it has an olive bronze sheen. The pelvic fins are olive or grayish black, and the other fins are indistinctly dark.

It bears a noticeable resemblance to the bigmouth buffalo, but it can be distinguished by a more compressed body and a more steeply arched back. It also possesses a smaller, subterminal mouth that lies laterally; the bigmouth buffalo's mouth lies at a slant. Characteristic of all suckers, the mouth extends downward, a noticeable feature when the smallmouth buffalo is feeding.

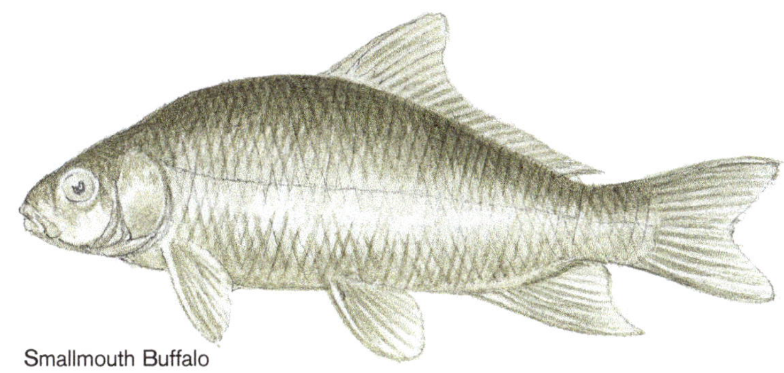
Smallmouth Buffalo

B

Size. Growing slower than the bigmouth, a smallmouth buffalo can reach 36 inches in length. The average commercially taken fish are in the 2- to 10-pound range, although some specimens weigh 15 to 20 pounds. The all-tackle world record for a smallmouth buffalo is 68 pounds, 8 ounces.

Distribution. Found only in North America, the smallmouth buffalo has a range similar to that of the bigmouth buffalo. It occurs in the Lake Michigan drainage and the Mississippi River basin, from Pennsylvania and Michigan to Montana and south to the Gulf of Mexico, and from Mobile Bay, Alabama, west to the Rio Grande in Texas and New Mexico. It is also found in Mexico and was introduced in Arizona. It is most abundant in the central states.

Habitat. Smallmouth buffalo inhabit pools, backwaters, large streams, main channels of small to large rivers, as well as warm lakes and reservoirs. They prefer slightly cleaner and deeper waters than do bigmouth buffalo, an explanation for relatively smaller numbers.

Life history/Behavior. Spawning and schooling habits are similar or identical to those of the bigmouth buffalo.

Food and feeding habits. Smallmouth buffalo feed on shellfish and algae, grinding it with the bony plates in their throats designed for that purpose; they eat more insects and bottom organisms than bigmouth buffalo do.

Angling. As with its bigmouth cousin, there is little concerted angling effort for this species.

See: Buffalo, Bigmouth; Suckers.

BUG

A type of floating fly.

See: Fly.

BUG TAPER

A specially designed type of weight forward fly line for casting large flies, deer hair bass bugs, and fly-rod poppers.

See: Flycasting Tackle.

BULKHEAD

An embankment or retaining wall along the waterfront, often made from wood but sometimes from metal or masonry. Bulkheads parallel the water and shoreline, and keep the water from eroding the shore behind it. They also serve as a buffer to boats and may be similar to a seawall. The water is usually moderately deep alongside a bulkhead, although this varies with tidal extremes. Bulkheads can be attractive to some species of fish and may be worth fishing along their length and at the corners.

See: Pier Fishing.

BULK SHOT

A number of split shot grouped at the same point on a fishing line.

See: Float; Sinker.

BULLHEAD, BLACK *Ameiurus melas.*

Other names—catfish, black catfish, yellow belly bullhead, horned pout; French: *barbotte noire.*

A smaller member of the catfish family, the black bullhead is very popular due primarily to its fine culinary appeal. It is often stocked in farm ponds and raised commercially. An excellent table fish, the black bullhead has flavorful white meat that is marketed by some as a delicacy. It is sold either fried, broiled, or smoked.

Identification. Although the name would imply something else, the "black" bullhead may actually be yellowish green, dark green, olive, brown, or black on the back, bronze or green on the sides, and bright yellow or white on the belly. The entire body possesses a lustrous sheen. Only the young and spawning males are truly black.

Distinguishing the black bullhead from brown or yellow bullhead can be done by noting the rear edge of the pectoral fin in the latter two, which have a spine that is serrated with numerous sharp, thorny protrusions; those found on the spine of the black bullhead's pectoral fin are much less prominent and may be absent altogether. The black bullhead has dark chin barbels that may be black-spotted, whereas the yellow bullhead has lighter ones. Also, the black bullhead has a chubby body that is deeper than the body of both the brown and yellow bullhead. Another distinguishing feature is the squarish tail, which contrasts with the distinctly forked tails of the channel catfish, white catfish, and blue catfish.

Size/Age. Black bullhead reportedly grow to $24^1/_2$ inches in length, but they are most common at 6 to 7 inches and are seldom larger than 2 pounds. The maximum life span for black bullhead is approximately 10 years, although most live only 5 years. The world-record rod-and-reel fish was an 8-pounder.

Distribution. The black bullhead is found from southern Ontario west to Saskatchewan and throughout the Great Lakes, Hudson Bay, St. Lawrence, and Mississippi River basins, extending to New York in the east, the Gulf of Mexico in the south, and Montana in the west. Introduced populations exist in Arizona, California, and other states.

Habitat. Black bullhead inhabit pools, backwaters, and slow-moving sections of creeks and small to large rivers; they also inhabit impoundments, oxbows, and ponds. They have a preference for muddy water and soft mud bottoms, and are able to tolerate polluted water better than other catfish do. They prefer water in the 75° to 85°F range and tend to avoid cooler, clearer water.

Spawning behavior. Spawning takes place in May, June, and July, usually at water temperatures between 66° and 70°F. In weedy sections, the female clears away debris and silt to prepare the nest. When the male joins her, the two proceed to butt and run their barbels over each other's bodies, after which the male wraps his tail around the female's head as she lays the eggs. Spawning up to five times an hour, the female releases roughly 200 eggs each time, fanning the eggs in between spawning. Both parents fan the eggs until they hatch, and guard the fry, which leave the nest in compact schools.

Food and feeding habits. Adults feed primarily at night, whereas the young are most active at dawn and dusk. Young black bullhead feed on immature insects, leeches, and crustaceans; adults eat clams, snails, plant material, and fish.

Angling. Bullhead are a frisky but not especially strong fish at the end of line; they tend to spin when landed and may be problematic to subdue. The spines at the base of the dorsal and pectoral fins can "lock" into an erect position, which evidently helps protect the fish from predators by making it much harder to swallow. When handling bullhead, anglers must be careful to grasp the fish by positioning the finger behind these fins to avoid being painfully stuck by these sharp protrusions.

Bullhead are not held in great esteem from a sporting standpoint and are primarily pursued for their table virtues. Thus, most bullhead that are caught are kept for consumption. This influences angling methods to some degree, as does their primarily bottom-scrounging nature. Most targeted bullhead fishing is done with some form of bait, either by bank and shore-based anglers, or from small boats in backwater environs.

Bullhead are disdained by many anglers for several reasons: Like all catfish, bullhead are rather ugly; they are not a dainty insect feeder like trout but a scrounger; the spines of their pectoral and dorsal fins can inflict painful wounds that heal slowly; they tend to swallow bait and be caught deep, making unhooking difficult; and they are very tough to clean for the table.

Many fish, in addition to bullhead, have to be handled carefully to minimize injury. If you intend to keep a catfish for consumption, then it doesn't matter if it is hooked deeply; if you don't want to keep it, then you have to detect a "strike" early on and set the hook sooner to avoid hooking the fish deeply. And once you learn how to properly clean a small catfish, and do it a few times, that chore won't seem so onerous.

Bullhead are a willing fish for anglers early in the season in northern climes as soon as the ice goes out. The best early-season angling is usually at the mouth of small tributaries to lakes and ponds. If the flow is moderate, bullhead will ascend creeks and streams and can be quite abundant. In the spring, when the water is warming, bullhead are caught all day long. Later, in the summer or when the water has warmed sufficiently, bullhead become nocturnal and are best caught after dark.

Black Bullhead

Bullhead and other small catfish are caught by anglers stillfishing with all sorts of baits. Nightcrawlers are the top natural baits for bullhead, and it is often worthwhile to put two on a hook, as bullhead possess a large mouth and a hefty appetite. Use a float or bobber on a bottom rig, with split shot and a long-shanked No. 1 or 1/0 hook, and get the bait just on or near the lake bottom. If fishing without a float or bobber, use a bell sinker with a couple of hooks spaced above it; some shore-based anglers use this setup for handlining because it can be cast a fair distance.

Bullhead are susceptible to a variety of other offerings, including many aimed at their larger catfish cousins and possessing scented characteristics. These include rancid cheese, doughballs, liver, fish, chunks of meat or fish, chicken entrails, congealed chicken blood, and an endless array of items that fall under the category of "stinkbait" *(see)*.

For the purposes of sport, most light to medium tackle is suitable, including 5- to 6-foot rods of light to medium action; 6- to 8-pound-test line is the norm. For purely food-procuring purposes, and where legal, bullhead and other catfish are caught on handlines, setlines, and trotlines.

See: Bullhead, Brown; Bullhead, Yellow; Catfish.

BULLHEAD, BROWN *Ameiurus nebulosus.*

Other names—bullpout, horned pout, brown catfish, mudcat, common bullhead, marbled bullhead, squaretail, minister; French: *barbotte brune.*

With its firm, pink flesh of excellent quality, the brown bullhead is an exceedingly popular species, sometimes included in the panfish category. Of moderate commercial importance, it is frequently stocked in farm ponds and can be prepared and cooked in many different ways.

Identification. The head of the brown bullhead is large for its round and slender body, and the skin is smooth and entirely scaleless. The coloring of the brown bullhead is not always brown, as the name would imply, but it may actually range from yellowish brown or chocolate brown to gray or olive with brown or black scattered spots; the belly is yellow or white. The young are jet-black and are

Brown Bullhead

often mistaken for black bullhead, and adults sport darker pigmentation during the breeding period.

The brown bullhead is distinguished from the yellow bullhead by its mottled coloring (the yellow fish has an even coloring) and its dark brown to nearly black chin barbels (the yellow bullhead has yellowish or white chin barbels). Color does not necessarily distinguish the different species of bullhead from one another. Instead, an inspection of the pectoral spine on the pectoral fin of brown and yellow bullhead reveals sharp, toothlike serrations, whereas the black bullhead shows very weak serrations or the absence of them. Also, the tail of brown and black bullhead is squarish or somewhat notched; the tail of the yellow bullhead is more rounded.

Size/Age. The average weight of the brown bullhead is less than a pound, and although fish in the 2- to 4-pound range are occasionally caught, this species seldom exceeds 3 pounds in weight. A 5-pound, 11-ounce fish was the largest ever caught on rod and reel. Brown bullhead can grow to 21 inches in length, although they are most commonly 8 to 14 inches long. Their life span is six or seven years.

Distribution. Brown bullhead range from Nova Scotia and New Brunswick to Saskatchewan, from North Dakota to Louisiana in the west, and from Maine to Florida in the east. Native to the eastern United States and southern Canada, they have been widely introduced elsewhere.

Habitat. Brown bullhead inhabit warm and even stagnant waters as well as sluggish runs over muddy bottoms. They occur in farm ponds, pools, creeks, small to large rivers, lakes, and reservoirs. Unlike other bullhead, they are found in large and deep waters, although they are able to withstand low oxygen concentrations and are known to bury themselves in mud to survive such conditions.

Spawning behavior. Spawning takes place in April and May. Nests are made by one or both sexes by fanning out dish-shaped hollows in mud or sand. The pair engages in a ritual of caressing each other with their barbels, facing opposite directions as they finally settle over the nest to spawn. Between 2,000 and 10,000 adhesive eggs are released in cream-colored clusters, hatching in six to nine days. The eggs are guarded by one or both parents, although some fish have been said to eat them. Young brown bullhead are jet-black and resemble tadpoles, forming large schools that swim in surface waters. The male continues to guard the young until they reach 2 inches in length and are able to protect themselves.

Food and feeding habits. Brown bullhead feed mainly at night on immature insects, worms, minnows, mollusks, crayfish, plankton, and offal.

Angling. See: Bullhead, Black.

See: Bullhead, Black; Bullhead, Yellow; Catfish.

BULLHEAD, YELLOW *Ameiurus natalis.*

Other names—yellow cat, creek cat, white-whiskered bullhead, greaser.

Although the least commercially important of the catfish, the yellow bullhead can provide decent angling and is a good food fish. The meat of this small catfish has been described as cream-colored and one of the best tasting of all panfish, but it is subject to quick deterioration if not iced immediately after the catch.

Identification. A moderately slim fish, the yellow bullhead has leathery skin without scales. The coloring ranges from yellowish olive to brown or almost black on the back with yellowish olive or brown sides, yellow or white on the belly, and dusky fins. Juveniles are dark brown or jet-black, making them difficult to distinguish from the young of black or brown bullhead.

The rounded tail helps to distinguish the yellow bullhead from other bullheads, which have squarish or truncated tails. On the back edge of the spine at the top of the pectoral fins, yellow and brown bullhead have sharp, toothlike serrations, whereas in the black bullhead the spine is only weakly serrated, if at all. Also, the chin barbels of the yellow bullhead are white, yellow, or pale pink, unlike the dark barbels of black and brown bullhead.

Size/Age. Yellow bullhead usually weigh less than a pound, although they sometimes reach a weight of 3 pounds. The most common length is between 7 and 11 inches, and they can be as much as 18.3 inches long. Because they have less of a tendency to overpopulate than do black bullhead, they are less likely to be stunted. The world-record fish is a 4-pound, 4-ounce specimen. They can live up to seven years.

Distribution. Yellow bullhead inhabit most of central and eastern North America, ranging in the east from New York to Florida and in the west from southern Quebec to central North Dakota and south to the Gulf of Mexico. As with other

Yellow Bullhead

bullhead, this fish has also been introduced outside its original range and is most common in the center of its range.

Habitat. With a preference for clear waters, gravel or rock bottoms, sluggish current, and heavy vegetation, yellow bullhead are found in pools, ponds, streams, small to large rivers, and small, shallow lakes. In comparison to the brown bullhead, they are more common in smaller, weedier, and shallower bodies of water. They are also more tolerant of polluted water and low oxygen levels than most other types of bullhead. They are most abundant at water temperatures between 75° and 80°F.

Spawning behavior. In May and June, sexually mature fish of 3 years and older move into shallow water at temperatures in the upper 60s or low 70s. After finding a suitable site, one or both of the parents constructs the nest, which consists of either a shallow depression in an open area or a 2-foot-deep burrow in the bank in a protected area. Clusters of cream-colored adhesive eggs, numbering from 2,000 to 6,000, are released and fertilized. The male guards the eggs and the fry hatch in 5 to 10 days, after which the young continue to be protected by the male in a tight group until they are able to protect themselves.

Food and feeding habits. Yellow bullhead are nocturnal scavengers that feed by smell and taste. They eat crustaceans, immature aquatic insects, snails, small fish, dragonfly nymphs, crayfish, mollusks, and bits of aquatic vegetation.

Angling. See: Bullhead, Black.

See: Bullhead, Black; Bullhead, Brown; Catfish.

BUMPER, ATLANTIC

Chloroscombrus chrysurus.

Other names—French: *sapater;* Spanish: *casabe.*

The Atlantic bumper and its Pacific relative *(Chloroscombrus orqueta),* are two of the smaller members of the jack family. Both species have not been greatly studied, and there is some speculation that they may be the same.

Identification. Although the bumper doesn't have a high back, it has an extended belly and a very thin body. With an overall silvery coloring, it has greenish tints on the back and yellow highlights on the sides and the belly. It also has a yellowish tail. There is a black spot on each gill cover and a black saddle on the base of the tail.

Size. Bumper rarely weigh more than half a pound and can reach a length of 10 inches in the western Atlantic or 12 inches in the eastern Atlantic.

Distribution. In the western Atlantic Ocean, Atlantic bumper are found north to Massachusetts, off Bermuda and south to Uruguay, as well as in the Caribbean Sea and the Gulf of Mexico. In the western Atlantic they range from Mauritania

Atlantic Bumper

to Angola. Bumper are said to be absent from the Bahamas and the Caribbean. The Pacific bumper ranges from Peru to California.

Habitat. Inhabiting brackish and saltwater, bumper occur over soft bottoms in shallow water. They are common in bays, lagoons, and estuaries.

Life history/Behavior. Small bumper have been observed in offshore waters, but they frequently range along sandy beaches. They travel in extensive schools, and juveniles are often found in association with jellyfish.

Angling. This fish is only an occasional and incidental catch by anglers. When caught, the bumper often emits a grunting noise.

See: Bumper, Pacific.

BUMPER, PACIFIC *Chloroscombrus orqueta.*

Other names—French, *sapater;* Spanish: *casabe.*

The Pacific bumper ranges from Peru to California and is a very similar species to the Atlantic bumper.

See: Bumper, Atlantic.

Pacific Bumper

BUNKER

A term for menhaden *(see).*

BUOY, MARKER

See: Marker Buoy.

BUOYS

Buoys are the principal daytime aids to navigation encountered by boaters. These are man-made objects strategically placed on navigable waterways by the United States Coast Guard and by appropriate state agencies on waters within the state boundary and without access to the sea. Buoys mark hazards, denote location, define routes, and conform to a standard color and numbering system. Most unlighted buoys are of the "can" or "nun" variety; some have lights, and some also have bells or gongs.

In many waters, buoys mark reefs, shoals, channels, and bars, and can be significant in helping to identify fishing areas depending on the species sought. In northern waters where ice may be encountered, buoys are removed for the winter and may not be returned until midspring; anglers who are on the water in late fall and early spring must proceed cautiously.

Other aids to navigation encountered by boaters include daybeacons, which are fixed structures; minor lights, which are the equivalent of lighted daybeacons; lighthouses; and channel markers. Channel markers are the least formal of all aids and may or may not have lights or painted signs.

Fishing around buoys. Some species of saltwater fish are attracted to buoys and channel markers, no matter how small the object or structure and its foundation or anchoring means might be. Cobia are often caught around these, as are tripletail, drum, snapper, amberjack, and, on occasion, other species.

Boaters should approach buoys and channel markers slowly, shutting the outboard motor off at a distance and allowing the boat to drift past the object or within reasonable casting distance of it. The shallower the water the more this is true. Engine noise will likely drive fish away. Consider the direction of wind and current in order to position the boat for a proper drift, and work the surface and near-surface water first, trying to draw an eager fish away from the buoy or marker. If you don't catch a fish immediately, try another drift or two, and try getting a little deeper, probably with a bucktail jig. If the water is deep and the current is too swift to make a good deep presentation while drifting, you may have to drop anchor well upcurrent to position the boat right next to the structure. Then you can fish a jig or bait.

Often, when the tide or current runs hard, there is little action at these locations. Keep trying. Sometimes buoys and channel markers produce fish when there is little or no water movement.

See: Navigation.

BURBOT *Lota lota.*

Other names—eelpout, pout, ling, cusk, lawyer, lingcod, gudgeon, freshwater ling, mud blower, lush (Alaska), maria (Canada); French: *lotte, lotte de riviére;* Spanish: *lota.*

The only freshwater member of the Gadidae family of codfish found in North America, Europe, and Asia, the burbot is often caught accidentally by anglers fishing for other species. Although it is a popular food fish in Europe, its ugly appearance makes it unappetizing to a fussy majority of Americans. It is mainly sold in salted form for ethnic consumption in North America, but is also a source of oil and is processed into fishmeal; the liver is high in vitamins A and D and is sold smoked or canned in Europe.

Identification. The elongate shape of the burbot resembles an eel or a cross between an eel and a catfish. It has been mistaken for a catfish, and in some places it is called an eel, although it is neither. It also looks like a smaller and slimmer version of the saltwater cod. Other distinctive features include tubular nostrils, a single chin barbel, and a rounded tail. The soft-rayed fins are also noteworthy in appearance: The pectoral fins are large and rounded, the first dorsal fin is small and short, and the second dorsal and anal fins start near the middle of the body and continue to the tail. It has a wide head, small eyes, and small, embedded scales that produce a slick skin.

The burbot has a mottled appearance, due to a dark brown or black pattern scattered over a yellow, light brown, or tan background; there may be regional color variations, including light brown, dark brown, dark olive, or even yellow. The anal fins have a dark edge to them.

Size/Age. Full-grown fish average 15 inches in length and less than a pound in weight. Burbot that are caught by anglers usually weigh several pounds and are occasionally in the 8-pound class, although they can grow much larger. An 18-pound, 11-ounce fish holds the all-tackle world record, but Alaska has produced larger fish, at least one of which was reportedly almost 60 pounds. Some are able to live for 20 years.

Distribution. The burbot is common throughout the circumpolar region above 40° north, especially in Alaska, Canada, the northern United States (including the Missouri and Ohio River drainages), and parts of Europe. It is absent from Scotland, Ireland, the Kamchatka Peninsula, the west coast of Norway, extreme western British Columbia, Nova Scotia, and the Atlantic Islands.

Habitat. Occurring in large, deep, cold rivers and lakes, the burbot are found in depths of up to almost 700 feet. It inhabits deep water in summer and moves shallower during summer nights.

Spawning behavior. By the time it is three years of age, the burbot is sexually mature. It is one of the few species that spawns in mid- or late winter under ice, doing so at night in shallow bays in 1 to 4 feet of water over sand or gravel; occasionally it will spawn in rivers in 1 to 10 feet of water. Burbot may produce more than a million spherical, amber eggs at one time, although the average amount is half that number. Without a nest or parental protection, the eggs hatch in four to five weeks.

Food and feeding habits. Young burbot feed on plankton and insects, graduating to a diet made up almost entirely of fish, especially perch, cisco, and whitefish. They will also eat mollusks, fish eggs,

Burbot

plankton, and crustaceans. Rocks and other indigestible items have been found in their stomachs.

Angling. Most burbot caught by anglers deliberately fishing for them are taken in the winter under the ice. Many are caught incidentally by ice anglers fishing for lake trout. Jigging spoons tipped with a minnow tail, and leadhead jigs tipped with a minnow, are the top producers. Applying luminescent paint on lures to make them glow in greater depths may be helpful. A dead minnow fished on the bottom also catches burbot in the winter. In early spring and late fall, when the water is cold, burbot remain shallow, and can be caught on a slowly worked lure. Some anglers in northern locales use cutbaits to stillfish for burbot in rivers on summer nights. Generally, however, they are deep and beyond the reach of most anglers once the water is warm.

Burbot are slow swimmers, and they don't chase after swiftly moving lures, which possibly explains why they are held in low regard by many anglers. Another explanation is their looks and a tendency to roll their eel-like tail around while squirming when an angler attempts to unhook them. Nevertheless, burbot are an excellent food fish, and some anglers find them preferable even to walleye. Their flesh and liver are held in high esteem in Europe, and the roe is consumed as well in Scandinavian countries.

See: Cod and Hake.

BURPING

A technique, usually used by fisheries professionals and occasionally by anglers, for relieving the pressure that has built in the air bladder of a fish that has been retrieved rapidly from deep water and is to be released. Burping is performed only on species that have a pneumatic duct connected to the air bladder, which allows them to expel air and make more extensive vertical movements; it is primarily used for lake trout and salmon.

See: Catch-and-Release.

BUTT CAP

The end covering at the base of a fishing rod. In fly rods this is often removable, covering a portal for the optional placement of a butt extension or fighting butt *(see).*

BUTTERFISH *Peprilus triacanthus.*

Other names—American butterfish, Atlantic butterfish, dollarfish, pumpkin scad, sheepshead; French: *stromaté fossette;* Spanish: *palometa pintada.*

The fatty and oily quality of the meat of the butterfish does not detract from its reputation as an excellent food fish. It is sold fresh, smoked, and frozen and may be prepared in many ways; the meat is white, tender, moist, and contains few bones. The fat content of the flesh varies greatly over time, at its minimum in August and its maximum in November.

Despite its culinary significance, the butterfish's importance to anglers is as a live or dead bait for larger saltwater gamefish and as natural forage for assorted species. The shape of the butterfish resembles that of some members of the jack family.

Identification. An oval fish, the butterfish has a very thin and deep body and a blunt head. The anal and dorsal fins are equally long. Butterfish are silvery fish with pale blue coloring on the back and upper sides, which often have irregular dark spots and usually possess 17 to 25 large pores directly underneath the dorsal fin.

Size/Age. The butterfish grows quickly, although it rarely exceeds more than 1 pound in weight or more than 12 inches in length. It is usually a short-lived fish, although it is thought to be capable of living longer than four years.

Distribution. Inhabiting the western Atlantic Ocean, butterfish occur in waters off eastern

Butterfish

B

Newfoundland and the Gulf of St. Lawrence in Canada, ranging down the North American coast to Palm Beach, Florida. They are also found in the Gulf of Mexico.

Habitat. Butterfish live and feed in large, dense schools along the coast in near-surface waters less than 180 feet deep and in the 40° to 74°F range. They may also inhabit brackish waters and in the winter may move into deeper water. Juveniles are usually associated with floating weeds and jellyfish.

Life history/Behavior. Sexual maturity is reached when butterfish are two years old and close to 8 inches in length. Spawning occurs once a year from May through August in offshore waters. The eggs float freely until they hatch within two days; juveniles enter coves or estuaries to conceal themselves in floating weeds and among jellyfish tentacles for protection from predators.

Food and feeding habits. Feeding primarily on jellyfish, butterfish are one of very few fish that eat such low-nutrition foods. Their diet also consists of assorted small worms, crustaceans, squid, shrimp, and fish.

Angling. The butterfish species is of no direct value to anglers other than as a baitfish. It is caught commercially in trawls along with squid, hake, scup, flounder, and skate, primarily in the spring and summer, when large schools migrate inshore and northward.

BUTTERFLYFISH *Chaetodontidae.*

There are 114 species and 10 genera that are classified under Chaetodontidae, although the entire family is better identified by its two main subfamilies, the butterflyfish and the angelfish (Pomacanthinae). These differ in size, the former being small, swift swimmers; the latter being larger and slower swimmers. Butterflyfish can also be distinguished from angelfish by their lack of spines, found on the preopercles of the angelfish.

Butterflyfish are brightly and strikingly colored, making them among the most beautiful fish in the sea and in aquariums. They earned the common name "butterflyfish" from their graceful movements and from their coloring; the scientific name *chaetodont* comes from the bristlelike teeth common to all family members.

Common shallow-water species include the foureye butterflyfish *(Chaetodon capistratus),* the spotfin butterflyfish *(C. ocellatus),* and the banded butterflyfish *(C. striatus).* Deeper-water species include the reef butterflyfish *(C. sedentarius),* the Caribbean butterflyfish *(C. guyanensis),* the bank butterflyfish *(C. aya),* and the longsnouted butterflyfish *(Prognathodes aculeatus).*

Identification. Conspicuous and brightly colored, butterflyfish are small, compressed fish that have disk-shaped bodies. They also have rounded to emarginate tails and densely scaled dorsal and anal fins. Among the butterflyfish is a variety of jaw sizes and shapes specially suited to different feeding methods. They have small mouths and lines of small, bristlelike teeth. Butterflyfish larvae have bony plates or armor that cover the entire region of the head.

Butterflyfish have several methods of protecting themselves from potential predators. Of note is the "eye spot" found near the tail on many species. The true eye is often camouflaged by a dark band to trick predators; some fish have even been seen swimming backward, which further confuses predators as to which end is the head. Also, the deep bodies and the dorsal and anal spines make them difficult for predators to consume, and their narrow width lets them slip into crevices.

Size/Age. Butterflyfish range from $3^1/_2$ inches to 12 inches, although most are less than 6 inches long.

Distribution. Found in the Atlantic, Indian, and Pacific Oceans, the majority of butterflyfish inhabit the Indo-Pacific region.

Habitat. Occurring in marine and brackish environments, these reef fish are found in tropical, subtropical, and warm temperate waters. Coral reefs and rocky bottoms are preferred habitats for butterflyfish.

Life history/Behavior. Butterflyfish have a prolonged larval stage that lasts two months or longer. The larvae have thin bony plates instead of head bones, which vary considerably in shape and design between butterflyfish. These fish ordinarily travel alone or in pairs, the pairs being described as nearly inseparable and thought to be exclusive throughout their lives.

Food and feeding habits. They are usually active by day, feeding on an assortment of crustaceans, small invertebrates, fish eggs, and algae;

Butterflyfish

some butterflyfish have more specific diets. The ornate butterflyfish is an example of one type of butterflyfish that has short jaws, used to pinch off pieces of coral polyps. The long-nosed butterflyfish *(Forcipiger flavissimus)* has a different type of mouth with elongated jaws that act as forceps and pick food from crevices in coral. Some species pluck parasites off larger fish, living in symbiosis with them.

Angling. Butterflyfish are an incidental catch for bottom anglers.

BUTT EXTENSION

See: Fighting Butt.

BUZZBAIT

See: Surface Lure.

BYCATCH

The portion of a commercial catch that is not targeted and is either economically undesirable or is governmentally regulated and, therefore, cannot be landed. Sometimes referred to as incidental catch, bycatch is discarded at sea and often results in nearly 100-percent mortality. The size of fish caught as bycatch is directly related to the shape and size of the mesh used for the targeted species. One example of the extent of the problem: In the Southeast and Gulf of Mexico shrimp fishery, trawls with small mesh are used to retain shrimp, causing as many as 10 pounds of undersize finfish bycatch to be taken for each pound of shrimp.

Although the impact of bycatch-induced mortality on stock recruitment is unknown, the unhealthy condition of many of the world's saltwater fisheries has focused attention on factors contributing to the decline of desirable stocks. Efforts have been intensified by the public to bring about a reduction in bycatch as a conservation measure, and in some cases by the commercial fishing industry as a means to avoid more restrictive regulations because bycatch caps are set for certain species. When the caps are met, the fisheries are closed even if the target species quota has not been landed.

Bycatch can include protected marine mammals, such as porpoises that get caught and killed by commercial tuna fishermen; smaller fish than can be harvested or marketed; and a host of assorted marine life that is not part of the target catch, such as small prey fish scooped up into shrimp nets. These are all incidental. Species that cannot be kept or that have no economic value at market are discarded, usually with total mortality. Coastal anglers have seen the dead small-fish bycatch of commercial trawlers littering the surface of the sea for great distances. In some places, recreational anglers buy or barter bycatch discards from shrimpers to use for their own angling purposes, or these anglers fish closely around shrimp boats because the discarded bycatch draws various species and sometimes provides good angling opportunity.

All of these small fish on the surface were discarded by the trawler on the horizon.

Bycatch can have serious implications to the food chain. Since each species has a role in the community, the removal of an important food item through bycatch could adversely affect species that eat that item. However, predators often eat a variety of food items. Reduction in the numbers of a single prey species may lead to an increase in another prey species that the predator will readily consume, although bycatch of prey species may lead also to the reduction in numbers of multiple prey species. It is generally thought that less bycatch, rather than more bycatch, is more desirable for maintaining a balance among the various species in a community.

Research on selective gear has caused changes in some commercial fishing practices. The development of a shrimp separator trawl used in North Atlantic waters, for example, reduces bycatch of small groundfish. As a result, many New England states have passed shrimping regulations requiring separator trawls to be used in state waters. However, a lot more must be done to reduce bycatch in these and other fisheries.

Relation to angling. For anglers, bycatch is a mixed blessing. On the one hand, it can contribute to the decline of some desirable fish stocks. On the other hand, the bycatch can be used to greatly assist angling. On balance, the former should outweigh the latter.

The most pernicious bycatch problem occurs with commercial shrimpers. Shrimp trawlers rake in a lot of bycatch. They are prevalent in the inshore and coastal waters frequented by anglers, some of whom habitually use and depend upon shrimp-boat bycatch for use in their daily angling activities, especially when fishing for tuna, shark, kingfish, and reef fish.

From a conservation standpoint, and for reasons previously noted, it is desirable to eliminate bycatch entirely and to avoid wasting important marine resources. When anglers use bycatch, they are indeed using something that would otherwise go to waste (discarded in the ocean), but they are also helping to support and subsidize commercial fishing, and even helping to make it more difficult to get bycatch reduced or eliminated. The ethics of using bycatch (usually as chum) are therefore muddy ones. Some people feel that it is more important to stop buying trawled shrimp so that there is no market for trawling, buying farm-raised shrimp instead. Others advocate catching your own bait or buying frozen bait rather than taking the shortcut of using bycatch.

See: Fisheries Management.

Conversion Charts

THE SYSTEM OF WEIGHTS AND MEASURES USED IN MOST COUNTRIES AND IN ALL SCIENTIFIC work is the International System of Units (SI), which is commonly referred to as the metric system. A notable and influential exception to this is the United States, where the general public, and non-scientific publications, use the U.S., or U.S. customary, system of weights and measures. Throughout the *Ken Schultz's Fishing Encyclopedia & Worldwide Angling Guide*, there is a liberal use of both metric and U.S. customary weights and measures without parenthetical conversions to equivalent weights or measures. Some anglers, especially those who travel widely and those who pay close attention to world-record fish weights and fishing line classifications, are accustomed to both systems, which are often found mixed at boat docks, fish camps, and tackle shops throughout the world. The following information is provided to help the reader make the conversion from one system to another.

U.S. To Metric Conversion Formulas

When You Know . . .	*Multiply By . . .*	*To Determine . . .*
Inches (in)	25.4	Millimeters (mm)
Inches (in)	2.54	Centimeters (cm)
Inches (in)	0.0254	Meters (m)
Square Inches (sq in)	645.0	Square Millimeters (sq mm)
Square Inches (sq in)	6.45	Square Centimeters (sq cm)
Square Inches (sq in)	0.00064	Square Meters(sq m)
Feet (ft)	30.5	Centimeters (cm)
Feet (ft)	0.305	Meters (m)
Feet (ft)	0.0003	Kilometers (km)
Square Feet (sq ft)	0.093	Square Meters (sq m)
Fathoms (fath)	1.827	Meters (m)
Fathoms (fath)	0.0018	Kilometers (km)
Yards (yd)	0.914	Meters (m)
Square Yards (sq yd)	0.836	Square Meters (sq m)
Statute Miles (mi) (5,280 ft)	1.61	Kilometers (km)
Nautical Miles (n mi) (6,020 ft)	1.852	Kilometers (km)
Square Miles (sq mi)	2.56	Square Kilometers (sq km)
Miles per hour (mph)	1.61	Kilometers per hour (kph)
Knots per hour	1.84	Kilometers per hour (kph)
Acres	0.405	Hectares
Ounces of Weight (oz)	28.3	Grams (g)
Ounces of Weight (oz)	0.0283	Kilograms (kg)
Ounces of Fluid (fl oz)	29.6	Milliliters (mL)
Pounds (lb)	454.0	Grams (g)
Pounds (lb)	0.454	Kilograms (kg)
Pints (pt)—U.S.	0.473	Liters (L)
Pints (pt)—Imperial	0.568	Liters (L)
Quarts (qt)—U.S.	0.946	Liters (L)
Quarts (qt)—Imperial	1.14	Liters (L)
Gallons (gal)—U.S.	3.79	Liters (L)
Gallons (gal)—Imperial	4.55	Liters (L)
degrees Fahrenheit (°F)	0.555 (after subtracting 32)	degrees Celsius (°C)

Metric To U.S. Conversion Formulas

When You Know . . .	*Multiply By . . .*	*To Determine . . .*
Millimeters (mm)	0.039	Inches (in)
Centimeters (cm)	0.394	Inches (in)
Centimeters (cm)	0.0328	Feet (ft)
Square Centimeters (sq cm)	0.155	Square Inches (sq in)
Meters (m)	39.37	Inches (in)
Meters (m)	3.281	Feet (ft)
Meters (m)	1.09	Yards (yd)
Meters (m)	0.547	Fathoms (fath)
Square Meters (sq m)	1.2	Square Yards (sq yd)
Kilometers (km)	3,279.0	Feet (ft)
Kilometers (km)	1,093.0	Yards (yd)
Kilometers (km)	546.0	Fathoms (fath)
Kilometers (km)	0.621	Statute Miles (mi)
Kilometers (km)	0.545	Nautical Miles (n mi)
Square Kilometers (sq km)	0.386	Square Miles (sq mi)
Kilometers per hour (kph)	0.621	Miles per hour (mph)
Kilometers per hour (kph)	0.545	Knots per hour
Hectares	2.47	Acres
Grams (g)	0.035	Ounces of Weight (oz)
Grams (g)	0.002	Pounds (lb)
Kilograms (kg)	35.2736	Ounces (oz)
Kilograms (kg)	2.2	Pounds (lb)
Milliliter (mL)	0.034	Fluid Ounces (oz)
Liters (L)	2.11	Pints (pt)—U.S.
Liters (L)	1.76	Pints (pt)—Imperial
Liters (L)	1.06	Quarts (qt)—U.S.
Liters (L)	0.880	Quarts (qt)—Imperial
Liters (L)	0.264	Gallons (gal)—U.S.
Liters (L)	0.22	Gallons (gal)—Imperial
degrees Celsius (°C)	1.8 (and add 32)	degrees Fahrenheit (°F)

Table Of Metric and U.S. Equivalent Line Strengths

Metric	*U.S. Customary*	*Metric*	*U.S. Customary*
1 kg	2.2 lb	10 kg	22.0 lb
2 kg	4.4 lb	15 kg	33.0 lb
3 kg	6.6 lb	24 kg	52.8 lb
4 kg	8.8 lb	37 kg	81.4 lb
6 kg	13.2 lb	60 kg	132.0 lb
8 kg	17.6 lb		

Table of Fish Weights

Metric	*U.S. Customary*	*Metric*	*U.S. Customary*
1 kg	2.2 lb	60 kg	132.0 lb
2 kg	4.4 lb	70 kg	154.0 lb
3 kg	6.6 lb	80 kg	176.0 lb
4 kg	8.8 lb	90 kg	198.0 lb
5 kg	11.0 lb	100 kg	220.0 lb
6 kg	13.2 lb	200 kg	440.0 lb
7 kg	15.4 lb	300 kg	660.0 lb
8 kg	17.6 lb	400 kg	880.0 lb
9 kg	19.8 lb	500 kg	1,100.0 lb
10 kg	22.0 lb	600 kg	1,320.0 lb
20 kg	44.0 lb	700 kg	1,540.0 lb
30 kg	66.0 lb	800 kg	1,760.0 lb
40 kg	88.0 lb	900 kg	1,980.0 lb
50 kg	110.0 lb	1,000 kg	2,200.0 lb

www.ingramcontent.com/pod-product-compliance
Lightning Source LLC
LaVergne TN
LVHW060635110826
845147LV00018B/990

* 9 7 8 1 6 8 4 4 2 7 6 4 2 *